Thought Without Language

SYMPOSIA OF THE FYSSEN FOUNDATION

Social Relationships and Cognitive Development
*Edited by Robert A. Hinde, Anne-Nelly Perret-Clermont,
and Joan Stevenson-Hinde*

Thought Without Language
Edited by L. Weiskrantz

Thought Without Language

Edited by
L. Weiskrantz

A Fyssen Foundation Symposium

CLARENDON PRESS · OXFORD
1988

DF
311
.T49
1988

Oxford University Press, Walton Street, Oxford OX2 6DP
Oxford   New York   Toronto
Delhi   Bombay   Calcutta   Madras   Karachi
Petaling Jaya   Singapore   Hong Kong   Tokyo
Nairobi   Dar es Salaam   Cape Town
Melbourne   Auckland
and associated companies in
Berlin   Ibadan

Oxford is a trade mark of Oxford University Press

Published in the United States
by Oxford University Press, New York

British Library Cataloguing in Publication Data
Thought without language.—(A Fyssen Foundation symposium).
1. Cognition
I. Weiskrantz, Lawrence   II. Series
155.4'13   BF311
ISBN 0-19-852180-4
ISBN 0-19-852177-4 Pbk

Library of Congress Cataloging in Publication Data
Thought without language/edited by L. Weiskrantz.
p. cm.—(A Fyssen Foundation sympmosium)
Report of the third Fyssen symposium held at the Trianon Palace Hotel, Versailles, France,
April 3–7, 1987.
Includes bibliographies and indexes.
1. Psycholinguistics—Congresses.   2. Cerebral dominance—Congresses.
3. Cognition—Congresses.   I. Weiskrantz, Lawrence.   II. Series.
BF455.A1T48 1988   153—dc 19
87–28323   CIP
ISBN 0-19-852180-4
ISBN 0-19-852177-4 Pbk

Set by The Alden Press, Oxford
Printed and bound
in Great Britain by Biddles Ltd
Guildford and Kings' Lynn

Preface

This is a report of the Third Fyssen Symposium, held at the Trianon Palace Hotel, Versailles, from 3 to 7 April 1987. It was officially opened with a welcoming introduction by Madame Fyssen, President of the Foundation. The origins of the idea to hold such a symposium go back to the period near the end of Mr Fyssen's life, when he became very interested in the functions of the 'silent' right cerebral hemisphere. The theme that has emerged is quite central to the aim of the Foundation, which is 'to encourage all forms of scientific enquiry into cognitive mechanisms, including thought and reasoning, underlying animal and human behaviour, and their ontogenetic and phylogenetic developments'.

The general organizational plan and administration of the meeting followed the exemplary model set by the organizers of the first symposium, Robert Hinde, Joan Stevenson-Hinde, and Anne-Nelly Perret-Clermont. Draft manuscripts were pre-circulated to participants. Final papers were prepared after the meeting to take account of points raised in the discussions. All questions put during the meeting were also recorded in writing at the meeting and used as a basis for written answers by the discussants. Further material was available from audio tapes. Edited summaries of the discussions appear after each Section.

Dr Marc Jeannerod offered very helpful advice on the planning of the symposium from its very inception, and he also co-chaired the meeting. Dr Michel Imbert also contributed to the initial planning. The tireless devotion, administrative efficiency, and useful experience of Madame Colette Leconte contributed immeasurably to the success of the meeting. Madame Colette Kouchner also helped with the pre-conference planning and the publication arrangements. To all of them I am pleased to express my gratitude.

I am also very grateful to my wife, Barbara, who assisted throughout the meeting, especially by keeping an account of and collating the multitude of exchanges during the extensive discussion periods, and also by helping with the preparation of the manuscript. The Oxford University Press have been very helpful and efficient at all stages of the publishing process, and it is a pleasure also to express thanks to them.

Madame Fyssen characteristically attended the whole of the meeting and contributed actively to it, and also played an important part in making it a gracious social and gustatory success. All of the participants are especially grateful to her.

Oxford   L.W.
August 1987

Contents

List of participants

Eduardo Bisiach (contributor)
Universita di Milano, Instituto di Clinica Neurologica, 20122 Milano—Via
F. Sforza N. 35, Italy.

Bernadette Brésard (contributor)
Groupe de Recherche sur les Anthropoïdes, Musée National d'Histoire
Naturelle, 57, rue Cuvier, 75231 Paris, Cedex 05, France.

George Butterworth (contributor)
Department of Psychology, University of Stirling, Stirling, FK9 4LA, United
Kingdom.

Alfonso Caramazza
Faculté de Psychologie et des Sciences de l'Education, Université De Genève,
24 rue du Général Dufour, 1211 Genève 4, Switzerland.

Jean-Pierre Changeux
Unite de Neurobiologie Moléculaire Institut Pasteur—Bâtiment des Biotech-
nologies, 28–28, rue du Docteur Roux, 75724 Paris, Cedex 15, France.

Georges Chapouthier
Départment de Psychophysiologie, CNRS—LPN, 91190 Gif-sur-Yvette,
France.

Jean Chavaillon
Directeur de Recherche, CNRS—5ème Circonscription, 1 Place Aristide
Briand, 92190 Meudon-Bellevue, France.

Leslie Cohen (contributor)
Department of Psychology, The University of Texas at Austin, Mezes Hall
330, Austin, Texas 78713–7789, USA.

Jean Decety
Laboratoire de Neuropsychologie Hôpital Neurologique, 59, Boulevard
Pinel, B.P. Lyon Montchat, 69394 Cedex 3, France.

Stanislas Dehaene
Ecole Normale Superieure, 45 rue d'Ulm, 75005 Paris, France.

Adele Diamond (contributor)

Department of Psychology, Washington University and the McDonnell Center for Studies of Higher Brain Function, Washington University School of Medicine, 202 Eads Hall, Box 1125, St Louis, Missouri 63136, USA.

Anthony Dickinson (contributor)

Department of Experimental Psychology, University of Cambridge, Downing Street, Cambridge, CB2 3EB, United Kingdom.

Colette Fabrigoule

Laboratoire de Neurosciences Fonctionnelles, CNRS—LNF U 1 bis, 31 Chemin Joseph-Aiguier, 13402 Marseilles, Cedex 09, France.

Mme. A. H. Fyssen

Foundation Fyssen, 194, Rue de Rivoli, Paris, 75001, France.

Michael Gazzaniga (contributor)

Department of Neurology, Division of Cognitive Neuroscience, The New York Hospital–Cornell Medical Center, 525 East 68th Street, New York, NY 10021, USA.

Maurice Godelier

Directeur d'Etudes, Ecole de Hautes en Sciences Sociales, 54, Boulevard Raspail, 75006 Paris, France.

Yves Guiard

CNRS—INP, 31 Chemin Joseph-Aiguier, 13402 Marseille, Cedex 09, France.

Didier Hannequin

Clinique Neurologique, Pavillon Felix-Deve, Hôpital Charles Nicolle, 1, rue de Germont, 76031 Rouen, Cedex, France.

Thierry Hasbroucq

Unite de Neurosciences Cognitives, CNRS—INP 3, 31 Chemin Joseph-Aiguir, 13402 Marseille, Cedex 09, France.

Robert Hinde

MRC Unit on the Development and Integration of Behaviour, Cambridge University, Madingley, Cambridge, CB3 8AA, United Kingdom.

Gabriel Horn (contributor)

Department of Zoology, University of Cambridge, Downing Street, Cambridge, United Kingdom.

Michel Imbert

Laboratoire des Neurosciences de la Vision, Université Pierre et Marie Curie, 9, Quai Saint-Bernard, Bâtiment C—6ème étage, 75230 Paris, Cedex 05, France.

Kalvis Jansons (contributor)
Department of Mathematics, University College London, Gower Street, London, WC1E 6BE, United Kingdom.

Marc Jeannerod (co-chairman)
Laboratoire de Neuropsychologie Expérimentale, Inserm U 94, 16, Avenue du Doyen Lépine, 69500 Bron, France.

Andrew Kertesz (contributor)
Department of Clinical Neurology, University of Western Ontario, St. Joseph's Hospital, London, Ontario, N6A 4V2, Canada.

Olivier Koenig
Faculté de Psychologie et des Sciences de l'Education, Université de Genève, 24, rue du Général-Dufour, 1211 Genève 4, Switzerland.

Alan Leslie (contributor)
MRC Cognitive Development Unit, 17 Gordon Street, London, WC1 0AH, United Kingdom.

Pierre Mounoud (contributor)
Faculté de Psychologie et des Sciences de l'Education, Université de Genève, 24, rue Général-Dufour, 1211 Genève 4, Switzerland.

Nicole Neuenschwander
Departement de Psychophysiologie, CNRS—LPN 11, 91190 Gif-sur-Yvette, France.

John Pearce (contributor)
Department of Psychology, University College, PO Box 78, Cardiff, CF1 1XL, United Kingdom.

Giuseppe Pellizzer
Faculté de Psychologie et des Sciences de l'Education, Université de Genève, 24, rue du Général-Dufour, 1211 Genève 4, Switzerland.

Jacques Perriault
Chargé de Mission, Ministère de l'Education Nationale, Centre National d'Enseignement à Distance, Tour, Paris-Lyon, France.

Bruno Poucet
Laboratoire de Neurosciences Fonctionnelles, CNRS—LNF, U 1 bis, 31, Chemin Joseph-Aiguier, 13402 Marseille, Cedex 09, France.

David Premack (contributor)
Department of Psychology, University of Pennsylvania, 3813-15 Walnut Street, Philadelphia 19194, USA.

David Schachter (contributor)
Department of Psychology, University of Arizona, Tucson, Arizona 85721, USA.

Justine Sergent (contributor)
Montreal Neurological Institute and Hospital, 3801 University, Montreal, Quebec, H3A 2B4, Canada.

Eric Sieroff
Laboratoire de Neuropsychologie Expérimentale, Inserm U 94, 16, Avenue du Doyen Lépine, 69500 Bron, France.

Elizabeth Spelke (contributor)
Department of Psychology, Cornell University, Uris Hall, Ithaca, NY 14853, USA.

Dan Sperber
Directeur de Recherche au CNRS, Laboratoire d'Ethnologie et de Sociologie Comparative, Université de Paris X, 200, Avenue de la République, 92001 Nanterre, Cedex, France.

Arlette Streri
Laboratoire de Psychologie Expérimentale, 28, rue Serpente, 75006 Paris, France.

Catherine Thinus-Blanc (contributor)
CNRS—LNF, U 1 bis, 31, ch. J. Aiguier, 13402 Marseille, Cedex 09, France.

Lawrence Weiskrantz (co-chairman and editor)
Department of Experimental Psychology, Oxford University, South Parks Road, Oxford, OX1 3UD, United Kingdom.

Andrew Young (contributor)
Department of Psychology, Fylde College, Bailrigg, Lancaster, LA1 4YF, United Kingdom.

Introduction: Three sides of a coin

The original impetus for focusing on the topic of this meeting came from Mr Fyssen's fascination with Luria's writings on the neuropsychology of the 'silent' right cerebral hemisphere, and the possibilities in it that he saw for an approach to non-verbal cognition. The importance of the left hemisphere for language has long been accepted, but it has taken rather longer for an appreciation to grow for those aspects of cognition that are controlled by systems in the brain that are independent and dissociable from those concerned with language. For non-verbal skills, especially perceptual and spatial, the right hemisphere comes into prominence. Also, recent advances in neuropsychology have revealed impressive perceptual and cognitive capacities in human subjects not necessarily accompanied by acknowledged awareness, and apparently divorced from verbal constructions or embellishment. These include studies both of patients with focal brain lesions as well as those in whom the connexions between the two hemispheres have been surgically severed. The neuropsychological literature, indeed the popular literature as well, is replete with characterizations of the components and the general features of the putatively non-verbal brain. This approach by itself could have offered ample material for a symposium in its own right.

But a more adventurous and novel challenge gradually presented itself, because it is clear that there are two other domains, equally rich in content, that approach the general issue of non-verbal cognition from quite different directions. One of these is the study of pre-linguistic human infants. Ingenious techniques have been devised by psychologists to allow access to the developing perceptual and mental capacities of infants in their first year, well before they have acquired language. The question of the interplay between non-verbal and verbal development is itself an important one, but notwithstanding there is a valuable harvest of enquiries that demonstrate impressive skills that do not rest upon language as a prerequisite.

The relevance of the third domain is also self-evident: it is the study of animal cognition. This is an area that has long been a source of both popular and scientific fascination, antedating Darwin's evolutionary linking of animal and human mentation. But in this domain, too, there has been a considerable development in recent years of techniques and conceptual frameworks that have been applied to cognitive skills of animals. The higher apes—although not them alone, nor indeed not only vertebrates—have been studied with sophisticated and novel methods and have yielded new insights.

Practitioners in these three domains have never, to our knowledge, come together specifically to consider this important common thread that runs through their subjects. But in organizing the meeting, a deliberate decision was taken to group the contributions and discussion *not* around the three domains separately, tempting and tidy as that was, but with the danger that the result might merely be a consolidation of their contrasting differences. Instead papers were organized around problems and cognitive realms on which there might be some convergence irrespective of particular origin of the field of study. These formed themselves into six areas (Sections A through F in this volume). The result was a fruitful interplay of discussion both of concepts and of techniques which patently could generalize beyond the particular field or experimental subjects.

The six areas ranged from the effect of social communication and symbolic training on the uncovering and subsequent growth of spatial and other cognitive skills in the human and the chimpanzee (A) to the interaction of verbal and non-verbal modes in brain-damaged patients, with special reference to the right hemisphere (F). There was considerable emphasis on categorical perception in animals and infants, with face perception having a particular focus (B). The perception and memory of space and place in animals and infants was another major area of interest (E), as well as the segmentation of objects and their causal interactions in the perception of a structured environment (C). Another group of papers (D) was concerned with types of implicit processing, especially with reference to different types of memory and knowledge, as revealed both by animal work on imprinting and by adult human neuropsychology.

Each Section is introduced by an Editorial that offers a commentary and summary of its highlights, together with an identification of some of the bridges between the Sections. A precis of the discussion follows each Section. Discussion, which was lively and far-reaching, occupied almost half of the time of the meeting, and so if completely reported would have considerably increased the number of words in this volume. Helpfully, points raised by questioners were also answered in writing after the meeting by the participants, often with considerable elaboration and careful thought, and the summaries are extracted largely from these considered written replies. Recordings of the discussion also helped to fill in some material. Hopefully the main points have been captured here that supplement the contributed papers themselves.

The final paper (G), by *Jansons*, is in a unique category: it deals not with experimental material or technique, but is a personal and gripping account by an accomplished mathematician whose dyslexia is so severe as to preclude normal reading and writing. He told of his educational tribulations as a schoolboy, and of his difficult but ultimately successful path to university and to professional distinction. He also revealingly describes some of the features of his mode of 'mathematical thought without words'.

One nettle was never resolutely grasped in the meeting, although several papers give it more than a glancing brush: the definition of 'thought' itself, its philosophical status, and what would constitute the minimal requirements for demonstrating 'thought' in the absence of language. Philosophers may well despair of this neglect, given its central place in modern philosophy. For some, indeed, it would seem that the medium *is* the message. 'A creature cannot have thoughts', wrote Davidson (1984, p. 157), 'unless it is an interpreter of the speech of another'. For Wittgenstein (1922, p. 5.62), . . . the limits of the language . . . mean the limits of my world'. Indeed, the attitude is not all that modern. Concerning animal cognition, Locke (1960, p. 126) seemed '. . . positive . . . that the power of abstracting is not at all in them; [it is] an excellency which the faculties of brutes do by no means attain to'. According to Dummett (1978, p. 458), in the analytical school of philosophy '. . . the study of *thought* is to be sharply distinguished from the study of the psychological process of *thinking* and . . . the only proper method for analyzing thought consists in the analysis of *language*'. In these terms, this symposium should perhaps have been entitled 'thinking without language'.

On the other hand, the question of how thought can be addressed without considering the subject of 'thinking' is a nettle that may be even more worthy of grasping, and its non-grasping continues to astound non-philosophers. It might be tidy or simplifying for one's beliefs about beliefs, or even as a matter of definition if it pleases, to deny the possibility of thought to other creatures or non-linguistic humans, or to those processes or capacities in human adults that can operate entirely divorced from verbal monitoring or commentary, but that only transfers the question of how to characterize whatever it is that is being denied that name. Whatever it is called, that is the subject of this book— what can be and has been discovered through empirical investigation about cognitive achievements in the absence of or independently of language as an essential crutch or constituent, the methodologies involved in studying them, the implications both for development and for comparative biology, as well as for understanding the organization of the mammalian nervous system. In one of his notebooks Darwin wrote that . . . 'he who understands baboons would do more towards metaphysics than Locke' (see Gruber 1974, pp. 317–18). At any rate, it might help.

Quite aside from the intrinsic interest of the findings in their own right, hopefully the published account of the meeting will lead to further cross-fertilization and convergence of methodological and conceptual approaches. Needless to say, it also includes a number of thoughts about thinking. If the volume leads to further thinking about thought, with or without language, so much the better.

References

Davidson, D. (1984). *Inquiries into truth and interpretation*. Clarendon Press, Oxford.

Dummett, M. (1978). *Truth and other enigmas*. Duckworth, London.
Gruber, H. E. (1974). *Darwin on man*. Wildwood House, London.
Locke, J. (1690). *An essay concerning human understanding. Vol. 1*. Dent, London.
Wittgenstein, L. (1922). *Tractatus logico-philosophicus*. Routledge and Kegan Paul,
    Andover, Hants.

Section A

Emergence and instruction

Editorial to Section A

Two of the major figures in the history of thought concerning the roots and development of thought in children are often contrasted, Piaget and Vytgotsy: the former saw thinking growing in stages out of the interaction of the infant with its physical environment, the latter out of social interactions. But as *Butterworth and Grover* point out in a helpful review of the respective theoretical positions, Piaget and Vytgotsy both accepted that thought did not originate in language and in this sense they both provide a suitable backdrop for the main theme of this volume. *Butterworth and Grover* saw the opportunity to combine both physical and social interactions to plot the pre-linguistic infant's progress in its comprehension of its space, by exploiting the important communicative value of a simple signal—the direction of gaze by an adult (typically its mother) to whom the infant is attending. This effects a redirection of gaze by the infant away from the adult to the target of the adult's gaze. The phenomenon is amenable to detailed experimental analysis of the spatial factors in the environment as well as of the social influence of the adult. Spatial computations, in and of themselves, are not all that remarkable as capacities: a simple computer program could no doubt extrapolate from an external object orientated in a particular direction to a distinct target that always had some fixed angular relationship to the object's orientation. The question is not the calculation itself, but what inferences can be drawn from the results. The prepotency of social communication is obviously one such inference, and the possible 'references' that are entailed in such communication. Another, less uncontroversial, is of an assumption by the infant of object permanence, and the 'permanent possibility of an object', which takes the infant's capacity well beyond what some traditional positions have maintained. Still another is the way in which the infant's co-ordinate system changes with development, suggesting the initiation of new mechanisms at various stages. *Butterworth and Grover* suggest that there are three successive phases through which the infant proceeds in its cognitive comprehension of signals and space between six and 18 months, and links these in turn to the development of language.

Stages of development are extended over a much broader sweep, for different domains of processes as well as over time, by *Mounoud.* He comes out of the Piagetian tradition, but sees a general process in which to place the emergence of various types of thought and cognitive skills in children. The process is recursive and repeating throughout development, the end point of each cycle serving as the initial starting point for the next. The new-born is interpreted as having an initial stage described in terms of sensori–motor co-ordinates determined by 'preformed representations'. Later there is a phase of new elementary representations based on segmentation and analysis. These, in turn, are integrated into new representations of semantic units, leading later again to segmentation and analysis of these units. He takes his examples from such widely different domains as the development of reaching behaviour, early speech production, word segmentation and learning to read, and the construction of tools. The scale of the outlook is broad, with a useful reference to the detailed investigations. '

The impact on cognitive development of instruction, which is after all an example of social communication *par excellence*, emerged most forcefully and directly, as it happened, not from the reports of human work but from *Premack*'s contribution on chimpanzee cognition. His long-term research project on the effect of 'language training' with arbitrarily designated plastic chips on a variety of cognitive skills has yielded fascinating results, quite aside from its bearing on issues of the nature of language itself and comparisons between the predispositions and propensities of apes and children. The implications of the research seem to be double-sided: language training *per se* does not confer strong cognitive advantages, even when the animal has learned the principle of matching of relations of 'plastic chips' to external relations of objects or events to which they refer in the real world. Animals without such training can also achieve, through sheer 'dogged' persistence, comparable success on some of the problems in the end. The chimpanzee in his view does not acquire formal syntactical language—that he considers to be species-specific to humans. But, nevertheless, especially instructive is the importance of a particular type of relation that emerges from training, namely, learning the meaning of 'same/different', which leads on to a strong advantage on success with solving analogies. Remarkable are some new findings; namely, the success of juvenile chimpanzees when set the problem of adding ratios, which they could manage even when the samples consisted of different types of items; e.g.

$$\tfrac{1}{4} \text{ apple plus } \tfrac{1}{2} \text{ bottle} = \tfrac{3}{4} \text{ disc or } \tfrac{1}{4} \text{ disc?}$$

Imaginal strategies could be ruled out in such a task. It is hard to conceive of the successful process not entailing abstract representations. While it happens that the crucial 'same/different' relationship emerged from 'language' training, the abstract representations and cognitive manipulations are seen in an animal without language, at least as we know it. *Premack*'s perspective and conclusions on this unique programme of research, stretch-ing back over almost 20 years, are concisely and eloquently summarized.

1

The origins of referential communication in human infancy

GEORGE BUTTERWORTH AND LESLEY GROVER

Introduction: classical theories of the relation between language and thought in human development: Piaget and Vygotsky

One approach to complex processes such as language and thought is to observe how they develop from their antecedents. The developmental approach, or 'genetic method', as Baldwin (1894) called it, also raises the question of the origins of thought and language and makes it natural that we should wish to consider the evidence from human infancy.

The classical accounts within developmental psychology concerning the origins of language and thought are those of Piaget (1926, 1954) and Vygotsky (1926). Theirs are often presented as mutually contradictory points of view, although, in fact, both agree that thought does not originate in language. The general theoretical background will first be reviewed before turning to the specific example of joint visual reference, a process of communication controlled by a succession of cognitive mechanisms during infancy which precedes the acquisition of language and is related to signalling by manual pointing. In fact, joint reference, or 'deictic gaze', as it has been called, illustrates that there are both social and individual precursors of reflective thought in infancy.

Piaget's theory

Piaget's (1926) approach is often characterized as individualistic since he traced the origins of thinking to the sensori–motor interactions of the baby with the physical environment. He argued that thought has its origins in a 'logic of action' which forms the necessary behavioural foundation for the mental operations that will emerge in the second year of life. The evidence from infancy, among his other investigations, led him to conclude that mental operations are derived from sensori–motor activities that give structure to thought and have primacy over language in development. In Piaget's usage thinking is defined in terms of the ability to reflect upon stored experience;

thought requires representation and transcends the 'practical', unreflective adaptation of the sensori–motor period.

Piaget (1954) described a universal sequence of stages in sensori–motor development culminating in the acquisition of the 'object concept'. The object concept includes the knowledge that objects exist independently of our own activities upon them, that they are permanent, and that they have their own unique identities. He described the object concept as the 'first invariant' of thought, the fulcrum of the cognitive system.

Piaget described the acquisition of the 'concept of the permanent object' in relation to the infant's search for hidden objects. The object concept develops in a sequence of stages which gradually take into account more and more of the objective properties of space, time, objects, and causes, and which culminate in mental representation. For purposes of the argument to be developed in this chapter the important points to note are that infants fail to search for a hidden object before stage IV (eight or nine months of age). It is not until stage V (about 12 months) that they become able to monitor the 'invisible displacements' of an object, i.e. movements that must be inferred rather than observed directly. The capacity to extrapolate unseen paths of movement will prove important for the arguments to be advanced. The fully formed object concept is revealed by the infant's persistent and successful search in the invisible displacement task, at around 18 months. Piaget took this achievement as the beginning of mental evocation of objects, for which he reserved the term 'representation'. His six stages of cognitive development during infancy are summarized in Table 1.1.

For the sake of simplicity the many qualifications to Piaget's description of infant cognitive development that have proved necessary in the light of modern research will be omitted (but see Butterworth 1981, 1985). Piaget certainly underestimated the perceptual sophistication of the young infant. His was a 'representationalist' realist theory of perception, as opposed to the 'presentationalist' theories of direct perception propounded by Michotte (1962) or Gibson (1966) and which have informed so much of the research on early infant perception of the last twenty years. The question of the ultimate roots of the operations of thinking, whether in the mechanisms of sensory perception or in sensori–motor action, has been re-opened by discoveries on the perceptual abilities of babies. Spelke (1988) has been instrumental in drawing our attention to the implications of the infant's perceptual sophistica- tion for theories of concept formation, and Leslie's evidence (1988) on the perception of causality in babies is also important for the question of origins. Mounoud's (Mounoud and Vinter 1981) revision of classical Piagetian theory is also relevant to questions of the status of early perception in the process of cognitive growth. For the moment it is sufficient to note that most researchers agree with Piaget that infants fail to search manually for hidden objects much before eight months and that infants can infer the invisible movements of objects at about one year.

Table 1.1 *Schematic outline of six stages in the development of the object concept*

Stage	Age (mths)	Search behaviour	Space	Action pattern
I	0–3	No search	Practical	Reflexes
II				Primary circular reactions
III	3–6	Extension of movement of eye and (later) of hand. Infant looks for object: (a) at place of disappearance (b) along trajectory of movement (c) at initial location	Subjective	Co-ordinated primary circular reactions Secondary circular reactions
IV	9–12	Manual search at first location at which an object was found	Objective/subjective	Co-ordinated secondary circular reactions
V	12–18	Search at last position object was visible	Objective/subjective	Tertiary circular reactions
VI	From 18	Persistent and successful search after invisible displacements	Objective	Representational solution to search problems

Piaget argued that precursors of thought can be observed in the baby's sensori–motor activities long before the child utters its first words (see Sinclair 1982). There is a great deal of evidence that infants' interactions with the physical environment do indeed become more systematic during the first 18 months of life. In addition to Piaget's own extensive observations reported in *The origins of intelligence in children* (1952), there now exists a massive corpus of work by Langer (1980, 1985) in which is summarized, month by month, the interactions of the baby with objects in the physical environment. Langer notes changes in the ways in which the baby can relate 'parts' and 'wholes' with simple play things. These he calls 'proto-operations' and they are said to lie at the roots of number and logico-mathematical thought.[1] Langer also maps changes in the way babies construct relations between means and ends. These he called 'proto-functions', said to lie at the roots of physical cognition, tool use, and reasoning about causality.[2] If such extensive observations on changes in the patterns of sensori–motor activity of babies are accepted as evidence of an emerging 'logic of action', then it seems likely that some operations that will prove fundamental to thought are available before the onset of speech and hence do not depend on language. Whether these operations are ultimately innately rooted in sensory perception or are constructed through action remains an important theoretical issue.

Vygotsky's theory

Vygotsky agreed with Piaget on the separate origins of thought from language. He argued that phylogenetic comparisons reveal a pre-linguistic phase in the evolution of thought (since the higher primates are capable of solving problems that require thought, but they do not speak). Also, a pre-intellectual phase can be observed in the evolution of speech (since, for example, parrots can imitate speech yet they have limited intellectual abilities in comparison to man and the primates).

A major difference, however, lies in Vygotsky's social approach to intellectual development. His general, theoretical position suggests that he would have considered the social foundations of language and thought, as

---

[1] For example, Langer argues that three basic types of logical operation can be observed in the activities of the infant: combinativity proto-operations (e.g. composing, decomposing, reforming, attaching); relational proto-operations (addition, subtraction, multiplication, and division); exchange, correlational, and negation proto-operations (e.g. replacing elements, establishing one-to-one correspondences between sets of elements, inversion of elements).

[2] Langer claims that elementary causal reasoning can be observed in the simple spatial constructions of two or three objects placed on a surface at six months. By 18 months, there is systematic variation of means and ends in the child's exploration of causality such that proto-functions have become ordered (e.g. pushing harder results in a cylinder rolling further; action dependencies show an increasing transitivity; also the infant by 24 months will construct a tower of four cylinders and then use a fifth cylinder to knock the bottom support away).

well as the sensori–motor precursors, to be observable in infancy. His famous aphorism is worth quoting:

Any function in the child's cultural development appears twice, or on two planes. First it appears on the social plane and then on the psychological plane. First it appears between people as an inter-psychological category and then within the child as an intra-psychological category. This is equally true with regard to voluntary attention, logical memory, the formation of concepts and the development of volition (1966, p. 41).

A second, important difference between the Piagetian and Vygotskian approaches concerns the interpretation of childhood egocentrism. The concept of egocentrism is not at all an easy one to define but it has two essential aspects: (i) a spatial aspect concerning the point of origin of experience and (ii) in Piaget's usage, it implies non-differentiation between the subject and object of experience. Flavell (1963, p. 60) defined Piaget's use of the concept as follows:

Egocentrism denotes a cognitive state in which the cognizer sees the world from a single point of view only, his own but without knowledge of the existence of viewpoints or perspectives and without awareness that he is a prisoner of his own [viewpoint].

Vygotsky (1962) made clear his disagreement with Piaget over the status of egocentrism in his description of thought in early childhood. Although he may have agreed that egocentrism implies an unconscious point of origin for experience, he would have denied that egocentrism implies solipsism indifferentiation of experience, or an inability to share in the experience of others.

Joint visual attention and referential communication

Having outlined the background it is now possible for us to move toward a more detailed consideration of some evidence from infancy which may help to reconcile the Piagetian intramental approach with Vygotsky's insistence that there should be intermental foundations to thought. There is little doubt that adults monitor very closely the infant's focus of attention and adjust their own gaze to maintain shared experience. Gaze following and gaze aversion are important in governing social interaction and in referential communication between the preverbal human infant and the caretaker. Most of the literature on joint visual attention between mothers and their babies has concentrated on the mother's behaviour in relation to the infant. Mothers monitor very closely the focus of their infant's attention; they vocalize at suitable moments in the interaction and create a tutorial environment. (Bruner (1983) called this the language acquisition support system (LASS).) Schaffer (1984) reviewed a number of studies which show that the majority of episodes of joint activity arise as a result of the mother monitoring the infant's line of gaze. These tutorial social interactions are said to foster the development of the referential and propositional aspects of language in the context of interactive games. Joint visual attention paves the way for deictic gestures which draw attention to a particular object by locating it for another person, as in referential pointing, by which time development has definitely moved into the realm of language (see Parker (1985) for an interesting review of the ontogenetic and phylogenetic literature on language acquisition).

Further evidence of the role of joint visual attention in pre-verbal communication comes from studies of 'emotional referencing', a term used to describe the transmission of affect from mother to child (or vice versa) in social interaction. Maternal emotional expressions may have the effect of attenuating or exaggerating the spontaneous emotional expression of the infant in pleasurable or stressful situations. Indeed, the emotional aspects of pre-verbal communication may form an extremely important link with the onset of speech. It has been suggested that the infant may show an increasing tendency to vocalization when attempting to regain the emotional security of the mother, as, for example, when she is out of sight (Campos and Stenberg 1980).

The importance of joint visual attention for purposes of this discussion lies in the discovery by Scaife and Bruner (1975) and by Churcher and Scaife (1982) that not only does the mother make use of the infant's line of gaze but also the infant redirects his line of gaze to share in the focus of the mother's attention. These investigators noted that babies from two months of age adjust their line of sight in response to a change in the focus of visual attention of an adult. They showed that the baby will adjust head and eyes to turn in the same direction as the mother, upon a change in the focus of her visual attention. Since the baby adjusts the focus of visual attention contingent upon a change in the focus of attention of an adult, this would seem to suggest less than total egocentrism; the baby perceives a change in *another person's* point of view. The observation is also important because it suggests that even the very young baby may be aware of an external, spatial objective of the mother's attention and this in turn may suggest that the infant perceives the mother's gaze as signalling the 'permanent possibility of an object' at the terminus of their joint lines of gaze. In other words, the phenomenon of joint visual attention involves a social, intermental dimension of early experience, it raises important questions about the status of egocentrism at the origins of development, and, last but not least, it raises the question of whether object permanence lies at the very root of cognitive development rather than being derived from it.

Subsequent studies have confirmed Scaife and Bruner's (1975) findings and extended our knowledge of how joint visual attention is possible between an adult and an infant. To establish precisely how the baby can 'look where someone else is looking' it was necessary to carry out systematically a series of experiments.

Butterworth and Cochran (1980) and Butterworth and Jarrett (1980) made an extensive series of studies in an attempt to establish the mechanisms serving joint visual attention. The studies were carried out under strictly controlled conditions in an undistracting environment, with identical targets placed at various positions relative to the mother and infant. These conditions allow relatively unambiguous conclusions to be drawn concerning how the baby is able to single out the referent of the mother's gaze, since distractions and other possible artifacts are eliminated. In these experiments the mother was instructed to interact naturally with the infant and then, on a signal, to turn, in silence and without pointing manually, to inspect a designated member of a set of targets placed at various positions relative to the mother and baby around the room; an example is shown in Fig. 1.1. Groups of babies aged 6, 12, and 18 months were studied.

We found evidence for three successive mechanisms of joint visual attention in the age range between 6 and 18 months. At 6 months, babies look to the correct side of the room, as if to see what the mother is looking at, but they cannot tell *on the basis of the mother's action alone* which of the two identical targets on the same side of the room the mother is attending to, even with angular separations as large as 60 degrees between the targets. Although the babies are accurate in locating the referent of the mother's gaze when the

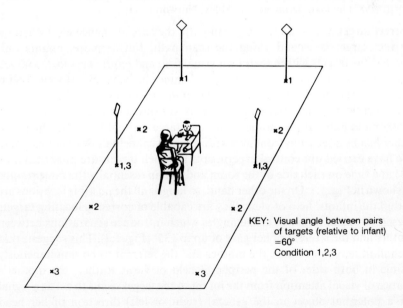

KEY: Visual angle between pairs
of targets (relative to infant)
=60°
Condition 1,2,3

Fig. 1.1

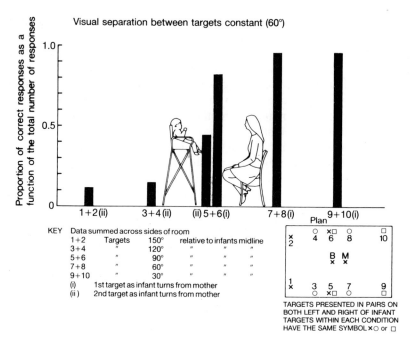

Fig. 1.2 Geometric compensation—6-month-old infants [reproduced from Butterworth (1983) by kind permission of Ablex, Norwood, NJ].

correct target is first along their scan path, they are at chance level when the correct target is second along the scan path. Furthermore, infants only localize the targets within their own visual field and hardly ever locate targets which the mother looks at in the region behind the baby, out of view. Figure 1.2 illustrates the data for 6-month-old infants in one of our studies in which four identical targets were presented at various locations relative to the mother and baby. If the mother looks at a target behind the baby, the infant either fixates a target in front and within the visual field or does not respond. We have carried out control experiments in which targets are presented only one at a time on each side of the room and obtain essentially the same results, as shown in Fig. 1.3. On the other hand, so long as all the possible locations are within the infants' field of view, they are capable of correctly locating targets presented one at a time at visual angles which introduce separations between mother and the referent of her gaze of up to 135° (Fig. 1.4). This suggests that the infant may not require the mother and the referent to be simultaneously visible in both sides of the peripheral field of view. Rather, the mother's change of visual attention from the infant to the target seems to act as a signal for a potential object in the general (right or left) direction of her head movement.

At 6 months, therefore, joint visual attention is restricted to targets within

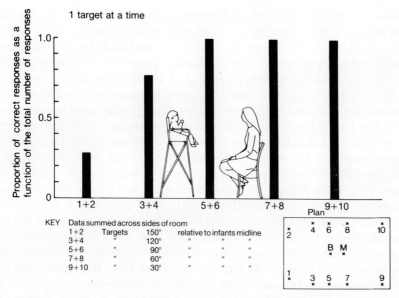

Fig. 1.3   Limits of accurate spacial localization—6-month-old infants.

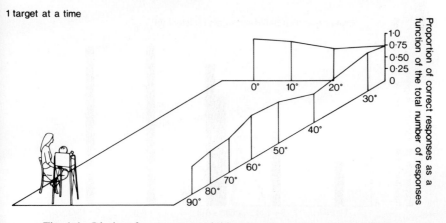

Fig. 1.4   Limits of accurate, spacial localization—6-month-old infants.

the infant's view (i.e. to targets that are not occluded by the baby's own body). Within the field of view, accurate localization of the referent seems to depend not only on the adult's signal but also on the intrinsic differentiating properties of the object being attended by the mother. Grover (1982) has demonstrated that the addition of movement to one of the otherwise identical targets is sufficient to lead the 9-month-old infant to fixate it. This earliest mechanism of joint visual attention we have called 'ecological', since we believe that it is the differentiated structure of the natural environment that completes for the infant the communicative function of the adult's signal. What initially attracts the mother's attention and leads her to turn is also likely, in the natural environment, to capture the attention of the infant. The ecological mechanism enables a 'meeting of minds' in the selfsame object.

By 12 months of age the infant is beginning to localize the targets correctly, whether first or second along the scan path, so long as the target is in the visual field (Fig. 1.5). The only information allowing this is the angular displacement of the mother's head and eye movement. It is interesting to note that the infant fixates intently on the mother while she is turning; then, when the mother is still, the infant makes a rapid eye and head movement in the direction of the target. The mean latency of response after the end of the mother's head movement is about one second (Butterworth and Cochran 1980, p. 268). This brief interval may be sufficient for the baby to register information about the angular orientation of the mother's head. We call this new ability the 'geometric mechanism', since it seems to involve extrapolation of an invisible line between the mother and the referent of her gaze, as plotted from the infants' position. In Piagetian terms the ability to extrapolate such an invisible line might be understood as an aspect of the ability to monitor invisible

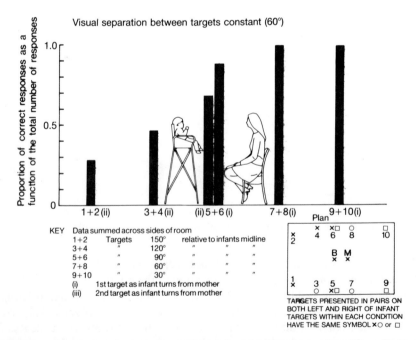

Fig. 1.5 Geometric compensation—12-month-old infants [reproduced from Butterworth (1983) by kind permission of Ablex, Norwood, NJ].

movements of objects, which generally appears at about 12 months, or at stage V. In his account of object concept development, Piaget (1954) demonstrated that babies of this age are able to infer the path of movement of an object whose trajectory was not directly observed, as for example when a person walks out of view behind a screen (e.g. obs. 104a, p. 185).

Despite this newfound geometric ability, however, babies at 12 months still fail to search for targets located behind them. Again, we have carried out control studies in which the visual field is emptied completely of targets, yet babies of one year do not turn behind them at the mother's signal. Instead they turn to scan to about 40° of visual angle and give up the search when they fail to encounter a target. It seems that if the geometric mechanism is available, it must still be restricted to the infant's perceived space.

By 18 months babies are as accurate when the correct target is first along their scan path from the mother, as when it is the second target they encounter. Figure 1.6 shows this. Furthermore, although the babies still do not search behind them when there are targets in the field of view, they will do so if the visual field is empty of targets. We found that head and eye movements to targets behind the baby would elicit turning to the correct target, so long as there was nothing in front of the 18-month-old infant, in the field of view. In

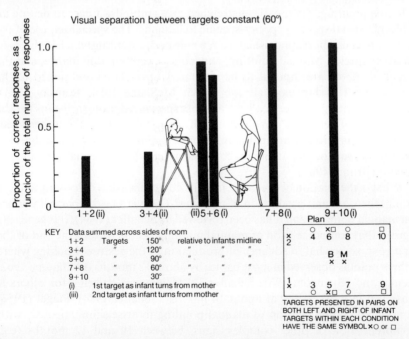

Fig. 1.6 Geometric compensation—18-month-old infants [reproduced from Butterworth (1983) by kind permission of Ablex, Norwood, NJ].

fact, the mother's eye movements alone are sufficient to lead the child to turn behind at 18 months, but infants do not respond so readily as when the signal involves head and eyes combined.

In summary, we have evidence in the first 18 months of life that three successive mechanisms are involved in 'looking where someone else is looking'. The earliest, 'the ecological mechanism', depends on completion of joint attention by the intrinsic, attention-capturing properties of objects in the environment, as well as on the change in mother's direction of gaze. At around 12 months, we have evidence for the beginning of a new mechanism, a 'geometric' process, whereby the infant from the mother's position extrapolates the line of her gaze to its intersection with a precise location in visual space. Finally, at some time between 12 and 18 months, there is an extension of joint reference to a 'represented' space which 'contains' the infant and leads to an awareness of the world that is out of view, behind the baby. Of course, by this stage most theorists would agree that language and thought have definitely made an appearance in development. How can we relate the capacity for joint visual attention to the origins of language?

Joint visual attention and manual pointing

Manual pointing, the use of outstretched arm and index finger to denote an object in visual space, is species-specific to humans. The specialized use of the index finger can be distinguished from whole body orienting which is observed in other species. Manual pointing, handedness, cerebral dominance, and the onset of speech are thought to be intimately interrelated and linked to the development of language (Bruner 1983; McShane 1980; Ramsay 1984). Manual pointing has been called 'the most specialized motoric means for the expression of reference' (Werner and Kaplan 1984). It is this specialized, referential function of manual pointing that is of interest here since this may be a precursor to, and an aid in, comprehending the referential functions of speech (Bruner 1983).

What is the relation between the infant's comprehension of looking and the comprehension and production of pointing? There is a fairly sparse literature on manual pointing and it has been reviewed by Schaffer (1984). It is generally agreed that comprehension of manual pointing occurs toward the end of the first year, somewhat in advance of production of the gesture. Looking where others point is observed in most babies by about 12 months (Guillaume 1962; Leung and Rheingold 1981; Schaffer 1984), whereas pointing for others is observed in most babies at about 14 months (Schaffer 1984). Piaget (1952) considered comprehension of manual pointing to arise simultaneously with comprehension of other complex signs, between 10 and 12 months (e.g. p. 249). To go on to link the comprehension of signs to the child's development of speech is indeed a difficult enterprise. However, Kaye (1982) has traced the long apprenticeship of the child in human symbolic communication to earlier forms of shared meaning through signals and gestures. His distinction between the different roles of index, sign, gesture, and symbol in sharing meaning is relevant to separating the specifically human aspects of language development from aspects of communication held in common with other species. It may also be necessary to rely heavily on such distinctions to explain how communication and language are ontogenetically related in early human development.

Theorists do not agree on the origins of production of the pointing gesture. Preyer (1896) included pointing in his discussion of expressive movements. He suggested that the use of the index finger must rest upon an hereditary co-ordination and that, in its original manifestation, it expresses a wish to seize. Vygotsky (1926) argued that pointing develops as a result of the mother's response to the infant's failed attempts to reach objects. He described early pointing as an unsuccessful grasping movement that becomes endowed with meaning by the mother. These seem unlikely explanations, however, since they neither account for the species-specificity of the response nor for its universality within the species. Millicent Shinn (1900, quoted in Schaffer 1984) suggested that manual pointing may develop out of an earlier, fine, conjoint, visuo–tactual inspection of objects. The infant of 8 or 9 months who is particularly interested in an object will simultaneously touch it with the index finger, while closely observing the exploration. She suggests that pointing begins soon after, as an extension of the conjoint, visual–tactual inspection to objects at more distant locations. On this account, pointing develops by the application to an extended space, of a pre-existing intersensory co-ordination between vision and touch used for fine inspection in near space.

It is worth noting, in passing, that the onset of manual pointing using the index finger may also be related to cognitive developmental changes that underly early instrumental behaviours and tool use. Index-finger–thumb opposition appears at about 28 weeks and increases to complete opposition at about 44 weeks. As Gesell and Halverson (1936, p. 349) noted, 'the thumb divorces itself from the forefinger in order that it may better cooperate with it'. This analysis offers another way in which to understand the manual posture involved in the pointing gesture. It can be understood as the *inverse* of the index-finger–thumb opposition involved in taking a precise grip; i.e. pointing involves activating the opposite movement pattern to the pincer grip and hence is not a simple extension of grasping. Our own research on mechanisms underlying the production of pointing has only just begun, and there is little to say so far except that these mechanisms clearly involve co-ordination of viewpoints, with the index finger 'holding' the position of the interesting object while the baby checks to see whether the mother has located the referent. We do have quite extensive data on the infant's comprehension of pointing, however, and this will now be reviewed.

Grover (1982) carried out a series of studies designed to provide more information about the baby's comprehension of pointing. She began with our previous observations on how the infant understands the mother's looking and tested the hypothesis that comprehension of gaze may serve to inform the baby about manual pointing. In her first study she compared the accuracy of 12-month-old babies in locating a target when the mother simply looked at it, versus when the mother looked and simultaneously pointed at it. The experimental situation was otherwise virtually identical to that already described for the studies by Butterworth and Cochran (1980) and by Butterworth and Jarrett (1980). Figure 1.7 shows the results, which are very similar to those obtained in our previous studies. Infants at 12 months fail to locate targets behind them, whether the mother looks or looks and points. They can correctly locate the mother's referent target within their own visual field whether the target is first or second on their scan path; in fact, they are slightly more accurate in singling out the second target when the point is added. The main effect of adding the manual point, however, is significantly to increase the probability that the infant will respond. Adding manual pointing to simple change of gaze has a compelling effect on the infants' attention. Figure 1.8 shows that the proportion of trials to which the infant responds when looking is accompanied by pointing increases to 96 per cent (from 59 per

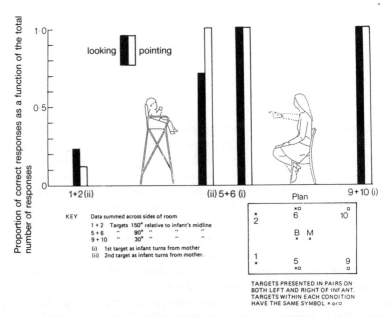

Fig. 1.7 Geometry of pre-verbal communication: comprehension of looking and pointing at 12 months of age [Grover 1982].

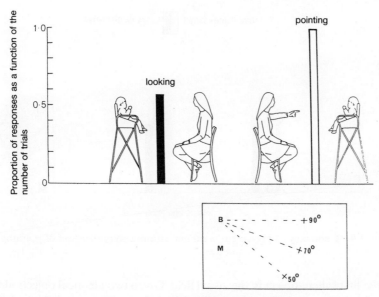

Fig. 1.8   Geometry of pre-verbal communication: comparison of mother looking or pointing on response rate of infants at 12 months of age (Grover 1982).

cent of trials when the mother only looks at the target). However, this does not result in an increase in accuracy to targets outside the field of view. The increase in responsiveness simply leads to a higher probability that the baby will single out a target inside the field of view when the mother points behind the infant.

In a later study Grover (1982) examined the development of comprehension of pointing at 6 months, 9 months, and 12 months. The experimental laboratory and cameras were arranged so that the direction of the infants gaze, whether toward the mother's hand or to the referent target, could be precisely measured. The results are summarized in Fig. 1.9. The results demonstrate that infants at 6 months and 9 months do not comprehend the manual pointing gesture. They are equally likely to fixate the mother's hand as the target to which she is pointing. By 12 months, 96 per cent of responses are to the target, and hand fixations are very few indeed. The 12-month-old infants have little difficulty in comprehending the manual point and they swiftly and smoothly look to the target being designated. They understand that they must look on from the hand toward the location in the visual field. By contrast, 6- and 9-month-old infants, if they locate the target, do so relatively slowly, in a two-step movement in which they first gaze at the mother's hand for a second or two before moving onto the target.

Grover (1982) has shown that the 12-month-old baby is not simply singling

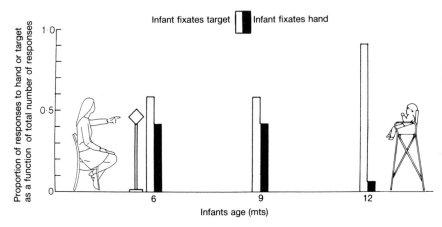

Fig. 1.9   Geometry of pre-verbal communication: comprehension of pointing.

out the first salient object in the visual field. Given two identical objects along the infant's scan path from the mother, the infant will sequentially fixate the first object and then correct the respose to alight on the target, second along the scan path. By 15 months the infant will often look straight to the correct place.

These experiments are important because they demonstrate that quite extensive experience in responding to mother's direction of gaze in the first 10 months of life does not help the infant with comprehension of her manual pointing. An apprenticeship in 'looking where someone else is looking' does not qualify the infant to 'look where someone else is pointing'. On the contrary, the evidence is much more consistent with the hypothesis that comprehension of looking changes from an 'ecological' to a 'geometric' mechanism and that this aspect of cognitive development allows comprehension of manual pointing.

If we now consider the series of experiments as a whole, babies begin to comprehend manual pointing at about 12 months, the age at which the new 'geometric' mechanism first becomes available. It seems that the ability to monitor invisible displacements in Piaget's terms, and the comprehension of looking and pointing as signals, leads these behaviours of adults to become acts of definite reference for the infant, which single out an object at a particular location in space.

Conclusion

This review of our research programme on comprehension of deictic gaze and manual pointing has provided a framework in which to examine the question

of the relation between language and thought in development. Our observations are relevant to at least four issues: (i) the status of perception in early
development as a means of comprehending reality; (ii) the relation between
precocious abilities such as comprehension of gaze and later appearing
abilities such as comprehension of pointing which are thought to be related to
language acquisition; (iii) the intermental aspect (in Vygotsky's terms) of
cognitive development; and (iv) the origins and status of childhood egocentrism whch has usually been considered as a limiting factor on cognition.

Our results make it clear that even the very young infant may enter into a
communicative network with others through comprehension of an adult's
direction of gaze; communication is not solely dependent on the greater
cognitive sophistication of the adult. At 6 months, the signal value of the
mother's head movement will indicate the general direction (left or right) in
which to look. Communication occurs because the easily distractible baby will
attend to the same attention compelling features of the objects in the
environment as the mother. When seen in a social context, the earliest
'ecological' mechanism of joint attention allows communication in relation to
publically shared objects through their common effects on intrinsic attention
mechanisms of mother and baby. This basic intermental process depends on
the fact that attentional mechanisms in infant and adult operate in much the
same way.

A more general theoretical implication concerns the infant's comprehension of object permanence. The infant clearly takes the mother's action to
signal the existence of a potentially interesting object somewhere in his own
visual field. That is, although the infant will not search manually for hidden
objects before 8 or 9 months, the mother's behaviour nevertheless signals the
'permanent possibility of an object' potentially *within the field of view*.
Looking for an object outside the field of view, on the basis of the mother's
signal, does not occur until the second year of life. This more advanced ability
seems to depend on the acquisition of a representation of space conceived as a
'container' within which the infant is located. The acquisition of this type of
spatial concept may be explained in terms of Piaget's stages of development in
the search for hidden objects (perhaps as a result of the child's own locomotor
development).

During the first year of life joint visual attention remains limited to
locations within the infant's own visual space. The baby behaves as if its own
field of vision is shared with the adult and this gives us an insight into infantile
egocentrism. On the one hand, the fact that the infant responds at all might
suggest that babies are not egocentric, since a change in the other person's
point of view has led them to respond. On the other hand, since under
circumstances when the mother looks behind the baby the infant assimilates
her line of gaze into his own visual field, this might be taken as evidence for
egocentrism. To resolve this paradox we need to move away from a solipsistic

theory of infant perception and toward a realist account. A theory of direct perception, such as that of Gibson (1966), enables us to understand that perception must originate at a particular viewpoint. This need not mean that the infant cannot perceive that others also have a perspective on a space that is common to several points of view. The phenomenon of joint visual attention is ultimately possible because perception, even in the infant, presupposes a world of objects that exist in a space that is held in common with others. The infant in the first year is limited by the boundaries of the immediate visual field, but this nevertheless allows intersubjectivity. Even though cognitive development of the participants in the interaction is at very different levels, the process of immediate perception provides a basis for agreement on the objects of experience.

Superimposed on this basic mechanism, with cognitive development, comes precise 'geometric' localization of the referent of the mother's gaze, a development that simultaneously allows comprehension of manual pointing. The geometric mechanism lessens the ambiguity of reference, since even targets that are identical in all respects except position can now be singled out by the infant. Once the geometric mechanism is available, communication does not require differential intrinsic properties of the objects being singled out; the infant will choose the correct object in relation to the angular displacement of the mother's head and arm. It seems likely that this ability arises from a cognitive developmental process of the Piagetian type, which allows invisible displacements to be monitored. Furthermore, this change also enables the comprehension of manual pointing, itself a pre-cursor of language. It seems quite likely that this will prove to be a general developmental change, perhaps related to frontal lobe maturation, that is implicated in other types of reasoning which require a solution by indirect means. The best known example is the detour task whereby a goal must be attained by an indirect route (Kohler 1925; see also Diamond 1988).

In conclusion, the evidence from infancy suggests that both social and cognitive precursors of thought and language can easily be observed. If thought is defined as a reflective activity, then the pre-reflective mechanisms available to the infant are nevertheless sufficient to ensure both communication and cognition in the absence of language.

Acknowledgements

The studies by Butterworth and Jarrett (1980) were carried out with the support of a grant from the Economic and Social Research Council, UK, and the extensions of this work by Grover (1982) were carried out under a doctoral studentship linked to the ESRC grant.

References

Baldwin, J. M. (1894). *Mental development in the child and the race*. Macmillan, New York.

Bruner, J. S. (1983). *Child's talk; learning to use the language*. Oxford University Press.

Butterworth, G. E. (ed.) (1981). *Infancy and epistemology*. Harvester Press, Brighton, Sussex.

—— (1983). Structure of the mind in human infancy. In *Advances in infancy research*, (ed. L. P. Lipsitt), Vol. 2. Ablex, New Jersey.

—— (1985). Events and encounters in infant perception. *The New Psychologist*, 3–7.

— and Cochran, E. (1980). Towards a mechanism of joint visual attention in human infancy. *International Journal of Behavioural Development*, **3**, 253–72.

— and Jarrett, N. (1980). The geometry of preverbal communication. Paper presented at the Annual Conference of the Development Psychology Section of the British Psychological Society, Edinburgh. Available from author.

Campos, J. J. and Stenberg C. R. (1980). Perception, appraisal and emotion. The onset of social referencing. In *Infant social cognition*, (ed. M. Lamb and L. Sherrod), pp. 273–314. Lawrence Erlbaum Associates, Hillsdale, NJ.

Churcher, J. and Scaife, M. (1982). How infants see the point. In *Social cognition: studies of the development of understanding*, (ed. G. E. Butterworth and P. Light), pp. 110–36. Harvester Press, Brighton, Sussex.

Diamond, A. (1988). Differences between adult and infant cognition: is the crucial variable presence or absence of language? In *Thought without language*, (ed. L. Weiskrantz), pp. 337–70. Oxford University Press.

Flavell, J. (1963). *The developmental psychology of Jean Piaget*. Van Nostrand, Princeton, NJ.

Gesell, A. and Halverson, H. M. (1936). The development of thumb opposition in the human infant. *Journal of Genetic Psychology*, **48**, 339–61.

Gibson, J. J. (1966). *The senses considered as perceptual systems*. George Allen and Unwin, Hemel Hempstead, Herts.

Grover, L. (1982). The comprehension and production of the pointing gesture in human infants. Paper presented to the 40th Annual Convention of the International Council of Psychologists, Southampton. Available from author.

Guillaume, P. (1962). *Imitation in children*. Chicago University Press.

Kaye, K. (1982). *The mental and social life of babies: how parents create persons*. Harvester Press, Brighton, Sussex.

Kohler, W. (1925). *The mentality of apes*. Routledge and Kegan Paul, Andover, Hants.

Langer, J. (1980). *The origins of logic: six to twelve months*. Academic Press, New York.

—— (1985). *The origins of logic: one to two years*. Academic Press, New York.

Leslie, A. M. (1988). The necessity of illusion: perception and thought in infancy. In *Thought without language*, (ed. L. Weiskrantz), pp. 185–210. Oxford University Press.

Leung, E. H. L. And Rheingold, H. (1981). Development of pointing as a social gesture. *Developmental Psychology*, **17**(2), 215–20.

McShane, J. (1980). *Learning to talk*. Cambridge University Press.

Michotte, A. (1962). *The perception of causality*. Methuen, Andover, Hants.

Mounoud, P. and Vinter, A. (1981). Representation and sensori-motor development.

In *Infancy and epistemology*, (ed. G. E. Butterworth), pp. 200–35. Harvester Press, Brighton, Sussex.

Parker, S. T. (1985). A social–technological model for the evolution of language. *Current Anthropology*, **26**(5), 617–39.

Piaget, J. (1926). *The language and thought of the child*. Harcourt Brace Jovanovitch, New York.

—— (1952). *The origins of intelligence in children*. International Universities Press, New York.

—— (1954). *The construction of reality in the child*. Basic Books, New York.

Preyer, W. (1896). *The senses and the will*. Appleton-Century-Crofts, New York.

Ramsay, D. (1984). Onset of duplicated syllable babbling and unimanual handedness in infancy: evidence for developmental change in hemispheric specialization? *Developmental Psychology*, **20**, 64–71.

Scaife, M. and Bruner, J. S. (1975). The capacity for joint visual attention in the infant. *Nature*, **253**, 265.

Schaffer, H. R. (1984). *The child's entry into a social world*. Academic Press, New York.

Sinclair, H. (1982). Piaget on language: a perspective. In *Jean Piaget: concensus and controversy*, (ed. S. Modgil and C. Modgil), pp. 167–77. London; Holt Rhinehart and Winston.

Spelke, E. S. (1988). The origins of physical knowledge. In *Thought without language*, (ed. L. Weiskrantz), pp. 168–84. Oxford University Press.

Vygotsky, L. S. (1962). *Thought and language*. M.I.T. Press: Cambridge.

—— (1966). Development of the higher mental functions. In *Psychological research in the USSR. Vol. 1*, (ed. A. Leontyev, A. Luria, and A. Smirnov), pp. 11–44. Progress Publishers, Moscow.

Werner, H. and Kaplan, B. (1984). *Symbol formation*. Lawrence Erlbaum Associates, Princeton, NJ.

2

The ontogenesis of different types of thought: language and motor behaviours as non-specific manifestations

PIERRE MOUNOUD

A symposium on the topic 'thought without language' should enable us to take stock of the present state of knowledge of a very complex problem which has intrigued scientists and philosophers for centuries and which, after a surge of interest at the beginning of this century, has now re-emerged as a topical issue, thanks particularly to recent developments in neuropsychology. Rather than to simply review the data on non-language-related behaviour, however, it would be more fruitful to make a general statement on different types of thought and, more specifically, to speculate upon what exactly thought with or without language might be.

To begin with, I will attempt to show that the first stages of language development are not different from those of the development of thought, contrary to Vygotsky's opinion, for one. Indeed, I believe that the manner in which a baby succeeds in knowing or in appropriating the complex object of language is the same as that in which he knows or appropriates any other object around him, including other people and even his own body. I will then try to demonstrate that the same is true for later stages of development. This approach leads us to the conclusion that we should substitute for the dichotomy of verbal and non-verbal thought a comparison of the different *types* of thought which characterize the phases of the construction of knowledge, including language.

At the beginning of this century, this symposium might have been called 'intelligence without language'; at the end of this century, 'cognition without language'! I admit that I am still not sure why the organizers chose to formulate the problem in terms of 'thought'. It may have been due to a certain weariness generated by the endless debates over the concept of intelligence— or it may represent a kind of challenge. At a time when many theories attempt to explain complex behaviour as consisting of properties emerging from the interaction of elementary systems (see, for example, Kugler *et al.* 1982), the choice of the term 'thought' seems indeed provocative. In spite of the difficulties involved in defining thought (or intelligence), there have been numerous efforts throughout this century to characterize its different forms in terms of simple dichotomies. Thought without language refers to one of these oppositions and gives reason to suppose that it is somehow distinct from thought with language.

The opposition between thought with or without language has a direct relationship to the opposition between practical and conceptual (or representative) intelligence (Köhler, Guillaume, Meyerson, Piaget, Wallon, etc.). This dichotomy, classical at the beginning of the century, is still alive under different labels such as non- or pre-symbolic thought vs. symbolic thought. The contrast that Piaget (1978) set up between 'success' and 'understanding' can be considered as a reformulation of the same question. Piaget's distinction is based upon the idea that our behaviour is guided by two different types of goals, one being direct adaptation to reality, i.e. the search for immediate success, and the other being more disinterestedly dedicated to knowledge as such, independent of any pragmatic motivations. Twenty years ago in my doctoral thesis on the child's construction of simple tools (Mounoud 1970), I criticized the dichotomy between practical and representative intelligence as a single chronological transition. At that time I considered it to have little relation to the absence or presence of language. I claimed, however, that, in contrast to conventional theory, at any stage of cognitive development there is a passage from a type of intelligence that can be described as practical to a representative or conceptual type—even during the sensori–motor stage.

To better understand this problem, I would like to briefly mention some of the dichotomies used by Piaget to characterize successive types of intelligence. First, Piaget (1952) divided the sensori–motor stage into six substages, defining three successive types of intelligence, respectively called 'practical', 'subjective', and 'objective'. When, later, he studied the concrete operational stage (for example, Piaget and Inhelder 1948), the third type of sensori–motor intelligence called 'objective' was renamed 'practical' in order to reconstitute the same relationship (practical vs. conceptual) at this stage. Finally, when he defined the stage of formal operations, he refocused on the opposition between concrete and formal (Inhelder and Piaget 1955). These shifts in terminology (from objective to practical, from conceptual to concrete) to characterize a single type of intelligence illustrate a major problem in developmental psychology: how to establish global comparisons between stages in terms of *types* of intelligence. As I will further discuss later on, I prefer to use these terms to qualify phases in a given stage (or the transformations in a given stage) as Piaget did for the sensori–motor stage rather than to differentiate between the stages themselves.

A few other oppositions along the same line are worth mentioning, such as the one between intuitive and rational thought, which was used extensively at the beginning of the century, by, for example, Piaget. This dichotomy has been taken up again, probably due to its similarity to the more recently introduced opposition between wholistic and analytic thought or between implicit and explicit knowledge. One criterion that has been used to compare these different types of thought concerns the goals attributed to them, including such goals as the necessity of immediate adaptation and the need to understand, know, and explain. A second criterion refers to the way they function: intuitive thought and thought without language are supposed to function 'wholistically', apply to bounded, unspecified elements of a given situation, use success and failure as criteria, and be basically data driven. Rational thought or thought with language, on the other hand, is supposed to function analytically, apply to unbounded, specified elements of a given situation, use truth and falsity as criteria, search for proof, and be basically conceptually driven. What seems clear to me is the complementarity of these various types of thought. The major problem is to understand their mutual and necessary relationship and their interdependency.

Human subjects are simultaneously oriented to different goals such as adaptation and understanding; moreover, in ontogenesis, there is no choice between these alternatives. Both understanding and adaptation are necessities tied by nature to each individual and in particular to our species as a whole. It is usually considered that through phylogeny humans are becoming able to escape, at least partially, the need for direct adaptation and satisfaction of needs in order to be able to engage in reflective activities (or thought!) that are supposed to give them access to the understanding of 'the possible'—origin of our hypothetical freedom!

A developmental framework

Let us now take a look at our conception of knowledge or thought construction. First of all, I consider cognitive development to be defined by a general process which is shared by all areas of knowledge, as opposed to the line of reasoning which postulates that there are specific processes for each domain of knowledge. Of course, in this view, the existence of a general process would not exclude specific underlying mechanisms. Second, I think that this general process is repeated several times during the course of development, and that the main developmental stages are thus defined. This general process can be defined as a process of thematizing (or of conceptualization) of the transactions that an organism has with his environment (physical, social, linguistic, etc.). It is related to what has been called 'objectivation', 'explicitation', 'awareness', or 'abstraction'. However, this process is not limited to simply rendering explicit or expressible or understandable that which has been experienced or expressed automatically: it is not only a question here of a process of meta-cognition where behaviours first *experienced* on one level of consciousness are then *conceptualized* on another level.

There are several reasons why the process of thematizing cannot be reduced to a simple grasp of consciousness. First and most important, there is a *qualitative transformation* of behaviour throughout the course of development. Between the new-born's automatic stepping and the voluntary walking of the one-year-old child, there is not only the simple addition of awareness. The same is true for the infant's early 'prehension' (reaching and grasping) and the one-year-old's 'late' prehension. There is, in these cases, a complete reorganization of the mode of interaction with the environment. We can make the same observation at other stages of development—such as, for example, the evolution of seriation or of classification skills in the three-year-old and in the 10-year-old (Mounoud 1986).

The second reason is that the phenomenon of *awareness is a transitory phenomenon*. It is true that during the course of his development the child analyses or becomes conscious of certain characteristics of his actions and of the objects he acts upon (as, for example, in the case of learning to walk, speak, write, etc.). It is also true that by the time the ability has been mastered to a certain degree, this consciousness disappears; we are unaware of or develop misconceptions about the rules governing our own behaviour (consider, for example, the grammatical rules of one's mother tongue).

The third reason is that of *progress*. While it may be commonly accepted that the child's development consists of steady improvements, we are far less certain when we consider the complexity of the *preceding* forms of knowledge. What is more, progress is sometimes accompanied by regression or even by a loss of competence. A case in point is the loss at the age of one year of the ability to discriminate between contrasting phonemes which do not exist in the baby's native language (Werker and Tees 1983). This may be due to an attentional deficit as Jusczyk (1985) has suggested. I believe, in fact, that all development and all transformations of knowledge take place within a context which we will call 'loss and gain'. The gains acquired in the accrued ability to plan and to control time and space compensate for losses in other areas (for example, neglecting dimensions previously taken into consideration).

It seems, therefore, that at each level of development, the child's behaviour illustrates a general process of thematizing (or conceptualization) which concerns not only the properties of objects but also the characteristics of his own actions. This process is at the origin of what is ususally called new forms of behaviour and which includes language. Our position is that this process depends on the child's capacities of symbolization (which includes both analogic representation usually qualified as non- or pre-symbolic and abstract or symbolic representation), and that several times in the course of development new symbolic capacities emerge (at birth, around age two, around age 10). We call capacity of symbolization the ability to translate or to transpose by means of a new coding system the current experiences of the organism which are initially determined by a different system of representation. In this perspective it is not possible to speak of thought without symbolization, language being just one of its expressions. The general process of thematizing is a complex one which involves several phases. Throughout these phases, it is possible to determine different types of thought, which is to say, different levels of knowledge and understanding or of planning and control.

The elaboration of new representations necessitates a new demarcation, a new segmentation—a new decomposition of information. The subject must therefore redefine the actions he produces and the objects with which he interacts, including his own body. In other words, he must carry out a new sampling of incoming and outgoing information in order to construct new representations. This translation seems to take place in two clearly distinct phases: the first one which we call semantic and during which the most important aspects would be semantic (or pragmatic), but also morphological, and a second phase called morphological during which the principal aspects would be morphological but also, of course, semantic.

These two phases consist of the translation, by means of a new code, of the different contents (objects, people, his own body) with which the child interacts from one level of representation to another. It is necessary to distinguish between several types of codes giving rise to representations on different levels. It is the appearance of new coding capacities, which I have suggested calling perceptual at birth, conceptual at around two years, and semiotic or formal at around 10 years, which determine the stages of cognitive development of the child. These new coding capacities constrain the child to reorganize, and to redetermine his behaviour (Mounoud 1981, 1983, 1985; Mounoud and Vinter 1981, 1985; Vinter 1985, 1987).

During the *first phase* of this process of thematizing (the first six to nine months for the sensori–motor stage), the objects and the subject's actions— given that they are initially determined by global representations (intersensori–motor coordinations)—are decomposed in terms of their components (segments, elements, organs), which will be defined and processed in the form of *elementary representations* (analogic). This first delimitation is pragmatic; that is, the components or segments taken into consideration consist of functional elementary units liable to have independent meanings. These different components or segments defined by elementary representations are at first isolated and juxtaposed with few relationships between them and few precise links to the configurations from which they have been abstracted and isolated. We can compare them to unbounded engrams (Harnad 1982). This first phase ends with the integration and co-ordination of the isolated components into *total representations* (non-decomposable, non-analysable) or functional totalities (bounded engrams). This last episode is similar to the operation of 'reduction' mentioned by Bisiach (1988) and can be compared to perceptual grouping or cognitive chunking of meaningful units. The first phase illustrates the type of information processing that Fodor *et al.* (1984) have called 'synthesis by analysis strategy'.

During the *second phase*, these integrated whole configurations or functional totalities defined by total representations (perceptuo–motor patterns or bounded engrams) are analysed according to their morphology in relation to more abstract dimensions whose variations are progressively mastered. These dimensions are not defined independently of the totalities as is the case during the first phase, but rather in relation to them. In other terms, in this second phase the rigid functional totalities constructed during the first phase are analysed either according to the relationships among their parts (intra-object relationships) or to their interrelationships (based on one of their dimensions and its variations). This second phase corresponds to what Fodor *et al.* (1974) call the 'analysis by synthesis strategy'.

As far as the sensori–motor stage (or stage of perceptual representations) is concerned, I have already described in detail and on several occasions (Mounoud 1983, 1987; Mounoud and Vinter 1981; Mounoud and Hauert 1982; Vinter 1986, in press) the development of reaching, imitation, face perception, and self-image. Here, I will only very briefly illustrate the general process of thematizing, taking reaching as an example.

Examples from infancy

The development of reaching behaviour

To gain a better understanding of the development of reaching, it is necessary to take into consideration the behaviours manifested by the baby during the first weeks of life. Several authors (Bower *et al.* 1970*a*, 1970*b*; Trevarthen *et al.* 1975; von Hofsten 1982) have demonstrated that infants are capable, during the first days of life, of a kind of reaching, which is quite surprising; they are able to project their arms in the direction of a visually perceived moving object. The new-born's reaching behaviour manifests his capacity to process certain categories of information related to the situation and to his own actions. Most, if not all, of the components of the movements of reaching are present in the first behaviours of the new-born in a remarkably well-organized form (such as, for example, the opening of the hand during transport or the fingertip–thumb grasp). The co-ordinated activities of the head-arm-hand will progressively dissociate to become elementary activities. These are only partially co-ordinated. This dissociation seemingly enables the baby to identify different segments or components in relation to different functions which they are apt to fulfil—hand opening and closing in relation to grasping or releasing an object; flexion and extension of the elbow according to the distance of the hand; wrist rotation based on different orientations and configurations of the hand; etc. (semantic or pragmatic phase). Correspondences can also be established between certain movements and their accompanying perceptions (for us, origin of the perceptual elementary representations). These elementary activities will then be progressively reintegrated, with the result that new globally organized reaching movements will appear (based on perceptual total representations). These movements are usually described as visually triggered, i.e. programmed before their execution, the hand opening during the course of the trajectory, closing again on the object. This brings us to the 24- to 32-week level which White *et al.* (1964) consider to represent the highest achievement, the 'top level' of reaching.

From this point, the 'late' reaching behaviour evolves (morphological phase); this involves more precise adjustments (the orientation of the arm; the opening and closing of the hand) based on the characteristics of the object to be seized (shape, size, weight, orientation). These adjustments will then lead to a complex reorganization of the activity of reaching as well as of its individual components. After 32 weeks, this non-decomposable, non-modulable collective activity constituting reaching gives rise to a complete reorganization which consists of controlling the different parts or units of this complex activity to adapt to the different conditions under which the activity is supposed to be able to be used. This second phase, which could be qualified as late evolution, has been remarkably described by Halverson (1931). In his study of the development of fine grasping, he maintains that at the age of 12 months the baby attains a level of prehension comparable to that of the adult, which has since been confirmed by more recent studies (von Hofsten and Rönnquist, in press). Adaptations to the reach as a function of different orientations of the object to be seized (Bushnell 1982; Lockman and Ashmead 1983; von Hofsten and Rönnquist, in press), as well as adaptations to the grasp as a function of the weights of objects (Mounoud 1973; Mounoud and Bower 1974), are other examples of the second level of organization beginning at around six to nine months and ending at around 16 months.

I have briefly summarized the evolution of reaching because it is among the domains I have studied in detail. Now we must examine the development of speech production in order to establish to what degree it is comparable to the process I have just described. Unfortunately, the complexity of this field, the limitations of our own knowledge, and the restrictions of space will confine us to a rather schematic discussion.

Early speech production

It is well known that around the age of one year the baby produces his first words, entering the phase known as the 'one-word period' which lasts around seven or eight months, that is, until about 18 months (see Dromi (1986) for a review of the question). This period has also been called the 'holophrase stage' by McNeill (1970). For McNeill these single-word utterances correspond to complete adult sentences, which has since been contested by numerous authors. This period is succeeded by the period of word combination productions or sentence construction (McShane 1980), which begins with the production of two-element utterances (Gregoire 1937; Braine 1963). The appearance of single words corresponds to the acquisition of lexical referential meanings (in other words, the constitution of symbols); that is to say, the possibility of relating meaning to defined sound sequences.

I take the position that the emergence of words represents the formation of totalities which are initially non-decomposable. This interpretation is akin to Studdert-Kennedy's (1986). For him, words are perceived as sequential and co-ordinated articulatory gestures and can be reproduced without considering the baby as having a concept of phonemic relationships or an articulated programme in which individual segments are concatenated. In the child's first word productions, Ferguson (1986) has demonstrated that it is the word which is the contrasted unit and not the phonetic segments.

This outcome may seem contradictory to the experimental data which show that quite early the baby is sensitive to the internal structure of words, at the level of phonetic segments (MacKain 1987; Mehler 1983). It is also known that just at the moment when the first words appear, the baby's discriminatory capacity diminishes in terms of its sensitivity to phonemic contrasts which are not from his native language (Werker and Tees 1983). In addition, as Jusczyk (1985) notes, several studies on phonetic perception (Edwards 1974; Garnica 1973; Shvachkin 1973) suggest that 'the one-year-old child is often unable to make many phonemic distinctions that appear to be well within the limits of the perceptual capacities of the average 2 month old' (p. 223).

In the model presented here, however, the phase which precedes the emergence of the non-decomposable totalities (in this case, words) is concerned with the elaboration of the components or elementary segments. From this point of view, the fact that words are not decomposable is not in contradiction to the baby's anterior production of components or segments smaller than the word. Contrary to what Studdert-Kennedy (1986) maintains, development does not always proceed from a level of undifferentiation to one of differentiation, or on the basis of 'analysis by synthesis strategy'.

During the period defined by the production of single words, babies seem to be actively involved in the improvement of the form of the words they produce. The initial productions are often only approximations, and, to succeed, the baby must modify certain parts of the totalities. During the one-word period, the transformations within the word forms recorded by Dromi

(1986) revolve around phonological changes, such as the addition of previously omitted phonemes, the modification of consonants and/or vowels, and the substitution of an appropriate phoneme for a distorted one, as well as around morphological markings, including inflections of number, gender and diminutives of nouns, and number, gender, and tenses of verbs. Dromi insists on the fact that phonological and morphological processes are highly correlated and may function in similar ways when adapted by the child for shaping his own production. According to the interpretation here, these transformations show that the baby is involved in an analysis or in a decomposition of the totalities which Menyuk and Menn (1979) call analysis of meaningful units. These analyses are thought to be carried out first on the basis of syllable-sized units, defined by their position in the word, and only later on the basis of phonetic segments (Menyuk and Menn 1979; Bever 1982). In addition, according to Mehler (1983), 'the response to phonetics or to distinctive features appears after access to lexicon when words are understood in and of themselves' (p. 141).

The description of the stage preceding the one-word period is certainly more difficult, and, what is more, most of the experimental data are inconclusive, especially concerning speech perception. One must also keep in mind, as Menyuk and Menn (1979) note, that the phonemic productions of the pre-speech period have not been seriously taken into consideration by linguists.

Let us finally take a look at the development of pre-speech vocal productions. By the age of three months, the baby begins to imitate and produce language sounds. According to Stark (1979), cooing sounds have often been described as vowel-like. In fact, they contain brief consonant elements. The sounds produced by the baby can be described as 'syllabic nasalized vowels' or as 'syllabic nasal consonants'. When cooing sounds first emerge they are produced as single segments. Subsequently, these segments are produced in series. This is an example of what Zlatin (1975) has called 'early syllabification'. The productions described as 'vocal play' also first appear as single segments in which babies prolong vowel- or consonant-like steady states, slowing down the rate of change. These vocal play segments are also produced later on in long series. From about six months on, the baby produces reduplicated babbling, defined as the production of series of consonant-vowel syllables in which the consonant is always the same. The syllable duration and that of the consonant-vowel syllables are close to adult speech. Nevertheless, precise temporal control still has not been achieved. Beginning at around nine months, non-reduplicated babbling emerges in which vowel-consonant-vowel and even consonant-vowel-consonant syllables appear. In short, it is possible to say that between the ages of three to 12 months, the baby produces isolated, juxtaposed, and reduplicated elementary segments, which are progressively better shaped, better controlled, and more complex.

Based on the experimental data cited here, I propose the following periods to characterize speech-processing. At birth, there is a global organization of speech-related activities (which I consider to be based on preformed representations). This global organization would be responsible for, among other things, temporal synchrony between the baby's lip (pre-speech) and arm movements and adult speech, prefiguring speech activity (Trevarthen 1979). Intersensori–motor co-ordination also allows the baby to localize sounds. This organization would also account for the discriminative ability of the new-born relative to auditory speech contrast.

During his first year, the baby elaborates (in addition to prosodic and suprasegmental aspects of speech, cf. Crystal 1979) *elementary segments or components* of a syllabic nature (isolated or juxtaposed or reduplicated), which come from a new perceptual encoding leading to elementary representations. These could be compared to the interpretative schemas as defined by Jusczyk (1985). These elementary representations which result from the perceptual encoding of visuo–auditory and proprioceptive information allow the baby to produce specific articulatory patterns at the syllabic level. Thus, at around one year, there is a co-ordination or integration of these segments or components which gives rise to words as *non-decomposable totalities*. Then, these totalities become decomposable, first into syllabic units defined by their relative positions in the word, and then into more abstract phonemic units. And finally, as Jusczyk (1985) notes, 'the process of building up a set of prototypical spectral representations commences . . . Building up such a dictionary is apt to be a long and arduous process' (pp. 219, 223).

Even if the present interpretation might be seen as stemming from a 'fortuitous realism' (one of the kinds of pre-causality described by Piaget), I consider the similarities between speech development and that of other types of behaviour, such as reaching, to be so close as to allow us to infer a general underlying process of construction. I have yet to consider what is for me the most striking aspect of the ontogenesis of behaviour in children: the repetition of this general process throughout the course of development. I will therefore briefly examine the 4- to 8-year-old child's capacity to analyse and segment words. And, finally, I will compare his progression in this area to his ability to construct simple tools. Once again, I will try to demonstrate the non-specificity of language development.

Examples from childhood

Word segmentation and learning to read

As far as learning to read is concerned, the question of readiness to learn was reformulated in an interesting way by Liberman and his colleagues (Liberman *et al.* 1974, 1977; Shankweiler and Liberman 1976), and was taken up again and developed by Alegria, Morais, and Content (Alegria and Morais 1979; Morais *et al.* 1987), among others.

According to Alegria and Morais (1979), learning to read within an alphabet system presupposes the capacity for explicit analysis (or segmentation) of speech in terms of phonemes. Now this capacity appears in the child at around 6 years of age. It increases rapidly at the onset of reading instruction and seems to be an important 'accelerator' of the ability to read. It is present in a small percentage (17) of 6-year-olds after three months of primary schooling, but reaches a high percentage (70) by the beginning of the second year of primary school. The authors think that instruction in reading or schooling has a 'net accelerator effect' on the capacity for phonemic segmentation.

Nevertheless, activities of segmenting or fractioning speech are carried out by children younger than 6 years, especially syllabic segmentation which is achieved by 46 per cent of 4-year-olds (4:10) (Liberman *et al.* 1974). Therefore, we are not dealing with a general impossibility for children under 6 years to fragment or decompose an auditorily (or visually) perceived continuum from a temporal (or spatial) point of view. These capacities for syllabic segmentation would explain why Japanese children learn, without systematic instruction, to read the 'katakana' before entering school (Sakamoto and Makita, 1973). It would also explain how Rozin and Gleitman (1977) managed to teach children who experienced difficulties with the alphabet to read syllabic writing without any notable effects on their capacity to read with the alphabetic system.

Syllabic segmentation seems to us to be possible because it is based upon units (elements or segments) which can have a reality of their own and may sometimes have their own meanings for the child, independent of the totalities into which they may be placed. In contrast, *phonemic segmentation* is based on 'units', which have been described as 'abstract' or 'formal', and which have no existence or meaning independent of the whole of which they are a part, as we have already pointed out. They can only result from breaking this totality into parts and have no existence outside these totalities. Expressed differently, *the phoneme* would only exist as a 'part' of a (bounded) whole and would not be accessible to 3-, 4-, or 5-year-olds at the conceptual level, whereas the syllable could exist on its own, independent of any larger entity which might include it as a segment. This does not mean, however, that *the syllable* has the same status when it is identified as an isolated entity as compared to when it is a part of a whole. These distinctions are, of course, only relative and correspond to what may be considered the subject's point of view at different steps in development. Liberman has shown that children can break words into syllables from the age of 4, while a more recent study by Bellefroid and de Ferreiro (1979) shows that the syllable becomes a 'part' of a word (with a defined position with respect to other parts) from the age of 6 years. As a part of a word, the syllable is thus 'defined with respect to the ensemble of word parts' by its relative position. Thus, during development, the syllable can have two fundamentally different statuses: (a) before 6 years it would have the status of an 'independent unit' (inseparable from meaning) which can be regrouped or juxtaposed with other syllables; (b) after 6 years it would have the status of 'part of a word', but essentially defined in terms of its relative position.

Using an example borrowed from psycholinguists, I have tried to show how the transformation of word segmentation capacities during learning to read at the stage of conceptual representations can now be explained by the general process of thematizing previously described and illustrated by early speech production at the stage of perceptual representations.

The existence of different systems of graphic transcription of languages (ideographic and phonographic) offers a supplementary demonstration that processes related to language (including written language) are expressions of a more general process. The ideographic system is related more to the first phase of the general process described as a first type of thought ('synthesis by semantical analysis strategy'), whereas the phonological system is closer to the second phase, considered to be a second type of thought ('morphological analyses by synthesis strategy'). This is one of the most convincing pieces of evidence that language-related phenomena are non-specific to language.

I would now like to briefly show how the general process manifests itself in relation to the way the child is able to define simple objects, such as tools, in problem-solving situations. This example will also allow me to demonstrate the capacity for integrating elements into a whole (the corollary of the capacity to segment).

The construction of tools

The general process of thematizing which describes the passage from a pragmatic or concrete organization to one which is formal or abstract can be illustrated by the results of some research carried out on the construction of simple tools by 4- to 8-year-old children (Mounoud 1970). In these studies, two radically different levels of analysis and problem-solving were demonstrated. These two levels seem to bear a close correspondence to the two phases of the general process.

A primary 'level' of analysing problem situations and of defining tools, typical of 4- and 5-year-old children, is based on a decomposition of the problem into tasks or elementary actions/properties; for example, in tasks involving reaching, reaching around, pushing, and seizing. These actions are used to define or to qualify different segments or pieces of a tool. Each segment thus has its own property: reaching, reaching around, pushing, taking, grasping, hooking, etc. This kind of segmentation can easily be called pragmatic or semantic.

At the 'second level', tools are defined by a general function or by a global transformation progressively specified by the relationships between different parts of the tool and of the situation. These parts only have meaning in relation to the whole (bounded whole), and the relationships are elaborated in reference to the signification of the entire tool. An example of such a tool would be an object designed to move a wood block while avoiding obstacles; another example is a tool constructed to remove a block with a hook on it from a jar. The defining properties of the tools are at the level of relationships such as the length, inclination, or curvature of different constituent parts. These parts are no longer defined in isolation by means of specific properties, but, rather, they are defined by their mutual relationships. Such a conception of the tool can be described as morphological, formal, or abstract and, therefore, corresponds to the formal or abstract capacities for analysing and segmenting words. The second level is characteristic 7- and 8-year-old children.

Segmentation and composition are possible at both levels, where they are completely different in nature. It is as if, for 4- and 5-year-old children, the tool is gradually defined by juxtaposition of segments or pieces, each one having a defined property or a direct relationship to the child's different actions (semantic aspect). This is reminiscent of the figural collections defined by Inhelder and Piaget (1964) in the realm of classifications (synthesis by semantic analysis strategy).

In contrast, at the second level for 7- and 8-year-olds, the tool is defined by a global transformation relative to certain constraints and conditions inherent in the situations. The tool is defined as a whole composed of parts (which only have meanings with respect to the whole) for which only the structural relationships between parts give it its function (morphological analysis by synthesis strategy).

The features of the tool, of the situation, and of the actions taken into consideration by 4- and 5-year-olds or 7- and 8-year-olds do not have the same status, despite their appearance or, especially, despite our adult observer's point of view. Both cases might deal with 'length', for example, but what the 4- and 5-year-old calls long or short will not have the same meanings as that for the 7- and 8-year-old. In the first case, with 4- and 5-year-olds, we would be in the presence of what Piaget called pre-concepts, where the object and what it signifies are not clearly dissociated. For these children, objects or instruments are characterized by isolated properties or components which may be juxtaposed to make up what we might call 'amalgams' (Wermus 1977). Object properties are directly dependent on the meaning of actions performed on them or for which they are substituted. Objects represent or stand for actions. They are a kind of transposition of actions, an analogue translation, a 'substitute'. Their definition will depend on the presence or absence of this or that segment to which a particular meaning is attached and where the whole is not taken into account.

With 7- and 8-year-old children, the instruments become the 'support' for meanings attributed to the whole, which are no longer relative to such and such particular actions but to one or several transformations of the whole. The instruments are no longer defined by the presence or absence of this or that isolated characteristic but uniquely by the relationships between their different parts.

The age of 6 years constitutes the transition between these two levels of organization. It is at around 6 years that the integration of previously isolated and juxtaposed elements with defined properties take place, which eventually give rise to wholistic meanings enabling transformations to be considered. I noticed that when the children succeeded in defining an instrument by means of a wholistic property, they were momentarily unable to construct or modify an instrument. They were only satisfied by the discovery of an instrument which had the whole set of anticipated characteristics.

Before 6 years it would be possible to say that objects do not exist 'conceptually' for the subject as wholes. Their sole conceptual existence would be linked to the current or previous actions associated with them and for which they act as a kind of extension or substitute. The objects would only have partial, local, and momentary 'conceptual' identity.

From (about) the age of 6, objects become identifiable in a stable and global way, and they have acquired a global identity without the relationships between parts of the object or between different objects having been mastered yet. Their identity no longer depends upon current contingencies of the action but is still limited by the degree of organization of the relationships the child is capable of mastering, both between the constituent parts of the object and between different objects.

It is noteworthy that Vinter and myself have found the two major steps of the general process in our research on the development of the self-image in the child from 3 to 11 years of age (Mounoud and Vinter 1985). This research studied the precision and stability of the child's image of his own face using a distorting mirror. In particular, we were studying the way in which children are affected by their initial confrontation with distortions of their face. Our findings were that, at age 6, children had a precise and faithful representation of themselves.

Similarly, in our research on the planning and control of movements, in the study of visuo–manual tracking of periodic signals in 3- to 9-year-old children (Mounoud 1982; Mounoud et al. 1985), we have described the passage from 'local control' to 'global control' of movement, which we interpret as the child's capacity for anticipating the 'to-and-fro' movements of the target and their arm movements as a totality, rather than locally, step-by-step, in a way which then permits the resolution of the problem of coincidence between target movements and their own movements.

Conclusion

In this presentation, I have tried to describe a general process which is not domain-specific in order to explain the successive emergence of different types of thought (semantic versus morphological) at each developmental stage. This process cannot be correctly understood without a definition of the initial stage. Given the recursive nature of this general process, any final state thus generated can itself become an initial state for the following one. Nevertheless, as far as ontogenesis is concerned, it is important to define the initial stage of the new-born (which can be considered as the final state of embryogenesis). I have described the initial state of the new-born in terms of intersensori–motor co-ordinations determined by what has been called preformed global representations (Mounoud and Vinter 1981).

During a first phase of thematizing, new *elementary representations* (analogic) based on meaningful components are constructed by means of a new encoding system (semantic segmentation or analysis). These elementary representations are either isolated or composed into particular unbounded configurations described as 'juxtaposed' or 'reduplicated'. These compositions or configurations can be called 'amalgams' (Wermus), 'appositions' (Bogen 1969), or 'figural collections' (Piaget).

Then the elementary representations are integrated or co-ordinated in *total representations* (symbolic), or bounded initially non-decomposable wholes resulting from 'perceptual grouping' or 'cognitive chunking' of semantic units. During a second phase, these total representations are progressively analysed from a morphological point of view into abstract units defined by the segmentation of their dimensions and their interrelationships (morphological segmentation or analysis).

Afterthoughts

After this presentation, we discovered an exciting paper by MacNeilage (1986), who with his colleagues has recently formulated an interesting hypothesis on the relationship between the beginnings of speech and bimanual co-ordination from an evolutionary perspective (MacNeilage *et al.* 1984). They suggest that left-hemisphere manual specialization may have evolved primarily for bimanual co-ordination rather than simply for manual functions in general. They also consider that the primary specialization of the left hemisphere is for a 'frame and content mode of organization' which is probably used both for bimanual co-ordination as well as for the phonological and syntactic level of speech production. Finally, they hypothesize that the frame and content mode of bimanual co-ordination and its associated hemispheric specialization is probably not specific to hominids but may also be present in Old World monkeys and perhaps also in great apes.

The hypothesis of the frame/content mode of organization at the phonological level of speech is based on an observation made by Shattuck-Hufnagel (1979) related to serial ordering errors in speech production. In particular, in order to explain exchange errors, it is necessary for the subject to separate syllabic structure (frame) from segments (content). Therefore, it is suggested that at the phonological level, speech production includes a stage in which phonological content elements—consonants and vowels—are inserted into syllable structure frames.

MacNeilage (1986) notes in Garret's study (1975) similar errors at the morphosyntactic level of speech: exchange position errors (inside a given syntactic context). These errors demonstrate the intervention of the frame/content mode of organization. In sum, for these authors, evolution would consist of the transposition of the frame/content mode of organization from bimanual co-ordinations to the phonological level of speech and then from the phonological to the syntactic level. Concerning the neurophysiological bases of this frame and content mode of organization, MacNeilage (1986) considers that the supplementary motor area (SMA) located in the superior frontal gyrus of the medial surface of the cerebral hemispheres, as well as other functionally related subcortical areas in the basal ganglia, ventral thalamus, and in the subthalamic nucleus, play a predominant role. These different cortical and subcortical areas show bilateral activities during unimanual tasks (continuous voluntary motor tasks involving actions more complex than single repeated gestures) as well as during speech production. He considers that the importance of the SMA in language has been underestimated.

I consider there to be important convergences between the hypotheses developed by MacNeilage and his colleages and those I have presented here and in previous publications (for example, Mounoud 1986). I have tried to compare the development of reaching to the first phases of speech production in order to characterize structural similarities between these two developmental sequences. More precisely, I have tried to demonstrate the appearance of a new type of segmentation of totalities and of the integration of segments at the beginning of the second year of life (morphological segmentation of totalities in abstract units and integration of elements in bounded totalities which are more than the sum of their parts). With MacNeilage, I am in favour of considering one-handed movements as a special subclass of bimanual control. I have also tried to emphasize the analogy between this new organization and the one that appears at around age six related to word segmentation when learning to read in the alphabetic system, in addition to its similarity to the organization at the morphosyntaxic level of speech (Mounoud 1986).

With regard to reading development, I was very impressed by Gladstone and Best's (1985, p. 98) hypothesis related to interhemispheric collaboration and what they call the time-integrated notion of callosal function, 'when callosal function is considered across diachronic [developmental] time'. As a brief reminder, the role of the callosum is both *facilitory* and *inhibitory*, regulating the flow of information *into* and *between* the cerebral hemispheres. The corpus callosum also forms an integral part of the system that regulates attentional capacities and attention balance. Finally, the anterior region of the callosum is involved in the co-ordination of bimanual motor skills. Gladstone and Best refer to the model of developmental change in hemispheric involvement in complex tasks (proposed by Goldberg and Costa 1981) based on differences in the cortical representation of novel versus acquired information. The right hemisphere would serve to code novel information, while the left hemisphere would be best suited for reporting *already acquired, compactly coded information*, the sequence of knowledge acquisition following a shift from right to left hemispheres. I suggest that the two-phase model I presented might be based on such a shift from right to left hemispheres or at least on a major change in interhemispheric collaboration. With regard to my model, this change in hemispheric involvement would be repeated several times in the course of development, mainly at around nine months and six years.

Acknowledgements

I would like to thank Stephanie Shine for translating the text, Françoise Schmitt for her valuable secretarial assistance, and A. Caramazza, C. A. Hauert, A. de Ribaupierre, D. Stern, A. Vinter, and G. Zanone for their very helpful comments.

References

Alegria, J. and Morais, J. (1979). Le développement de l'habileté d'analyse phonétique consciente de la parole et l'apprentissage de la lecture. *Archives de Psychologie*, **47**, 251–70.

Bever, T. G. (1982). Regression in the service of development. In *Regressions in mental development: basic phenomena and theories*, (ed. T. G. Bever), pp. 153–88. Lawrence Erlbaum Associates, Hillsdale, NJ.

Bisiach, E. (1988). Language without thought In *Thought without language*, (ed. L. Weiskrantz), pp. 464–84. Oxford University Press.

Bogen, J. E. (1969). The other side of the brain III: an appositional mind. *Bulletin of the Los Angeles Neurological Society*, **34**, 135–62.

Bower, T. G. R., Broughton, J. M., and Moore, M. K. (1970a). The coordination of visual and tactual input in infants. *Perception and Psychophysics*, **8**, 51–3.

——, Broughton, J. M., and Moore, M. K. (1970b). Demonstration of intention in the reaching behavior of neonate human. *Nature*, **228**, 679–81.

Braine, M. D. (1963). The ontogenesis of English phrase structure: the first phraze. *Language*, **39**, 1–14.

Bushnell, E. W. (1982). Visual-tactual knowledge in 8, 9½, and 11 month-old infants. *Infant Behaviour and Development*, **5**, 63–75.

Crystal, D. (1979). Prosodic development. In *Language acquisition: studies in first language development*, (ed. P. Fletcher and G. Garman). Cambridge University Press.

de Bellefroid, B. and Ferreiro, E. (1979). La segmentation du mot chez l'enfant. *Archives de Psychologie*, **47**, 1–35.

Dromi, E. (1986). The one-word period. In *Stage and structure*, (ed. I. Levin), pp. 220–45. Ablex, Norwood, NJ.

Edwards, M. L. (1974). Perception and production in child phonology: the testing of four hypothesis. *Journal of Child Language*, **1**, 205–19.

Ferguson, C. A. (1986). Discovering sound units and constructing sound systems: it's child play. In *Invariance and variability of speech processes*, (ed. J. S. Perkell and D. H. Klatt), pp. 36–57. Lawrence Erlbaum Associates, Hillsdale, NJ.

Fodor, J. A., Bever, T. G., and Garrett, M. (1974). *Psychology of language*. McGraw-Hill, New York.

Garnica, O. (1973). The development of phonemic speech perception. In *Cognitive development and the acquisition of language*, (ed. T. E. Moore), pp. 215–22. Academic Press, New York.

Garrett, M. (1975). The analysis of sentence production. In *The psychology of learning and motivation*, vol. 9, (ed. G. Bower), pp. 133–77. Academic Press, New York.

Gladstone, M. and Best C. T. (1985). Developmental dyslexia: the potential role of interhemispheric collaboration in reading acquisition. In *Hemispheric function and collaboration in the child*, (ed. C. T. Best), pp. 87–118. Academic Press, New York.

Goldberg, E. and Costa, L. (1981). Hemispheric differences in the acquisition and use of descriptive systems. *Brain and Language*, **14**, 144–73.

Gregoire, A. (1937). L'apprentissage du langage: les deux premières années. Bibliothèque de la Faculté de Philosophie et Lettres, Liège.

Halverson, H. M. (1931). An experimental study of prehension in infants by means of systematic cinema records. *Genetic Psychology Monographs*, **12**, 107–285.

Harnad, S. (1982). Metaphor and mental duality. In *Language, mind, and brain*, (ed. T. W. Simon and R. J. Scholes), pp. 189–211. Lawrence Erlbaum Associates, Hillsdale, NJ.

Inhelder, B. and Piaget, J. (1955). *De la logique de l'enfant à la logique de l'adolescent*. Presses Universitaires de France, Paris.

—— and —— (1964). *The early growth of logic in the child*. Norton, New York.

Jusczyk, P. W. (1985). On characterizing the development of speech perception. In *Neonate cognition: beyond the blooming buzzing confusion*, (ed. J. Mehler and R. Fox), pp. 199–229. Lawrence Erlbaum Asociates, Hillsdale, NJ.

Kugler, P. N., Kelso, J. A. S., and Turvey, M. T. (1982). On the control and coordination of naturally developing systems. In *The development of movement control and coordination*, (ed. J. A. S. Kelso and J. E. Clarke), pp. 5–78. John Wiley, Chichester, Sussex.

Liberman, I. Y., Shankweiler, D., Fischer, F. W., and Carter, B. (1974). Reading and the awareness of linguistic segments. *Journal of Experimental Child Psychology*, **18**, 201–12.

——, ——, Liberman, A. M., Fowler, C., and Fischer, F. W. (1977). Phonetic segmentation and reading in the beginning reader. In *Toward a psychology of reading*, (ed. A. S. Reber and D. L. Scarborough), pp. 000. John Wiley, New York.

Lockman, J. J. and Ashmead, D. H. (1983). Asynchronies in the development of manual behavior. In *Advances in infancy research*, vol. 2, (ed. L. P. Lipsitt and C. K. Rovee–Collier), pp. 113–36. Ablex, Norwood, NJ.

MacKain, K. S. (1987). Filling the gap between speech and language. In *The emergent lexicon: the child's acquisition of a linguistic vocabulary*, (ed. M. D. Smith and J. L. Locke). Academic Press, New York.

MacNeilage, P. F. (1986). Bimanual coordination and the beginning of speech. In *Precursors of early speech*, (ed. B. Lindblom and R. Zetterström), pp. 189–201. Stockton Press, Oslo.

——, Studdert-Kennedy, M., and Lindblom, B. (1984). Functional precursors to language and its lateralization. *American Journal of Physiology*, **246**, (Regulatory Integrative Comp. Physiol. 15), R912–R914.

McNeill, D. (1970). *The acquisition of language: the study of developmental psycholinguistic*. Harper and Row, New York.

McShane, J. (1980). *Learning to talk*. Cambridge University Press.

Mehler, J. (1983). La connaissance avant l'apprentissage. In *Le développement dans la première année* (ed. S. de Schönen), pp. 129–55. Presses Universitaires de France, Paris.

Menyuk, P. and Menn, L. (1979). Early strategies for the perception and production of words and sounds. In *Language acquisition: studies in first language development*, (ed. P. Fletcher and M. Garman), pp. 49–70. Cambridge University Press.

Morais, J., Alegria, J., and Content, A. (1987). The relationships between segmental analysis and alphabetic literacy: an interactive view. *Cahiers de Psychologie Cognitive*, **7**, 415–38.

Mounoud, P. (1970). *Structuration de l'instrument chez l'enfant*. Delachaux and Niestlé, Paris.

—— (1973). Les conservations physiques chez le bébé. *Bulletin de Psychologie*, **312**(13–14), 722–8.

—— (1982). Psychological revolutions during childhood. In *Regressions in mental development: basic phenomena and theories;* (ed. T. G. Bever), pp. 119–31. Lawrence Erlbaum Associates, New York.

—— (1981). Cognitive development: construction of new structures or construction of internal organizations. In *New directions in piagetian theory and practice*, (ed. I. E. Sigel, D. M. Brodzinsky, and R. M. Golinkiff), pp. 99–114. Lawrence Erlbaum Associates, Hillsdale, NJ.

—— (1983). L'évolution des conduites de préhension comme illustration d'un modèle du développement. In *Le développement dans la première année*, (ed. S. de Schönen), pp. 75–106. Presses Universitaires de France, Paris.

—— (1985). Similarities between developmental sequences at different age periods. In *Stage and structure*, (ed. I. Levin), pp. 40–58. Ablex, Norwood.

—— (1986). Action and cognition. Cognitive and motor skills in a developmental perspective. In *Motor development in children*, (ed. M. G. Wade and H. T. A. Whiting), pp. 373–90. Nijhoff, Dordrecht.

—— (1987). L'utilisation du milieu et du corps propre par le bébé. In *Encyclopédie de la Pléiade. La psychologie*, (ed. J. Piaget, P. Mounoud, and J. P. Bronckart), pp. 563–601. Gallimard, Paris.

—— and Bower, T. G. R. (1974). Conservation of weight in infants. *Cognition*, **3**(1), 29–40.

—— and Hauert, C. A. (1982). Development of sensori–motor organization in young children: grasping and lifting objects. In *Action and thought: from sensori–motor schemes to symbolic operations*, (ed. G. Forman), pp. 3–35. Academic Press, New York.

—— and Vinter, A. (1981). Representation and sensori–motor development. In *Infancy and epistemology: an evaluation of Piaget's theory*, (ed. G. Butterworth), pp. 200–35. Harvester Press, Brighton, Sussex.

—— and —— (1985). Development of self-image in 3 to 11 years-old children. In *The future of Piagetian theory: the neo-Piagetians*, (ed. V. Shulman, L. C. R. Restaino, and L. Butler), pp. 37–69. Plenum Press, New York.

——, Viviani, P., Hauert, C.-A., and Guyon, J. (1985). Development of visuo–manual tracking in 5- to 9-year-old-children. *Journal of Experimental Child Psychology*, **40**, 115–32.

Piaget, J. (1952). *The origins of intelligence in children*. International University Press, New York.

—— (1978). *Success and understanding*. Routledge and Kegan Paul, Andover, Hants.

——, and Inhelder, B. (1948). La représentation de l'espace chez l'enfant. Presses Universitaires de France, Paris.

Rozin, P. and Gleitman, L. R. (1977). The structure and acquisition of reading 2: the reading process and the acquisition of the alphabetic principle. In *Toward a psychology of reading*, (ed. A. S. Reber and D. L. Scarborough), pp. 55–142. John Wiley, New York.

Sakamoto, T. and Makita, K. (1973). Japan. In *Comparative reading: cross-national studies of behavior and process in reading and writing*, (ed. J. Downing), Macmillan, New York.

Shankweiler, D. and Liberman, I. Y. (1976). *Exploring the relations between reading and speech*. Haskins Laboratories Status Report on Speech Research, SR-45/46, 1–16.

Shattuck-Hufnagel, S. (1979). Speech errors as evidence for a serial ordering mechanism in sentence production. In *Sentence processing: psycholinguistic studies presented to Merril Garrett*, (ed. W. E. Cooper and E. C. T, Walker), pp. 91–127. Lawrence Erlbaum Associates, Hillsdale, NJ.

Shvachkin, N. K. (1973). The development of phonemic speech in early childhood. In *Studies of child language development*, (ed. C. A. Ferguson and D. I. Slobin), pp. Holt, Rinehart and Winston, New York.

Stark, R. E. (1979). Prespeech segmental feature development. In *Language acquisition: studies in first language development*, (ed. P. Fletcher and M. Garman), pp. 15–32. Cambridge University Press.

Studdert-Kennedy, M. (1986). Sources of variability in early speech development. In *Invariance and variability of speech processes*, (ed. J. S. Perkell and D. H. Klatt), pp. 77–84. Lawrence Erlbaum Associates, Hillsdale, NJ.

Trevarthen, C. (1979). Communication and cooperation in early infancy: a description of primary intersubjectivity. In *Before speech: the beginning of interpersonal communication*, (ed. M. Bullowa), pp. 321–47. Cambridge University Press.

—— Hubley, P., and Sheerman, L. (1975). Les activités innées du nourrisson. *La Recherche*, **56**, 447–58.

Vinter, A. (1985). *L'imitation chez le nouveau-né*. Dalachaux et Niestlé, Paris.
—— (1986). The role of movement in eliciting early imitations. *Child Development*, **57**, 66–71.
—— (1987). Les fonctions de représentation et de communication dans les conduites sensori–motrices. In *Encyclopédie de la Pléiade. La psychologie*, (ed. J. Piaget, P. Mounoud, and J. Bronckart), pp. 417–62. Gallimard, Paris.
—— (in press). Sensory and perceptual control of action in early development. In *Perception and action relationships: current approaches*, (ed. W. Prinz and O. Neuman).
Von Hofsten, C. (1982). Eye–hand coordination in the newborn. *Development Psychology*, **18**, 450–61.
—— and Rönnqvist, L. (in press). Preparation for grasping an object: a developmental study. *Journal of Experimental Psychology*.
Vygotsky, L. S. (1962). *Thought and language*. MIT Press, Cambridge, MA.
Werker, J. F. and Tees, R. C. (1983). Developmental changes across childhood in the perception of non-native speech sounds. *Canadian Journal of Psychology*, **37**, 278–86.
Wermus, H. (1977). Essai de développement d'une prélogique à partir des foncteurs partiels. *Archives de Psychologie*, **45**, 85–100.
White, B. L., Castle, P., and Held, R. (1964). Observation on the development of visually directed reaching. *Child Development*, **35**, 349–64.
Zlatin, M. (1975). Explorative mapping of the vocal trad and primitive syllabification in infancy: the first six months. Paper presented at the American Speech and Hearing Association Convention, Washington DC, pp. 18, 20–1, 26.

3

Minds with and without language
DAVID PREMACK

Introduction

If individuals who speak different languages actually differ in how they think (Whorf's hypothesis), how great then must be the difference between a group that has language and one that does not. Does the specific grammar one acquires in learning a particular language transform one's mode of thinking? Then what of the mind that acquires no grammar at all? This difference between it and all speaking minds must be very great indeed. This issue reminds us that the comparison we should most wish to make is that between two human minds that do and do not speak. For what we really want to know is this: how much of what is unique about the human mind is owed to language?

Consider the proto-human mind before and after the addition of language. How did the addition of speech alter the existing mind? What specifically were the changes? Of course, there are no existing groups whose simple direct comparison would enable us to answer this question. Fortunately, however, we can find approximations that will give us at least a partial answer. For example, we can compare the pre- and post-language child; the deaf child and the speaking one; the chimpanzee and the young child; the chimpanzee who has and has not been language-trained. None of these comparisons is a pure case of what we are after; in each case, the linguistic factor is confounded with others. Yet the totality of these comparisons may help us to answer the general question: how does language transform a mind? In this chapter, I will concentrate on two of the possible comparisons that one can make between creatures with and without language. I shall compare chimpanzees and young children, and also chimpanzees that have and have not been taught an artificial language.

Overlapping vs concentric circles

In comparing one species with another, we encounter two opposing views and one that is intermediate. At one extreme, we can maintain that species simply cannot sensibly be compared. Each species is *sui generis*, a unique adaptation to a special niche. What sense could there be, for example, in comparing bees and beavers? On the other hand, there are obviously groups such as the primates where the species are indisputably related by both current and fossil evidence and where homologues with regard to both anatomy and behaviour are well established. For groups of this kind, we have options. A conservative one in which, for example, human, ape, and monkey intelligence is represented by overlapping circles; the intersection of each group with the other represents the elements they share, and the non-intersecting area the elements that are unique to each group. Alternatively, we can represent the intelligence of these groups with concentric circles, the human as the largest circle, the ape as a subset of the human, and the monkey as a subset of the ape. Then the ape has no elements not found in the human and the monkey no elements not found in the ape; only the human has unique elements. This is clearly the more provocative option, the one that is more challenging to maintain.

A standard view of the difference among primates is that conveyed by neoteny. The monkey enters the world with nearly all its adult brain, the chimpanzee with roughly 60 per cent, the human with less than 30 per cent. From the point of view of monkey and ape, the human neonate is a fetus and should have remained where it was until reaching more respectable adult proportions. This view emphasizes the protracted helplessness of the human infant, the long period of dependence during which the child acquires human culture.

In point of fact, the traditional neoteny ordering—monkey, ape, human—holds only for a short interval, about the first 10 months of the human infant life. In that period, quite as neoteny requires, monkey exceeds ape and ape exceeds child on virtually any measure that can be applied. Of course, these measures concern primarily sensori–motor behaviour—the ability to grasp an object, to reach for an object, to sit up unassisted, etc. (Perhaps in that early period, the 'old' or Piagetian model of ontogeny may still apply; that is, the difference between a one-, six-, and 10-month-old infant may truly be a difference in 'mental machinery', not merely a difference in knowledge as the 'new' model of ontogeny would have it.)

By the tenth or eleventh month, and ever more markedly thereafter, the human infant no longer lags the other primates, it leads them. Much of the gross sensori–motor development is complete by this time; hence we turn to more cognitive measures. Suppose, for example, we turn to the social gesture of pointing. We note that an 11-month-old human infant, sitting in the living room with his grandfather, startled by the sudden closing of the kitchen door—cutting off the infant's view of his mother—points alarmedly in the direction of the kitchen, maintaining eye contact with the grandfather while doing so. And we wait in vain for pointing to emerge in the non-human primates. The chimpanzee, unless specially trained, does not point; it comprehends pointing (looking not at the end of the finger but at its trajectory) but does not produce pointing (cf. Woodruff and Premack 1979). Does the monkey even comprehend pointing?

Far from being a misleading example, pointing is a harbinger of all the differences to come. Cognitive differences among the three primates soon become so marked that we can no longer compare the three groups as we did earlier. Most of the competences the child achieves spontaneously never appear in the ape or monkey at all. Hence we can continue the comparison only by changing the question: Which of the child's spontaneous competences can be 'brought out' by special training in the ape or monkey?

Consider, for example, the various ways in which the child's spontaneous behaviour gives evidence of the type-token distinction. Most of the child's achievements are so well known, I mention them only to emphasize that virtually none of them appear in the ape. For instance, the child separates, say, red blocks from green ones (neglecting the green ones at this early stage), though slightly later separating both, red tokens in one pile, green ones in another. Spatial sorting is never seen in the ape (not even the weak form). The ape shows only temporal sorting, picking up like objects consecutively, a form that appears earlier in the child, some weeks in advance of spatial sorting. In reaching only to temporal sorting, the ape resembles certain retarded children (Down's syndrome) who themselves resemble the normal child at an earlier stage of development. Whereas the ape never spontaneously carries out a single act in which it manipulates the spatial distribution of physical similarity, sorting is only the first of many such operations in the child. Later, rather than separating the blocks into piles, the child makes a 'line' of the red ones and then places one green one into coincidence with each red one. In thus carrying out one–one correspondence, the child does not abandon the earlier dispositions. For instance, the blocks it arranges into a line, rather than being a mixture of red and green, are all red, and thus are an instance of spatial sorting, even as picking them up consecutively is an instance of temporal sorting. Complex skills, ever being added in the normal child, do not eliminate simpler ones, but are interwoven. We see little such interweaving in the ape.

Match to sample

Though the ape does not spontaneously group like items, it can be taught to do so. Given an object as a sample, two or more alternatives, one like the sample (in any of indeterminately many respects), the ape can be taught to put the two like items together. We compared 18-month-old human and ape infants on this task, training them in an identical fashion. The humans reached criterion in an average of eight trials, the apes in 800. The difference is foreshadowed, of course, in the spontaneous behaviour of the two species. (Indeed, that the child required eight trials to reach criterion is a comment on our ineptitude; arranging a smoother transition between what we require of the child and what it does naturally should eliminate all errors.)

Despite the contrast between the child's instant success and the ape's belaboured one, once the two species reached criterion they performed equally well on new items. Both showed perfect transfer, the apes preserving their 85 per cent correct training level on all new items, the children their 98 per cent correct training level. The transfer was of special interest because both groups were deliberately trained on a narrow inductive base. Only two objects had been used, a cup and a lock (so that on all trials, either cup or lock was sample, cup and lock the alternatives). Yet when tested on new items—foods, swatches of cloth, plastic objects—both children and apes showed perfect transfer; i.e. preserved their training levels (Oden *et al.* in press). Does this mean that extensive training brought the chimpanzee to the child's level so that the transfer capacities of the two species are now equal? In fact, only a relatively slight change will disclose that the transfer capacities are not equal.

The results from the transfer tests suggested that both species had learned the same rule: 'Put like items together'. The question is, however, what constitutes an 'item'? Notice that all the items used in the transfer tests are objects, more than that, normal objects. Thus, we had two alternatives, either to shifts from *object* to *event* (which would require a modality change, e.g. vision to audition) or from normal to non-normal object (which would not require a modality change). We elected to try the latter, and we did so by physically changing the normal make-up of the objects.

In one approach, we mutilated normal objects, e.g. squashed them in a vice, cut them in various ways, etc. In another, we formed non-normal objects, not by mutilating but by combining normal ones. After first collecting a set of normal objects (for which both species showed perfect transfer) we arbitrarily divided them into 'small' and 'large' objects, and then glued one small object to the top of each large one. With the new objects produced in this way—a–B, c–D, f–G, . . . , etc.—we then carried out ordinary match to sample, e.g. a–B appeared as the sample, a–B and c–D as the alternatives.

On this case and all others, the children performed exactly as they had on normal objects: about 98 per cent correct. But the apes did not. They suffered a 20–40 per cent loss, depending on the case. The loss was temporary; after being restored to criterion (in form 20 to 100 training trials) they then passed the very first transfer test, one based, of course, on new non-normal objects produced by exactly the same distortion procedure (Premack, Oden, and Durlach, unpublished data).

I call these changes distortions to distinguish them from transformations, such as a change in orientation (A–$\succ$) or a change in size (A–A). Transformations (unlike distortions) do not violate the normal character of an object: a rotated or miniaturized object is still a normal object. In testimonial of this difference, apes were no more impaired by the two transformations we studied than were the children. Both groups performed perfectly. In sum, the child's response to the distorted objects showed that it is a more powerful perceptual system than the ape. The child detects the equivalence of distorted objects as accurately as that of normal ones. The ape, in contrast, is temporarily derailed by the non-normal object; it cannot detect equivalence in this case, and requires some number of trials to develop a new subroutine, one for every new distortion (to be sure, we did not discover any distortions for which the ape was incapable of developing a subroutine, though we did not press the issue). Although transformations are not sufficiently 'strong' to distinguish ape from child—and we had to resort to distortions—transformations are evidently sufficiently strong to differentiate less-related groups, e.g. primates from pigeons. Cerella (1977) found that pigeons failed both the transformations mentioned here, rotation and change in size. The perceptual power of a species, is, I think an important albeit neglected, aspect of its intelligence; I will return to this issue in a later section.

Picture–object

Further evidence of the child's cognitive advantage is shown in the matching of objects to their two-dimensional representations. Children of 18 months require no training to match objects to their photographs (e.g. Hochberg 1980), whereas apes of the same age fail even after prolonged training. The normal test offers, say, a banana as sample, pictures of banana and of apple as alternatives (or picture of banana as sample, apple and banana as alternatives). A more interesting test can be arranged by putting certain dispositions into competition. Let us give, say, banana as sample, picture of banana and an actual shoe as alternatives (or picture of banana as sample, banana and picture of shoe as alternatives). When tested in this manner, the ape matches banana to shoe, and picture of banana to picture of shoe. The conventional test teaches us only that apes are unable to match pictures and objects; the unconventional one tells us something more interesting. The similarity the ape finds between two objects (or two photographs)—*any* two objects (or photographs)—is greater than the similarity it finds between an object and its photograph. Is this so bizarre a condition that we shall never find it in the child? Were it so, we would refute the model of concentric circles, for that model requires the ape to have no unique elements, neither strengths nor weaknesses.

Because children readily pass the conventional test, we typically do not give them the unconventional one—and in this way we miss the interesting fact that children, when young enough (12 to 18 months) display the same 'weakness' as the ape. When given the unconventional test, young children too match object with object and (to a lesser extent) photograph with photograph. They do so only briefly, however, sometimes only for the duration of a 16-trial session. Nevertheless, the comparison is a representative one. All the 'weaknesses' we have so far found in the chimpanzee can also be found in the normal child, albeit in lesser degree, simply by reducing the age of the child; the 'weaknesses' can also be found in retarded children. In strikingly many cases, apes and children appear to pass through similar stages—the ape later than the child on cognitive measures (reverse neoteny); in addition the ape resembles the retarded child in the sense of aborted development.

The measures we have considered so far concern operations on physical similarity, some gross some subtle, but always physical similarity. We can add to this conclusion in a simple way. Suppose we highlight one object such as an apple, and then offer the child an array of alternatives, e.g. another apple, a patch of red, an orange, a shoe, etc. If we allow the child to examine the highlighted object and then choose freely among the alternatives, we have only to record the *order* of his choices to discover that the child has a preferred mode of operation, one that changes over age. The young child (two to three) is preoccupied with identity; he will choose first the apple, then the red patch, next the orange, and last the shoe. When slightly older, however, the red patch will supplant the apple, the orange and shoe remaining the same. Now the featural match takes priority over simple identity. And perhaps in a somewhat older child, the orange will make its 'move', supplanting the red patch, category membership taking priority over featural matching. The details are less important than the general argument. Identity, featural matching, category membership are all variants of physical similarity: the child is a specialist in this dimension. A natural specialist, for only laborious training brings the ape to a point even remotely comparable to the spontaneous achievements of the pre-language child. Some of the earliest evidence for the biological separation of the two species thus lies in the child's mastery of physical similarity.

We can easily picture, however, a species more evolved than our own. The children of this species would commence like human children, manipulating varieties of physical similarity in increasingly subtle ways. But then they would move on to yet another level of equivalence. After putting, say, two red blocks together and two green blocks, they would then put together the two cases of *same*, the two red blocks with the two green ones. Or after putting together a red block and a green one, as well as a square one and a round one, they would then put together these two cases of *different*. The equivalences here are not those of physical similarity. Two red blocks do not look like two green ones in the simple sense in which one red block looks like another, one square looks like another, etc. The equivalence is not one between objects but between relations. In a species more evolved than our own, the children would move spontaneously from similarity beween objects to relations between relations. But this transition is not maturational in the human child; it occurs only as the product of pedagogy, after the child has attended school. A transition that could have been brought about by biological evolution has been achieved instead by cultural evolution.

For all of the child's advantage in physical similarity, as regards conceptual equivalence (relations between relations), child and ape are essentially in the same boat. Neither species makes such computations spontaneously, the child no more than the ape. School brings such computations out in the child. And, as we shall see, school has a similar effect on the ape. By 'school' I mean, in the case of the ape, dogged drill on each of the exercises (which is not what we mean by 'school' in the case of the child). Interestingly, there is a second way in which to teach the ape conceptual equivalence. This is not by dogged drill on each exercise, but by teaching the ape language.

Effect of language training

We began comparing apes and children in 1969 with the attempt to teach language to an ape. After training three animals, we found that, while the ape acquired far more than we had thought possible, the ape's system shows no evidence of grammatical (as opposed to semantic) classes, recursion, or structure-dependent rules. The ape cannot be a significant drawing board for the study of human language. This does not dash the comparative programme, however. From about 1974 on we turned to the study of non-language competence; e.g. 'theory of mind', analogies, mental representation, and the like.

In the course of general cognitive testing, we found that language- and non-language-trained animals differed; the former had an advantage over the latter on certain kinds of tests (and not on others). This serendipitous finding made it advisable to return to language training (LT), not for purposes of studying language, but to study the possible secondary benefits of such training. Specifically, we needed a formal comparison, one that would establish three points. *First*, was the apparent effect genuine? *Second*, if it was, what was the nature of the benefit—how do the tasks that profit differ from those that do not? *Third*, LT is a highly heterogeneous procedure; what part of it is vital?

To prepare for the formal comparison we arranged two sets of tasks, one which LT did, and another which it did not, appear to benefit. The underlying theme of the former or diagnostic set was conceptual equivalence (as opposed to physical similarity). The non-diagnostic set, tasks which LT did not benefit, included spatial inferences of several kinds and various tests of 'natural reasoning' (Premack 1983). The point was to compare LT and non-LT apes on the two sets: if LT conferred an advantage, the animals should differ on the one set but not on the other. How should we make the comparison?

Given only four animals (each of which costs thousands of dollars), it was not sensible to train two, not train the other two, and then compare the two groups. This is not only a dubious comparison but also one that is extraordinarily wasteful of resources. Instead we trained all four animals but trained one group ahead of the other. Moreover, we fist divided LT into four steps, brought the lead group to criterion on step one and then tested both the lead and lag groups on the diagnostic and non-diagnostic tasks. Next we brought the lag group to criterion on step one, repeated the testing, and proceeded in this manner through the four steps of LT. The four steps into which we divided LT were: lexicon, 'sentences', the words same/different, and competence in the interrogative.

Our main findings are these. *First*, LT does confer an advantage. The strongest example is the analogy test where the LT animal has a definite edge. *Second*, but it is not the first two steps of LT—lexicon and 'sentences'—that confer the advantage. Rather, it is the introduction of the plastic words 'same/different'. *Third*, although LT is a sufficient condition for passing the diagnostic set, it is not a necessary one. The animal can be taught at least some members of the set simply by dogged training (Premack, unpublished data).

The effect of LT on analogies was established by using a strictly non-verbal format so that both groups could be tested. Four plates were arranged in an analogical format, one item was placed in each of three plates, and the animal was required to fill in the fourth plate from the two alternatives given it, i.e.

Alternatives: B',C

The possible use of similarity was definitively ruled out: both the correct (B') and incorrect alternative (C) differed from B by one transformation, A by two transformations, while B' differed from A' by three transformations and C by only one transformation. Hence, if an animal were to choose between the alternatives on the basis of their similarity to the elements in the analogy—taken either singly or in any combination—it would perform at chance level. In fact, the lead group passed at a high level (90 to 95 per cent correct) whereas the lag group performed at chance level (Matsuzawa and Premack, unpublished data). The success of the two lead animals was especially gratifying because, prior to these tests, Sarah was the only animal to have done analogies.

That the introduction of 'same/different' proves the vital step is an interesting finding not only because these words do not appear in the analogy test but, more important, the words same/different (as we used them) referred only to physical similarity, e.g. two apples were called 'same', a banana and an apple 'different'. Nevertheless, labelling the sameness and differences of (mere) *objects* enabled the animals to deal with the sameness and difference of *relations*. Although steps one and two of LT do not themselves enable the animal to do analogies, they may be an indirect prerequisite. The ape has difficulty acquiring its first words (even when they are names of objects) and probably could not acquire same/different as first words.

Even the words same/different can be omitted if the animal is given prolonged training on each of the tasks. For instance, if given repeated match-to-sample trials on like proportions of different objects (e.g. 1/4 apple to 1/4 glass of water), hundreds of such trials over a period of one to three years, it will gradually improve, finally reaching a criterion of 80 per cent correct or better and passing transfer tests. The dogged training is of special interest for two reasons. First, the success that it confers on one task in the set does not transfer to any other member of the set (whereas LT facilitates all members of the set). Second, the training involves no differential feedback—the animal is praised for all choices, incorrect as well as correct. Consider that members of the diagnostic set differ from the ordinary tasks given animals—e.g. if the light is red, turn right; if green, turn left—in that they all have intrinsic right answers. For instance, AA does match BB (not CD), EF does match GH (not LL); $\frac{1}{2}$ apple does match $\frac{1}{2}$ glass of water (not $\frac{1}{4}$ glass), etc. The ape can detect conceptual equivalence without benefit of feedback; indeed, comparison of trials with and without feedback (in an ABBA design) shows that feedback confers no advantage.

'Advanced cognition'

In this section I turn to three more advanced topics of cognition—metacognition, mental representation, and level of analysis—and ask whether the functions that each involve depend on language. In metacognition, the individual gains access to some aspect of his own performance so that where formerly he processed only the outside world he now in addition processes his own performance. Does this depend on language? In considering mental representation, we are surprised to find the ape engaging in mental operations that appear to make the use of imaginal strategies wholly inadequate. Does this imply that the ape must therefore have internal representation of a language-like form? Yes, provided there are only two alternatives: internal representation that is either word-like or image-like. But, as we shall see, the work suggests that there are other alternatives. In the final topic, levels of analysis, I have in mind some issues that have yet to achieve traditional status. When humans examine scenes, they ask questions about them that move from superficial to deep. Superficial or outside questions naturally concern appearance; e.g. the type of house, whether the garden is lush or thin, whether the cherries are ripe, etc. Deep or inside questions concern plans, intentions, motivation, e.g. Why does the individual garden during the worst heat of the day? Why was so lavish a house built so close to the road? etc. What is interesting about such questions, about the human ability to ask them, is not only the rich social attribution that they presuppose, but even more the flexibility that enables the human to move from one level of analysis to another. Does this flexibility depend on language?

Metacognition

In a traditional approach to metacognition, we have asked: When an ape performs well on a test, does it understand the conditions upon which its success depends? If we were to degrade those conditions, would the animal simply fail or would it take steps to overcome our interference and restore the required conditions?

A simple way of addressing this question was presented recently by four young apes who were at an early stage of LT, acquiring 'words'. All four had learned not simply to rush into the room but to look at the plastic word the trainer placed on the writing board before setting out to find the object (one of four) that corresponded to the word. At this early stage of training, the animals returned with the correct object about 70 to 80 per cent of the time. Did they understand the basis of their success?

We arranged probe trials, interspersed between regular ones, on which the trainer no longer presented the plastic word in the usual way. She greatly reduced the visibility of the word, turning the writing board either 90° (so the word faced to the side) or 180° (so that the word faced into her chest and could not be seen at all). One animal was visibly disturbed by the change: he whimpered and fussed. But he did not appear to understand the source of his disturbance, and did nothing to rectify the situation. Two other animals, showing no upset of any kind, immediately rectified the situation either in whole or in part. One animal grasped the board and pulled it into its proper position. The other animal, rather than touching the board, changed her own position, adopting a novel posture to see the turned board and peeking over the top for a glimpse of the concealed word. The fourth animal was neither disturbed by the change nor took any steps to restore the impaired visibility of the word. She went into the room as she did on any other trial and chose among the four objects as though she knew which was correct; of course, she performed at chance level. Interestingly, we found no relation between the animal's accuracy on the vocabulary problem and its behaviour on probe trials. For example, the animal who showed neither upset nor corrective behaviour on probe trials was tied for the best performance on the vocabulary problem.

A second form of metacognition lies in the individual's ability to judge the accuracy of his own performance. After sufficient experience with a set of problems, he should no longer need the trainer's feedback to tell him when he was correct; he should be able to make the judgement himself. With increased self-knowledge, he should be able to anticipate his success. Simply examining a problem should enable him to predict whether or not he could do it.

All of our attempts to find evidence for this type of competence in Sarah have gone unanswered. For example, when offered a choice between doing an easy or a difficult problem, Sarah failed to demonstrate a consistent preference for the easy problem. Similarly, when offered the opportunity to escape doing either a difficult or even an unsolvable problem simply by meeting a time criterion, she failed to consistently meet the criterion.

We were therefore surprised by recent positive evidence that emerged from an experiment not explicitly designed to produce such evidence. Years earlier Sarah had successfully completed incomplete analogies (Gillan *et al.* 1981); more recently she was given the task of constructing them from scratch (Oden and Premack, in preparation). She was given either four or five elements, a different set on each trial, along with the analogy board, and praised for whatever she did. Unlike younger animals who simply play with the elements, Sarah used them properly, arranging them on the board. Her arrangements resulted in analogies significantly more often than chance; e.g. chance level for the four-element case is 33 per cent, and she performed at the 58 per cent level ($p < 0.05$). More important for our present purposes, she sometimes 'edited' or corrected earlier arrangements of the board before going on to complete the analogy. In going over the video-tapes, Oden found that she made 15 such changes in 240 trials. For instance, on one occasion she has made an A/B arrangement and then placed B′ adjacent to A in the same row on the board. This arrangement blocked the possibility of an analogy; there is no way a fourth element could be successfully added. After examining the board, Sarah moved B′, placing it adjacent to B, and then completed the analogy. While she made relatively few such changes—leaving many erroneous cases uncorrected—11 of her 15 corrections were correct. Moreover, on 14 of the 15 cases, she was well advised to make the change. An analogy could not have been formed had she left the elements as they were.

Using proportions to study internal representation

In a conference devoted to thought without language the nature of internal representation in the ape, a languageless animal, is of special interest. Is the ape's internal representation either word-like or image-like, or are there preferable alternatives, closer perhaps to the patterns of interconnections among elements in connectionist models? Questions of this kind, concerning specifically the form of the ape's internal representation, may be not merely difficult but impossible to answer (Anderson 1978). Fortunately, our aim is more modest. We shall consider the form of the ape's internal representation only in so far as it is implicated by the functional capacity of the system. I shall describe some recent work showing that the functions the ape can compute are rather more powerful than we had anticipated. To be sure, surprises of this kind are becoming ever more commonplace; evidently we poorly estimated animal capacity in the first place. However, in the present case the accomplishment may seem surprising even to the most jaded.

The work concerns the ape's ability to make judgements about proportions.

The ape's ability to carry out this task was extended by teaching it language, as already noted. The non-language-trained ape readily matched, say, $\frac{1}{4}$ apple to $\frac{1}{4}$ apple (or $\frac{1}{4}$ bottle of water to $\frac{1}{4}$ bottle of water); but the language-trained ape also matched $\frac{1}{4}$ apple to $\frac{1}{4}$ bottle of water (Woodruff and Premack 1981), a form of non-sensory or conceptual matching which the non-language-trained ape failed (Premack 1983). Although this is the first (and weakest) of the three steps making up the present demonstration, it already raises questions concerning internal representation. Comparing physically like objects poses no problem; but how does an animal manage to compare the proportions $\frac{1}{4}$, $\frac{1}{2}$, $\frac{3}{4}$, and 1 when they are instantiated by different objects (somehow the animal is able to compare apples and onions!)? The question is raised still more forcibly by the next step.

In the second step we expanded on what was presented in the sample, no longer limiting it to one item. Now we gave samples consisting of two (e.g. $\frac{1}{4}$ and $\frac{1}{2}$ apple), three (e.g. $\frac{1}{4}$, $\frac{1}{4}$, and $\frac{1}{4}$ apple) or even four objects (e.g. $\frac{1}{4}$, $\frac{1}{4}$, $\frac{1}{4}$, and $\frac{1}{4}$ apple), requiring the animal to match the 'sum' of the sample with the corresponding proportion. Moreover, we retained the practise of using different objects as samples and alternatives. For example, on a representative trial, the sample consisted of $\frac{1}{4}$ and $\frac{1}{2}$ apple; the alternatives of $\frac{3}{4}$ and $\frac{1}{4}$ bottle of water on some trials ($\frac{3}{4}$ and $\frac{1}{2}$ bottle on others). There are a total of six possible ways in which to combine the proportions $\frac{1}{4}$, $\frac{1}{2}$, and $\frac{3}{4}$ so that their sum does not exceed one; three consist of two items, and two others of three and four items respectively. We gave the animal all possible permutations of these six combinations, varying the objects that were used as sample and as alternatives. We used two natural objects, apples and potatoes, and two unnatural ones, bottles of coloured fluid and wooden discs milled in the instrument shop. Sometimes we placed the objects in the sample adjacent to one another, other times as much as three inches apart.

An important control we observed was to equate the surface area or volume of the two objects that served as alternatives on any trial. The equating was exact in the case of the unnatural objects, approximate in the case of the natural ones. For example, we equated the alternatives $\frac{3}{4}$ and $\frac{1}{4}$ apple by using an appropriately larger apple to produce $\frac{1}{4}$ than to produce $\frac{3}{4}$. The discs were constructed according to formula so that every proportion in the set was exactly the same volume or surface area. Finally, we used non-differential feedback throughout, i.e. the animal was praised for incorrect and correct responses alike, and was given a small portion of food at the end of the test session.

All three juveniles passed all of the tests given them, one combination of objects as readily as the other. Moreover, they were successful from the beginning, performing as well on the first test in the series as on the last. Items placed three inches apart in the sample were 'summed' as accurately as those placed next to each other. Tests in which the bottle appeared were not performed more accurately than others, although one might suppose they would be. Even when the bottle is only partly filled, one can always see the whole bottle, whereas when given part of an apple, potato, or disc, in order to determine the proportion represented by the part one must somehow picture or reconstruct the whole object. Nevertheless, bottles were not judged more accurately than other objects.

In the third and final step, we continued the practice of giving multiple-object samples, but now the objects in the sample were no longer of the same kind. In other words, we eliminated yet another constraint on the test procedure, moving from the homogeneous to the heterogeneous sample. For example, the sample might consist of $\frac{1}{4}$ apple and $\frac{1}{2}$ bottle of liquid; or $\frac{1}{4}$ apple, $\frac{1}{4}$ bottle, $\frac{1}{4}$ apple, $\frac{1}{4}$ bottle; etc. In all cases, the alternatives consisted of yet a third object, e.g. $\frac{3}{4}$ and $\frac{1}{4}$ disc in the first example, $\frac{1}{4}$ and one disc in the second. Now the animal was required not only to combine proportions but proportions of different objects. Combining $\frac{1}{2}$ apple with $\frac{1}{2}$ apple may no longer seem so difficult (now that we know the animal can do it). But combining $\frac{1}{2}$ apple with $\frac{1}{2}$-filled bottle seems quite another matter. For example, if the object we 'see' when combining $\frac{1}{2}$ apple with $\frac{1}{2}$ apple is a whole apple, what is the object we 'see' when combining $\frac{1}{2}$ apple with $\frac{1}{2}$-filled bottle?

No doubt the animals, too, found this a puzzling question, for on the first session (16 trials) of this new kind they all fell to chance level. However, they recovered by the second session—despite the absence of differential feedback—and thereafter performed at about the 85 per cent correct level, the same level of accuracy as on the earlier phases of the test. In this series, we confined the objects in the sample to combinations of apple and bottle, using the discs as alternatives. Of the permutations afforded by the four values of proportion, the two objects, the two positions, we gave 64, counterbalanced for number, position, etc. over the course of four 16-trial sessions. Two of three animals performed consistently over the four sessions; the third, our one male subject, was less consistent, though he too performed well above chance level ($p < 0.01$) on the whole.

How does the animal combine the separate pieces in the sample? If we consider only the homogeneous sample (step two), we may be led to suppose that the animal uses an imaginal strategy, mentally 'moving' one piece into alignment with another just as one would physically move the actual pieces into alignment with one's hand. However, in the case of the heterogeneous sample, this imaginal strategy would produce 'monsters', e.g. $\frac{1}{4}$ apple 'appended' to a bottle $\frac{1}{4}$-filled, and would be of no use. Moreover, notice that the imaginal strategy, even when applied to the homogeneous case, would not solve the animal's problem, but only delay its solution. For after producing, say, $\frac{3}{4}$ apple by mentally combining $\frac{1}{2}$ and $\frac{1}{4}$ apple, the $\frac{3}{4}$ apple must be converted to a more abstract representation such that it could be compared with the $\frac{3}{4}$ disc. Since a conversion to abstract representation must take place at some point, perhaps the animal makes the conversion 'early', *before* it combines the pieces (and thus combines not physical pieces but their abstract representations). This view is compatible with the finding that pieces separated by three inches were combined as accurately as adjacent pieces.

What could the 'abstract representation', which we have been discussing, consist of? Relative area or volume seem the most plausible candidates. Either of these measures would seem highly suitable for such objects as bottle where the whole object or its frame is always present. With objects of this kind, the part/whole ratio defining either relative area or relative volume could be interpreted as a directly perceivable Gibson-type property (1966). There is, however, a large class of objects to which this proposal would not apply. These are all those objects like apple, potato and disc where, for proportions less than one, there is no frame or outline of the whole object. In such cases, the part/whole ratio could not be perceived directly; the whole would somehow have to be computed before the ratio could be perceived.

How able is the chimpanzee to compute the whole of an object from its part? The chimpanzee must have some ability of this kind, for without such ability it is not clear how it could have solved the present problems. Projecting the whole of an object from a segment is part of the subject matter of group theory (Warren and Shaw 1984), the theory that deals with predicting the 'visible from the invisible', the unseen back from the front, one side from another, the top from the bottom, etc. The ability to make projections of this kind is, I think, an important aspect of intelligence, though unfortunately a largely neglected one. It will be important for the sake of more adequate theories of intelligence, both ontogenetic and phylogenetic, to correct this neglect.

Levels of analysis

When a human looks at a scene, he can ask questions about the scene at a number of levels. For example, in looking at a scene he may detect a problem, and then ask: What caused the problem? as well as: What might solve the problem? If we doubt that the individual is really asking questions of *cause* and *solution*, we can ask a control question: 'Tell me, what is neither cause nor solution (of the problem) but merely an associate (a more or less accidental associate)?' That humans analyse scenes in this fashion, raising questions that concern both past (What caused the problem?) and future (How can the problem be solved?) is beyond doubt. What is in doubt is whether non-humans also make analyses of this kind.

Fortunately, to determine whether non-humans are capable of analysing scenes in a similar fashion we require neither a language-trained animal nor scenes of great complexity. For example, we can show an ape a video-tape no more complex than this: a human actor discovers a small fire of paper burning on the floor; he looks concerned, intent on putting the fire out. By a procedure that I will describe in a moment, we ask the ape: What could cause the fire? What could put it out? What is neither cause nor solution but merely an associate of the fire? If the ape can answer this triplet of questions for the present scene and others like it, we can conclude that the animal resembles the human in the important sense of making causal analyses of what it sees.

To interrogate both children and apes in a non-verbal manner we associate a distinctive marker with each of the intended questions (basically by associating the marker with a set of alternatives that could constitute an answer to the question). The procedure can be used in a number of settings, some simpler than others. Consider the setting in which the procedure was first introduced to Sarah. We were concerned with the basic thematic concepts of actor, object, and instrument of the action, and whether the ape observes these distinctions. To find out, we showed Sarah video-tapes of simple actions, and required her to identify examples of the thematic concepts in each of them. For instance, one video-tape showed Henry cutting an orange, another Bill painting a fence, yet another John washing an apple. Sarah was given different pieces of sticky paper, and trained to apply them to the TV monitor—the red pieces to Henry, Bill, John (agents of the action); green pieces to orange, fence, apple (objects of the action); and blue pieces to knife, brush, water (instruments of the action). Transfer tests then established whether or not Sarah had associated the three markers with the proper referents and thus whether the markers served to ask the intended questions: Who is the agent? What is the object? (on which he is acting?) What is the instrument he is using? Sarah was generally successful in answering the questions posed by the three markers (Premack 1986).

The procedure is similar in the case of the causal analysis and the distinctions between *cause*, *solution*, and (mere) *associate*. For instance, when shown the video-tape of the small fire, she is presented with a red square accompanied by photographs of three alternatives: (matches, knife, clay); a green triangle accompanied by photographs of three alternatives (water, Scotch tape, eraser); and a blue circle with three alternatives (pencil, apple, blanket). She is trained to choose matches (possible cause) in the case of the red square, water (possible solution) for the green triangle, and pencil (actual associate) for the blue circle. Matches can cause fire, water can put it out, and pencil which is neither a possible cause nor solution is an actual associate in that Sarah has often scribbled on paper (the material of the fire) with a pencil. After being trained in this fashion, she was given transfer tests to determine whether or not she had formed the desired associations. She was unsuccessful on our first attempt and we have not yet made a second. Unfortunately, we have not yet applied the procedure to children either, and therefore cannot properly assess the difficulty of the task. Is it one that even a four-year-old child would fail? If so, then Sarah's failure would be no surprise.

That children may succeed where Sarah failed is suggested by the results for another task which is similar to though simpler than the preceding one. Here the child (and Sarah) were again shown a simple video-tape, e.g. a human actor jumping up and down (presumably) to obtain bananas out of reach overhead, and asked this trio of questions: What does the actor look like? What is he doing? Why is he doing it? Here too a distinctive marker identified each question. To introduce the most superficial question ('What does he look like?' —specifically 'What is the actor's shirt pattern?' we presented a red square accompanied by three photographs of coloured patterns (one like the actor's shirt). To establish the behavioural question. 'What is the actor doing?'), we presented a blue triangle accompanied by three photographs of different actions (a man jumping, washing, and cutting); and to introduce the question concerning intentions '(Why is he doing it?), we presented a green circle accompanied by three photographs showing possible solutions to the problem—a man stepping up onto a chair, reaching out with a stick, etc.

After the children succeeded on the individual questions they were advanced to pairs of questions, and finally to the grand assembly of individual materials: three markers and six alternatives presented together in the presence of new video-tapes. Five-and-a-half- to six-year-old children, including retarded ones (Down's syndrome), were remarkably successful (confirming that the difficulty of a visual problem can seldom be conveyed by verbal description). There was an interesting difference between the order in which the normal and retarded children answered the three questions. Although in all children the predominant order of answering was shirt pattern, action, intention, this order was exaggerated in the retarded children. For example, only 6 per cent of the retarded children answered the question of intention first, 12 per cent of the normal children; conversely, 75 per cent of the retarded children answered the superficial (shirt pattern) question first, only 56 per cent of the normal children ($p < 0.01$). Sarah did not enjoy the children's success on this level of analysis, though her testing is preliminary and needs to be repeated.

Why did Sarah fail on this problem when she succeeded on another one that is in many respects comparable? In the successful paradigm Sarah was given objects in an intact and transformed state and required to choose from a set of alternatives the instrument that could account for the transformation. For instance, she was given an intact apple and a cut one, along with the alternatives knife, water, pencil, and required to choose the knife. Her impressive performance on problems of this kind (both when the object–instrument pairs were novel and even anomalous, e.g. severed ping-pong balls, apples that were written on, etc.) (Premack 1976) shows that she can recognize, in an essentially arbitrary sequence of objects, a representation of action, and answer the question: What caused this? She was, moreover, no less adept at handling cases where the change was in the opposite direction, i.e. the object was not deflected from base but rather returned to it. For instance, when given paper-cut paper, she chose scissors; but when given the reverse, cut paper-paper, she chose Scotch tape. These results indicate not only that she could take order of the sequence into account but, more important for present purposes, that she could handle both cause and solution. For if we treat the deflection of an object from base as an example of cause of a problem, we may reasonably treat its restoration as an example of the solution of a problem. Why was she consummately successful in handling cause/solution in the one paradigm and thoroughly unsuccessful in the other?

The paradigms differ immensely in their difficulty. In the easy case she is given a concrete example of a change and required to do no more than select the instrument that could account for it. In the difficult case, she is given a condition, such as the burning paper, that represents a moment in time, and asked to picture, on the one hand, how the condition might have been caused, and, on the other, how it might be corrected. In effect, she must imagine a condition that preceded the one she is shown, e.g. paper that is not yet on fire, and choose an instrument such as matches that could change the imagined condition into the one she is shown. Similarly, she must picture the future, the condition that lies on the 'other side' of the one she is shown, the extinguished fire, and again chose an instrument such as water that could change the imagined condition into the one she is shown.

The causality or action paradigm is vastly simpler: it does not require her to imagine anything. She has only to choose an instrument that could causally link two objects, both of which are shown to her. That she can do quite nicely. What she evidently cannot do is imagine conditions that come before and after the one she is shown. Children of five to six can do this, I believe; pilot data suggest they can, though we have yet to make the full-scale study.

Notice that the non-verbal approach to interrogation used in the difficult paradigm is not one that makes the question explicit. On the contrary, the question is left altogether implicit and the individual must discover it for himself. While looking both at the scene and at the alternatives, he must ask himself: what is the question for which one of these alternatives could be an answer? For what question about burning paper could matches be an answer? For what question could water be an answer? Could pencil be an answer? The individual is given no guidance except the scene and the alternatives, and must discover the question himself. Sarah evidently cannot; perhaps children can.

The cause/solution/associate test is also appreciably more difficult than the description/behaviour/intention test. In the latter, two of the three alternatives can be chosen merely by matching them with some aspect of the video-tape: the coloured pattern with the actor's shirt, the act of jumping with the actor's behaviour. It is only the inferential question, the actor's intention, that cannot be answered in this simple manner. Stepping up onto a chair, for example, does not appear in the video-tape, and must be chosen on a more inferential basis. The greater difficulty of this question is reflected in the comparison between the normal, and the Down's syndrome children: the latter pass the first two question but largely fail on the last one.

Conclusions

1. The consequences of teaching language to an ape are based neither on a deep change, such as a change in internal representation, nor strictly speaking on the language *per se*. Rather, the advantage is conferred simply by teaching the words 'same/different'. These words evidently call the ape's attention to the distinction, increasing its awareness of the distinction and thus its ability to use it. The distinction itself, however, is one the ape can recognize without any training. This is shown by at least two factors. First, habituation procedures with 18-month-old infant apes establish that the ape can detect not only the sameness/difference of objects but also of relations (e.g. not only the sameness of A to A, but also that of AA to BB, CD to EF); however, it cannot make instrumental use of the sameness/difference of relations (e.g. though it can match A to A, it cannot match AA to BB or CD to EF) (Premack, Oden, and Durlach, unpublished data). Second, the ape can be taught to make instrumental use of the sameness/difference of relations simply by dogged training, without differential feedback.

2. How do the words 'same/different' contribute to the ape's success with analogies? Though used only to refer to physical similarity between objects, the words none the less enable the ape to make the judgements about the relation between the relations. We can understand this effect if we assume that the animal can recognize the analogy between the sameness/difference of objects, on the one hand, and that of relations, on the other. That is, evidently the animal can recognize:

$$(A/A' \text{ same } B/B') \text{ SAME } (CC/DD \text{ same } EE/FF),$$

i.e. analogies based on objects are the same as those based on relations. An individual who could recognize this simple identity would be close to using analogies in the manner claimed for the human adult (e.g. mapping one model of the world onto another model) and would have the potential at least for the recursive use of analogies. The same assumption will account for a similar outcome in the child, viz. the beneficial effect that the use of language has on the child's ability to do conceptual matching. The normal four- to five-year-old child fails conceptual matching just as does the ape. Moreover, differential feedback—corrections for putting CD with AA, EF with BB— helps the child no more than it does the ape. Yet we can alleviate the child's problem in a moment, simply by telling him that AA is a case of 'same', CD a case of 'different'; he succeeds immediately and goes on to pass transfer tests like a college sophomore. The child's success can be understood in the same terms as the ape's. Though the child too uses 'same/different' to refer only to the physical similarity of objects, he too grasps the analogy between sameness/difference of objects and of relations.

3. The human infant is a specialist in physical similarity, spontaneously matching like objects in an impressive variety of ways, greatly exceeding the ape whose spontaneous behaviour of this kind is limited to mere temporal sorting. Yet the human infant does not show a comparable superiority over the ape in computing conceptual equivalence. While the ape does not spontaneously match *either* objects or relations, the human spontaneously matches only the former.

4. Both the human and the ape can learn to compute conceptual equivalence. But both require school, special experience. The human species has invented culture, i.e. the institutions which automatically provide most children with the needed experience. Hence most children progress 'naturally' from physical similarity to conceptual equivalence, i.e. they progress by merit of the cultural evolution which is the inheritance of virtually every child. Apes, not having invented culture, do not progress naturally from one level of information processing to another, and, unless they fall into human hands, remain at the level of physical similarity.

The difference between ape and human is therefore not entirely a difference in malleability: provided they are given special experience both species can make the same transition (albeit to a different degree). But only in one species is this experience the inheritance of every child. The difference between ape and human intelligence lies not in the ability to profit by school; it lies rather in the ability to have invented school (Premack 1984).

5. The thoroughgoing superiority of the pre-language child on every measure used indicates that the cognitive advantage to the human is not one introduced by language. One cannot view the human as an ape to which language has been added. By as early as the eleventh month the human infant has already reversed the traditional neoteny ordering—monkey, ape, human. From that time on the human infant does not lag; rather it leads the non-human primates, evermore as one progresses from sensori–motor to cognitive measures. What are the evolutionary implications of these findings? The addition of language to the proto-human did not create a difference but amplified one that already existed. For proto-human intelligence already greatly exceeded that of the ape.

References

Anderson, J. R. (1978). Arguments concerning representations for mental imagery. *Psychological Review*, **85**, 249–77.

Cerella, J. (1977). Absence of perspective processing in the pigeon. *Pattern Recognition*, **9**, 65–8.

Gibson, J. J. (1966). *The senses considered as perceptual systems*. Houghton Mifflin, Boston, MA.

Gillan, D. J., Premack, D. and Woodruff, G. (1981) Reasoning in the chimpanzee: I. Analogical reasoning. *Journal of Experimental Psychology: Animal Behaviour Processes*, **7**, 1–17.

Hochberg, J. E. (1980). Pictorial functions and perceptual structures. In *The perception of pictures, vol. 2*, (ed. M. A. Hagen). Academic Press, New York.

Oden, D., Thompson, R. I., and Premack, D. (in press). Match-to-sample in infant chimpanzees. *Journal of Experimental Psychology: Animal Behavior Processes*.

Premack, D. (1976). *Intelligence in ape and man*. Lawrence Erlbaum Associates, Hillsdale, NJ.

—— (1983). The codes of man and beasts. *The Behavioral and Brain Sciences*, **6**, 125–67.

—— (1984). Pedagogy and aesthetics as sources of culture. In *Cognitive neuroscience*, (ed. M. Gazzaniga), pp. 15–35. Plenum Press, New York.

—— (1986). *Gavagai! Or the future history of the animal language controversy*. MIT Press, Cambridge, MA.

Warren, W. H. and Shaw, R. E. (1984). Events and encounters as units of analysis for ecological psychology. In *Persistence and change*, (ed. W. H. Warren and R. E. Shaw). Lawrence Erlbaum Associates, Hillsdale, NJ.

Woodruff, G. and Premack, D. (1979) Intentional communication in the chimpanzee: the development of deception. *Cognition*, **7**, 333–62.

—— and —— (1981) Primitive mathematical concepts in the chimpanzee: proportions and numerosity. *Nature*, **293**, 568–70.

Discussion, Section A

Extrapolations in space and from space

Some methodological and procedural points arose during discussion concerning the pointing/eye gaze experiments. *Kertesz*, for example, asked what duration of gaze was accepted as being directed towards a target location. *Butterworth* said that the judgements of gaze direction were based on inter-observer agreement: 'In some cases the duration of gaze was very fleeting indeed, while in others it was more extended. Coding was based primarily on the direction in which the child was looking rather than on duration of gaze'. *Jeannerod* wanted to know what the cue is that is used by babies to locate where the mother is looking. Could it be arranged for mothers to move the eyes only, or eyes and head? *Butterworth* answered that he was able to compare eye movements only with eye movements and head movements for the 18-month-old infants. He found that eye movements alone were sufficient to elicit a response, but the probability of the infant looking where the mother was looking was increased by eye and head movements in combination.

Why do the infants not look behind them? *Premack* asked about the role of (a) losing sight of mother (necessitated by turning around) and (b) a reluctance to turn around? *Butterworth's* response was that he believed that they fail to look behind them 'because they lack a representation of space that allows them to understand themselves to be "contained" within the room. When the mother looks behind the baby she refers to a location which the infant has no means of comprehending, certainly during the first year of life. I do not think this failure to search behind can be explained simply as a result of the infant losing sight of the mother. We have tested the mother and baby in different seating arrangements, and infants even as young as six months are capable of correctly locating a target within the visual field at a separation of 135° of visual angle from the mother. If the mother is available in vision she can only be perceived in the extreme periphery under these circumstances, yet this does not interfere with correct localizations. There is no difficulty with turning round *per se*. The infants do not have any motor problems with the task of turning to look behind them and indeed this is often one of the first things a baby will do when seated in the laboratory. The problem is one of interpreting the mother's signal as referring to a space outside the field of view'.

Various issues arose concerning the possible inferences that could be drawn from gaze/pointing experiments and also the relation of pointing to other cognitive functions. *Caramazza* said that there seemed to be 'a very large inferential leap' between the observations and the notion of 'object permanence'. What assumptions are necessary to make us accept the link between the observations and the conclusions? *Butterworth* said he would justify the reference to object permanence in terms of Michotte's (1962) writings. 'He pointed out that when we perceive a room suddenly illuminated, we do not experience the furniture as coming into existence but rather as being located in an indefinite past. In the same way, the posture of our head and eyes reveals only a portion of the environment to us. The portion that is presently invisible is nevertheless potentially visible and can be rendered so merely by a change of posture. Visual perception presupposes the permanent possibility of objects and I think it is in that sense possible to relate joint visual attention to this fundamental category of experience'.

Leslie said that pointing was a way of calculating an imaginary line in space between eye or pointing finger and a target. Did the calculation simply become more precise and more complex without a fundamental change from 'ecological' to geometric? He followed the question with a suggestion that 'a similar computation seems to be involved in understanding "lines of transmission" in various causal-mechanical phenomena by pre-schoolers (e.g. Shultz 1982). This suggests that, following eye gaze, pointing may be part of the child's causal understanding; in particular, the child's causal understanding of perception. There is evidence from work on the child's "theory of mind" (e.g. Flavell, Schultz, and others, including some of my own work) that seeing is understood by the child early on and is understood as a causal relation between people and objects before it is understood as a mental state. Given the nature of the computations involved it would perhaps be rather odd if these infantile abilities and the pre-schoolers' theories were not related'.

Butterworth said that he did not think the child's calculation of an imaginary line in space simply becomes more precise with age: 'Our experiments with the six-month-old infants show that they are unable to identify which of two identical targets the mother is looking at even when the angular separation between them is as great as 60°. Yet the one-year-old infant is easily capable of locating the correct target and our recent unpublished research suggests that the angular separation can be as small as 35° without causing the baby any difficulty. However, once the geometric ability is available then your suggestion that the calculation becomes more precise may have some force. It seems very likely that there is a relationship between these abilities and pre-schoolers' theories of mind'.

The relationship, if any, of pointing to language was raised by a number of participants. *Premack*, for example, said that chimpanzees, though not pointing naturally, do so under relatively minimal experimental pressure. Yet chimpanzees do not acquire language. The moral is that pointing is a *precursor* but not a sufficient condition for the subsequent appearance of language. *Butterworth* said that he was very careful to define manual pointing as species-specific and involving a specialized posture of the arm, hand, and index finger. 'Other organisms, such as chimpanzees, do not use the hand in this specialized fashion to refer to objects, even though they may orient with the whole hand or, as in the case of dogs, with the head and body. The evolutionary record shows changes in the proportion of the index finger relative to the remaining fingers in the period from 4 million to 1.7 million years ago which are consistent with the beginnings of tool use and the acquisition of speech (Hilton 1986). I do not wish to argue that the onset of manual pointing causes language. However, it does seem to be more intimately related to speech in our species than are other forms of orienting also observed in species that do not acquire language. The problem of the specific causal relationship between pointing and language is indeed difficult ... There are general cognitive changes that come about at the age of 10 months or so which may reasonably be considered precursors of language and which enable manual pointing. To isolate a particular cause of language may be impossible; perhaps all we can do is establish developmental pathways and make arguments about the genesis of language in terms of family resemblances between behaviours organized at different levels. In this case the important resemblance is in terms of the referential functions of pointing and of speech'.

A closely related issue was raised by *Chapouthier*, who said that language involved very specific aspects such as 'semantics'. Was it possible to study 'precursors of semantics' with the models discussed here or are the logical processes completely different? *Butterworth* said it was a very difficult question to answer. He had put the view that the referential functions of gaze and pointing can be related to the referential functions of language. However, there was much controversy over the extent to which other aspects of parent/ infant interaction can be related to linguistic structures, and the extent to which there was a continuity of pre-linguistic with linguistic processes.

Other ontogenetic processes

The relation to social referencing of *affective* stimuli was raised by *Hinde*, who pointed out that it occurs somewhat earlier in man than spatial referencing, and also occurs in vervet monkeys. *Butterworth* referred to the work on emotional referencing by Campos and his colleagues at the University of Colorado. The mother is trained to register a particular emotion when a radio-controlled toy car enters the room. 'Babies will readily alter their emotional expression to conform with the expression of the mother. For example, if the mother seems alarmed, the baby will rapidly switch from an expression of joy to one of fear of the toy car. . . . It is very clear that joint visual attention serves the purpose of communication'.

Kertesz asked *Butterworth* and *Mounoud* how social interaction, à la Vigotsky, could be separated from the psychological level. The answer was that the contrast between Piaget and Vigotsky makes the point that both the individual and social aspects of cognitive growth had to be taken into account. But having contrasted these positions, it is extremely difficult to separate them, except as theoretical perspectives.

He also asked about the evidence relating to the 'language acquisition support system (LASS)'. Was it a necessary prerequisite for language development? There is contrary evidence. *Butterworth* replied that the problem is that the evidence relies largely on anecdotal accounts to support the assertion that the LASS is not necessary. 'Rather than take these isolated extreme cases of child rearing under unusual conditions, where we have little control or understanding of the influences that have had an effect, I would rather take another approach which is more painstaking but requires us to consider all the factors that may eventually culminate in language. From this perspective, it is clear that some pre-natal experiences, such as hearing the mother's voice in the womb, may contribute to the child's comprehension of the pattern of sound, but this is not yet language. The innate coordination that can be observed between seeing and hearing may also contribute but is not itself language. Nevertheless, detailed examination of many constituent abilities under development may enable us to solve the problem of where language comes from. We may also answer the question of the necessity of a LASS by a *reductio ad absurdum*. If there were no social interaction at all, then clearly no language would be acquired. Presumably the quality of the language acquired will bear a systematic relation to the quality of the social interaction which is the vehicle for transmission of speech from adult to child'.

Changeux, while acknowledging the importance of psychological and behavioural tests to probe the ontogenesis of thinking, expressed surprise to see so little reference to neurological data in *Butterworth's* and *Mounoud's* presentations. 'Synapse formation in cerebral cortex is taking place throughout the first year of life in a particularly dramatic manner and, of course, continues up to adolescence. To what extent is the early performance of the infant (e.g. recognition of the mother's voice, early categorization, etc.) related to the maturation of the cerebral cortex? Lesion studies and the use of infants with birth defects (e.g. anencephaly, lissencephaly) might bring important information to bear on this issue'.

Butterworth replied that there is a tendency to assume that the cortex is not functional in the new-born infant. But 'Visser *et al.* have made systematic comparisons between an anencephalic infant (where the cortex is completely missing), and the new-born normal infant, and they show differences in the modulation of sucking and looking patterns which suggest that the cortex must be serving some function right from birth. Lissencephalic infants constitute an intermediate case since layers one to four of the cortex are present but not layers five and six. The overall behavioural capacities of this group would presumably reflect the extent to which subcortical processes interact with processes served by layers one to four of the cortex. It may be the case that the majority of behaviours of the new-born are subcortically mediated, but there is no need to suppose that the infant, under normal circumstances, is effectively decorticate. In the case of the older baby, say from 10 months onwards, a great deal of converging evidence suggests that maturation of the prefrontal cortex is involved in the acquisition of new abilities, such as the geometric ability that I have described (see the contribution from *Diamond* in this volume). (The editor would also raise the point that "cognition" is not necessarily just "cortical", even in the human adult, let alone in the infant. Subcortical mechanisms are strongly implicated in memory systems and in spatial aspects of vision; cf. Weiskrantz 1986, 1987.)

Symbolic training in chimpanzee

Cohen wondered what specifically it was about 'language training' that conferred an advantage on the chimpanzees who went through the regime. Could it be that it was indirectly teaching the animals 'same–different'?

Premack went into some further detail about the actual stages of language training. All the chimpanzees went through it, but some before the others, and so the design allowed a comparison between groups as well as a comparison before and after training. But he graphically stressed that language training did *not* confer an advantage on the range of '*diagnostic tests*' when they were only taught the names of objects, actions, etc. using the plastic chips. Even teaching the meanings of *combinations* of plastic words conferred no advantage. That is, 'learning the correspondence between plastic descriptions of the world and the real world itself, the learning of relations to relations, conferred no benefit'. This had been disquieting to him, but it was too neat a view to think that it might have been a crucial key. 'But throw in "same–different" and there is a big effect; the animals go from 60 per cent to 95 per cent. Dogged training helps the animals to solve the "same–same" judgments but not "different–different". Teach them "same–different" and it helps "different–different", and in comes the ability to do analogies'.

A possible reason for the origin of the inability of the chimpanzee to learn grammar was pursued by *Changeux*. In the field, he said, it appears that chimpanzees have an exceptional spatial memory for the environment in which they live. Grammar involves temporal organization and memory. Do chimpanzees not learn grammar because they have poor temporal abilities? *Premack* thought not. He had carried out studies of the ability of the chimpanzee to make judgements about order in which the animals were taught to make judgements of spatial order, temporal order, or 'mixtures' of the two orders, using sets of three items. (The mixture case was one of showing the chimpanzee the items spatially and then testing them temporally, or vice versa.) They could manage all of them moderately well, 78 per cent correct for spatial and temporal order judgements, about 68 per cent for the mixture case.

'But', he went on, 'the important thing is that order is not *salient* for the chimpanzee. It took about one-and-a-half years for the animals to reach the point where they recognized that you are asking them about order. But in just moments they will learn the meaning of questions about amounts and the like. And so it is not entirely correct that chimpanzees cannot learn about order and that this is why they cannot learn grammar. They cannot learn language because language is a species-specific thing. You are looking at the wrong species if you want language'.

References

Campos, J. J. and Stenberg, C. R. (1980). Perception, appraisal and emotion. The onset of social referencing. In *Infant social cognition*, (ed. M. Lamb and L. Sherrod). Laurence Erlbaum Associates, Hillsdale, NJ.

Flavell, J. H., Flavell, E. R., & Green, F. L. (1983). Development of the appearance–reality distinction. *Cognitive Psychology*, **15**, 95–120.

Hilton, C. E. (1986). Hands across the old world: the changing hand morphology of the hominids. Unpublished manuscript, Department of Anthropology, University of New Mexico.

Michotte, A. (1962). *The perception of causality*. Methuen, Andover, Hants.

Shultz, T. R. (1982). Rules of causal attribution. *Monographs of the Society for Research in Child Development*, **47**(1), 1–51.

Visser, G. H. A., Laurini, R. N., DeVries, J. I. P., Bekedam, D. J., and Prechtl, H. F. R. (1985). Abnormal motor behaviour in anencephalic fetuses. *Early Human Development*, **12**, 173–83.

Weiskrantz, L. (1986). *Blindsight: a case study and implications*. Oxford University Press.

—— (1987). Neuroanatomy of memory and amnesia: a case for multiple memory systems. *Human neurobiology*, **6**, 93–105.

Section B

Categorical perception

Editorial to Section B

The eye is exposed to an infinite set of patterns of stimulation that vary in size, contrast, wavelength, retinal location, and yet the brain achieves perception of objects whose identity is stable over all these variations. How it does this is still not fully understood. Not only that, but classes of objects can be recognized as belonging to the same category. Animals such as pigeons have been shown by Herrnstein and others to have a remarkable and efficient capacity to learn to respond correctly to pictures of objects such as trees, fish, people, as each belonging to the same class. *Pearce* takes off from this point by considering two theoretical alternative explanations, either by the learning of specific instances and grouping by stimulus generalization, or by representing a class by a 'prototype'. He shows how the issue can be tackled by careful logical and experimental analysis in the pigeon. The conclusion from his own experiments favours memory for specific instances, and stimulus generalization from them as new stimuli are encountered. Whether this conclusion itself will generalize to other situations and species arises later as a very moot point in Section C, when a quite different set of behavioural measures are used by *Cohen* to investigate precisely the same issue in human infants. The infant research suggests that exemplars are genuinely classified into categories. The difference highlights the methodological demands and niceties involved in reaching a general conclusion, if indeed there be one that applies both to pigeons and to human infants. But equally compelling are the findings themselves, which demonstrate in both species a capacity to negotiate with large sets of objects and two-dimensional stimuli in the external world that was not suspected before the present era of research.

However they do it, pigeons and infants do not judge similarity or form groups by using verbal labels. Human adults obviously *do* attach verbal labels to perceived categories. One issue, therefore, is how to disentangle categorical perception from linguistic support. Faces work very well in this regard, because they are notoriously difficult to encode verbally if adequate care is taken to remove distinguishing features such as beards, hair-style, etc. from the exemplars. They also have special biological importance in social interactions, and there is even evidence that a unique set of neurons in the primate brain respond selectively to faces. Finally, there is evidence that has led many to consider that, at least for humans, the two cerebral hemispheres have quite different roles to play in the processing of perception and memory of faces. All of these issues arise in the chapters by *Young* and *Sergent*.

Young's chapter, in addition to setting out the conditions for a processing model for faces, also leads nicely into a later section (D) on implicit processing by citing highly instructive evidence from the neuropsychology of agnosia, a condition caused by brain damage in which there is a loss of meaning of objects. There are several varieties of agnosia, and the way in which they ramify and dissociate highly specifically provides an important insight into how the brain organizes its acquired knowledge. It is unusual for agnosia for a particular type of object to be pure, i.e. usually more than one category is affected. But the fact that the different categories are very unequally and differentially affected leads one to conclude that there are a number of identifiable categories into which knowledge is organized that are potentially independent. One such category of agnosia is for faces, prosopagnosia. The prosopagnosic patient does not recognize *familiar* faces, although he need have no loss in his discriminative or perceptual capacity as such. *Young* and his colleagues illustrate very nicely the way in which specific disorders lead to theoretical constructions about the cognitive processes involved, together with conjectures about the point in the model at which the disability arises. Beyond that, they show that despite the unavailability of the information to the patient himself in controlling his everyday behaviour, nevertheless one level of the nervous system is still processing the familiarity of the faces normally. The issue of implicit processing, that is, a capacity or a process of which the subject is unaware and which is divorced from verbal commentary or intervention, is taken up much more fully in Section D. Here, it is interesting to note that this important but strongly non-verbal medium shows itself to have an internal categorical property, which, in turn, can be further removed in patients from even any awareness of the property itself.

Sergent's chapter also tackles the requirements for human face perception and processing, both for perception and for memory of specific exemplars. She does this in terms of manipulation of the specific features than might be involved, as well as their configurational properties. The latter remain even when the high-frequency components are filtered out of the visual display, and suffice for face recognition. All of these considerations are linked to the specific issue of differences between the two cerebral hemispheres. The matter is still not entirely uncontroversial, but the evidence is increasingly favouring the view that the right hemisphere is typically more important than the left for face perception, and indeed for perceptual information in general. There are cases of prosopagnosia in which the damage is apparently restricted to the right hemisphere (despite the more common but undecisive collection of patients who have bilateral damage). *Sergent* offers a broad characterization of the differences between the two hemispheres based on the spatial frequency spectrum. The inputs to striate cortex, at the earliest cortical visual receiving stage, cover a wide band of spatial frequencies, from less than a cycle/degree to 40 cycles/degree or higher. She suggests that the right hemisphere, at stations beyond the striate cortex, filters this information such that it is biased towards the low-frequency end of the spectrum, and the left hemisphere is biased towards the high frequencies. Faces are especially dependent on low spatial frequencies and hence are more vulnerable to right-hemisphere damage. This characterization, she suggests, also provides a way of making quantitative the general view that the right hemisphere is more 'holistic' and the left more 'analytic'. Whether this characterization, which emerged largely from modern work on 'split-brain' patients, really is as firm as all that is taken up in a later section (F) by *Gazzaniga*. But a number of particular predictions emerge from this spatial frequency filtering or biassing approach. *Sergent* also speculates about the origins of hemispheric specialization and links the spatial frequency hypothesis to the evidence that the right hemisphere develops earlier than the left, and does so at a period when the macular region of the retina is still immature and acuity is not fully developed. Hence there is a possibility that this developmental difference in maturity produces an initial bias in the right hemisphere for the low-frequency end of the spectrum, as it receives no high-frequency input at birth. While this analysis is applied mainly to the relatively early stages of visual inputs, the consequences are suggested to follow through to the upper reaches of higher perceptual and mnemonic processing. The approach illustrates how a relatively simple filtering of information can have, in principle, widespread implications for functional processing and categorization, and especially for the non-verbal domain in which faces are so important.

4

Functional organization of visual recognition
ANDREW W. YOUNG

Introduction

Visual recognition involves an interesting example of how linguistic and non-linguistic abilities must interface with each other. We need to recognize the appearances of seen objects and relate these to our stored knowledge, which may be in linguistic form (e.g. object names) or non-linguistic form (e.g. how the object would be used).

When we look about us we see an orderly arrangement of things in three-dimensional space, and we can usually recognize other people, everyday objects, and printed words without difficulty. Our visual experience has such a unified quality that it is initially surprising to learn that brain injury can sometimes lead to quite specific impairments of one aspect of visual experience or another (Cowey 1985). Sometimes these impairments affect what we might consider to be fairly basic visual abilities, such as ability to see colour (Damasio et al. 1980) or movement (Zihl et al. 1983). Specific impairments of 'higher' visual abilities are, however, also found. Thus dissociations can be observed between impairments affecting pattern recognition and space perception. Patients experiencing object recognition difficulties may be relatively unimpaired on spatial tasks, and patients who are spatially disoriented may yet remain able to identify objects without difficulty.

Newcombe and Russell (1969), for instance, studied a group of men with brain lesions due to shrapnel and gunshot wound injuries sustained some 20 years previously. They found that men with right hemisphere injuries could show severe problems in spatial tasks (such as maze learning) or in pattern-processing tasks (such as Mooney's visual closure), but that these deficits did not relate to each other. Newcombe et al. (1987) present post-mortem findings on two individual cases drawn from this series, one with each type of impairment, and relate their findings to work on the separation of cortical visual systems responsible for object recognition and spatial perception in the monkey (Ungerleider and Mishkin 1982).

Even more surprisingly, perceptual impairments can be not only specific to pattern recognition, but specific to particular types of visual pattern. We might group them roughly into those in which patients complain primarily of difficulties in recognizing faces, objects, or words, though this is by no means a complete list. In this chapter I will discuss some of the things we have learnt about the functional organization of visual recognition from studies of brain-injured patients and studies of normal subjects. I will concentrate mostly on face recognition, and make comparisons between face, word, and object recognition.

Dissociable impairments of visual recognition

The most common specific pattern recognition impairment is inability to read words. There are a number of different types of word recognition impairment, but the most pertinent to present purposes is the condition neurologists call pure alexia, or alexia without agraphia. Patients with pure alexia can write quite well (to dictation, for example), but show seriously impaired reading. They can, however, recognize without difficulty spoken words or words that are spelt aloud, and can usually also identify raised letters and words felt by touch or 'written' onto the palm of the hand. Thus the word recognition disorder does seem to be specific to the visual modality.

Damasio and Damasio (1983) reviewed 16 cases of pure alexia. Most of their patients could recognize seen objects and faces without difficulty, despite their seriously impaired word recognition ability. Thus the recognition deficit is both specific to the visual modality *and* specific to a particular class of material (words) within that modality.

Although it is often convenient to discuss neurological conditions such as pure alexia as if they were unitary in nature, this is not really the case. There are both neurological and behavioural differences between individual patients. In particular, some pure alexic patients are unable to identify seen words or letters, whereas others are able to identify letters and can thus read words 'letter-by-letter' (Hécaen and Kremin 1976). The existence of letter-by-letter reading emphasizes still further the specificity of the deficit to visual word recognition. These patients are able to identify individual letters, yet do not seem able to take in a word 'as a whole'. Even letter-by-letter reading can itself, however, be divided into different variants (Warrington and Shallice 1980; Patterson and Kay 1982; Shallice and Saffran 1986).

Patients with word recognition impairments, then, may remain able to recognize everyday objects and familiar faces. Conversely, patients with impaired ability to recognize both objects and faces may remain able to recognize seen words without apparent difficulty (Albert *et al.* 1975; Levine 1978). Thus there is a double dissociation between impairments affecting word recognition and impairments affecting the recognition of other visual stimuli (including everyday objects and familiar faces).

There is also evidence of dissociable deficits of object recognition (visual object agnosia) and familiar face recognition (prosopagnosia). These deficits are often found together, but not invariably. There have been a number of reports of prosopagnosic patients who do not experience difficulty in recognizing everyday objects (e.g. Pallis 1955; Bruyer *et al.* 1983; De Renzi 1986*a*). The converse pattern, in which face recognition is spared whilst object recognition is impaired, has been less convincingly established but does seem to occasionally happen. The only published reports of cases in which face recognition seemed to be fully preserved despite severe object recognition impairments were those of Hécaen *et al.* (1974) and Ferro and Santos (1984). Hécaen *et al.*'s patient was able to recognize hospital staff and all photographs of celebrities presented to him, despite his object agnosia. Ferro and Santos' patient was also able to identify all of the faces shown to him, though he could not always name them. However, he could often mime the use of objects presented to him, so that it is unclear whether this is a case of optic aphasia (Beauvois 1982) rather than visual agnosia *per se*. In two other cases face recognition was not fully preserved, but the object recognition impairment was more severe (Albert *et al* 1985; McCarthy and Warrington 1986). Albert *et al.*'s patient however, was rapidly regaining his ability to recognize objects during the period in which he was being tested. Thus the most convincing cases are those of Hécaen *et al.* (1974) and McCarthy and Warrington (1986), but in neither of these was the dissociation between face and object recognition impairments subjected to further investigation.

Why should disorders of word, object, and face recognition dissociate from each other in such a way that ability to recognize one class of material may be affected whilst ability to recognize the other classes remains intact? I suspect that part of the answer lies in the different demands that are placed on the recognition mechanisms involved. There are several reasons why organization into functionally separable modules may be a useful response to differing demands, including economy of nerve connections and the possibility of modifying one process without affecting others (Marr 1982; Cowey 1985)

In recognizing objects, for instance, we usually need to assign them to broad categories that maximize the functional and visual similarities of the objects within each category (cats, cups, chairs, etc.). Rosch *et al.* (1976) refer to these as 'basic level' categories. Although the members of these basic level categories may possess a number of common visual features, the task facing the perceptual system is often one of assigning different stimuli (different cats, different cups, or different chairs) to the appropriate category (cat, cup, or chair). This categorization process has to operate across a wide range of different views, and a plausible idea is that computation of the seen object's three-dimensional structure plays an important part (Marr 1982).

For face recognition the task is quite different. In Rosch *et al.*'s (1976) terms faces themselves form a kind of basic level category, but what we are primarily interested in is the differences between the individual members that allow us to identify specific people (Ellis 1981). These differences might only be slight, so that the axis-based descriptions proposed by Marr (1982) for object recognition would not seem particularly suited to the task of recognizing faces. For faces, too, their relation to semantic categories is relatively arbitrary. Appearance alone is a good guide to whether an unfamiliar object is a tool or a piece of furniture, since the object's shape is in part determined by the functions it must perform, whereas appearance is most unlikely to indicate whether a face is that of a politician or a stockbroker.

Face recognition, then, demands identification *within* a class of rather homogeneous stimuli on the basis of any difference in individual features or their arrangement. The range of transformations of viewpoint across which face recognition needs to operate is also probably relatively restricted in comparison to other objects, since people usually stand with their heads more or less upright, and will often be looking toward you. Thus the demands made on face recognition mechanisms are in some ways more reminiscent of the demands of word recognition than object recognition. With written words, however, the range of potential distinguishing features is limited to the set of letters in the language, and the crucial spatial arrangement is in the form of a sequence.

The idea that object recognition usually requires us to assign the things we see to different basic level categories, whereas face recognition always demands within-category discrimination, raises questions as to the extent to which prosopagnosia is specific to faces. Is the difficulty in recognizing familiar faces simply a reflection of a more general problem in identifying individual members of a visually homogeneous stimulus category? This hypothesis has been advanced by Damasio *et al.* (1982), who maintain that the primary defect in prosopagnosia is one of 'contextual evocation'. Prosopagnosic patients know that a face is a face; their problem is that they do not know *whose* face it is. Similarly, Damasio *et al.*, argue that, although these patients can recognize a pen as a pen or a chair as a chair, they would fail if asked whose pen or whose chair it is. Under such circumstances Damasio *et al.* claim that a prosopagnosic patient 'will be just as incapable of evoking the history of a familiar object as he will be of evoking the history of a familiar face' (1982, p. 337).

This is an important argument, and there are several observations of prosopagnosic patients having other types of within-category recognition difficulty, including problems with foods, animals, and different types of cars (Pallis 1955; MacRae and Trolle 1956; Damasio *et al.* 1982; Blanc-Garin 1984). This is not, however, inevitably the case. One of De Renzi's (1986*a*, 1986*b*) patients could not recognize faces yet was able to pick out his own belongings when these were mixed in with distractor objects chosen to resemble them. He could also identify samples of his own handwriting among samples of the same sentence written by other people, recognize his own car in a car-park, sort domestic (Italian) coins from foreign ones, and pick out a Siamese cat among photographs of other cats. The patient was himself convinced that his difficulties related only to face recognition, and De Renzi was unable to find any evidence to contradict this assertion. Conversely, Assal *et al.* (1984) report that a prosopagnosic farmer who was initially also unable to recognize his cows later regained his ability to recognize familiar faces yet remained unable to recognize his cows. This case forms a neat double dissociation when set alongside Bruyer *et al.*'s (1983) patient, also a farmer, who had problems in recognizing familiar faces but could identify his livestock.

Inability to recognize familiar faces is not, then, inevitably linked to difficulties in recognizing individual members of other visually homogeneous stimulus categories. It seems that recognition problems involving only faces can occur.

Why should there be recognition mechanisms specific to faces? I think that the answer probably lies in a combination of their social and biological significance (Ellis and Young in press). We use faces not only to identify familiar people, but also to assist in assessing the age and sex of unfamiliar people, to interpret feelings from facial expressions, to regulate social interaction through eye contact and other facial gestures, and to assist in speech comprehension (hearing adults make use of lip-reading to a considerable extent, though they are not generally aware of this; e.g. McGurk and MacDonald 1976).

There is evidence that new-born babies are attentive to face-like stimuli (Goren *et al.* 1975), that they can discriminate facial expressions (Field *et al.* 1982), and that they can imitate facial gestures (Meltzoff and Moore 1977, 1983; Vinter 1985). These innate face-processing abilities probably facilitate the acquisition of a number of social skills, and the attentiveness to faces will ensure that infants get plenty of opportunity to acquire the information on which recognition of individual faces will later be based. I am not, however, aware of any evidence that would suggest 'hard-wiring' of the face recognition system itself; in fact young infants are able to recognize people's voices (Mills and Melhuish 1974; De Gasper and Fifer 1980) before they can recognize their faces (Fagan 1979; Bushnell 1982). In addition, it is known that 'face-like' properties such as vulnerability to the effect of inversion (Yin 1969, 1970) accrue to other types of configurational stimuli if we become sufficiently expert at identifying them (Diamond and Carey 1986).

The development of a specific face recognition ability is thus probably due to a combination of specific demands made by face recognition, the degree to which the ability is practiced because of its social importance, and the need to co-ordinate recognition with other aspects of face processing which do seem to show a degree of innate determination. The force of this type of argument can perhaps be seen more clearly for visual word recognition, where material-specific recognition mechanisms are again apparently involved, yet there can not be innately specified cerebral mechanisms for reading. The skill is simply too recent a development in evolutionary terms, and was not in any case widespread until this century. I would argue that the existence of material-specific recognition mechanisms for words is due to a combination of specific demands made by word recognition, the degree of practice at the skill, and the need to integrate it with other aspects of language processing.

Cerebral hemisphere differences

One of the most intriguing aspects of visual recognition mechanisms is that they do not seem to be symmetrically represented in the left and right cerebral hemispheres of the human brain.

Like other language disorders, pure alexia is associated with left-hemisphere lesions. These are typically located in the left occipital lobe, and either extend into the splenium of the corpus callosum or disrupt nerve connections from the splenium (Damasio and Damasio 1983). Equivalent right-hemisphere lesions do not usually lead to impairments of word recognition.

Face recognition, in contrast, has often been thought to be a right-hemisphere function. Studies have shown the importance of the right hemisphere both in recognizing familiar faces (Hécaen and Angelergues 1962; Warrington and James 1967) and in the ability to match and remember unfamiliar faces (De Renzi and Spinnler 1966a; Warrington and James 1967; De Renzi et al. 1968).

The right hemisphere may not, however, necessarily make an exclusive contribution to race recognition. Meadows (1974) noted that prosopagnosic patients tend to have bilateral cerebral lesions, with the right-hemisphere lesion in the region of the occipito–temporal junction. Bilateral lesions have been found in all cases that have come to autopsy (Meadows 1974; Damasio et al. 1982, 1986). The left-hemisphere lesion is not always anatomically symmetric with the right-hemisphere lesion, but it is usually in the same region, and thought to be affecting the same part of the visual system (Damasio et al. 1982). This suggests that whilst the right hemisphere may be more important to face recognition, the left hemisphere is not without face recognition ability. This conclusion is supported by studies of split-brain patients (Levy et al. 1972; Gazzaniga and Smylie 1983), patients with unilateral cerebral lesions (Benton 1980), and normal subjects (Sergent 1982, 1984a). The only inconsistent evidence comes from reports of prosopagnosic patients with only right-hemisphere lesions (De Renzi 1986b; Landis et al. 1986). Such reports are initially surprising, since it is known that in other cases right occipito–temporal lesions have not produced prosopagnosia. The reports implicating the right hemisphere exclusively are based on CT scans rather than on post-mortem findings, so that it is conceivable that left-hemisphere lesions have not been detected. Alternatively (and more interestingly), however, individuals may differ in their degree of cerebral asymmetry for face recognition, so that the same unilateral lesion might lead to prosopagnosia in open person and not in another.

The evidence for some degree of bilateral involvement in face recognition raises the question of whether the left and right hemispheres make qualitatively different contributions. This has often been thought to be the case, with several people suggesting that the right hemisphere is able to make use of the configuration of facial features whereas the left hemisphere relies on a more analytic, feature-by-feature strategy (e.g. Levy *et al.* 1972; Sergent 1982). The attraction of this idea is that it would allow cerebral asymmetries for face recognition to be mapped onto other phenomena attributed to hypothesized cerebral hemisphere differences in mode of information-processing. It would not, however, be compatible with the idea of individual differences in the degree of right-hemisphere involvement in face recognition; if the left hemisphere has access to a qualitatively different face recognition strategy one would expect it to be always used when needed.

It is difficult to find ways of empirically disentangling the claims of qualitative or quantitative differences in left- and right-hemisphere face recognition mechanisms, but what evidence there is suggests that the differences are in fact quantitative. One way of approaching the question is by making use of a distinct pattern that emerges when recognition of familiar and unfamiliar faces is compared. Ellis *et al.* (1979) showed that when faces have to be recognized from internal features (eyes, nose, and mouth) performance is better to familiar than to unfamiliar faces, whereas for recognition based on external features (hair, face shape, chin) there is no difference between familiar and unfamiliar faces. The same pattern of findings can be observed in matching tasks using a reaction time measure (Young *et al.* 1985c). We might then expect that any qualitative cerebral hemisphere difference in face recognition ability would be associated with deviation from this pattern that characterizes normal performance. However, studies of both normal and brain-injured people have shown that the same pattern is found for both right- and left-hemisphere performance, but that the right hemisphere achieves a better overall level of performance (Young 1984; de Haan and Hay 1986). It thus seems that both hemispheres use the same type of recognition mechanism, but that the right hemisphere is more efficient. Sergent (1984a), too, has found that both the right and left cerebral hemispheres are capable of processing faces as configurational stimuli.

Because both cerebral hemispheres can make some contribution to face recognition, a central issue becomes that of identifying the information-processing stage or stages at which cerebral hemisphere differences arise. The underlying assumption here is that recognition is dependent on separable functional components which may themselves be differentially lateralized. Persuasive explanations of this approach are given by Moscovitch (1979, 1986) and Allen (1983), and its application to understanding cerebral hemisphere differences for face recognition has been developed by Ellis (1983) and Rhodes (1985). It is not the only possible approach, and I should mention Sergent's (1983, 1984*b*, 1988) emphasis on how information is extracted from the visual input as an important alternative, but my own sympathies lie with the functional components approach.

Moscovitch (1979, 1986) has argued that cerebral asymmetries are not found for early stages of stimulus analysis. This was initially demonstrated for faces by Moscovitch *et al.* (1976) in a study of normal subjects, and much the same point can be seen in Gazzaniga and Smylie's (1983) study of split-brain patients. Gazzaniga and Smylie (1983) noted that the split-brain patient V.P. learnt dissimilar faces equally well with either hemisphere, but that when tested on similar faces her right hemisphere's performance was considerably better than that of her left hemisphere. This demonstrates that the basic perceptual mechanisms needed to discriminate between dissimilar faces are available to the left hemisphere. Comparable findings have also been made in a study of normal subjects by Young *et al.* (1985*b*). In this study we asked people to discriminate faces from non-faces under conditions in which the non-faces were moderately scrambled, highly scrambled, or everyday objects (see Fig. 4.1). The advantage of this face vs. non-face decision task is that no memory component is involved, and it thus gives a relatively pure measure of ability to construct facial representations. Right-hemisphere superiority (in the form of faster responses) was only found to faces when these had to be discriminated from the most 'face-like' of the non-faces (moderately scrambled non-faces). Again, the left hemisphere is able to perform basic perceptual discriminations (faces vs. highly scrambled non-faces, or faces vs. objects) as efficiently as the right hemisphere, but falls behind as more sophisticated discriminations are required.

Such evidence does not imply, however, that construction of facial representations is the *sole* locus of right-hemisphere superiority for face-processing. Instead, I suspect that there are a number of separable components involved. There is evidence that right-hemisphere superiorities for expression analysis, familiar face recognition, and matching of unfamiliar faces can be separated from each other (e.g. Warrington and James 1967; Etcoff 1984, 1985).

The same approach of trying to pin-point the loci and nature of cerebral hemisphere differences can be applied to word recogntion, as Moscovitch (1979, 1981) has demonstrated; detailed reviews are given in Chiarello (1987) and Young (1987). Again, substantial cerebral hemisphere differences are not found for early stages in the visual analysis of words. Pure alexia, for instance, is often accompanied by right hemianopia, so that seen words are projected to

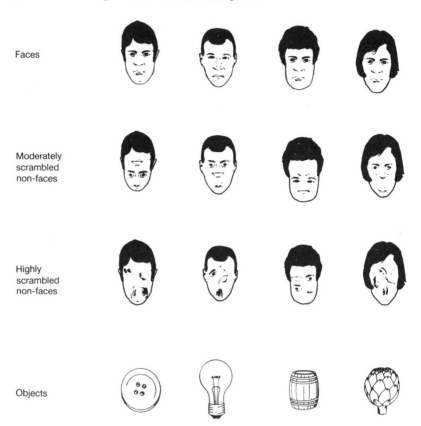

Faces

Moderately
scrambled
non-faces

Highly
scrambled
non-faces

Objects

Fig. 4.1   Examples of stimuli used by Young *et al.* (1985*b*).

the visual cortex of the right hemisphere. Yet, as I have already noted, many such patients remain able to identify the constituent letters of words. Similarly, studies of normal subjects indicate that both cerebral hemispheres are capable of identifying unpronounceable strings of letters, but that the left hemisphere is better able to make use of the higher order 'word-likeness' of pronounceable strings (Young *et al.* 1984).

Word recognition is unlike face recognition, however, in that the cerebral hemisphere differences found are qualitative in nature. In addition to being unable to make effective use of spelling–sound correspondences (Young *et al.* 1984), the right hemisphere relies on a method of lexical access that is not normally used by the left hemisphere (Brand *et al.* 1983; Young and Ellis 1985). Young and Ellis showed that recognition ability for words initially presented to the right cerebral hemisphere declines with increasing word length, whereas the left hemisphere's performance remains relatively unaffected by the length of words in conventional format. Both the left and right hemispheres are, however, equally sensitive to the length of non-words and to the length of words in unusual formats. Hence there seems to be a specialized (length-insensitive) form of lexical access available for conventionally formatted words presented to the left cerebral hemisphere. This method of lexical access is not available to words initially presented to the right hemisphere. regardless of whether the right hemisphere is seen as accessing words in the left hemisphere's lexicon or words in a lexicon of its own.

The functional components approach is also being successfully applied to understanding cerebral hemisphere differences in object recognition. As with other basic visual abilities, there is no evidence of any substantial cerebral hemisphere differences for early stages of object recognition (Young and Ratcliff 1983). Warrington and her colleagues, however, have built upon earlier findings of De Renzi and Spinnler (1966b) and De Renzi et al. (1969) to develop the view that higher order stages are lateralized, with the right hemisphere being primarily involved in perceptual categorization and the left hemisphere in semantic categorization of seen objects (Warrington and Taylor 1973, 1978; Warrington 1982; McCarthy and Warrington 1986).

The most puzzling question about cerebral asymmetries is why they should exist at all, and it is an indication of how little we understand the phenomena concerned that we really do not know the answer. My own guess is that asymmetries have evolved in response to competition for cortical 'space', and that they will be found wherever there is a combination of competition between different functional modules and no need for a particular module to be bilaterally represented. From this standpoint it might be more useful to ask ourselves what pressures tend to maintain symmetric organization, where this is known to occur, than to ask what asymmetry is for.

An interesting aspect of cerebral asymmetries for visual recognition skills, however, is that they may be more or less entirely parasitic on other asymmetries. By following the argument set out in the preceding section to account for the existence of material-specific recognition mechanisms, I would claim that the reason why the left hemisphere is so much better at visual word recognition must be that reading is developed to interface with other language skills that are already highly lateralized. Conversely, I suspect from the developmental evidence already discussed that the 'wired-in' (though I do not mean to imply unmodifiable) aspects of face-processing may lie more toward attentional and expressive functions than toward recognition itself. On this view the right-hemisphere superiority for face recognition arises from its being developed in co-ordination with other aspects of face-processing for which the right hemisphere is intrinsically specialized.

Studies of the ontogeny of cerebral hemisphere differences fit this conception well, since they reveal that there is little change across age in the pattern of cerebral hemisphere differences (Witelson 1977; Young 1982, 1983, 1986). This is as true for face recognition, a skill learnt early in life, as for visual word recognition, which is a comparatively late acquisition. The absence of developmental change is consistent with the view that these skills are developed to be directly co-ordinated with the existing abilities that are themselves lateralized because of underlying anatomical specializations present in the infant brain (Witelson 1983).

Perhaps the neatest demonstration of this point comes, however, not from the developmental literature but from Campbell *et al.*s (1986) study of dissociable impairments of lip-reading and facial expression analysis following brain damage. Campbell *et al.* described two patients showing a double dissociation between impairments affecting ability to read speech sounds from movements of the lips and tongue and ability to identify facial expressions. The patient with the impairment in analysing expressions had a right-hemisphere lesion, and was also prosopagnosic. In contrast, the patient with the lip-reading impairment had a *left*-hemisphere lesion and was also alexic. Thus lip-reading is organized (and lateralized) in a way that brings it into correspondence with other language skills, despite the fact that the necessary information is read from the face. Interestingly, and entirely in line with the view I have offered, there is evidence to suggest that lip-reading is organized in the left hemisphere even whilst the skill is being acquired in infancy (MacKain *et al.* 1983; Studdert-Kennedy 1983).

Functional models

I have shown that a useful approach to understanding cerebral asymmetries lies in considering visual recognition systems as involving a number of separable functional components, each of whch may be differentially lateralized. The success of this enterprise is dependent on the availability of functional models that are sufficiently clearly specified to make it possible to design studies that can isolate effects arising from each functional component. A number of suitable models exist for word recognition (Allport 1979; Morton 1979; Coltheart 1981; Patterson 1981; Carr and Pollatsek 1985) and object recognition (Marr 1982; Ratcliff and Newcombe 1982; Warrington 1982; Humphreys 1987), but when I began working on face recognition there was no obvious equivalent (Ellis 1975). For this reason my colleagues and I have tried to develop a functional model of face recognition (Hay and Young 1982; Young *et al.* 1985*a*; Ellis *et al.* 1987*b*), and a similar approach has been pursued by other workers, most notably Bruce (Bruce 1979, 1983) and Ellis (Ellis 1981, 1986). Our aims are to provide a model that can describe the functional components involved in face recognition and also specify how recognition relates to other aspects of face-processing, such as analysis of facial expressions. We intend to account not only for the findings of studies of normal subjects, but also for the different types of impairment that can follow brain injury. This will make it possible to use such models to investigate questions concerning the localization (and lateralization) of particular functions, though we do not assume that precise localization of functional components will necessarily exist (see Morton 1981).

I will use Bruce and Young's (1986) model as an example of this approach. This is shown in schematic form in Fig. 4.2. This kind of representation is convenient simply because it highlights the ways in which different processes are held to interact with each other. In essence we propose that following structural encoding of a seen face's appearance, different types of information can be extracted in parallel. Thus lip-reading, expression analysis, recognition of familiar faces, and the directed visual processing needed to compare unfamiliar faces to each other are all independently achieved. Recognition of a familiar face involves a match between the products of structural encoding and previously stored structural codes describing the appearance of familiar faces, held in face recognition units. Each recognition unit contains the description of the face of a known person, and the recognition unit will signal to a decision system the extent to which the seen face resembles its stored

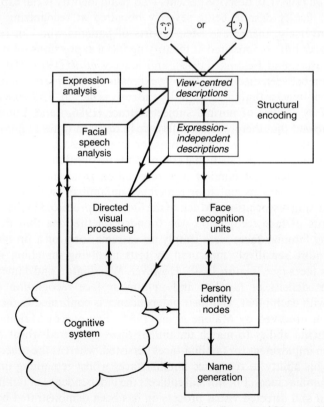

Fig. 4.2   Model of face-processing proposed by Bruce and Young (1986).

description. Activation of the recognition unit indicates that the seen face seems familiar. The face recognition unit can then access semantic information about the person seen via a person identity node, and finally the person's name. The person identity node would also be accessible from other types of input such as the voice or the written or spoken name; these other methods of person recognition are not shown in Fig 4.2, which deals only with face-processing.

Studies of normal subjects and studies of the effects of brain injuries are both consistent with Bruce and Young's (1986) model. I have already mentioned Campbell et al.'s (1986) demonstration of a double dissociation between impairments affecting facial speech analysis (lip-reading) and expression analysis. Their patient with impaired expression analysis, however, was also prosopagnosic.

This combination of impaired recognition of familiar faces and defective identification of facial expressions is found for some prosopagnosic patients, but not all. Hécaen and Angelergues (1962), Shuttleworth et al. (1982), and Bruyer et al. (1983) all describe patients who could identify facial expressions without difficulty despite being severely impaired at recognizing familiar faces. Conversely, there have been reports of patients who can recognize familiar faces but are impaired at identifying facial expressions by Bornstein (1963), Kurucz and Feldmar (1979), and Kurucz et al. (1979). The double dissociation between disorders affecting expression analysis and familiar face recognition suggests that these are independently achieved. This conclusion is supported by studies of normal subjects. Bruce (1986a) and Young et al. (1986c) showed that there was no difference in reaction times to familiar and unfamiliar faces in tasks requiring expression analysis, as would be expected if this is independent from functional components involved in face recognition.

The independence of familiar face recognition from the directed visual processing necessary to match or remember unfamiliar faces is among the more surprising dissociations. Much of the literature produced in the 1960s on impairments of face recognition was founded on the idea that deficits in recognizing familiar faces were simply an extreme form of a problem that could be more sensitively measured by tests involving matching views of unfamiliar faces (see Benton 1980). However, Warrington and James (1967) found that deficits of familiar and unfamiliar face recognition did not correlate with each other, and their independence is confirmed in the double dissociation observed by Malone et al. (1982). For one of Malone et al.'s (1982) patients ability to match unfamiliar faces recovered whilst a severe recognition impairment for familiar faces persisted, whereas the other patient recovered his ability to recognize familiar faces whilst remaining unable to match unfamiliar faces. For normal subjects the independence of familiar face recognition and directed visual processing has been demonstrated by Bruce (1979).

Separation of the system that identifies familiar faces into sequentially accessed face recognition units, person identity nodes, and name generation is supported by studies of everyday errors and by experiments with normal subjects. A common type of everyday error is to know that a face is familiar, but to be unable to bring to mind any information concerning whose face it is (Young *et al.* 1985*a*). Thus it is possible to recognize the face's surface form as corresponding to that of a familiar person without being able to access any stored semantic information about that person, as the separation of face recognition units and person identity nodes would imply. Similarly, in experiments with normal subjects different factors affect reaction times for familiarity (familiar vs. unfamiliar) and semantic (politician vs. non-politician) decisions to faces, suggesting that different functional components underpin each type of discrimination (Young *et al.* 1986*d*).

Another common experience is to see a face and know who the person is but to be unable to remember the person's name (Yarmey 1973; Reason and Lucas 1984; Young *et al.* 1985*a*; Cohen and Faulkner 1986). When in this state we can usually remember where we met that person, who her or his friends are, and so on; only the name remains elusive. This suggests that names are accessed indirectly from seen faces via person identity nodes, and this idea is bolstered by the observation that we never seem to remember a name without knowing who the person is (Young *et al.* 1985*a*). We do not find ourselves thinking: 'There's Paul McCartney, but who is he?' Such an error would be perfectly possible if names were retrieved directly from face recognition units, but it could not happen if names are accessed indirectly via identity nodes that specify who the person is.

Formal experiments also support this conception. Reaction times to name faces are longer than reaction times for categorizing them by occupation (Young *et al.* 1986*b*), as would be expected if semantic information provided by the person identity node is accessed from a familiar face before the person's name. Names, in fact, can be remarkably more difficult to learn than other types of semantic information. Cohen and Faulkner (1986) showed that people's names were poorly recalled in comparison to place names, occupations, or hobbies, and McWeeny *et al.* (1987) found that it was harder to learn the same items if they were presented as names (Mr Carpenter, Mr Farmer, etc.) than if they were presented as occupations (the carpenter, the farmer, etc.).

Automatic aspects of recognition

Some aspects of visual recognition proceed quite automatically. We cannot look at Margaret Thatcher's face and will ourselves not to recognize it, however much some of us might want to. An interesting way of examining these automatic aspects of recognition is to use priming tasks. I will briefly discuss repetition priming and semantic priming.

Repetition priming tasks investigate the facilitatory effect of having recently encountered a particular stimulus on subsequent recognition. The facilitatory effects found are usually reasonably long-lasting; they can be measured across delays of several minutes, hours, or even days. They are also material-specific. Thus visual recognition of a particular word is primed to a greater extent by seeing the word than by hearing it (Clarke and Morton 1983) or saying it in response to a definition (Winnick and Daniel 1970). Similarly, visual recognition of a particular object is primed by seeing an object of the same type but not primed by reading the object's name (Warren and Morton 1982).

Repetition priming effects on face recognition are also material-specific. The decision that a particular face is familiar is more quickly taken if that face has been recently seen, but is unaffected by having seen the person's name or even his or her (clothed) body (Bruce and Valentine 1985; Ellis *et al.* 1987*a*). The fact that there is no priming from names or bodies rules out person identity nodes as a possible source of repetition priming effects, and suggests instead that they arise from repetition of structural encoding processes or from the persistence of activation in face recognition units. This view is also supported by the finding that priming effects are material-specific for semantic (politician vs. non-politician) as well as for familiarity decisions (Young *et al.* 1986*d*); hence the person identity nodes do not seem to contribute to repetition priming even in a task (semantic decision) that requires their involvement.

The reason why repetition priming effects are material-specific is probably that they are based on physical similarity between the previously seen and test stimuli. Ellis *et al.* (1987*a*) showed that repetition priming will transfer from one photograph of a face to a different photograph of the same face, but only in proportion to the extent to which the second photograph is similar to that initially seen. Priming is maximal to the same photograph, less to a similar photograph of the same face, and less again to a dissimilar photograph of that face. Thus names and bodies do not prime later recognition of the same people's faces because their names and bodies do not look like their faces.

An important implication of material specificity is that repetition priming effects are not based on deliberately remembering who was in the initial (pre-training) phase of the experiment. Normal subjects can remember the faces, names, bodies, or whatever other items they encountered during the pre-training phase, but of these only the faces affect their subsequent reaction times for face recognition. Thus there is an independence between memory for the pre-training items and repetition priming effects. Schacter (1987) reviews several lines of evidence pointing to the same conclusion.

In semantic priming tasks the influence of one stimulus on the recognition of a different stimulus is investigated. Recognition of related stimuli is facilitated. Thus seeing the word 'doctor' primes recognition of the word 'nurse', seeing a loaf of bread primes recognition of a piece of cheese, and seeing Prince Charles's face primes recognition of Princess Diana (Meyer and Schvaneveldt 1971; Sperber *et al.* 1979; Bruce and Valentine 1986).

Semantic priming effects differ from repetition priming effects, however, in that they cross from one type of material to another (for example, from a seen object to word recognition; Sperber *et al.* 1979; McCauley *et al.* 1980) and they are comparatively short-lived, usually dissipating within a matter of seconds (Dannenbring and Briand 1982; Bruce 1986*b*). Clearly, there are different loci for repetition and semantic priming effects.

The most commonly used paradigm for investigating semantic priming is to present stimuli in pairs in which a prime stimulus is followed by a target stimulus to which subjects respond. The relation between the prime and target stimuli can be varied, and different interstimulus intervals examined.

Bruce and Valentine (1986) used this paradigm to investigate semantic priming of face recognition. Their first experiment included related pairs (such as Ernie Wise's face preceded by Eric Morecambe's; these were a British comedy duo), neutral pairs (Ernie Wise preceded by an unfamiliar face), and unrelated pairs (Ernie Wise preceded by Prince Charles). Reaction times to recognize the second face in each pair as familiar were faster for related than for neutral pairs, even when the prime face preceded the target face by only 250 msec, but there was no difference between neutral and unrelated conditions. The semantic priming effect is thus one that facilitates the recognition of related stimuli without inhibiting recognition of unrelated stimuli. In terms of Posner and Snyder's (1975) influential two-process theory of expectancy, this type of effect is automatic in nature, since the use of conscious anticipatory strategies would have produced evidence of inhibitory effects. This is consistent with Bruce and Valentine's (1986) finding of facilitation without inhibition at the 250 msec prime-target interval, at which use of explicit expectancies would be most unlikely.

Repetition and semantic priming effects are automatic in nature, then, but they arise in different ways. I suspect that repetition priming arises from residual activation in the recognition system, whereas semantic priming affects decision thresholds (Ellis *et al.* 1987*b*; Young and Ellis, in press).

Recognition and awareness

An important feature of repetition and semantic priming is that such effects are not consciously mediated. Normal subjects are aware, of course, of recognizing the stimuli involved, but this awareness is not what is determining their performance.

This point is perhaps most clearly seen in studies of the effects of different types of brain injury. Amnesic patients, for instance, can show 'normal' priming effects for repetition and for broadly comparable tasks such as fragment completion, despite being unable to explicitly recognize or recall items as having been recently seen (Warrington and Weiskrantz 1968, 1970; Shimamura 1986; Schacter 1987). The previously seen stimuli are affecting their performance even though they are not aware that they have seen them before. Semantic priming of word recognition can be shown for patients with substantial comprehension impairments (Milberg and Blumstein 1981).

Dissociations of recognition mechanisms and different aspects of awareness have also been found in other clinical conditions (see Schacter *et al.* 1988). Only relatively basic recognition abilities have as yet been demonstrated within parts of the visual field that are blind on standard clinical tests (Weiskrantz 1986), but patients who 'extinguish' (i.e. do not report) the leftmost of two stimuli when one is presented in each visual field have been found to be able to accurately compare the stimulus presented in the extinguished left visual field to a simultaneously presented (and reportable) right visual field stimulus (Volpe *et al.* 1979). Shallice and Saffran (1986) have shown that a pure alexic patient who achieved overt recognition of words with a letter-by-letter strategy was able to make lexical decisions and some types of semantic decision at above-chance levels to words presented too briefly for him to be able to name them.

Covert recognition can also be shown in prosopagnosia. Bauer (1984) found that electrodermal responses were greater to presentation of the correct than of an incorrect name when his patient was viewing a familiar face that he could not recognize overtly, and Tranel and Damasio (1985) found that electrodermal responses were greater to familiar than to unfamiliar faces despite absence of overt recognition.

The underlying theme to all of these demonstrations is that certain aspects of visual recognition can remain intact without the patient's being aware that this is the case. Often the preserved capacities can only be revealed in tasks that test recognition implicitly.

We have recently carried out a detailed investigation of a prosopagnosic patient who shows covert recognition of familiar faces that he cannot identify explicitly (de Haan *et al.* 1987*a*, 1987*b*). Our patient, P.H., was involved in a motor-cycle accident. He sustained serious injuries, including a severe closed head injury and the loss of his right arm. His language skills are well preserved (verbal IQ = 91; consistent with his previous education), and he is still able to read small print (N5), but he shows impairments on tests of visual recognition and of memory.

In 'short-term' memory tasks P.H.'s performance is normal for both verbal and non-verbal material, but his performance on 'long-term' memory tasks is seriously impaired (score of 0 for recall of Wechsler Memory Scale stories after 60 minutes delay, and unable to reproduce any components of Rey-Osterrieth figure after 45 minutes delay). The severity of his memory impairment on formal tests is a little surprising, since he is well oriented and readily engages in conversation about what he has been doing recently, his holidays, and so on.

P.H.'s visual recognition problems are very severe, but he also shows some impairments of basic visual abilities. His visual fields are constricted, and he experiences impaired contrast sensitivity for all spatial frequencies greater than 1.5 cycles per degree. We do not, however, think that these impairments are sufficient to account for his visual recognition problems; other patients with more serious impairments of basic visual abilities do not show substantial recognition impairments.

P.H. complains of his inability to recognize faces in everyday life. We have shown him hundreds of photographs of famous faces, but only once was one of them overtly recognized. Neither can he sort faces into those that belong to familiar or unfamiliar people (18/36 correct). On tests that require him to match views of unfamiliar faces or to identify expressions he performs less well than control subjects, but is none the less well above chance level.

P.H. also experiences difficulties in identifying individual members of other visually homogeneous categories such as cars (3/33) or flowers (0/26), and there is also some object agnosia. His recognition deficits cannot be explained as a direct consequence of his memory problems, however. Although he cannot overtly recognize familiar faces, for example, he continues to be able to identify familiar people from their names; in other words, he has not forgotten who they are.

Because P.H. performs so poorly on even the simplest of overt face recognition tasks, we have made use of tasks in which familiarity might exert its effect implicitly. These include matching tasks, interference tasks, and learning tasks.

In matching tasks P.H. is asked to determine whether two simultaneously presented photographs show the same person or different people. When the photographs were of complete faces, P.H.'s responses were faster to familiar than to unfamiliar people. Reaction times and error rates for P.H. and normal subjects of the same age are shown in Table 4.1. P.H.'s reaction times are slow compared to those of normal subjects, but the difference between familiar and unfamiliar faces remains proportional to the overall increase. Slow times were found for all of our reaction time work with P.H. (we are measuring manual responses made with his left hand, not vocal reaction times), and they arose even in tasks he performed without difficulty (such as name classification). Slow performance of choice reaction time tasks is not unusual after closed head injury (van Zomeren and Deelman 1978). The key point is that, like normal subjects, P.H. matched familiar faces faster than unfamiliar faces, despite his inability to overtly identify them. Moreover, when the matching task was changed so that it demanded use of either internal or external features, P.H.'s reaction times for familiar faces were only faster than his reaction times to unfamiliar faces for internal feature matches. This pattern is again comparable to that seen in normal subjects (Young et al. 1985c).

Table 4.1 *Mean reaction times (msec) and percentage error rates for familiar and unfamiliar face matching by P.H. and 16 normal subjects of comparable age. [Data for P.H. from de Haan et al. (1987a); for normal subjects from Young et al. (1986c).]*

	Familiar	Unfamiliar
P.H.		
Mean reaction time	2550	2762
Error rate	18.7	16.4
Normal subjects		
Mean reaction time	977	1045
Error rate	1.6	3·9

The interference tasks we have used with P.H. involved simultaneous presentation of a face and a printed name. P.H. was instructed to carry out a semantic classification of the name (politician's vs. non-politician's name) and to ignore the face. Normal subjects find in tasks like this that they cannot ignore the faces, and their responses are longer when the irrelevant face belongs to a category that is inconsistent with the name they are classifying. In three separate interference tasks, P.H.'s reaction times showed precisely this pattern (De Haan *et al.* 1987a, 1987b). I will use De Haan *et al.*'s (1987b) study as an example.

De Haan *et al.* (1987b) used faces and names of four politicians and four non-politicians chosen to be of comparable age and appearance. A pre-test was used to establish that P.H. could not achieve accurate overt classification of the faces as those of politicians or of non-politicians (30/48 responses correct). He was then asked to classify the names as being those of politicians and of non-politicians, and given 32 trials with the names to practice the task. After this practice session the name + face stimuli were presented. These stimuli formed three conditions in which the name was accompanied by the same person's face (Same person), by the face of a different person from the same occupational category (Related), or by the face of a person from the other occupational category (Unrelated). There were 64 trials for each condition, with P.H. continuing to classify the names. The important feature of the design is that the same names and faces were used in each condition, only the way in which the names and faces were combined with each other differed across conditions.

Table 4.2 *Mean reaction times (msec) for name classification by P.H. The names are presented together with the face of the same person, a related face (from the same semantic category as the name), or an unrelated face (from the opposite semantic category to the name)*

Same person	Related	Unrelated
1059	1122	1234

P.H.'s reaction times for this interference task are shown in Table 4.2. They were longer for the unrelated than for the related condition, but the difference between the same person and related conditions was not significant. This corresponds exactly to the pattern found in equivalent studies of normal subjects (Young *et al.* 1986*a*). Hence, despite his inability to achieve accurate overt classification of the faces, P.H. none the less experienced covert recognition to a degree sufficient to interfere with a name classification task.

We adapted the idea of using learning tasks to investigate covert recognition from Bruyer *et al.* (1983). The basic paradigm involves learning to associate correct or incorrect information with photographs of familiar (but not overtly recognized) faces. In tasks of this type P.H. learnt correct names or correct occupations much more readily than incorrect names or occupations. This was even so for faces of people who have only become familiar to him since his accident. We found that he learnt to associate our names with photographs of our own faces much more readily than he could learn to associate our names with faces of unfamiliar people of the same age and sex and of comparable appearance (De Haan *et al.* 1987*a*). P.H. thus showed covert recognition of faces he has never recognized overtly; his face recognition system has continued to build representations of the new people it encounters.

In various different types of task, then, P.H. shows 'recognition without awareness'. He is, of course, perfectly well aware that he is looking at a face, and he can assess the person's age, sex, and so on reasonably reliably, but he has lost the sense of knowing who the person is. Yet, as we have seen, his recognition mechanisms are in many ways surprisingly intact. We might make an analogy with Weiskrantz's (1986) discussion of blindsight and say that it is as if face recognition mechanisms have been disconnected from other functional systems that might have allowed P.H. to comment on his recognition abilities.

Such neuropsychological phenomena offer considerable promise for clarifying the relation between recognition mechanisms and awareness, and I will briefly discuss three of the issues that they raise. These involve the extent to which covert effects are typical of disordered recognition, the level at which covert recognition produces its effects, and the relation between perceptual and memory impairments. Work on covert recognition is sufficiently recent that I have no firm views as yet, and have already changed my mind on some points.

First, whether covert effects are typical of all cases of disordered recognition: I think this unlikely. Shallice and Saffran (1986), for instance, noted that previous studies of letter-by-letter readers by Warrington and Shallice (1980) and Patterson and Kay (1982) did not reveal the kind of effects they found with their patient. Similarly our own work with the patient M.S., who has a severe object agnosia and complete prosopagnosia on clinical tests (for further description see Newcombe and Ratcliff 1974 and Ratcliff and Newcombe 1982) indicates that he does not show covert recognition of faces or of objects (Young et al. 1987). We thus prefer to think in terms of covert recognition being characteristic of certain types of recognition disorder and not others.

This working hypothesis raises the question as to the level at which covert recognition produces its effects. We have seen that P.H. can show effects of semantic category in interference tasks and in learning to associate faces with occupations. These initially led us to suspect that he had achieved covert recognition of familiar faces to a level corresponding to person identity nodes. This would be problematic for models such as that of Bruce and Young (1986), since the person identity nodes are held to be common to face and name recognition; it would be hard to explain why the same identity node can be accessed overtly from the name but only covertly from the face. This problem would, of course, disappear if we stipulated that separate stores of semantic information are accessed from faces and names, but I now prefer instead to think that the covert effects arise at the recognition unit level. What I think we are seeing is the continued operation of automatic aspects of recognition mechanisms, and for this reason I am keen to explore the parallel between covert recognition following brain injury and those aspects of recognition that function automatically in normal people (see the discussion in the preceding section). To account for these automatic effects in the way I have outlined it will be necessary to postulate more organization at the recognition unit level than Bruce and Young (1986) had in mind, but our more recent pronouncements are in any case tending to move in this direction in order to account for semantic priming (Ellis et al. 1987b; Young and Ellis, in press).

I explained earlier that P.H.'s face recognition impairment is not simply due to his other memory problems, because he has not forgotten who familiar people are. The way in which his performance takes on a normal pattern as soon as it is tested implicitly is, however, reminiscent of many of the findings with amnesic patients. This would probably be expected by those who have argued that one form of prosopagnosia can be considered to be a material-specific amnesia (e.g. Warrington and James 1967; De Renzi 1982; Tiberghien and Clerc 1986). There is probably no hard and fast line to be drawn between perceptual and memory impairments, and this emphasizes the need to conceptualize the different types of deficit in terms of explicit functional models.

Summary

In this chapter I have discussed a wide range of findings concerning visual recognition. The following summary of what I think are the key points may help the reader to digest the rather stodgy resultant mixture.

1. Higher visual functions are organized, no less than basic functions, into modular subsystems. Dissociable disorders affecting only word, object, or face recognition can occur, and for each class of material a number of different types of impairment can be observed. Much of the reason for this type of organization probably lies in differences in the demands that are placed on recognition mechanisms by different types of material.

2. Some aspects of visual recognition are highly lateralized. A promising approach to disentangling the complex underlying arrangement is to formulate explicit functional models and to try to identify which components are involved using the techniques of experimental psychology.

3. Functional models can be developed from studies of normal and clinical subject populations. An adequate functional model should be able to account for the different types of impairment that can occur, and observed patterns of impairment can in turn be used to refine functional models.

4. Visual recognition mechanisms can operate automatically. Repetition and semantic priming provide good examples of automatic effects, but they arise in different ways. Repetition priming probably reflects residual activation in the recognition system, whereas semantic priming may affect decision thresholds.

5. Automatic processes involved in recognition may continue to function after brain injury, despite the patient's being unaware that this happens. Investigation of such cases promises to yield important insights into the mechanisms responsible both for recognition and for awareness itself.

Acknowledgements

My views on recognition disorders have been heavily influenced by discussions with Vicki Bruce, Edward de Haan, Andy Ellis, Hadyn Ellis, Dennis Hay, and Freda Newcombe, though I would not wish to hold any of these people responsible for my mistakes. The support provided by grants from ESRC (C 0023 2323), MRC (G8519533), and the Nuffield Foundation is gratefully acknowledged.

References

Albert, M. L., Reches, A., and Silverberg, R. (1975). Associative visual agnosia without alexia. *Neurology*, **25**, 322–6.

Allen, M. (1983). Models of hemispheric specialization. *Psychological Bulletin*, **93**, 73–104.

Allport, A. (1979). Word recognition in reading. In *Processing of visible language, 1*, (ed. P. A. Kolers, M. E. Wrolstad, and H. Bouma), pp. 227–57. Plenum, New York.

Assal, G., Favre, C., and Anderes, J. P. (1984). Non-reconnaissance d'animaux familiers chez un paysan: zoo-agnosie ou prosopagnosie pour les animaux. *Revue Neurologique*, **140**, 580–4.

Bauer, R. M. (1984). Autonomic recognition of names and faces in prosopagnosia: a neuropsychological application of the guilty knowledge test. *Neuropsychologia*, **22**, 457–69.

Beauvois, M-F. (1982). Optic aphasia: a process of interaction between vision and language. *Philosophical Transactions of the Royal Society, London*, **B298**, 35–47.

Benton, A. L. (1980). The neuropsychology of facial recognition. *American Psychologist*, **35**, 176–86.

Blanc-Garin, J. (1984). Perception des visages et reconnaissance de la physionomie dans l'agnosie des visages. *L'Année Psychologique*, **84**, 573–98.

Bornstein, B. (1963). Prosopagnosia. In *Problems of dynamic neurology*, (ed. L. Halpern), pp. 283–318. Hadassah Medical School, Jerusalem.

Brand, N., van Bekkum, I., Stumpel, M., and Kroeze, J. H. A. (1983). Word matching and lexical decisions: a visual half-field study. *Brain and Language*, **18**, 199–211.

Bruce, V. (1979). Searching for politicians: an information-processing approach to face recognition. *Quarterly Journal of Experimental Psychology*, **31**, 373–95.

—— (1983). Recognizing faces. *Philosophical Transactions of the Royal Society, London*, **B302**, 423–36.

—— (1986a). Influences of familiarity on the processing of faces. *Perception*, **15**, 387–97.

—— (1986b). Recognising familiar faces. In *Aspects of face processing*, (ed. H. D. Ellis, M. A. Jeeves, F. Newcombe, and A. Young), pp. 107–17. Martinus Nijhoff, The Hague.

—— and Valentine, T. (1985). Identity priming in the recognition of familiar faces. *British Journal of Psychology*, **76**, 373–83.

—— and Valentine, T. (1986). Semantic priming of familiar faces. *Quarterly Journal of Experimental Psychology*, **38A**, 125–50.

—— and Young, A. W. (1986). Understanding face recognition. *British Journal of Psychology*, **77**, 305–27.

Bruyer, R. *et al.* (1983). A case of prosopagnosia with some preserved covert remembrance of familiar faces. *Brain and Cognition*, **2**, 257–84.

Bushnell, I. W. R. (1982). Discrimination of faces by young infants. *Journal of Experimental Child Psychology*, **33**, 298–308.

Campbell, R., Landis, T., and Regard, M. (1986). Face recognition and lipreading: a neurological dissociation. *Brain*, **109**, 509–21.

Carr, T. H. and Pollatsek, A. (1985). Recognizing printed words: a look at current models. In *Reading research: advances in theory and practice, 5*, (ed. D. Besner, T. G. Waller, and G. E. Mackinnon). pp. 1–82. Academic Press, New York.

Chiarello, C. (1987). Lateralization of lexical processes in the normal brain: a review of visual half-field research. In *Studies in neuropsychology*, (ed. H. A. Whitaker and A. Caramazza). Lawrence Erlbaum Associates, Hillsdale, NJ.

Clarke, R. and Morton, J. (1983). Cross modality facilitation in tachistoscopic word recognition. *Quarterly Journal of Experimental Psychology*, **35A**, 79–96.

Cohen, G. and Faulkner, D. (1986). Memory for proper names: age differences in retrieval. *British Journal of Developmental Psychology*, **4**, 187–97.

Coltheart, M. (1981). Disorders of reading and their implications for models of normal reading. *Visible Language*, **15**, 245–86.

Cowey, A. (1985). Aspects of cortical organization related to selective attention and selective impairments of visual perception: a tutorial review. In *Attention and performance, XI*, (ed. M. I. Posner and O. S. M. Marin), pp. 41–62. Lawrence Erlbaum Associates, Hillsdale, NJ.

Damasio, A. R. and Damasio, H. (1983). The anatomic basis of pure alexia. *Neurology*, **33**, 1573–83.

——, Yamada, T., Damasio, H., Corbett, J., and McKee, J. (1980). Central achromatopsia: behavioral, anatomic and physiologic aspects. *Neurology*, **30**, 1064–71.

——, Damasio, H., and Van Hoesen, G. W. (1982). Prosopagnosia: anatomic basis and behavioral mechanisms. *Neurology*, **32**, 331–41.

——, ——, and Tranel, D. (1986). Prosopagnosia: anatomic and physiologic aspects. In *Aspects of face processing*, (ed. H. D. Ellis, M. A. Jeeves, F. Newcombe, and A. Young), pp. 268–72. Martinus Nijhoff, The Hague.

Dannenbring, G. L. and Briand, K. (1982). Semantic priming and the word repetition effect in a lexical decision task. *Canadian Journal of Psychology*, **36**, 435–44.

De Casper, A. J. and Fifer, W. P. (1980). Of human bonding: newborns prefer their mothers' voices. *Science*, **208**, 1174–6.

De Haan, E. H. F. and Hay, D. C. (1986). The matching of famous and unknown faces, given either the internal or the external features: a study on patients with unilateral brain lesions. In *Aspects of face processing*, (ed. H. D. Ellis, M. A. Jeeves, F. Newcombe, and A. Young), pp. 302–9. Martinus Nijhoff, The Hague.

——, Young, A., and Newcombe, F. (1987a). Face recognition without awareness. *Cognitive Neuropsychology*, **4**, 385–415.

——, ——, and Newcombe, F. (1987b). Faces interfere with name classification in a prosopagnosic patient. *Cortex*, **23**, 309–16.

De Renzi, E. (1982). Memory disorders following focal neocortical damage. *Philosophical Transactions of the Royal Society of London*, **B298**, 73–83.

—— (1986a). Current issues in prosopagnosia. In *Aspects of face processing*, (ed. H. D. Ellis, M. A. Jeeves, F. Newcombe, and A. Young), pp. 243–52. Martinus Nijhoff, The Hague.

—— (1986b). Prosopagnosia in two patients with CT scan evidence of damage confined to the right hemisphere. *Neuropsychologia*, **24**, 385–9.

—— and Spinnler, H. (1966a). Facial recognition in brain damaged patients. *Neurology*, **16**, 145–52.

—— and —— (1966b). Visual recognition in patients with unilateral cerebral disease. *Journal of Nervous and Mental Disease*, **142**, 515–25.

——, Faglioni, P., and Spinnler, H. (1968). The performance of patients with unilateral brain damage on face recognition tasks. *Cortex*, **4**, 17–34.

——, Scotti, G., and Spinnler, H. (1969). Perceptual and associative disorders of visual recognition: relationship to the side of the cerebral lesion. *Neurology*, **19**, 634–42.

Diamond, R. and Carey, S. (1986). Why faces are and are not special: an effect of expertise. *Journal of Experimental Psychology: General*, **115**, 107–17.

Ellis, A. W., Young, A. W., Flude, B. M., and Hay, D. C. (1987a). Repetition priming of face recognition. *Quarterly Journal of Experimental Psychology*, **39A**, 193–210.

——, ——, and Hay, D. C. (1987b). Modelling the recognition of faces and words. *Modelling cognition*, (ed. P. E. Morris), pp. 269–97. John Wiley, Chichester, Sussex.

Ellis, H. D. (1975). Recognizing faces. *British Journal of Psychology*, **66**, 409–26.

—— (1981). Theoretical aspects of face recognition. In *Perceiving and remembering faces*, (ed. G. M. Davies, H. D. Ellis, and J. W. Shepherd), pp. 171–97. Academic Press, London.

—— (1983). The role of the right hemisphere in face perception. In *Functions of the right cerebral hemisphere* (ed. A. W. Young), pp. 33–64, Academic Press, London.

—— (1986). Processes underlying face recognition. In *The neuropsychology of face perception and facial expression*, (ed. R. Bruyer), pp. 1–27. Lawrence Erlbaum Associates, Hillsdale, NJ.

—— and Young, A. W. (in press). Are faces special? In *Handbook of research on face processing*, (ed. A. W. Young and H. D. Ellis). North-Holland, Amsterdam.

——, Shepherd, J. W., and Davies, G. M. (1979). Identification of familiar and unfamiliar faces from internal and external features: some implications for theories of face recognition. *Perception*, **8**, 431–9.

Etcoff, N. L. (1984). Selective attention to facial identity and facial emotion. *Neuropsychologia*, **22**, 281–95.

—— (1985). The neuropsychology of emotional expression. In *Advances in Clinical Neuropsychology, 3*, (ed. G. Goldstein and R. E. Tarter). Plenum, New York.

Fagan, J. F. III (1979). The origins of facial pattern recognition. In *Psychological development from infancy*, (ed. M. H. Bornstein and W. Kessen), pp. 83–113. Lawrence Erlbaum Associates, Hillsdale, NJ.

Ferro, J. M. and Santos, M. E. (1984). Associative visual agnosia: a case study. *Cortex*, **20**, 121–34.

Field, T. M., Woodson, R., Greenberg, R., and Cohen, D. (1982). Discrimination and imitation of facial expressions by neonates. *Science*, **218**, 179–81.

Gazzaniga, M. S. and Smylie, C. S. (1983). Facial recognition and brain asymmetries: clues to underlying mechanisms. *Annals of Neurology*, **13**, 536–40.

Goren, C. G., Sarty, M., and Wu, P. Y. K. (1975). Visual following and pattern discrimination of face-like stimuli by newborn infants. *Pediatrics*, **56**, 544–9.

Hay, D. C. and Young, A. W. (1982). The human face. In *Normality and pathology in cognitive functions*, (ed. A. W. Ellis), pp. 173–202. Academic Press, London.

Hécaen, H. and Angelergues, R. (1962). Agnosia for faces (prosopagnosia). *Archives of Neurology*, **7**, 92–100.

—— and Kremin, H. (1976). Neurolinguistic research on reading disorders resulting from left hemisphere lesions: aphasic and 'pure' alexias. In *Studies in neurolinguistics, Vol. 2*, (ed. H. Whitaker and H. A. Whitaker). Academic Press, New York.

——, Goldblum, M. C., Masure, M. C., and Ramier, A. M. (1974). Une nouvelle observation d'agnosie d'objet. Deficit de l'association ou de la categorisation, specifique de la modalité visuelle? *Neuropsychologia*, **12**, 447–64.

Humphreys, G. W. (1987). Objects, words, brains and computers. *Bulletin of the British Psychological Society*, **40**, 207–10.

Kurucz, J. and Feldmar, G. (1979). Prosopo-affective agnosia as a symptom of cerebral organic disease. *Journal of the American Geriatrics Society*, **27**, 225–30.

——, ——, and Werner, W. (1979). Prosopo-affective agnosia associated with chronic organic brain syndrome. *Journal of the American Geriatrics Society*, **27**, 91–5.

Landis, T., Cummings, J. L., Christen, L., Bogen, J. E., and Imhof, H-G. (1986). Are unilateral right posterior cerebral lesions sufficient to cause prosopagnosia? Clinical and radiological findings in six additional patients. *Cortex*, **22**, 243–52.

Levine, D. N. (1978). Prosopagnosia and visual object agnosia: a behavioral study. *Brain and Language*, **5**, 341–65.

Levy, J., Trevarthen, C., and Sperry, R. (1972). Perception of bilateral chimeric figures following hemispheric disconnexion. *Brain*, **95**, 61–78.

McCarthy, R. A. and Warrington, E. K. (1986). Visual associative agnosia: a clinico-anatomical study of a single case. *Journal of Neurology, Neurosurgery and Psychiatry*, **49**, 1233–40.

McCauley, C., Parmelee, C., Sperber, R., and Carr, T. (1980). Early extraction of meaning from pictures and its relation to conscious identification. *Journal of Experimental Psychology: Human Perception and Performance*, **6**, 265–76.

McGurk, H. and MacDonald, J. (1976). Hearing lips and seeing voices. *Nature*, **264**, 746–8.

MacKain, K. S., Studdert-Kennedy, M., Spieker, S., and Stern, D. (1983). Infant intermodal speech perception is a left hemisphere function. *Science*, **219**, 1347–9.

MacRae, D. and Trolle, E. (1956). The defect of function in visual agnosia. *Brain*, **79**, 94–110.

McWeeny, K. H., Young, A. W., Hay, D. C., and Ellis, A. W. (1987). Putting names to faces. *British Journal of Psychology*, **78**, 143–9.

Malone, D. R., Morris, H. H., Kay, M. C., and Levin, H. S. (1982). Prosopagnosia: a double dissociation between the recognition of familiar and unfamiliar faces. *Journal of Neurology, Neurosurgery, and Psychiatry*, **45**, 820–2.

Marr, D. (1982). *Vision*. W. H. Freeman, San Francisco, CA.

Meadows, J. C. (1974). The anatomical basis of prosopagnosia. *Journal of Neurology, Neurosurgery and Psychiatry*, **37**, 489–501.

Meltzoff, A. N. and Moore, M. K. (1977). Imitation of facial and manual gestures by human neonates. *Science*, **198**, 75–8.

—— and —— (1983). Newborn infants imitate adult facial gestures. *Child Development*, **54**, 702–9.

Meyer, D. E. and Schvaneveldt, R. W. (1971). Facilitation in recognizing pairs of words: evidence of a dependence between retrieval operations. *Journal of Experimental Psychology*, **90**, 227–34.

Milberg, W. and Blumstein, S. E. (1981). Lexical decision and aphasia: evidence for semantic processing. *Brain and Language*, **14**, 371–85.

Mills, M. and Melhuish, E. (1974). Recognition of mother's voice in early infancy. *Nature*, **252**, 123–4.

Morton, J. (1979). Facilitation in word recognition: experiments causing change in the logogen model. In *Processing of visible language, 1*, (ed. P. A. Kolers, M. Wrolstad, and H. Bouma), pp. 259–68. Plenum, New York.

—— (1981). The status of information processing models of language. *Philosophical Transactions of the Royal Society, London*, **B295**, 387–96.

Moscovitch, M. (1979). Information processing and the cerebral hemispheres. In *Handbook of behavioural neurobiology, vol. 2: neuropsychology*, (ed. M. S. Gazzaniga), pp. 379–446. Plenum, New York.

—— (1981). Right-hemisphere language. *Topics in Language Disorders*, **1**, 41–61.

—— (1986). Afferent and efferent models of visual perceptual asymmetries: theoretical and empirical implications. *Neuropsychologia*, **24**, 91–114.

——, Scullion, D., and Christie, D. (1976). Early versus late stages of processing and their relation to functional hemispheric asymmetries in face recognition. *Journal of Experimental Psychology: Human Perception and Performance*, **2**, 401–16.

Newcombe, F. and Ratcliff, G. (1974). Agnosia: a disorder of object recognition. In *Les syndromes de disconnexion calleuse chez l'homme*, (ed. F. Michel and B. Schott), pp. 317–41. Colloque International de Lyon, Lyon.

—— and Russell, W. R. (1969). Dissociated visual perceptual and spatial deficits in focal lesions of the right hemisphere. *Journal of Neurology, Neurosurgery and Psychiatry*, **32**, 73–81.

——, Ratcliff, G., and Damasio, H. (1987). Dissociable visual and spatial impairments following right posterior cerebral lesions: clinical, neuropsychological and anatomical evidence. *Neuropsychologia*, **25**, 149–61.

Pallis, C. A. (1955). Impaired identification of faces and places with agnosia for colours. *Journal of Neurology, Neurosurgery and Psychiatry*, **18**, 218–24.

Patterson, K. E. (1981). Neuropsychological approaches to the study of reading. *British Journal of Psychology*, **72**, 151–74.

—— and Kay, J. (1982). Letter-by-letter reading; psychological descriptions of a neurological syndrome. *Quarterly Journal of Experimental Psychology*, **34A**, 411–41.

Posner, M. I. and Snyder, C. R. R. (1975). Facilitation and inhibition in the processing of signals. In *Attention and performance, V*, (ed. P. M. A. Rabbitt and S. Dornic), pp. 668–82. Academic Press, London.

Ratcliff, G. and Newcombe, F. (1982). Object recognition: some deductions from the clinical evidence. In *Normality and pathology in cognitive functions*, (ed. A. W. Ellis), pp. 147–71. Academic Press, London.

Reason, J. T. and Lucas, D. (1984). Using cognitive diaries to investigate naturally occurring memory blocks. In *Everyday memory, actions and absentmindedness*, (ed. J. Harris and P. E. Morris), pp. 53–70. Academic Press, London.

Rhodes, G. (1985). Lateralized processes in face recognition. *British Journal of Psychology*, **76**, 249–71.

Rosch, E., Mervis, C. B., Gray, W. D., Johnson, D. M., and Boyes-Braem, P. (1976). Basic objects in natural categories. *Cognitive Psychology*, **8**, 382–439.

Schacter, D. L. (1987). Implicit memory: history and current status. *Journal of Experimental Psychology: Learning, Memory and Cognition*, **13**, 501–18.

——, McAndrews, M. P., and Moscovitch, M. (1988). Access to consciousness: dissociations between implicit and explicit knowledge in neuropsychological syndromes. In *Thought without language*, (ed. L. Weiskrantz), pp. 242–78. Oxford University Press.

Sergent, J. (1982). About face: left-hemisphere involvement in processing physiognomies. *Journal of Experimental Psychology: Human Perception and Performance*, **8**, 1–14.

—— (1983). Role of the input in visual hemispheric asymmetries. *Psychological Bulletin*, **93**, 481–512.

—— (1984a). Configural processing of faces in the left and right cerebral hemispheres. *Journal of Experimental Psychology: Human Perception and Performance*, **10**, 554–72.

—— (1984b). Inferences from unilateral brain damage about normal hemispheric functions in visual pattern recognition. *Psychological Bulletin*, **96**, 99–115.

—— (1988). Face perception and the right hemisphere. In *Thought without language*, (ed. L. Weiskrantz), pp. 108–31. Oxford University Press.

Shallice, T. and Saffran, E. (1986). Lexical processing in the absence of explicit word identification: evidence from a letter-by-letter reader. *Cognitive Neuropsychology*, **3**, 429–58.

Shimamura, A. P. (1986). Priming effects in amnesia: evidence for a dissociable memory function. *Quarterly Journal of Experimental Psychology*, **38A**, 619–44.

Shuttleworth, E. C. Jr., Syring, V., and Allen, N. (1982). Further observations on the nature of prosopagnosia. *Brain and Cognition*, **1**, 307–22.

Sperber, R. D., McCauley, C., Ragain, R. D., and Weil, C. M. (1979). Semantic priming effects on picture and word processing. *Memory and Cognition*, **7**, 339–45.

Studdert-Kennedy, M. (1983). On learning to speak. *Human Neurobiology*, **2**, 191–5.

Tiberghien, G. and Clerc, I. (1986). The cognitive locus of prosopagnosia. In *The neuropsychology of face perception and facial expression*, (ed. R. Bruyer, pp. 39–62). Lawrence Erlbaum Associates, Hillsdale, NJ.

Tranel, D. and Damasio, A. R. (1985). Knowledge without awareness: an autonomic index of facial recognition by prosopagnosics. *Science*, **228**, 1453–4.

Ungerleider, L. G. and Mishkin, M. (1982). Two cortical visual systems. In *Analysis of visual behaviour*, (ed. D. J. Ingle, M. A. Goodale, and R. J. W. Mansfield), pp. 549–86. MIT Press, Cambridge, MA.

van Zomeren, A. H. and Deelman, B. G. (1978). Long term recovery of visual reaction time after closed head injury. *Journal of Neurology, Neurosurgery and Psychiatry*, **41**, 452–7.

Vinter, A. (1985). La capacité d'imitation a la naissance: elle existe, mais que signifie-t-elle? *Canadian Journal of Psychology*, **39**, 16–33.

Volpe, B. T., LeDoux, J. E., and Gazzaniga, M. S. (1979). Information processing of visual stimuli in an 'extinguished' field. *Nature*, **282**, 722–4.

Warren, C. and Morton, J. (1982). The effects of priming on picture recognition. *British Journal of Psychology*, **73**, 117–29.

Warrington, E. K. (1982). Neuropsychological studies of object recognition. *Philosophical Transactions of the Royal Society, London*, **B298**, 15–33.

—— and James, M. (1967). An experimental investigation of facial recognition in patients with unilateral cerebral lesions. *Cortex*, **3**, 317–26.

—— and Shallice, T. (1980). Word-form dyslexia. *Brain*, **103**, 99–112.

—— and Taylor, A. M. (1973). The contribution of the right parietal lobe to object recognition. *Cortex*, **9**, 152–64.

—— and —— (1978). Two categorical stages of object recognition. *Perception*, **7**, 695–705.

—— and Weiskrantz, L. (1968). New method of testing long-term retention with special reference to amnesic patients. *Nature*, **217**, 972–4.

—— and —— (1970). Amnesia: consolidation or retrieval? *Nature*, **228**, 628–30.

Weiskrantz, L. (1986). *Blindsight: a case study and implications*. Oxford Psychology Series 12. Oxford University Press.

Winnick, W. A. and Daniel, S. A. (1970). Two kinds of response priming in tachistoscopic recognition. *Journal of Experimental Psychology*, **84**, 74–81.

Witelson, S. F. (1977). Early hemisphere specialization and interhemisphere plasticity: an empirical and theoretical review. In *Language development and neurological theory*, (ed. S. J. Segalowitz and F. A. Gruber), pp. 213–87. Academic Press, New York.

—— (1983). Bumps on the brain: right-left anatomic asymmetry as a key to functional lateralization. In *Language functions and brain organization*, (ed. S. J. Segalowitz), pp. 117–44. Academic Press, New York.

Yarmey, A. D. (1973). I recognize your face but I can't remember your name: further evidence on the tip-of-the-tongue phenomenon. *Memory and Cognition*, **3**, 287–90.

Yin, R. K. (1969). Looking at upside-down faces. *Journal of Experimental Psychology*, **81**, 141–5.

—— (1970). Face recognition by brain-injured patients: a dissociable ability? *Neuropsychologia*, **8**, 395–402.

Young, A. W. (1982). Asymmetry of cerebral hemispheric function during development. In *Brain and behavioural development*, (ed. J. W. T. Dickerson and H. McGurk), pp. 168–202. Blackie, Glasgow.

—— (1983). The development of right hemisphere abilities. In *Functions of the right cerebral hemisphere*, (ed. A. W. Young), pp. 147–69. Academic Press, London.

—— (1984). Right cerebral hemisphere superiority for recognising the internal and external features of famous faces. *British Journal of Psychology*, **75**, 161–9.

—— (1986). Subject characteristics in lateral differences for face processing by normals: age. In *The neuropsychology of face perception and facial expression*, (ed. R. Bruyer), pp. 167–200. Lawrence Erlbaum Associates, Hillsdale, NJ.

—— (1987). Cerebral hemisphere differences and reading. In *Cognitive approaches to reading*, (ed. J. R. Beech and A. M. Colley), pp. 139–68. John Wiley, Chichester, Sussex.

—— and Ellis, A. W. (1985). Different methods of lexical access for words presented in the left and right visual hemifields. *Brain and Language*, **24**, 326–58.

—— and Ellis, H. D. (in press). Semantic processing. In *Handbook of research on face processing*, (ed. A. W. Young and H. D. Ellis). North-Holland, Amsterdam.

—— and Ratcliff, G. (1983). Visuospatial abilities of the right hemisphere. In *Functions of the right cerebral hemisphere*, (ed. A. W. Young), pp. 1–32. Academic Press, London.

——, Ellis, A. W., and Bion, P. J. (1984). Left hemisphere superiority for pronounceable nonwords, but not for unpronounceable letter strings. *Brain and Language*, **22**, 14–25.

——, Hay, D. C., and Ellis, A. W. (1985a). The faces that launched a thousand slips: everyday difficulties and errors in recognising people. *British Journal of Psychology*, **76**, 495–523.

——, ——, and McWeeny, K. H. (1985b). Right cerebral hemisphere superiority for constructing facial representations. *Neuropsychologia*, **23**, 195–202.

——, ——, ——, Flude, B. M., and Ellis, A. W. (1985c). Matching familiar and unfamiliar faces on internal and external features. *Perception*, **14**, 737–46.

——, Ellis, A. W., Flude, B. M., McWeeny, K. H., and Hay, D. C. (1986a). Face–name interference. *Journal of Experimental Psychology: Human Perception and Performance*, **12**, 466–75.

——, McWeeny, K. H., Ellis, A. W., and Hay, D. C. (1986b). Naming and categorising faces and written names. *Quarterly Journal of Experimental Psychology*, **38A**, 297–318.

——, ——, Hay, D. C., and Ellis, A. W. (1986c). Matching familiar and unfamiliar faces on identity and expression. *Psychological Research*, **48**, 63–8.

——, ——, ——, and —— (1986d). Access to identity-specific semantic codes from familiar faces. *Quarterly Journal of Experimental Psychology*, **38A**, 271–95.

——, de Haan, E. H. F., and Newcombe, F. (1987). Object agnosia and prosopagnosia without covert recognition. Paper presented at the EPS Meeting, Nottingham.

Zihl, J., von Cramon, D., and Mai, N. (1983). Selective disturbance of movement vision after bilateral brain damage. *Brain*, **106**, 313–40.

5

Face perception and the right hemisphere

JUSTINE SERGENT

Introduction

One indispensable capacity that social animals must possess is the ability to discriminate between other members of the group and to recognize them, and there is no doubt that, for humans, the face is the most effective and reliable cue for this purpose. This is somewhat paradoxical because a face is not a rigid and static object and it takes so many different expressions and poses that its appearance is ever changing. In addition, faces are morphologically very similar to one another, and, therefore, potentially prone to confusions. Recognizing faces must thus require a powerful device able to encode information contained in a face, extract the physiognomic invariants that uniquely define an individual, and store this information in an accurate manner. No computer has yet surpassed the brain in this respect, and our capacity to discriminate between faces, although it develops over time, requires no formal training and is acquired quasi-automatically. By contrast with speech which begins as a process of mimicking the words heard in association with a particular experience, face recognition is not acquired through imitation and is in fact a private experience, almost uncommunicable to others. Indeed, every attempt so far to increase our capacity to identify and remember the faces of other people has resulted in failure, at least for faces of our own race, and training has even sometimes reduced the subjects' capacity to recognize faces (Baddeley 1979). This does not mean that one could not improve this skill, but two factors may prevent this improvement. One is that we still do not understand how we perceive and recognize faces, and it is therefore difficult to improve the efficiency of a function whose basic mechanisms are unknown. The second factor is that our ability to deal with faces is already at a very high level and there may be no room for improvement. As noted by Ellis (1981), our capacity for discriminating and identifying faces may represent the ultimate in our classificatory abilities, and there is practically no other class of visual objects, having such a similarity among its members, which is dealt with as efficiently as faces.

Whether the face constitutes a special class of visual object has been the matter of considerable debate. Certainly, few, if any, other categories carry with them such social, personal, communicative, and affective importance that we need pay as much attention to them as we do to faces. Identification is but one aspect of what we can do with the information contained in a face, and we also make inferences about character and personality, sex, age, race, mood and feelings. As pointed out by Yin (1978), the potential uniqueness of face perception is that people derive a great deal of information from the face on the basis of very slight differences. In as much as faces represent a biologically relevant category of visual objects, specific neural mechanisms may have evolved that would be uniquely dedicated to their processing. This, of course, implies a particular view of how the brain organizes its functions, and one must examine empirical evidence to determine whether such an organization would correspond to the functional architecture of the brain. It is, in fact, equally plausible that faces are treated by some 'general-purpose' neural mechanisms, involved in the processing of all visual stimuli, but that would have become particularly well tuned to faces because of their relevance for an individual and of their frequent appearance.

While much speculation has surrounded this issue, it remains that we still know very little about the processes underlying face perception. Among the many useful and interesting approaches to understanding this problem that have been developed, the one I have chosen addresses only some of the relevant questions and bears on perceptual processes and the nature of the representations on which operations are performed. In the context of this symposium devoted to 'thought without language', the problem of the processes underlying face perception and recognition may appear marginal. However, taken in its broad sense, thought may be conceived as a process involving an organized hierarchy of associations, symbols, or labels, and, in the process of thinking, one acts to organize information initially not clearly coherent so that it may become understood. Thought is thus a means of reality manipulation and of deduction, which also characterizes the processes inherent in perceiving and remembering faces. As noted by Gregory (1970, p. 147), 'human thought is an outgrowth of the sort of distal, multidimensional perception which is characteristic of vision', and the type of processes involved in face perception may reflect some basic properties of thought without language.

Processes underlying face perception

Despite the apparent automaticity typical of face perception and recognition, a considerable number of difficulties have to be solved by the brain in order to extract the invariant features necessary to access the identity of an individual from the initial array of intensities that depend on viewpoint, distance, and illumination. Among the questions worth asking in this respect, I have retained three: What are the rules governing the combination of facial features in order to give rise to the emergence of a meaningful percept? What attributes of the face convey the relevant information? How is facial information stored for further recognition?

The rules governing the extraction and combination of facial information are obviously well incorporated within visual-processing mechanisms, to the point that we have little control over their operations. It seems to be established by now that these processes do not require a verbal encoding of the various aspects of the face. For instance, speechless infants as well as monkeys possess the capacity to discriminate and recognize faces (Carey 1981; Rosenfeld and van Hoesen 1979), and research on normal adults shows that there is no correlation between the number of verbal descriptions made on a face and subsequent recognition (Goldstein *et al.* 1979). The availability or the use of verbal codes has little or no positive effect on face recognition. The saying that a picture is worth one thousand words is in fact quite appropriate in this case as can be illustrated by the typically poor match between a face drawn from verbal descriptions and the actual face (e.g. Davies 1981). Thus a face does not readily lend itself to accurate verbal descriptions, and, for a verbal contribution to be of some help to face recognition, it would also be necessary to have descriptions of every possible transformations to which a face can be subjected, as a function of distance and angle of view, of lighting conditions and shading, and of modifications of the facial configuration during the expression of emotion. All this can be readily achieved by visual mechanisms. For example, most people to whom the face shown in Fig. 5.1 has been presented had no difficulty in identifying it even though the particular instance of that face has never been seen before.

How then are the component features integrated to give rise to the percept of a face, and how are they used for discriminating between different faces? Although this issue is far from settled, two main answers have been proposed. One suggests that faces are analysed in terms of their component features which are processed sequentially and usually in a top-to-bottom order. Thus the way a particular face could be recognized would be through a serial comparison of each feature with a stored representation of the face. It is interesting to note that Leonardo da Vinci advised his students to remember faces according to such an analytic method by which each component is treated independently of the other (Gombrich 1972). The second suggestion is that faces are treated as a whole or a *Gestalt*, in terms of their configuration. Irrespective of the actual underlying processes, it seems to be established that we develop a basic facial schema resulting from our frequent exposures to upright faces that enables us to access consistent encoding dimensions which facilitate perception and memory (Goldstein and Chance 1981; Diamond and Carey 1986). The brain shapes its representational and operational capacities

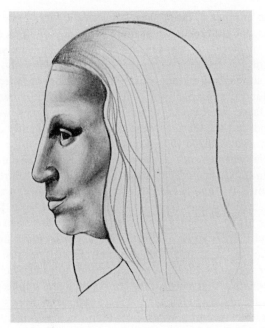

Fig. 5.1   Unusual view of a well-known face (I am grateful to François Massé for this drawing).

as a function of the individual's needs, and some type of implicit or meta knowledge may thus be incorporated within visual mechanisms to guide the processing of faces and determine which attributes to operate on and which attributes to leave in the background. One possible illustration of this, elegantly demonstrated by Thompson (1980) and by Diamond and Carey (1986), is our difficulty at recognizing upside-down faces and even at treating the features of such faces as being inverted. Facial features in inverted faces are in fact processed by mechanisms adapted to deal with upright faces, and we often fail to notice incongruities in upside-down faces.

Some empirical evidence

It was thought for a long time that faces were processed through some form of serial analytic scanning, with each feature treated independently of the other. The experimental method used in these investigations consists in presenting, either simultaneously or successively, two faces and in examining the time taken to decide whether the faces are the same or different. By varying the number of differences between the two faces, the analysis of reaction times can reveal whether the features are compared according to an analytic strategy or to a holistic one. Typically, an analytic strategy implies that reaction times will decrease as the number of differences between the faces increases, since it is faster to detect one difference when there are many differences between the faces than when there are few. On the contrary, a holistic strategy, which implies that all the features are processed simultaneously, predicts that reaction times should be constant whatever the number of differences. In most cases it was found that reaction times decreased as the number of differences between the faces increased, suggesting that the faces were compared analytically and that the features were treated independently of one another (e.g. Bradshaw and Wallace 1971; Smith and Nielsen 1970).

Discrete facial features such as the eyes, the nose, or the chin are certainly critical in defining a face. The visual system is particularly sensitive to variations in intensity, and these variations are typically concentrated in the facial features, which makes them important physical bases for processing. However, this does not mean that they constitute relevant units for recognition and there is some evidence that face perception and recognition may be achieved without processing discrete facial features. For instance, faces are better recognized following instructions to remember them according to characteristics that necessitate considering the whole physiognomy. When subjects are requested to examine faces in terms of honesty, personality, or likeableness, they recognize more faces than when paying attention only to the physical attributes. Qualities such as honesty or likeableness are not conveyed by any single feature independent of the others, and the faces must then be treated as a 'unit' (Bower and Karlin 1974; Patterson and Baddeley 1977). That facial features as such are not indispensable for recognizing a face can also be illustrated with the picture of Mona Lisa shown in Fig. 5.2, which is a coarsely quantized representation of the original face. In this face, no single part conveys enough information for identification, and it is only the interrelationship among the blurred components that allows for recognition. This suggests that a face has both component and configurational properties, and a configuration stems from the interaction of the components. The configuration becomes the most salient property of the face when the components are blurred or, in other words, when the high spatial frequency contents of the face have been filtered out. This does not mean, however, that the configuration is removed when the components are not blurred, and, in a normal face, component and configural properties coexist.

As a consequence, it becomes difficult to identify the relevant parameters when facial features are manipulated in laboratory studies. Since configural properties emerge from components, and since components are the characteristics that are directly manipulated, performance in face recognition is analysed as a function of the components which are considered the critical variables, but this is not justified. Let us take a simple example. Each of the three stimuli presented in Fig. 5.3 is made of a circle and two spokes, and the left spoke is the only dimension to be manipulated. The normal practice is thus

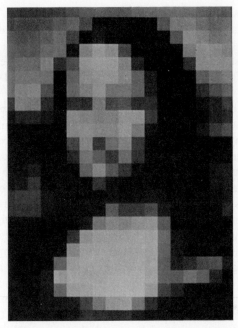

Fig. 5.2   Coarsely quantized representation of Mona Lisa (Courtesy of Ed Manning).

Fig. 5.3   Three circles with two spokes each.

to consider the left spoke as the source of difference between the three stimuli, and to explain any variation in performance as the result of the manipulation of this dimension. Yet it is obvious that changing a single dimension also modifies the interrelationship between the components and, therefore, the configuration of the stimuli. In this particular example the critical variable may not be the left spoke as such but the spaces described by the spokes within the circle, even though these spaces are not directly manipulated. Thus changing or manipulating a feature in a visual pattern also changes its configuration, and variations in performance following manipulation of a feature is not necessarily due to processing the feature as such. This also applies to faces, as illustrated by Haig (1984, 1986), who used a computer-driven display system to make a single slight alteration to a target face. The faces thus generated can readily be perceived as different, even though it is difficult, at least for some of the faces, to identify what local change has been made.

Thus, finding that reaction times decrease when the number of differences between faces increases does not necessarily imply an analytic mode of processing. It may as well suggest that increasing differences between faces enhances their configural dissimilarity, which in turn reduces the comparison time. The fact that this comparison time varies depending on which feature is manipulated—for example, it is usually faster to compare two faces that differ only by the hair-styles than two faces that differ only by the nose—may thus reflect the different contribution of each feature to the configuration itself.

This question was investigated in laboratory experiments through multi-dimensional scaling analysis of reaction times in the comparison of faces (Takane and Sergent 1983). Such an approach offers two advantages over classical analyses of reaction time data. One is that it allows an identification of the rules by which the component features are combined, and thus to specify the nature of the underlying processes. The other is the possibility to derive a spatial representation of the stimuli that shows the relative weight of the features in the comparison process and possible interactions among these features. The patterns of reaction times obtained in this experiment showed the typical decrease in latency with an increase in the number of differences, but this was not due to an analytic process, as suggested by the comparison of different models of similarity relations postulating specific combinations of the features. Of four possible models tested, the Euclidean model provided the best fit of the data, suggesting that the faces were compared on the basis of their overall configuration rather than of their features treated independently of one another. Figure 5.4 shows the representation of eight face stimuli in a Euclidean space derived from the multidimensional scaling analysis. The unequal distances separating faces that differ on the same feature suggest that features interact between one another and do not contribute equally and similarly depending on the particularities of the other features composing the face. In addition, the finding that four dimensions best accounted for the pattern of reaction times, when only three dimensions were actually manipulated, suggests some form of combination of the facial features, indicating an emergent property of the face not explainable by an independent treatment of the facial features. Thus features contribute differently to the overall configuration, and adding differences between faces enhances their configurational dissimilarity, which reduces the comparison time.

The involvement of this configurational and interactive processing of faces can be more directly illustrated with one example. The two pairs of eyes shown

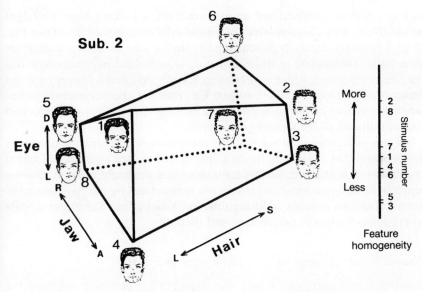

Fig. 5.4   Derived representation of eight faces in a three-dimensional Euclidean space. The fourth dimension is shown on the right (from Takane and Sergent 1983).

Fig. 5.5   (a) Two identical pairs of eyes; (b) the two pairs embedded in a different facial context. (After Luckiesh (1965) with permission from the publisher.)

in Fig. 5.5(a) are identical and we perceive them as looking directly straight ahead. Now, if we place each pair of eyes in a different facial context [see Fig. 5(b)], it becomes extremely difficult not to perceive them as looking in different directions. The context in which a feature is embedded influences how this feature is perceived, which is a clear indication that facial features are not treated independently of one another. This example also suggests that, even when one focuses on one component of a face, the remainder is also processed and contributes to the meaning of percept.

At this point, one may say that the perception of faces involves complex mechanisms that are automatically acquired without the assistance of verbal mediation. It is characterized by a simultaneous treatment of many components in a configurational and interactive manner and by the involvement of transformations capable of fitting different views of the same face despite alterations, changes in perspective, and shading.

Spatial frequency composition of facial representations

Another aspect worth mentioning with respect to face perception concerns the representations of facial information as they can be elaborated by the visual system. Recent evidence that the visual system filters information contained in a display into separate bands of spatial frequencies has provided a new way of describing visual patterns in terms of physical attributes consonant with the properties of early neural processing (Shapley and Lennie 1985). Results of the application of filtering processes to the human face suggest that much of the relevant information necessary for face recognition is conveyed by the low frequencies (Ginsburg 1978). This was already shown earlier with the spatially quantized face of Mona Lisa and can be further illustrated in Fig. 5.6. Here, a face is represented in terms of gradually increasing spatial frequency contents, and it is clear that the lower range of spatial frequencies already contains relevant information about an individual. In laboratory experiments with faces, like face e here, that contains six cycles per width, subjects familiar with the faces had no difficulty in identifying them. However, their performance could be significantly improved when higher frequencies were available, such as with face h and i, but this was the case only in a face identification task and not in a male/female categorization.

Further discussion of empirical evidence is beyond the scope of this chapter (see Sergent, in press), but some implications of the spatial frequency approach are worth pointing out. First, the early filtering taking place in the visual system provides the brain with several representations of the incoming information, each with different spatial frequency contents which are not equally useful depending on the type of operations to be carried out; for example, identification benefits from the availability of high frequencies (e.g. Fiorentini *et al.* 1983; Sergent 1985) while other tasks can be carried out as

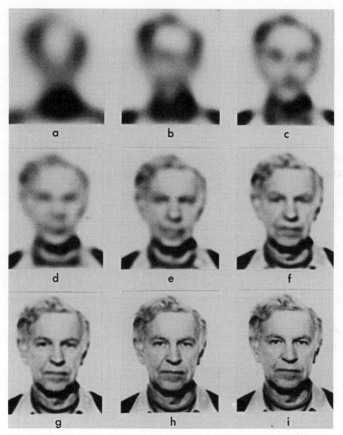

Fig. 5.6 Increasing spatial frequency facial contents by 0.5 octave. As a reference, face *b* and face *e* contains 3.1 and 6.2 cycles per face width, respectively.

efficiently on low as on high frequencies. Second, low frequencies convey the basic configuration of the face but provide little information about the details of the features, as can be shown here with face e. In addition, because low frequencies are resolved faster, and are less affected by any type of degradation than high frequencies, they provide the initial information and a more stable basis for processing. Third, the nature of the operations that can be carried out on faces is partly determined by the composition of the representations on which these operations have to be performed. Representations containing essentially low frequencies make an analytic type of processing difficult to achieve since the facial features are not sufficiently distinct to provide specific detailed information about their shape. A last point concerns the fate of physical attributes in memory representations of faces. As pointed out by Estes (1980), human memory, unlike computer memory, has been designed to sacrifice high fidelity in favour of a capacity to maintain large amounts of approximate information. In the case of faces, this suggests that details about features are less likely to be stored in a highly accurate manner, and there is evidence that the less-salient aspects of a face decay more rapidly (Walker-Smith 1978). An interesting series of experiments by Harvey (1986) has attempted to specify the spatial frequency composition of faces stored in memory using a matching procedure with stimuli similar to those shown in Fig. 5.6. He found that memory representations of faces were essentially a function of the lower range of spatial frequencies, and, at the size the faces were presented, the information contained in the memorized face was about of the order of that contained in faces e and f. This may indicate that any operation calling on memory representations of faces may be primarily dependent on their low spatial frequency contents.

In conclusion, several factors converge toward making the processing of faces primarily dependent on the lower range of spatial frequencies which convey much of the relevant facial information and which are less susceptible to degradation than high frequencies. The evidence that the visual system encodes information through semi-independent channels tuned to narrow bands of spatial frequencies may thus provide one way of addressing the question of the respective contribution of the cerebral hemispheres to the processing of faces.

Contribution of the right hemisphere to the processing of faces

Evidence of a dominant contribution of the right hemisphere to face and pattern recognition, and to visuo-spatial functions in general, is now overwhelming and comes from research on normal subjects and brain-damaged patients. It is becoming clear, however, that the left hemisphere is not simply a silent partner in these processes, and this raises the question of the respective contribution of the cerebral hemispheres and the basis for their joint participation.

Research on normal subjects

Before discussing what neuropsychological investigation on normal subjects can tell us about the contribution of the cerebral hemispheres to the processing of faces, it is necessary to point out some of the characteristics of the lateral tachistoscopic technique of stimulus presentation. The appropriateness of this technique is based on the anatomical property of the visual system whereby the left half of each retina projects to the left hemisphere and the right half to the right hemisphere. Thus information can be sent initially to only one hemisphere by presenting the visual stimulus in the retinal periphery for a duration short enough to prevent eye movements that would expose the stimulus to the two hemispheres. While this technique allows an initial segregation of information to one side of the brain, it also creates particular viewing conditions unlike those prevailing in normal situations.

It is a truism that the visual system and the brain have not evolved to perceive and process visual information seen for a fraction of a second outside the area of highest acuity, and the interpretation of results obtained through lateral tachistoscopic presentation requires that account be taken of the particular viewing conditions determined by this technique. This type of presentation produces some form of functional sensory deficit since the stimuli cannot be resolved as well as they would be if they were presented in the fovea for an unlimited duration. One implication is that the high frequencies contained in the stimulus are attenuated, especially when the contrast between the various components is relatively low as is often the case in black-and-white photographs, which in turn implies a greater reduction of the information about single facial features than about the configural property of the face. This makes the capacity to discriminate between different shades of grey a critical factor, which is of importance for performance since Benton and Gordon (1971) have found a significant positive correlation between the ability to recognize faces and the capacity to discriminate between different patterns of shading.

Research on cerebral lateralization of functions in normal subjects has yielded a considerable amount of information, and the diversity of the results is such as to support almost any hypothesis by the manner relevant findings are selected. When one examines the particular experimental variables involved in these studies, several factors seem to be necessary for the emergence of a right-hemisphere superiority in the processing of faces. A detailed review of these experiments is beyond the scope of this chapter (for reviews see Ellis 1983; Sergent 1986), and Table 5.1. summarizes the particular experimental conditions that favour the emergence of a right- or left-hemisphere superiority in tachistoscopic studies with normal subjects (see Sergent 1986).

None of the variables presented in this table is by itself sufficient to determine the superiority of one hemisphere over the other, and it is their conjoint influence that makes one hemisphere more efficient than the other. One outcome that is evident from research in normals is that both hemispheres appear to be capable of processing faces, and the main task becomes to succeed in characterizing the conditions that allow one hemisphere to be more efficient, not in terms of these experimental variables, but in terms of the effects of particular values of these variables on cerebral and neural processing.

At the outset it may thus be suggested that the particular competence of the right hemisphere cannot be reduced to an exclusive specialization of this

Table 5.1 *Experimental factors contributing to the emergence of a right-hemisphere-dominant involvement in processing faces in lateral tachistoscopic studies with normal subjects*

Experimental factors

More favourable*	Less favourable*
Upright faces	Inverted faces
Emotional faces	Neutral faces
Facial identity (different views of same face)	Physical identity (same view of same face)
Set of highly dissimilar faces	Set of highly similar faces
Black-and-white photographs	Schematic or line-drawing faces
Unfamiliar faces	Familiar faces
Low stimulus energy	High stimulus energy
Low-pass faces	High-pass faces
Successive presentation	Simultaneous presentation
Recognition accuracy	Response latency

* To a right-hemisphere superiority in face perception

hemisphere in the processing of faces. It can also be suggested that both hemispheres have the capacity to extract the physiognomic invariants from different views of the same face and access its identity, as suggested by several studies on face identification that showed left-, right-, or no-hemisphere superiority depending on the experimental conditions (Bertelson *et al.* 1979; Marzi and Berlucchi 1977; Sergent 1985).

One explanation for the functional asymmetry in processing faces is concerned with the specific processing competence of the cerebral hemispheres, and the 'dominant' view suggests that the right hemisphere is specialized in holistic or configurational operations and the left in analytic processing. This is probably the idea most often used to account for empirical data, having started with Levy-Agusti and Sperry (1968) from their research with split-brain patients, and recently supported by Bradshaw and Nettleton (1981). A quotation from Sperry (1974) may summarize this view:

'The left and right hemispheres apprehend and process things in different ways. In dealing with faces, the right hemisphere seems to respond to the whole face directly as a perceptual unit, whereas the left hemisphere seems to focus on salient features and details to which labels are easily attached, and then used for discrimination and recall' (p. 14).

This type of interpretation has often been successful in providing a convenient account of results, and many empirical findings seem to be quite consistent with this view.

The major problem with this interpretation is that it has little objective basis in the data, and the main concepts of this dichotomy have not been defined in operational terms that would allow testable predictions. As noted by Bertelson (1982) and by Marshall (1981), any finding can be made consistent with the analytic–holistic dichotomy whose explanatory successes are essentially *post hoc*. To examine the nature of the processes underlying the perception of faces as a function of the hemisphere to which the stimuli are initially projected, an experiment was carried out using a design that allowed the determination of the rules by which the component dimensions of a face are combined (Sergent 1984*a*). Although four different models were specifically tested, I will only discuss two of them. One is the serial self-terminating model, which is the typical analytic model suggesting that two stimuli are compared in terms of their individual dimensions until a difference is detected; the other is the Euclidean distance metric model, which implies that two stimuli are compared in terms of their overall similarity or configuration that encompasses their component dimensions. The task involved reaction times and 'same–different' judgements, and the results were subjected to multidimensional scaling analysis. The results showed a considerably better approximation of the reaction time data by the Euclidean model in the two hemispheres of each subject, and they suggested that a purely analytic mode of comparison was too simple a process to account for the operation taking place in the left hemisphere.

Figure 5.7 shows the three-dimensional spatial representation of the eight faces for the left and the right visual field of one subject. While the same configural process was found to underlie performance in the right and the left hemispheres, the perceived dissimilarities between the faces were none the less significantly different in the two hemispheres. The important characteristic in this figure is the interaction between the component features. Consider, for example, the pair 7–8 and the pair 3–4. There is only a difference in hair between the faces of each pair, and the distance separating faces 7 and 8 is much shorter than that between faces 3 and 4. An analytic independent process would predict equal distance between the faces of these two pairs. Instead, the other features of the face influenced how the difference in hair was perceived. This implies simultaneous and interactive processing of the component dimensions, and these are typical properties of a *Gestalt* mode of perception which both hemispheres may thus be capable of mediating.

If the two hemispheres perform basically the same type of process, what then can explain the overwhelming evidence of functional hemispheric asymmetry in the perception and recognition of faces? One possible explanation may be in terms of the representation and description of visual

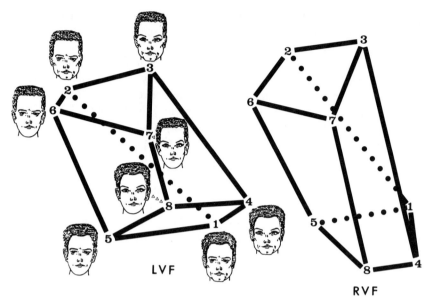

Fig. 5.7 Derived representation, for left visual field (LVF) and right visual field (RVF) presentation, of eight faces differing on three features of two values each (from Sergent, 1984a).

information in the brain, which may not be similar in the two hemispheres. As noted by Marr (1982), for example, a representation is a formal system for making explicit certain entities or types of information, and how information is represented can greatly affect how easy it is to do different things with it.

This makes it necessary to consider the type of representation that can be elaborated from a lateral tachistoscopic presentation of a face. A tachistoscopic presentation allows only some aspects of the physical characteristics of the face to be accurately encoded, which makes the representation of information in the brain essentially in terms of low spatial frequency components of a face. It is therefore the hemispheric system that is the more capable of dealing with these low frequencies that will be the more efficient at processing the incoming information in very brief tachistoscopic presentations, and there is some evidence indicating that the right hemisphere may be more sensitive than the left hemisphere to the outputs of the low spatial frequency channels of the visual system. This is suggested by the frequent finding of right-hemisphere superiority at very brief exposure duration as well as by recent evidence that faces from which the high frequencies have been removed are processed much more efficiently in the right hemisphere in tasks that yield a left-hemisphere superiority when a broad range of spatial frequencies is available for processing (Sergent 1985).

A consequence of this differential sensitivity of the cerebral hemispheres is that the representations elaborated in the brain may not emphasize the same attributes of the face in the two hemispheres. A description in terms of the low to intermediate spatial frequencies may characterize the representations on which the right hemisphere preferentially operates, while, in the left hemisphere, the representations may emphasize the intermediate to high spatial frequencies. This may give the illusion that the hemispheres perform different types of process, whereas they may operate similarly on different attributes of the information.

Research on brain-damaged patients

Research on brain-damaged patients has yielded much less-equivocal findings than the study of normal subjects and it has strongly contributed to the view that the right hemisphere is specialized at processing faces. All but two studies (Grafman *et al.* 1986; Hamsher *et al.* 1979) found a significantly greater impairment in right- than in left-hemisphere damaged patients, whether the task was purely perceptual or called for memory mediation, and whether the faces were familiar or unfamiliar to the patients. It must be noted, however, that impairments after right-hemisphere injury are relative rather than absolute, and the patients do not specifically complain and exhibit gross difficulties at recognizing faces. In fact, there are reasons to believe that complete disruption of face recognition, that is, prosopagnosia, may require a bilateral lesion: out of 15 cases of prosopagnosia for which autopsy could be performed, only one was found to have damage restricted to the right hemisphere (Damasio and Damasio 1986).

While a large body of data has accumulated with respect to the deficits displayed by right-hemisphere-damaged patients, very little is known as to how such deficits come to the fore, and two main problems need to be investigated: (1) What is the impact of a localized damage on the functioning of the whole brain? and (2) What is the nature of the contribution of the right hemisphere that gives it such primordial importance in face perception?

The characterization of the functional specialization of the cerebral hemispheres requires consideration, at least in general terms, of the properties of cerebral processing. Each hemisphere is an integral part of a highly interactive nervous system and its functions cannot be understood irrespective of its relations with the other hemisphere and the rest of the brain. Because of the interactive and distributed nature of cerebral processing, a series of functional changes in the brain are to be expected as a result of the destruction of one of its components, at least within a given modality (see Sergent 1984*b*). As pointed out by Powell (1981, p. 62), 'activity in one area in the normal brain or some disturbance in the abnormal will inevitably and invariably affect the function of several other parts, if not the whole, of the cortex in the same or both sides'.

For example, there is evidence that a lesion within cortical areas involved in visual processing has detrimental effects on the spatio–temporal integration of the incoming information, and it is therefore necessary to determine whether the particular representations generated in the presence of brain damage are still compatible with the sensitivity of the structures not invaded by the lesion. If the right hemisphere plays a crucial role in processing information that lacks its usual redundancy, a right-sided injury may then deprive the brain of structures normally involved in dealing with qualitatively altered information. Kobayashi et al. (1985) showed that the contrast sensitivity function of patients with right posterior lesion was significantly impaired compared with left-damaged patients. I have also found this to be the case and, although not all patients conformed to the general pattern, none displayed results in the opposite direction. I recently observed a right-hemispherectomized patient who had a marked deficit in the resolution of low spatial frequencies and who was considerably impaired in tasks involving the processing of faces. This may suggest that the cerebral hemispheres are not equally competent at processing information of reduced redundancy, and that the right hemisphere may play a critical role in such conditions by its being less affected than the left hemisphere by an input that is deprived of high frequencies and whose spatio–temporal characteristics are altered.

In the context of the foregoing considerations, one may enquire about the nature of the contribution of the right hemisphere to face perception. Right-hemisphere damage produces, on the one hand, impairments in elementary visual functions (de Renzi 1982; Hécaen and Albert 1978; Sergent 1984b) and, on the other, deficits in face and object recognition, but there has been so far almost no attempt at determining whether the two types of deficits were related. Is the deficit in face recognition by right-hemisphere patients one of general impairment in visual functions, one produced by the destruction of structures specifically involved in higher order cognitive operations, or one resulting from interactions between disrupted representations and impaired operations?

When one considers some of the underlying representations and operations involved in face recognition and some of the characteristics of the experimental tasks to which the patients are subjected, there are several coincidences between the requirements of the tasks and the nature of the deficits displayed by right-hemisphere patients. As noted earlier, Benton and Gordon (1971) found a significant positive correlation between facial recognition and the ability to discriminate patterns of shading, and the latter has been shown to depend predominantly on right-hemisphere integrity (de Renzi 1982). Similarly, changing the illumination of a face modifies the contrast between the various facial features and introduces shadowed areas not initially present (e.g. the Benton face recognition test). Moreover, as noted earlier, tasks that involve a memory representation of faces make more demands on the processing of low-frequency contents. If the capacity to process such characteristics is impaired—and it is in right-hemisphere patients—this may be one source of the deficit in face recognition. In addition, most research on face recognition in brain-damaged patients has been carried out with black-and-white photographs in matching tasks, and those are some of the characteristics that have been found to contribute to a right-hemisphere superiority in normal subjects (Sergent 1986). It is also the case that the examination of categorization of objects presented in an unconventional view uses black-and-white photographs often containing shadows that make more difficult the extraction of the relevant information. As noted by Humphreys and Riddoch (1984), the particular patterns of shading on these unconventional views of objects convey depth cues that right-hemisphere patients fail to utilize. It may be that it is its capacity to extract the invariant information from an input of reduced quality and redundancy that predisposes the right hemisphere to play a crucial role in the processing of faces and objects.

This unequal capacity of the cerebral hemispheres to deal with different spatial frequency band-widths is not sufficient, however, to account for all the findings, and a patient I recently saw produced results interesting in this respect. This 34-year-old woman had undergone surgery at age 13 in 1965 for a right hemispherectomy. She was severely prosopagnosic, to the point that she behaved as if she had no idea that faces could be used to identify people. To my knowledge, this is the first case of prosopagnosia in a hemispherecto-mized patient, and, although she may be atypical in that her left hemisphere shows signs of enlarged ventricules, her patterns of results proved interesting in many respects. She showed a marked deficit in contrast sensitivity restricted to the lower range of spatial frequencies. Below 3 cycles per degree of visual angle she required a contrast of at least 0.4 to start seeing a grating, which is 7 standard deviations higher than normals. She had no deficit in high spatial frequency resolution and her Snellen acuity was normal. When she was required to match a photograph of a face with its low-pass version, she performed at chance and mentioned that she barely saw the face, while she had no difficulty performing the same task with highly contrasted photographs. She was also unable to match a face with its spatially quantized version, even when she had to chose between only two faces. On the other hand, when tested on Mooney's faces, her performance was above the mean of the control group in both speed and accuracy, and this was the case when she had to discriminate between faces and non-faces and when she had to tell the sex and the approximate age of these faces. She also performed almost perfectly in telling the age of 16 unfamiliar faces and in ordering the faces according to their age. When presented with Ekman faces and asked to tell the emotion expressed by the faces, she was accurate only in telling whether it was a positive or a negative emotion, and always recognized the happy faces. She could not match the faces of the same individuals when they expressed different emotions, and she performed barely above chance when matching front view with three-quarters view of the same individual.

She had no object and colour agnosia but she had considerable difficulty discriminating and naming 15 green vegetables presented on colour photographs. She could not recognize doctors and nurses, and she never recognized me other than by my voice, accent, or clothes. She had not lost the notion of identity of people, and she could provide the name of the last six US presidents, but she was unable to identify any on a photograph.

Obviously the left hemisphere of this patient was unable to subserve the operations necessary to access the identity of an individual from his face, even though it could carry out operations specific to the processing of faces such as telling the age, sex, or emotion of a face. The exact nature of her deficit at recognizing faces is rather elusive, however, but it is not reducible to her impairment at low-frequency resolution as the presentation of high-resolution faces did not modify her performance. There is no simple explanation of her prosopagnosia, especially in view of the fact that no such deficit has yet been reported among about 100 cases of hemispherectomy (Damasio and Damasio 1986). One particularity of her deficit, however, is her lack of awareness that she is missing the capacity to recognize faces. All prosopagnosic patients described in the literature either complain about, or comment on, their impairment, while this patient never did.

Conclusion

When one considers the type of functions to which the contribution of the right hemisphere seems to be critical, certain characteristics are worth pointing out: these functions require no formal training, are acquired early in life, involve little verbal mediation, and do not require a high level of resolution. In fact, spatial orientation and object and face recognition can be performed quite efficiently even on degraded information, while the sort of visual information on which the left hemisphere typically operates more efficiently, such as written words, is normally characterized by high contrast and high spatial frequencies.

How the specialized competences of the hemispheres are established has been a matter of debate and controversy, and there are reasons to believe that cerebral lateralization, as it is observed in the adult normal brain, is the result of the cumulative influence of internal and external factors (e.g. Corballis 1983; Michel 1981) that combine to overdetermine the particular patterns of functional asymmetry. The visual modality may be used to illustrate how the conjunction of a yet unknown primary internal factor and environmental influences may contribute to the emergence of hemispheric specialization of the sort described earlier.

One first element to consider is the fact that the corpus callosum is non-functional at birth (Selnes 1974). It does not start myelinating before three weeks after birth (Volpe 1977) and may not be completely functional before puberty (Yakovlev and Lecours 1967). This indicates that, at least during the first months of life, processes taking place within one hemisphere may not be directly influenced by the processes going on in the other.

A second element to consider is that, although some properties of cortical cells are certainly built in (e.g. Rakic 1981), others seem to develop during the first weeks of life. Blakemore (1974) has shown that the final organization and sensitivity of neural cells in the visual cortex is determined by the young animal's early visual experience. The tuning of neural cells to the environment has a distinct critical period after which adaptation is no longer optimal, and this critical period extends over several years for spatial vision (Harwerth et al. 1986). Thus the properties of cortical cells are, at least in part, dependent upon the visual environment as well as upon the maturation of the infant's sensory receptors during the first months of life.

There are several sources of evidence, recently reviewed by Geschwind and Galaburda (1985), that the right hemisphere may develop earlier than the left hemisphere. In new-born humans, the right hemisphere seems to be the only hemisphere activated by light flashes (Crowell et al. 1973) and shows a higher contrast sensitivity (Lewis et al. 1978). In addition, the macular region of the retina is immature at birth (Mann 1964), and visual acuity develops slowly, with the higher spatial frequency resolved by six months of age being only of 6 cycles per degree. This indicates that, during the first months, the visual representations on which an infant can perform any type of processing are composed essentially of low spatial frequencies (see Dobson and Teller 1978).

Now, cortical cells which, in the 'association' cortex, process the sensory output may become optimally tuned to the components of the visual representations received from the sensory area. As the resolving power of the visual system increases, more detailed information from the visual scene may become available. Yet the right hemisphere, developing earlier, may not adapt as easily to the increasingly higher frequencies now available. Indeed, for adaptive purposes and for continuity of processing, the right-hemisphere cortical cells and structures may maintain the same type of tuning and organization, while the 'lagging' left hemisphere may continue its development by adapting to the more detailed information which can be provided by the sensory receptors. That is, at equivalent levels of cortical development, the left hemisphere receives higher frequency components than the right hemisphere and has to deal with it. The myelination of the commissures during the first year of life may also have some influence in preventing the hemispheres from 'competing' with each other for the same type of tuning. In this sense, the tuning of the right hemisphere may have developed on the basis of early processing capacity and built on it. On the other hand, the later development of the left hemisphere may have allowed a neural sensitivity and representation to develop in accordance with the higher-frequency components of a visual scene; that is, a greater ability to deal with information of a high level of sensory resolution.

This may have predisposed the right hemisphere toward subserving biologically relevant functions, on the basis of information that can be resolved by the visual system at an early age, specifically the lower range of spatial frequencies, while limiting its capacity to operate on the higher range of spatial frequencies. Because low frequencies convey much of the relevant information for face and object recognition, as well as for most visuo-spatial operations, are less prone to degradation, and are resolved earlier than high frequencies, these functions may be represented in such a way that the right hemisphere keeps playing the critical role in the early operations and provides the frame within which the left hemisphere performs more refined operations. In this sense, the efficient contribution of the left hemisphere to the processing of faces, most evident in studies with normal subjects, may depend on a preliminary processing by the right hemisphere. By contrast, a non-functional right hemisphere may prevent the left hemisphere from operating efficiently, not because it is deprived of the necessary equipment but because it needs some pre-processing by the right hemisphere to exploit all its resources. Although this scenario is admittedly speculative, it may offer one way of conceiving how the two hemispheres operate in co-operation by treating different aspects of the same information.

References

Baddeley, A. (1979). Applied cognitive and cognitive applied psychology: the case of face recognition. In *Perspectives on memory research*, (ed. L. G. Nilsonn). pp. 367–88. Lawrence Erlbaum Associates, Hillsdale, NJ.

Benton, A. L. and Gordon, M. C. (1971). Correlates of facial recognition. *Transactions of the American Neurological Association*, **96**, 146–50.

Bertelson, P. (1982). Lateral differences in normal man and lateralization of brain function. *International Journal of Psychology*, **17**, 173–210.

——, van Haelen, H., and Morais, J. (1979). Left-hemifield superiority and the extraction of physiognomic invariants. In *Structures and functions of the cerebral commissures*, (ed. S. Russell, I. Van Hof, and G. Berlucchi), pp. 400–10. MacMillan, London.

Blakemore, C. (1974). Developmental factors in the formation of feature extracting neurons. In *The neurosciences: third study program*, (ed. F. O. Schmitt and F. G. Worden), pp. 105–14. MIT Press, Cambridge, MA.

Bower, G. H. and Karlin, M. B. (1974). Depth of processing pictures of faces and recognition memory. *Journal of Experimental Psychology*, **103**, 751–7.

Bradshaw, J. L. and Nettleton, N. C. (1981). The nature of hemispheric specialization in man. *Behavioural and Brain Sciences*, **4**, 51–91.

—— and Wallace, G. (1971). Models for the processing and identification of faces. *Perception and Psychophysics*, **9**, 443–8.

Carey, S. (1981). The development of face perception. In *Perceiving and remembering faces*, (ed. G. Davies, H. Ellis, and J. Shepherd), pp. 9–38. Academic Press, London.

Corballis, M. C. (1983). *Human laterality*. Academic Press, New York.

Crowell, D. H., Jones, R. H., Kapunia, L. E., and Nakagawa, J. K. (1973). Unilateral cortical activity in newborn infants: an early index of cerebral dominance? *Science*, **80**, 205–8.

Damasio, A. R. and Damasio, H. (1986). The anatomical substrate of prosopagnosia. In *The neuropsychology of face perception and facial expression*, (ed. R. Bruyer), pp. 268–72. Lawrence Erlbaum Associates, Hillsdale, NJ.

Davies, G. M. (1981). Face recall systems. In *Perceiving and remembering faces*, (ed. G. Davies, H. Ellis, and J. Shepherd). pp. 227–50. Academic Press, London.

De Renzi, E. (1982). *Disorders of space exploration and cognition*. John Wiley, Chichester, Sussex.

Diamond, R. and Carey, S. (1986). Why faces are and are not special: the effect of expertise. *Journal of Experimental Psychology: General*, **115**, 107–17.

Dobson, V. and Teller, D. Y. (1978). Visual acuity in human infants: a review and comparison of behavioural and electrophysiological studies. *Vision Research*, **18**, 1469–83.

Ellis, H. D. (1981). Theoretical aspects of face recognition. In *Perceiving and remembering faces*, (ed. G. Davies, H. Ellis, and J. Shepherd). pp. 171–97. Academic Press: London.

—— (1983). The role of the right hemisphere in face perception. In *Functions of the right cerebral hemisphere*, (ed. A. W. Young), pp. 33–64. Academic Press, London.

Estes, W. K. (1980). Is human memory obsolete? *American Scientist*, **68**, 62–9.

Fiorentini, A., Maffei, L., and Sandini, G. (1983). The role of high spatial frequencies in face perception. *Perception*, **12**, 195–201.

Geschwind, N. and Galaburda, A. M. (1985). Cerebral lateralization. *Archives of Neurology*, **42**, 428–59, 521–52, 634–54.

Ginsburg, A. (1978). *Visual information processing based on spatial filters constrained by biological data*. Report No. 78–129, Volumes I and II, Aerospace Medical Research Laboratory, Wright Patterson Air Force Base, OH.

Goldstein, A. G. and Chance, J. E. (1981). Laboratory studies of face recognition. In *Perceiving and remembering faces*, (ed. G. Davies, H. Ellis, and J. Shepherd), pp. 81–104. Academic Press, London.

——, Johnson, K. S., and Chance, J. E. (1979). Does fluency of face description imply superior face recognition? *Bulletin of the Psychonomic Society*, **13**, 15–18.

Gombrich, E. H. (1972). The mask and the face: the perception of physiognomic likeness in life and art. In *Art, perception, and reality*, (ed. E. H. Gombrich, H. Hochberg, and M. Black), pp. 32–74. John Hopkins University Press.

Grafman, J., Salazar, A. M., Weingartner, H., and Amin, D. (1986). Face memory and discrimination: an analysis of the persistent effects of penetrating brain wounds. *International Journal of Neuroscience*, **29**, 125–39.

Gregory, R. L. (1970). *The intelligent eye*. MacGraw Hill, New York.

Haig, N. D. (1984). The effect of feature displacement on face recognition. *Perception*, **13**, 456–63.

——. (1986). Investigating face recognition with an image processing computer. In *Aspects of face processing*, (ed. H. Ellis, F. Newcombe, M. Jeeves, and A. Young), pp. 410–25. Martinus Nijhoff, The Hague.

Hamsher, K., Levin, H. S., and Benton, A. L. (1979). Facial recognition in patients with focal brain lesions. *Archives of Neurology*, **36**, 837–9.

Harvey, L. O. (1986). Visual memory: what is remembered? In *Human memory and cognitive capabilities*, (ed. F. Klix and H. Hagendorf), pp. 173–87. Elsevier, Amsterdam.

Harwerth, R. S., Smith E. L. III, Duncan, G. C., Crawford, M. L., and von Noorden, G. K. (1986). Multiple sensitive periods in the development of the primate visual system. *Science*, **232**, 235–8.

Hécaen, H. and Albert, M. (1978). *Human neuropsychology*. John Wiley, New York.

Humphreys, G. W. and Riddoch, M. J. (1984). Routes to object constancy: implications for neurological impairments of object constancy. *Quarterly Journal of experimental Psychology*, **36A**, 385–415.

Kobayashi, S., Mukuno, K., Ishikawa, S., and Takashi, Y. (1985). Hemispheric lateralization of spatial contrast sensitivity. *Annals of Neurology*, **17**, 141–5.

Levy-Augusti, J. and Sperry, R. W. (1968). Differential perceptual capacities in major and minor hemispheres. *Proceedings of the National Academy of Sciences*, **61**, 1151.

Lewis, T. L., Maurer, D., and Kay, D. (1978). Newborn's central vision: whole or holes? *Journal of Experimental Child Psychology*, **26**, 193–203.

Luckiesh, M. (1965). *Visual illusions*. Dover Publications, New York.

Mann, I. (1964). *The development of the human eye*. British Medical Association, London.

Marr, D. (1982). *Vision*. W. H. Freeman, San Francisco, CA.

Marshall, J. C. (1981). Hemispheric specialization: what, how and why. *Behavioral and Brain Sciences*, **4**, 72–3.

Marzi, C. and Berlucchi, G. (1977). Right visual field superiority for accuracy of recognition of famous faces in normals. *Neuropsychologia*, **15**, 751–6.

Michel, G. F. (1981). Right-handedness: A consequence of infant supine head-orientation preference? *Science*, **212**, 657–8.

Patterson, K. E. and Baddeley, A. D. (1977). When face recognition fails. *Journal of Experimental Psychology: Human Learning and Memory*, **3**, 406–17.

Powell, T. P. S. (1981). Certain aspects of the intrinsic organization of the cerebral cortex. In *Brain mechanisms of perceptual awareness and purposeful behavior*, (ed. O. Pompeiano and C. Ajmone-Marsan). pp. 53–72. Raven Press, New York.

Rakic, P. (1981). Development of visual centers in the primate brain depends on binocular competition before birth. *Science*, **214**, 928–31.

Rosenfeld, S. A. and van Hoesen, G. W. (1979). Face recognition in the rhesus monkey. *Neuropsychologia*, **17**, 503–9.

Selnes, O. (1974). The corpus callosum: some anatomical and functional considerations with special reference to language. *Brain and Language*, **1**, 111–40.

Sergent, J. (1984a). Configural processing of faces in the left and the right cerebral hemispheres. *Journal of Experimental Psychology: Human Perception and Performance*, **10**, 554–72.

—— (1984b). Inferences from unilateral brain damage about normal hemispheric functions in visual pattern recognition. *Psychological Bulletin*, **96**, 99–115.

—— (1985). Influence of input and task factors on hemispheric involvement in face processing. *Journal of Experimental Psychology: Human Perception and Performance*, **11**, 846–61.

—— (1986). Methodological constraints on neuropsychological studies of face perception in normals. In *The neuropsychology of face perception and facial expression*, (ed. R. Bruyer, pp. 91–124. Lawrence Erlbaum Associates, Hillsdale, NJ.

—— (in press). Structural processing of faces. In *Handbook of research on face perception*, (ed. H. Ellis and A. W. Young), Elsevier, Amsterdam.

Shapley, R. and Lennie, P. (1985). A spatial frequency analysis in the visual system. *Annual Review of Neuroscience*, **8**, 547–83.

Smith, E. E. and Nielsen, G. D. (1970). Representation and retrieval in short term memory: recognition and recall of faces. *Journal of Experimental Psychology*, **85**, 397–405.

Sperry, R. W. (1974). Lateral specialization in the surgically separated hemispheres. In *The neurosciences: third study program*, (ed. F. O. Schmitt and F. G. Worden), pp. 5–19. MIT Press, Cambridge, MA.

Takane, Y. and Sergent, J. (1983). Multidimensional scaling models for reaction time and same–different judgments. *Psychometrika*, **48**, 393–423.

Thompson, P. (1980). Margaret Thatcher: a new illusion. *Perception*, **9**, 483–4.

Volpe, J. J. (1977). Symposium on neonatal neurology. *Clinics in Perrinatology*, **4**, 17–38.

Walker-Smith, G. J. (1978). The effects of delay and exposure duration in a face recognition task. *Perception and Psychophysics*, **24**, 63–70.

Yakovlev, P. I. and Lecours, A. R. (1967). The myologenetic cycles of regional maturation in the brain. In *Regional development of the brain in early life*, (ed. A. Minkowski), pp. 3–70. Blackwell Scientific Publications, Oxford.

Yin, R. K. (1978). Face perception: a review of experiments with infants, normal adults, and brain injured patients. In *Handbook of sensory physiology, volume 8*, (ed. R. Held, H. W. Leibowitz, and H.-L. Teuber), pp. 593–608. Springer Verlag, Berlin.

6

Stimulus generalization and the acquisition of categories by pigeons

JOHN M. PEARCE

Introduction

A fundamental aspect of human thought is the ability to organize experience into categories. This skill allows us to treat a variety of events in the same way, even though they may differ considerably among themselves. The concern of this chapter is with the capacity of one non-human species, the pigeon, to categorize its experiences. It may seem perverse to study the operation of a human mental process in this way, but the theme of this symposium provides one very good reason for doing so. There appears to be a close relationship between language and our skills of categorization. Unless we could form categories, the meaning of many words would be extremely restricted; and syntactic rules would be impossible to apply without such grammatical classes as subject, verb, and object. But to what extent does categorization depend upon language? This is not an easy question to answer by studying people, but important insights may be gained by studying non-linguistic animals. Once we have understood the fundamental processes of categorization in non-humans, then we may be in a better position to understand how they are embellished by language in our own species.

In fact the impression has been created by several authors that animals are incapable of forming categories. Two quotations, cited by Herrnstein (1984, p. 233), should suffice to make this point. According to Hunt (1982, p. 48), 'human beings . . . are concept-making creatures. Unlike any other animal, we have a natural ability to group objects or events into categories'. While Howard and Campion (1978, p. 32) maintain that 'the human visual is the only effective pattern classification system known'.

There is now, however, ample evidence showing that some animals are very good at categorizing their experiences (for reviews, see Herrnstein 1984; Lea 1984), and a study by Herrnstein et al. (1976) provides a good example. In each session pigeons were presented with a set of 80 different slides, half of which contained pictures of trees. The trees were not especially prominent in the slides, rather the slides were of scenes that contained trees. The remaining slides were of similar scenes but without trees. Slides were presented one at a time and subjects were rewarded for pecking a response key whenever one showing a tree was present; responses in the presence of the remaining slides were never rewarded. The slides were selected from a pool containing more than 500 pictures and eventually most subjects were discriminating accurately between the two sets. Similar findings have been reported, also with pigeons, when the relevant feature of the slides consists of water, a specific person, or even underwater scenes containing fish (Herrnstein 1984).

One theoretically trivial explanation for the success of this training is that the subjects remembered the individual slides and their significance. The use of a pool of 500 slides makes such a suggestion unlikely, and it is contradicted by the finding that the discrimination transfers very well to a set of novel photographs (Herrnstein *et al.* 1976). This would be impossible if discrimination learning depended on remembering each of the slides associated with food. The behaviour of animals, therefore, can be controlled not just by a specific stimulus but by a collection of stimuli that belong to a category. The main purpose of this chapter is to examine the processes responsible for this control.

There are at least two ways in which pigeons might learn about categories. Studies of category formation by humans have led to the suggestion that exposure to a variety of instances results in the formation of a prototype. This is said to reflect the central tendency, or average, of the instances and is believed to be used in all future judgements as to whether or not an item belongs to that category (e.g. Franks and Bransford 1971; Posner and Keele 1968, 1970; Reed 1972). Such a claim raises the intriguing possibility that animals too may form a prototype as a result of being exposed to a number of instances of a category.

In contrast to this possibility, we can look to conventional conditioning theory to understand the way animals form categories. The last two decades have seen a considerable improvement in our knowledge about the learning processes of animals when they are confronted with simple tasks. The value of this work would be enhanced considerably if it could be used to help in our understanding of the learning that takes place in more complicated procedures, such as those involving a discrimination between different categories of stimuli. In fact, the results to be described in this chapter are likely to disappoint those looking for new mental mechanisms in animals, but they may provide some encouragement for advocates of conditioning theory.

Do animals acquire prototypes?

Evidence that humans form prototypes comes from studies in which the stimulus that corresponds to the presumed prototype is never presented while the category is being taught. On test trials it is often found that people are significantly better at classifying the prototype when they are first exposed to it than they are at classifying other novel members of the category (e.g. Posner and Keele 1968, 1970).

The use of this technique for discovering whether or not animals form prototypes is obviously difficult when they are trained with photographs of natural objects. The pictures are generally so complex that it is impossible to determine what a prototype of a tree, for example, should look like. Moreover, even if this could be determined, there remains the problem of constructing a picture of this prototype so that subjects can be tested with it. A more successful approach might be to study category learning with artificial stimuli such as patterns. As studies with humans have revealed (e.g. Neumann 1977; Posner and Keele 1968, 1970; Reed 1972), this should make the specification and construction of the prototype relatively straightforward.

To my knowledge, with artificial stimuli there has been only a single study to explore the role of prototypes in learning about categories by animals. Lea and Harrison (1978) trained pigeons in a discrimination in which patterns constructed from three features signalled whether or not reward was available for pecking a response key. The patterns consisted of two shapes (A1 or A2), which varied in brightness (B1 or B2), and were presented against backgrounds of different colours (C1 or C2). The pattern composed of the features A1, B1, and C1 was designated as the ideal instance for the category signalling reward, while the ideal instance for the non-rewarded category was composed of A2, B2, and C2. During training only two features at a time were presented from the relevant category, so that a signal for reward might consist of A1, B1, and C2, while non-reward might be signalled by A2, B1, and C2. Once the discrimination between the two categories had been learned, testing was conducted with the ideal instances. Although subjects discriminated successfully between these patterns, their accuracy was slightly worse than for the training patterns. This outcome would not be expected if the original training resulted in the formation of a prototype that was used to identify the category to which a specific item belonged. Such a prototype should consist of the three relevant features for a category, and thus make the classification of the ideal instances easier than for any other pattern.

There are, however, a number of reasons for questioning whether this study provides an adequate test for the involvement of a prototype in category learning. The very nature of the design ensured that there were only three training instances for each category. Perhaps experience of a greater number of training stimuli is needed before a prototype is constructed. Alternatively, it is conceivable that a prototype did develop, but the generalization decrement engendered by the encounter with the novel test pattern more than outweighed any advantage conferred upon this pattern because it matched the prototype.

The first experiments to be described explore whether or not category learning by pigeons depends upon the formation of a prototype. In the hope of overcoming the problems that have just been identified, the number of training instances in each category was considerably larger then that used by Lea and Harrison (1978).

The apparatus used in all of the experiments described in this chapter consisted of standard pigeon test chambers, which were modified to accommodate a microcolour television with a rectangular screen. The screen was placed 4 cm behind a clear Perspex response key. A BBC microcomputer was used to generate patterns that were shown on the television screen, and two examples of the patterns that were employed are presented in Fig. 6.1. They consisted of three vertical coloured bars (yellow, red, and white going from left to right). The bars were presented against a blue background and within a rectangular frame consisting of a white line. For the purposes of the computer program, the bars were measured in units that were equivalent to 0.5 cm on the television screen. The width of each bar was 0.8 units and their maximum height was 7 units, which was also the height of the frame. For the first two experiments the patterns were constructed according to two criteria. The combined height of the bars for each member of the *short* category was always 9 units, with each bar never deviating from its mean height of 3 by more than 2 units. A similar constraint applied to all members of the *tall* category, except that the combined bar height was always 15 units and the mean height of each bar was 5 units. An example of a short pattern is 4–1–4 (left-hand panel) and of a tall pattern is 7–5–3 (right-hand panel), where the numbers refer, respectively, to the heights of the left, centre, and right bars.

The method of training was autoshaping. In conventional experiments based on this technique a response key is illuminated for about 10 sec and then food is made briefly available to a hungry pigeon. These conditioning trials occur approximately once every minute. Subjects are not required to peck the

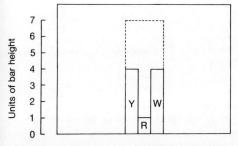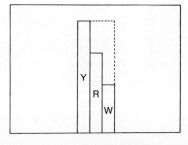

Fig. 6.1 Examples of a short, 4–1–4 (left-hand side), and a tall, 7–5–3 (right-hand side), pattern used in the initial studies of category learning. The bars were coloured yellow (Y), red (R), and white (W). They were presented within a frame provided by a white line (dotted line) and against a blue background.

key in order to receive food, but after a number of trials they generally do so and at a high rate. This response is regarded as a conditioned response (CR) due to the Pavlovian pairing of the key-light (conditioned stimulus, CS) with food (unconditioned stimulus, US). For the experiments described below a similar procedure was adopted, except that, instead of a single stimulus signalling food, discrimination training was given in which patterns from one category, short bars, were paired with food while patterns from the other category, tall bars, were followed by nothing. If subjects are able to discriminate between the two categories then eventually they should peck the response key rapidly whenever a short pattern is presented, whereas they should peck it slowly in the presence of a tall pattern.

There were two groups, with four pigeons in each, for the first experiment. Group 'category' received the training just described, with 18 short patterns signalling the delivery of food and 18 tall patterns being presented alone. They were presented in a random sequence and each pattern was shown twice in every session. The same patterns were presented to group 'random', but the delivery of food was not signalled by a particular category. Instead, nine short and nine tall patterns were consistently paired with food, while the remaining patterns were followed by nothing. The results are portrayed in Fig. 6.2, which shows for each group, in two-session blocks, the mean rate of responding in the presence of the patterns that signalled the occurrence or absence of food.

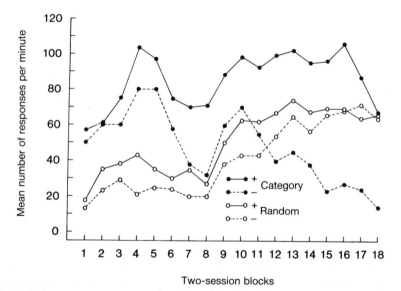

Fig. 6.2   The mean rate of responding in the presence of patterns that signalled either the occurrence (+) or non-occurrence (−) of food for pigeons in group 'category' and group 'random'.

Turning first to group 'category', it is apparent that as training progressed these subjects learned the discrimination. Eventually the rate of responding during the short patterns was substantially faster then during the tall patterns. This was true for all four subjects in each of the last eight sessions. One explanation for this successful discrimination is that the patterns were treated as if they were completely unrelated and subjects learned about the significance of each of the 36 patterns to which they were exposed. Such a possibility, however, is challenged by the results of group 'random'. In this group the relationship between each pattern and the outcome of the trial was constant, yet there was no evidence of successful discrimination learning. Thus, by the end of training, the rate of responding during the patterns signalling food was much the same as during those that signalled its absence. One unexpected outcome from this study was the difference between the rates of responding by the two groups during the initial sessions of training. There is no obvious reason for this result, which has not occurred in other studies using a related design.

In an attempt to understand the performance of group 'category', a number of test sessions were given after the completion of the above training. These were conducted in the manner just described except that occasionally a trial was included in which patterns that had not appeared during training was presented. The patterns used were as follows: 0–0–0, 1–1–1, 3–3–3, 4–4–4, 5–5–5, and 7–7–7. The 3–3–3 and 5–5–5 patterns constitute the averages of the short and tall patterns that were used throughout conditioning. As such they might be expected to correspond closely to any prototype that resulted from this training and be treated as ideal instances of the two categories. If category training can result in the formation of a prototype, then the rate of responding in the presence of the 3–3–3 pattern should be higher than to any other test pattern, or to the training stimuli also presented in the test session. Conversely, the response rate to the 5–5–5 pattern should be lower than to any other pattern.

The results from the test session, depicted in Fig. 6.3, lend little support to this analysis. The left-hand pair of histograms shows the mean rate of responding during the test sessions to the short (+) and tall (−) training patterns. The right-hand histograms reveal the response rates recorded in the presence of the test patterns. The important features to note are that highest rate of responding, for all four birds, was not to the 3–3–3 but to 1–1–1 pattern; and the lowest response rate was to the 7–7–7, rather than to the 5–5–5, pattern (this was true for three birds). In addition, for all four birds, the rate of responding to the 1–1–1 pattern was faster than to the short training patterns, while it was slower to the 7–7–7 pattern than to the tall training patterns. The finding of a higher response rate to 1–1–1 than to the training patterns is of special interest because it indicates that with this method of category training the introduction of a novel stimulus does not necessarily result in a generalization decrement.

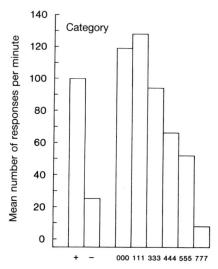

Fig. 6.3 The mean rate of responding to various patterns for group 'category' during the generalization test sessions. The left-hand pair of histograms depicts the rate of responding during the reinforced short (+) and non-reinforced tall (−) training patterns. The remaining histograms show the results for the patterns introduced for the generalization tests.

There is, therefore, no suggestion from this study that pigeons treat stimuli which constitute the average of their training patterns in a special way. Instead, it seems that the patterns they best discriminate between are those that are rather different to the ones used for training.

A stimulus generalization model for category learning

The failure to confirm the most direct prediction from an account of category learning which assumes the formation of prototypes raises the question of how the present findings should be explained. There are several ways of approaching this problem, but the one I shall adopt is based on a model that was developed originally to account for the effects of stimulus generalization in Pavlovian conditioning (Pearce 1987). It will become apparent that many of the ideas that are developed are not original but stem from a theory of discrimination learning that was developed some 50 years ago (Spence 1936).

According to Pearce (1987), animals possess a buffer of limited capacity that is always full and represents the overall pattern of stimulation to which they are exposed. The main principle of the model, for Pavlovian conditioning, is that whenever a US is presented then an association will be formed in long-term memory (LTM) between representations of the US and the contents of the buffer prior to its delivery. The strength of this associative bond is assumed to grow with repeated conditioning and to influence directly the strength of the CR. If the contents of the buffer should change, even slightly, from one trial to the next, then a new CS–US association will be formed in LTM.

On every trial the contents of the buffer are compared with all the CS representations in LTM. This comparison will then result in each representation being activated to a degree which is directly related to its similarity with the contents of the buffer. Once it is activated, a representation can contribute to the overall strength of conditioned responding by exciting the US representation with which it is associated. The level of this excitation is determined by the product of the strength of the CS–US association and the degree of activation of the CS representation. Thus the greater the similarity between the contents of the buffer and the representations in LTM, the stronger will be the CR that is performed.

For the sake of simplicity, assume that conditioning is conducted with only the short patterns and that they are all paired with food. This will result in connections being formed in LTM between representations of each pattern and food. When a novel pattern, such as 3–3–3, is presented its similarity to all the training patterns will ensure that they are strongly activated and a vigorous CR will be observed. But if a novel tall pattern, say 5–5–5, is presented then it will have less of an influence on the patterns stored in LTM and a correspondingly weaker CR will be recorded. These views are summarized in Fig. 6.4. The abscissa represents a gradient of similarity of the

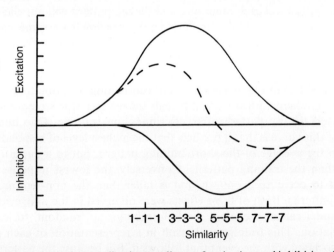

Fig. 6.4 Hypothetical generalization gradients of excitation and inhibition that might result from discrimination training between reinforced short patterns and non-reinforced tall patterns; the dotted line reflects net response strength and was derived by subtracting the inhibitory from the excitatory gradient.

patterns used in the above experiment, ranging from 1–1–1 at one end to 7–7–7 at the other. The ordinate in the upper half of the figure represents excitatory response strength which determines the strength of the CR. A conventional bell-shaped curve, which has its centre above 3–3–3, depicts the generalization gradient that will result after training with the short patterns. When a pattern that is similar to the average of the training patterns is presented a strong CR will be recorded; but when a very different pattern is used the strength of the CR will be negligible.

If discrimination training is now introduced, with tall patterns signalling the non-occurrence of food, then initially their slight similarity to the short patterns will result in a CR being performed in their presence. The model assumes, however, that if a stimulus elicits a CR but it is not paired with a US then an inhibitory association will be formed in LTM. This association will be between a representation of the contents of the buffer and what Konorski (1967) refers to as a no-US representation. The details of such a representation need not be of present concern (but see Pearce and Hall 1980); all that needs to be stipulated is that when an inhibitory CS is presented it will exert an influence that counteracts the effects of any concurrently activated CS representations that are associated with the US. Thus as a result of discrimination training the presentation of a tall pattern will activate strongly the representations of the tall patterns in LTM and arouse a level of inhibition. Of course, the pattern will also activate the representations of the short patterns, but to a lesser degree, and arouse a measure of excitation. When discrimination training is complete the simultaneously aroused excitation and inhibition will cancel each other out, and the tall pattern will not elicit a CR. There is no reason why inhibition should not generalize in the same manner as excitation, and the curve in the lower panel of Fig. 6.4 shows the inhibitory generalization gradient, centred on the 5–5–5 pattern, which can be expected as discrimination training approaches completion.

The dotted line in Fig. 6.4 is a result of subtracting the inhibitory from the excitatory gradients. Effectively, it reveals the net response strength that can be expected to any pattern after discrimination training. One interesting feature of this curve is that it predicts that the highest level of responding will not be to the average of the short training pattern, but to a pattern that is shorter than the training patterns. Conversely, the lowest response rate is predicted to occur to a pattern that is taller than the non-reinforced tall training patterns. Both of these effects were observed in the above study.

The model can also explain the failure by group 'random' to learn the discrimination. This training will result in a representation of each pattern being associated with the event that follows it. But because the patterns were not organized into categories, each one will closely resemble some that were paired with food and some that were not. As a consequence, although a particular pattern may be correctly associated with the trial outcome, it will elicit an intermediate rate of responding because of the generalization of excitation and inhibition from the patterns to which it is similar.

Two experimental tests of the model

One prediction to follow from the model is that it should not be necessary to train subjects extensively with a large number of short and tall patterns in order for them to discriminate between them. Instead, it should be sufficient to give discrimination training with only a single member of each category. Once the discrimination has been learned the gradients of excitation and inhibition around the training patterns should be similar to those depicted in Fig. 6.3. Presenting a novel member from the short category will then activate the representation of the excitatory short pattern in LTM to a far greater extent than the representation of the inhibitory tall pattern, and a substantial CR will be recorded. On the other hand, presenting a tall pattern will have the converse effect and result in very little responding. To test this prediction an experiment with two groups of eight pigeons was conducted. Group 'category' ($n=6$) was trained in much the same way as its namesake described above, while for the first 34 sessions of training group 'instance' ($n=7$) received discrimination training in which a member of the short category (4–2–3) signalled food while a member of the tall category (5–3–7) was presented alone. The results for the six birds in group 'category' and the seven in group 'instance' that learned the discrimination are shown in Fig. 6.5. Despite the larger number of stimuli shown to group 'category', these subjects mastered the discrimination at much the same rate as group 'instance'.

For the next stage of the experiment group 'instance' was introduced to the patterns with which group 'category' had been trained from the outset. It is apparent from the right-hand side of Fig. 6.5 that this change had little impact on responding. In the presence of the short patterns, group 'instance' immediately responded at a rate that was comparable to that shown by group 'category'. There was some indication that group 'instance' initially responded more rapidly than group 'category' to the tall patterns, but even this difference soon disappeared. Examination of the results for the first session in which they were exposed to the two categories indicated that all subjects in group 'instance' responded more rapidly in the presence of the short than the tall patterns, thus indicating successful transfer from training with two instances to the entire range of patterns.

A rather similar finding to this has been reported by Cerella (1979). In his experiments the silhouette of a single oak leaf was repeatedly presented among 40 slides showing the silhouettes of non-oak broad leaves. This discrimination was learned readily and showed little disruption when the original oak leaf was replaced by 40 different oak leaves.

The next experiment to be described tests a prediction of the model

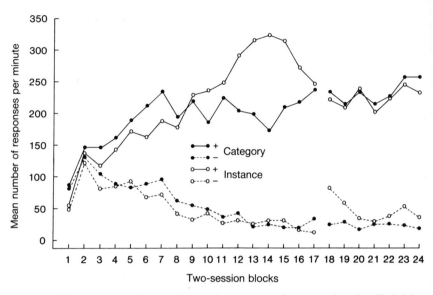

Fig. 6.5   The mean rate of responding in the presence of patterns that signalled either the occurrence (+), or non-occurrence (−), of food for piegeons given 34 sessions of discrimination training between one short and one tall pattern (group 'instance') or between the short and tall categories. The right-hand portion of the figure shows the mean response rates for both groups when they were both given discrimination training between the categories.

concerning the effects of extinction. Inspection of Fig. 6.3 reveals that, following discrimination training, in which food is presented after members of the short but not the tall category, the greatest net level of excitation will be aroused by a pattern with a mean bar height that is less than the average of the short training patterns. The results from group 'category' of the first experiment confirmed this prediction with the 1–1–1 pattern, and the next experiment was designed to examine the effect of repeatedly presenting this pattern in extinction after discrimination training. According to the account developed above, this will result in the growth of an inhibitory association to a representation of the 1–1–1 pattern. For the extinction training to be effective, the strength of this association will have to be considerable if it is to overcome the combined generalization of excitation to this stimulus from all the short patterns used during training. When one of the original short training patterns is then presented again, the generalization of the high level of inhibition from the 1–1–1 pattern will counteract the excitation aroused by this pattern and lead to a low level of responding in its presence. Consequently, for group 'category', extinction training with the 1–1–1 pattern should not only eliminate responding in the presence of this pattern, it should also result in the elimination of responding to all patterns. This prediction, it should be noted, holds for those patterns that themselves were paired directly with food, and even though the 1–1–1 pattern had never taken part in conditioning.

To test this prediction, group 'category' of the first experiment received, after its original training, three extinction sessions in which the 1–1–1 pattern was repeatedly presented by itself. There was then a single test session in which four presentations of the 1–1–1 pattern were followed by a single exposure to each of the 36 patterns that were used for the category training. Food was not presented in this session. The left-hand panel of Fig. 6.6 shows that the mean rate of responding to the 1–1–1 pattern, in the test session, was relatively low as a result of the extinction sessions. It is further apparent, from the right-hand side of this panel, that this training virtually abolished responding to the original patterns, and that there was no longer any difference between the levels of responding to the short and tall categories.

The right-hand panel of this figure shows the results for group 'random', which was treated in exactly the same way as group 'category' for this stage of the experiment. These subjects also responded very slowly to the 1–1–1 pattern in the test session, but there was a considerable recovery in responding when the training patterns were shown again. The rate of responding to the patterns that previously signalled food was significantly faster for group 'random' than for group 'category' [Mann-Whitney $U(4,4) = 1$, $p < 0.05$; and the equivalent difference for the non-reinforced patterns was also significant, $U(4,4) = 0$, $p < 0.05$]. The relatively high rate of responding to the training patterns in group 'random' can be readily explained by the generalization

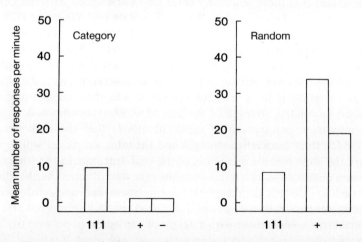

Fig. 6.6 The mean rate of responding for group 'category' and group 'random' of the first experiment, during an extinction test session, to the 1–1–1 pattern and to the previously reinforced (+) and non-reinforced (−) training patterns. Prior to this session they received three sessions of non-reinforced exposure to the 1–1–1 pattern.

model. Since half the patterns that signalled food were tall, it is likely that the generalization of inhibition from the 1–1–1 pattern would have less of a disruptive influence on the overall rate of responding than for group 'category', where only short pattern signalled food. Figure 6.6 indicates that in the test session group 'random' responded more rapidly to the reinforced than to the non-reinforced patterns. This difference, however, is by no means significant: half the subjects in the group actually responded more rapidly to the non-reinforced patterns.

Before leaving this experiment, we should note that its results again lend little support to the idea that pigeons form a prototype as a result of being exposed to a variety of patterns. In particular, it is not clear why extinction training with a pattern that should not correspond to the prototype will abolish responding to the entire category. Perhaps the failure of reveal the existence of prototypes in pigeons should not be too surprising, as there are also grounds for doubting their involvement in the acquisition of artificial categories by humans (Hintzman 1986; Medin and Schaffer 1978).

The configural basis of category learning

According to the account of category learning developed above, conditioning results in the formation of an association between a representation of the entire pattern of stimulation that is present on a trial and the US. In contrast to this proposal, most contemporary theories of conditioning regard the pattern of stimulation accompanying each trial to consist of a number of elements, and that these separately enter into associations with the US (e.g. Mackintosh 1975; Pearce and Hall 1980; Rescorla and Wagner 1972). As a consequence, when this sort of theory is applied to the present experiments it provides a rather different explanation for their results. Specifically, it might be predicted that, as training progresses, representations of the different heights of the bars will individually enter into associations with the US. The level of responding to a particular pattern will then depend upon the combined associative strength of the bars of which it is composed.

An important assumption of these theories is that the elements must compete for their associative strength and the most successful will be those that are the most reliable predictors of the trial outcome. In the studies that have been described so far, it has been the case that different bar heights are correlated to different degrees with reinforcement and non-reinforcement. For example, bars with a height of 3 occurred on both reinforced and non-reinforced trials, while those with a height of one occurred only on trials that were accompanied with food. Given such an arrangement, it is likely that the bars with a height of one gained greater associative strength than those with a height of 3, and this would explain the superior responding to the 1–1–1 than to the 3–3–3 pattern that was observed in the generalization test of the first experiment. A similar argument can be developed to explain the slower responding that was recorded during this session to the 7–7–7 than to the 5–5–5 pattern.

Despite this different approach, elemental theories of conditioning make a number of similar predictions to the account developed here. Indeed it may be very difficult to choose unequivocally between them. But there is at least one prediction that follows naturally from the generalization model and which is not in keeping with the spirit of elemental models of conditioning.

According to elemental theories of conditioning, features that are irrelevant to the solution of a discrimination will ultimately possess no associative strength. As a consequence, if these features are modified in some way after the discrimination has been learned then this should have no influence on performance. In a test of this prediction a group of six pigeons was used which had received extensive discrimination training (49 sessions) between short patterns signalling food and tall patterns signalling nothing. They were then given test trials in which two tall (6–4–5 and 4–7–4) and two short (2–2–5 and 3–1–5) training patterns were occasionally presented in a distorted form during an otherwise standard training session. For all four patterns the normally contiguous bars were separated by a gap of one unit. The red bar remained in the centre of the screen, but the yellow and white bars were displaced towards their respective sides, with the blue background occupying the space between the bars. Since the position of the bars was never of any relevance to the trial outcome, the most direct interpretation from elemental theories of conditioning is that this distortion should not influence the discrimination. On the other hand, the model of category learning proposed above makes a different prediction. Distorting the short patterns will reduce their ability to activate the representations of short patterns in LTM and result in a weaker CR than when a normal short pattern is presented. Conversely, the distortion of a tall pattern will reduce its capacity to activate the inhibitory tall representations, and the corresponding weaker level of inhibition that it generates will result in a stronger CR than that elicited by a normal tall pattern.

The results supported this analysis. With the tall patterns, the mean rate of responding to the normal configuration was 17 responses/min, while to the distorted versions responding increased to 175 responses/min. This increase was shown by all subjects. The rate of responding to the normal short patterns was 264 responses/min, which was reduced to 194 responses/min by the distortion. In this case the decline in responding was shown by all but one subject [Student's $t(5) = 2.0$, $p = 0.05$]. Although these findings do not readily follow from elemental theories of conditioning, they can be explained by them but in a somewhat arbitrary fashion. According to these theories the irrelevant features will be without influence only when learning is at asymptote. It is conceivable that this state had not been reached after 49 sessions and that the features relating to the position of the bars retained a measure of associative strength. Moving the bars might destroy these features and eliminate their contribution to the overall rate of responding. By itself, however, this interpretation is inadequate since separating the bars of a tall pattern led to an increase in responding, while the same manipulation with a short pattern led to a reduction in responding. To explain these opposing outcomes it must be assumed that the distortions influenced different features and that these features possessed different associative properties. Unfortunately, until we have a precise theory of the way in which patterns are analysed in terms of features, this type of account will be very difficult to test rigorously.

The next experiment to be described also suggests that pigeons remember the overall configuration created by a training stimulus, but it employed a pattern that has not been considered so far. A single group ($n = 8$) of pigeons was given discrimination training with four patterns. Patterns 3–6–4 and 7–3–5 were consistently paired with food, while 3–3–4 and 7–6–5 were never followed by food. The reason for selecting these patterns was that none of them contains a feature that uniquely signals the trial outcome. For each of the three coloured bars, a given height is followed by food on half the occasions on which it occurs. Thus if the only means that animals have at their disposal for solving discriminations is by learning about those elements that reliably signal the outcome of a trial, then they should find this discrimination insoluble. In contrast, if animals learn about the entire pattern of stimulation then the discrimination should present them with little difficulty since the four stimuli clearly create four very different patterns. In particular, food is signalled by patterns in which the two side bars are either lower or higher than the centre bar. The results from this study are depicted in Fig. 6.7, which shows quite clearly that subjects experienced little difficulty with the discrimination. From session 5 onwards the rate of responding was significantly faster in the presence of the patterns that signalled food.

Additional support for the claim that the subjects learned about the patterns created by the training stimuli comes from a further stage of the experiment. After the original training, the procedure was changed so that in each session 40 different patterns were presented. The patterns were all based on the four training patterns but the height of each bar was increased or reduced by a maximum of 2 units. In addition, all of the 20 patterns based on the 3–6–4 and 7–3–5 originals retained the overall shape of the side bars, being either lower or higher than the centre bar. None of the instances derived from the 3–3–4 and 7–6–5 patterns was of these general shapes. Food was signalled by the variants of the 3–6–4 and 7–3–5 patterns, and the selection of bar heights ensured that no single feature could indicate the trial outcome.

The right-hand side of Fig. 6.7 shows that the origial training transferred reasonably well to the novel patterns. In fact, despite the slight decrement in the discrimination, responding to the patterns paired with reward was

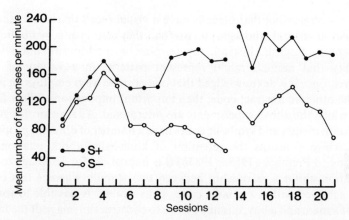

Fig. 6.7   The left-hand side shows the mean rate of responding by a single group of pigeons in the presence of two patterns, 3–6–4 and 7–3–5, that signalled food (S+), and two, 3–3–4 and 7–6–5, that signalled nothing (S−). The mean rates of responding during patterns that were based on these training stimuli is shown in the right-hand side.

significantly faster than to the others, even on the first session of this stage [$t(7) = 2.5$, $p < 0.05$]. One explanation for this outcome is that, as a result of their original training, the pigeons classified the novel patterns on the basis of their overall configuration or shape.

The relational basis of category learning

If it is accepted that remembering individual patterns forms the basis of the category discriminations described above, we must then identify how the pattern is represented. One way of approaching this problem is to adopt a distinction that is frequently made concerning the representation of knowledge by humans. It has been suggested that we store information either as an image or symbolically (e.g. Anderson 1985), and it is conceivable that these separate means are also available to pigeons. The information about the training patterns might then be stored in such a way that it is equivalent to a mental snapshot. This image-like representation would permit the retrieval of information about the elements that were present in each pattern, as well as about their spatial configuration. Alternatively, the information might be stored in a more abstract way and represented by a symbolic code. For example, a pattern could be represented by the sentence: 'Three tall bars against a blue background'. Provided the symbolic representation was sufficiently precise then it too should be able to encode information about features and their relationship to one another.

I am not suggesting that pigeons have a visual recall that allows them to experience a mental photograph, or that they can use a symbolic code equivalent to English. Instead, my purpose is to draw attention to the possibility that animals might represent patterns in a variety of ways. Moreover, once it is acknowledged that one of these ways employs an image, while the other an abstract code, then important implications follow for the way in which the above experiments are interpreted. As a means for storing information images and symbolic codes have a number of different properties, one of which concerns the retention of knowledge about relationships. According to Premack (1983a, 1983b) it is impossible for an image to store information about a relatioship between two stimuli, whereas this can be readily achieved with a symbolic code. Thus while it is possible to form an image of a man, and a boy, it is impossible to construct an image of the father–son relationship between them. Of course, information about this relationship can be readily encoded symbolically.

Consider the patterns that were used in the first experiment (see p. 135). The solution of the discrimination depended upon information about the absolute height of the bars, and this can be retrieved from either an image or a symbolic representation of the training stimuli. But consider now the patterns depicted in Fig. 6.8. Representations of these patterns as images would contain the information that one consisted of two tall bars, and the other a short and a tall bar. In addition to this information, a symbolic representation could encode the fact that the bars on the left are the *same* height, while on the right they are of a *different* height. In the next experiment pigeons were given a category discrimination with patterns similar to those in Fig. 6.8. For half the trials, the bars were of the same height and these signalled the delivery of food. The remaining patterns, which were never followed by food, were composed of

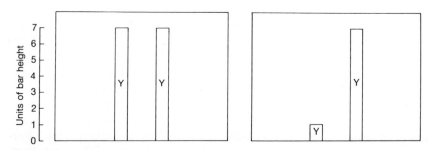

Fig. 6.8 Examples of two patterns employed in a study to determine if pigeons can discriminate between categories with bars of either the same or different heights. The yellow (Y) bars were presented against a blue background and separated by a distance of 1.3 units.

bars of different heights. If the only way in which animals store information about these sorts of figures is as images, then their inability to encode information about a relationship will make it difficult to solve the discrimination. On the other hand, if a symbolic representation is employed then this could readily encode information about the relationship between the two bars and be used in the solution of the discrimination.

Two groups of eight pigeons were used for this study. Group 'variable' was exposed to the seven possible configurations with the bars at the same height and to 20 patterns with the bars at a different height. Group 'instance' was shown only four patterns: the two depicted in Fig. 6.8 (7–7 and 1–7) and their counterparts (1–1 and 7–1). For both groups food was delivered after patterns containing bars of equal height. There were an equal number of reinforced and non-reinforced trials in each session.

The results for the 20 sessions of this training are shown in the left-hand section of Fig. 6.9. There was no indication of the birds in group 'variable' learning the discrimination. Throughout the experiment the rate of responding to the *same* patterns was virtually identical to that for the *different* patterns. The results from group 'instance' suggest that this failure was not due to subjects being unable to perceive the stimuli. They found the discrimination difficult, but not impossible, so that on sessions 7, 11–13, and

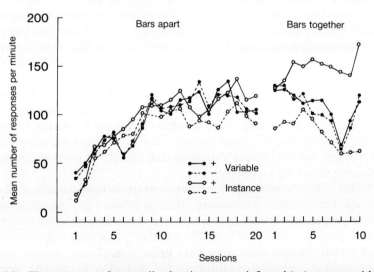

Fig. 6.9   The mean rate of responding by pigeons to reinforced (+) patterns with bars of the same height and to non-reinforced (−) patterns with bars of different heights. Group 'variable' received six 'same' patterns and 20 'different' patterns, while group instance was shown two patterns from each category. During the first 20 sessions the bars were separated, but for the remaining 10 sessions they were adjacent.

16–18 responding was significantly faster for the 1–1 and 7–7 patterns than for the 1–7 and 7–1 patterns [$ts(7) > 2.25$, $ps < 0.05$].

For the final 10 sessions of the experiment the bars were placed side-by-side in the centre of the screen. There was no sign of any improvement in the performance of group 'variable', even though this had a profound influence on the discrimination by group 'instance'. In every session of this stage all subjects in group 'instance' responded more rapidly to the same than to the different patterns.

Perhaps it would be foolish to draw any firm conclusions from a single study, especially one that includes a null result. None the less, the failure by members of group 'variable' to solve the discrimination suggests that they were unable to encode information about the relationship between the two bars in the various patterns to which they were exposed. Such a conclusion in turn implies that the way in which a pattern is encoded is as an image rather than symbolically.

There is nothing in the results obtained from group 'instance' to challenge this conclusion. The training would result in the growth of excitatory associations with the 1–1 and 7–7 patterns, and inhibitory associations with the 1–7 and 7–1 patterns. Since any one pattern contains a bar height that is present in both members of the other category, the similarity between the members of the two categories is likely to be high. This will result in a considerable amount of generalization among the instances and will interfere with the learning of the discrimination. Eventually, however, the associative strength of each pattern should be sufficient to counteract the disruptive effects of generalization from the other patterns, and the discrimination will be mastered. A similar analysis can be applied to group 'variable', but at the same time the question is raised as to why these subjects were incapable of solving the discrimination. Presumably the answer rests with the far greater number of patterns that were used, so that many more sessions would be needed before learning about each instance was complete. If this interpretation is correct then the performance of 'group variable' may eventually have shown some improvement, but this would have been due entirely to learning about the significance of the individual patterns.

Whether or not the results of this experiment are surprising will depend very much upon the readers perspective. Human adults (and my six-year-old daughter) experience no difficulty whatsoever when they are given the group 'variable' problem and asked to predict whether or not food will occur at the end of a trial. Indeed, those who have never conditioned pigeons express astonishment at their failure to solve this discrimination. In contrast, humans find considerable difficulty with the patterns used in the first experiment. This may be due in part to them searching for a relational rule—for instance, 'left bar taller than the centre bar'—which will interfere with the discovery of the correct solution. Of course, if pigeons lack a symbolic means for representing patterns, they would not adopt this misleading strategy.

Those who have attempted to train pigeons to solve match-to-sample problems may perhaps be less than surprised by the above findings. In a typical experiment a colour, say red, is projected onto the centre key of a three-key panel. Once the bird has pecked this key the side keys are illuminated by two different colours, red and green. To gain reward, the pigeon must peck the side key that is the same colour as the centre key. One way of solving this discrimination is by learning to peck the side key that is the same colour as the centre key. To test whether pigeons employ such a relational rule when solving these problems a number of experiments have examined the transfer of matching to novel stimuli (e.g. Cumming and Berryman 1961). The use of a relational rule should permit very good transfer in these circumstances, but the general finding is that this change in procedure results in a drop to near chance levels of responding. Moreover, there are good reasons for believing that, on those occasions where positive transfer has been demonstrated, this is not due to a use of the relational rule (Wilson *et al.* 1985). The findings from match-to sample studies, then, join the present results in suggesting that, at the very least, pigeons find it difficult to use relationships when solving discriminations. And one reason for this might be that they lack the means for storing knowledge symbolically.

Concluding comments

One of the reasons for conducting these experiments was to determine whether it is possible to account for category learning in terms of conditioning theory. Drawing from a model that was developed to explain the effects of stimulus generalization in Pavlovian conditioning, an account of category learning was developed which assumes that: (1) animals remember each training pattern and its significance; (2) the response to a test item is determined by its similarity to the stored patterns. This account has proved successful in explaining performance to novel test patterns. It can also explain the effects of extinction training with an individual instance after a discrimination between two categories has been learned.

Despite these successes there remains a need for further development of the model and for additional experiments to test it. A number of the predictions from the model were based on the generalization gradients depicted in Fig. 6.3. However, the slopes of these gradients were derived from the common assumption that generalization curves are bell-shaped, and the gradients of excitation and inhibition were made similar, simply for reasons of parsimony. Ideally these assumptions need to be justified theoretically and supported by experiment.

Another problem with the model is that it does not specify how the similarity between two patterns should be computed. In analysing the results of the first experiment the assumption was made that similarity is determined by comparing the average height of the bars in different patterns. Of course, subjects may not have relied specifically on this method. Similarity could be equally well judged by focusing on the area occupied by the bars, or on the amount of blue background above them. The adoption of any of these strategies would lead to the patterns being organized along the scale of similarity represented in Fig. 6.3.

The fact that the results from the first experiment were consistent with predictions derived from Fig. 6.3 suggests that determinations of similarity were strongly influenced by at least one of the above strategies. But the results of the configural experiment suggest that these may not be the only way in which the similarity between the training patterns is computed. In that experiment subjects were initially given trials in which the 3–6–4 and 7–3–5 patterns signalled food, and the 3–3–4 and 7–6–5 patterns were followed by nothing. They were then introduced to training in which food was signalled by patterns that bore the same general shape to the 3–6–4 and 7–3–5 patterns; that is, the centre bar was either taller than or shorter than both side bars. Non-reward was signalled by patterns that were of a different shape. For this stage of the experiment, the average bar height of the patterns paired with food varied from 2.66 to 5.33 units, while for the other patterns the range was from 1.66 to 7.00 units. Although the successful discrimination on the first test session must have been due to generalization from the training patterns, given such overlap it is unlikely that the degree of this generalization was determined by the average heights of the training and test patterns. Instead, we must look for some additional means by which similarity can be judged. An obvious candidate is the shape of a pattern, but we must then specify how different shapes are compared. All shapes are composed of features and it is not unreasonable to assume that the number of features that two shapes have in common determines their similarity.

Once it is acknowledged that similarity is judged on the basis of a number of dimensions it then becomes necessary to specify how this information is combined to derive the overall similarity of two patterns. A solution to this problem is offered by Medin and Schaffer (1978; see also Medin 1975), who propose that a parameter, s, is used to reflect the similarity on each of the various dimensions that two sitimuli have in common. The value of s can vary from 0 to 1 and the greater its magnitude the closer is the similarity on the chosen dimension. Once the values of s have been computed for the common dimensions, they are then combined multiplicatively to determine the overall degree of similarity.

Before leaving this discussion of the generalization model some mention should be made of its relevance to our understanding of discrimination learning involving natural categories, such as trees. There is no compelling reason, as yet, why the approach advocated here should not also be applied to these categories. Obviously the means of assessing the similarity between two photographs will be more complex than for artificial patterns constructed according to simple rules. However, it has been suggested that learning about natural categories involves processes that will not operate where artificial categories are concerned. For example, Herrnstein *et al.* (1976) have suggested that 'pigeons tend innately to infer a tree category from instances of a tree' (p. 301). If this is correct then it might be claimed that the use of computer-generated patterns will be of little value for the study of learning about natural categories. But it is only once we have fully understood the processes involved in learning with artificial categories that it will be possible to evaluate whether there is indeed something special about natural categories.

Pigeons, it would appear, are readily capable of learning the significance of categories of stimuli and of transferring this learning to novel stimuli. In this respect the thought processes of animals appear to resemble those of humans. This conclusion has also been reached elsewhere (e.g. Estes 1985; Medin and Schaffer 1978) and it is supported by the fact that the generalization model for category learning developed above has much in common with at least two models of human category learning (Hintzman 1986; Medin and Schaffer 1978).

Where the thought processes of pigeons and people appear to part company is with the representation of relationships. No one would doubt that humans have little difficulty in comprehending relationships, but the results of the final experiment indicate that this is a skill that may be beyond the capacity of the pigeon.

Acknowledgements

This work was supported by a grant from the UK Science and Engineering Research Council. I should like to thank Louis Collins for his help with the experiments, and Anthony Dickinson and Paul Wilson for their comments on the manuscript.

References

Anderson, J. R. (1985). *Cognitive psychology and its implications.* W. H. Freeman, New York.

Cerella, J. (1979). Visual classes and natural categories in the pigeon. *Journal of Experimental Psychology: Human Perception and Performance,* **5,** 68–77.

Cumming, W. W. and Berryman, R. (1961). Some data on matching behavior in the pigeon. *Journal of the Experimental Analysis of Behavior*, **4**, 281–4.

Estes, W. K. (1985). Some common aspects of models for learning and memory in lower animals and man. In *Perspectives in learning and memory*, (ed. L. G. Nilsson and T. Archer), pp. 151–66. Lawrence Erlbaum Associates, Hillsdale, NJ.

Franks, J. J. and Bransford, J. D. (1971). Abstraction of visual patterns. *Journal of Experimental Psychology*, **90**, 65–74.

Herrnstein, R. J. (1984). Objects, categories, and discriminative stimuli. In *Animal cognition*, (ed. H. T. Roitblat, T. G. Bever, and H. S. Terrace), pp. 233–62. Lawrence Erlbaum Associates, Hillsdale, NJ.

——, Loveland, D. H. and Cable, C. (1976). Natural concepts in pigeons. *Journals of Experimental Psychology: Animal Behavior Processes*, **2**, 285–311.

Hintzman, D. L. (1986). 'Schema abstraction' in a multiple-trace memory. *Psychological Review*, **93**, 411–28.

Howard, J. M. and Campion, R. C. (1978). A metric for pattern discrimination performance. *IEEE Transactions on Systems, Man, and Cybernetics*, **8**, 32–7.

Hunt, M. (1982). How the mind works. *New York Times Magazine*, 24 January issue, p. 30ff.

Konorski, J. (1967). *Integrative activity of the brain*. University of Chicago Press.

Lea, S. E. G. (1984). In what sense do pigeons learn concepts. In *Animal cognition*, (ed. H. T. Roitblat, T. G. Bever, and H. S. Terrace), pp. 263–76. Lawrence Erlbaum Associates, Hillsdale, NJ.

—— and Harrison, S. N. (1978). Discrimination of polymorphous stimulus sets by pigeons. *Quarterly Journal of Experimental Psychology*, **30**, 521–37.

Mackintosh, N. J. (1975). A theory of attention: variations in the associability of stimuli with reinforcement. *Psychological Review*, **82**, 276–98.

Medin, D. L. (1975). A theory of context in discrimination learning. In *The psychology of learning and motivation. Vol. 9*, (ed. G. H. Bower), pp. 263–314. Academic Press, New York.

Neumann, P. G. (1977). Visual prototype formation with discontinuous representation of dimensions of variability. *Memory and Cognition*, **5**, 187–97.

Pearce, J. M. (1987). A model for stimulus generalization in Pavlovian conditioning. *Psychological Review*, **94**, 61–73.

—— and Hall, G. (1980). A model for Pavlovian learning: variations in the effectiveness of conditioned but not of unconditioned stimuli. *Psychological Review*, **87**, 532–52.

Posner, M. I. and Keele, S. W. (1968). On the genesis of abstract ideas. *Journal of Experimental Psychology*, **77**, 353–63.

—— and —— (1970). Retention of abstract ideas. *Journal of Experimental Psychology*, **83**, 304–8.

Premack, D. (1983a). Animal cognition. *Annual Review of Psychology*, **34**, 351–62.

—— (1983b). The codes of man and beasts. *The Behavioral and Brain Sciences*, **6**, 125–67.

Reed, S. K. (1972). Pattern recognition and categorization. *Cognitive Psychology*, **3**, 382–407.

Rescorla, R. A. and Wagner, A. R. (1972). A theory of Pavlovian conditioning: variations in the effectiveness of reinforcement and nonreinforcement. In *Classical conditioning II: current research and theory*, (ed. A. H. Black and W. F. Prokasy), pp. 64–99. Appleton-Century-Crofts, New York.

Spence, K. W. (1936). The nature of discrimination learning in animals. *Psychological Review*, **43**, 427–49.

Wilson, B. J., Mackintosh, N. J. and Boakes, R. A. (1985). Matching and oddity learning in the pigeon: transfer effects and the absence of relational learning. *Quarterly Journal of Experimental Psychology*, **37B**, 295–311.

Discussion, Section B

Prosopagnosia and models of face-processing

Kertesz asked *Young* about the specificity of his neuropsychological evidence for faces *per se*. Young replied; 'It is true that P.H. has other visual recognition problems, but we know that these can dissociate from prosopagnosia in other patients . . . P.H. does not report having any problems recognizing other objects he encounters in his daily life'.

The inference that, despite the lack of overt recognition of faces, the 'face module' is still intact in *Young*'s neuropsychological cases was pursued by Caramazza, who asked: 'Why not just posit damage to the recognition module itself?' Young replied: 'We are impressed by the fact that P.H.'s *pattern* of performance on tasks that tap recognition implicitly always looked normal. He matches familiar faces faster than unfamiliar faces'. *Schacter* followed this up by remarking: 'To show that the facial module is intact, P.H.'s slowing must be general and not specific to faces'. *Young* said that the slowing was general to all reaction time tasks. *Weiskrantz* pressed further regarding the model and asked: 'Why do you say the semantic system is disconnected when you can show implicit use of semantic information?' *Young*'s answer was: 'We do find implicit use of semantic information . . . but our recent work indicates that the kind of semantic information he can covertly access in such tasks is not very precise'. *Caramazza* wanted justification for the distinction between 'cognitive system' and 'semantics' and 'recognition module' in the model. *Young* answered: 'I agree that the reason for taking 'person identity modes' outside the 'cognitive system' is simply theoretical convenience. Vicki Bruce and I were quite clear on this point [Bruce and Young 1986, pp. 312–13], but for reasons of space I didn't emphasize it in my paper here'.

Poucet asked whether another type of agnosia, failure of recognition of familiar places, could be approached with a similar type of model, and it was thought that there were both similarities and differences. (For a review of dissociations among various types and experimental analyses of agnosia, see Warrington 1982, 1985—ed.)

Premark asked about priming: 'Does seeing one part of a face prime recognition of a different part?' *Young* replied: 'Yes. This is interesting because repetition priming does not transfer from seeing a person's body to recognizing that person's face [Ellis *et al.* 1987], but it will transfer from one part of the face to another'.

Changeux asked: 'How large is the repertoire of faces recognized by an individual, on average?' *Young* replied that we are able to *name* about 700 faces (Ellis 1986), but that the number we can recognize must be much larger.

Pursuing a different type of theoretical approach, *Dickinson* asked *Sergent* whether parallel-distributed associative networks have been usefully applied to the problems of face recognition. Sergent did not know of any that had done so in a detailed manner. (But see Rolls 1987, in press—ed.).

Hemisphere differences and spatial frequency

Weiskrantz asked how the two hemispheres might be said to use different ranges of spatial information when the inputs to the striate cortex in both hemispheres are equal with respect to spatial information. *Sergent* replied fully by saying: 'This may be achieved by a differential sensitivity of hemispheric structures underlying cognition to the outputs of spatial-frequency channels'. She added that, in the striate cortex: 'Structurally identical neurons are selectively activated by signals conveying information of different spatial-frequency band-widths. Such a selective sensitivity can very well extend beyond the striate cortex'. She went on to consider similar explanations in other modalities. In audition, for example, 'Molfese (1978) has shown an equal capacity of the left and right sensory areas to detect formats of all band-widths and temporal frequencies. The discrimination of duration is equal in the two hemispheres but becomes superior in the left when the intervals are 50 msec or less. Schwartz and Tallel (1980), using stop consonant-vowel syllables that subjects had to label, observed an accuracy decrement in left-hemisphere performance and an improvement in right-hemisphere performance as the duration transition increased from 40 to 80 msec'. And, in the tactile mode, she considered that the right-hemisphere bias in tactile tasks 'may be due to the coarse spatial discriminative power of skin receptors which provide the brain only with low spatial frequency information. Thus, rather than extraction of low spatial information as such, it may be a preferential hemispheric sensitivity of neural cells to different frequency contents that provides a basis for the two hemispheres to develop and subserve different processing competences'.

Pursuing a similar issue, *Young* remarked: 'One of the first demonstrations of a dissociable face deficit was by Elizabeth Warrington, who, if I remember correctly, showed that patients with right temporal lesions had difficulty recognizing familiar faces, and patients with right parietal lesions had problems with matching unfamiliar faces. How do you account for such a dissociation given that all the patients had right-hemisphere lesions?'

Sergent answered: 'Familiar and unfamiliar faces, and an identification and a matching task, impose different demands in terms both of the particular facial features that have to be processed for efficient performance and of the stored knowledge that has to be reactivated. That temporal damage affects the identification of famous faces is consistent with the role of this area in object recognition, while the impairment following parietal damage may reflect a perceptual deficit to which a matching operation typically may be vulnerable'.

Chapouthier wondered whether one should expect a different cerebral organization for face-processing in left-handers. *Sergent* said it was an interesting question that had no clear answer as yet: 'Bryden (1982) has suggested that there is no difference between right- and left-handers. On the other hand, Levy (1984) has presented data showing different patterns of laterality in right- and non-inverted left-handers on face perception'. The issue needs more investigation.

Caramazza raised with Sergent a methodological issue for face discrimination experiments: 'Before one can interpret the data you reported as support for your conclusion, one should first demonstrate that the features by which pairs of faces differ are equally easily discriminable or otherwise equally easy to process. Otherwise, the notion of 'feature' would include differences among pairs of faces that differ in unequal ways'. *Sergent* acknowledged that this raised an important methodological problem. She described how facial features were not equally discriminable, for at least two reasons, one objective and the other in terms of communicative significance. For her experiments the first factor had to be controlled: 'The procedure I used was to conduct a control experiment in which the subjects compared each pair of features (two sets of eyes, nose, mouth, etc.) to assess their respective discriminability. I then used the reaction times of these comparisons in a covariance analysis on the face comparison task, to cancel out the feature discriminability factor. Thus the results of the face comparison task are not "contaminated" by the unequal differences of the facial features'.

Mounoud doubted whether the stages of acquisition for face discrimination and language acquisition were so different. *Sergent* replied that she contrasted the two because 'the acquisition of face recognition skills required no formal training and was a very private experience not subjected to any control. A better comparison might have been with "language comprehension", but I am not aware of any empirical study that has systematically compared the development of the two functions'.

Categorical perception by animals

Various participants raised procedural questions about the pigeon categorization experiments. Thus *Caramazza* commented that *Pearce* 'arbitrarily referred to one task as "same–different" and the others as "category learning". However, the so-called "same–different task" may be characterized as a category learning task, where the criterion was whether or not the tops of the bars were level'. *Pearce* replied: 'The important feature of the final experiment is that the solution to the discrimination depended upon the relationship between the two bars. It is impossible to solve the discrimination by learning about the significance of a single feature, or of a combination of features. Instead, it is the relationship between two features that provides the solution. ... Whatever terms are used to describe this relationship, the principal conclusion to be drawn from the experiment is that pigeons experience great difficult in learning about relationships.'

Both *Fabrigoule* and *Premack* wondered whether stimulus generalization could handle all examples of categorization by animals. Thus *Fabrigoule* agreed that, while it could account for *Pearce*'s data, but perhaps not for Herrnstein's, 'the stimuli are numerous and they do not share any common feature. Perhaps one way of categorizing in animals is to put into the same class the objects or stimuli that lead to the same consequence'. *Pearce* answered: 'While a collection of slides depicting trees may not possess a single feature that is identical in all of them, they may share a number of features that vary along relatively simple dimensions . . .; e.g. leaves that vary in size and colour, tree trunks that vary in height, width, and colour, and branches that vary in a similar fashion. Perhaps pigeons learn to attend to these features, so that generalization could then occur along the dimensions they provide. Of course, the problem then remains of specifying how pigeons identify the features to which they must attend. This is a difficult problem to solve with such complex stimuli as photographs, but studies involving artificial patterns may reveal the way in whch this change is brought about. As for the suggestion that animals treat stimuli that signal the same outcome as equivalent, it is possible; but it does not explain how discrimination training can transfer to novel stimuli'.

Premack cited the evidence by Cerella (1979) of a study in which pigeons were trained to discriminate between pictures of 'Charlie Brown' and other *Peanuts* characters—'Linus', 'Snoopy', etc: 'Test trials were then conducted in which distorted versions of Charlie Brown were presented. For example, the feet and head may have been transposed. Despite this distortion, the discrimination was not disrupted. This outcome appears to contradict your suggestion that animals learn about the significance of a pattern, since modifying the pattern did not destroy the discrimination'. *Pearce* thought not: 'Although the configuration of Charlie Brown was modified to some extent, many of the relationships between groups of features remained intact. Thus the face was never rearranged. It is conceivable that a more determined attempt to distort the Charlie Brown pattern, by destroying the relationship between all the features of which it is composed, would have seriously influenced the discrimination. Hence, although this result suggests that a discrimination can withstand some modification of the training pattern, it does not demonstrate that the discrimination can survive the complete destruction of the pattern. Until this can be shown, I think it will be worth pursuing the possibility that configural learning forms the basis of category discriminations'.

Hasbroucq asked how *Pearce*'s model would explain the overtraining reversal effect (the more animals are overtrained initially in discrimination tasks, the easier they find it to reverse their discriminations). *Pearce* said that his model does not predict this effect as such, but to his knowledge it has never been demonstrated with categorical learning. 'But if it should be demonstrated, then it would suggest that an additional, perhaps attentional, process would have to be incorporated. . . . One possibility would be to adopt Medin and Schaffer's [1978] suggestion that the attention paid to different dimensions on which similarity is judged can vary. If extended training results in an increase of attention to the relevant dimension, and a loss to the irrelevant dimension, then this should facilitate reversal learning [see also Mackintosh 1975; Sutherland and Mackintosh 1971].'

Hinde asked *Pearce* how his model differed from what used to be called stimulus generalization. Pearce agreed that he was proposing that categorization depends entirely on stimulus generalization: 'Where my account differs from a number of previous accounts of this process is in the assumption that animals learn about the significance of the configuration of stimuli to which they are exposed, rather than learning about the significance of individual elements'.

References

Bruce, V. and Young, A. W. (1986). Understanding face recognition. *British Journal of Psychology*, **77**, 305–27.

Bryden, M. P. (1982). *Laterality. Functional asymmetry in the intact brain.* Academic Press, New York.

Cerella, J. (1979). Visual classes and natural categories in the pigeon. *Journal of Experimental Psychology: Human Perception and Performance*, **5**, 68–77.

Ellis, H. D. (1986). Processes underlying face recognition. In *The neuropsychology of face perception and facial expression*, (ed. R. Bruyer), pp. 1–27. Lawrence Erlbaum Associates, Hillsdale, NJ.

—— et al. (1987). Repetition priming of face recognition. *Quarterly Journal of Experimental Psychology*, **39A**, 193–210.

Levy, J. (1984). A review, analysis, and some new data on hand–posture distributions in left-handers. *Brain and Cognition*, **3**, 105–27.

Mackintosh, N. J. (1975). A theory of attention: variations in the associability of stimuli with reinforcement. *Psychological Review*, **82**, 276–98.

Medin, D. L. and Schaffer, M. M. (1978). Context theory of classification learning. *Psychological Review*, **85**, 207–38.

Molfese, D. L. (1978). Left and right hemisphere involvement in speech perception: Electrophysiological correlates. *Perception and Psychophysics*, **23**, 237–43.

Rolls, E. T. (1987). Information representation, processing and storage in the brain: analysis at the single neuron level. In *The neural and molecular bases of learning*, (ed. J.-P. Changeux and M. Konishi), pp. 503–40. Wiley, Chichester.

—— (in press). Visual information processing in the primate temporal lobe. In *Models of visual perception: from natural to artificial*, (ed. M. Imbert). Oxford University Press, Oxford.

Schwartz, J. and Tallal, P. (1980). Rate of acoustic change may underlie hemispheric specialization for speech specialization. *Science*, **207**, 1380–1.

Sutherland, N. S. and Mackintosh, N. J. (1971). *Mechanisms of animal discrimination learning*. Academic Press, New York.

Warrington, E. K. (1982). Neuropsychological studies of object recognition. *Philosphical Transactions of the Royal Society, London*, **B298**, 15–33.

—— (1985). Agnosia: the impairment of object recognition. In *Handbook of clinical neurology*, (ed. J. A. M. Frederiks), pp. 333–49. Elsevier, Amsterdam.

Section C

The ontogeny of perceptual
and causal knowledge

Editorial to Section C

The human infant may not locomote or speak, but its eyes are very active. Its fascination with the external world can be 'read' tellingly by experimentalists. Here they tell of some of their results. The answers, not surprisingly perhaps, reveal much more about their skill in asking penetrating questions than in their sheer accumulation of recorded responses. The main techniques are 'looking time' towards a stimulus display (sometimes combined with a choice of stimuli, so that preferences can be assessed) and habituation. The infant gradually looks less and less at the same stimulus (habituation) and will look more at a novel one (dishabituation). The method allows one to make inferences about what the infant treats as the same or different from the stimulus to which it had habituated, and from this one can go a long way to reconstruct the character of its perceived world.

Habituation has both a long history and a current popularity in biology, but more commonly in another context, namely, the study of 'memory'. If repeated exposure to a stimulus has an enduring effect in reducing responsiveness to it, it would seem that a substrate for a memory of that stimulus has been established. But, as *Cohen* cogently points out, the fact that even worms and mollusks—indeed, practically all forms of animal life—show habituation of simple reflexes makes one skeptical about this application of the technique to uncover an intellectually rich mnemonic life of a creature. Habituation, it may be worth stressing in passing, when applied to memory research, can be logically no more than enduring fatigue or sensory adaptation and dishabituation no more than sensitization, i.e. enduring elevations in thresholds or their lowering, and these need have nothing to do with representations or traces (although there are special examples of habituation that *do* have such an implication). This does not diminish its great importance as an adaptive biological mechanism, but it is worth emphasizing that its application in the present research context is to demonstrate *discrimination*, not endurance. It is a method for examining *structure*, and the results are both fascinating and surprising.

Spelke reviews a body of her research on how infants see objects. They do not, she finds, always perceive the 'unity, boundaries, and persistence' of objects in the same way that adults do. Two *stationary* adjacent objects, for example, may be perceived as a single unit even if they differ in colour and texture. On the other hand, the infant do very well with regard to the 'correct' segregation and unity of objects that move or are spatially separated. Even if an object is partly occluded it will be perceived as unitary. And so the perceptual world is neither strictly constructivist or *Gestalt*-like in its operation. Similar considerations apply to objects perceived by touch, and, moreover, the infants appear to live in a single unitary 'amodal' world because their visual responses are directly controlled by immediately prior haptic exposure to them. The evidence also reveals that even four-month-old infants assume the persistence of hidden objects, contrary to what is commonly believed. *Spelke* places all of the varied results in the context of the infants having an early developing 'theory of the physical world' by which objects are organized, based on cohesion, boundaries, substance, and spatio–temporal continuity, the same factors that are very much at the heart of adult perception. Further develpment produces theory enrichment and refinement, not theory replacement. Whether one would wish to apply the term 'theory of the physical world' to a seeing robot designed on human principles (none exists as yet, of course) is perhaps a moot point, but it is one way of encapsulating those principles.

Leslie applies essentially the same methodology, but to a quite different set of questions about infants, the perception of causation. The stimuli are generated from filmed simulations of events like billiard balls hitting each other, the same class of stimuli used so effectively in the classical experiments on adult perception by Michotte. Infants habituate to such events, as they do to others, and the question in the test phase is whether it is specifically the perceived *causal* aspect in the event that is important. The experimental control required to analyze this question is demanding and intricate, and the constructions are ingenious. The conclusion is that young infants *can* perceive a specifically causal relation *per se*. It is not just the spatio–temporal properties to which they habituate. *Leslie* also links his findings to those of others, especially Baillargéon, on the perception of hidden objects, because these too involve the nature of the physical cause that brings about the occlusion. The evidence suggests that infants not only understand 'where a hidden object is, what its orientation is, whether it is compressible or not', but that they can use 'this rich representation to make judgements about "likely" and "unlikely" outcomes for mechanical interactions, even though some of these are also hidden from view'. All of this evidence he puts in the context of contemporary debate on computational vs. parallel-connectionistic models, and supports rule-driven computations and symbolic processing, even in infancy: 'A language of thought appears before a "language of talk" '.

The richness of scope for these techniques is further illustrated in

Cohen's chapter. He used them to pursue discrimination of transforms and classes of stimuli. He was also interested in how perception changes progressively in infancy. Do infants, for example, match identical stimuli when they have different orientations? Do they respond to subparts of stimuli or to the overall configuration? Forming a direct link with issues in Section B, he also asked whether infants could form *categories* of objects. Are they able to group all examples, say, of stuffed animals as belonging to the same class or, in controlled experiments, to drawings having certain properties in common? The main outcome was that indeed they can; that is, they dishabituate less to a member of the same class than they do to a member of a different class (with appropriate balancing of control groups). The same issue arises, of course, as in categorization exeriments with animals—are they remembering specific instances, plus stimulus generalization (as *Pearce* concluded), or forming genuine prototypes? In the Discussion (see end of Section), *Cohen* advances the reasons for favouring the latter alternative for infants. But the progressive aspects of the findings were intuitively unexpected: the infants appear to go through a sequence of developmental changes such that at seven months of age they had more difficulty discriminating than did infants either of four or 10 months of age. The interpretation, drawn from a number of different experiments, was that the younger infants tended to select isolated features, and the older ones the configuration or class relationships among stimuli. In between there was a period of ambiguity in which dependence was primarily on single, unique stimuli in isolation from the class.

Given that even older children are often considered to be less endowed than young infants studied with the techniques reported here, one may either consider, as *Mounoud* suggests, that there are recurrent and repeating cycles of growth, each end point serving as the starting point for the next, or that genuinely new mechanisms intrude, perhaps with progressive myelinization and neuronal maturation. Some of *Cohen's* evidence, in fact, of changes in infants from four to 10 months, might be said to fit the former notion. But the difference between earlier findings and those reviewed here is much more likely to stem from the sensitivity of methods together with the pointedness of the questions raised. As *Spelke* mentions in her paper, traditional approaches invariably involve observing infants' co-ordinated search for objects. It may be the co-ordinated visuo–motor search, with its attendant motor, strategic, and memory demands, that sets the limits rather than perceptual and cognitive competence. Dishabituation reveals an infant not only attending to the world but also evaluating it.

7

The origins of physical knowledge

ELIZABETH S. SPELKE

Overview

My research has focused on the ability of young infants to organize the perceptual world into physical objects. Infants, we have found, have considerable abilities to apprehend objects in visual scenes: they can sometimes perceive the unity and continuity of an object that is partly hidden, the boundaries between two objects that send overlapping images to the eyes, and the persisting identity of an object that moves fully out of view. Our evidence suggests, however, that infants do not perceive the unity, boundaries, and persistence of objects under all the conditions that are effective for adults. This finding is of special interest, because a consideration of the nature and limit of infants' abilities could shed light on the mechanism by which objects are apprehended, by mature humans as well as by infants. Our research suggests that this mechanism is surprisingly central—so central that it may be misleading to say that objects are *perceived*. Objects may be known, instead, by virtue of an early developing *theory* of the physical world. This chapter will review some of the research that has led to this suggestion, and then it will attempt to characterize the infant's physical theory and its role in apprehending objects. Finally, I will consider some of the ways in which the infant's theory might be changed by the acquisition of further physical knowledge, with and without benefit of language.

Perceiving objects as unitary and bounded

At its outset, our research was guided by the view that visual arrays are organized into objects at an early point in perceptual analysis. Two plausible, competing theses concerning the nature and development of this capacity appeared to be the thesis that objects are constructed from a structureless visual tableau through activities such as visually guided reaching (e.g. von Helmholtz 1885; Piaget 1954) and the thesis from gestalt psychology that objects are perceived by virtue of a general, unlearned tendency to organize experience into the simplest and most regular configuration (e.g. Koffka

1935). In an attempt to test these theories, Kellman and I investigated young infants' perception of partly hidden objects (Kellman and Spelke 1983). We asked whether infants below the age of visually guided reaching perceive a centre-occluded object as two separate visible fragments or as one unit that is continuous behind its occluder.

Our studies used a habituation of the looking time method. Four-month-old infants were presented repeatedly with an object that was partly hidden by a second object (Fig. 7.1(a)). On each of the series of trials, the objects were presented for as long as an infant looked at them; such presentations were repeated until the infant's looking time declined to half its original level. Then the infants were presented with two non-occluded object displays on alternating trials: a complete object and a broken object with a gap where the occluder had been (Fig. 7.1(b)). The complete object corresponded to the object adults report seeing in the partial occlusion display; the broken object corresponded to the visible areas of the object in the occlusion display. Looking time to these two test displays was measured, on the assumption that infants would generalize habituation to the display corresponding to what they had previously seen and would look longer at the other display (see Kellman and Spelke (1983) and Spelke (1985) for a discussion of these assumptions and of the evidence to support them).

A number of different occlusion displays were presented in different experiments to determine whether, and under what conditions, centre-

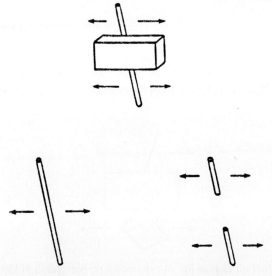

Fig. 7.1 Schematic drawings of the habituation and test displays for an experiment on the perception of the unity of a partly hidden object (from Kellman and Spelke 1983).

occluded objects are perceived as continuous units. These studies provided evidence that infants perceive a partly hidden object as a connected unit if the ends of the object move together behind the occluder (Kellman and Spelke 1983). Any unitary translation of the rod in three-dimensional space leads infants to perceive a continuous object: vertical translation and translation in depth have the same effect as lateral translation (Kellman *et al.* 1986). These findings provided evidence against the constructivist view, and they appeared to support the gestalt thesis. Further findings, however, have called the gestalt analysis into question. Infants do not appear to perceive the continuity of a partly hidden object by analysing the static configurational properties of a display in accord with the gestalt principles of similarity, good continuation, closure, and good form. For example, experiments have provided evidence that infants perceive a connected object just as strongly when they view a moving display that is irregular in its gestalt properties (Fig. 7.2) as when they view a moving display with regular gestalt properties such as that in Fig. 7.1 (Kellman and Spelke 1983). When infants were presented with a stationary object that was regular in form and homogeneous in colour (Fig. 7.3), moreover, their perception appeared to be indeterminate between a connected object and two object fragments: infants dishabituated equally to these test displays (Schmidt and Spelke 1984; also, see Schmidt *et al.* 1986). These findings contrast with the reports of adults who were shown the same displays. Adults' apprehension of centre-occluded objects is affected both by motion and by static gestalt properties (Kellman and Spelke 1983; Schmidt, unpublished thesis, 1985), whereas infants appear to be affected by motion alone.

Similar conclusions follow from research on infants' perception of object boundaries. Infants were presented with two objects in arrangements such as that in Fig. 7.4. Perception of the boundary between the objects was investigated by means of methods assessing object-directed reaching (von Hofsten and Spelke 1985), number detection (Prather and Spelke 1982),

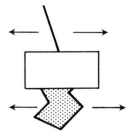

Fig. 7.2   Habituation display for an experiment on perception of the unity of partly hidden moving objects with irregular shapes and colouring (from Kellman and Spelke 1983).

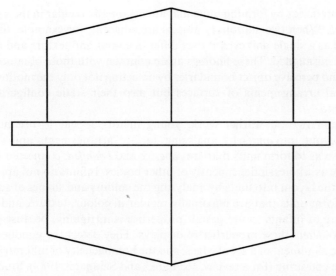

Fig. 7.3 Habituation display for an experiment on perception of the unity of partly hidden stationary objects (from Schmidt and Spelke 1984).

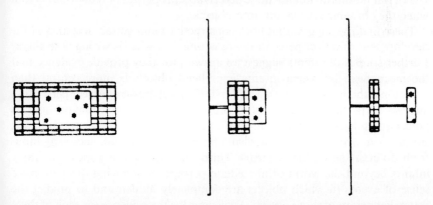

Fig. 7.4 Front and side views of the habituation display for an experiment on perception of the boundaries of adjacent objects (from Kestenbaum *et al.* 1987).

surprise reactions (Spelke *et al.*, unpublished manuscript, 1983), and habituation–dishabituation (Kestenbaum *et al.* 1987). Infants were tested at three to five months of age. All the experiments provided evidence that infants perceive two objects as separate units when (a) either object moves relative to the other, or (b) the objects are stationary and are spatially separated in any dimension, including separation in depth. In contrast, infants do not appear to perceive object boundaries by forming units that are maximally regular in their gestalt properties. When two stationary objects are adjacent, for example, they are perceived as a single unit even if they differ in colour and texture and if their edges are misaligned. These findings again contrast with those obtained with adults, who perceive object boundaries by detecting not only the motions and the spatial arrangements of surfaces but also their static configurational properties.

To summarize our earlier work, young infants appear to organize the surface layout into units by analysing surface arrangements and surface motions so as to form units that are *cohesive* and *bounded*: connected bodies that move as wholes, independently of other bodies. Infants do not appear to organize the layout into units by analysing the colours and shapes of surfaces so as to form units that are maximally regular in colour, texture, and form. The failure of infants to use gestalt properties is intriguing, because young infants do *detect* these properties of displays. They detect the goodness of a figure, the alignment of a set of edges, and the homogeneity or inhomogeneity of surface colouring (for a review, see Banks and Salapatek 1983). Studies by Schmidt provide evidence that infants detect gestalt properties of the very displays we present in our object perception studies (Schmidt and Spelke 1984). But infants do not *use* these perceivable properties of the surface layout when they organize the layout into objects.

These findings suggest that both constructivist and gestalt accounts of the development of object perception are wrong, but what is wrong with them? Further studies of infants suggest an answer, for they provide evidence that the mechanism by which infants apprehend objects is more central than traditional theories had envisaged. First, the mechanism of object perception appears to perform an analysis of properties of the surface layout as it is perceived; it does not operate directly on patterns of optic, acoustic, or haptic stimulation. Second, the mechanism appears to be amodal, accepting input from different perceptual systems. Third, the mechanism appears to carry infants beyond the world of immediate perception, allowing them to make sense of events in which objects are completely hidden and to predict the future behaviour of those objects. I will describe the evidence for each of these conclusions in turn.

The information for object unity

Evidence that the mechanism for apprehending objects operates on a representation of the perceived layout comes from an experiment by Kellman *et al.* (1987). The experiment investigated whether infants apprehend the unity of a moving, partly hidden object by detecting *proximal* or *distal* motion: patterns of two-dimensional displacement in the immediate optic array or patterns of three-dimensional displacement through the perceived surface

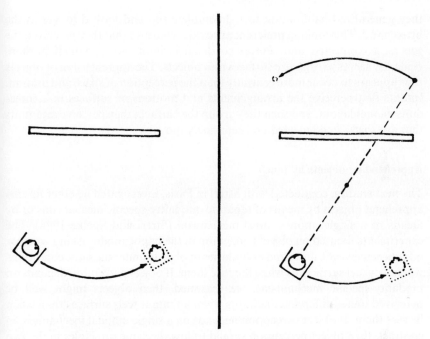

Fig. 7.5 Top view of the experimental situation in the proximal motion condition (left) and the distal motion condition (right) of an experiment on perception of partly occluded objects by a moving observer (from Kellman *et al.* 1987).

layout. To distinguish proximal from distal displacements, infants were presented with a centre-occluded object while they themselves were in motion (Fig. 7.5): they faced a rod and block display while sitting in a chair that moved back and forth in an arc. The rod was stationary in one condition, and thus its image was displaced in the visual field as the baby moved. The rod moved conjointly with the infant in the other condition, so as to cancel this image displacement. The extent and the speed of the infant's motion were such that the first condition presented about the same amount of proximal displacement, and the second condition presented about the same amount of distal displacement, as in the earlier experiments with stationary infants and moving objects. Perception of the continuity of the rod was investigated by means of the habituation method.

Infants in the proximal motion condition of this experiment showed the same looking patterns as infants in the previous experiments with stationary objects: they looked equally at the complete and broken test rods. This looking pattern provides evidence that the infants did not perceive the rod as complete. In contrast, infants in the distal motion condition showed the same looking patterns as infants in the previous experiments with moving objects:

they generalized habituation to the complete rod and looked longer at the broken rod. This looking preference provides evidence that they perceived the rod as a connected unit. Perceived distal motion, not proximal motion, evidently serves to organize surfaces into objects. The apprehension of objects thus appears to occur more centrally than the perception of space and motion. Infants first perceive the arrangements and motions of surfaces in a three-dimensional layout, and then they group the surfaces they perceive into units that are spatially connected and separately movable.

Apprehending objects by touch

The next studies, conducted with Streri in Paris, investigated whether infants apprehend objects by means of separate, modality-specific mechanisms or by means of a single, more central mechanism (Streri and Spelke 1988). The experiments focused on object perception in the haptic mode, asking whether infants perceive the unity and boundaries of objects under the same conditions when they feel surfaces as when they see them. If object perception depends on modality-specific mechanisms, we reasoned, then objects might well be perceived under different conditions when an infant feels surfaces than when he sees them. If object perception depends on a single amodal mechanism, in contrast, then object perception should follow the same principles in the two input modes.

Four-month-old infants held two rings, one in each hand, under a cloth that blocked their view of the rings and of their own bodies. In our first experiments, the rings either could be moved independently or they could only be moved rigidly together. Figure 7.6 depicts the display of rigidly movable objects. Infants were allowed to move the rings at will, and they did so quite actively. (Few infants ever touched the area between the rings; those who did could be eliminated from the analysis without changing the results.) To investigate whether infants perceived the independently movable rings as separate objects and the rigidly movable rings as a single connected object, half the infants were habituated to each haptic display, and then the infants were shown alternating visual displays of connected and separated rings undergoing no distinctive motion. Looking time was measured as in the previous habituation experiments.

In these experiments, habituation to the independently movable rings was followed by greater generalization to the separated display, providing evidence that infants perceived the independently moving rings as distinct objects. In contrast, habituation to the rigidly movable rings was followed by greater generalization to the connected display, providing evidence that infants perceived the commonly moving rings as a single object. Motion therefore appears to specify the unity and boundaries of objects in the haptic mode as it does in the visual mode. Our most recent research suggests,

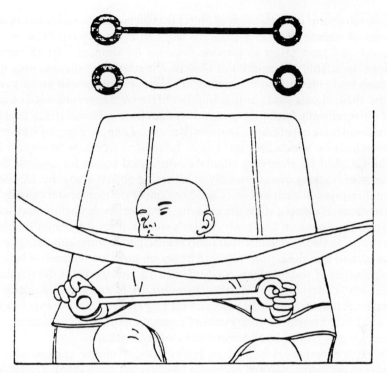

Fig. 7.6 Objects and apparatus for experiments on haptic perception of objects (from Streri and Spelke 1988).

moreover, that gestalt configurational properties fail to influence infants' organization of felt arrays, as they fail for visual arrays (Streri and Spelke, in prep.). Infants perceive the unity of two rigidly movable surfaces that differ in texture, substance, and form just as readily as they perceive the unity of two rigidly movable surfaces of the same texture and substance and of one simple form. These findings provide evidence that objects are perceived under the same conditions whether they are seen or felt. Objects do not appear to be apprehended by separate visual and haptic mechanisms but by a single mechanism that operates on representations arising either through vision or through touch.

Inferring the behaviour of hidden objects

The last experiments investigated whether infants apprehend objects in situations beyond the domain of immediate perception, making inferences about the behaviour of objects that move fully out of view and about the identity or distinctness of objects encountered at different places and times.

The development of knowledge of object persistence and identity has been a subject of intense study ever since the work of Piaget (1954). Most of this research has been taken to provide evidence for dramatic developmental changes in infants' conceptions of objects: it is generally believed either that humans begin life with no conception of object persistence and identity (e.g. Piaget 1954; Harris 1983) or that humans begin with conceptions of objects that differ radically from the conceptions of adults (e.g. Bower 1982). I am led to question these conclusions, however, because of one problematic feature of the research on which they are based. Infants' conceptions of objects are usually studied by observing infants' co-ordinated search for objects: their patterns of tracking objects visually or retrieving objects manually. Developmental changes in such activities need not imply developmental changes in conceptions of objects, since the capacity for co-ordinated action may itself undergo development. Curiously, Piaget's studies of sensori–motor development provide strong evidence that action capacities do grow and change over infancy, and that the actions required by search tasks are themselves beyond the capacities of young infants (Piaget 1952). To investigate the development of infants' conceptions of objects, therefore, it is necessary to focus on behaviours that are within the young infant's repertoire. Our own experiments have begun to investigate young infants' conceptions of object persistence and object identity by means of preferential looking methods.

Our first experiments focused on five-month-old infants' apprehension of objects as persisting over full occlusion (Baillargéon *et al.* 1985). The critical events in this study involved a stationary block behind a rotating screen. As the screen rotated upward, it hid the object completely. Then the screen either rotated until it reached the place the block had occupied (Fig. 7.7(a)) or it rotated 180° through that place (Fig. 7.7(b)). To adults, the first of these events is expected and the second is surprising, since one object cannot pass

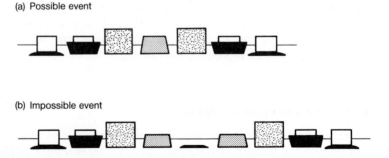

(a) Possible event

(b) Impossible event

Fig. 7.7 Test displays for an experiment on knowledge of object persistence (from Baillargéon *et al.* 1985).

through a place occupied by another object. To investigate how infants conceive these events, the events were embedded in an experiment in which infants were first habituated to the screen rotating 180° with no block present. Then infants were tested with the block and the screen undergoing the novel but possible rotation and the familiar but impossible rotation. Infants looked longer at the impossible rotation. With appropriate controls (see Baillargéon et al. 1985), this experiment provided evidence that infants represent the continuous existence of the block behind the screen.

Further research by Baillargéon (in press a) provided evidence that even three- and four-month-old infants perceive objects as persisting over full occlusion. In studies with older infants, she has found that infants represent not only the existence of a hidden object but also its motion in relation to other hidden objects (Baillargéon 1986), its orientation (Baillargéon, in press b), and its height (Baillargéon, in prep.). Her experiments provide evidence that infants conceive of objects both as persisting and as substantial: objects exist continuously and move only through unoccupied space.

Current studies with Macomber and Keil provide further evidence that infants conceive of objects as persisting and substantial (Macomber et al., in prep.). In one study, four-month-old infants were habituated to an event in which an object was dropped behind a screen on an open stage, and then the screen was lifted to reveal the object on the ground of the stage. Infants then were tested with events in which a table was placed on the stage in the object's path of motion, the object was again dropped behind the screen, and the screen was lifted to reveal the object either in a new position on top of the table or in its old position below the table (Fig. 7.8). The infants looked longer when the object was in its old position beneath the table, in accord with the principle that objects cannot move through solid surfaces. This finding converges with the findings of Baillargéon, providing evidence that infants, like adults, represent hidden objects and make inferences about the behaviour of such objects in accord with the notion that objects are substantial.

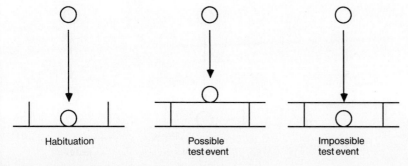

Habituation   Possible   Impossible
                     test event   test event

Fig. 7.8 Habituation and test displays for an experiment on knowledge of object substance (from Macomber et al., in prep.).

A further study by Macomber suggests a limit to young infants' physical knowledge: infants below five months do not appear to conceive of objects as subject to gravity. Four-month-old infants were habituated to an event in which an object fell behind a screen and then was revealed at rest upon a table: the possible test event of the first experiment. Then infants were tested with events in which the table was removed and the object either came to rest in a new position on the floor of the display or in its former position, now unsupported in mid-air (Fig. 7.9). Adults report that the latter event is surprising, since the object stops moving without any visible support. Infants, in contrast, showed little interest in this event: they generalized habituation to the unsupported object and looked longer at the supported object in the new position. Young infants may fail to predict where and how objects will move in accord with the notions that objects are subject to gravity and must be stably supported.

Consider, finally, infants' apprehension of the identity of objects that move in and out of view. One way of apprehending object identity, much discussed in philosophy, is to trace the apparent continuity or discontinuity of object motion (e.g. Hirsch 1982). For adults, physical objects must move on continuous paths; they cannot jump from one place to another. Our first experiments investigated whether four-month-old infants apprehend the identity or distinctness of objects over occlusion in accord with this principle (Spelke and Kestenbaum 1986). Following research by Moore et al. (1978), infants were presented with events involving two screens, as in Fig. 7.10. In one event, a single object moved continuously across the display, disappearing behind each screen in turn. The second event was identical except that no object appeared between the screens: an object disappeared behind the first screen and then, after a pause, an object reappeared from behind the second screen. In both events, the motions were slow enough that adults do not report that they 'perceive' a continuously persisting object, as in the case of apparent

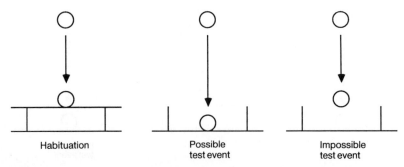

Habituation   Possible   Impossible
                     test event   test event

Fig. 7.9 Habituation and test displays for an experiment on knowledge of gravity (from Macomber et al., in prep.).

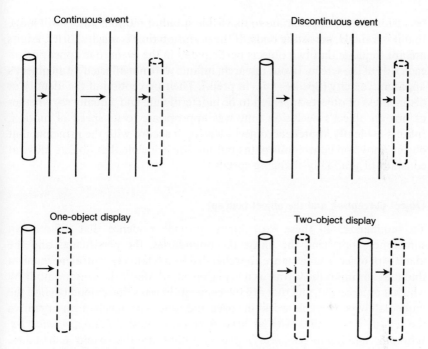

Fig. 7.10   Habituation and test displays for experiments on infants' knowledge of spatio–temporal continuity (from Spelke and Kestenbaum 1986).

motion or amodal completion (Michotte 1963). Nevertheless, adults judge that the first event involves one object and the second event involves two objects (Spelke *et al.*, in prep.). These judgements follow from the notion that objects move on continuous paths.

In three experiments, separate groups of infants were habituated to each event, and then all the infants were given test trials in which one or two objects appeared without the occluders, undergoing no distinctive motion. The infants who were habituated to the continuous event generalized more to the one-object display, providing evidence that they perceived the continuous event as involving one object. In contrast, the infants who were habituated to the discontinuous event generalized more to the two-object display, providing evidence that they perceived the discontinuous event as involving two objects. Infants appear to apprehend the identity of objects by analysing the apparent continuity or discontinuity of paths of motion, in accord with the principle that objects move on spatio–temporally continuous paths.

Our last experiments suggested that infants fail to apprehend the persisting identity of objects under one set of conditions that are effective for adults. If an object moves in and out of view on alternate sides of one wide screen, and if its occlusion time is appropriate to its visible speed of motion, adults will judge that it is a single, persisting body. If the occlusion time is much shorter, adults are apt to judge that two objects participated in the event, one appearing on each side of the screen. In our research, infants were not affected by an object's apparent velocity (Spelke *et al.*, in prep.). Their perception of the identity or distinctness of objects appeared to be indeterminate and, equally so, whether or not an object's occlusion time was appropriate to its speed of motion. Infants evidently apprehend object identity in accord with the principle that objects move on continuous paths but not the principle that objects move at constant or gradually changing speeds.

Object perception and the object concept

To summarize, all these experiments provide evidence that infants can sometimes apprehend the unity, the boundaries, the persistence, and the identity of objects. Objects are apprehended by a relatively central mechanism that takes as input the layout as it is perceived, whatever the sensory mode by which it is perceived, and that organizes events in ways that extend beyond the immediately perceivable world in space and time. This mechanism organizes the layout into bodies with at least four properties: *cohesion, boundaries, substance*, and *spatio–temporal continuity*. Infants are able to find such bodies, because these properties limit were surfaces stand and how they move with respect to one another. The surfaces of a cohesive body must be connected and they must remain connected over the body's free motions; the surfaces of a bounded body must be distinct from the surfaces around them and they must move independently of their surroundings; the surfaces of a substantial body must move through unoccupied space; and the surfaces of a spatio–temporally continuous body must move on connected paths. Infants apprehend objects by analysing the arrangements and the motions of surfaces, I suggest, because they conceive the physical world as populated with bodies whose properties constrain surface arrangements and motions.

Infants may fail to apprehend objects by analysing gestalt relationships, support relationships, or velocity relationships, because they do not conceive the physical world as populated with bodies whose properties constrain such relationships. The relationships are perceived, and they may be used by other central mechanisms for other purposes. Object form, for example, may be used by an early developing mechanism for representing space and guiding navigation, as Cheng and Gallistel (1984; also see Cheng 1986) and Landau (see Landau *et al.* 1984) have proposed. Object support and object velocity may be used to guide early object-directed reaching (Bresson and de Schönen 1976–7; von Hofsten 1979; Piaget 1954). These relationships will not be used for purposes of apprehending objects, however, until children learn that objects tend to be regular in substance and form, that objects are subject to gravity, and that objects tend to move at gradually changing speeds.

I suggest that the infant's mechanism for apprehending objects is a mechanism of thought: an initial *theory* of the physical world whose four principles jointly define an initial *object concept*. This suggestion is motivated not only by evidence of the centrality of the mechanism for apprehending objects, but also by a consideration of the principles governing its operation. The principles of cohesion, boundedness, substance, and spatio-temporal continuity appear to stand at the centre of adults' intuitive conceptions of the physical world and its behaviour: our deepest conceptions of objects appear to be the notions that they are internally connected and distinct from one another, that they occupy space, and that they exist and move continuously (for further discussion, see Spelke 1983, 1987). These conceptions are so central to human thinking about the physical world that their uniformity sometimes goes unremarked. In studies of intuitive physical thought, for example, much attention is paid to the idiosyncratic and error-ridden predictions adults sometimes make about the motions of objects (e.g. McCloskey 1983). It is rarely noted, however, that adults predict with near uniformity that objects will move as cohesive wholes on connected paths through unoccupied space. This conception, at least, is clear and central to our thinking; it appears to have guided our thinking since early infancy.

The centrality, for adults, of the initial conception of objects suggests that the spontaneous development of physical knowledge is a process of *theory enrichment*, in which an unchanging, core conception of the physical world comes to be surrounded by a periphery of further notions. It is not difficult to see, in outline, how theory enrichment could occur. If an initial theory of the physical world allows children to single out objects, then children will be able to acquire further knowledge about objects by following them through time and observing their behaviour. The initial theory will perpetuate itself over the learning process, because the entities the child learns about will be just the entities that his initial theory has specified. Theory enrichment seems likely to occur whenever humans acquire knowledge spontaneously in an innately structured domain. In domains where humans have no initial theory, systematic knowledge may not develop spontaneously at all.

Language and conceptual development

In this context, one may consider the possible role of language in the development of physical knowledge. Our research provides evidence, counter to the views of Quine (1960) and others, that the organization of the world into objects precedes the development of language and thus does not depend upon it. I suspect, moreover, that language plays no important role in the spontaneous elaboration of physical knowledge. To learn that objects tend to move at smooth speeds, for example, one need only observe objects and their motions; one need not articulate the principles of one's theory or communicate with others about it. It is possible, nevertheless, that language influences conceptual development at certain critical times, when the child or adult finds himself on the edge of a domain of entities that his initial theories do not single out and cannot describe. When we recognize the need to reorganize the physical world from a realm of objects into a realm of matter, for example (see Smith *et al.* 1985), or from a realm that is three-dimensional into a realm of higher dimensionality, we may do so by modifying our theories explicitly or by bringing to bear theories of other domains. Communicating with others who have made this leap, and/or articulating the principles of the new theory to be applied, may play critical roles in this process of conceptual change.

The distinction between development as the spontaneous enrichment of theories and development as the laboured reorganization of theories may point to a general role of language in thought and to a general difference between human adults, on the one hand, and human infants and non-human species, on the other. As adults, we may transcend current theories of the world when we reach their limits, and this ability may be unique to us. I am struck, nevertheless, by what I think is a profound similarity between adults and infants, and probably between humans and many other animals. Infants, like adults, appear to conceive the world in terms of physical bodies and to use this conception to support inferences and predictions about physical events. In content, the infant's conception of the physical world appears to constitute the core of our physical conception as adults. This conception may first reveal itself when infants apprehend objects and make sense of their behaviour in the perceived spatial layout.

Acknowledgements

This work was supported by NSF grant BNS 83-18156 and NIH grant 08-R1H023103A. I thank Frank Keil and Janet Macomber for comments.

References

Baillargéon, R. (1986). Representing the existence and the location of hidden objects: object permanence in 6- and 8-month-old infants. *Cognition*, **23**, 21–42.
—— (in press *a*). Object permanence in 3.5- and 4.5-month-old infants. *Developmental Psychology*.
—— (in press *b*). Young infant's reasoning about the physical and spatial properties of a hidden object. *Cognitive Development*.
—— (in prep.). Qualitative and quantitative reasoning about the height of a hidden object in 6.5-month-old infants.
——, Spelke, E. S. and Wasserman, S. (1985). Object permanence in five-month-old infants. *Cognition*, **20**, 191–208.
Banks, M. S. and Salapatek, P. (1983). Infant visual perception. In *Handbook of child*

psychology. Volume 2: Infancy and developmental psychobiology, (ed. P. Mussen), pp. 435–57. John Wiley, New York.

Bower, T. G. R. (1982). *Development in infancy*, (2nd edn). W. H. Freeman, San Francisco.

Bresson, F. and de Schönen, S. (1976–7). A propos de la construction de l'espace et de l'object: la prise d'un object sur un support. *Bulletin de Psychologie*, **30**, 3–9.

Cheng, K. (1986). A purely geometric module in the rat's spatial representation. *Cognition*, **23**, 149–78.

—— and Gallistel, C. R. (1984). Testing the geometric power of an animal's spatial representation. In *Animal cognition*, (ed. H. L. Roitblat, T. G. Bever, and H. S. Terrace). Lawrence Erlbaum Associates, Hillsdale, NJ.

Gentner, D. and Stevens, A. L. (1983). *Mental models*. Lawrence Erlbaum Associates, Hillsdale, NJ.

Harris, P. (1983) Infant cognition. In *Handbook of child psychology. Volume 2: Infancy and developmental psychobiology*, (ed. P. Mussen), pp. 689–782. John Wiley, New York.

Hirsch, E. (1982). *The concept of identity*. Oxford University Press, New York.

Kellman, P. J. and Spelke, E. S. (1983). Perception of partly occluded objects in infancy. *Cognitive Psychology*, **15**, 483–524.

——, ——, and Short, K. (1986). Infant perception of object unity from translatory motion in depth and vertical translation. *Child Development*, **57**, 72–86.

——, Gleitman, H., and Spelke, E. S. (1987). Object and observer motion in the perception of objects by infants. *Journal of Experimental Psychology: Human Perception and Performance*, **13**, 586–93.

Kestenbaum, R., Termine, N., and Spelke, E. S. (1987). Perception of objects and object boundaries by three-month-old infants. *British Journal of Developmental Psychology*, **5**, 367–83.

Koffka, K. (1935). *Principles of gestalt psychology*. Harcourt, Brace and World, New York.

Kuhn, T. (1962). *The structure of scientific revolutions*. University of Chicago Press.

Landau, B., Spelke, E. S. and Gleitman, H. (1984). Spatial knowlege in a young blind child. *Cognition*, **16**, 225–60.

Macomber, J., Spelke, E. S., and Keil, F. (in prep.). Early development of the object concept: knowledge of substance and gravity.

McCloskey, M. (1983). Naive theories of motion. In *Mental models*, (ed. D. Gentner and A. L. Stevens). Lawrence Erlbaum Associates, Hillsdale, NJ.

Michotte, A. (1963). *The perception of causality*, (trans. T. R. Miles and E. Miles). Methuen, Andover, Hants.

Moore, M. K., Borton, R. and Darby. B. L. (1978). Visual tracking in young infants: evidence for object identity or object permanence? *Journal of Experimental Child Psychology*, **25**, 183–98.

Piaget, J. (1952). *The original of intelligence in childhood*. International Universities Press, New York.

—— (1954). *The construction of reality in the child*. Basic Books, New York.

Prather, P. and Spelke, E. S. (1982). Three-month-old infants' perception of adjacent and partly occluded objects. Paper presented at the International Conference on Infant Studies, Austin, TX.

Quine, W. V. O. (1960). *Word and object*. MIT Press, Cambridge, Massachusetts.
Schmidt, H. (1985). The development of gestalt perception in children. Unpublished Ph.D. thesis. University of Pennsylvania.
—— and Spelke, E. S. (1984). Gestalt relations and object perception in infancy. Paper presented at the International Conference on Infant Studies, New York.
——, ——, and LaMorte (1986). The development of Gestalt perception in infancy. Paper presented at the meeting of the International Conference on Infant Studies, Los Angeles, CA.
Smith, C., Carey, S., and Wiser, M. (1985). On differentiation: a case study of the development of the concepts of size, weight, and density. *Cognition*, **21**, 177–238.
Spelke, E. S. (1983). *Cognition in infancy. MIT Occasional Papers in Cognitive Science*, No. 28.
—— (1985). Preferential looking methods as tools for the study of cognition in infancy. In *Measurement of audition and vision in the first year of post-natal life*, (ed. G. Gottlieb and N. Krasnegor), pp. 323–64. Lawrence Erlbaum Associates, Hillsdale, N.J.
—— (1987). Where perceiving ends and thinking begins: the apprehension of objects in infancy. In *Perceptual development in infancy. Minnesota symposia in child psychology*, (ed. A. Yonas), pp. 197–234. Lawrence Erlbaum Associates, Hillsdale, NJ.
—— and Kestenbaum, R. (1986). Les origines du concept d'objet. *Psychologie Franciase*, **31**, 67–72.
——, Born, W. S., Mangelsdorf, S., Richter, E., and Termine, N. (1983). Infant perception of adjacent objects. Unpublished manuscript.
——, Kestenbaum, R. and Wein, D. (in prep.). Spatiotemporal continuity and object indentity in infancy.
Streri, A. S. and Spelke, E. S. (1988). Haptic perception of objects in infancy. *Cognitive Psychology*, **20**.
—— and —— (in prep.). Effects of movement and gestalt relations on haptic perception in infancy.
von Helmholtz, H. (1885). *Treatise on physiological optics*, Vol. 3. (trans. J. P. S. Southall). Dover, New York.
von Hofsten, C. (1979). Development of visually directed reaching. The approach phase. *Journal of Human Movement Studies*, **5**, 160–78.
—— and Spelke, E. S. (1985). Object perception and object-directed reaching in infancy. *Journal of Experimental Psychology: General*, **114**, 198–212.

8

The necessity of illusion: perception and thought in infancy

ALAN M. LESLIE

Introduction

I am going to discuss three examples of the way in which events are understood early in development. In the first example, infants perceive a specifically causal property of a simple event. In the second, infants show a thoughtful reaction to a more complex causal situation. In the final case, full-blown counterfactual causal reasoning is involved at the start of childhood.

These examples of 'surprising' early abilities are interesting in their own right. We can add them to the growing catalogue of such things. But my motive here goes beyond this. I think these cases can give us insight into how the infant mind is organized. Recent advances in experimentation have led to the collapse of the sensori–motor theory of infancy, but they have not automatically produced a framework to replace it. A new theoretical understanding of the mental architecture of infancy, however, is very much on the agenda (Leslie 1986, 1987; Mandler, in press; Spelke 1987, 1988).

One view of the infant mind is that it is essentially homogeneous, without differentiated powers, and without symbolic processes—a single network that acquires structure gradually through associative learning or through some other principle of equal generality.

I want to discuss a quite different framework for infant cognition. This framework argues for an infant with a wide variety of mental structures and powers (Leslie 1986, 1987; Leslie and Keeble 1987; Spelke 1987, 1988). It is this variety of specific mechanisms and the overall design into which they fit that holds the key to understanding the competence of the infant and his powers to develop.

Each of the three examples of causal understanding I shall deal with illustrates a different level of mental organization. Each level has its own distinct tasks and mechanisms suited to their execution. Carrying out these tasks requires symbolic representation and creates systems of knowledge with logical and conceptual structure. In building this knowledge, the role of perception is to provide thought with a conceptual identification of current input from the environment (Fodor 1983; Sperber and Wilson 1986). I shall argue that recent results from the study of infancy reveal that this mental architecture is the basis for development, and not its outcome.

The significance of illusions

Part of my method in addressing infant cognitive organization will be to consider the nature and existence of illusions. The essence of a perceptual illusion is that a bit of the world appears to us in a way we know is not or cannot be the case but which, despite such knowledge, appears this way repeatedly and incorrigibly. Illusions are important because they reflect inherent limitations either in the models of the world that brain mechanisms build, or in the way the mechanisms build them, or in the way these mechanisms interact (Coren and Ward 1979; Gregory 1974, ch. 30; Robinson 1972).

A strong case can be made that perceptual mechanisms are organized on a modular basis (Fodor 1983; Marr 1982; Ullman 1984). The computational task of maintaining a detailed description of current input to the organism appears to be broken down into a number of independent subtasks. These are then carried out by devices dedicated to these subtasks, operating automatically, independently of other devices, and without access to knowledge or information represented centrally.

The modularity of perception provides an explanation both for the existence of illusions and for their incorrigibility in the face of what we know about the distal stimulus. Illusions are an inevitable consequence of automatic computation of limited solutions to limited problems with limited information access (Leslie 1986). But the incorrigibility of illusion implies something more than simply the impenetrability of input-processing. Illusions often create incongruities in a perceived situation. We lack the ability to modify the percept, but we do have the ability to detect the incongruities. The mechanisms of thought that detect such incongruities must have a different character from those that created them.

My aim is to exploit such phenomena to prise apart the hidden seams of perception and thought in infancy and to understand their relationship to one another in development.

A causal illusion

To suggest that there is such a thing as a *perceptual illusion* of causality is to imply that there is a rather humble perceptual mechanism operating automatically and incorrigibly upon the spatio–temporal properties of events[1] yet producing abstract descriptions of their causal structure. It also implies that the idea of cause and effect does not originate in prolonged learning. It was Michotte (1963) who discovered that adults are, under certain circumstances, subject to just such an illusion. I have been trying to determine whether or not young infants are subject to a similar illusion (Leslie 1982, 1984). I have recently obtained evidence which indicates that they are (Leslie 1986; Leslie and Keeble 1987).

Experimental studies: a first question

My investigation of a causal illusion in infants has gone in a number of steps, each using the habituation–dishabituation of looking technique. The infant watches a film of a red object colliding in a variety of ways with a green object. The film is presented repeatedly until the infant begins to lose interest as measured by the length of succeeding unbroken looks. After this, a variety of slightly changed events can be presented and any recovery of interest, measured in the same way, can be compared with a base-line established with an unchanged event. The pattern of recovery across a number of event comparisons can then provide a basis for inferring how the events are being perceived.

The basic event of these studies I call *direct launching*. This corresponds to a billiard ball collision type event where one object launches another by colliding with it (see Fig. 8.1(a)). The first question was: Can infants distinguish the *submovements* involved in direct launching or is it simply perceived as a single unanalysable 'whoosh' going from one side of the screen to the other?

I argued (Leslie 1984) that if direct launching is seen as an event with a particular internal structure (i.e. composed of submovements), then reversing the event, by playing the film backwards, should rearrange that structure. If, however, an event has *no* submovements, then reversing it would affect only properties such as spatial direction which do not depend upon structured subcomponents.

The idea then was to use reversal to probe for the infant's perception of structure in direct launching. I compared the effect of reversing direct launching with the effect of reversing a single movement made by a single object (see Fig. 8.1 (a) and (b)). Since a single movement has no subcomponents, reversal will change only its spatial direction. Using the looking technique, one can predict the following from the subcomponent hypothesis: those infants habituated to direct launching and tested on its reversal will

---

[1] Such a device could also consider properties of the objects involved, if it operated sufficiently late in the input systems (i.e. after object recognition). Unfortunately, the evidence bearing on whether it does or not is scanty (for discussion, see Leslie 1986).

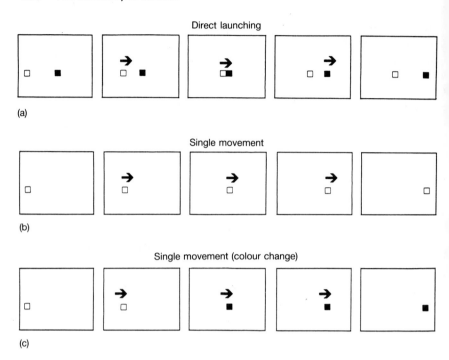

Fig. 8.1   Illustration of films used by Leslie (1984) to test for the perception by infants of internal structure in direct launching (from Leslie and Keeble 1987).

recover their looking *more* than those habituated to a single movement and tested on its reversal. The results of this experiment (Leslie 1984, experiment 1A) showed, as predicted, little recovery in the single movement group and significantly higher recovery in the direct launching group.

Despite this finding, the possibility remained that direct launching was perceived as a single movement but with differently coloured halves—as a single moving entity that changes colour from red to green half-way across. I made a film in which exactly this happened (see Fig. 8.1(c)). If infants do see direct launching this way, they should not readily discriminate these two sequences. In a new experiment, however, infants easily made this discrimination (Leslie 1984, experiment 1B). Taken together, these two studies showed that six-month-olds did detect internal structure, and thus parsed the submovements, in direct launching.

A question about connections

I now asked what kind of internal structure, beyond submovements, infants could perceive in direct launching. Two further experiments (Leslie 1984, experiments 2 and 3) tried to find out how they perceive the relationship between the submovements. Do they perceive causal relationships or simply spatio–temporal properties?

I want to skip over many of the details here so that I can get to broader issues. Suffice it to say that a set of films were prepared which varied the spatio–temporal relations between the submovements. One version had a short delay between the impact of one object and the reaction of the other, another had a small gap between the objects so that they did not actually make contact, while yet another had both the delay and the gap combined. These sequences are illustrated in Fig. 8.2. Only the first sequence, direct launching, appears directly causal to adult observers.

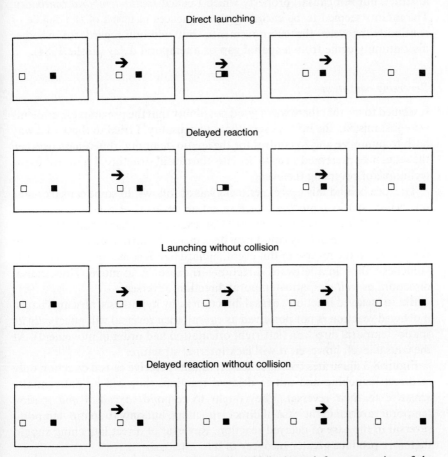

Fig. 8.2 Illustration of films used by Leslie (1984) to test infant perception of the relation between submovements in collision events (from Leslie and Keeble 1987).

All the possible comparisons between pairs of sequences were presented to the infants. Would a given contrast in spatio–temporal parameters be more effective in producing recovery of interest when it involved a causal contrast than when it did not? For example, in direct launching vs. delayed reaction without collision (see Fig. 8.2) a delay and a gap are introduced in going from a 'causal' to a 'non-causal' sequence. A delay plus a gap is also the difference between delayed reaction and launching without collision, but here both sequences are 'non-causal'. Would the infants perceive a greater difference between the first pair than between the second? It seems they did, suggesting a causal property had been perceived.

The other comparisons, however, did not support a causal conclusion. In fact, the overall results seemed simpler to account for in terms of a fairly abstract, but not causal, property which I called *spatio–temporal continuity*. The infants seemed to be encoding the sequences in terms of the degree of continuity between the submovements, but without regard for whether discontinuity came from a spatial gap or a temporal delay (Leslie 1984).

Reversing causation

It seemed to me that there was a good possibility that the previous experiments were just missing the infant's sensitivity to causality. I tried to think of a way both to minimize and to control for the spatio–temporal differences between the sequences presented so as to 'isolate' the causal structure. I returned to the technique of reversing the event.

The idea behind this new experiment was as follows. In some causal events, reversal of spatio–temporal direction entails reversal of causal direction as well. Launching is such an event. For example, billiard ball A directly launches billiard ball B by colliding with it in a rightward direction—A causes B to move. In the reverse of this event, billiard ball B comes back and directly launches ball A in a leftward direction—B causes A to move. Thus, causal direction, *as well as* spatio–temporal direction, reverses.

But in 'delayed reaction', causal direction is, by hypothesis, absent. That is, if delayed reaction is not perceived as causal, then reversal will affect *only* its spatio–temporal direction (left/right orientation and order of movement). At the causal level, however, it will lack internal structure.

Figure 8.3 illustrates the sequences. If infants perceive causal direction only in direct launching and not in delayed reaction, they will be differentially sensitive to their reversal. They ought to respond to causal *and* spatio–temporal reversal in the case of direct launching, but only to spatio–temporal reversal in the case of delayed reaction. Reversal of direct launching should therefore produce greater recovery of interest.

This is exactly what we found (Leslie and Keeble 1987). Infants around 27 weeks recovered more to reversal of an apparently causal event than to the

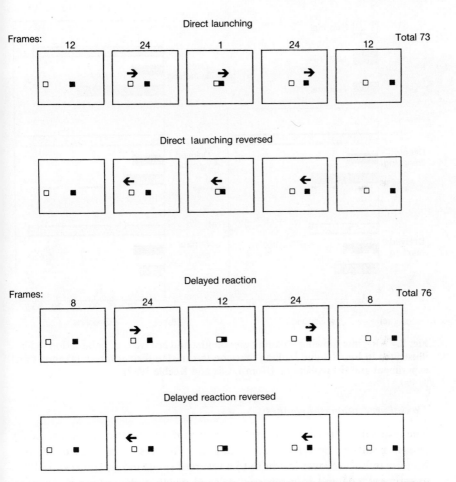

Fig. 8.3 Illustration of films used by Leslie and Keeble (1987) to test for infant perception of causal direction (from Leslie and Keeble 1987).

reversal of an apparently non-causal event. Figure 8.4(a) shows the mean looking times obtained on first look to stimulus, last look following habituation and first look following reversal of the stimulus. Both groups were similar on last look to their respective films. But when these films were reversed, the direct launching group increased its looking significantly more.

The results of a replication were even clearer (Fig. 8.4(b)). We included a control group with no reversal to check that its looking would stay at the same level on the test trial and it did. As predicted, reversal of direct launching produced the most recovery.

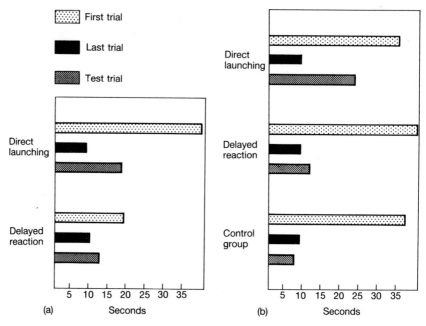

Fig. 8.4 Results showing looking times on first and last trials of habituation to films illustrated in Fig. 8.3 and looking times on test trial to their reversal. (a) shows first experiment and (b) replication (from Leslie and Keeble 1987).

Causal perception: a hypothesis

The reversal experiments suggest that young infants can perceive a specifically causal relation. Because spatio–temporal changes were controlled, and because infants recover less both to a reversed single movement (Leslie 1984, experiment 1A) and to a reversed delayed reaction, we require a *structural* explanation. I have proposed (Leslie 1986; Leslie and Keeble 1987) that at 27 weeks there is a visual mechanism already operating which is responsible for organizing a causal percept. Taking input from lower level motion-processing, this device will parse submovements, produce higher level descriptions of the spatio–temporal properties of the event, and produce a description of its causal structure.

A working hypothesis about the output of this mechanism is illustrated in Fig. 8.5. Multiple representations are computed for the same event. Succeeding representations become more abstract and a higher level description is computed from a lower one. At the first level, the spatial and temporal relations between the submovements are computed and represented orthogonally. This allows a redescription of launching and its variants in terms of continuity at the second level, produced by summing the values of the

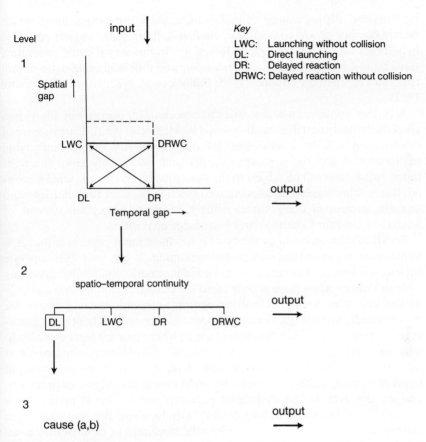

Fig. 8.5 A working hypothesis concerning the output from a module for analysing launching events (from Leslie and Keeble 1987).

parameters at level one. The second-level description then allows the selection of highly continuous events for redescription at the last level. Causal roles may be described at this third level. Further investigation of this level is at present under way.

Modular perception and development

Why should there be such a visual mechanism and why should it be operational at 27 weeks of age? The answer could be that this mechanism forms part of a major learning system. The module for perceiving launching automatically provides a conceptual identification of its input for central thought. There are a number of specific contributions such a device might make (Leslie and Keeble 1987). For example, it could help analyse visible mechanisms, distinguishing causally connected events from those which merely co-vary or are coincidental. Its descriptions could suggest plausible hypotheses for central thought to follow up. In this way it could promote a rapid build-up of mechanical understanding and thus help explain pre-school children's competence (Bullock 1985; Bullock *et al.* 1982; Kun 1978; Schultz 1982).

A further implication is that this same mechanism operates in adults and gives rise to the causal illusion discovered by Michotte (1963). The existence of this illusion will be a side-effect of the modularity of the underlying mechanism: it will operate automatically and incorrigibly given the right input. Infants too will be subject to the same illusion and for the same reasons adults are. This suggests an important connection between adult illusions and infantile perceptual competence: namely, modular perceptual systems of adults are ideal for fostering early knowledge acquisition.

Recall that an essential property of a modular input process is that it is impervious to general knowledge and reasoning. It can, and does, operate without the benefit of either of these. Such a mechanism is ideal for operating early in infancy when there is little or no encyclopaedic knowledge and only limited reasoning ability. It can provide an automatic starting engine for encyclopaedic knowledge. Because it operates independently of such knowledge and reasoning, it can function at a time when these are just beginning to develop, and it can do so without suffering any disadvantage whatsoever. It can provide a conceptual identification of input from the environment, in terms of cause and effect, in exactly the right format for inferential processes, and do this even in the absence of past experience. This is perfect for a mechanism whose job is to help produce development. But do infant input systems actually feed into central inferential mechanisms, or must they await the development of thought processes which can exploit perceptual descriptions?

A causal principle

Baillargéon has made an important discovery about the young infant's understanding of mechanics (Baillargéon 1986, 1987*a*, *b*; Baillargéon *et al.* 1985). In the basic experiment, five-month-old infants watch a screen which starts flat on a table and rotates backwards in a drawbridge type movement until it is flat on the table again (Baillargéon *et al.* 1985). This is repeated until the infants habituate. With the screen back in its starting position, they are shown a box being placed behind the screen. The infants then watch the same movement of the screen as before. After the screen reaches 30° to the upright, the box is occluded from the infant's view for the remainder of its rotation.

The results showed that those infants who were tested on the impossible event in which the screen made the same movement but appeared to rotate *through* the hidden box recovered interest and appeared to be surprised.

Meanwhile, the infants who saw the new but possible event in which the screen stopped when it reached the hidden object showed less recovery of interest.

It is hard to fit this result within the standard framework of habituation–dishabituation theory. In particular, it is hard to see how the infant's dishabituation could have been the result of an automatic process of perceptual discrimination and local stimulus recognition (see Mandler, in press). It seems rather to reflect the central evaluation of the significance of a change in the real world. For it is only possible to understand why the infants dishabituate by considering the stimulus as an *event* in a sequence of events in a world where things have to make sense in certain ways.

These results have since been extended to cover a third object moving behind the screen. In this case, the hidden box is either blocking the moving object's trajectory or merely alongside it. Infants are surprised only when the moving object appears to have passed through the blocking box's position (Baillargéon 1986). In another variation on the original set-up, a compressible object is hidden behind the screen. This time the infants are not surprised when the screen rotates all the way back. Furthermore, infants' surprise is also contingent upon the orientation of the hidden object: it must be oriented such that it will be in the right place to block the screen's backward rotation (Baillargéon 1987a).

The infants in these studies understand where the hidden object is, what its orientation is, whether it is compressible or not, and retain fairly accurate information about its spatial exent. The infants use this rich representation to make judgements about the likely outcomes for mechanical interactions, even though some of these are also hidden from view.

I said these results imply an important evaluative act of understanding from infant central thought. Since the very existence of thought in young infants has traditionally been doubted, this hunch must be given very careful consideration. If correct, there will be major consequences for a theory of infant cognitive architecture. The remaining parts of this section address this question. First, I consider whether these results could stem entirely from the operation of infant input systems and therefore not imply thought. Some will find the assumptions I make about the powers of infant input systems rather liberal. Even so, evidence from illusions leads me to conclude that input systems are not responsible for the crucial feature of Baillargéon's results. I then consider what properties of infant thought account for the results.

Illusions and impossible events

Let us assume that input systems function to build and maintain a model of the perceptual world that is rich enough to allow a conceptual identification of input. At the least, this implies a description of a perceptual situation that extends far enough in time and space to allow a local identification of objects and causal interactions. Thus the infant's input systems would pass information to central systems about, for example, the size, shape, and locations of objects, their displacements through space, and some inherent properties like solid or compressible. They would also describe the mechanical interactions of objects.

Next assume that representations built by input systems can include descriptions of objects which are no longer visible or otherwise sensible, as well as for objects traditionally celebrated as being present to the senses. There is evidence that the visual system can construct illusory invisible objects: in experiments on apparent motion, for example, a shape can appear to move and 'hide' behind another (Ramachandran and Anstis 1986). It is very likely then that input systems can describe situations with hidden objects. The results of Bower (1967) indicate that this is likely in the case of infants too.

With these assumptions in mind, let us consider again what seems to be happening in Baillargéon's experiments. The infant is surprised when an apparently impossible event occurs. A block is seen in a certain position behind a screen. The screen rotates upwards but the box is stationary as it is occluded. Then either the screen or some other object appears to move through the space still occupied by the box. This sequence of events creates an incongruity between one representation that says that a certain region of space is occupied by a rigid solid object and another representation that says that another solid object has just passed through that space. The detection of such incongruities will be the task of a system which seeks to maintain consistent and non-superficial models of a region of space through time.

Is this task carried out by the input systems themselves? One might try the following argument. Since these systems work bottom-up and without access to central information, they will not be able to access the earlier representation of the blocking object when the later passing-through event takes place. They would therefore not be able to detect the contradiction. This will require instead the use of central memory resources. However, avoiding the problem of not having access to earlier representations may have led to a solution in which input systems are specifically designed by evolution to hold onto representations of the objects in the current space. In which case, input systems would be able to detect such incongruities. This sort of *a priori* argument, then, is too weak to be of much use to us.

Much better would be evidence that input systems are actually quite happy with the idea of one object passing through another. Here evidence from illusions is, for obvious reasons, crucial. And, in fact, an illusion does exist where one object appears to pass through another (Ramachandran 1985). However, there are two immediate problems with citing this particular illusion as evidence in our case. The illusion involves the apparent motion of a light through a hand. First, there may be something special about apparent as opposed to real movement (e.g. Kolers 1964), and, second, a light is not a solid object.

Sperber, speaking in the discussion period, has put the following point to me: 'Part of the function of input modules is to filter out most information and to filter *in* potentially relevant information. Incongruities in the environment are typically relevant to the organism and should therefore be filtered in to become objects of central attentive processes'. This suggests a simple explanation: the infant's input systems detect the incongruity in Baillargéon's experiment and alert central systems to pay more attention. Nothing of interest would follow as regards infant thought.

It is not the case, however, that input systems always filter in incongruities. sometimes they resolve conflicts and produce new illusions as a result. For example, stereograms can be used to create an incongruence between interposition and binocular information for the relative positions in depth of two planes (Zanforlin 1982). In this case, the visual system resolves the contradiction by bending one of the planes round the other.

The power of input systems to resolve incongruities can also be seen in intermodal illusions. In the 'McGurk effect' a listener is exposed to an auditory 'ga' while watching the speaker make the lip movements for 'ba'. Under these circumstances the looker/listener hears neither 'ba' nor 'ga' but an intermediate 'da' (McGurk and Macdonald 1976). The incongruity between visual and auditory input is resolved by the input systems in a striking illusion.

So it would be of great interest if the perceptual resolution of an incongruity resulted in an illusion of one object passing through another. It would suggest that this was more acceptable to vision than the original incongruity. The Ames trapezoidal window with rod illusion might fit this bill. In this a trapezoid seems to rotate back and forth while a rod projecting through the centre seems to rotate continuously through 360°. According to Rock (1983), however, it is not clear exactly what is seen at the moment when the rod should pass through the side of the window. Rock also points out that the conflicting interposition information is available to the visual system only very briefly at this instant. This illusion too, then, is not quite what we are looking for.

The following kind of evidence is needed: a robust and clearly describable illusion in which one solid rigid object is seen to pass through another solid rigid object; the illusion arises from the visual system's attempt to resolve an incongruity; and it occurs despite the continuous availability of perceptual information that conflicts with the resolving (illusory) percept. This is quite a complex specification and I despaired of ever finding such a phenomenon. Then Wilson and Robinson (1986) published their observations on the Pulfrich double pendulum illusion.

Seeing is not believing
The Pulfrich double pendulum (PDP) illusion is actually a set of simultaneous illusions. Wilson and Robinson (1986) constructed two pendulums using rigid metal rods with plastic detergent bottles filled with sand on the end. The

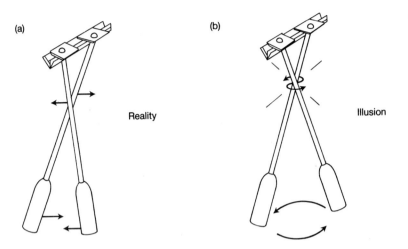

Fig. 8.6   The Pulfrich double pendulum illusion: (a) what really happens, and (b) how the illusion appears to an observer viewing with reduced luminance to one eye (direction of apparent rotation depends upon which eye).

pendulums are then mounted so that they swing in parallel, one slightly behind the other. The arrangement is viewed in fairly dim light with the pendulums set to swing in opposite phase in a frontal plane (see Fig. 8.6). The observer holds a neutral density filter over one eye but looks with both. The reduced luminance to one eye creates a time delay in signals from it and thus a stereoscopic discrepancy in the position of the pendulum which varies with the velocity and direction of swing. Stereoscopic fusion interprets this discrepancy as a variation in depth and the pendulum is seen to swing in an ellipse. With two pendulums in opposite phase, two elliptical paths are seen and the pendulum bobs appear to be chasing each other around without, somehow, the rods twisting round each other.

Wilson and Robinson (1986) also describe a concomitant size illusion due to inappropriate size constancy scaling with the pendulum bobs appearing to grow as they recede and shrink as they approach. What Wilson and Robinson do not describe, however, is what observers see happening to the rods. They say that observers do *not* see them twisting round each other, but they do not say what observers *do* see. How does the visual system resolve the incongruity in the overlapping orbits of the two pendulum swings created by the stereoscopic illusion? It seemed there might be a chance that it would have the rods pass through each other. Robinson (pers. comm.) confirmed that Wilson and Robinson (1986) had not studied this aspect of the illusion.

I have therefore investigated this myself with a similarly constructed PDP.

The results were clear (Leslie, in preparation *a*). First, I can confirm that the PDP illusion as reported by Wilson and Robinson, including the elliptical paths, the 'chasing round', and the size illusion, is striking and easily obtained. Equally striking is the clear perception of the rigid solid rods passing through each other. Most observers were able to find an angle of view where even the pendulum bottles appear to pass through one another despite their large size and marked surface texture.

The PDP illusion satisfies the conditions I laid down. First, the illusion is robust and easily described, most viewers spontaneously offering the observation that the rods were passing through each other. Second, this seems to arise from the visual system resolving a perceptual conflict which is itself due to an illusion. Most impressively, however, there is conflicting interposition, convergence, and retinal size information continuously available that the pendulums are not varying in depth and not passing through each other. Presumably, the visual system could have resolved this in some other way; for example, by bending the rods and momentarily twisting and untwisting them, or by simply not specifying clearly what happens at the cross-over point, or indeed by suppressing the stereoscopic illusion altogether. Instead, an illusion of passing through occurs. This suggests that the visual system is really rather happy with the idea of solid objects passing through one another.

Baby knows better

Let us return to the infants in Baillargéon's experiments. These infants seem to have knowledge that solid objects cannot cohabit the same space even temporarily. The adult visual system, on the other hand, despite a great deal of time to detect this regularity about the behaviour of objects in the familiar world—despite never having seen a counterexample in 40 years—does not seem to have learned it and is perfectly prepared to advance this bizarre percept as soon as it is shown the PDP illusion. Such obstinate ignorance would be difficult to understand if input systems were simply mechanisms of associative learning. Instead it points to a different kind of organization—one which is designed to provide central learning mechanisms with the right conceptual identification of input. Such identifications may carry an *implication* of mechanical incongruity which input systems cannot detect, nor resolve.

A *central* learning mechanism is, I believe, the key to understanding Baillargéon's results. First the infant input systems provide central thought with the representation that a solid rigid object is in a certain location throughout. Then a little later they advance the representation that another solid rigid object has just passed through this location. So far there is no contradiction. Contradiction only arises in conjunction with a third proposition, namely, that solid objects cannot occupy the same space. But the results from the PDP illusion show that, unlike the other two, the source of this third proposition cannot be perception.

Yet infant thought does appear to apply a principle of no cohabitation to solid objects. What I have to do now is to try to understand how this principle is embodied and applied in thought. I shall follow Sperber and Wilson (1986) and assume that central thought employs a general system of spontaneous *deductive* inferences.

An engine of development

I think the reason the principle of no cohabitation exists in the form it does is that there is a central system which, in conjunction with input mechanisms, maintains a consistent and non-superficial model of the infant's current environmental situation. We all need this bit of architecture no matter what age. But the same system has another related function which is particularly important in development. This function is to build encyclopaedic knowledge and common-sense theories about the mechanics of the physical world.

I am going to postulate two parts to this system. First, a set of spontaneous deductive inferences, and, second, a set of principles which enter into these inferences along with other representations. These other representations may include further principles, perceptual representations, and encyclopaedic knowledge. This system in Baillargeon's infants detects the *logical* contradiction in holding three things to be simultaneously true: (a current perceptual representation that) one solid object has traversed a certain trajectory, (a representation received previously and now in memory that) another solid object has all the while sat astride that trajectory, and (a principle representation that) solid objects cannot share the same space.

What distinguishes principles from other representations, aside from their origins, is their inviolability. That is, in the face of apparent counterevidence principles are not disconfirmed. Instead such evidence is immediately doubted or the system looks for other ways to escape from interpretations that lead detectably (by spontaneous deduction) to contradiction of a principle. In short, apparent violation of a principle creates paradox and not disproof.

The privileged status of no cohabitation gives this principle its power in the learning system—the engine of development—that builds and constrains the child's encyclopaedic knowledge and common-sense theories about the physical world. This system is apparently functioning by four months of age (Baillargéon 1987*b*) and probably serves us in essentially the same role throughout life.

Spelke's objecthood principles: distinguishing perception and thought

Spelke (1987, 1988) has made important proposals regarding the infant's core concept of an object. According to her theory, this core concept consists of four principles: *boundedness, cohesion, spatio-temporal continuity*, and *substance*. This last principle is what I have discussed as 'no cohabitation', though Spelke may not agree with my proposals for how it is embodied.

Spelke is skeptical about past attempts to distinguish perception from thought, and in particular about the role that the notion of modular organization might play in such a distinction. She argues that if there is any principled distinction between perception and thought it will be that they deliver different kinds of knowledge. Perception delivers knowledge about the continuous surface layout of the world in continuous change—producing representations like Marr's (1982) $2\frac{1}{2}$-D sketch. Thought breaks this continuous layout up into units—into objects and events—and finds relations between these units. The units and relations thought finds in the world are intimately related to the theories thought builds and entertains about the world. The infant's object constructing principles are an example of this function of central thought.

I cannot hope to do justice to Spelke's ideas and results here, but I do want to respond briefly to her arguments on the differences between perception and thought. For the sake of argument, I shall assume Marr's (1982) view of the organization of visual perception. According to this, early vision culminates in a viewer-centred representation of surface layout which Marr called a '$2\frac{1}{2}$-D sketch' (Marr 1982; Marr and Nishihara 1978). This representation is arrived at entirely bottom-up as a function simply of the retinal array. This kind of early recoding of retinal arrays can be thought of, therefore, as a kind of extended *sensory analysis*. It is to this, however, that Spelke wants to restrict the term *perception*.

The next level of representation in Marr's account is the object-centred representation called the '3-D model'. This goes beyond sensory analysis in the sense that representations at this level are only partial functions of retinal arrays. Additional information, for example, from a catalogue of three-dimensional object shape descriptions, is used to disambiguate viewer-centred representations and to categorize objects (Marr and Nishihara 1978). There is neuropsychological evidence that a 'pure visual' object recognition module operates independently of and prior to a module for recognizing object function or 'meaning' (Warrington and James 1986). Also at this level, according to Ullman's (1984) theory of visual routines, there are processes of visual analysis which are responsive in highly restricted ways to goals set by central attention. For example, 'optional' visual analyses, like fast curve-tracing, can be performed in support of the recognition of particular objects or other special tasks (Jolicoeur *et al.* 1986), while the influence of set on the perception of illusory contours (Coren *et al.* 1986) suggests that this class of illusions may involve some kind of central triggering information. Let us call this level of input processing *perceptual analysis*.

It is the level of perceptual analysis, interfacing sensory analysis and thought, that results in a conceptual identification of input. Physical objects and physical events are parsed and related at this level. Mandler (in press) uses the term perceptual analysis in a somewhat similar way; I do not want to suggest, however, that this represents the highest level of infant cognition, as the previous discussion of Baillargéon's findings should have made clear. On the other hand, it does seem likely that some of Spelke's objecthood principles are implemented at the level of perceptual analysis. For example, boundedness and cohesion would seem to be required for Marr–Nishihara-type object recognition. By contrast, the principle of substance or no cohabitation must belong to central thought if the arguments presented earlier are accepted. This means that infants construct concrete objects over a number of cognitive levels.

Causal inference and metarepresentation

Toward the end of infancy a capacity for a new kind of internal representation emerges. This first shows itself in the ability to pretend. Instead of being directed at representing the world in a faithful and literal way, as perception and the kind of thought we have been considering are, pretence involves a deliberate distortion of the way the real situation is understood. I have been trying to understand the cognitive mechanisms that make this possible but will not say much about this aspect here (see instead, Leslie 1987a, in press a). I do want to describe briefly a study of inferential processes with respect to imaginary states of affairs in two-year-olds (Leslie, in preparation b). This study demonstrates counterfactual causal reasoning and has important implications for early mental architecture.

Sharing pretence with young children can be turned into a flexible experimental method. I require the child to follow what I am pretending, encouraging him to join in as much as possible. For example, I show the child two empty toy cups, a toy bottle, and some toy animals and I describe the setting, giving a birthday party for one of the animals, as a cover story for later 'events'.

I ask the child to 'pour out' some 'water' into the two cups. I then pick up one of the cups and turn it upside-down for a moment or two and then replace it. I ask the child which cup is empty/full. The child can either point, say which one, or 'refill' the 'empty' cup (both are really empty). To get this right, the child has to keep track of the pretend status of the two cups. He must watch what I do and interpret my actions with respect to the pretend world we jointly create. Somehow he must calculate the 'consequences' of those actions in the pretend world, as well as perceive the actual results in the real world. Children of around two-and-a-half years seem to enjoy this task and are very good at making appropriate causal inferences.

During the 'birthday party' a regrettable incident takes place in which one of the animals picks up a cup which the child has recently 'filled' with 'water' and proceeds to upturn the cup above the head of another animal, holding the cup upside-down in this position. I ask the child what has happened. The children usually answer that the water has gone all over the victim or that the victim is wet. Again causal inferences appropriate to the pretend but not to the real state of affairs are made. Some children draw a different conclusion and 'refill' the cup.

One regrettable incident leads to another, and soon the child has inferred that one of the animals has become 'muddy' by rolling on a certain region of the table I have designated as a muddy puddle. I suggest that the animal is in need of a bath (the children never seem to think of this themselves) and make a 'bath' using four toy bricks arranged to produce a cavity. I place the animal in this cavity and roll it around a few times, then remove it. The child might then pick up a 'towel' to 'dry' the animal. I say, 'Watch this' and pick up one of the toy cups. I then put the toy cup into the cavity formed by the bricks and make a single scooping motion. I then ask the child, 'What's in here?', pointing to the empty cup. The child replies, 'Water'.

The language of thought in pretence

The two-year-old is following the pretend scenario which we jointly construct by representing imaginary events, imaginary objects, and properties and by calculating the imaginary consequences of imaginary states of affairs. But the inferences used by the two-year-old to do this are real world inferences—they are not just fantastic and random leaps from one pretend state of affairs to another. This is interesting for several reasons. First, it shows that even early pretending involves highly constrained thought processes. It also demonstrates counterfactual reasoning which employs the same knowledge used in understanding and predicting the real world. This is exactly what was expected on the basis of the cognitive model of pretense proposed in Leslie (1987a, in press a).

These results further show that the two-year-old's real world knowledge is not represented in such a way that it is bound to specific contexts. The perceptual support provided by my pretend scenarios is minimal. The props used and my actions and words at best *suggest* a story-line, but this story-line cannot be simply perceived nor be computed from perception by central thought in the normal way (see Leslie 1987a). The inferences used, while being drawn from the set of real world inferences the child can make, nevertheless have to apply to different representations than those that arise in understanding the real current situation. They have to apply to representations of the pretence and not to representations of what is really happening. They must also produce other pretense representations as their output, and not serious ones (Leslie 1987).

Inferential processes are only one part of this complex cognitive activity in two-year-olds. One must also consider the nature of the representations that are being processed. I will outline some main points here (but, for more extended discussion, see Leslie 1987a, in press a, in press b).

Pretence representations have computational properties that distinguish them not only from representations of actual situations but from any serious, literal representation, even ones considered false. They belong to the class of *metarepresentations*—that is, the class of representations that relate agents to representations of representations. Sentences which report direct speech are a natural model for metarepresentations. So, for example, in *John said, 'Computer hardward is infallible'*, John is related to a sentence or representation. But because this sentence or representation is quoted and not asserted, one cannot make normal inferences from it—in particular one cannot infer that computer hardware does not break down.

In fact, there is a detailed correspondence between the inferential properties of another related class of sentences in language and the inferential properties of pretence (Leslie 1987a). These are sentences like *John believes computer hardware is infallible*—sentences which report mental states. This correspondence suggests that pretending and mental state reporting depend cognitively upon the same underlying form of representation. This form of representation must have certain crucial inferential properties.

Consider the following as thoughts:

(1) the cup is full of water;
(2) the empty cup is full of water;
(3) I pretend the empty cup is full of water;
(4) I pretend the cup is both empty and full of water.

There are internal contradictions in (2) and (4) but not in (1) and (3). I do not think that we or young children can have (2) and (4) as thoughts in the ordinary way because the logical contradiction is so blatant and is soon picked up by spontaneous deduction. The puzzle is why (3) does not suffer this defect while (2) and (4) do.

The answer I give is roughly this (see Leslie 1987a, in press a). The internal representation of the thought (3) has more structure than is apparent in the way it is written down. Part of the expression is actually quoted or, as I say, *decoupled*:

(5) I pretend the empty cup 'it is full of water'.

Inferential processes have to respect this structure. Suppose there was a causal inference to do with what happens when things that contain water are turned upside-down. If this were to apply to (1) it might output something like (6):

(6) the water pours out and makes something wet—the container becomes empty.

Used in pretence, this inference would apply to the decoupled part of (5). Since the input to the inference is decoupled, its output too will be decoupled. This ensures that the 'conclusion' is part of the pretence and not a prediction about the real world. Thus one of the 'conclusions' when the inference is applied to (5) would be:

(7) I pretend the empty cup 'it is empty'.

The thought (7) is not a mere tautology. In fact, it is a particularly interesting case of pretence because it shows that pretend representations are not merely marked as false (see Leslie, in press *a*). In the extended pretence going from 'filling' the cup with 'water' to 'emptying' it to 'refilling' it again, of which (7) is a part, the cup really is empty throughout. If parts of pretend representations were simply marked as false, they could not be used to produce this kind of pretence. Leslie (in press *a*) gives further reasons why a 'mark as false' account of pretence will not work.

Recall the *spontaneous deductive* inferences, discussed in the middle part of this chapter (p. 200), which detected the contradiction between the location of one object, the trajectory of another, and the principle of no cohabitation. These spontaneous inferences will not detect a contradiction in (5) since the elements which would have been incongruous are at different levels; i.e. decoupled and non-decoupled. However, if I write out (4) in full, to give

(8) I pretend the empty cup 'it is both empty and full of water',

one can see that here the contradictory elements are at the same level—as they also are in (2). Spontaneous deduction should immediately detect this within-levels contradiction. This is why one never finds children who think like (2) or pretend like (8).

Inferences in pretence: evidence for symbolic processing
One of the most fundamental questions about infant mental architecture concerns the computational organization of the processing hardware. Recently it has been claimed that cognitive psychology has been mistaken when it assumed that (all or any) adult computational processes involved the manipulation of symbolic codes (e.g. Rumelhart *et al.* 1986). The suggestion is based on the study of a quite different computational architecture from the familiar serial processing, by rules, of symbol strings read from and written to a memory store (Newell 1980). In 'connectionist' systems, there are no symbolic representations, no representation of the processing rules, and no distinct memory stores containing symbols. Yet these connectionist systems have interesting powers of associative learning. The question arises whether in the early stages of development a connectionist architecture might provide the entire basis for cognition.

I think that the existence of a capacity for pretence rules out this possibility. Connectionist architecture, while it may be able to simulate pretence, is, as far as I can see, inherently incapable of providing a principled explanation for the most important properties of pretence cognition and related phenomena. Whatever the hardware, it must keep serious and pretence-related cognitions apart and distinct. An organism that confused its serious knowledge of the world with its pretence would be in trouble. Because pretence is part of the capacity to represent different mental models of the world, it is a special case of a much more general system of cognition underlying our ability to model other minds (Leslie 1987*a*, *b*, in press *a* and *b*). There are thus equivalent requirements to keep apart and distinct (representations of) my pretend from your pretend, my beliefs from your beliefs, your hopes from my beliefs, my beliefs from my beliefs about my beliefs, my hopes about your beliefs from my beliefs about your hopes, and so on and on. To handle these different representational 'spaces' and the differences in their content will require in connectionist machinery functionally distinct networks.

Using functionally distinct networks would probably allow a simulation to be built. In simulation one could attempt to construct networks whose 'contents' had shared properties. On the other hand, it would be just as easy to construct networks whose 'contents' were arbitrarily different. There is nothing in connectionist architecture to prevent functionally distinct networks from differing arbitrarily. But this fact will deprive us of a principled explanation should it be the case that different 'mental spaces' are *always* related in their content.

Unfortunately for connectionist models, the contents of metarepresentational states are always deeply and systematically related to one another. In fact, this is the first thing any theory in this domain must account for. These states are individuated in three important ways: first, in terms of whose state it is; second, in terms of the relation involved (e.g. *pretend, believe, hope, expect* and so on); and third, in terms of the content of the state—whether I believe that it is raining, or that Edinburgh is a beautiful city, or that Leslie discovered the connection between heat and light. Two states then may differ but share exactly the same content: there is a non-arbitrary relationship between *pretending it is raining* and *believing it is raining*. What they have in common is the proposition *it is raining*. Or one content may be the negation of another: *believing it is not raining*. And so on with endlessly many relations.
relations.

These facts—both the differences between different metarepresentational states and the systematic relations between their possible contents—can be parsimoniously accounted for using a system of symbolic computation (Pylyshyn 1984; Leslie 1987*a*). For example, the differences between serious and pretense-related cognition can be captured by the differences between the forms of the underlying representations. Their systematic relations meanwhile are given by relations between subexpressions in the symbolic code. So the *full of water* that features in pretense is the same *full of water* that features in serious cognition. Since all the different 'mental spaces' use the same symbolic code, systematic relations of this sort are ubiquitous and inevitable.

Finally, the fact that both types of representation are subject to the same computational processes (e.g. the same rules of inference) also receives a principled explanation in a symbolic processing account. In connectionist machines there are no computational processes identifiable independently of the network. So different networks are perfectly free to vary in, for example, the rules of inference they implement. This deprives such architectures of a principled explanation of the fact that in human children pretence employs the same inferential processes as serious cognition. In symbolic processing architectures, however, it is fundamental that there are computational processes which apply to symbolic expressions and which are sensitive to the structure of those expressions; that is what a symbolic computation system is. We can therefore readily find an explanation for why the same inferences apply and why these inferences respect the structural differences, as well as the structural similarities, between primary representations and metarepresentations.

Pretence, then, provides powerful evidence in favour of an infant mental architecture that includes symbolic processing. Because metarepresentation presupposes primary representation, it is likely that symbolic processing devices have been operating throughout most of infancy. The arguments and evidence discussed earlier in this chapter, regarding the relationship between perception and thought in infancy and the logical properties of infant representations, confirm and support the existence of a symbolic processing architecture during human infancy.

Conclusion

The main organizational features of the adult mind appear to be present in infancy. I have argued for a modular organization in infant perception and pointed to its advantages for development. Central thought processes appear to operate early and, like perception, are richly structured, presumably by biological endowment. They employ powerful inferential processes which are sensitive to the logical properties of infant symbolic representation.

Towards the end of infancy, thought acquires the power to represent itself recursively and thereby to reason imaginatively. This will provide the basis for the conceptual distinction between appearance and reality (Leslie in press a). This distinction will allow central processes to theorize about those things in experience that are incorrigibly not what they seem. The necessity of illusion comes home to roost.

Figure 8.7 summarizes the argument of this chapter. The main conclusion appears to be that human mental architecture provides the basis for development and not its outcome. Should this seem strange, we should reflect that acquiring theoretical knowlege of the world—in the sense both of common sense and of more specialized scientific and religious theories—is

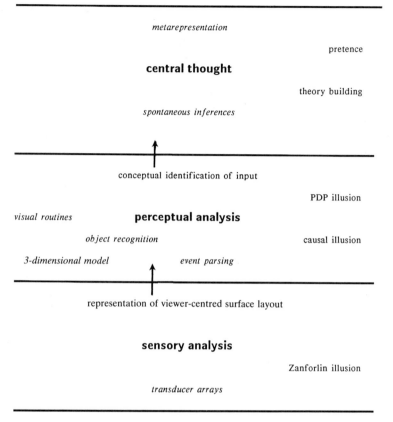

Fig. 8.7   Summary of main arguments concerning mental architecture in infancy.

uniquely the point of human development. The basic organization of the infant-adult mind is highly designed for this task.

Acknowledgements

I am grateful to John Morton for comments on an earlier draft, and to Jean Mandler and Elizabeth Spelke for highly relevant discussion.

References

Baillargéon, R. (1986). Representing the existence and the location of hidden objects: object permanence in 6- and 8-month old infants. *Cognition*, **23**, 21–41.
—— (1987a). Young infant's reasoning about the physical and spatial properties of a hidden object. *Cognitive Development*, **2**, 179–200.
—— (1987b). Object permanence in 3.5- and 4.5-month-old infants. *Developmental Psychology*, **23**, 655–64.

——, Spelke, E. S., and Wasserman, S. (1985). Object permanence in five-month-old infants. *Cognition*, **20**, 191–208.
Bower, T. G. R. (1967). The development of object permanence: some studies of existence constancy. *Perception and Psychophysics*, **2**, 74–6.
Bullock, M. (1985). Causal reasoning and developmental change over the preschool years. *Human Development*, **28**, 169–91.
——, Gelman, R., and Baillargéon, R. (1982). The development of causal reasoning. In *The developmental psychology of time*, (ed. W. Friedman), pp. 209–54. New York.
Coren, S. and Ward, L. M. (1979). Levels of processing in visual illusions: the combination and interaction of distortion-producing mechanisms. *Journal of Experimental Psychology: Human Perception and Performance*, **5**, 324–35.
——, Porac, C., and Theodor, L. H. (1986). The effects of perceptual set on the shape and apparent depth of subjective contours. *Perception and Psychophysics*, **39**, 327–33.
Fodor, J. A. (1983). *The modularity of mind.* MIT Press, Cambridge, Ma.
Gregory, R. L. (1974). *Concepts and mechanisms of perception.* Duckworth, London.
Jolicoeur, P., Ullman, S., and Mackay, M. (1986). Curve tracing: a possible basic operation in the perception of spatial relations. *Memory and Cognition*, **14**, 129–40.
Kolers, P. A. (1964). The illusion of movement. *Scientific American*, **211**, 98–106.
Kun, A. (1978). Evidence for preschoolers' understanding of causal direction in extended causal sequences. *Child Development*, **49**, 218–22.
Leslie, A. M. (1982). Discursive representation in infancy. In *Knowledge and representation*, (ed. B. de Gelder), pp. 80–93. Routledge and Kegan Paul, Andover, Hants.
—— (1984). Spatiotemporal continuity and the perception of causality in infants. *Perception*, **13**, 287–305.
—— (1986). Getting development off the ground: modularity and the infant's perception of causality. In *Theory building in development*, (ed. P. van Gest), pp. 405–37. North-Holland, Amsterdam.
—— (1982a). Pretense and representation: the origins of 'theory of mind'. *Psychological Review*, **94**, 412–26.
—— (1987b). The child's understanding of the mental world. In *The Oxford companion to the mind*, (ed. R. L. Gregory), pp. 139–42. Oxford University Press.
—— (in press a). Some implications of pretense for mechanisms underlying the child's theory of mind. In *Developing theories of mind*, (ed. J. Astington, D. Olson, and P. Harris). Cambridge University Press.
—— (in press b). A 'language of thought' approach to early pretense. *Cahiers de la Fondation Archives Jean Piaget.*
—— (in prep. a). *Further observations on the Pulfrich double pendulum illusion.* MRC Cognitive Development Unit, University of London.
—— (in prep. b). *Causal inferences in pretense: evidence for symbolic processing in two year olds.* MRC Cognitive Development Unit, University of London.
—— and Keeble, S. (1987). Do six-month-old infants perceive causality? *Cognition*, **25**, 265–88.
Mandler, J. (in press). How to build a baby: on the development of an accessible representational system. *Cognitive Development.*

Marr, D. (1982). *Vision*. (W. H. Freeman, San Francisco, CA).
—— and Nishihara, H. K. (1978). Representation and recognition of the spatial organization of three-dimensional shapes. *Proceedings of the Royal Society of London, B,* **200**, 187–217.
McGurk, H. and Macdonald, J. (1976). Hearing lips and seeing voices. *Nature,* **264**, 746–8.
Michotte, A. (1963). *The perception of causality*. Methuen, Andover, Hants.
Newell, A. (1980). Physical symbol systems. *Cognitive Science,* **4**, 135–83.
Pylyshyn, Z. W. (1984). *Computation and cognition: toward a foundation for cognitive science*. MIT Press, Cambridge, MA.
Ramachandran, V. S. (1985). The neurobiology of perception. *Perception,* **14**, 97–103.
—— and Anstis, S. M. (1986). The perception of apparent motion. *Scientific American,* **255**, 80–7.
Robinson, J. O. (1972). *The psychology of visual illusion*. Hutchinson, London.
Rock, I. (1983). *The logic of perception*. MIT Press, Cambridge, MA.
Rumelhart, D. E., Hinton, G. E., and McClelland, J. L. (1986). A general framework for parallel distributed processing. In *Parallel distributed processing: explorations in the microstructure of cognition. Vol. 1,* (ed. D. E. Rumelhart and J. L. McClelland), pp. 45–76. MIT Press, Cambridge, MA.
Shultz, T. R. (1982). Rules of causal attribution. *Monographs of the Society for Research in Child Development,* **47**, No. 1.
Spelke, E. S. (1987). Where perceiving ends and thinking begins: the apprehension of objects in infancy. In *Perceptual development in infancy. Minnesota symposia on child psychology,* (ed. A. Yonas), pp. 197–234. Lawrence Erlbaum Associates, Hillsdale, NJ.
—— (1988). The origins of physical knowledge. In *Thought without language*, (ed. L. Weiskrantz), pp. 168–83. Oxford University Press.
Sperber, D. and Wilson, D. (1986). *Relevance: communication and cognition*. Blackwell Scientific Publications, Oxford.
Ullman, S. (1984). Visual routines. *Cognition,* **18**, 97–159.
Warrington, E. K. and James, M. (1986). Visual object recognition in patients with right-hemisphere lesions: axes or features? *Perception,* **15**, 355–66.
Wilson, J. A. and Robinson, J. O. (1986). The impossibly twisted Pulfrich pendulum. *Perception,* **15**, 503–4.
Zanforlin, M. (1982). Figure organization and binocular interaction. In *Organization and representation in perception,* (ed. J. Beck), pp. 251–67. Lawrence Erlbaum Associates, Hillsdale, NJ.

9

An information-processing approach
to infant cognitive development
LESLIE B. COHEN

Along with other participants at this meeting, I consider myself to be a developmental psychologist; more specifically a developmental psychologist interested in understanding the mechanisms underlying infant perception, memory, and categorization. For any developmental psychologist, the major challenge is not just to uncover the infants' capabilities at ony one particular age, but to discover the ways those capabilities change as infants become older and more sophisticated. Distinguishing what changes from what does not change is a more difficult issue than at first it may appear, and in this chapter I would like to share with you some of our attempts to examine it. While it goes without saying that an understanding of infant development requires extensive examination of human infants at several different ages, I also hope to illustrate that additional valuable information about infant development can be obtained from an examinaton of adult human and animal literatures as well.

Consider first the case of infant habituation. For years, we and others have been devising better and better ways to bore babies. For example, by repeatedly presenting the same visual pattern we can produce a decrease (or habituation) in infant looking and by subsequently presenting a novel pattern we can produce a resurgence (or dishabituation) in that same looking. The results of an idealized habituation experiment are presented in Fig. 9.1. In this figure are illustrated both habituation of infant visual attention to some repeated stimulus, A, and subsequent dishabituation to some novel stimulus, B. Note that the experiment is divided into separate habituation and test phases. Demonstration of true habituation requires more than a decrease in responding. It also requires selective dishabituation to a novel, but not to the familiar, stimulus in the test. Without this selective dishabituation, one could not know if the preceding decrease during the habituation phase resulted from repeated presentations specifically of the familiar stimulus, A, or from a more generalized fatigue on the part of the infant.

In the late-1960s and 1970s those interested in learning about infant cognition found this habituation paradigm to be just what was needed. After

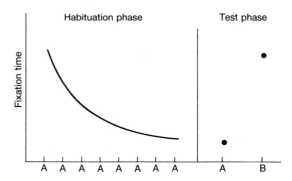

Fig. 9.1 Idealized habituation–dishabituation experiment under the assumption that infant fixation times are habituated to stimulus A and then tested for dishabituation with stimuli A and B.

all, it could be argued, assuming appropriate controls for fatigue, the reason infants habituated to a particular stimulus had to be because they had experienced that stimulus before. In other words, habituation, by definition, implied some type of memory. And memory, as everyone knew, was a paradigmatic cognitive process; almost every book on cognition devoted considerable space to the discussion of memorial processes. So, from this type of argument it followed naturally that habituation should be a simple and convenient way to explore infant cognition.

Drawing upon the literature from older children and adults, investigators began asking the same types of questions about the memory of infants that had been asked about the memory of more mature subjects. By varying the number or duration of habituation trials one could examine how quickly infants could remember. By varying the time interval between habituation and test, one could examine how long infants could remember, and, by inserting different numbers or types of stimuli in that interval between habituation and test, one could attempt to interfere with that memory (see Cohen and Gelber (1975) or Olson and Sherman (1983) for reviews of this literature). The results were almost uniformly positive. These early investigations reported that infants as young as two months of age could remember and those as young as four or five months of age appeared to have excellent long- and well as short-term memories (e.g. Fagan 1973, Martin 1973). The human infant, therefore, seemed to be more sophisticated cognitively than had previously been believed. More recent investigations not only have confirmed these demonstrations of infant memory but have extended the evidence to younger and younger ages. In the last few years convincing demonstrations have been provided of habituation and dishabituation by the new-born (e.g. Slater *et al.* 1983), and even by the intact fetus (Madison *et al.* 1986).

Results on infant habituation were intriguing from a developmental perspective as well. While it was evident that very young infants (and now perhaps even fetuses) could habituate, it also was evident that younger infants usually looked longer at the same pattern than did older infants. The younger ones also habituated less rapidly than did the older ones. Thus, while it was clear that infants at any age might have the 'cognitive' ability to remember, there also appeared to be some developmental improvement in this ability over the first several months of life. A central, but usually neglected, issue is how to explain these changes both in visual attention and in habituation rate over age. Another possible explanation for changes in attention and habituation over age shall be presented later in this chapter.

Disillusionment with the necessity of a cognitive interpretation of habituation came, in part, from an examination of habituation studies with animals and simple physiological preparations. There appeared to be abundant evidence that decorticate cats, decerebrate earthworms, or even simple neuronal reflexes in the mollusk habituated (Tighe and Leaton 1976). If that was the case, what type of cognition could be inferred from the mere fact that an organism or a preparation habituated? Certainly, one could still argue that habituation implied some type of memory, but this habituation memory system seemed to be more a broad-based adaptive mechanism available to a wide variety of species or preparations than it was any thoughtful cognitive act. In spite of earlier assumptions about the intimate tie between habituation and cognition, one seemed to be placed in the dilemma either of concluding that habituation *per se* was not necessarily 'cognitive' or that the definition of cognition must be broadened considerably to include changes in simple neuronal mechanisms.

Furthermore, if habituation was that simple and basic, why should there be these developmental progressions in infancy of decreased looking time to the same pattern and more rapid habituation over the first several months of life? Certainly a new-born infant is more complex neurologically than a mollusk. The answer that memory improves over age is inadequate. For one thing it seems circular. It asserts little other than what it is trying to explain; namely, that habituation will improve over age. For another, it does not handle the equally dramatic changes in overall attention to a stimulus over age; i.e. that younger infants usually tend to look longer than older ones. Finally, and probably most devastating, is the fact that the memory improvement explanation is incompatible with the occasional, but reliable, finding that under certain circumstances older infants will habituate *less* readily than younger ones (Cohen and Younger 1985). One answer both to the question of the relationship between cognition and habituation and to what develops over age could be that *how quickly* an infant habituates and remembers may be less important cognitively and developmentally than *what* an infant remembers. In fact, evidence from our own laboratory provides several demonstrations that the very same stimulus may be processed in different ways by infants at different ages and that what they process can determine how rapidly or slowly they habituate (Younger and Cohen 1986). From this point of view, the most productive use of the habituation procedure in assessing cognitive development may not be to investigate parameters of infant memory, but to investigate the mechanisms of infant perception and information-processing.

The idealized data from the habituation paradigm shown in Fig. 9.1 were discussed previously from the point of view of infant memory. One could also look at them from the point of view of infant visual perception or infant visual information-processing. Dishabituation to a novel stimulus, B, but not to the familiar one, A, in the test means more than just memory for A. It also indicates the ability to differentiate between A and B, and that, in turn, provides clues as to what type of information about A has been processed and remembered. By far the most frequent use of the infant habituation paradigm today involves manipulation of novel and familiar test items to determine what infants are encoding or processing.

Furthermore, it is not always clear that what the experimenter thinks is being presented really is being seen by the infant. Consider, for example, the experimenter who shows a picture of a face to both younger and older infants. From this experimenter's perspective it is the same picture of a face shown to both ages. It may even be considered a study of infants' 'face' perception. However, the identical face may not be perceived in the same way by infants at different ages. Some work from our laboratory suggests that whereas young infants may process a complex pattern in terms of a series of discrete features, older infants may integrate those same features into a single configuration or gestalt (Younger and Cohen 1986). If that interpretation is correct, one may question whether the younger infants are, in fact, perceiving a face. Furthermore, the frequent reports that younger infants look longer and habituate more slowly to a face or other complex pattern could occur because the younger ones are not seeing a face, but are perceiving a number of independent features. Younger infants may look longer at a complex pattern because they have more to look at. They may habituate more slowly, not because they have poorer memories, but because they have more to remember. From this point of view, one would even predict that under certain circumstances, i.e. when the features remain the same but the overall gestalt changes, older infants actually should habituate to a pattern more slowly than should younger ones. Data supporting this prediction will be presented shortly.

First, it is necessary to consider the evidence for a developmental change in perceptual organization. Support for our view of increased perceptual integration over age comes, in part, from an experiment we conducted on infant perception of angular relations (Cohen and Younger 1984). The angular relations study was an explicit attempt to examine, in one small domain, that infants first process independent features and later integrate those features into more complex patterns. The study was based upon a monograph by Schwartz and Day (1979). In a series of experiments Schwartz and Day had habituated 2- to 4-month-old infants to one angle (or simple shape) and had examined dishabituation to a variety of transformed angles (or shapes). Overall, they found that when the relationship between the lines forming the angle changed (i.e. when the size of the angle changed) the infants dishabituated, but when the orientation of the angle as a whole changed (thus preserving the size of the angle) the infants did not dishabituate. Their conclusion was that the ability to perceive an angle as a whole must be innate.

We took issue with Schwartz and Day's (1979) conclusion on two grounds. First, in some of their experiments the infants would have responded the same way if they had just attended to the orientation of one of the angle's line segments. Second, and more generally, it was quite possible, based upon evidence from other investigators, that infants younger than 2 months of age might not have responded in the same way as Schwartz and Day's infants.

To test these ideas further we designed the experiment shown in Fig. 9.2. Six- and 14-week-old infants were tested with a procedure and apparatus identical to that used by Schwartz and Day (1979). However, in our study the stimuli were slightly different. We varied both the orientation of particular line segments and the size of the angle.

Half the subjects were presented with the stimuli shown on the top line, the other half with the stimuli shown on the bottom line. In comparison to the habituation stimulus the first test stimulus was familiar in both angle and line orientation (A_FO_F); the second was familiar in angle but novel in line orientation (A_FO_N), etc. If infants were processing the angle, they should dishabituate to the *third* and *fourth* test stimuli, but not to the first two. If they were processing the orientation of the lines but not the relationship between the lines (i.e. the angle), they should dishabituate to the *second* and *fourth* items but not to the first and third. Results for the 6- and 14-week-olds are

Habituation   **Test**

A_FO_F A_FO_N A_NO_F A_NO_N

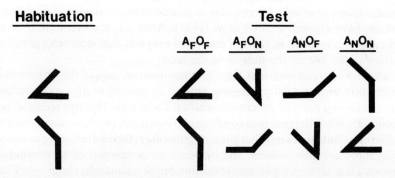

Fig. 9.2 Design of the Cohen and Younger (1984) angular relations experiment. [Reproduced by kind permission of Ablex, Norwood, NJ.]

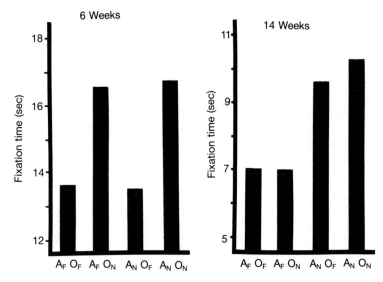

Fig. 9.3 Test Results for 6- and 14-week-old infants on the Cohen and Younger (1984) angular relations experiment. [Reproduced by kind permission of Ablex, Norwood, NJ.]

shown in Fig. 9.3. As one can see, the 14-week-olds performed as had Schwartz and Day's (1979) subjects. They dishabituated only when the angle changed. The 6-week-olds, on the other hand, seemed to ignore the angle and dishabituated only to a change in line orientation.

Thus, contrary to Schwartz and Day's (1979) assumption about the innateness of the perception of angularity, our subjects clearly showed a change over age from processing the separate line segments to processing the relationship between the segments. I am not asserting from results such as these that infant perceptual development undergoes a change from processing raw sensations or absolute properties of stimuli to processing relational ones as some have claimed (Antell *et al.* 1985). After all, the orientation of a particular line segment is, itself, a relational property that depends upon the position of the line on the slide or in the room.

I also am not claiming that there is some kind of unique developmental transition in information-processing around $1\frac{1}{2}$ months of age, a transition from processing parts to processing wholes. To be sure, that age seems to be appropriate when the task is to combine two independent line segments into a single angle. But angles or other simple figures may, themselves, serve as parts of yet more complex wholes, and evidence on perception of these wholes suggests a similar developmental transition but at a somewhat later age. For example, as I mentioned earlier, there seems to be a development trend in the ability of infants to perceive a face as a whole. Estimates of the age at which the

A   B   C

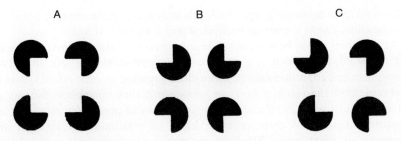

Fig. 9.4 Examples of stimuli similar to those used by Bertenthal *et al.* (1980) to examine infant perception of subjective contours. Pattern A produces the illusion of a square. Patterns B and C do not, even though they contain the same four simple forms as A.

switch occurs from processing separate facial features to processing the entire facial configuration vary depending upon the nature of the procedure and stimuli shown to the infants. However, there seems to be reasonable consensus for a transition somewhere between two and four months of age (see Maurer (1985) for an excellent review of this literature).

Another example of a part–whole transition has been reported in studies of infant perception of subjective contours or Kanizza illusions (Bertenthal *et al.* 1980). In these illusions non-existent contours can be seen that are totally dependent upon the arrangement of simple two-dimensional forms. Therefore perception of the illusion requires the ability to integrate information across these forms, a task that, from our point of view, should be more difficult than perceiving the individual forms themselves. Figure 9.4 illustrates the types of stimuli used by Bertenthal *et al.* in their study of infant perception of subjective contours.

Pattern A produces the illusion. As an adult, one clearly sees a white square superimposed over four black circles. One even can discern the apparent, but non-existent, contour of the square against the white background. On the other hand, neither patterns B nor C, which contain the same forms as A, but rotated in different directions, produce the illusory square. The question Bertenthal *et al.* (1980) raised was at what age infants also could perceive that square. At 7 months of age, infants who were habituated to pattern A dishabituated to both B and C. But those who were habituated to C, only dishabituated to A. That pattern of results would be consistent with the view that pattern A was somehow special for the 7-month-olds, and that the infants could perceive the illusion. A hint of the same effect was found for the 5-month-olds, but it was not nearly as compelling.

If one combines these results with the abundant evidence that well before 5 months of age infants can perceive the individual forms, then as a whole the evidence lends additional support to the information-processing view that infants go from processing separate forms to processing the interrelationships among those forms sometime between 4 and 7 months of age.

At this point it may be worthwhile to summarize the main points covered so far. First, I have been arguing that developmental changes in infant perception and cognition may be more closely related to *what* infants process and remember than to *how easily* or *permanently* they remember. Second, at all ages infants seem to be sensitive to some types of perceptual relations; an important task is to discover what kinds of relational information are available at what ages. Third, a recurring developmental trend keeps appearing, from an ability to process independent parts to an ability to process some higher order integration of those parts. This constructivist trend appears at different ages, and items that serve as a perceptual 'whole' at one age may serve as only a 'part' of some more elaborate 'whole' at a subsequent age.

So far my discussion of developmental changes in infant information-processing has dealt primarily with infants' perception and memory of relatively simple, black-and-white, two-dimensional line drawings of forms or patterns. Even most of the face literature is based upon infants' reactions to black-and-white drawings of schematic faces. While it might be agreed that infant habituation and memory *per se* are not necessarily good examples of cognitive activity, it might also be argued that neither is the processing of simple two-dimensional patterns. Most people, however, would agree that concept acquisition and category formation do fall within the generally accepted domain of cognition. The remainder of this chapter will be a discussion of recent attempts to examine infants' categorization ability. As the discussion proceeds, we shall discover that we inevitably will be led back to a consideration of the perception of independent vs. interrelated features.

The essence of a concept or category is that one treats as equivalent items that are clearly discriminably different. Thus robins and ostriches are both birds; a high chair and a bean bag chair are both chairs, etc., but one has no trouble distinguishing a robin from an ostrich or a high chair from a bean bag. Much of our recent research effort has been directed toward an examination of the conditions under which infants, like older children and adults, also are able to form categories. As we have shown several times in our research, it is possible to modify the standard habituation procedure to examine infant acquisition of perceptual categories (e.g. Cohen and Younger 1983). Instead of presenting a single stimulus during habituation, all one needs to do is present a series of different stimuli, all of which belong to a single class or category. If infants habituate to the series and then do not dishabituate to a novel member of the class, but do dishabituate to a non-member, one has evidence of categorization.

A case in point would be the study we ran on infants' categorization of toy stuffed animals (Cohen and Caputo 1978). Seven-month-old infants were randomly assigned to one of three groups. During the habituation phase of the experiment, those infants in the 'same group' were repeatedly shown a colour slide of a single stuffed animal. Those in the 'changing group' were shown different slides on each trial, but the pictures were always examples of stuffed animals. Finally, those in the 'objects group' also received slides that changed from trial to trial, but there was no obvious way to group the pictures into any single category. Thus they would see a toy car, a ball, a stuffed animal, a telephone, etc. In the subsequent test phase all three groups were shown a novel stuffed animal, one they had not seen before, and a totally different picture such as a rattle.

The results for both habituation and test phases were quite revealing and are shown in Figs 9.5 and 9.6. Considering habituation first, as one can see in Fig. 9.5, looking times for the same and changing groups habituated rapidly, while very little habituation occurred for the objects group. Our interpretation was that for both the same and changing groups the set of slides during the habituation phase included some invariant property that the infants could process and remember. For the same group it could have been one or more specific features of the particular stuffed animal they had seen. For the changing group the specific features varied from trial to trial; only the category remained invariant. Thus those infants probably habituated to the more abstract category of 'stuffed animal in general'. In contrast to these two groups, both specific features and general categories varied from trial to trial

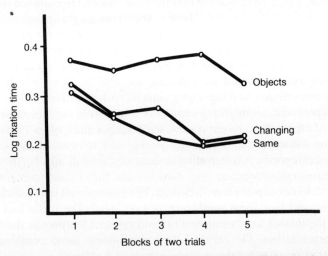

Fig. 9.5   Habituation phase of Cohen and Caputo (1978) stuffed animal experiment. [Reproduced from Younger and Cohen (1985) by kind permission of Academic Press, New York.]

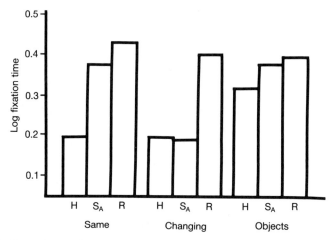

Fig. 9.6 Test phase of Cohen and Caputo (1978). H, S_A, and R refer to last habituation trial, novel stuffed animal, and rattle, respectively. [Reproduced from Younger and Cohen (1985) by kind permission of Academic Press, New York.]

for the objects group; there was little that remained invariant enough for this group to process and remember, so there was no basis for habituation.

Our interpretation of the different information available for the three groups was confirmed by the results of the test phase. As shown in Fig. 9.6, infants in the same group dishabituated both to the novel stuffed animal and to the rattle, a pattern indicating that they had indeed remembered something about a specific stuffed animal. Those in the changing group dishabituated to the rattle but not to the novel stuffed animal, indicating that for them the novel stuffed animal in the test was somehow familiar or equivalent to the other stuffed animals they had seen before (i.e. it was perceived as a member of the same category). As would be expected, the objects group which had not habituated continued looking a long time at both test items.

This experiment, along with a number of others from our laboratory as well as those of others (for a recent review, see Younger and Cohen 1985), present convincing evidence that infants as young as 7 months of age can form perceptual categories. As interesting as these experiments may be, they are still only demonstration studies; they demonstrate that infants can form categories, but do not explain how they do it. For example, all the stuffed animals were furry and had some semblance of eyes, while the rattle had neither. Perhaps the infants were using one or both types of features as the basis for their categorization. Or perhaps they were using some combination of features that represented the stuffed animals as a class.

As was the case a decade earlier in the study of infant memory, it now became important to examine the literature on adult categorization to obtain clues as to the cognitive processes involved in infant categorization. It quickly became clear that to examine these processes one had to use artificially constructed objects or pictures so that the types and combinations of features present in the category items could be manipulated.

For instance, one of the central issues in the adult categorization literature is whether individuals represent a category in terms of some summary representation of 'prototype'. Assuming some type of prototype is formed, a related question is whether it is based upon the average values of the features experienced or the most frequently occurring values. Strauss (1979, 1981) examined these same issues in his studies of 10-month-old infants. He familiarized infants to a series of line drawings of faces. The facial features such as nose length, separation between the eyes, etc. varied from face to face. The questions he asked were whether infants, like adults, would be able to form a prototype and, if they did, would the prototype be based upon the average of the most frequent values of the features they had seen? His results clearly indicated that 10-month-old infants formed an *average* prototype and responded to that prototype as highly familiar even though they had never seen it during familiarization. Recently Younger (1985) has found that 10-month-old infants form average prototypes when viewing line drawings of animals. And Bomba and Sequiland (1983) and Younger and Gotlieb (1987) have both found that infants as young as three months of age will form prototypes of simple dot patterns.

Another research issue taken from the adult literature is whether infants can learn 'ill-defined' categories. Most object categories cannot be defined in terms of a single feature or set of features that all category members share. For example, not all chairs have backs or four legs. Not all birds can sing or fly. As Rosch (1978) has argued, most categories are constructed from items that have sets of partially overlapping features. Those items whose features overlap the most are considered better members of the category than those whose features overlap less. Thus for adults a desk chair is considered a 'better' example of a chair than a bean bag, and a robin is a 'better' example of a bird than an ostrich. Husaim and Cohen (1982), using line drawings of animals, found that 10-month-old infants could form an ill-defined category and could differentiate between two categories even though both were ill-defined.

A final adult issue we have examined extensively with infants is whether the features infants use in category formation are processed independently or in relationship to one another (Younger and Cohen 1983, 1986). Although we did not fully realize it when we began this type of research, the issue we were raising was practically identical to the one raised in the angle study presented earlier in this chapter. To test for infants' sensitivity to correlational information artificial animals were constructed such as the ones shown in Fig. 9.7.

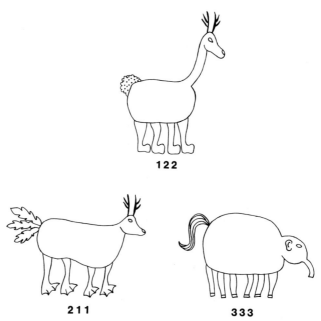

122

211   **333**

Fig. 9.7 Examples of stimuli used in the correlated attribute experiments. [Reproduced from Younger and Cohen (1983) by kind permission of the Society for Research in Child Development, Chicago, IL.]

As one can see from this figure, the animals varied on three attributes, type of body, tail, and feet. Four-, 7-, and 10-month-old infants were habituated to one of the two sets shown in Table 9.1. Inspection of set A, for example, shows that two of the three attributes (*a* and *b*) were correlated. That is to say, whenever *a* had a value of 1, *b* had a value of 1; and whenever *a* had a value of 2, *b* had a value of 2. The third attribute, *c* was uncorrelated with either *a* or *b*. In the test, infants were shown an animal that maintained the correlation (C), one that violated the correlation (U), and a totally novel animal with different features (N).

Our argument was that if infants had processed independent features, across examples, they would have received an equal number of 1's and 2's for each attribute and, therefore, should not dishabituate either to C or U since both were constructed from those same 1's and 2's. The infants should dishabituate to N, however, since N contained novel features, 3's. On the other hand, if infants had processed the correlation between features, they should dishabituate to U as well as to N, since U constituted a new arrangement that violated the previously experienced correlation.

Our results are shown in Fig. 9.8. Comparing first the data for 4- and 10-month-old infants, one can see that the findings were strongly supportive of

Table 9.1   *Habituation and test stimuli for experiment 2*
[*from Younger and Cohen 1986*]

Stimuli	Set A	Set B
	a b c	*a b c**
Habituation		
1	1 1 1	1 2 1
2	1 1 2	1 2 2
3	2 2 1	2 1 1
4	2 2 2	2 1 2
Test		
Correlated	2 2 2	2 1 1
Uncorrelated	2 1 1	2 2 2
Novel	3 3 3	3 3 3

* Values 1, 2, and 3, respectively, for each of the three attributes, *a*, *b*, and *c*, were as follows: giraffe, cow, and elephant body; feathered, fluffy, and horse tail; webbed, club, and hoofed foot.

the information-processing theory mentioned earlier. Both ages habituated, but they responded very differently in the test. The 4-month-olds were down to both C and U, suggesting that they had processed independent features. In contrast, the 10-month-olds were down only to C, indicating that they took into account the correlation among the features. Thus we had found another instance of a transition from processing independent features to processing the relationship among features; this time that transition is occurring at some point between 4 and 10 months of age.

The most intriguing data came from the 7-month-olds. These infants neither habituated nor showed any differential responding in the test. This is such a remarkable and unusual finding that we felt it necessary to attempt a replication with another group of 7-month-olds. Both the original data (solid squares) and the replication data (open circles) are shown in Fig. 9.8. As one can see, the results from both studies agree. For some reason the 7-month-olds were having more trouble with this task than either the 4- or 10-month-olds.

One implication of this 'habituation to no habituation to habituation again' developmental shift already has been alluded to in this chapter. Unless one believes that 7-month-olds have temporarily lost their memories one must conclude that rate of habituation depends upon factors in addition to memory, factors such as the type of information-processing available at different ages. Our interpretation, based upon these results as well as upon

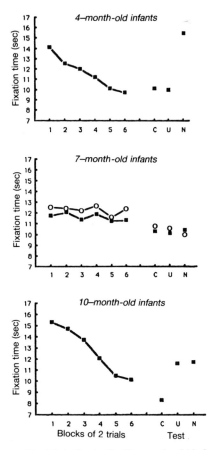

Fig. 9.8 Habituation and test data for 4-, 7-, 10-month-old infants from experiment 2 of the Younger and Cohen (1986) experiment. [Reproduced by local permission of the Society for Research in Child Development, Chicago, IL.]

studies on pattern perception, was that infants at 7 months of age could perceive individual animals as wholes or units and thus were sensitive to correlations or relations among features, but that they could not go beyond the individual animal to use this correlational information in the formation of categories. Thus for 7-month-olds, each of the line drawings was a unique animal. The task for them was not unlike that for the unrelated objects group in the stuffed animal experiment described earlier.

Two additional experiments supported this view. Since we had used a fixed number of habituation trials in these studies, one could argue that 7-month-olds may have poorer memories than 10-month-olds. If we had given the 7-month-olds a greater number of trials, perhaps they too would have habituated and responded in the test like their older counterparts. So in one experiment we *forced* 7-month-olds to habituate by running them to a criterion of habituation rather than for a fixed number of trials. If all they needed was additional familiarization during habituation, they should now respond like 10-month-olds in the test. The results did not support this conclusion. Instead, when forced to habituate, the 7-month-olds appeared to 'regress' and process only independent features. They responded just like our 4-month-olds, dishabituating only to the novel test animal, N.

In the other study we simplified the task to see if 7-month-olds would now respond to the correlation. We ran essentially the same study shown in Table 9.1 except that attribute c also was correlated with a and b. In other words, the habituation phase was reduced to seeing repeated examples of 1 1 1 and 2 2 2. Under these conditions, in which the 7-month-olds only had to remember two discrete animals, they dishabitated to both the U and C test items; that is, they *were* able to respond to the relationship among the features.

Additional studies have replicated the results described above. We also have shown that 10-month-olds acquired categories more readily if the features were correlated than if they were not, and that the 10-month-olds did not respond to the C test stimulus as more familiar simply because they saw it previously during habituation (see Cohen and Younger (1983) or Younger and Cohen (1985) for reviews of this literature).

It is clear from the evidence cited above that infants like adults can form categories and that they do so in a very sophisticated manner. It also is apparent that the developmental change evident in pattern perception from processing independent features to processing more abstract relations among features applies to the formation of categories as well.

It may be noted that the bulk of evidence for infant categorization has come from infants 7 months of age or older. This does not mean that younger infants are incapable of forming categories. In fact, as was mentioned with respect to some of the prototype studies, there is growing evidence for categorization (or something like categorization) with infants as young as 3 or 4 months of age. However, it is interesting to note that with 3- or 4-month-olds the types of categories learned were themsleves simple features, such as the objective shape of a single object (Caron *et al.* 1979), or they were simple forms constructed from patterns of dots (Bomba and Siqueland 1983; Younger and Gotlieb 1987). Thus, what may vary over age is not the ability to categorize in general, but the ability to use certain types of information in the formation of categories. If the young infant's perception is restricted to simple feature like information, then his categories should represent different examples of those features, and if the older infant can integrate those features into more complex objects and events, then his categories should represent classes of those objects and events.

These demonstrations of early categorization reinforce the view that the young human infant is a cognitive organism. But before one becomes too enamoured of the cognitive sophistication of the infant, one should examine the animal literature on categorization, as has been done in the case of habituation and memory. While I know of no demonstrations of categorization in simple neural preparations, considerable evidence has been accumulated by Herrnstein and others on the ability of pigeons to categorize. Both Herrnstein (1982, 1984) and Lea and Harrison (1978) also have reported what appears to be pigeons' sensitivity to correlational information. More recently, Kluender and Diehl (1986) have found categorization by Japanese quail. Lea (1984) goes so far as to assume that even responses to simple colours or line orientations by the pigeon may be considered more parsimoniously as instances of concept formation than as simpler forms of discrimination. Thus, once again, we seem to be drawn to the conclusion that categorization, like habituation and memory, is a basic adaptive mechanism available to a wide variety of species. That does not minimize the importance of categorization or its utility in cognitive activity. It just suggests for those of us interested in the early development of cognition that what is remembered and categorized may be a more critical developmental question than at what age infants can first remember or categorize anything.

In summary, in this chapter I raised the question of what changes and what does not change in infant cognitive development. I have attempted to illustrate how an answer to that question requires more than an examination of infants *per se* in that both the adult human and animal literatures can provide important clues to the processes and limitations of infant cognition. The ubiquity of memory and categorization across species suggests that these abilities may be better considered as basic adaptive mechanisms than as anything uniquely human. One may or may not assert that memory and categorization represent true cognitive abilities, but the resolution of that issue may turn out to be more semantic than real.

The central question for a developmental psychologist is what changes over age. One answer to that question seems to be that it is the way information is processed. The ability to turn off, or habituate to, irrelevant stimuli, to learn and remember stimuli that have been experienced previously, and to group similar stimuli together into a common class or category undoubtedly all are essential to an organism's survival and probably are available to an infant at birth or even before birth. However, we and others are finding that it is the perceived nature of the stimuli ignored, remembered, or grouped together that changes dramatically during the first year of life. Important goals for developmental psychologists should be to identify the types of stimuli or, perhaps more appropriately, the types of perceptual and cognitive relations infants at different ages can process, and to try to derive a developmental taxonomy of those relations. Then, perhaps, we shall all be in a better position to understand how infants at different ages come to perceive and interpret objects and events in the world around them.

Acknowledgements

The research presented in this chapter was supported in part by grant HD-15035 from the National Institute of Child Health and Human Development.

References

Antell, S. G., Caron, A. J., and Myers, R. S. (1985). Perception of relational invariants by newborns. *Developmental Psychology*, **21**, 942–8.

Bertenthal, B. I., Campos, J. J., and Haith, M. M. (1980). Development of visual organization: the perception of subjective contours. *Child Development*, **51**, 1072–80.

Bomba, P. C. and Siqueland, E. R. (1983). The nature and structure of infant form categories. *Journal of Experimental Child Psychology*, **35**, 294–328.

Caron, A. J., Caron, R. F., and Carlson, V. R. (1979). Infant perception of the invariant shape of an object vaying in slant. *Child Development*, **50**, 716–21.

Cohen, L. B. and Caputo, N. F. (1978). Instructing infants to respond to perceptual categories. Paper presented at the Midwestern Psychological Association Convention, Chicago, IL.

—— and Gelber, E. R. (1975). Infant visual memory. In *Infant perception: from sensation to cognition: basic visual processes. (Vol. 1)*, (ed. L. Cohen and P. Salapatek), pp. 347–403. Academic Press, New York.

—— and Younger, B. A. (1983). Perceptual categorization in the infant. In *New trends in conceptual representation* (ed. E. Scholnick), pp. 197–220. Lawrence Erlbaum Associates, Hillsdale, NJ.

—— and —— (1984). Infant perception of angular relations. *Infant Behavior and Development*, **7**, 37–47.

—— and —— (1985). Developmental change in infant categorization. Paper presented at the meeting of the Society for Research in Child Development, Toronto, Canada.

Fagan, J. F., III. (1973). Infants' delayed recognition memory and forgetting. *Journal of Experimental Child Psychology*, **16**, 424–50.

Herrnstein, J. R. (1982). Stimuli and the texture of experience. *Neuroscience and Biobehavioral Reviews*, **6**, 105–17.

—— (1984). Objects, categories, and discriminative stimuli. In *Animal cognition*, (ed. H. L. Roitblat, T. G. Bever, and H. S. Terrace), pp. 253–61. Lawrence Erlbaum Associates, Hillsdale, NJ.

Husaim, J. S. and Cohen, L. B. (1982). Infant learning of ill-defined categories. *Merrill-Palmer Quarterly*, **27**, 443–56.

Jouen, F. (1984). Visual-vestibular interactions in infancy. *Infant Behavior and Development*, **7**, 135–45.

Kluender, K. R. and Diehl, R. L. (1986). Japanese quail categorize[d] across talker and allophonic variation. *Journal of the Acoustical Society of America Supplement 1*, **80**, 5110.

Lea, S. E. G. (1984). In what sense do pigeons learn concepts? In *Animal cognition*, (ed.

H. L. Roitblat, T. G. Bever, and H. S. Terrace), pp. 263–76. Lawrence Erlbaum Associates, Hillsdale, NJ.

—— and Harrison, S. N. (1978). Discrimination of polymorphous stimulus sets by pigeons. *Quarterly Journal of Experimental Psychology*, **30**, 521–37.

Madison, L. S. *et al.* (1986). Fetal response decrement: true habituation? *Journal of Developmental and Behavioral Pediatrics*, **7**, 14–20.

Martin, R. M. (1973). Long-term effects of stimulus familiarization. Paper presented at the meeting of the Society for Research in Child Development, Philadelphia, PA.

Maurer, D. (1985). Infants' perception of facedness. In *Social perception in infants*, (ed. T. M. Field and N. A. Fox), pp. 73–100. Ablex, Norwood, NJ.

Medin, D. L. and Schaffer, M. M. (1978). A context theory of classification learning. *Psychological Review*, **85**, 207–38.

Olson, G. M. and Sherman, T. (1983). Attention, learning, and memory in infants. In *Handbook of child psychology. (Vol. 2) Infancy and developmental biology*, (ed. P. H. Mussen), pp. 1001–80. John Wiley, New York.

Rosch, E. (1978). Principles of categorization. In *Cognition and categorization*, (ed. E. Rosch and B. Lloyd), pp. 27–48. Lawrence Erlbaum Associates, Hillsdale, NJ.

Schwartz, M. and Day, R. H. (1979). Visual shape perception in early infancy. *Monographs of theSociety for Research in Child Development*, **44**, (7, Serial No. 182).

Sherman, T. (1981). Categorization skills in infants. Paper presented at the meeting of the Society for Research in Child Development, Boston, MA.

Slater, A., Morison, V., and Rose, D. (1983). Locus of habituation in the human newborn. *Perception*, **12**, 593–8.

Strauss, M. S. (1979). Abstraction of prototypical information by adults and 10-month-old infants. *Journal of Experimental Psychology: Human Learning and Memory*, **5**, 618–35.

—— (1981). Infant memory of prototypical information. Paper presented at the meeting of the Society for Research in Child Development, Boston, MA.

Tighe, T. and Leaton, R. N. (ed.). (1976). *Habituation: perspectives from child development, animal behavior and neurophysiology*. Lawrence Erlbaum Associates, Hillsdale, NJ.

Younger, B. A. (1985). The segregation of items into categories by ten-month-old infants. *Child Development*, **56**, 1574–83.

—— and Cohen, L. B. (1983). Infant perception of correlations among attributes. *Child Development*, **54**, 858–67.

—— and —— (1985). How infants form categories. In *The psychology of learning and motivation: advances in research and theory*, (ed. G. Bower), pp. 211–47. Academic Press, New York.

—— and —— (1986). Developmental change in infants' perception of correlations among attributes. *Child Development*, **57**, 803–15.

—— and Gotlieb, S. J. (1987). Development of categorization skills: changes in the nature or structure of infant form categories? Paper presented at the meeting of the Society for Research in Child Development, Baltimore, MD.

Discussion, Section C

Origins of physical knowledge

Given the claims based on habituation, rather than on action indices, *Dickinson* said that inferences are made that the infant represents its experience on the level of objects and other features of the physical world: 'As this level of representation has no implications for action, is it appropriate to attribute object representations without direct evidence that they will support actions?'

Thinus-Blanc interjected that, from the viewpoint of habituation studies in animals, she did not think they 'lacked content'. She used habituation in investigations of exploration. Its adaptive value is to reduce the stress of novelty. Equally, in the infant, there is visual exploration and curiosity, and habituation as novelty decreases. There *is* content.

Spelke remarked that she completely agreed: 'The simple exploratory activities we have studied [have] functional significance. In so far as the infant's conceptions guide such activities, those conceptions have functional/behavioural significance as well'. But she went on to say, however: 'I believe the importance of behavioural significance can be overestimated in studies of cognition and cognitive development. For me the most important aspect of human beliefs and thought processes is not that they guide behaviour but that they interact to produce further beliefs: they support inferences. Our experiments with infants ask them, in effect, to make such inferences: they must predict how an array of objects will move, figure out what the unseen parts of an object look like, or infer where an object has gone and what it is doing when it moves fully out of view. To the extent that we obtain evidence for such inferences, I believe we have evidence for underlying conceptions of the world'.

The special importance of motion for infants prompted *Kertesz* to wonder why infants do not use their discriminatory ability of surface pattern to distinguish the unity of objects. *Spelke* distinguished between 'perception' and 'knowledge', the implication being, presumably, that habituation is based on the latter: 'If objects were products of some perceptual function, such as a function that minimized heterogeneity or irregularity as the gestalt psychologists proposed, then one would expect infants to use all the perceptible properties of the surface layout to organize the layout into objects. The fact that the infants do not do this is one reason for suspecting that objects are products of a mechanism of a diffrent kind—a mechanism of thought. . . . We are frequently in situations in which we perceive some property of an object . . . and yet that property is uninformative for us because we do not know its relevance. You may be looking for a stranger who is to meet you at a train, he may be wearing a red carnation, and you may see this. You will not conclude that the person with the red carnation is the person you seek, unless you expect him to be wearing one. Similarly, I suggest, an infant who sees two adjacent objects perceives that they differ in colour, texture, shape, and pattern, and he perceives that the configuration taken as a whole is less regular than the configuration of each object considered alone. Because the infant does not know that objects tend to be uniform in colour, texture, shape, and pattern, however, he does not use these observed properties as information that the two objects are distinct'.

Hinde raised the question of the status of an even earlier age group: 'Does the listing of basic principles imply that experience before three to four months does not matter?' There were two respondents. *Leslie* said that he always had two problems with a question like that: 'First is to understand what is meant by "experience". Sometimes people mean "exposure" which can be determined from the outside; sometimes what is meant is the result of psychological processes which respond to exposure and sometime people just conflate the two. My other problem is with understanding what is meant by "matter"!

'The general goal of cognitive developmental theory is to understand the mechanisms which acquire, or contribute to, the acquisition of knowledge which ordinary adult human beings possess. A principles approach is really about getting the most—in terms of encyclopaedic knowledge and common sense theory—out of whatever exposure history (however ambiguous, incongruous, inconsistent, and arbitrary that would be without principles) an infant may have.

'The fact that solid objects do not cohabit is one of the most regular patterns one is exposed to. Yet if the visual system simply tunes itself to patterns and regularities in information in ambient energy, and if it also has special mechanisms for picking up information from collision events, then is it not a wonder that it never seems to learn the regularity about cohabitation? I think the question of what matters in experience has to be answered in relation to an understanding of the overall learning system, its organization into parts, its tasks and subtasks, and its major computational properties'.

Spelke, in responding to *Hinde*'s question, acknowledged that all evidence suggests a tremendous amount of learning in the first four months: 'Early experiences may, therefore, yield some of the principles about objects we see at four months. . . . To date, however, there have been no studies of the physical conceptions of younger infants, so I can only respond to the question in two ways. First, studies of four-month-old infants are interesting whether or not the capacities are innate, because they still have a great deal to learn. . . . The findings suggest that certain physical conceptions are more basic than others, regardless of their ultimate source. Second, . . . I do not believe that all of the principles are learned, for reasons that have been discussed in the psychological literature on perception (e.g. Koffka 1935) and the philosophical literature on identity. . . . If no such principles guided us from the start, it is utterly mysterious how any of our experiences could inform us that objects were there, such that we could observe them and induce principles governing their behaviour'.

There was considerable interest in philosophical issues raised by the interpretation of infants' perceptions. Thus *Leslie* said that there was no reference to object sorts of types among *Spelke*'s four principles, nor any reference to causal laws constraining possible changes in an object while still being judged by us to retain its identity: 'Such changes have been claimed as core conceptions by philosophers like Wiggins (1980). Do you think infants employ such a principle as well?' *Spelke* offered a very full reply, summarizing Wiggins' views that how one singles out an object and follows it through time depends on what kind of thing one takes the object to be; identity cannot be equated by a general conception of physical object. While acknowledging that the concept of physical object will not provide unique specifications, she nevertheless rejected Wiggins' conclusions: 'There is a core conception, *physical object*, of which sortal concepts such as "table" and "horse" are specific examples, and this conception does the major work of singling out physical bodies and tracing them through time'. If Wiggins' conclusions were valid, then the acquisition of sortal concepts such as 'book' would be a mysterious process: 'There must be some way of apprehending books and following them through time that does not itself depend on an already developed sortal concept. It is reasonable to suppose that a general conception of *physical object* fulfills this function'. She went on to trace the argument through, in terms both of object names and of judgements about object persistence in time, claiming that linguistic usage of sortal terms like 'cups and saucers, nuts and bolts . . . makes sense if the initial conception of physical objects has served as the basis for acquiring sortal terms'. She also argued that 'intuitions about persistence and change concern changes that destroy properties of physical objects; they are just the changes that are relevant to the general conception of physical objects and independent of particular sortal concepts. If we could find a way to ask infants about persistence and change through time, these are the changes I would expect to matter for them'.

Butterworth asked whether we should be referring to 'innate knowledge'— does it presuppose what we set out to explain? 'Perhaps there is information in the world and inate mechanisms for detecting this information which can give rise to knowledge. It is a logical error to confuse "mechanisms" and "knowledge".' *Spelke* replied that, although we often speak about what infants 'know' and the 'origins of knowledge', she saw the real role of cognitive psychology to be the study not of knowledge but of human conceptions: 'In my own work, I suggest that humans come into the world with certain conceptions about what it contains. Whether these conceptions deserve to be called "knowledge" depends on what the world is really like, and on the nature of our encounters with it'.

Perception of causation

Questions arose concerning the *level* of explanation. *Butterworth* said that he liked *Leslie*'s description of an illusion as the outcome of a contradiction between a substantiality and a causality detecting mechanism: 'However, shouldn't you retain the realist vocabulary in describing Michotte's own demonstration? He had *captured* the information at the retina that gives rise to the causal experience, not discovered a new illusion'. In reply, *Leslie* said that a lot of the time Michotte seems to be have been interested in arriving at phenomenological descriptions of perception: 'I'm not sure that Michotte captured the information on the retina as you suggest. It seems to me that to do that you have to give a precise description of the mathematical properties of the intensity array over time that are used to compute the descriptions at the causal level. In other words, you would need a good theory, from the retina upwards, of the input to the module I hypothesize. But even if he had captured this, no amount of realist vocabulary would get around the fact that he had discovered a new and important illusion'.

Spelke also asked about the processing level: 'Does the infant *perceive* your events to be causal or *judge* them to be so? The issue is peripheral vs. central processes, and I have qualms about the idea that any early developing, well-structured domain is of the former kind'. *Leslie* gave a full reply, acknowledging that he shared her qualms: 'However, I think we can ask in what way are the early developing domains structured in perception and structured in thought. I think there are likely to be differences between the two, even when the information involved is the same or highly similar. For example, I think it quite likely that the *cohesion* of an object is calculated by object recognition processes. This does not pre-empt, however, a similar notion being represented in central thought as well and being available to me, for example, to guide my intuitions about distinct objects making up some complex artifact. Given the different computational tasks of perception and central thought, however, the one to give a conceptual identification of input, the other to build conceptual theories about the world, this same notion is likely to be represented in quite different ways at these different levels.

'My answer to the first part of your question, then, would be that probably the infant judges some of my events to be causal because he perceives them to be causal. However, if my proposals about the infant's mental architecture are along the right lines, then while the infant is bound to *perceive* the events that way, he is not bound so to *judge*. There's some freedom to thought that you won't find an entirely modular system. When the capacity for recursive thought (including pretence) and for constructing theories about mind itself develops, yet more freedom is granted'.

Infant categorization

Weiskrantz asked what happens, in the experiment reported with angles in different orientations, if the infant is tilted instead of the lines? *Cohen* said that he had not done that particular experiment; the closest one he knew of was by Jouen (1984) on infant visual–vestibular interactions and responses to line orientation. Two-month-old infants showed some sensitivity to the objective orientation of the lines, and four-month-olds were still more sensitive. Expanding the issue to the general question of objective vs. retinal properties of stimuli, work on shape constancy (Caron *et al.* 1979) and relational visual information (Antell *et al.* 1985) 'suggest that within the limits of their restricted visual acuity, even very young infants are capable of perceiving objective characteristics of patterns or objects'.

The importance of motion for classification in object matching for the chimpanzee was emphasized by *Premack*: 'E.g., we hang fruit from the ceiling, using long strings. An apple is the sample, banana and apple the alternatives. If the apple (sample) and banana are set into motion, about 40 per cent of the time the young ape matches moving apple to moving banana (rather than to unmoving apple). That is, it matches "moving" rather than apple to apple'.

Cohen agreed that such 'functional properties' of objects can play an important role in infant categorization, and movement is certainly a highly salient cue for infants. The question is to specify its precise role: 'It could just act like any other highly salient feature. It could act to highlight and make more salient those features that move as opposed to those that do not move. Of it could act to enhance natural correlations among features that together define an object; i.e. features that move in synchrony tend to represent characteristics of the same object. One can find evidence in the infant literature for all three of these positions. We are planning research that will go into the matter further'.

There was considerable discussion concerned with specifying the determinants and status of categorization. *Sergent* asked whether an attempt had been made to manipulate the physical attributes *within* a putative category to examine what properties were important. A category had to be based on visual similarities in the absence of language or a semantic network. *Cohen* said that both similarities and differences were important. If, for example, all 'dogs' could not be distinguished, one could argue that responding was based solely on primary physical generalization and, therefore, no true category would have been learned: 'In our work we try to distinguish between an infant's response to a new stimulus that could be based in primary stimulus generalization vs. one that would be based upon some higher order equivalence. In fact, we have defined categorization as a recognized equivalence among stimuli, objects, or events that are discriminably different (Cohen and Younger 1983). Operationally, what this means is that in order to demonstrate infant categorization we require both that infants' habituation generalizes to a novel exemplar, but not to a non-exemplar, and that this generalization occurs even though the infants *can* discriminate the novel exemplar from the set of previously seen habituation exemplars. . . . My answer to your question is that, for the reasons cited above, we usually try to make the individual exemplars quite different from one another and therefore we don't manipulate their physical similarity within a category. One study by Strauss (1979) on infant prototype formation did do such a manipulation and found that adults were more sensitive to similarity differences than were infants'.

Premack commented that the formation of a category 'seems a peculiar matter. Shall we suppose that the individual is disposed to detect a certain level of similarity? If we assume this, the categories an individual formed might depend on the exemplars given to him'. *Cohen* responded by agreeing that it is not a well-understood matter. Some people use the term 'equivalence class' instead of category, because equivalence implies substitutability rather than identity: 'It is also true that according to many views of categorization the nature of a category depends upon one's experience with specific examples . . . Older children might have different categories than younger ones. One might then ask why so many of our categories seem to be widely shared rather than idiosyncratic. The answer may lie in part on the overlap of our experiences and in part on the predetermined nature of the features which are both characteristic of objects and events and to which we, as human beings, are sensitive'.

Caramazza pressed the issue, specifically with regard to the experiments reported here: 'What leads you to consider the data you have described (the line drawings of animals) to be relevant to "category" formation?' He saw no particular reason to consider them as category formation or processing. *Cohen* explained that he had only presented a subset of the categorization studies with line drawings, and he could understand the confusion. Other studies in the set were clearer demonstrations of categorization: 'By way of recapitulation, in order to demonstrate infant category formation, we have set the following criteria: (1) that our infants be exposed to multiple exemplars in habituation; (2) that, in a subsequent test, the infants generalize to novel exemplars but not to non-exemplars; and (3) that this generalization occurs even though the infants can discriminate these novel exemplars from the exemplars they received in habituation or training. All three conditions are met in our stuffed animal and other demonstration studies'. But he said that the line drawing studies presented here for illustration only satisfied two of the three conditions. But in earlier research using more varied material (five features, each having a value of 1 or 2, rather than three features), all three conditions were met (Younger and Cohen 1983).

Pearce, not surprisingly, followed up an alternative possibility that had emerged from the pigeon work: 'Is there any evidence which forces the view that children form prototypes over one which asserts that categorization depends upon the formation of multiple memories?' *Cohen* gave a full reply. There was abundant evidence consistent with prototype formation that infants of three to 12 months of age will generalize more to an item they have never seen before if it is a good representative of the category than to an item they have actually seen. The question is why they are doing it. Medin and Schaffer (1978) had the view that each example of a category is remembered individually, and that a new item's membership is determined by its similarity to those previously remembered exemplars. This can fit some of the cases. But there were two lines of evidence from the infant categorization field that argue against the 'exemplar' view: 'First, some evidence, including data from our own correlation attribute studies, suggests that infants have a difficult time remembering more than two or three specific examples, yet they can form prototypes after having seen brief presentations of as many as 14 examples. Furthermore, Sherman (1981) has shown that if infants are forced to remember more than two or three items, they seem to lose the ability to form a prototype. The evidence as a whole seems to indicate that formation of a prototype accompanies incomplete processing of many exemplars, rather than complete processing of only a few. . . .'.

'Second, in one of our own correlation studies with 10-month-old infants (Cohen and Younger 1985) we specifically tested whether the infants were remembering the correlation among subset of features vs. the exemplars as a whole, as Medin and Schaffer (1978) would predict. The stimuli and procedure were the same as that shown in Table 9.1, except that the infants were not habituated to stimulus of *set A* (or stimulus three of *set B*). Under these conditions the correlated test item should be more familiar if infants had processed the correlation between *a* and *b*, whilst the uncorrelated test item should be more familiar if they had processed the exemplars as a whole and were basing their response upon overall similarity. The evidence was unequivocally against the exemplar theory and for the processing of correlations'.

While much of the evidence may still be circumstantial, he said, it seems to be uniformly in support of young infants' ability to form a summary representation or prototype: 'Since this prototype has never been experienced, it must be abstracted or constructed by the infants from what has been experienced. Thus evidence for infant prototype formation also appears to be an additional source of evidence for a constructivistic view of infant perception and cognition.

References

Antell, S. G., Caron, A. J., and Myers, R. S. (1985). Perception of relational invariants by newborns. *Developmental Psychology*, **21**, 942–8.

Caron, A. J., Caron, R. F., and Carlson, V. R. (1979). Infant perception of the invariant shape of an object varying in slant. *Child Development*, **50**, 716–21.

Cohen, L. B. and Younger, B. A. (1983). Perceptual categorization in the infant. In: *New trends in conceptual representation*, (ed. E. Scholnick), pp. 197–220. Lawrence Erlbaum Associates, Hillsdale, N.J.

—— and —— (1985). Developmental change in infant categorization. Paper presented at a meeting of the Society for Research in Child Development, Toronto, Canada.

Jouen, F. (1984). Visual–vestibular interactions in infancy. *Infant bebavior and development*, **7**, 135–45.

Koffka, K. (1935). *Principles of gestalt psychology*. Harcourt, Brace and World, New York.

Medin, D. L. and Schaffer, M. M. (1978). A context theory of classification learning. *Psychological Review*, **85**, 207–38.

Michotte, A. (1962). *The perception of causality*. Methuen, Andover, Hants.

Sherman, T. (1981). Categorization skills in infants. Paper presented at a meeting of the Society for Research in Child Development, Boston, MA.

Strauss, M. S. (1979). Abstraction of prototypical information by adult and 10-month-old infants. *Journal of Experimental Psychology: Human Learning and Memory*, **5**, 618–35.

Wiggins, D. (1980). *Sameness and substance*. Basil Blackwell, Oxford.

Younger, B. A. and Cohen L. B. (1983). Infant perception of correlations among attributes. *Child Development*, **54**, 858–67.

Section D

Implicit processing and intentionality

Editorial to Section D

This set of contributions provides a fresh and powerful experimental approach to some classical issues. One of these is the question of types of awareness, and interestingly this is addressed both on the human and on the animal levels. In one sense, the question is not only is there 'thought without language' but is there cognition without conscious thought? Or, more conservatively, what is the character of cognitive processes, such as memory and discrimination, in the absence of acknowledged awareness, and what would be the functional homologies in animal behaviour? A second issue is how does one address experimentally whether an animal might be said to have a belief and, if so, what is its content. If a non-linguistic animal can be said to have a belief, obviously this cannot be based on an internalized language.

Both of these types of issues are, of course, old and crusty, but the approach summarized here is new. Neuropsychological evidence is reviewed by *Schacter et al.* demonstrating that in certain forms of brain damage a clear and striking dissociation can occur between, on the one hand, a capacity to discriminate or to learn and, on the other, any knowledge by the patients that they possess the specific results of the operation of such capacities. The lack of such knowledge is by no means trivial—the patients may well be severely incapacitated. Nevertheless, it can be shown, for example, that amnesic subjects, who in everyday life show no evidence of being able to form new memories, can actually acquire information and store it, and that the information can be retrieved by appropriate experimental manoeuvres. But the information, when retrieved, is not recognized by the patient as a 'memory'. Similarly, in certain forms of agnosia, a patient may patently fail to recognize objects or faces, and yet it can be readily demonstrated that they 'unknowingly' (to them) possess such evidence. Similarly, some patients rendered blind in parts of their visual field by damage to the visual cortex can nevertheless make visual discriminations in the absence of visual experience, 'blindsight'. *Schacter et al.* muster neuropsychological evidence from a variety of domains on this type of dissociation, showing how such 'implicit' processes can be uncovered by ingenious experimental techniques. They also show that new information can be fed into the implicit level, arguing against such a system consisting merely of old information being temporarily re-activated. They also related implicit processing to theoretical distinctions in the information-processing domain, and speculate about possible neurological bases. Judging from the almost epidemiological character of new evidence now coming forward about implicit processing both in normal and in brain-damaged human subjects, we seem almost to be at a new experimental frontier of an old territory previously only explored anecdotally and allegorically.

Needless to say, workers at the animal level had been approaching the neural bases of memory and perception from quite a different angle. *Horn* presents some of the experimental evidence that he and his colleagues have gathered over many years on the neural mechanism of one form of rapid and early learning, namely 'imprinting'. This makes an exciting new and important frontier in its own right. But from the point of view of this volume, what is splendid is the emerging convergence between dissociations seen at the animal level between multiple types of memory systems and the dissociation between 'implicit' and 'explicit' processing seen at the human level—and, moreover, the hope of identifying the underlying neural circuitry of these dissociations. Thus the difference between the acquisition of stable discriminatory habits and 'recognition' or 'familiarity' appears to have a clear neurological basis both in birds and in mammals, although the precise anatomical homologies between them remain to be worked out. At this level of argument, the cross-fertilization between work at the human and animal levels is nurturing several fruitful lines.

The debate about 'thoughtful' or 'rational' processes in animals is also ancient. *Dickinson* develops a closely reasoned dissection of some of the logical questions that surround intentionality and beliefs in animals and advances experimental evidence to assist in decisions at critical points. He deliberately remains at the level of conditioning, where there can be the *appearance* of intentionality but where the numbers of factors in the formulation can be kept within manageable limits. He shows how, both in classical and in instrumental conditioning, the mere appearance of 'intentionality' is not only inadequate but can be seriously misleading; there are forms of such behaviour that can be handled entirely without any such assumption. He nevertheless concludes that some examples of simple instrumental conditioning do support an intentional characterization. He does so on the basis of empirical evidence deliberately designed to address this issue, and, aside from the skillfulness of the experimental construction, the approach is a departure from more general and more familiar dissections from the armchair. Indeed, as he argues, in any particular case of a behavioural episode the decision cannot be made in advance on *a priori* grounds, but has to be put to a sophisticated experimental test. Such skillful experimental dissection is perhaps more commonly put at the service of a reductionist exercise, but there is a thoughtful account as to why entertaining an intentional stance might be pragmatically and theoretically helpful. What emerges from the debate and the discussion is the realization of an experimental approach to a conclusion, which, if accepted, demands and reinforces the assumption of beliefs and purposeful 'rational' states in animals that cannot be based on internalized linguistic systems. If they cannot be based on language, all the more reason why it is challenging to consider a non-linguistic mode of representation that would provide a common link between speaking and non-speaking creatures or even between speaking and non-speaking modes within creatures that possess language.

10

Access to consciousness: dissociations between implicit and explicit knowledge in neuropsychological syndromes

DANIEL L. SCHACTER, MARY PAT McANDREWS, AND MORRIS MOSCOVITCH

Neuropsychological analyses of cognition rely heavily on observations concerning the preserved and impaired abilities of brain-damaged patients. Perhaps the most striking and important lesson that has been learned from neuropsychological investigation of such patients is that specific cognitive functions can be disrupted selectively. For example, patients with lesions restricted to specific regions of the left hemisphere are typically impaired on various linguistic tasks and are unimpaired on spatial tasks, whereas the opposite is true of patients with lesions restricted to specific regions of the right hemisphere; damage to particular areas within the left hemisphere impairs certain linguistic functions and spares others; patients with lesions to the hippocampus and medial temporal regions are severely amnesic for recent events yet perform normally on tests of intelligence, perception, and language. Many other similar dissociations could be cited, and they have been used by neuropsychologists from the nineteenth century onward in attempts to fractionate cognition into isolable components or subsystems.

During the past decade or so, a growing number of neuropsychological studies have provided evidence of a dissociation that is somewhat different from the sort of dissociations noted above. The general form of this dissociation is similar across a variety of tasks and patient groups. A patient with a particular lesion and corresponding cognitive impairment is asked to perform a task that requires direct or explicit use of his impaired function; as expected, performance is extremely poor. The patient is then asked to perform another task that also taps the impaired function, but in an indirect or implicit manner. Now, the patient's performance may be quite good—in some cases entirely normal—even though he does not have conscious access to the knowledge required to perform the task. Variants of this striking dissociation—normal or near-normal knowledge together with severely impaired explicit knowledge—have been observed in patients with disorders of memory, language, visual perception, facial recognition, reading, and other cognitive functions.

The purposes of this chapter are to review evidence concerning dissociations between implicit and explicit knowledge in various neuropsychological syndromes, to discuss relevant empirical and conceptual issues, and to delineate the theoretical implications of the observed phenomena. It is our contention that the dissociations to be discussed in this chapter have important implications for understanding the relations among cognition, language, and consciousness both in normal and in brain-damaged populations.

The remainder of the chapter consists of four main sections. In the first, we review the evidence concerning dissociations between implicit and explicit expressions of knowledge in a variety of neuropsychological syndromes. In the second, we consider more closely the nature of and relations among the various phenomena described in the former section, and pay particular attention to the criteria used to assess patients' 'conscious awareness' of different types of information. In the third, we consider possible theoretical accounts of the reported dissociations and, in the fourth, we outline a model of implicit/explicit dissociations.

Before considering the relevant evidence, some brief remarks concerning our terminology should be made. In this chapter, implicit knowledge refers to knowledge that is expressed in performance without subjects' phenomenal awareness that they possess it, whereas explicit knowledge refers to expressed knowledge that subjects are phenomenally aware that they possess. We sometimes use the phrase 'failure to gain access to consciousness' to describe those situations in which implicit knowledge is expressed in the absence of explicit knowledge. Although the exact definition and assessment of implicit knowledge differs in the various clinical and experimental situations that we consider, the emphasis in all cases is on patients' lack of reflective awareness of knowledge that is revealed in task performance.

Implicit/explicit dissociations: a survey

We now examine evidence for dissociations between implicit and explicit knowledge in six neuropsychological conditions: amnesia, blindsight, prosopagnosia, dyslexia, aphasia, and hemi neglect. We then note briefly additional relevant observations that have been made in anosognosia, visual agnosia, and split-brain patients. Since we will be considering a wide variety of phenomena in diverse patient groups, it should be stated at the outset that we are aware that some of these phenomena may turn out to be related to one another only superficially. It will be evident to the reader that certain phenomena represent clearer and more compelling instances of implicit/ explicit dissociations than do others. We have deliberately cast a rather wide net, however, because we think it is important to bring together as much *potentially* relevant evidence as possible. There have only been a few prior attempts to relate the various phenomena discussed here to one another (e.g. Marcel 1983; Schacter 1987; Weiskrantz 1977, 1980), and no detailed, comprehensive treatments exist. We would rather err by including some examples that in the end may not be genuine implicit/explicit dissociations than by omitting possibly relevant phenomena.

Amnesia

Amnesic patients suffer from a severe and selective inability to remember recent experiences and to learn various types of new information, despite preservation of most perceptual, linguistic, and intellectual skills. Lesions to either the medial temporal or diencephalic regions of the brain are typically necessary to produce a full-blown amnesic syndrome, although the critical damage can be produced by any number of aetiologies, including encephalitis, bilateral infarction, ruptured aneurysms, Korsakoff's disease, head injury, and others (for a review, see Hirst 1982; Moscovitch 1982; Schacter and Crovitz 1977; Squire and Cohen 1984; Weiskrantz 1985).

Amnesic patients' striking inability to remember recent experiences across even brief retention intervals (i.e. minutes) is usually revealed by laboratory tests that require *explicit* remembering, such as free recall, cued recall, and recognition. On these tests, subjects are instructed to deliberately 'think back' to a specific study episode and to produce information that they remember from the episode (recall), or to indicate whether they remember that a particular test item had been presented during a prior study episode (recognition).

Despite amnesic patients' poor performance on tests of explicit memory, it has been known for some time that they show implicit memory for recent experiences. For example, in one of Korsakoff's (1889) original papers on alcoholic amnesia, he described a patient who had been given an electrical shock and was later exposed to a case that contained the shock apparatus. Although this patient did not explicitly remember any shock experience, when he saw the case '. . . he told me that I probably came to electrify him, and meanwhile I knew well that he had only learned to know that machine during his illness' (1889, p. 512). Other clinical observations of this kind have been reported (e.g. Claparède 1951; MacCurdy 1928), but only recently have the implicit memory abilities of the amnesic patient been subject to careful experimental studies. These studies have shown that amnesic patients perform relatively well—and sometimes normally—on a variety of implicit memory tests in which subjects are not required to think back to any prior episode, and conscious or explicit recollection of previous experiences is not necessary for successful performance. Since much of this evidence has been reviewed elsewhere (e.g. Cohen 1984; Moscovitch 1982, 1984; Parkin 1982; Schacter 1985; Schacter and Graf 1986*b*; Shimamura 1986; Squire and Cohen 1984), we do not provide a detailed review here. The point we wish to highlight is that amnesic patients show implicit memory for recent experiences across a wide variety of tasks and materials.

Perhaps the earliest and best known example of implicit memory in amnesic patients is the research on motor skill learning in the densely amnesic patient H.M. reported by Milner and Corkin and their colleagues (Corkin 1965, 1968; Milner 1962; Milner *et al.* 1968). They found that H.M. showed excellent learning and retention of tasks such as pursuit rotor and mirror tracing across trials and sessions. Each time he performed one of these tasks, however, H.M. failed to recollect any previous experience with it. Similiar findings of preserved motor skill learning in other densely amnesic patients have been reported (e.g. Eslinger and Damasio 1985; Starr and Phillips 1970). It has also been demonstrated that amnesic patients can learn various other kinds of skills that are acquired gradually across multiple trials. For example, Cohen and Squire (1980) and Moscovitch *et al.* (1986) used a task introduced by Kolers (1975) which involves reading of mirror inverted script. Normal subjects become progressively faster at this task with practice. Both Cohen and Squire (1980) and Moscovitch *et al.* (1986) reported that amnesic patients acquired the skill of reading the transformed script at about the same rate as did control subjects. The amnesics, however, performed poorly on tests that required explicit remembering of the prior occurrence of the target materials. Nissen and Bullemer (1987) used a serial learning task in which subjects were exposed to a spatial array of lights and simply had to press a key beneath a light when it was activated. They found that when lights were activated according to a repeated serial pattern, both amnesic patients and control subjects responded more quickly than when a random pattern was used. Amnesic patients learned this task at a normal rate despite their severe impairment when asked to remember explicitly the sequence of lights in the repeating pattern.

Although the foregoing studies and others like them (e.g. Brooks and Baddeley 1976; Kinsbourne and Wood 1975; Martone *et al.* 1984) demonstrate implicit retention on skill learning tasks that are acquired gradually and rather slowly, a good deal of recent research has documented normal implicit memory for single episodes in amnesic patients. This line of research was initiated by the classic studies of Warrington and Weiskrantz (1968, 1970, 1974, 1978). In one experiment, for example, Warrington and Weiskrantz (1974) showed amnesic patients a list of familiar words and tested memory for the words with a standard yes/no recognition test, and with a task in which patients were given three-letter cues and were asked to indentify the words represented by the cues. As expected, amnesics performed disastrously on the explicit recognition test. However, they showed entirely normal retention on the letter cueing test: amnesics and controls completed the letter cues with about the same number of study list targets. More recently, Graf *et al.* (1984) showed that the implicit/explicit nature of test instructions is a critical determinant of performance in the Warrington and Weiskrantz paradigm. They found that when subjects were instructed to use three-letter word stems in order to *remember* study list items (explicit memory instructions), amnesics were impaired relative to control subjects. However, when subjects were instructed to write down the first word that came to mind (implicit memory instructions), amnesics and controls showed similar facilitations of test performance (similar results have been reported by Graf *et al.* 1985; Schacter 1985; Shimamura and Squire 1984). Such a performance facilitation is now referred to as direct or repetition priming (cf. Cofer 1967).

It has been established that amnesic patients show intact priming effects on a variety of implicit memory tasks in addition to stem completion. These tasks include word identification, in which subjects attempt to 'see' briefly exposed items (Cermak *et al.* 1985); lexical decision, in which subjects decide whether or not a letter string constitutes an English word (Moscovitch 1982); and free association to the initial words of highly related paired associates (e.g. 'table–chair'; Shimamura and Squire 1984) and linguistic idioms (e.g. 'sour grapes'; Schacter 1985). In these and other priming experiments discussed thus far, the critical items were familiar units (i.e. words, idioms) that are in some sense represented in memory prior to exposure on a study list. Recently, several investigators have examined whether amnesic patients also show priming effects on implicit memory tests for novel information that is not represented in memory as a single unit prior to experimental presentation. Cermak *et al.* (1985) found that Korsakoff amnesics do not show priming effects for non-words on a perceptual identification test, and Diamond and Rozin (1984) reported similar findings in a variety of patients with the stem completion test. Other studies, however, indicate that at least some amnesic patients do show implicit memory for novel information. In an experiment by Graf and Schacter (1985), subjects studied unrelated word pairs (e.g. 'window–reason') and were then given a stem completion test in which some items were presented in the same context as on the study list (i.e. 'window–rea—') and other items appeared in a different context (i.e. 'officer–rea—'). Graf and Schacter reasoned that implicit memory for a new association would be demonstrated if subjects completed more stems in the same context condition than in the different context condition. They observed an equivalent same/different context effect in amnesic patients and control subjects. In a subsequent study using the same paradigm, Schacter and Graf (1986b) found evidence of implicit memory for new associations in mildly amnesic patients, but not in severely amnesic patients.

Evidence from other priming studies indicates that even severely amnesic patients can show implicit memory for new associations. Moscovitch *et al.* (1986) assessed implicit memory with a task that involved reading and rereading unrelated pairs of degraded words in same and different context conditions. They found that patients with severe memory disorders, like control subjects, reread same context pairs faster than different context pairs, thereby indicating normal implicit memory for a new association. McAndrews *et al.* (1987) presented amnesics and controls with novel, difficult-to-comprehend sentences (e.g. 'The haystack was important because the cloth ripped') and asked them to generate the critical word that made the sentence comprehensible (e.g. *parachute*); critical words were provided if they were not generated. Sentences were shown again at delays of 1 min, 10 min, 1 hr, 1 day, and 1 week, and subjects were asked again to think of the critical word. McAndrews *et al.* found that severely amnesic patients showed substantial priming at all test delays, as indicated by enhanced generation of key words on the second presentation of a sentence relative to the first. However, these patients had virtually no explicit memory for the sentences: they performed at chance levels on a yes/no recognition test.

In addition to the various types of skill learning and priming effects that we have considered, amnesic patients have shown implicit memory for recent experiences in other experimental paradigms. Several studies have shown that amnesic patients can acquire new factual information, even though they do not explicitly remember having learned any facts and claim no familiarity with the information that they do retrieve (e.g. Schacter *et al.* 1984). Glisky *et al.* (1986*b*) examined whether amnesic patients could acquire complex factual knowledge necessary to operate, program, and interact with a microcomputer in a study that involved extensive repetition across numerous learning sessions. They found that a densely amnesic patient could learn to write programs, edit them, and use disk storage and retrieval operations. Yet this patient did not explicitly remember having learned anything about the computer, and claimed at the beginning of each session that he had never worked on a computer before. It has also been demonstrated that amnesic patients can acquire preferences for simple melodies that they do not explicitly recognize (Johnson *et al.* 1985), show classical conditioning of an eye-blink response without remembering prior conditioning sessions (Weiskrantz and Warrington 1979), produce bits and pieces of recently presented stories that they do not recollect having been told (Luria 1976), and show an increased skin conductance response (SCR) to previously studied emotional words that are not recognized explicitly (Nishio 1984, cited in Moscovitch 1985).

Blindsight

The term 'blindsight' was introduced by Weiskrantz *et al.* (1974) to describe the residual visual capacities of cortically damaged patients with blindness for a part of the visual field. Blindsight refers to the ability to make certain classes of responses, in the absence of explicit perceptual awareness, to stimuli presented in blind visual fields. For example, a patient who accurately points to the location of a bright light presented within his blind region may claim to have had no conscious visual experience of the stimulus and assert that he is 'guessing' the location.

The investigation of blindsight in humans was stimulated by primate research that showed that complete ablation of primary visual cortex does not result in permanent blindness. In the past decade there have been a number of compelling demonstrations that a similar type of residual visual function is also present in hemianopic humans with cortical damage. The most widely used paradigm involves localization of a stimulus presented briefly to one of several regions of the blind field along a chosen meridian. A cue is given to initiate the response, which requires the patient to 'guess' where the target had been. Under these conditions, hemianopic patients have been shown to make reasonably accurate localization judgements by pointing or reaching toward the target position (e.g. Perenin and Jeannerod 1975, 1978; Weiskrantz 1980; Weiskrantz et al. 1974; Zihl 1980) and making a verbal response such as 'top' or 'bottom' (e.g. Barbur et al. 1980; Weiskrantz 1980). In these studies accuracy was invariably poorer for stimuli presented within the scotoma than for stimuli in the intact visual field, and the effect was usually confined to locations between $0°$ and $45°$ eccentricity from the fixation point (but see Weiskrantz et al. (1974) for reports of a larger range). Yet however limited the effect, it is striking that any correlation between the target location and 'guessed' location is obtained, given that patients do not report an experience comparable to 'seeing' the stimuli in intact visual regions.

Weiskrantz (1980) argued that specific practice or shaping of the response is required for demonstrating blindsight localization. He reported that patients may initially fail the localization task unless they are initially trained on a relatively easy version, such as presentation of only the two extremes of the stimulus range. Using a five-position saccadic localization task, Zihl (1980) found that accuracy of blind-field localization responses increased over a few hundred trials to the point where it was indistinguishable from performance on intact-field presentations. Campion et al. (1983) have argued that the need for training, coupled with the fact that discrimination for blind-field stimuli is rarely normal, seriously weakens the argument that blindsight performance is based on a spared visual system that is functionally independent of normal (striate) vision. However, there are data demonstrating detection and use of information in the blind field that is equivalent to intact-field performance under conditions in which practice plays little or no role. Singer et al. (1977) found that the detection threshold for a part of the intact visual field which had been elevated by adaptation could be reset by 'adapting' a mirror-symmetric region in the blind field. These findings suggest that the mechanisms for location-specific detection and recruitment of visual attention are preserved in residual vision (cf. Singer et al. 1977). Although the neural mechanisms may be fully functional at the outset of localization training, it appears that subjects must learn to monitor and interpret their outputs in order to organize a response.

Aside from localization it has been reported that hemianopic patients can make various other visual discriminations when forced to guess. Weiskrantz (1980; also see Weiskrantz et al. 1974) has demonstrated that patients can discriminate between gratings of reasonably high spatial frequencies and an equally luminous homogeneous patch in the blind field and that acuity in some regions can surpass that in more eccentric regions of the normal visual fields. The same studies reveal that some patients can discriminate very simple figures (X vs. O, straight-sided vs. curved triangles) and line orientations (horizontal vs. vertical, vertical vs. diagonal) at accuracy levels well above chance. However, Perenin and Jeannerod (1975) failed to find evidence of pattern discrimination in hemidecorticate subjects using a more demanding task that required discrimination among eight alternatives. It has been suggested that orientation discrimination may be relatively well preserved in blindsight patients, whereas form identification remains impaired (Weiskrantz 1980). Indeed, Weiskrantz (1980) has reported double dissociation of detection and form discrimination for the blind and normal fields of one patient, with form judgements always worse in the blind field relative to the normal field even when detection is better in the scotoma.

Two additional sets of studies have shown that information presented to the blind field can influence patients' responses to stimuli presented in the intact field. The first case involves the completion effect, where simple geometric forms such as circles are presented with half the form in the sighted field and half in the scotoma. Bender and Teuber (1946) and Torjussen (1978) demonstrated that subjects often reported that the complete figure had been presented, whereas they failed to report any form when half-figures were presented to the blind field only and did not show completion when half-figures were presented to the intact field. The observed lack of completion when there is no objective stimulus delivered to the blind field provides crucial support for an interpretation of the completion phenomenon as residual vision rather than as inference or visual confabulation. Evidence of confabulatory completion has been found for hemianopic patients (e.g. Gassel and Williams 1963), but it appears to be confined to patients with damage involving the parietal area (Warrington 1962). A second type of interaction between normal and blind-field stimulation was reported by Richards (1973). He found that patients were able to discriminate between monocular presentation of a light or dark bar and binocular stimulation with two stereoscopically presented bars which were positioned symmetrically about the border of the scotoma. Discrimination performance in this 'straddle' condition was equivalent to discrimination when both bars were presented to intact regions. The completion and stereopsis studies suggest that further research on the modification of responses to visible stimuli by information presented in the 'unseeing' regions may be helpful in determining the limits of residual vision in humans.

What do patients 'perceive' under conditons where stimulation in the blind field produces accurate responding, and how are these perceptions and awarenesses different from those of conscious visual experience? The verbal reports of patients clearly indicate a strong phenomenal distinction between blindsight and normal vision. Investigators typically claim that patients virtually never report noticing that a stimulus has been presented to the blind region and they believe that they are 'just guessing', responding on the basis of a 'gut reaction' (e.g. Poppel *et al.* 1973; Weiskrantz 1980). However, most researchers have noted that some patients, on some trials, do indicate awareness of some kind of stimulation, and it is instructive to examine how they describe these experiences. A few patients studied by Richards (1973) reported sensations of a 'pinprick' or 'gunfire at a distance' when light bars were flashed to the blind field. Weiskrantz' patient D.B. stated that he sometimes had a 'feeling' that a figure was smooth or jagged when asked to discriminate between 'O' and 'X' (Weiskrantz *et al.* 1974), and another patient sensed 'a definite pinpoint of light' but, upon further probing, claimed that it did not 'actually look like a light [but] . . . nothing at all' (Weiskrantz 1980, p. 378). The hemidecorticate subjects studied by Perenin and Jeannerod (1978) reported feeling that a bright light had been turned on in the impaired field and was spreading toward the intact field, although they had no conscious idea about the stimulus location or form. After considerable practice and training, subjects appear to develop a heightened awareness or sensitivity to information presented in the blind region, particularly with moving, or otherwise salient, stimuli. Thus D.B. now is reported to be 'aware' that something has been presented and roughly where it was (Weiskrantz 1980). Similarly, two of Zihl's (1980) patients were sometimes able to 'feel' the correspondence between eye movement and target position, and were able to indicate the relative accuracy of their localization responses after several hundred trials.

These occasional reports of awareness of some event in the blind field have been seized upon by critics of the blindsight phenomenon, who claim that it is simply a matter of cautious responding on the basis of near-threshold vision produced by scattered light (e.g. Campion *et al.* 1983). Although we are in agreement with the view that blindsight 'awarenesses' are profoundly different from the 'awareness' of conscious visual experience (e.g. Weiskrantz 1977, 1980, 1986), it may appear somewhat paradoxical to acknowledge that blindsight patients have some 'awareness' of 'unseen' stimuli. Natsoulas (1982) offers the analogy of a sleepwalker manoeuvring in an unfamiliar environment as a way of revolving this conceptual paradox:

For, in order for the sleepwalker to manoeuvre in this way, he must have some perceptual awarenesses of the environment. But, of course, such a person remains a sleepwalker; he does not know what he is doing, or that he intends to do anything, or that he is having perceptions in his environment while sleepwalking. The acts of consciousness which are his perceptual awarenesses during the episode are not conscious acts of consciousness (p. 88).

Similarly, the perceptions or awarenesses of hemianopic patients in a localization task do not appear to be 'conscious' perceptions. These patients do not experience the environment as 'appearing to' them, and they lack the capacity to comment upon, monitor, and manipulate their blind-field visual world.

It is also difficult to see how explanations such as those proposed by Campion *et al.* (1983) can account for an inability to discriminate form in an area of the scotoma characterized by good visual acuity, or why it would predict that thresholds for detection, orientation discrimination, and localization can themselves be dissociated (Weiskrantz 1980). The force of these criticisms is also weakened by a recent demonstration of an analogue to blindsight in the tactile modality (Paillard *et al.* 1983). A patient with hemianaesthesia of the right side due to damage to parietal sensory cortex was often able to point to locations on the 'unfeeling' limb touched by the experimenter, although the authors noted that her tactile deficit was so severe that she could cut or burn herself without noticing. However, it should also be noted that not all patients who are tested demonstrate residual vision in blindsight paradigms (e.g. Weiskrantz 1980) and that the degree of awareness of stimuli presented in the blind field varies over patients (cf. Campion *et al.* 1983). Some of these discrepancies are likely attributable to the precise locus and extent of cortical and subcortical damage in different patients. Patients are typically selected solely on the basis of visual field defects, rather than on the basis of lesion site and extent. The generally accepted anatomic basis for residual vision following destruction of striate cortex involves midbrain input to prestriate cortex (e.g. Trevarthen 1970), and destruction of these areas and projections in naturally occurring brain lesions is a likely source of confusion in the existing literature.

The nature and extent of blindsight are still a matter of some dispute, and it is not clear whether the phenomenon demands the interpretation originally given to it (e.g. a form of non-striate vision). However, we think that there is sufficient evidence to indicate that, at the phenomenal level, blindsight represents a genuine dissociation between implicit and explicit perceptual knowledge.

Prosopagnosia

Prosopagnosia refers to a deficit in ability to recognize and identity familiar faces; it is typically produced by bilateral lesions to occipito-temporal cortical regions, but a significant number of cases have been reported with unilateral right-hemisphere lesions (for a review, see Damasio 1985). Although there is some debate about whether prosopagnosic patients' difficulties are restricted entirely to *facial* recognition (e.g. Damasio 1985; Damasio *et al.* 1982), nearly all investigators would agree that the cardinal sign of prosopagnosia is a lack of familiarity with faces that ought to be recognized easily by the patient (e.g. spouse, children, friends). Recently, both psychophysiological and behavioural studies have revealed that prosopagnosic patients possess implicit knowledge of faces that they cannot recognize explicitly.

Consider first the psychophysiological evidence. Bauer (1984) reported a case study in which a prosopagnosic patient was shown pictures of famous faces (e.g. actors, politicians) and family members. While viewing an individual face, the patient was read a series of five names—one was the correct name of the exposed face, and the other four were lures. For the famous faces, lure names were drawn from the same category as the target (i.e. another actor or politician); for the family faces, lure names were other family members. Skin conductance responses (SCRs) to the names were recorded. Bauer found that the prosopagnosic patient failed to name any of the familiar faces spontaneously, and selected the correct name at a chance level (20 per cent correct), whereas control subjects' performance was almost perfect. However, the patient exhibited a maximal SCR on each trial to 60 per cent of the correct names, which was significantly above chance expectation; control subjects exhibited maximal SCRs to 90 per cent of correct names. In a subsequent study, Bauer *et al.* (1986) replicated the results of the famous faces–names task with a different prosopagnosic patient: despite selecting names for famous faces at a chance level, the patient showed maximal SCRs on individual trials to over 60 per cent of the correct names. By contrast, they observed no evidence of preserved electrodermal responding on a task involving *unfamiliar* faces.

Tranel and Damasio (1985) also reported psychophysiological evidence of implicit recognition of faces in prosopagnosia. They exposed two prosopagnosic patients to familiar and unfamiliar faces and recorded SCRs. One patient completely failed to recognize explicitly any of the familiar faces. However, she showed consistently larger SCRs to the familiar faces than to the unfamiliar faces. The second patient was able to recognize explicitly familiar faces of people she knew prior to the illness that led to her prosopagnosia (encephalitis), but could not recognize faces of people she had met since her illness (e.g. hospital staff). Nevertheless, this patient showed larger and more consistent SCRs to familiar than to unfamiliar faces from both time periods.

Behavioural evidence suggestive of implicit knowledge of faces in prosopagnosia was reported initially by Bruyer *et al.* (1983). Bruyer *et al.* devised a task that required a prosopagnosic patient to match names with famous faces;

the names were either arbitrarily assigned to the faces or were correct names. Even though the patient did not explicitly recognize the famous faces and could not name them, he had more difficulty learning to match the faces with arbitrary names than with real names. This interference effect indicates that some information about the faces was available, although the patient was unable 'to gain conscious access to these stored data' (1983, p. 280). It should be noted, however, that Bruyer *et al.*'s patient was not completely prosopagnosic, so interpretive caution must be exercised regarding the implicit/explicit nature of his preserved knowledge. In more extensive and systematic studies, described in detail elsewhere in this volume (see Young 1988), de Haan *et al.* (1987) reported results that are consistent with and extend the observations of Bruyer *et al.* They studied the performance of a young man (P.H.) who became prosopagnosic after a closed head injury on a variety of facial processing tasks involving familiar (i.e. famous) and unfamiliar (i.e. unknown) faces. Although P.H. did not explicitly recognize any of the familiar faces, his performance benefitted from familiarity in a manner similar to that observed in normal subjects. For example, on a matching task that required subjects to make same–different judgements regarding the identity of two simultaneously exposed faces, P.H., like normal controls, responded more quickly when a judgement involved famous faces than when it involved unknown faces. Similarly, like Bruyer *et al.*, de Haan *et al.* found that P.H. was slower to learn name–face pairings when a name was incorrectly paired with a familiar face than when it was correctly paired with the true face. De Haan *et al.* also observed evidence of interference from unrecognized familiar faces in a Stroop-like paradigm. For example, when asked to decide whether a visually presented name is that of a pop star (e.g. Mick Jagger), P.H. showed a pattern of interference effects on this task that was identical to that observed in control subjects.

The only notable difference between P.H. and controls is that he was consistently slower to respond on all facial processing tasks, perhaps because of generalized response slowing. However, the patient's *pattern* of response across experimental conditions was influenced by familiarity in the same manner as was controls' performance, thereby indicating that information about a face's familiarity was accessible to, and exerted an influence on, facial processing. Indeed, P.H. appears to have access to much the same informaton about facial familiarity as normal subjects do. The difference, however, is that P.H.'s knowledge of familiar faces is entirely implicit, and does not give rise to the phenomenal experience of familiarity reported by neurologically intact individuals.

Dyslexia

Studies on reading without awareness form a substantial subset of the literature on perception without awareness. Claims about various aspects of the phenomenon, including its very existence, continue to be as controversial today as they have been for as long as the phenomenon has been studied (for reviews, see Dixon 1971, 1982; Eriksen 1960; Marcel 1983; Cheesman and Merikle 1985; Holender 1986). Some authors, such as Marcel, have turned to the neuropsychological literature for evidence in support both of the phenomenon and of particular models used to explain it.

With regard to reading, the neuropsychological evidence is weak but tantalizing. Though much has been written in the past few years about a variety of acquired dyslexias, most especially deep and surface dyslexia (Coltheart *et al.* 1980; Patterson *et al.* 1985), very few studies speak directly to the issue of reading without awareness. What they do provide is evidence about the existence and organization of component processes involved in normal and pathological reading, as well as some indirect evidence about access of the output of those processes to consciousness. The only studies concerned directly with the issue of reading without awareness deal with the syndrome of alexia without agraphia caused by a lesion to the left occipital and posterior temporal cortex and to the splenium of the corpus callosum. Some of the patients who suffer from this syndrome have lost the ability to recognize whole words visually and must resort, instead, to a letter-by-letter decoding strategy in order to read. Three recent reports, by Landis *et al.* (1980), Shallice and Saffran (1986), and Coslett (1986), claim that these subjects have implicit lexical knowledge of visually presented words in the absence of explicit identification of them.

In each of these studies, words were presented in the intact left visual field at exposure durations that were too short for the subjects to decode the words letter-by-letter. Despite claiming to be unable to identify words, Landis *et al.*'s (1980) subject was able to choose 'intuitively' (p. 49) and correctly from a large array on a table those objects that were denoted by different target words on five out of seven trials. The objects were selected so that for every target object there was another object whose name began with the same letter as that of the target. Only when the subject consciously tried to decode the word letter-by-letter and based his choice on the first (and only) letter he could decode, did his performance deteriorate. Landis *et al.* concluded that explicit 'visual–verbal reading' (p. 52) interferes with 'iconic reading' in which the unconscious associations between a word and its corresponding image are activated. Iconic reading allows for automatic access to semantic information which then influences the subject's 'intuitive' choices in a word–object matching task.

Shallice and Saffran (1986) investigated more thoroughly the preserved whole-word reading abilities of their patient. On a binary semantic classification task for words he could not read explicitly, their subject performed correctly on some categories and poorly on others. He also performed well above chance on a lexical decision task. In both the semantic tasks performance was not dependent on his ability to identify the first couple of letters of the word nor on his knowledge of sequential dependencies among letters in the word. Though he was insensitive to the appropriateness of word affixes, his performance supported the conclusion that he based his lexical and semantic decisions on 'morphemic properties of the string and not on orthographic familiarity alone' (1986, p. 444). It should be noted, finally, that his performance with visual presentation, though impressive in light of his inability to identify the words explicitly, was none the less inferior to his performance with auditory presentation. Coslett (1986), in a brief abstract, described findings similar to those of Shallice and Saffran. He reported that three patients with alexia without agraphia performed at above-chance levels on a lexical decision test under conditions in which explicit word identification was precluded. He also reported that all patients were capable of semantic categorization of non-identified words. In contrast to the results reported by Coslett and by Shallice and Saffran, however, other patients with similar syndromes could neither distinguish words from non-words, semantically classify the words (Patterson and Kay 1982), nor match the words to a picture (Warrington and Shallice 1980) if they could not first identify the word explicitly. Why such a discrepancy in performance should exist among the various patients remains to be determined.

There is also a report of an effect that could be considered the converse of letter-by-letter reading, namely implicit letter recognition in the absence of explicit letter identification or naming. Friedman (1981) showed that subjects who could not name letters, nor match lower with upper case letters, were none the less able to distinguish orthographically acceptable non-words from unpronounceable letter strings. Because the two types of non-words were equivalent in their similarity to real words, decisions about orthographic acceptability must have been based implicitly on letter identification.

The evidence from these two classes of patients suggests that failure to gain access to consciousness can probably occur at either high or low levels in the hierarchy of processes involved in word recognition. It also suggests that some caution must be exercised in ascribing the patients' deficit to an impairment of a particular subsystem in reading rather than to the output of that subsystem, or to some other system whose representational content can be manipulated voluntarily and apprehended consciously. The implications of this statement to studies of deep and surface dyslexia should be clear. Until implicit knowledge of phonology or word form is assessed, one cannot conclude safely that the phonological and lexical routes to reading are impaired in deep and surface dyslexia, respectively.

Aphasia

The two classical aphasic syndromes, Broca's aphasia and Wernicke's aphasia, have as one of their main symptoms an impairment in processing syntactic and semantic information, respectively. Agrammatism in Broca's aphasia, initially thought to occur primarily in speech production, has in the last 15 years been shown to be a feature of speech comprehension as well. Patients who are agrammatic in speech also have difficulty appreciating the syntactic structure of sentences. Similarly, the semantic deficit of Wernicke's aphasics is reflected both in language reception and in language production. Their speech, though fluent and often grammatically correct, is characterized by a paucity of appropriate content words, by frequent circumlocutions and semantic paraphasias, and by occasional neologisms. Until recently the agrammatism in Broca's aphasia was thought to result from damage to a syntactic parser that decodes incoming sentences and confers grammatical structure on speech output. The semantic deficit in Wernicke's aphasia was believed to arise from an impairment or loss of semantic representation of words. Recently, both interpretations have been challenged by new evidence showing that syntactic and semantic abilities of both Broca's and Wernicke's aphasics, respectively, seem to be far better preserved than had previously been suspected. As we will show below, a brief review of this evidence suggests that, in part, the deficits of both types of aphasic patients may be described as a failure in access of syntactic and semantic information to consciousness.

Consider first the evidence concerning Broca's aphasia. In an interesting and neglected study, Andrewsky and Seron (1975) asked an agrammatic, French aphasic to read or complete sentences with words that could either be functors or content words (this patient is also a deep dyslexic; J. Marshall, personal communication). For example, the French word 'car' could mean either 'bus' or 'because' depending on how its role or position is specified in a sentence. In a variety of tests, they showed that the patient would either misread or omit the word when it was a functor, but read or supply it correctly when it was a substantive. They concluded that Broca's aphasics act like grammatical filters that pass semantic, but delete syntactic, information. Whatever the correct interpretation of this phenomenon, the aphasic subject's performance presupposes some implicit grammatical knowledge. How else would he know when to supply or omit the target word?

Andrewsky and Seron's (1975) demonstration resembles other similar observations suggesting that agrammatic aphasics retain implicit knowledge of grammars, despite the fact that their behaviour on explicit tests of comprehension and production indicated that they were generally insensitive to syntactic structure (Goodglass et al. 1970). It was Frederici's (1982) and especially Linebarger et al.'s (1983) observations, however, that focused attention on just how well preserved the agrammatic aphasics' syntactic abilities seem to be.

Instead of only testing the agrammatic patients' language comprehension and production, Linebarger et al. and Frederici had them make judgements of syntactic well-formedness of sentences. In general, Linebarger et al.'s and

Frederici's subjects scored between 80–100 per cent correct on most of the types of rule violation, suggesting that some syntactic abilities were preserved. This performance contrasted with the patients' generally poor ability to use this information in the comprehension and production of sentences. Unlike Andrewsky and Seron's (1975) findings, Frederici's and Linebarger et al.'s do not fit the mould that implicit grammatical knowledge is preserved. Judgements of grammatical acceptability seem to be no less explicit than apprehension of sentence meaning based on syntax, and thus do not represent a failure to gain access to consciousness as such. Rather, these observations indicate an inability to use preserved information in the service of higher order functions, such as language comprehension and production, which may occur because the output of a syntactic parser is disconnected from some processes but not others.

Several studies of patients with Wernicke's aphasia conform more closely to the notion that only implicit linguistic knowledge is preserved. In a series of experiments using lexical decision tasks, Milberg and Blumstein (1981; see also Blumstein et al. 1982; Milberg et al. in press) showed that Wernicke's aphasics appear to have sensitivity to semantic aspects of words despite being impaired in their ability to use that information on explicit tests of comprehension and on explicit judgements of semantic relatedness. Thus, when required to make yes/no judgements regarding the semantic relatedness of word pairs, a task that requires explicit knowledge of semantic information, Wernicke's patients performed at chance levels. A quite different pattern of results was observed on the lexical decision task, which requires the subject to decide whether a letter string forms a word in the lexicon. Response latencies to words are faster when the target item (e.g. *money*) is preceded by a related word (e.g. *bank*) than when it is preceded by an unrelated word (e.g. *tree*) or a non-word string (e.g. *bukler*). Like normal people, patients with Wernicke's aphasia had shorter response latencies in the related than in the unrelated word condition, both when the items were presented visually (Milberg and Blumstein 1981) and when they were presented acoustically (Blumstein et al. 1982). The consistency with which they showed a 'related' advantage was as high as in normal people, and did not correlate at all with the aphasics' performance on explicit tests of auditory comprehension, reading, and judgements of semantic relatedness, all of which correlated significantly with each other.

In a subsequent experiment, Milberg et al. (in press) showed that the Wernicke's aphasics' representations are not restricted to highly associated or related items without reference to their meanings, but rather include the semantic knowledge necessary for disambiguating words. In a modification of a lexical decision task first used by Schvaneveldt et al. (1976), Milberg et al. asked subjects to indicate whether the third item of an auditorily presented triplet was a word or not. In the critical condition, the second word of each triplet was a semantically ambiguous word, such as 'bank'. In Wernicke's aphasics, as in normal people, lexical decisions to the target word 'money' were shorter when the interpretation of the middle word was concordant with the target (coin–bank–money) than when it was not (river–bank–money).

Wernicke's aphasics, as Broca's aphasics, seem to have far greater linguistic knowledge than they can put to use in comprehension and production. However, we cannot be certain that the implicit/explicit dichotomy provides an adequate account of the preserved and impaired abilities of these patients; the observed dissociations may be explicable with reference to different types of linguistic processes. We include these phenomena to highlight the possibility that the implicit/explicit distinction is relevant to them, and thereby encourage future research that explores the issue directly. We believe that, in the final analysis, the role of conscious processes in aphasic disorders will have to be taken into account by linguistic models.

Hemineglect

This syndrome is characterized by an impaired ability to attend to the egocentric side of space contralateral to the damaged hemisphere. The syndrome takes its severest form following right parietal lobe lesions, but can also occur following left-sided lesions and also unilateral lesions to other areas of the brain (Mesulam 1981; Gainotti *et al.* 1986). The question relevant to the concerns of this chapter is whether there is evidence that the subject is influenced by information in the neglected field, information which, by definition, does not reach conscious awareness. The evidence, though rather sparse and sometimes anecdotal, generally favours the view that in hemineglect, as in other syndromes, the patient has available much more information than he exhibits on explicit tests.

Informal observation during recovery from the severe, acute phase of the syndrome indicates that patients can sometimes report stimuli from the neglected side of space but mistakenly locate them in the intact field. Even when unilateral neglect is complete, there is a strong suggestion that the spatial extent of the neglected region may influence the size or extent of the region over which attention is allocated, at least in some subjects. Thus, given a piece of paper on which to draw, a patient will confine his drawing to the right of an imaginary line, which will shift, sometimes dramatically, as the width of the piece of paper changes. Similar observations are made with regard to a patient's copy of drawings. It is the size and symmetry of the target object that determines, in part, what is neglected and what is attended.

These anecdotal observations are supported by a more formal study of line bisection in patients with unilateral neglect of the left side of space. By looking at where the subjective midpoint was, Bisiach *et al.* (1983) calculated that for some patients the inferred extent of a line grew as the length of the line increased, whereas for other patients it remained constant. One interpretation of the performance of the first class of patients is that information from the neglected part of the line biases the subject's estimate of the line's length. By contrast, the performance of patients who perceive a line of constant length is influenced by information only from the attended field.

Other evidence for the influence of unattended information on the neglected side comes from a study by Volpe *et al.* (1979) concerning the phenomenon of extinction to double simultaneous stimulation. This occurs when presentation of a single stimulus anywhere in the visual field results in an accurate description of it, but simultaneous presentation of two stimuli to the left and right visual fields results in accurate description of only the right visual field stimulus. Volpe *et al.* observed the extinction phenomenon in four patients with right parietal lobe tumours who were shown either pictures of common objects or familiar words simultaneously in the two visual fields. In addition, they required patients to make same/different judgements regarding the two stimuli. All four patients performed the same/different task at high levels of accuracy, ranging from 88 to 100 per cent correct judgements. Two patients 'felt that something had appeared' in the left field, but 'were unable to characterize it' (1979, p. 723); the other two patients 'were completely unaware that anything had been presented' (p. 724) to the left field. Yet, as indicated by their accurate same/different judgements, these patients had implicit knowledge of stimuli that they could not explicitly identify. Similar conclusions are suggested by studies of reading. Both Kinsbourne and Warrington (1962) and Bisiach *et al.* (1983) report that reading ability of patients with right parietal lesions varies according to the type of orthographic information that is available on the left. Thus, if required to read a word, the patient will tend to neglect the letters on the left, but the number of letters neglected changes according to whether they are pronounceable or not; or, if pronounceable, on the function they serve in determining the pronunciation or meaning of the non-neglected portion of the word.

It should be noted that the phenomena of hemineglect can be viewed in two ways. One view, that makes hemineglect analogous to the other phenomena we have considered, is that the deficit is one in which spatially coded information from one side fails to gain access to consciousness automatically, much as various other types of information can fail to do so. This places spatially coded information on the same level as visual, facial, or linguistic information. A second possibility, however, is that the deficit does not entail a failure of a specific type of information to gain access to consciousness, but rather involves difficulties in engaging attentional mechanisms that are necessary for bringing various types of information from one side to conscious awareness. In effect, the second view places the deficit closer to the level of consciousness itself, rather than at the level of an input path to consciousness from a particular informational system. Thus it should be kept in mind that observations of implicit knowledge in hemineglect patients may demand a different interpretation than similar observations in other syndromes.

Other observations

Although the foregoing descriptions present the bulk of the evidence concerning implicit/explicit dissociations in neuropsychological syndromes, scattered observations suggestive of similar phenomena can be found in other types of patients. Recent research conerning inter hemispheric transfer in split-brain patients suggests that some high-level information may be exchanged between the hemispheres though neither side is explicitly aware of the information that has been transferred. For example, when information is presented directly to the left hemisphere the patient can name it, and when it is projected directly to the right hemisphere the patient can point to it. Performance on these explicit tests is at chance if each hemisphere is asked to report on information received by its neighbour. Nevertheless, through implicit measures such as priming, each hemisphere can reveal that it possesses information received from the other (e.g. Holtzman *et al.* 1981; Sergent in press; Zaidel 1982).

Another kind of implicit/explicit dissociation has been reported briefly by Margolin *et al.* (1983). They found that a patient with severe visual object agnosia could derive some meaning from stimuli that were not explicitly recognized. Although he recognized and named only three of 24 pictures of common objects, he was able to make accurate judgements concerning the size of the real-life object and state whether it was living or inanimate in 22 instances. Margolin *et al.* argued that their study '. . . emphasizes the importance of differentiating between the awareness of knowledge and knowledge which is preconscious' (1983, p. 242). Warrington (1975) reported a somewhat different type of evidence suggestive of preserved implicit knowledge in visual agnosia. She observed that two agnosic patients showed better short-term memory for real words than nonsense words—yet the patients did not explicitly recognize the real words and could not state their meaning.

Clinical observations concerning the phenomenon of anosognosia—unawareness and/or denial of deficits following hemiplegia, hemianopia, and other neuropsychological disorders—suggest that anosognosic patients may possess implicit knowledge of deficits that they deny explicitly. Weinstein *et al.* (1964), for example, argued that:

. . . the term 'anosognosia', meaning 'lack of knowledge', is not wholly accurate. The patient indicates knowledge of the neglected extremities by referring to them in such expressions as a 'dummy' and a 'rusty piece of machinery'. Patients who deny that they are ill subscribe to hospital routine and express no surprise when they are told, for example, that they are to have a craniotomy. The very fact of the selectiveness indicates some knowledge of the deficit . . . (p. 384).

Weinstein and Friedland (1977) made similar observations, describing a patient with left hemiplegia who denied that his left arm was paralysed, yet referred to it as '. . . a canary claw, yellow and shrivelled' (p. 60).

Characteristics of implicit/explicit dissociations

The studies reviewed in the previous section indicate clearly that patients who are characterized by a variety of neuropsychological deficits show implicit knowledge under conditions in which explicit knowledge is poor or entirely absent. The quality and quantity of evidence for implicit/explicit dissociations varies widely, from isolated and rather loosely controlled clinical and experimental observations to rigorous studies that have been replicated under a variety of conditions. Thus, while we cannot be certain that each and every one of the cited observations represent genuine, replicable dissociations between implicit and explicit expressions of knowledge, we think that there is sufficient evidence to support the general proposition that implicit/explicit dissociations can be observed across a variety of patients, tasks, and stimuli. The critical question, of course, concerns the proper interpretation of these phenomena: How can we best characterize the observed implicit/explicit dissociations? To what extent and in what sense are they related to one another? And what can these dissociations teach us about normal cognition and consciousness? To set the stage for addressing these questions we will delineate some of the critical characteristics of the evidence that has been discussed thus far.

Since the phenomena of interest have been observed in widely disparate patients and paradigms, it is important to try to point out some of the similarities and differences among them. We can begin by noting that four broadly different types of evidence for implicit knowledge have been cited. The first comes from situations in which similar or identical types of information are being tapped on implicit and explicit tests, but the responses required from the patient differ. For example, in blindsight studies patients deny explicitly perceiving a particular stimulus attribute (e.g. location) and then show implicit access to that attribute on various types of forced-choice tests. Similarly, Milberg and Blumstein's studies of Wernicke's aphasia (Blumstein et al. 1982; Milberg and Blumstein 1981; Milberg et al., in press) indicate that information concerning semantic relatedness can be revealed implicitly by associative priming effects, though the same or similar information cannot be used on explicit tests of semantic relatedness.

A second, similar type of evidence for implicit knowledge derives from studies in which patients' task performance is affected by experimental variables whose influence presupposes access to information that the patient cannot express explicitly. De Haan *et al.*'s (1987) demonstration that a prosopagnosic's performance is affected by variations in facial familiarity, Bisiach *et al.*'s (1983) finding that extending the length of a line in a patient's neglected field influences line bisection performance, and Warrington's (1975) finding that word meaning influences agnosic patients' short-term memory performance are examples of this kind of evidence.

The third type of evidence for implicit knowledge, which is not always easy to distinguish unequivocally from the first two, comes from studies in which an implicit test can be performed on the basis of different information than is needed for successful performance on an explicit test. Many studies of amnesic patients are of this type. For example, implicit memory can be revealed on a skill learning task that taps a quite different kind of information than is required for explicit remembering of a recent experience. Similarly, patients can show priming of familiar words on a stem completion test, even though they fail to remember these words on cued recall tests that require explicit access to contextual information regarding the occurrence of a word in a particular time and place. Other results, however, are more difficult to classify. For example, the finding that some amnesic patients show implicit memory for newly acquired associations on stem completion (Graf and Schacter 1985; Schacter and Graf 1986b), serial learning (Nissen and Bullemer 1987), and reading tests (Moscovitch *et al.* 1986) could be interpreted as indicating that these patients have implicit access to contextual information, but cannot gain explicit access to it. Alternatively, it is possible that different types of contextual information are required for implicit and explicit memory of new associations (e.g. Schacter and Graf 1986a). The fourth type of evidence is provided by studies in which implicit knowledge has been revealed by *physiological* measures, such as in the SCR studies of prosopagnosia by Bauer (1984) and Tranel and Damasio (1985).

The foregoing classificatory scheme may not enable us to place each relevant study unambiguously into one and only one of the four categories, but it does provide at least a rough taxonomy of the kinds of evidence that we have considered. However, some further issues must be considered in order to provide a basis for discussing alternative accounts of the observed dissociations. The first issue concerns whether or not patients' performance on the task or measure used to assess implicit knowledge was normal with respect to that of control subjects. Several studies have provided evidence for normal access to implicit knowledge. Perhaps the strongest evidence comes from studies of amnesic patients which have demonstrated normal priming effects on various implicit memory tests (e.g. Graf *et al.* 1984, 1985; Graf and Schacter 1985; Moscovitch *et al.* 1986; Schacter 1985; Shimamura and Squire 1984; Warrington and Weiskrantz 1970, 1974) and which have also shown normal perceptual and motor skill learning (e.g. Brooks and Baddeley 1976; Cohen and Squire 1980; Eslinger and Damasio 1985). Normal performance on an implicit measure has also been observed in some studies of blindsight (e.g. Singer *et al.* 1977; Richards 1973). In several studies which used reaction time as a dependent measure, ascertaining whether patients perform normally on an implicit task is not entirely straightforward. Studies of serial pattern learning in amnesia (Nissen and Bullemer 1987), semantic priming in aphasia (Blumstein *et al.* 1982; Milberg and Blumstein 1981), and facial processing in prosopagnosia (de Haan *et al.* 1987) have all demonstrated that patients and controls show identical *patterns* of performance on implicit tests, but also indicate that patients' overall response latencies are significantly slower than those of controls. If one attributes these elevated latencies to generalized response slowing that is unrelated to the specific functions tapped by an implicit test, which we believe is a reasonable inference in the cited studies, then these data, too, can be considered as evidence for normal access to implicit knowledge.

However one classifies the reaction time experiments, the majority of studies that we have reviewed do not provide evidence of normal performance on an implicit measure; rather, they simply indicate that patients have *some* access to implicit knowledge. In several studies, data from normal controls were not presented, so it is not possible to evaluate whether patients' implicit knowledge is normal (Bisiach *et al.* 1983; Bruyer *et al.* 1983). In other studies, however, the data reveal that patients' performance on an implicit measure, though above baseline, is impaired with respect to controls' performance. Conforming to this description are prosopagnosic patients' SCR responses (Bauer 1984; Tranel and Damasio 1985); many of the 'guesses' made by blindsight patients (e.g. Pöppel *et al.* 1979; Weiskrantz *et al.* 1974); alexic patients' lexical decisions and semantic categorizations (Coslett 1986; Friedman 1981; Landis *et al.* 1980; Shallice and Saffran 1986); neglect patients' same/different judgements (Volpe *et al.* 1979); and some implicit memory phenomena in amnesics, including acquisition of factual knowledge (Glisky *et al.* 1986*a*, 1986*b*; Schacter *et al.* 1984), classical conditioning (Weiskrantz and Warrington 1979), and some reports of skill learning (Brooks and Baddeley 1976; Milner *et al.* 1968). The theoretical implications of normal vs. impaired access to implicit knowledge will be discussed shortly.

The second point concerns the nature of the evidence and criteria that were used to support statements such as 'the patient was not consciously aware of X' or that a certain type of information 'failed to gain access to consciousness'. In the majority of cases, lack of explicit or conscious knowledge was inferred from patients' subjective verbal reports. Thus, in blindsight and hemineglect, patients' claims that they do not see anything in a specific portion of the visual field are taken as evidence that they lack conscious perceptual knowledge; in prosopagnosia, lack of explicit knowledge of facial familiarity is inferred from patients' reports that they do not recognize a face as familiar; in alexia without agraphia, patients' reports that they cannot read a word are the basis for arguing that they lack explicit knowledge of its identity; and, in many studies of amnesia, lack of explicit memory is based on patients' yes/no judgements that they do not remember the prior occurrence of a test stimulus. However, reliance on yes/no judgements is not the only way in which lack of explicit knowledge has been inferred. In studies of Broca's aphasia, for example, patients' chance performance on forced-choice matching tests is one basis for concluding that they do not possess explicit knowledge of syntax (e.g. Schwartz *et al.* 1980), and, in some studies of amnesia (e.g. Squire *et al.* 1985; Warrington and Weiskrantz 1974), patients perform at chance or near-chance levels on explicit tests of memory. As we shall see in the next section of the chapter, the fact that lack of explicit knowledge has been revealed on both yes/no and forced-choice tests has significant implications for theoretical accounts of implicit/explicit dissociations.

The third important point to note about dissociations between implicit and explicit knowledge is that they are *domain-specific*. By 'domain-specific' we mean that patients generally do not have serious problems gaining explicit access to information in cognitive domains outside of their deficit. For example, amnesic patients have no difficulty on explicit tests of perception, language, comprehension, or reading. Similarly, Wernicke's aphasics would have little or no difficulty on the explicit perceptual tests that blindsight and prosopagnosic patients cannot perform, whereas these two types of patients would experience little difficulty on the explicit tests of semantic comprehension that the Wernicke's aphasic cannot perform (assuming, of course, that the test was adminstered in the appropriate modality).

In asserting that implicit/explicit dissociations are domain-specific, we do not wish to imply that each of the patient groups we have discussed is entirely free of cognitive deficits in all domains outside of their primary impairment. What we do want to stress, however, is that implicit/explicit dissociations do not represent *global* disorders of consciousness or awareness.

Theoretical accounts of implicit/explicit dissociations

We now consider alternative theoretical views of the phenomena we have reviewed. Since few investigators have considered these phenomena as a group, there is a corresponding lack of theories directed at all or even most of the relevant observations. Accordingly, we will consider ideas that have been discussed with respect to a subset of the relevant phenomena and that we think merit consideration. Our discussion concerns three possible accounts of implicit/explicit dissociations which we will argue are inadequate. In the next section, we outline a general approach that we think will prove to be more fruitful.

Conservative response bias?

As is well known, signal detection analyses of perception and memory separate performance into two components: d', which reflects an observer's sensitivity to a particular signal, and β, which reflects the response criterion used to make a judgement concerning the presence or absence of that signal. Given the identical signal, an observer with a cautious response criterion would make a negative judgement regarding its presence while an observer with a lenient criterion would make a positive judgement. It is conceivable that implicit/explicit dissociations arise because patients have an extremely cautious response criterion: they are unwilling to acknowledge the presence of a signal that they can, in fact, detect. As noted earlier, such an argument has been made by Campion *et al.* (1983) regarding phenomena of blindsight. They contended that blindsight patients have access to degraded perceptual information and, as sometimes occurs when only a degraded signal is available, are quite cautious about acknowledging its presence. This kind of argument has not yet been advanced to account for other cases of apparent implicit/explicit dissociations, but it merits some consideration.

Although it may be applicable to certain cases, the response bias argument advanced by Campion *et al.* can be rejected as a general account of implicit/explicit dissociations on both empirical and logical grounds. First, as discussed in the previous section, there are reports in which lack of access to explicit knowledge is indexed by performance on forced-choice tests, and a response bias argument cannot account for these results. Second, the notion that the cautious criterion is attributable to patients' dependence on 'degraded' information is only tenable when patients' performance on an implicit test is impaired with respect to that of control subjects. Yet we have pointed out that a number of different instances of *normal* performance on implicit test have been documented. Where is the 'degraded' information in these cases?

In addition to these empirical considerations, there are logical and conceptual difficulties with this view. Even when failure on an explicit test is documented by yes/no procedures and success on an implicit test is revealed by forced-choice procedures, it is not clear what it means to invoke a response criterion argument: Does one wish to imply that the patient 'really does' have explicit access to the information that he denies perceiving, understanding, or remembering? This question has been raised by several commentators in discussions of blindsight (Natsoulas 1982; Underwood 1983; Weiskrantz 1983) and of perception without awareness in normal subjects (Bisiach 1986; Fowler 1986; Paap 1986; Wolford 1986). We, like they, think that a positive answer to the question misses the very essence of the phenomena under consideration. And even if the question makes some sense when directed at phenomena such as perception without awareness, where extremely brief stimulus exposures are given and subjects may sometimes be 'unsure' of whether or not they saw anything, it is less applicable to many of the dissociations that we have discussed, where information is made available to the subject without any artificial restrictions. For example, to assert that the Wernicke's aphasic 'really understands' the semantic relations between a presented pair of words or that the prosopagnosic is 'really familiar' with a face that he has unlimited time to inspect is not a terribly satisfying account of these phenomena. The difference between the concept of implicit knowledge and cautious response criterion is illustrated nicely by Weiskrantz' (1986) description of the 'blindsight' experiences of patient D.B. within his scotoma, and the 'degraded vision' experiences of D.B. in amblyopic regions of the visual field:

... the qualitative difference between the seeing field and the scotoma was reported as being very clear by D.B. Thus, in the spared amblyopic crescent in the left half-field while vision was fuzzy he nevertheless reported it as *vision*. Measured visual acuity was, in fact, poorer in that region of the field than it was in the scotoma ... but despite this the subjective experience in the crescent was reported to be definitely and unambiguously of 'seeing', in contrast to the scotoma, where he said he was not even aware of the bright back-projected display within which the grating was generated (1986, p. 147).

Disturbance of consciousness or language?

We have noted that the primary, though not the sole source of evidence for lack of explicit or conscious knowledge is the patient's report of his subjective experience. This report is usually expressed verbally. It is therefore possible that the various dissociations are best described not as failures to gain access to consciousness but rather as failures to gain access to language production mechanisms. Perhaps the patient is in some sense 'consciously aware' of the information that we have referred to as 'implicit', but is unable to express this awareness verbally. Dissociations of this kind, in which language production mechanisms are isolated from specific processing systems, are familiar in neuropsychology and have been considered at great length by Geschwind (1965) in his well-known discussion of disconnection syndromes.

   There are several reasons why we do not think that a disruption or disconnection of language production mechanisms plays an important role in implicit/explicit dissociations. First, implicit knowledge can itself be expressed verbally. For example, an amnesic patient who completes the stem 'tab—' with the recently experienced word 'table', without any explicit memory for having seen the word before, is expressing implicit memory for a recent experience with a verbal response. Similarly, forced-choice judgements of various kinds that reveal implicit knowledge involve verbal stimuli and require linguistic responses. Weiskrantz (1986, p. 169) noted specifically that the 'blindsight guesses' of his patient D.B. could be expressed verbally or non-verbally. Second, lack of explicit knowledge can be shown without requiring a verbal response. For example, some severely amnesic patients who show implicit memory effects perform at chance levels on two-alternative forced-choice recognition tests for recently exposed non-verbal materials (i.e. faces) in which they could show explicit memory by simply pointing to the correct face (e.g. Warrington and Weiskrantz 1982). Third, in those neuropsychological syndromes in which impairment of language production mechanisms is crucial, such as naming disorders, the phenomenology of the disturbance is quite different from what we have described. For example, an anomic patient who cannot explicitly produce the name of a familiar object in a picture will often have explicit access to many kinds of information about it, and state that he 'knows' perfectly well what the object is and does. This phenomenal experience of 'knowing' contrasts sharply with the absence of such experiences when knowledge is expressed implicitly in the studies that we have considered.

While we certainly do not want to suggest that language and consciousness are unrelated, and also recognize that language is the principal vehicle for expressing and communicating conscious, explicit knowledge, we do not think that disrupted access to language mechanisms plays a significant role in implicit/explicit dissociations. It is instructive in this regard to compare the phenomena discussed here with some of those observed in split-brain patients. As noted earlier, when stimuli are confined to the left visual field and thus projected to the right hemisphere, patients may not state verbally what they see. However, if allowed to use their left hand to select the presented stimulus from a number of alternatives, patients can do so with a high degree of accuracy (e.g. Gazzaniga and LeDoux 1978). But we would not want to call this a dissociation between implicit and explicit knowledge. Rather, the dissociation appears to reflect the right hemisphere's limited ability to express its knowledge and experience verbally together with its ability to express itself non-verbally. A variety of observations (e.g. Sperry et al. 1979) suggest that the right hemisphere possesses extensive conscious awareness but has difficulty organizing a verbal response and thus cannot express its 'awareness' through language when it is disconnected from the verbal mechanisms in the left hemisphere. This kind of phenomenon demands a different theoretical interpretation than the implicit/explicit dissociations that we have discussed. Indeed, Weiskrantz (1986, p. 169) has pointed out that split-brain patients do not show implicit/explicit dissociations when given the same experimental tasks that produce such dissociations in D.B. and other blindsight patients. However, as discussed earlier, there are reports of implicit knowledge of information transferred between the hemispheres in split-brain patients. This evidence, like other phenomena we have discussed, cannot be accounted for in terms of a verbal/non-verbal distinction.

Different systems for implicit and explicit knowledge

A quite different explanatory approach than the foregoing ones is to attempt to identify implicit and explicit expressions of knowledge with distinct and dissociable neural systems. By this view, each of the dissociations we have discussed would indicate the presence of two different systems within a particular domain; one of them can produce conscious, explicit knowledge and one of them cannot. Thus dissociations in blindsight would be interpreted in terms of two different visual systems, a conscious, explicit system that is impaired and an unconscious, implicit system that is preserved; dissociations in prosopagnosia would lead to the postulating of two different facial recognition systems; dissociations in Wernicke's aphasia would be explained in terms of the two different comprehension systems; dissociations in amnesia would require postulation of two separate memory systems; and so on. This 'multiple systems' approach to explaining implicit/explicit dissociations has been pursued most vigorously in the amnesia literature (cf. Cohen 1984; Moscovitch 1982; Schacter and Tulving 1982; Squire and Cohen 1984).

To illustrate what we believe are the strengths and weaknesses of this approach, let us consider the distinction between procedural and declarative memory systems that has been discussed extensively in amnesia research (Cohen 1984; Squire and Cohen 1984). The distinction was proposed to account for the dissociation between preserved skill learning/priming and impaired explicit remembering in amnesic patients. Normal skill learning in amnesics was attributed to a spared procedural system, in which learning is expressed as on-line modifications of procedures or processing operations that are not accessible to conscious awareness. By contrast, amnesics' inability to remember recent experiences and to learn new facts was attributed to an impaired declarative system, which represents facts and events in a manner that permits them to be consciously remembered. By this view, conscious or explicit remembering is a *property* of the declarative system.

Although this distinction accounts reasonably well for preserved skill learning in amnesic patients, it has difficulty accounting for some properties of priming effects (for a discussion, see Schacter, 1987). More importantly, it is extremely difficult to attribute all of the diverse implicit memory phenomena observed in amnesic patients to the procedural system. For example, amnesic patients can learn various types of factual information, yet do not explicitly remember having learned any facts (e.g. Glisky *et al.* 1986*a*, *b*; Schacter *et al.* 1984). It does not seem reasonable to attribute implicit memory phenomena of this kind to a procedural system, since acquisition of factual knowledge is allegedly the responsibility of declarative memory. Similarly, it would not make much sense to attribute implicit memory for affect in amnesic patients (Johnson *et al.* 1985) to the procedural system. The critical point is that manifestations of implicit memory in amnesic patients are simply too diverse to be attributed to a particular memory system that lacks the capacity for conscious remembering. Although *some* of these phenomena (e.g. perceptual and motor skill learning) may reflect the operation of a dissociable memory system (cf. Sherry and Schacter 1987), amnesic patients can express implicit memory for recent experiences in ways that do not fit with such a view.

Returning to implicit/explicit dissociations outside of amnesia, it is the sheer diversity of situations in which implicit expressions of knowledge can be observed that leads us to believe that postulation of multiple processing or memory systems in each situation—one responsible for implicit knowledge, the other for explicit knowledge—is likely to be of limited value.

Toward a model of implicit/explicit dissociations

Having discussed and found wanting several possible accounts of the reviewed phenomena, we close the chapter by sketching the outline of a general approach to implicit/explicit dissociations that we think is worth exploring further. Our purpose here is not to provide a detailed model of the various dissociations, but rather to suggest the broad outlines of an appropriate model and to target key issues that will have to be addressed by such a model.

There are two critical observations that motivate our approach. The first is the *generality* of implicit/explicit dissociations: They have been observed across different types of stimulus information, response requirements, cognitive functions, and subject populations. The fact that similar dissociations are observed in such diverse circumstances persuades us that it is useful to seek a common explanation for them, rather than attempt to postulate different explanations to account for each of the dissociations individually. This general idea has been suggested previously regarding some of the phenomena we have discussed by Marcel (1983), Schacter (1987), and Weiskrantz (1977, 1980, 1986). The second critical observation concerns the *selectivity* of the dissociations. Patients' inability to gain access to explicit knowledge is domain-specific and does not represent a global disorder of conscious awareness.

In view of these considerations, we hypothesize that (a) conscious or explicit experiences of perceiving, knowing, and remembering all depend in some way on the functioning of a common mechanism, (b) this mechanism normally accepts input from and interacts with a variety of processors or modules that handle specific types of information, and (c) in various cases of neuropsychological impairment, specific modules are disconnected from the conscious mechanism.

The idea that conscious experiences depend in some way on the functioning of a specific mechanism has been proposed by several investigators. This mechanism has been referred to as a commentary system (Weiskrantz 1978, 1986), conscious processing system (Posner 1978), selector input (Shallice

1972), high-level operator (Johnson-Laird 1983), output of a left-brain interpreter (Gazzaniga 1985), and executive system (Hilgard 1977). Each of these and other conceptualizations of a 'conscious mechanism' differ in various ways that will not be discussed here. They are similar, however, in so far as they all subscribe to the general notion that conscious awareness of a particular stimulus requires involvement of a mechanism that is different from the mechanisms that process various attributes of the stimulus, a notion that makes neurobiological as well as psychological sense (Dimond 1976). If, as numerous theorists have argued recently, processing of different kinds of information is handled by specialized modular systems (e.g. Fodor 1983; Gazzinga 1985; Shallice 1981), it is a short and straightforward step to suggest that in some cases of neuropsychological impairment a conscious mechanism is disconnected selectively from a specific module. Such a disconnection need not involve damage to the conscious mechanism itself, and thus would not result in a global disruption of conscious awareness; it would produce the kind of domain-specific impairments that were observed in the studies reviewed earlier. Note also that the idea of 'disconnection' as used here need not imply a disconnection of fibre tracts that link various brain structures, as in the classical discussions by Geschwind (1965). Rather, our use of disconnection refers more generally to a failure of a processor or module to gain access to a conscious mechanism, and does not make any assumptions about the nature of the neurological disruption that produces the access failure.

The foregoing is no more than a summary sketch of an approach to implicit/explicit dissociations (for a more detailed exposition, see Schacter, in press). However, even these rather general ideas raise some difficult problems. For example, assuming a basic separation between modular processing systems and conscious experience, one could still hypothesize that *multiple* conscious mechanisms exist or, similarly, that each modular system is associated with its own conscious mechanism. The notion of a disconnection between modular processing and conscious mechanisms could be invoked as easily in this scenario as in a scenario involving just a single conscious mechanism. But how could we distinguish between these two scenarios? At the present time we see no unequivocal way of doing so, and think that the matter ought to be left open for the time being. However, there is one consideration that favours the idea of a single conscious mechanism. In a system composed of multiple modules that operate in parallel and largely independently of one another, a critical function of a conscious mechanism is to *integrate* the various modular outputs (e.g. Baars 1983; Johnson-Laird 1983). If each module were associated with its own conscious mechanism, the integrative function of consciousness could not be served; one would have to postulate a yet higher level conscious mechanism that integrates the output of the module-specific conscious mechanisms. Though such a possibility should not be dismissed out of hand, it may be more parsimonious to assume a single conscious mechanism until the data dictate otherwise.

A second problem that will have to be confronted by models of the kind we advocate is related to the notion that implicit/explicit dissociations in neuropsychological syndromes are attributable to a *disconnection* between a specific module and the conscious mechanism. Another possibility is that the dissociations are attributable to damage at the modular level. It is conceivable that damaged modules send degraded outputs to a conscious mechanism, outputs which are sufficient for implicit but not explicit expressions of knowledge. Alternatively, it is possible that a module needed for performance on an explicit task is damaged, and that a different module supports performance on an implicit task, a module that does not normally have access to the conscious mechanism. Though these possibilities cannot always be readily distinguished from the disconnection idea, we can suggest some guidelines for differentiating between them. To support the notion that a particular implicit/explicit dissociation reflects disconnection of a conscious mechanism from the output of modular processing, two kinds of evidence would appear to be critical. First, patients should show normal or near-normal performance on an implicit task. If patients perform normally on an implicit task, it is difficult to argue that implicit knowledge is based on the degraded output of a damaged module. Second, patients should perform normally on implicit tasks that tap the same kind of information that is tapped by an explicit task. If it can be shown that patients have access to the same kind of information that control subjects do, and lack only conscious awareness of it, it is difficult to argue that different modules are needed to perform the two types of tasks. Although various pieces of evidence discussed here conform to one of these two criteria, and some data come reasonably close to fulfilling them both, the results required by our hypothesis remain to be demonstrated unambiguously. Documentation of such results thus represents an important challenge for future research.

Whatever the strength of evidence for the present view, it seems quite unlikely that all instances of implicit/explicit dissociations will be attributable to 'pure' disconnection between a specific module and a conscious mechanism. Undoubtedly, many cases will involve both disconnection and damage at the modular level. Moreover, it is likely that the interaction between individual modules and an hypothesized conscious mechanism is not all or none (i.e. absolute disconnection vs. normal communication); different degrees of disruption of this interaction are surely possible. Consideration and investigation of the hypothesis proposed here, however, should provide further insight into the basis of implicit/explicit dissociations and thereby contribute to our understanding of the nature of conscious awareness.

Acknowledgements

The work described in this chapter was supported by a Special Research Program Grant from the Connaught Fund, University of Toronto, and by the

Natural Sciences and Engineering Research Council of Canada, Grant U0361 to D. L. Schacter. We thank Edoardo Bisiach, Alfonso Caramazza, Peter Graf, John Marshall, Dan Tranel, and Andy Young for useful comments and criticisms, and thank Carol A. Macdonald for help with preparation of the manuscript.

References

Andrewsky, E. L. and Seron, X. (1975). Implicit processing of grammatical rules in a classical case of agrammatism. *Cortex*, **11**, 379–90.

Baars, B. J. (1983). Conscious contents provide the nervous system with coherent, global information. In *Consciousness and self-regulation. Vol. 3*, (ed. R. J. Davidson, G. E. Schwartz, and D. Shapiro), pp. 41–79. Plenum, New York.

Barbur, J. L., Ruddock, K., and Waterfield, V. A. (1980). Human visual responses in the absence of the geniculo-calcarine projections. *Brain*, **103**, 905–28.

Bauer, R. M. (1984). Autonomic recognition of names and faces in prosopagnosia: a neuropsychological application of the guilty knowledge test. *Neuropsychologia*, **22**, 457–69.

——, Verfaellie, M., and Valenstein, E. (1986). Autonomic recognition of faces in prosopagnosia depends upon premorbidly stored representations. Paper presented to the meeting (February) of the International Neuropsychological Society, Denver, Col.

Bender, M. B. and Teuber, H.-L. (1946). Phenomena of fluctuation, extinction and completion in visual perception. *Archives of Neurology and Psychiatry*, **15**, 627–59.

Bisiach, E. (1986). Through the looking-glass and what cognitive psychology found there. *The Behavioral and Brain Sciences*, **9**, 24–6.

——, Bulgarelli, C., Sterzi, R., and Vallar, G. (1983). Line bisection and cognitive plasticity of unilateral neglect of space. *Brain and Cognition*, **2**, 32–8.

Blumstein, S. E., Milberg, W., and Shrier, R. (1982). Semantic processing in aphasia: evidence from an auditory lexical decision task. *Brain and Language*, **17**, 301–15.

Brooks, D. N. and Baddeley, A. D. (1976). What can amnesic patients learn? *Neuropsychologia*, **14**, 111–22.

Bruyer, R. *et al.* (1983). A case of prosopagnosia with some preserved covert remembrance of familiar faces. *Brain and Cognition*, **2**, 257–84.

Campion, J., Latto, R., and Smith, Y. M. (1983). Is blindsight an effect of scattered light, spared cortex, and near-threshold vision? *The Behavioral and Brain Sciences*, **6**, 423–86.

Cermak, L. S., Talbot, N., Chandler, K., and Wolbarst, L. R. (1985). The perceptual priming phenomenon in amnesia. *Neuropsychologia*, **23**, 615–22.

Cheesman, J. and Merikle, P. M. (1985). Word recognition and consciousness. In *Reading research: advances in theory and practice. Vol. 5*, (ed. D. Besner, T. G. Waller, and G. E. Mackinnon), pp. 311–52. Academic Press, New York.

Claparède, E. (1951). Recognition and 'me-ness'. In *Organization and pathology of thought*, (ed. D. Rapaport), pp. 58–75. Columbia University Press.

Cofer, C. C. (1967). Conditions for the use of verbal associations. *Psychological Bulletin*, **68**, 1–12.

Cohen, N. J. (1984). Preserved learning capacity in amnesia: evidence for multiple memory systems. In *Neuropsychology of memory*, (ed. L. R. Squire and N. Butters), pp. 83–103. Guilford Press, New York.

—— and Squire, L. R. (1980). Preserved learning and retention of pattern-analyzing skill in amnesia: dissociation of 'knowing how' and 'knowing that'. *Science*, **210**, 207–9.

Coltheart, M., Patterson, K. E., and Marshall, J. C. (ed.) (1980). *Deep dyslexia*. Routledge and Kegan Paul, Andover, Hants.

Corkin, S. (1965). Tactually-guided maze learning in man: effects of unilateral cortical excisions and bilateral hippocampal lesions. *Neuropsychologia*, **3**, 339–51.

—— (1968). Acquisition of motor skill after bilateral medial temporal-lobe excision. *Neuropsychologia*, **6**, 255–65.

Coslett, H. B. (1986). Preservation of lexical access in alexia without agraphia. Paper presented at the 9th European Conference (June) of the International Neuropsychological Society, Veldhoven, The Netherlands.

Damasio, A. R. (1985). Disorders of complex visual processing: agnosias, achromatopsia, Balint's syndrome, and related difficulties of orientation and construction. In *Principles of behavioral neurology*, (ed. M. M. Mesulam), pp. 259–88. F. A. Davis, Philadelphia, PA.

——, Damasio, H., and Van Hoesen, G. W. (1982). Prosopagnosia: anatomic basis and behavioral mechanisms. *Neurology*, **32**, 331–41.

De Haan, E. H. F., Young, A., and Newcombe, F. (1987). Face recognition without awareness. *Cognitive Neuropsychology*, **4**, 385–415.

Diamond, R. and Rozin, P. (1984). Activation of existing memories in the amnesic syndrome. *Journal of Abnormal Psychology*, **93**, 98–105.

Dimond, S. J. (1976). Brain circuits for consciousness. *Brain, Behaviour and Evolution*, **13**, 376–95.

Dixon, N. F. (1971). *Subliminal perception: the nature of a controversy*. McGraw-Hill, Maidenhead, Berks.

Dixon, N. F. (1981). *Preconscious processing*. John Wiley, New York.

Eriksen, C. W. (1960). Discrimination and learning without awareness: a methodological survey and evaluation. *Psychological Review*, **67**, 279–300.

Eslinger, P. J. and Damasio, A. R. (1985). Severe disturbance of higher cognition after bilateral frontal lobe ablation: patient EVR. *Neurology*, **35**, 1731–41.

Fodor, J. A. (1983). *The modularity of mind*. MIT Press, Cambridge, MA.

Fowler, C. A. (1986). An operational definition of conscious awareness must be responsible to subjective experience. *The Behavioral and Brain Sciences*, **9**, 33–5.

Frederici, A. D. (1982). Syntactic and semantic processes in aphasic deficits: the availability of prepositions. *Brain and Language*, **15**, 245–58.

Friedman, B. R. (1981). Preservation of orthographic knowledge in aphasia. *Brain and Language*, **14**, 307–14.

Gainotti, G., d'Erme, P., Monteleone, D., and Silveri, M. C. (1986). Mechanisms of unilateral spatial neglect in relation to laterality of cerebral lesions. *Brain*, **109**, 599–612.

Gassel, M. M. and Williams, D. (1963). Visual function in patients with homonymous hemianopsia-III. The completion phenomenon: insight and attitude to the defect and visual functional efficiency. *Brain*, **86**, 229–60.

Gazzaniga, M. S. (1985). *The social brain*. Basic Books, New York.

—— and LeDoux, J. E. (1978). *The integrated mind*. Plenum, New York.

Geschwind, N. (1965). Disconnexion syndromes in animals and man. *Brain*, **88**, 237–94.

Glisky, E. L., Schacter, D. L., and Tulving, E. (1986a). Computer learning by memory-impaired patients: acquisition and retention of complex knowledge. *Neuropsychologia*, **24**, 313–28.

——, ——, and —— (1986b). Learning and retention of computer-related vocabulary in memory-impaired patients: method of vanishing cues. *Journal of Clinical and Experimental Neuropsychology*, **8**, 292–312.

Goodglass, H., Gleason, J., and Hyde, M. (1970). Some dimensions of auditory language comprehension in aphasia. *Journal of Speech and Hearing Research*, **13**, 595–606.

Graf, P. and Schacter, D. L. (1985). Implicit and explicit memory for new associations in normal and amnesic subjects. *Journal of Experimental Psychology: Learning, Memory, and Cognition*, **11**, 501–18.

——, Squire, L. R., and Mandler, G. (1984). The information that amnesic patients do not forget. *Journal of Experimental Psychology: Learning, Memory, and Cognition*, **10**, 164–78.

——, Shimamura, A. P., and Squire, L. R. (1985). Priming across modalities and priming across category levels: extending the domain of preserved function in amnesia. *Journal of Experimental Psychology: Learning, Memory, and Cognition*, **11**, 385–95.

Hilgard, E. R. (1977). *Divided consciousness*. John Wiley, New York.

Hirst, W. (1982). The amnesic syndrome: descriptions and explanations. *Psychological Bulletin*, **91**, 435–60.

Holender, D. (1986). Semantic activation without conscious identification in dichotic listening, parafoveal vision, and visual masking: a survey and appraisal. *The Behavioral and Brain Sciences*, **9**, 1–66.

Holtzman, J. D., Sidtis, J. J., Volpe, B. T., Wilson, D. H., and Gazziniga, M. S. (1981). Dissociation of spatial information for stimulus localization and the control of attention. *Brain*, **104**, 861–72.

Humphrey, N. K. (1970). What the frog's eye tells the monkey's brain. *Brain, Behaviour and Evolution*, **3**, 324–37.

Johnson, M. K., Kim, J. K., and Risse, G. (1985). Do alcoholic Korsakoff's syndrome patients acquire affective reactions? *Journal of Experimental Psychology: Learning, Memory, and Cognition*, **11**, 27–36.

Johnson-Laird, P. N. (1983). *Mental models*. Harvard University Press.

Kinsbourne, M. and Warrington E. K. (1962). A variety of reading disability associated with right hemisphere lesions. *Journal of Neurology, Neurosurgery, and Psychiatry*, **25**, 208–17.

—— and Wood, F. (1975). Short term memory and the amnesic syndrome. In *Short-term memory*, (ed. D. D. Deutsch and J. A. Deutsch), pp. 258–91. Academic Press, New York.

Kolers, P. A. (1975). Memorial consequences of automatized encoding. *Journal of Experimental Psychology: Human Learning and Memory*, **1**, 689–701.

Korsakoff, S. S. (1889). Etude médico-psychologique sur une forme des maladies de la mémoire. *Revue Philosophique*, **5**, 501–30.

Landis, T., Regard, M., and Serrant, A. (1980). Iconic reading in a case of alexia without agraphia caused by a brain tumor: a tachistoscopic study. *Brain and Language*, **11**, 45–53.

Linebarger, M. C., Schwartz, M. F., and Saffran, E. M. (1983). Sensitivity to grammatical structure in so-called agrammatic aphasics. *Cognition*, **13**, 361–92.

Luria, A. R. (1976). *The neuropsychology of memory*. V. H. Winston, Washington, DC.

McAndrews, M. P., Glisky, E. L., and Schacter, D. L. (1987). When priming persists: long-lasting implicit memory for a single episode in amnesic patients. *Neuropsychologia*, **25**, 497–506.

MacCurdy, J. T. (1928). *Common principles in psychology and physiology*. Cambridge University Press.

Marcel, A. J. (1983). Conscious and unconscious perception: experiments on visual masking and word recognition. *Cognitive Psychology*, **15**, 197–237.

Margolin, D., Friedrich, F., and Carlson, N. (1983). Visual agnosia and optic aphasia: a continuum of visual-semantic dissociation. *Neurology*, **33**, 242.

Martone, M., Butters, N., Payne, M., Becker, J., and Sax, D. S. (1984). Dissociations between skill learning and verbal recognition in amnesia and dementia. *Archives of Neurology*, **41**, 965–70.

Mesulam, M. A. (1981). A cortical network for directed attention and unilateral neglect. *Annals of Neurology*, **10**, 309–25.

Milberg, W. and Blumstein, S. E. (1981). Lexical decision and aphasia: evidence for semantic processing. *Brain and Language*, **14**, 371–85.

——, ——, and Dworetzky, B. (in press). Processing of lexical ambiguities in aphasia. *Brain and Language*.

Milner, B. (1962). Les troubles de la mémoire accompagnant des lésions hippocampiques bilatérales. In *Physiologie de l'hippocampe*. Centre National de la Recherche Scientifique, Paris.

——, Corkin, S., and Teuber, H. L. (1968). Further analysis of the hippocampal amnesic syndrome: 14 year follow-up study of H.M. *Neuropsychologia*, **6**, 215–34.

Mohler, C. W. and Wurtz, R. H. (1977). Role of striate cortex and superior colliculus in visual guidance of saccadic eye movements in monkeys. *Journal of Neurophysiology*, **40**, 74–94.

Moscovitch, M. (1982). Multiple dissociations of function in amnesia. In *Human memory and amnesia*, (ed. L. S. Cermak), pp. 337–70. Lawrence Erlbaum Associates, Hillsdale, NJ.

—— (1984). The sufficient conditions for demonstrating preserved memory in amnesia: a task analysis. In *Neuropsychology of memory*, (ed. L. R. Squire and N. Butters), pp. 104–14. Guilford Press, New York.

—— (1985). Memory from infancy to old age: implications for theories of normal and pathological memory. *Annals of the New York Academy of Sciences*, **444**, 78–96.

——, Winocur, G., and McLachlan, D. (1986). Memory as assessed by recognition and reading time in normal and memory-impaired people with Alzheimer's disease and other neurological disorders. *Journal of Experimental Psychology: General*, **115**, 331–47.

Natsoulas, T. (1982). Conscious perception and the paradox of 'blind-sight'. In *Aspects of consciousness*, (ed. G. Underwood), pp. 79–109. Academic Press, New York.

Nissen, M. J. and Bullemer, P. (1987). Attentional requirements of learning: evidence from performance measures. *Cognitive Psychology*, **19**, 1–32.

Paap, K. R. (1986). The pilfering of awareness and guilt by association. *The Behavioral and Brain Sciences*, **9**, 45–6.

Paillard, J., Michel, F., and Stelmach, G. (1983). Localization without content: a tactile analogue of 'blind sight'. *Archives of Neurology*, **40**, 548–51.

Parkin, A. (1982). Residual learning capability in organic amnesia. *Cortex*, **18**, 417–40.

Patterson, K. E. and Kay, J. (1982). Letter-by-letter reading: psychological descriptions of a neurological syndrome. *Quarterly Journal of Experimental Psychology*, **34A**, 411–41.

——, Marshall, J., and Coltheart, M. (ed.) (1985). *Surface dyslexia in adults and children*. Lawrence Erlbaum Associates, New York.

Perenin, M. T. and Jeannerod, M. (1975). Residual vision in cortically blind hemifields. *Neuropsychologia*, **13**, 1–17.

—— and —— (1978). Visual function within the hemianopic field following early cerebral hemidecortication in man: I. Spatial location. *Neuropsychologia*, **16**, 1–13.

Poppel, E., Held, R., and Frost, D. (1973). Residual visual function after brain wounds involving the central visual pathways. *Nature*, **243**, 295–6.

Posner, M. (1978). *Chronometric explorations of mind*. Lawrence Erlbaum Associates, Hillsdale, NJ.

Richards, W. (1973). Visual processing in scotomata. *Experimental Brain Research*, **17**, 333–47.

Schacter, D. L. (1985). Priming of old and new knowledge in amnesic patients and normal subjects. *Annals of the New York Academy of Sciences*, **444**, 41–53.

—— (1987). Implicit memory: history and current status. *Journal of Experimental Psychology: Learning, Memory, and Cognition*, **13**, 501–18.

—— (in press). On the relation between memory and consciousness: dissociable interactions and conscious experience. In *Varieties of memory and consciousness: essays in honor of Endel Tulving*, (ed. H. L. Roediger and F. I. M. Craik). Erlbaum Associates, Hillsdale, NJ.

—— and Crovitz, H. F. (1977). Memory function after closed head injury: a review of the quantitative research. *Cortex*, **13**, 150–76.

—— and Graf, P. (1986a). Effects of elaborative processing on implicit and explicit memory for new associations. *Journal of Experimental Psychology: Learning, Memory, and Cognition* **12**, 432–44.

—— and —— (1986b). Preserved learning in amnesic patients: perspectives from research on direct priming. *Journal of Clinical and Experimental Neuropsychology*, **8**, 727–43.

—— and Tulving, E. (1982). Memory, amnesia, and the episodic-semantic memory distinction. In *The expression of knowledge* (ed. R. L. Isaacson and N. E. Spear), pp. 33–65. Plenum Press, New York.

——, Harbluk, J. L., and McLachlan, D. R. (1984). Retrieval without recollection: an experimental analysis of source amnesia. *Journal of Verbal Learning and Verbal Behavior*, **23**, 593–611.

Schvaneveldt, R. W., Meyer, D. E., and Becker, C. A. (1976). Lexical ambiguity, semantic context, and visual word recognition. *Journal of Experimental Psychology: Human Perception and Performance*, **2**, 243–56.

Schwartz, M. F., Saffran, E. M., and Marin, O. S. M. (1980). The word order problem in agrammatism. I. Comprehension. *Brain and Language*, **10**, 249–62.

Sergent, J. (in press). A new look at the human split brain. *Brain*.

Shallice, T. (1972). Dual functions of consciousness. *Psychological Review*, **79**, 383–93.

—— (1981). Neurological impairment of cognitive processes. *British Medical Bulletin*, **37**, 187–92.

—— and Saffran, E. (1986). Lexical processing in the absence of explicit word identification: evidence from a letter-by-letter reader. *Cognitive Neuropsychology*, **3**, 429–58.

Sherry, D. F. and Schacter, D. L. (1987). The evolution of multiple memory systems. *Psychological Review*, **94**, 439–54.

Shimamura, A. P. (1986). Priming effects in amnesia: evidence for a dissociable memory function. *Quarterly Journal of Experimental Psychology*, **38A**, 619–44.

—— and Squire, L. R. (1984). Paired-associate learning and priming effects in amnesia: a neuropsychological study. *Journal of Experimental Psychology: General*, **113**, 556–70.

Singer, W., Zihl, J., and Poppel, E. (1977). Subcortical control of visual thresholds in humans: evidence of modality specific and retino-topically organized mechanisms of selective attention. *Experimental Brain Research*, **29**, 173–90.

Sperry, R. W., Zaidel, E., and Zaidel, D. (1979). Self recognition and social awareness in the deconnected minor hemisphere. *Neuropsychologia*, **17**, 153–66.

Squire, L. R. and Cohen, N. J. (1984). Human memory and amnesia. In *Proceedings of the Conference on the Neurobiology of Learning and Memory*, (ed. J. McGaugh, G. Lynch, and N. Weinberger), pp. 3–64. Guilford Press, New York.

——, Shimamura, A. P., and Graf, P. (1985). Independence of recognition memory and priming effects: a neuropsychological analysis. *Journal of Experimental Psychology: Learning, Memory, and Cognition*, **11**, 37–44.

Starr, A. and Phillips, L. (1970). Verbal and motor memory in the amnestic syndrome. *Neuropsychologia*, **8**, 75–88.

Torjussen, T. (1978). Visual processing in cortically blind hemifields. *Neuropsychologia*, **16**, 15–21.

Tranel, D. and Damasio, A. R. (1985). Knowledge without awareness: an autonomic index of facial recognition by prosopagnosics. *Science*, **228**, 1453–4.

Trevarthen, C. (1970). Experimental evidence for a brain stem contribution to visual perception in man. *Brain, Behaviour and Evolution*, **3**, 338–52.

Underwood, G. (1983). Verbal reports and visual awareness. *The Behavioral and Brain Sciences*, **3**, 463–4.

Volpe, B. T., LeDoux, J. E., and Gazzaniga, M. S. (1979). Information processing of visual stimuli in an 'extinguished' field. *Nature*, **282**, 722–4.

Warrington E. K. (1962). The completion of visual forms across hemianopic field defects. *Journal of Neurosurgery and Psychiatry*, **25**, 208–17.

—— (1975). The selective impairment of semantic memory. *Quarterly Journal of Experimental Psychology*, **27**, 635–57.

—— and Shallice, T. (1980). Word form dyslexia. *Brain*, **103**, 99–112.

—— and Weiskrantz, L. (1968). New method of testing long-term retention with special reference to amnesic patients. *Nature*, **217**, 972–4.

—— and —— (1970). Amnesia: consolidation or retrieval? *Nature*, **228**, 628–30.

—— and —— (1974). The effect of prior learning on subsequent retention in amnesic patients. *Neuropsychologia*, **12**, 419–28.

—— and —— (1978). Further analysis of the prior learning effect in amnesic patients. *Neuropsychologia*, **16**, 169–76.

—— and —— (1982). Amnesia: a disconnection syndrome? *Neuropsychologia*, **20**, 233–48.

Weinstein, E. A. and Friedland, R. P. (1977). Behavioral disorders associated with hemi-inattention. In *Advances in neurology. Vol. 18*, (ed. E. A. Weinstein and R. P. Friedland), pp. 51–62. Raven Press, New York.

——, Cole, M., Mitchell, M. S., and Lyerly, O. G. (1964). Anosognosia and aphasia. *Archives of Neurology*, **10**, 376–86.

Weiskrantz, L. (1977). Trying to bridge some neuropsychological gaps between monkey and man. *British Journal of Psychology*, **68**, 431–5.

—— (1978). A comparison of hippocampal pathology in man and other animals. In *Functions of the septo-hippocampal system*, Ciba Foundation Symposium 58, pp. 373–87. Elsevier, Amsterdam.

—— (1980). Varieties of residual experience. *Quarterly Journal of Experimental Psychology*, **32**, 365–86.

—— (1983). Evidence and scotomata. *The Behavioral and Brain Sciences*, **3**, 464–7.

—— (1985). On issues and theories of the human amnesic syndrome. In *Memory systems of the brain: animal and human cognitive processes*, (ed. N. Weinberger, J. McGaugh, and G. Lynch), pp. 380–415. Guilford Press, New York.

—— (1986). *Blindsight*. Oxford University Press, New York.

—— and Warrington, E. K. (1979). Conditioning in amnesic patients. *Neuropsychologia*, **17**, 187–94.

——, ——, Sanders, M. D., and Marshall, J. (1974). Visual capacity in the hemianopic field following a restricted occipital ablation. *Brain*, **97**, 709–28.

Wolford, G. (1986). A review of the literature with and without awareness. *The Behavioral and Brain Sciences*, **9**, 49–50.

Young, A. W. (1988). Functional organization of visual recognition. In *Thought without language*, (ed. L. Weiskrantz), pp. 78–107. Oxford University Press.

Zaidel, E. (1982). Reading by the disconnected right hemisphere: an aphasiological perspective. In *Dyslexia. Neuronal, cognitive and linguistic aspects*, (ed. Y. Zotterman), pp. 67–91. Pergamon Press, Oxford.

Zihl, J. (1980). 'Blindsight': improvement of visually guided eye movements by systematic practice in patients with cerebral blindness. *Neuropsychologia*, **18**, 71–7.

11

What can the bird brain tell us about thought without language?

GABRIEL HORN

Although I have studied the brain and the behaviour of the domestic chick (*Gallus gallus domesticus*) for some two decades and am an ardent champion of its neural and behavioural capacities, I concede that the chick has no skill with words, and that its communicative capacities fall short of those that can be achieved through the use of human language. In the context of the present meeting, however, these concessions are not made reluctantly. If chicks think at all, it follows that they do so without the benefit of (human) language; and in this sense a study of their behaviour is likely to throw more light on the subject of 'thought without language' than is the study of human behaviour. I recognize, however, that there is a problem with this view: it is necessary to understand, and if possible to agree, the meaning of the word 'thought'.

Descartes (1912, p. 229) was clear enough on this issue: 'By the term *thought*, I comprehend all that is in us, so that we are immediately conscious of it'. This definition is anthropocentric and subjective, and a notion of consciousness is central to it. Since Descartes denied consciousness to non-human animals ('animals') it followed that they could not be capable of thought. Unlike Descartes, who saw discontinuity between humans and animals, Darwin (1882, p. 126) saw continuity. He wrote: '. . . the difference in mind between man and the higher animals, great as it is, certainly is one of degree and not of kind'. There thus seems to be an *impasse* between the Cartesian and Darwinian views.

A way forward, one that has been taken by several of the contributors to this symposium, is to avoid defining the word 'thought' and to study the processes which it subsumes, such as intentionality (Dickinson 1988), orientation in space and time (Thinus-Blanc 1988), attention, awareness (Schacter *et al.* 1988), the ability to organize experience into categories (Cohen 1988; Pearce 1988), memory (Cohen 1988, Schacter *et al.* 1988), and object, particularly face recognition (Sergent 1988; Spelke 1988; Young 1988). By adopting this approach it becomes possible to consider the cognitive capacities not only of humans with impaired linguistic abilities (Kertesz 1988), but also of animals which have no (human) linguistic abilities at all. It also becomes possible to enquire whether there are continuities between the cognitive capacities of humans and animals, remembering that, for both, cognition is not directly observed but is inferred from behaviour. With these considerations as background, we may ask what the chick brain has to tell us about thought without language. I will address issues which have recurred in this symposium, particularly memory processes and face recognition, and will conclude by making some general remarks about 'thought' and 'consciousness'.

Recognition through exposure

Soon after hatching, young domestic chicks follow their mothers. This following response is not only elicited by the natural mother: a chick will approach a wide range of visually conspicuous objects, especially if they are moving. If the chick continues to be exposed to such an object the chick forms a social attachment to it. When this 'training' or 'imprinting' object is near, the chick emits soft calls, and if the object is moving the chick follows it. In addition, instead of approaching other conspicuous objects, as it would have done in the naïve state, the chick may now avoid them. As a result, when the chick is given a choice between a novel object and the one it had previously seen, the chick prefers the familiar object, and, in this sense, the chick recognizes it. This pattern of behaviour suggests that the chick has learned the characteristics of the object by having been exposed to it. The learning process is known as imprinting. It occurs in precocial species, that is, in those species in which the young are capable of well-coordinated locomotor activity within a few hours of birth or hatching.

There are many advantages in using chicks to analyse the neural basis of the recognition memory of imprinting. For example, young chicks are not dependent on their mothers for feeding. By using chicks, therefore, the experimenter circumvents the problem, which may arise in the study of precocial mammals, of the young becoming imprinted on maternal odours (for example, see Porter and Etscorn 1974) rather than on an object selected by the experimenter. Furthermore, by rearing chicks in darkness before training them the experimenter may be confident that no information derived from visual experience has been stored in the brain. In addition, the chick's behaviour changes dramatically as a result of exposing the young bird to the training object. For example, if a dark-reared chick is placed, when a mere 20 hours old, in a running wheel and exposed to an illuminated, rotating box, the chick may run the equivalent of one kilometre in an hour, as it attempts to approach the training object.

The evidence that chicks recognize a stimulus they have previously seen is that they prefer it to a novel object, moving toward the former and avoiding the latter. The evidence that human subjects recognize a stimulus they have previously seen is that they make an appropriate movement or give an appropriate verbal, or autonomic (Tranel and Damasio 1985), response when they see the stimulus again. In both chicks and humans we infer from the selectivity of the response that a neural representation of the object has been established as a result of exposure to it; and in both cases the inferred recognition memory is formed in the absence of any obvious reward. To these extents there are continuities between these examples of learning in chicks and learning in humans. Whether these continuities are merely superficial or whether they have a deeper significance, for example reflecting continuities at the neural level, is still an open question, but, as we shall see, it is one which will recur.

A brain region involved in imprinting

In an effort to characterize the neural bases of the storage processes implicated in imprinting, chicks are trained by exposing them to a visually conspicuous object. A variety of such objects have been used (see Fig. 11.1). Although the finer details of the training procedure have varied in different experiments, the general pattern is similar. After hatching, chicks are reared in darkness until they are between 20 and 30 hours old. The chicks are then placed individually in running wheels, the centre of which stands some 50 cm from the imprinting stimulus. The chicks are exposed to the stimulus for approximately one to two hours. A chick's preference is subsequently measured by exposing the chick to the familiar object and to a novel object.

Through the use of a variety of techniques, biochemical, electrophysiological, and pharmacological, a region of the brain has been identified as being implicated in, and probably used for, the storage of information acquired through imprinting (for a review, see Horn 1985, 1986). The region lies within the medial part of the hyperstriatum ventrale, and is localized to the intermediate extent of this structure. The region is referred to as IMHV. If the region is lesioned prior to training the chicks fail to acquire a preference through imprinting; that is, after training, chicks with lesions of IMHV do not prefer the imprinting object to a novel object, whereas sham-operated controls do (McCabe *et al.* 1981). IMHV is also necessary for the retention of a preference acquired through imprinting. Chicks with bilateral lesion placed in IMHV shortly after training perform at chance level in a preference test. In contrast, sham-operated controls have a strong preference for the imprinting object. The deficiency in the IMHV-lesioned birds cannot be attributed to some non-specific consequence of brain damage: chicks with lesions of similar size placed in certain other brain regions prefer the training object to a novel one (McCabe *et al.* 1982).

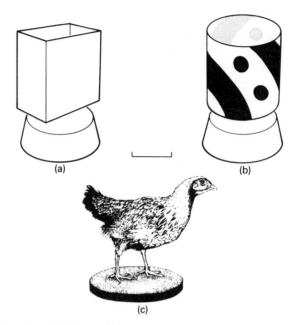

(a)   (b)

(c)

Fig. 11.1   Examples of objects which have been used as imprinting stimuli in various experiments described in the text. Stimulus (a) consists of a 12V 45W lamp over which is placed a coloured filter and round which rotates a plastic box. The two larger surfaces of the box are translucent and the other surfaces are blacked out. The object shown in (b) has a similar construction to that shown in (a), but is surrounded by a translucent plastic cylinder painted with two diagonal black stripes between which are two black circular patches. The stuffed fowl (c) is illuminated by a spotlight, and rotates on a stand. Scale bar 10 cm. (From Horn 1985.)

The poor performance of the IMHV-lesioned chicks in the preference test could be accounted for if, for example, some sensory or motor functions were impaired by the lesion, or if the chicks lacked the motivation to approach the training object. A relatively superficial examination of the chick's behaviour provides no evidence to support either explanation. Chicks with bilateral lesions of IMHV peck at objects no less accurately than do sham-operated controls, and when a control and a lesioned bird are placed together on a bench-top in the laboratory, and a 'clinical' impression formed of their behaviour, the birds cannot be distinguished from one another. Even a more detailed study of IMHV-lesioned chicks does not support a sensori–motor/ motivational explanation of their behaviour in the preference test (see the next two sections below; also see Horn 1985 for a review). It seems more likely that the IMHV-lesioned chicks have a defect of recognition memory.

Some dissociations

Human organic amnesics, who may have medial temporal lobe and/or diencephalic lesions, perform poorly when they are required to remember recent experiences, as when they are required to say whether they recognize a picture or an object they have seen before—a test of 'explicit' memory (see Schacter *et al.* 1988). In spite of this deficiency, which may be very severe, these patients are capable of learning some things, and hence are capable of storing some information (the 'implicit' memory of Schacter *et al.*). For example, the patient H.M., who has a severe defect of recognition memory, is able to learn new motor skills, such as mirror drawing (Milner 1962; Milner *et al.* 1968); and Weiskrantz and Warrington (1979) were able to establish reliable, stable, classically conditioned eye-blink responses in their amnesic patients who, like H.M., also had a defect of recognition memory.

Do operationally similar dissociations occur in chicks with appropriate brain lesions? The question is a reasonable one to ask because imprinting involves recognizing objects which have been seen before, and because lesions to IMHV impair this ability. Do these lesions of the chick brain spare certain other forms of learning, as do medial temporal lobe lesions in primates? This question was addressed in the following study.

Four groups of chicks were used: one group of IMHV-lesioned chicks, one group of sham-operated controls, and two groups of chicks with lesions in either the Wulst region of the forebrain or in the lateral parts of the cerebral hemispheres. The chicks, which were between 2.5 and three days old at the time of training, were required to discriminate between two visual patterns to obtain a reward of warm air. The apparatus is illustrated in Fig. 11.2. The experiment was conducted at 12°C. Above each goal box was a fan by means of which a stream of warm air could be introduced into the box. Half of the chicks were rewarded if they approached the blue-and-black pattern (right-hand pattern in Fig. 11.2), the remaining birds being rewarded if they approached the other pattern. The position of the stimulus to be rewarded was varied from right to left goal box on a quasi-random basis. Twenty-four trials were run for each bird. The groups did not differ (i) in the time taken to leave the start box and run down the alley, (ii) in the proportion of chicks giving correct and incorrect responses in the first and last trials, (iii) in the proportions of chicks achieving a criterion of eight out of 10 consecutive correct responses, or (iv) in the number of trials taken to reach this criterion. Thus, as evidenced by a variety of criteria, all groups of chicks learned the visual discrimination task within 24 trials; and there were no significant differences between any of these groups for any of the criteria (McCabe *et al.* 1982).

It does not follow that IMHV can be destroyed with impunity in all forms of associative learning (for example, see Patterson *et al.* 1986; Davies *et al.*, in

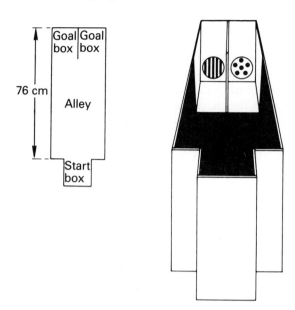

Fig. 11.2   Apparatus for the heat-reinforcement experiment. The dimensions in the left inset are scaled relative to the length of 76 cm. The floor and side walls of the goal box were painted white and the alley and start box black. The stimulus patterns were back-projected onto the Perspex rear walls as circles of light 10 cm in diameter. One stimulus pattern comprised black bars 1.3 cm wide separated by the same interval on a yellow background. The other stimulus pattern was composed of black spots, each 2.5 cm on a blue background. (After McCabe *et al.* 1982).

press). Nor could it be argued that IMHV plays no part in the visual discrimination learning described above: IMHV may play a role in such learning, but its role may not easily be detected. To illustrate the point (see Horn 1985). suppose that two things happen when a chick learns to associate a particular discriminative stimulus (for example, a pattern in a goal box (Fig. 11.2)) with a reward:

   (i) A habit is established. The neural basis of the habit need consist of little more than the strengthening of the connections between the receptors activated by the discriminative stimulus, and the neurons controlling the chick's approach response. The memory on which this habit is based would be comparable to the procedural memory of Cohen and Squire (1980) or the implicit memory of Schacter *et al.* (1988), and would be represented by the strengthened, 'peripheral', sensori–motor connection.

   (ii) The chick also stores information about a variety of aspects of the training situation, the context in which the training occurred, a further neural representation of the discriminative stimulus, and a representation of the outcome of the behavioural response. This information may be retained in a central storage system. A storage system of this kind probably corresponds to Warrington and Weiskrantz's (1982) 'mediational' memory system, to Cohen and Squire's (1980) 'declarative' memory system, and to Schacter *et al.*'s (1988) 'explicit' memory system. If the central store lies in parallel with the peripheral store, then destruction of the central store need not impair the ability of the chick to acquire a habit, such acquisition *ex hypothesi* being dependent on the strengthened peripheral sensori–motor link.

Evidence that a central store had been destroyed would only be obtained if the chick were required to read information out of this store. Such information could be used, for example, for reversal learning and for the transfer of learning. However, the only task we have so far devised for studying such functions in associative learning relates to the outcome of an operant response, and involves object recognition (Johnson and Horn 1986).

The learning abilities of IMHV-lesioned chicks were investigated by analysing their performance on an operant task. Day-old, visually naïve chicks quickly learn to press a pedal in order to be presented with either a red or a blue flashing light (Bateson and Reese 1969). As the chicks learn to associate the pedal-press with a view of the object, the chicks also learn the characteristics of this object: when presented with it, after having reached criterion on the operant task, they prefer it to be a novel object. The two processes of recognition and association occur concurrently. This training procedure, therefore, appeared to be an appropriate one to use when enquiring whether or not the process of recognition and operant learning could be dissociated by lesions of IMHV (Johnson and Horn 1986).

The operant training apparatus used is illustrated in Fig. 11.3. Three walls of the box were painted matt black. The remaining side was made of wire mesh in front of which stood the reinforcing object, either the rotating flashing red box (Fig. 11.1(a)) or the rotating stuffed fowl (Fig. 11.1(c)). In the floor of the box were set two conspicuous pedals painted in a black-and-white chequer-board pattern. The chick could press a pedal merely by stepping on it. Pressing one of the pedals activated a relay which resulted in the illumination and rotation of the reinforcing object for so long as the chick remained on the pedal. The 'activated' object was now attractive to the chick, which moved toward it and, in so doing, moved off the pedal. As a result, the object ceased to be illuminated and stopped rotating. Pressing the other pedal had no effect. To counteract any left/right bias the position of the 'active' pedal was varied systematically between different birds. For a given bird the active pedal was consistently on the right or the left side of the floor of the box. Thus the chicks were required to go to a certain place in order to be rewarded by a view of the activated object.

Two groups of chicks were used, sham-operated controls and chicks with

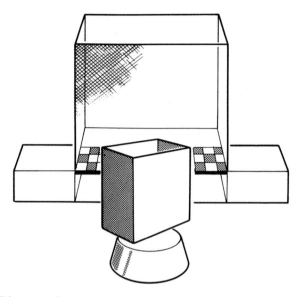

Fig. 11.3 Diagram of the operant training apparatus with one of the reinforcing stimuli in front of the open mesh side. The mesh side measures 42 cm × 30 cm. The stimuli were placed 35 cm in front of the apparatus. For a discussion, see text. (After Bateson and Reese 1969.)

lesions placed bilaterally in IMHV. The operations were carried out when the dark-reared chicks were approximately 12 hours old. Operant training began when the chicks had fully recovered from surgery and were 20–24 hours old. For half of the chicks the reinforcing object was the red box; for the other half it was the stuffed fowl. The chicks were given two training sessions, the second session beginning approximately two hours after the end of the first.

The two groups of chicks did not differ in the mean time taken to make the first pedal-press (Fig. 11.4(a)). Some 70 per cent of the birds in each group reached the criterion of nine out of 10 successive presses of the active pedal in one of the two training sessions (Fig. 11.4(b)). There were no significant differences in the mean time taken by each group of chicks to reach the criterion, and in both groups it was reached sooner in the second operant training session than in the first (Fig. 11.4(c)). Furthermore, the two groups of chicks did not differ in the amount of time spent on the active pedal. Thus chicks with lesions in IMHV did not differ significantly from the sham-operated controls in any measure of performance, and both groups learned to press the pedal in order to gain a view of the training object, which they approached.

Two hours after the second session in the operant training apparatus the chicks were given a simultaneous choice test (Bateson and Wainwright 1972).

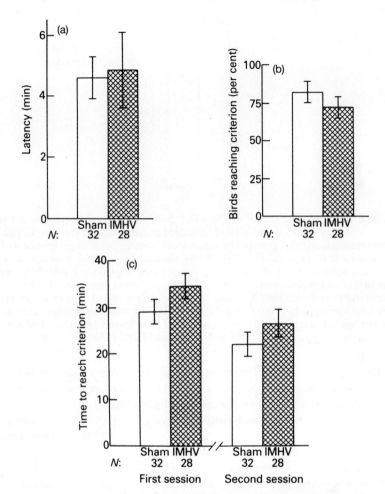

Fig. 11.4 Operant training task. Means ± standard errors of the mean (SEM), (a) Latency to make first pedal-press. (b) Percentage of birds reaching criterion in one of the two training sessions. The birds came from seven batches and the percentage of birds, in each batch, to reach criterion was calculated. The overall mean and standard error of the seven mean values were calculated and are shown. (c) Time taken to reach criterion according to training session. The mean time taken in the second session was significantly shorter than that in the first session for both the sham-operated controls and for the IMHV-lesioned chicks ($p < 0.005$). N is the number of chicks in each group. (After Johnson and Horn 1986.)

A preference score was calculated which provided a measure of the percentage of the total activity in the test which was directed toward the training object. The sham-operated chicks preferred the object which had been used as a reinforcer; chicks with bilateral lesions of IMHV performed at chance,

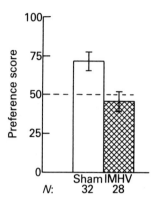

Fig. 11.5 Preference scores of chicks which had been trained on the operant task. Means ± SEM. The objects which had been used as the reinforcers (either the red box or the rotating fowl) were both placed equidistant from the chick. A preference score of 100 implies that all a chick's activity was directed toward the training object, a preference score of 0 that all the activity was directed toward the novel object, and a score of 50 that the chick preferred neither one object to the other. The sham-operated control chicks preferred the object they had previously seen and their mean preference score was significantly greater than 50 ($p < 0.01$). The mean preference score of the lesioned birds was significantly less than that of the controls ($p < 0.01$), and was not significantly different from 50. (After Johnson and Horn 1986.)

showing no greater preference for the reinforcing object than for the novel object. The mean preference score achieved by the controls was significantly greater than that achieved by the lesioned birds (Fig. 11.5).

The failure of the lesioned birds selectively to approach the reinforcing object in a preference test could be accounted for in many ways, though explanations in terms of changes in arousal, attention, motor and sensory functions are not consistent with the available evidence (see Horn 1985) or with the lack of the impairment in the operant task itself. In particular, when the sham-operated control chicks stood on the active pedal, and the object was illuminated and rotated, the chicks moved off the pedal to approach the object. Not only did the IMHV-lesioned chicks learn to press the active pedal as quickly as the controls, but they also stepped off the pedal as quickly; that is, the activated object appeared to be as effective in eliciting approach responses from the lesioned chicks as from the controls. The lesioned chicks were no less active in the preference test than were the controls; but unlike the controls the lesioned chicks did not direct their movements more to the reinforcing object than to the novel object. They behaved as if they were *unfamiliar* with the reinforcing object and did not recognize it.

The dissociation by brain lesions of the ability of chicks to learn a habit (procedural or implicit memory) from their ability to recognize an object which had been used in the operant conditioning procedure (mediational, declarative, or explicit memory) is reminiscent of the behaviour of human patients suffering from certain forms of organic amnesia. H.M. acquired the skill to perform a mirror drawing task, but this learning was unaccompanied by any feeling of *familiarity* (Milner 1962); Weiskrantz and Warrington's (1979) patients could be conditioned, but they appeared to be *unfamiliar* with the essentials of the conditioning procedures, and appeared not to recognize the apparatus used in the training experiments (also see Claparède 1911 quoted by MacCurdy 1928). This operational similarity between the performance of human organic amnesics on the one hand and IMHV-lesioned chicks on the other is consistent with the view that more than one memory system may be formed during learning, with a peripheral memory represented as the strengthening of some sensori–motor link and one or more central stores lying in parallel. In the chick IMHV may be, or be part of, the mediational (declarative or explicit) memory system.

There is evidence from mammals that makes the notion of parallel stores more than a 'neuro-logical' one. An air puff delivered to the cornea of the eye of rabbits or cats elicits an eye-blink and a contraction of the nictitating membrane, a third cartilaginous eyelid. If the air puff is presented together with a tone a sufficient number of times, the eye-blink/nictitating membrane response comes to be elicited by the tone alone. The conditioned response can be learned by cats and rabbits without the cerebral cortex, including the hippocampus (see Thompson *et al.* 1983). Nevertheless, the activity of neurons in the rabbit hippocampus is modified in a highly specific way during the course of training (Berger and Thompson 1978). These findings together suggest that the hippocampus is involved in the learning process and that it lies in parallel with the neural structures necessary for the formation of the sensori–motor component of the conditioned response (these structures include the cerebellum—see Thompson *et al.* 1983; Yeo *et al.* 1985).

It is not being suggested that, for mammals, the hippocampus is a central store, only that it, and other structures in the medial temporal lobe are implicated in learning and recognition processes (see Murray and Mishkin 1986; Zola-Morgan and Squire 1984). Damage to structures in this lobe disconnects the input to the store, which may be in the frontal lobes and which may correspond to the mediational memory store of Warrington and Weiskrantz (1982). The IMHV of chicks is 'upstream' of the avian hippocampus, though whether IMHV corresponds to the cortex of the primate prefrontal lobe is not known (see Horn 1985). It is, however, attractive to speculate that early in the history of terrestrial vertebrates a circuit for efficiently storing information evolved and has been retained by natural selection. Clearly there is no way such an hypothesis can be tested, but it is worth remarking that many structures, from the molecular to the anatomical levels of complexity, have been preserved in the course of evolution, sometimes with little or no modification.

Is there a predisposition to respond to faces?

It has been established for some time that young precocial birds have a tendency to approach some objects rather than others, but the suggestion that objects resembling the natural mother of the young bird are particularly effective in eliciting approach (Hinde 1961; Gaioni et al. 1978) has not been extensively investigated. The evidence that led us to begin such an investigation came from a series of four experiments involving lesions to IMHV. In these experiments two objects were used as imprinting stimuli: the rotating, flashing, red box (Fig. 11.1(a)) and a rotating, stuffed fowl (Fig. 11.1(c)). In each of these studies, an analysis of variance had been performed on the preference scores contributed by the lesioned and control groups of chicks. These scores were not significantly affected by the nature of the training object. However, when data for all the lesion studies were combined, a clear effect appeared: lesions to IMHV profoundly affected the preference of chicks exposed to the box, but had a smaller, though significant, effect on chicks that had been trained on the fowl (Horn and McCabe 1984). A similar pattern of results was obtained by Davies et al. (1985). They found that the acquisition of a preference for the box was severely impaired following the administration of the neurotoxin DSP4. This neurotoxin was found to reduce the concentration of noradrenaline in the chick forebrain by approximately 60 per cent. The effect of this drug, like the effect of lesions to IMHV, was comparatively small, though significant, for chicks, trained on the stuffed fowl. In contrast, the preference for the fowl, but not for the box, was correlated with plasma testosterone concentration; and the administration of exogenous testosterone enhanced the acquisition of a preference for the fowl, but was without effect on the acquisition of a preference for the box (Bolhuis et al. 1986). These results taken together suggest that some neural structures and mechanisms involved in imprinting on the red box are different from those that are involved in imprinting on the fowl.

In the light of the findings described above, it seemed curious that no behavioural evidence of a stronger preference for the fowl or a selective predisposition to approach it had been found over the years of studying intact chicks. Such a predisposition may have been present but have gone undetected if the sequential test of preference, which had been used in all save one of the lesion studies, was insufficiently sensitive. A simultaneous choice test is more sensitive and may reveal more subtle changes in preference than does the sequential test (see Horn 1985). Using the simultaneous choice test, we found that dark-reared chicks that had spent some two hours in the running wheels when they were approximately 24–27 hours old, later preferred the fowl to the red box. This preference could be detected when the chicks were given the choice test 24 hours after having been removed from the wheel. If only two hours elapsed after being removed, the chicks showed no preference for one stimulus over the other. This emerging preference appeared even though the chicks had been in darkness until they were given the choice test; that is, until this time the chicks had seen neither of the test objects before (Bolhuis *et al.* 1985; Johnson *et al.* 1985). Apart from the two hours spent in the running wheels the chicks remained housed in individual compartments within an incubator. Control chicks, which had remained in the incubator until the choice test, showed no preference for one object over the other. Thus handling, or being in the wheel, or some other factor associated with this experience, appears to be necessary for the predisposition to 'surface'. What the crucial factors are is not yet known, nor is it clear why such a long time after the experience of the running wheel needs to elapse before the preference for the fowl appears (for a discussion, see Bolhuis *et al.* 1985). We have enquired, however, what features or characters of the stuffed fowl cause it to be preferred over the red box (Johnson and Horn, in press).

In these experiments chicks were maintained in darkness from the time of hatching until they were given a simultaneous choice test. When the chicks were approximately 24 hours old they were placed individually in running wheels for a total of two hours. At all other times the chicks remained in the dark incubator. The chicks were tested *either* two hours (test I) after having been removed from the wheel *or* 24 hours (test II) afterwards. One of the two objects was always the stuffed fowl (Fig. 11.1 (a)). The other 'test' object varied between different experiments. During the choice test these objects were illuminated and rotated on their base. When the test object was the red box, the chicks preferred the fowl at test II, but not at test I, as expected from the earlier studies. When the test object was an inverted, anatomically unusual stuffed fowl (Fig. 11.6(a)) no preference for either object appeared at either test (Fig. 11.6(b)). When the test object was a cut-up pelt of a fowl (Fig. 11.7(a)), stuck on the side of a rectangular box, the chicks preferred the intact fowl at test II (Fig. 11.7(b)).

In an effort to identify which component of the fowl was attractive to the chicks the test object illustrated in Fig. 11.8(a) was used. This object was found to be as attractive to the chicks as the intact fowl (Fig. 11.8(b)). In the next experiment only the head and neck region of the object illustrated in Fig. 11.8(a) remained on the box. When given the choice between this object and the intact fowl the chicks showed no preference for either object (Fig. 11.9); that is, the head and neck region was as attractive to the chicks as was the intact fowl. When the test object was another species (a Gadwall duck) no preference developed. These results suggest that the 'target' of the predisposition is the configuration of features contained within the head and neck region, and that this configuration is not species specific.

In the natural situation, where the chick is exposed to patterned light and is able to move around freely, the predisposition may emerge very rapidly (Bolhuis *et al.* 1985). In the natural environment the predisposition may serve

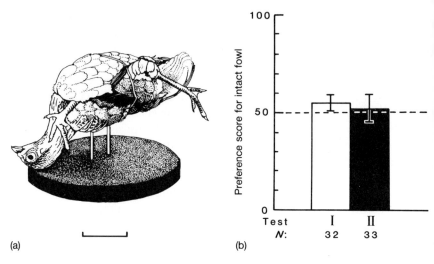

(a)   (b)

Fig. 11.6 (a) The disarticulated stuffed fowl used as the test object against the intact fowl [see Fig. 11.1(c)]. Scale bar 10 cm. (b) The mean and standard error preference scores of the two groups of chicks at the two testing times. Test I was conducted two hours and test II 24 hours after chicks had been removed from running wheels. The preference score is expressed, in percentage terms, as a preference for the intact fowl. This preference score is calculated in such a way that activity directed solely toward the intact fowl is given a score of 100, activity directed solely toward the test object, a score of 0, and when the chicks run equally to the two objects the preference score is 50 (no preference). The number (N) of chicks used in each test is given below each bar of the diagram. (After Johnson and Horn in press.)

to ensure that the chick approaches an appropriate object, normally the chick's own mother. The chick may then learn her characteristics and so come to recognize her (see also Spelke 1988). IMHV is probably implicated in this learning process but not in the emerging predisposition (Horn and McCabe 1984; Johnson *et al.* 1985; Bolhuis *et al.* 1985). Two predictions arise from this proposal. First, ablation of IMHV should not impair the emerging predisposition. This prediction was confirmed by Johnson and Horn (1986): IMHV-lesioned chicks which had been exposed to the fowl or box behaved like intact dark-reared birds in the choice test; that is, the lesioned chicks all showed an emerging preference for the intact fowl relative to the box. Second, chicks, with lesions of IMHV should be unable to learn the characteristics of individuals. This prediction has also been confirmed (Johnson and Horn 1987). These authors showed that if young, dark-reared chicks are placed in a running wheel and exposed to a stuffed fowl (see Fig. 11.1(c)) for a few hours, they prefer it to another stuffed fowl in a choice test. Chicks with lesions of IMHV perform at chance in this test.

The failure of chicks with lesions of IMHV to recognize particular

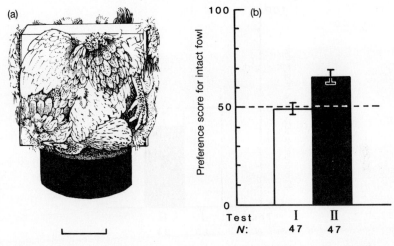

Fig. 11.7 (a) The cut-up pelt mounted on the box. Scale bar 6 cm. (b) The mean (±SEM) preference scores of the two groups of chicks at the two tests. (After Johnson and Horn, in press.)

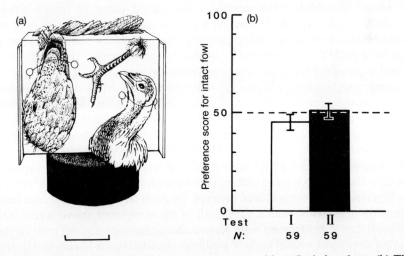

Fig. 11.8 (a) The 'scrambled' fowl pelt used as test object. Scale bar 6 cm. (b) The mean (±SEM) preference scores of the two groups of chicks at the two tests. (After Johnson and Horn, in press.)

individuals has implications for the ability of these chicks to select a mate in later life. When choosing a mate, females of some species may prefer an individual that differs slightly from those with which the female has been raised (Bateson 1978). The developmental process involved in establishing

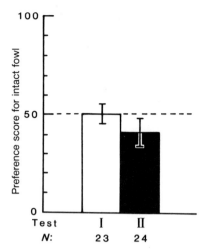

Fig. 11.9   The mean ($\pm$ SEM) preference scores of the two groups of chicks at the two tests (see text for discussion). (After Johnson and Horn, in press.)

such preferences is known as sexual imprinting. The effects of IMHV lesions on sexual imprinting have recently been studied using 32 female chicks (Bolhuis *et al.*, in prep.). The chicks were dark-reared until they were anaesthetized 6–10 hours after hatching. Sixteen chicks received bilateral lesions to IMHV and 16 served as sham-operated controls. The chicks were raised in groups. Each group contained four females, either all controls or all lesioned, and two normal males from the same hatch. After six weeks one of these males was removed from each group, leaving the four females with one male. The sexual preferences of the females were measured when the birds were 12 weeks old. In the choice test two males were placed in separate enclosures behind Perspex screens. The test female was able to see both males. An observer, unaware of the identity of the test female, recorded the time spent by the females next to each of the two males. On the first day of testing the females were given a choice between the male with which they had been reared (familiar white) and a novel male of the same strain (novel white). On the second day, the females were given a choice between a novel male of the rearing strain and a novel male of a different strain, Rhode Island Red (novel brown). The sham-operated birds spent significantly more time with the novel white than they did with the familiar white or the novel brown. There were no such differences for the lesioned females.

The results of the experiment described above provide clear evidence of selectivity in mate choice in the intact female domestic hen: males that were slightly different from the individual with which the female had been reared were most preferred. The absence of this finding in the lesioned birds is very unlikely to be attributable to some general impairment of behaviour that made them less able to perform the choice tests. These birds preferred a novel white male to an artificial stimulus, a rotating red box. Furthermore, the lesioned females approached the test males; and, although not selective in their choice, the mean time spent by these females in close proximity to the test males was not significantly different from that of the sham-operated controls.

Both filial and sexual preferences are based on learning processes which involve recognition, of a parent in the former case and of sibs in the latter. The results of these experiments suggest that the learning processes have a common neural substrate which includes IMHV, and demonstrate that lesions of this region have relatively lasting effects on these proceses.

The evidence presented in this section indicates that the emerging predisposition is for the head and neck region, and that a system lying outside IMHV may be responsible for controlling this predisposition. The possibility that some features of the head and neck may activate, in this system, neurons with properties resembling 'face' neurons in the temporal cortex of monkeys (Bruce et al. 1981; Perrett et al. 1982) is an attractive one.

When, in the course of filial imprinting, the predisposition directs the young chick's attention to the head and neck of its own mother, the chick may learn specifically about the features in this region and come to recognize her on the basis of these features. It is therefore of interest that Scott (unpublished thesis 1980) found that the head region was particularly important for the recognition of adult quail by their chicks, and Candland (1969) found that combinations of features associated with the head are particularly important in the recognition of other individuals by adult chickens.

The notion of a predisposition directing the newly hatched chick's attention towards stimuli resembling the head or face of conspecifics may have parallels in other species. For example, it is known that human new-borns are prepared to track a schematic face rather than a variety of 'scrambled' faces (Goren et al. 1975). It is possible that this predisposition ensures that characteristics of faces are learned very quickly by infants (Johnson, in press).

Language and thinking

It might be argued that by using the device of analysing some of the processes subsumed by the word 'thought' I have avoided addressing the problem of whether thought may occur without language, and the subsidiary question of whether animals can think. However, provided a comprehensive list of these processes is set out, then the word 'thought' is defined (the list of processes given on p. 279 is not, of course, comprehensive). The central question is whether the list, to be complete, must include human symbolic language as an item. To insist on its inclusion would be to imply that visual thinking, in humans, cannot occur unless such language is used as the medium of the imagery. Yet studies of brain-damaged patients show that damage to the right, linguistically impoverished hemisphere produces handicaps in the ingredients of visual thinking—in visual recognition, especially of objects, faces, and places, and in visual memory (Newcombe 1969; Warrington 1982; Newcombe *et al.* 1987; Sergent 1988). Furthermore, some patients with right-hemisphere lesions report that their visual imagery and visual memory become faint and sketchy and some report that they have ceased to dream (Humphrey and Zangwill 1951). From such considerations Zangwill (1976, p. 308) concluded that there is '... *prima facie* evidence that the right hemisphere has an important part to play in what might loosely be called visual thinking'.

In the light of the more recent evidence about the visual functions of the right hemisphere provided by studies of commissurotomized patients (see Sperry 1984) and of patients with other brain damage (see Warrington 1982; Newcombe *et al.* 1987; Sergent 1988), the *prima facie* case can probably now be regarded as substantive. Therefore symbolic language may be omitted from the list of conditions that must be met if 'thinking' is to be inferred from human behaviour. Whilst symbolic language may enormously extend the power and range of thinking, it is not a necessary condition for thinking (see Kertesz 1988; Jansons 1988). There seem no good grounds, therefore, for denying this activity to non-human animals and to a range of animals that extends beyond the primate order to which humans belong.

Thought and consciousness in humans and other animals

It is not, I suppose, wholly inappropriate to make some concluding remarks about thought and consciousness since, for Descartes, the two were inextricably entwined and I began this chapter by referring to his views. Like Descartes I assume that I am conscious. When other human beings behave in particular ways I assert that they too are conscious. By and large this concession is mutual: others seem to be willing to admit that I am conscious. Difficulties appear to arise when an animal, about which an opinion is being sought as to its state of consciousness, is not human; and the further the animal is away from resembling a human the greater appears to be the difficulty. In an attempt to resolve this difficulty it might be worth identifying the kinds of behaviour which, when present, would widely be accepted as evidence that a human is conscious. An easy way to begin is to consider an instance where there may be general agreement that a person is *unconscious*. There would probably be a consensus that a patient in deep, clinical coma is unconscious—a person, that is, who is inert, cannot be aroused by any stimulus, however vigorous, and who on recovery has no recollection of events which occurred during the coma. In the course of recovery such patients show periods, increasing in duration, when they make co-ordinated movements, become increasingly more alert to events going on around them, are attentive, recognize objects and faces, use objects appropriately, show purposive behaviour, become orientated in space and time, are able to remember past events, and are able to learn. When this whole repertoire of capacities is present many would agree that the patient is conscious. The transition from unconsciousness to consciousness is not abrupt; during the recovery period the patient may be described as being 'partly conscious'.

One element implicit in the above description of recovery from coma relates to the state of awareness—for example, the patient is often said to 'become increasingly aware of his surroundings'. Indeed a notion of awareness is central to the meaning of the word 'conscious'. Recent studies of blindsight have provided important clues about certain of the criteria used for inferring awareness in humans.

Blindsight refers to the residual capacities of patients with damage to the visual cortex to respond to visual stimuli in the 'blind' part of the visual field (Sanders *et al.* 1974). Although these patients may respond to such a stimulus, they characteristically say they have seen nothing; that is, they respond to the visual stimulus, but appear to be unaware of that stimulus. Thus response and awareness are dissociated. Perhaps this dissociation characterizes the behaviour of animals: do they behave like Cartesian automata, responding to stimuli without being aware of them?

In patients with blindsight accuracy in localizing stimuli within the blind region, the scotoma, is poorer than for stimuli presented in the intact visual field; and whilst orientation discrimination for stimuli presented within the scotoma may be reasonably well preserved, pattern discrimination and form identification may be severely impaired (for a review, see Schacter 1988; Weiskrantz 1986). Thus a patient with blindsight not only appears to be unaware of visual stimuli presented within the scotoma but also *his capacities to make visual discriminations within the scotoma are differentially impaired in striking ways.* How might we judge whether a human subject is aware of a stimulus to which he responds if the subject is not able, or not permitted, to give a verbal response when presented with the stimulus? If the subject were able to detect and to discriminate visual stimuli over a range similar to that of a normal human who asserts that he is aware of such stimuli, we might conclude that the subject too was aware of the stimuli. But if the subject's abilities to detect and discriminate stimuli resembled those which characterize a patient with blindsight, we might reasonably conclude that the subject, like the patient, was unaware of the stimuli. There is no reason why similar criteria for inferring the existence of awareness should not be applied to animals. The evidence available, mainly from studies of the visual abilities of vertebrates, including macaques, rats, chickens, and pigeons (for example, see Hinde 1970), gives no support to the view that the visual capacities of these animals resemble those of humans with blindsight, and no reason, therefore, to infer that these animals are unaware of the stimuli to which they respond.

Patients with blindsight respond to certain visual stimuli without being aware, or 'conscious', of them. The neural basis of the dissociation is not known. It is worth considering, however, possible neural bases of the syndrome if only to provide hypotheses for future empirical work and to throw light on the possible neural mechanisms of awareness.

Perception may involve the comparison of a currently presented stimulus with previous experience, stored in memory, of that stimulus or of similar stimuli. This view is hardly new. James (1950, Vol. 2, p. 103) wrote:

Enough has now been said to prove the general law of perception, which is this, that *whilst part of what we perceive comes through our senses from the object before us, another part* (and it may be the larger part) *always comes out of our head.*

James implied that the contribution from the head was the memory of the stimulus and of its context—a memory, that is, of other events that were occurring at the same time as the stimulus was experienced, as well as when the experience occurred: 'We apprehended it, in short, with a cloud of associates . . .' (1950, Vol. 2, p. 81). And he also wrote:

Each of its associates becomes a hook to which it hangs, a means to fish it up by when sunk beneath the surface. Together, they form a network of attachments by which it is woven into the entire tissue of our thought (1950, Vol. 1, p. 662).

Is it possible that the activation of this 'network of attachments'—which may correspond to information-storing networks of neurons in mediational memory (see p. 285)—is necessary for a human (or an animal) to be aware of a currently present stimulus, and that if this stimulus fails to activate these networks it would not have 'a hook' on which to hang and the human (or animal) would be unaware of the stimulus? Such a failure to activate the networks could be achieved by, for example, disconnecting them from the sensory analysers of the input. Another possibility is that the current stimulus may be encoded in the central nervous system in such a way that the network storing information about previous experience of that or other similar inputs may not be activated. In the case of blindsight part of the visual cortex is destroyed. The intact visual pathways which subserve the residual visual response in blindsight may encode information in a different way from that of the visual cortex. This form of encoding may be ineffective in activating the memorial networks established before the lesion and which operated on a code generated by the output of the previously intact visual cortex.

Mediational memory is, by implication, a system in which contextually rich information of previous experiences is stored (Warrington and Weiskrantz 1982). If this is so, it may be that the degree of awareness is a function of the storage capacity of this system. In nervous systems where this capacity is small or non-existent the ability to store contextually rich information would, correspondingly, be small or non-existent. If small, (i) information about all objects may be stored in a contextually impoverished manner or (ii) information of great survival value (e.g. about parents, home, foraging sites) may be stored with contextual embellishment whereas other information may be stored without such embellishment.

An implication of the arguments set out above would be that animals without mediational memory systems respond to stimuli in the environment without being aware of them. Such animals may learn to respond selectively to these stimuli, but the acquired response would be little more than a habit, and the memory system a 'peripheral' one, corresponding to implicit or procedural memory (see pp. 284–5). The arguments given above also imply that animals with nervous systems that are able to store contextually rich information are aware of the stimuli to which they respond, and that the magnitude, or level of awareness, varies with the storage capacity of the mediational memory system. Just which animals possess this system and which do not, and whether there are continuities or discontinuities in the capacity of these systems between species, are empirical questions that have still to be resolved.

Studies of blindsight have provided valuable clues about object awareness, but no direct information about self-awareness. If it is conceded that a human, or a particular animal, is aware of objects, what additional criteria are needed to clarify whether that individual is self-aware? The issue of self-awareness is central to the Cartesian view of consciousness. Descartes' dictum, 'I think therefore I am', posits an 'I'. 'I' is an autobiographical word: it summarizes verbally the history of an individual. This autobiographical information depends critically on at least two abilities: (i) the ability to distinguish self from other objects which occupy space and (ii) the ability to store contextually rich autobiographical information. We may assume that humans have these abilities; do animals have them?

If an animal were not aware of its body some very odd things would be expected—mice would probably get stuck in holes that were too small for them to get through, a kitten might never cease to chase its tail, and self-mutilation would be common. In practice, of course, mice tend not to get stuck in holes, kittens stop chasing their tails, and although I know of no quantitative studies, self-mutilation appears to be rare in nature. It therefore seems reasonable to infer that many animals are able to distinguish their own bodies from other objects that occupy space (Horn 1952). In humans the ability to make this distinction is facilitated by the organization of the central nervous system, especially of the brain. 'Labelled lines' transmit to particular brain regions information about events occurring on the body surface (somatic sensory signals), information about the position and movements of parts of the body relative to each other (proprioceptive), and of the orientation of the body in gravitational space (vestibular), and indicate when the body surface has been damaged (pain). Other labelled lines and other brain regions are specialized for transmitting and analysing respectively, e.g.

visual, auditory, and olfactory signals which are usually initiated by events remote from the body. It seems reasonable to suppose that the labelled lines and the corresponding brain regions are part of the neural machinery which allows events impinging directly on or occurring within the individual's body (intrapersonal space) to be distinguished from events occurring in extrapersonal space. This labelled-line organization is found widely amongst vertebrates. And although the structural organization of invertebrate nervous systems is radically different from that of vertebrates, many invertebrate nervous systems have labelled lines which preserve the identity of signals evoked by events occurring on or within the body, as well as by events occurring outside the body (see Bullock *et al.* 1977). Thus the nervous system of a wide range of animals, like that of humans, is organized in a way that may permit an individual to distinguish between self and not-self.

Autobiographical memory is the thread that holds together the beads of an individual's episodic sensory experiences. Some animals, probably very many, have autobiographical memory just as humans have. Autobiographical memory may be short-lasting as in the case of working memory (for example, see Olton and Samuelson 1976; Kamil 1978); and autobiographical memory may be long-lasting as when animals recognize objects and places after relatively long delays (Beritashvili 1972; Hess 1973; Overman and Doty 1980; Sherry *et al.* 1981; Vander Wall 1982; Sherry 1984). We need to know whether the contextual richness of autobiographical memory varies between species. Nevertheless the evidence already available suggests that autobiographical memory is not the prerogative of human beings.

If the various criteria for judging the state of consciousness in other human beings are applied to an animal, and it is not found wanting, it is difficult to deny the animal that state; so when an animal behaves in such a way as to satisfy these criteria it seems logically capricious to argue that it is not conscious.

Just as symbolic language must greatly extend the range and power of thinking, so must it greatly enrich the state of consciousness. But I suspect that the time will come that the view that humans alone are conscious will be regarded as ignorantly anthropocentric as the view that the sun revolves around the earth.

References

Bateson, P. (1978). Sexual imprinting and optimal outbreeding. *Nature*, **273**, 659–60.
—— and Reese, E. P. (1969). The reinforcing properties of conspicuous stimuli in the imprinting situation. *Animal Behaviour*, **17**, 692–9.
—— and Wainwright, A. A. P. (1972). The effects of prior exposure to light on the imprinting process in domestic chicks. *Behaviour*, **42**, 279–90.
Berger, T. W. and Thompson, R. F. (1978). Neuronal plasticity in the limbic system

during classical conditioning of the rabbit nictitating membrane response. *Brain Research*, **145**, 323–46.

Beritashvili, I. S. (1972). Phylogeny of memory development in vertebrates. In *Brain and human behavior*, (ed. A. G. Karczmar and J. C. Eccles), pp. 341–51. Springer, New York.

Bolhuis, J. J., Johnson, M. H., and Horn, G. (1985). Effects of early experience on the development of filial preferences in the domestic chick. *Develop. Psychobiol.*, **18**, 299–308.

——, McCabe, B. J., and Horn, G. (1986). Androgens and imprinting: differential effects of testosterone on filial preference in the domestic chick. *Behav. Neurosci.*, **100**, 51–6.

——, Johnson, M. H., Horn, G., and Bateson, P (in prep.). Sexual imprinting in domestic chicks impaired by the brain lesion which affects filial imprinting.

Bruce, C., Desimone, R., and Gross, C. G. (1981). Visual properties of neurons in a polysensory area in superior temporal sulcus of the macaque. *J. Neurophysiol.*, **46**, 369–84.

Bullock, T. H., Orkand, R., and Grinnell, A. (1977). *Introduction to nervous systems*, W. H. Freeman, San Francisco, CA.

Candland, D. K. (1969). Discrimination of facial regions used by the domestic chick in maintaining the social dominance order. *J. Comp. Physiol. Psychol.*, **69**, 281–5.

Claparède, E. (1911). Récognition et moïïë. *Archs. Psychol.*, **11**, 79–90.

Cohen, N. J. and Squire, L. R. (1980). Preserved learning and retention of pattern analyzing skill in amnesia: dissociation of knowing how and knowing that. *Science*, **210**, 207–9.

Cohen, L. B. (1988). An information-processing approach to infant cognitive development. In *Thought without language*, (ed. L. Weiskrantz), pp. 211–28. Oxford University Press.

Darwin, C. (1882). *The descent of man*, (2nd edn). J. Murray, London.

Davies, D. C., Horn, G., and McCabe, B. J. (1985). Noradrenaline and learning: the effects of the noradrenergic neurotoxin DSP4 on imprinting in the domestic chick. *Behav. Neurosci.*, **99**, 652–60.

——, Taylor, D. A., and Johnson, M. H. (in press). The effects of hyperstriatal lesions on l-trial passive avoidance learning in the chick. *J. Neurosci.*

Descartes, R. (1912). *A discourse on method*. (trans. J. Veitch). J. M. Dent and Sons Ltd., London.

Dickinson, A. (1988). Internationality in animal conditioning. In *Thought without language*, (ed. L. Weiskrantz), pp. 305–25. Oxford University Press.

Gaioni, C. C., Hoffman, H. S., and de Paulo, P. (1978), Imprinting in older ducklings: some tests of a reinforcement model. *Anim. Learn. & Behav.*, **6**, 19–26.

Goren C. C., Sarty, M., and Wu, P. Y. K. (1975). Visual following and pattern discrimination of face-like stimuli by newborn infants. *Pediatrics, Springfield*, **56**, 544–9.

Hess, H. E. (1973). *Imprinting: early experience and the developmental pscychobiology of attachment*. Van Nostrand Reinhold, New York.

Hinde, R. A. (1961). The establishment of the parent–offspring relation in birds, with some mammalian analogies. In *Current problems in animal behaviour*, (ed. W. H. Thorpe and O. L. Zangwill), pp. 175–93. Cambridge University Press.

—— (1970). *Animal behaviour*, (2nd edn). McGraw-Hill, New York.

Horn, G. (1952). The neurological basis of thought. *Mermaid*, **18**, 17–25.

—— (1985). *Memory, imprinting, and the brain*. Clarendon Press, Oxford.

—— (1986). Imprinting, learning and memory. *Behav. Neurosci.*, **100**, 825–32.

—— and McCabe, B. J. (1984). Predispositions and preferences. Effects on imprinting of lesions to the chick brain. *Animal Behaviour*, **32**, 288–92.

Humphrey, M. E. and Zangwill, O. L. (1951). Cessation of dreaming after brain injury. *J. Neurol. Neurosurg. Psychiat.*, **14**, 322–5.

James, W. J. (1950). *The principles of psychology*. Dover Publications, New York.

Jansons, K. M. (1988). A personal view of dyslexia and of thought without language. In *Thought without language*, (ed. L. Weiskrantz), pp. 498–503. Oxford University Press.

Johnson, M. H. (1987). Brain maturation and the development of face recognition in early infancy. *Behav. Brain Res.* **26**, 224.

—— and Horn, G. (1986). Dissociation of recognition memory and associative learning by a restricted lesion of the chick forebrain. *Neuropsychologia*, **24**, 329–40.

—— and —— (1987). The role of a restricted region of the chick forebrain in the recognition of individual conspecifics. *Behav. Brain Res.*, **23**, 269–75.

—— and —— (in press). Development of filial preferences in the dark-reared chick. *Animal Behaviour*.

——, Bolhuis, J. J., and Horn, G. (1985). Interaction between acquired preferences and developing predispositions during imprinting. *Animal Behaviour*, **33**, 1000–6.

Kamil, A. C. (1978). Systematic foraging by a nectar-feeding bird, the amakihi (*Loxops virens*). *J. comp. physiol. Psychol.*, **92**, 388–96.

Kertesz, A. (1988). Cognitive function in severe aphasia. In *Thought without language*, (ed. L. Weiskrantz), pp. 451–63. Oxford University Press.

McCabe, B. J., Horn, G., and Bateson, P. P. G. (1981). Effects of restricted lesions of the chick forebrain on the acquisition of filial preferences during imprinting. *Brain Research*, **205**, 29–37.

——, Cipolla-Neto, J., Horn, G., and Bateson, P. (1982). Amnesic effects of bilateral lesions placed in the hyperstriatum ventrale of the chick after imprinting. *Exp. Brain Res.*, **48**, 13–21.

MacCurdy, J. T. (1928). *Common principles in psychology and physiology*. Cambridge University Press.

Milner, B. (1962). Les troubles de la mémoire accompagnant des lésions hippocampiques bilatérales. In *Physiologie de l'hippocampe*, Colloques Internationaux No. 107, pp. 257–72. CNRS, Paris.

——, Corkin, S., and Teuber, H.-L. (1968). Further analysis of hippocampal amnesic syndrome: 4 year follow-up study of H.M. *Neuropsychologia*, **6**, 215–34.

Murray, E. A. and Mishkin, M. (1986). Visual recognition in monkeys following rhinal cortical ablations combined with either amygdalectomy or hippocampectomy. *J. Neurosci.*, **6**, 1991–2003.

Newcombe, F. (1969). *Missile wounds of the brain. A study of physiological deficits*. Oxford University Press.

——, Ratcliffe, G., and Damasio, H. (1987). Dissociable visual and spatial impairments following right posterior cerebral lesions: clinical, neuropsychological and anatomical evidence. *Neuropsychologia*, **25**, 149–61.

Olton, D. S. and Samuelson, R. J. (1976). Remembrance of places passed: spatial memory in rats. *J. exp. Psychol.: Anim. Behav. Proc.*, **2**, 97–115.

Overman, W. H. Jr. and Doty, R. W. (1980). Prolonged visual memory in macaques and man. *Neurosci.*, **5**, 1825–31.

Patterson, T. A., Alvarado, M. C., Warner, I. T., Bennett, E. L., and Rosenzweig, M. R. (1986). Memory stages and brain asymmetry in chick learning. *Behav. Neurosci.*, **100**, 856–65.

Pearce, J. M. (1988). Stimulus generalization and the acquisition of categories by pigeons. In *Thought with language*, (ed. L. Weiskrantz), pp. 132–55. Oxford University Press.

Perrett, D. I., Smith, P. A. J., Potter, D. D., Mistlin, A. J., Head, A. S., Milner, A. D., and Jeeves, M. A. (1982). Visual cells in the temporal cortex sensitive to face view and gaze direction. *Proc. R. Soc. Lond. B.*, **223**, 293–317.

Porter, R. H. and Etscorn, F. (1974). Olfactory imprinting resulting from brief exposure in *Acomys cahirinus*. *Nature*, **250**, 732–3.

Sanders, M. D., Warrington E. K., Marshall, J., and Weiskrantz, L. (1974). 'Blindsight': vision in a field defect. *Lancet*, 20 April, issue, pp. 707–8.

Schacter, D. L., McAndrews, M. P., and Moscovitch, M. (1988). Access to consciousness: dissociations between implicit and explicit knowledge in neuropsychological syndromes. In *Thought without language*, (ed. L. Weiskrantz), pp. 242–78. Oxford University Press.

Scott, A. J. (1980). Filial and sexual imprinting in chicks and Japanese quail. Unpublished Ph.D. thesis. Univeristy of Cambridge.

Sergent, J. (1988). Face perception and the right hemisphere. In *Thought without language*, (ed. L. Weiskrantz), pp. 108–31. Oxford University Press.

Sherry, D. F. (1984). Food storage by black-capped chicadees: memory for the location and contents of caches. *Animal Behaviour*, **32**, 451–64.

——, Krebs, J. R., and Cowie, R. J. (1981). Memory for the location of stored food in marsh tits. *Animal Behaviour*, **29**, 1260–6.

Spelke, E. S. (1988). The origins of physical knowledge. In *Thought without language*, (ed. L. Weiskrantz), pp. 168–83. Oxford University Press.

Sperry, R. (1984). Consciousness, personal identity and the divided brain. *Neuropsychologia*, **22**, 661–73.

Thinus-Blanc, C. (1988). Animal spatial cognition. In *Thought without language*, (ed. L. Weiskrantz), pp. 371–95. Oxford University Press.

Thompson, R. F., Berger, T. W., and Madden, J. IV. (1983). Cellular processes of learning and memory in the mammalian CNS. *Am. Rev. Neurosci.*, **6**, 447–91.

Tranel, D. and Damasio, A. R. (1985). Knowledge without awareness: an automatic index of facial recognition by prosopagnostics. *Science*, **228**, 1453–4.

Vander Wall, S. B. (1982). An experimental analysis of cache recovery in Clark's nutcracker. *Animal Behaviour*, **30**, 84–94.

Warrington, E. K. (1982). Neuropsychological studies of object recognition. *Phil. Trans. R. Soc. Lond. B.*, **298**, 15–33.

—— and Weiskrantz, L. (1982). Amnesia: a disconnection syndrome? *Neuropsychologia*, **20**, 233–48.

Weiskrantz, L. (1986). *Blindsight. A case study and implications.* Clarendon Press, Oxford.

—— and Warrington, E. K. (1979). Conditioning in amnesic patients. *Neuropsychologia*, **17**, 187–94.

Yeo, C. H., Hardiman, M. J., and Glickstein, M. (1985). Conditioning of the nictitating membrane response of the rabbit. 1. Lesions of the cerebellar nuclei. *Experimental Brain Research*, **60**, 87–98.

Young, A. W. (1988). Functional organization of visual recognition. In *Thought with language*, (ed. L. Weiskrantz), pp. 78–107. Oxford University Press.

Zangwill, O. L. (1976). Thought and the brain. *Brit. J. Psychol.*, **63**, 301–14.

Zola-Morgan, S. and Squire, L. R. (1984). Preserved learning in monkeys with medial temporal skills: sparing of motor and cognitive skills. *J. Neurosci.*, **4**, 1072–85.

12

Intentionality in animal conditioning
ANTHONY DICKINSON

Ever since Brentano (1973) argued that the mental could be distinguished from the physical by intentionality, this property has been taken as a hallmark of cognition. In this technical sense intentionality refers to the property of mental states by which they possess a content or, in Searle's (1983) words, are 'directed at or about or of objects and states of affairs in the world' (p. 1). Typical of such states are the so-called propositional attitudes in which the agent takes a certain psychological relationship to a propositional content, such as believing that 'action A causes outcome O' and desiring that 'outcome O occurs'. Although some motivational and emotional states do not have propositional content, intentionality would appear to be a universal property of cognitive states; if we are to have a thought, it must be a thought about something.

Thus a central issue in the study of cognition must be the nature of the representations that carry the propositional content of mental states. A number of reasons have been given for why the obvious candidate, some internalized form of natural language, will not do, at least one of which appeals to comparative evidence. Given that the intentionality of our beliefs and desires is displayed in the purposive nature of our actions, a number of cognitive theorists (e.g. Fodor 1976, p. 56; Searle 1983, p. 5) have argued that the comparable goal-directedness manifest in the behaviour of other animals challenges the claim that intentionality is founded upon natural language. And I think that there is little doubt that the competence shown by Premack's apes, even in the absence of language training, warrants an account in intentional terms (see Premack 1988). I shall argue, however, that a more basic feature of animal behaviour, namely simple instrumental conditioning, will also support an intentional interpretation and may represent one of the most primitive markers of cognition.

Disputes about the intentional status of animal conditioning will produce, I am sure, a sense of *dejà-vu* and possibly even *ennui* in those who recall the time 30 or 40 years ago when this issue dominated the study of learning. Throughout the heyday of stimulus–response behaviourism Tolman (e.g. 1932, 1951, 1959) consistently argued for the purposive nature of conditioned responses and actions, a tradition that culminated in Irwin's (1971) formal presentation of the logic of the intentional states underlying conditioning. For Tolman a conditioned response was the product of a belief ('means–end readiness') or expectation about an environmental contingency[1] and a desire ('valence') for a particular outcome or goal. It is true that Tolman was often unclear about the ontological status of these mental states. By identifying them as intervening variables in what he claimed was a behavioural theory, he often seemed to adopt a position akin to the so-called intentional stance recently espoused by Dennett (1979). This stance simply attributes beliefs and desires to a system in cases where it is found that to do so enables us to predict and, at some level, explain certain aspects of the system's actions without ascribing a reality to these states that transcends the structure and potentialities of the system's behaviour. By contrast, as Amundson (1986) has recently pointed out, an inspection of Tolman's substantive theoretical statements often leads to the conclusion that he thought of intentional states as real, causal factors in the control of behaviour.

I do not intend in this chapter to discuss the reality of mental states in animals. Rather my aim is more limited, namely to re-examine some of the original evidence upon which the intentional interpretation of conditioning was first based without making any commitment to the ontological or causal status of such states. Specifically, the question of concern is simply whether the classic evidence that was advanced for an intentional account of conditioning in fact supports such an interpretation. This issue, although more limited, is prior to that of whether animal conditioning actually requires an intentional explanation; unless we can determine that the basic phenomenon of conditioning will sustain an interpretation in terms of beliefs and desires, there is no need to raise the question of whether intentionality in animal behaviour can be reduced to mechanistic processes of either the psychological or neurophysiological variety. What I shall argue is that the phenomena that were originally taken as evidence for intentionality in conditioning do not justify such an interpretation; even so, Tolman's conclusion about the purposive nature of animal action is, at least in certain cases, correct and can be supported by further, contemporary investigations of the same effects.

In many ways the conditioning procedure represents an ideal paradigm for investigating the basic intentionality of animal behaviour. During conditioning we present the animal with evidence which will support a belief about the relationship between two (or possibly three) terms. In simple excitatory classical or Pavlovian conditioning this evidence warrants the belief that 'the conditioned stimulus predicts the occurrence of the reinforcer', whereas a simple instrumental conditioning schedule of positive reinforcement provides

[1] In fact Tolman (e.g. 1959) distinguished between beliefs in the form of means–ends readinesses and expectations in that an expectation for Tolman was an activated means–end readiness. Stripped of its mechanistic interpretation, this distinction can be characterized by regarding an expectation as the occurrent mental state by which the dispositional state of belief interacts with other mental states, such as desires.

evidence to support the proposition that 'the instrumental action causes the occurrence of the reinforcer'. Correspondingly, we can control the animal's desires by manipulating the quality and quantity of the reinforcer relative to its current need or drive state. Thus a desire that the reinforcer occurs would be supported by a state of hunger and the use of a palatable food as the reinforcer.

In general, I assume that an intentional account of behaviour is justified if that behaviour can be shown to be dependent on, in the sense of being a rational consequence of, a set of beliefs and desires about the world. In the present context this translates into the requirement that conditioned actions are reasonable with respect to beliefs and desires whose content matches the conditioning schedule, reinforcer type and drive state. To be reasonable this behaviour must serve to bring about the occurrence of the reinforcer if it has positive value for the animal (and its non-occurrence when it has negative value) in a way that conforms with the content of the belief supported by the conditioning schedule. Moreover, if an intentional account is to be anything more than a redescription of behaviour, the animal must, when faced with a change of conditioning schedule, reinforcer type, or drive state, adjust its actions to maintain their goal-directedness in a way that conforms to the content of the beliefs and desires supported by the new state of affairs. All this, of course, is folk psychology, but how could it be otherwise; common-sense explanations of behaviour are intentional in kind.

Manifest intentionality

The main problem with folk psychology lies not so much with the nature of its implicit theory but rather with the attribution of intentionality on the basis of inadequate evidence. Often it seems to be assumed that cognition is manifest directly in behaviour. The manner in which oyster catchers open mussels (e.g. Griffin 1984), or, for that matter, hungry rats traverse mazes that lead to food and press levers that dispense it, is taken as evidence for the intentional status of these actions. In fact Good and Still (1986) argued recently that Tolman's original attribution of intentionality to conditioned responses was based upon the purposiveness that was apparent in their execution. Just as, for example, Michotte (1963) claimed that causality is an irreducible perceptual feature of visual impacts, so they argued that intentionality can also be directly perceived in behaviour.

But if conditioned behaviour manifests intentionality, why was this compelling feature ignored in the initial accounts of conditioning? The reason appears to lie, at least in part, with theoretical prejudices of the early students of conditioning. It was Pavlov's preference for mechanistic accounts which led him to restrict his measurement to salivation. In fact he was fully aware of the manifest intentionality of conditioned behaviour but consciously took great care that he should have as little chance as possible to see it. As he noted when discussing the motor activities accompanying salivary conditioning, '. . . a very important point in favour of secretory reflexes is the much smaller tendency to interpret them in an anthropomorphic fashion—*i.e.* in terms of subjective analogy' (Pavlov, 1927, p. 18). In fact, when Zener (1937) released his dogs from the restraining harness of the Pavlovian procedure, he observed that they both oriented towards and approached the food dish during the conditioned stimulus, a behaviour he readily interprets in terms of an intentional state of expectation that the food will be delivered.

There is little doubt that most would agree that to human eyes, at least, animal behaviour does manifest goal-directedness. The question is, however, whether this is sufficient to warrant an intentional explanation. Pavlov, I think, was right about this issue, but for the wrong reason. Pavlov wanted to rule out this type of account by fiat, whereas there is good empirical evidence, at least for his form of conditioning, that the resultant behaviour just will not sustain an intentional interpretation, however purposive the behaviour may at first sight appear. Perhaps the most telling argument against the validity of manifest intentionality is the fact that Pavlovian conditioned responses lose their goal-directed character when trained on an omission schedule.

This point can be illustrated by reconsidering those motor activities generated by Pavlovian conditioning which Zener thought displayed intentionality. If a short tone signals to a rat (rather than to a dog in this case) the delivery of a food pellet to a magazine, then, not surprisingly, the animal comes to approach the magazine during the tone. An intentional account might attribute the behaviour to the belief that 'approaching the magazine in the presence of the tone causes receipt of food' plus a desire for food or some such combination. Whatever the specific content of the belief, it must relate to the contingency between approaching the magazine and receipt of the food if the behaviour is to be regarded as goal-directed, and thus sustain an intentional interpretation. The fact that approach can be established on an omission schedule, however, shows that this contingency is not necessary for conditioning. Holland (1979) found that rats would come to approach the magazine during the tone even though every time they performed this response the food was omitted at the end of the tone. Thus for these animals access to the food could never have been experienced following approach during the tone and therefore could not have supported a belief that approach caused receipt of food. And yet the animals acquired this approach response. As Fig. 12.1 shows, the level of conditioned approach under the omission schedule was sustained above that in a control group which received unpaired presentations of the tone and food.

Thus the behaviour of Holland's (1979) rats under this omission contingency failed to meet the criterion for intentionality, namely that it should exhibit goal-directedness that is in accord with the content of the belief supported by the conditioning schedule. To gain the food under the omission schedule, the animals should have refrained from approaching the magazine

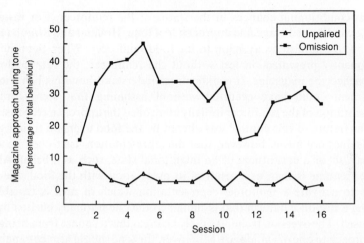

Fig. 12.1 The acquisition of magazine approach during a tone when the tone was paired with the delivery of food if the rat did not approach during the tone (omission condition), and when the tone and the delivery of food were unpaired (unpaired condition). The strength of magazine approach is expressed by the percentage of all behaviours observed during the tone that consisted of approaching the magazine, (After Holland 1979.)

in the presence of the tone; in fact by continuing to approach the magazine they lost a significant proportion of the available food. It would appear that the manifest intentionality of the approach response deceived us about its true intentional status just as Michotte's (1963) perceived causality misleads observers about the nature of the interaction between the elements of his display.

The development and maintenance of a conditioned response under an omission schedule is not peculiar to the rat's approach behaviour but is characteristic of Pavlovian appetitive conditioning in general. Moreover, the failure of apparently purposive behaviour to preserve its intentional character when faced with changing environmental conditions is not restricted to laboratory tasks and procedures. Ever since Fabre's classic (1916) observations that even minor perturbations in the stimulus configuration during nest provisioning by solitary wasps could disrupt the whole behavioural ritual, the dangers of attributing intentionality to an animal on the basis of the manifest goal-directedness of its behaviour, however sophisticated that might be, have been clear.

The identification of a particular behaviour as non-intentional does not rule out a role for psychological processes in its generation. It is now generally argued that a Pavlovian conditioned response, such as magazine approach by the rat, is often mediated by a process involving what might be regarded as some form of internal representation of the reinforcer. One of the most compelling sources of evidence for this claim comes from studies of the effect of post-conditioning changes in the status of the reinforcer. For instance, having conditioned magazine approach to a tone, Holland and Straub (1979) went on to establish an aversion to the food reinforcer. When the tone was subsequently presented on test without the reinforcer, the rats no longer approached the magazine. It is difficult to understand how this behavioural adjustment could have occurred without assuming that some form of representation of the reinforcer initially controlled the approach response and that the nature of this control was altered by the food aversion training.

This does not mean, however, that the representation has to be of a form that can act as a constituent of an intentional state, such as a belief. All we have to assume is that, as a result of its association with the food, the tone comes to activate a reinforcer representation which in turn is capable of exciting a response pattern that is similar to the one normally elicited by the food itself. The aversion training simply changes this response from being one of approach to one of avoidance. Moreover, the tone should also be capable of activating the reinforcer representation under an omission schedule; until the approach response is conditioned, the tone will be paired with the reinforcer and, even after the response occurs on a certain proportion of trials, the tone will still be paired with the food on those occasions when the animal does not approach during the tone. Thus a simple, non-intentional account provides a ready explanation of why a conditioned response develops under an omission contingency.

Although such an account refers to representations, the processes that operate upon these entities, such as excitation or activation, are mechanistic, albeit of a psychological kind, in that they gain their explanatory force by analogy to processes of physical causation. These psychological mechanisms must be distinguished from the processes that operate on the representational content of intentional mental states; to explain an action in terms of the agent's beliefs and desires is to demonstrate that the action is rational with respect to the content of those mental states, an explanation that could be couched in a causal form by viewing an action as the consequence of a process of practical inference operating upon this content. Although this is not the place to discuss the vexed problem of 'reasons as causes', it is clear that practical inference and excitation or activation are not the same type of causal process, at least at this level of analysis.

In conclusion, my general contention is that manifest intentionality, however beautifully adapted a behaviour might be for some functional purpose, is an unreliable index of the operation of an intentional process on mental states. Pavlovian conditioning, I should argue, is misleading in this respect; although such conditioned responses usually appear to be adaptive, it turns out that when analysed by omission schedules these responses are not rationally related to the beliefs supported by the environmental contingencies, a fact that points to a mechanistic rather than intentional account.

Instrumental conditioning

At first sight instrumental conditioning would seem to be a much better candidate for an intentional interpretation. Actions, if they are to be instrumental, must manifest at least rationality with respect to the belief supported by the action-reinforcer contingency, for they are by definition sensitive to this relationship; an instrumental action is one that is strengthened and maintained only when the performance of this action causes the occurrence of the reinforcer. (This discussion will be restricted to positive reinforcement. Seligman and Johnston (1973) have presented an intentional account of negative reinforcement or avoidance conditioning couched in terms of Irwin's (1971) theory.) Thus an instrumental action under this definition must exhibit goal-directedness that is in accord with the content of a belief that represents upon the instrumental contingency.

But if an intentional account is to be anything more than a redescription of the behaviour, we have to show that instrumental actions also retain their purposive character across changes in conditions that should on this account alter an animal's desires. It has long been thought that the classic latent learning effects, studied so intensively 30 or 40 years ago, provide just such evidence. This point can be illustrated by a recent study of our own (Dickinson and Dawson 1987a) which used the most popular of the latent learning designs, namely that for studying irrelevant incentive learning. Two groups of hungry rats were initially trained to press a lever, one for a reward of sucrose solution and the other for food pellets. Both groups were then simply tested for their propensity to press the lever in the absence of any reinforcement while they were thirsty.

An intentional account requires that instrumental performance on test should conform to the interaction between beliefs and desires supported by the current state of affairs. Thus test performance should be based upon beliefs established during training to the effect that 'lever pressing causes the delivery of the sucrose solution' for one group but '... food pellets' for the other, whereas the shift in drive state from hunger to thirst should lead to a change in the relative desirability of the two reinforcers. During training under hunger the two reinforcers were equally desirable, but under thirst the sucrose solution, being a fluid, should be preferred to the food pellets. Thus, on test, the animals trained with the sucrose solution should press on test more than those trained with the food pellets. The absence of the reinforcers during the test is important because, if they were actually presented, any variations in performance could be attributed to differences in their direct impact under the test drive state. Figure 12.2 shows that test performance did in fact conform to the intentional account, in that the rats trained with the sucrose solution pressed more than those trained with the pellets. No such difference was observed when the value of both of the reinforcers was maintained by testing the animals hungry.

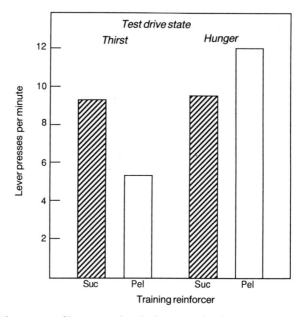

Fig. 12.2   Mean rates of lever pressing during an extinction test under either thirst or hunger following reinforcement of lever pressing by either the sucrose solution (Suc) or the food pellets (Pel).

The theoretical implication of the classic latent learning studies for the nature of instrumental conditioning has been largely ignored over the intervening years by students of animal learning, at least in part, because it has been antithetical to the traditional mechanistic perspective of this area of psychology. Instead, they concentrated on determining the learning processes that mediate Pavlovian conditioning, an enterprise that has been conducted without making a commitment to the nature of the underlying knowledge. The analysis of instrumental conditioning was left in the hands of the radical behaviourists, whose aim of uncovering formal laws relating instrumental performance to contingencies of reinforcement allowed them to ignore the phenomenon. It seemed to be generally believed that latent learning warranted an intentional account in one form or another, although most theorists appeared to be uncomfortable with this conclusion and reluctant to develop it.

But we might well question whether the classic irrelevant incentive effect really does indicate intentionality. The problem is that the training schedules were not such as to justify the claim that the effect is based upon a belief about instrumental contingency, namely that the action produces a particular type of reinforcer. In our experiment, as in all the classic studies, the groups differed not only in the particular beliefs that were supported by the conditioned schedules but also in the fact that they received differential exposure to the reinforcers during training. The potential significance of this fact can be illustrated by considering an alternative training schedule.

Suppose that instead of training the hungry animals just to lever press, we also give them the opportunity to perform another action, say chain pulling, at the same time on a concurrent schedule. We can now arrange equal exposure to the two reinforcers while maintaining the different instrumental consequences of pressing the lever in the two groups. Thus for one group lever pressing is reinforced with the sucrose solution and chain pulling with the food pellets, whereas the other group experience the opposite action-reinforcer assignment. Under an intentional account this change in the training schedule should make no difference to the outcome of a test for lever pressing alone under thirst; those animals given evidence for the belief that lever pressing produces the sucrose solution should press more than those for whom this action produced food pellets during training.

Whenever we have tried this experiment in one form or another, we have never succeeded in detecting an irrelevant incentive effect. After concurrent training the amount of lever pressing on test is unaffected by whether or not this action produced the sucrose solution during training. The results of one of these experiments (Dickinson and Dawson 1987a) is illustrated in Fig 12.3, which shows the comparable performance following concurrent training with the two reinforcers. To check that our failure to detect an irrelevant incentive effect following concurrent training was not due to the specific schedule of

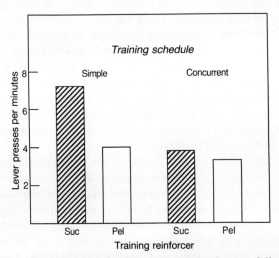

Fig. 12.3 Mean rates of lever pressing during an extinction test following reinforcement by either the sucrose solution (Suc) or the food pellets (Pel). In one condition the animals received simple lever-press training, whereas in the other lever pressing was reinforced concurrently with chain pulling during training.

reinforcement for lever pressing, a second pair of groups received identical training with the lever except for the fact that the chain was not present so that the animals could not gain access to the reinforcer contingent upon this action. Now the standard effect emerged (see Fig. 12.3); when lever pressing was reinforced with the sucrose solution rather than with food pellets during training, the rats pressed more on test following a shift from hunger to thirst.

This finding is potentially devastating for the intentional interpretation of the basic effect. What appears to be important during training is not that the animal is provided with evidence that an instrumental action produces a particular type of reinforcer but rather that it is exposed selectively to the reinforcers, a conclusion that undercuts any explanation based upon a belief about the instrumental contingency. The insensitivity of the irrelevant incentive effect to the instrumental contingency is not peculiar to this particular drive shift from hunger to thirst, for it is also observed following a shift from thirst to either hunger (Dickinson and Dawson 1986) or to a sodium appetite (Dickinson 1986). Moreover, it does not appear to be due to generalization between the two actions because the effect also fails to occur following training with the lever alone as long as the schedule ensures equal exposure to the two reinforcers (Dickinson and Nicholas 1983).

Mechanistic processes in instrumental conditioning

The failure of the simple irrelevant incentive effect to support an intentional interpretation of instrumental conditioning suggests that the effect is mediated by some form of mechanistic process. A possible candidate is that embodied in two-factor theory (e.g. Rescorla and Solomon 1967), which appeals to the role of the Pavlovian association between the reinforcer and the cues that are present when the instrumental response is executed and the reinforcer delivered. As we have already noted, such an association should enable these cues to activate a representation of the reinforcer, which, Rescorla and Solomon (1967) argue, can enhance or motivate the performance of the instrumental response.

The single reinforcer training used in the simple irrelevant incentive procedure ensures that only in the group receiving the sucrose solution are the contextual cues associated with a reinforcer whose representation should be capable of being activated under the test drive state and so be able to enhance performance. Following concurrent training, however the contextual cues are equally associated with the sucrose solution and food pellets, whatever reinforcer is used to train the target instrumental action. As a result, the motivating influence of these cues should be equated on test after all training conditions. In the next study we attempted to determine whether such a motivational influence operates in our procedure.

A role for a Pavlovian process in instrumental performance is usually justified on the basis of the outcome of Pavlovian–instrumental transfer studies. In such a study instrumental performance and Pavlovian conditioning are established independently before testing the effect of presenting the conditioned stimulus while the animals are performing the instrumental action. An enhancement of performance during this stimulus is then attributed to the motivating properties of this stimulus acquired through its Pavlovian association with the reinforcer.

We (Dickinson and Dawson 1987b) used a Pavlovian–instrumental transfer design in which we trained hungry rats under a complex schedule with three different conditions. In two of the conditions, each of which was signalled by a different stimulus, the animals received either sucrose solution or food pellets non-contingently with the lever withdrawn. Thus in both these conditions the animals experienced a Pavlovian association between one of the stimuli and one of the reinforcers. Each training session consisted of a series of presentations of these two conditions in alternation. The presentations of the Pavlovian conditions were separated by a third, instrumental condition in which the lever was inserted and the animals could earn food pellets by pressing it. Finally, unrewarded lever pressing was tested in the presence of the two Pavlovian stimuli, one of which had been associated with the sucrose solution and the other with the food pellets, while the rats were thirsty.

If a cue can exert a motivating effect on instrumental performance simply as a result of being associated with a reinforcer that is relevant to the current drive state of the animals, we should expect them to press most vigorously during the sucrose stimulus. Figure 12.4 shows that just such an effect was observed; the stimulus that had been associated with the sucrose solution maintained a higher rate of lever pressing than the one that had signalled the food pellets. A comparable effect was not seen when a control group of animals was tested hungry.

This finding suggests that the simple irrelevant incentive effect can be mediated by a purely mechanistic, Pavlovian process. In fact we have evidence from a further study that the effect is probably due solely to such a process. In this study hungry rats were trained with two Pavlovian stimuli, one signalling the sucrose solution and the other food pellets as in the previous experiment. In addition, there were also two instrumental discriminative stimuli whose presentations were intermixed among those of the Pavlovian signals. The levers were inserted only during the instrumental stimuli and pressing was rewarded with the sucrose solution in the presence of one of the stimuli and with food pellets in the presence of the other. Thus the animals experienced two stimuli associated with each type of reinforcer, one Pavlovian signalling the free delivery of the appropriate reward and the other, the instrumental or discriminative stimulus, signalling that pressing the lever would be reinforced

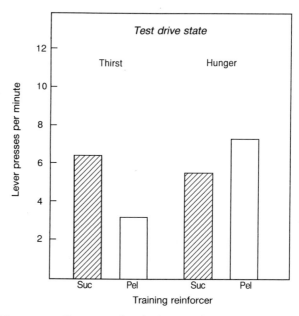

Fig. 12.4   Mean rates of lever pressing during an extinction test in the presence of a Pavlovian conditioned stimulus that had been paired with either the sucrose solution (Suc) or the food pellets (Pel) during training. Different groups of animals were tested under thirst and hunger.

with this reward. Finally, all animals were tested for lever pressing without any reinforcers in the presence of all four stimuli while they were thirsty.

The difference between test performance in the two discriminative stimuli indicates the size of the instrumental effect. If this effect is entirely due to the Pavlovian relationship between these stimuli and the reinforcers that is embedded in instrumental training, we should have observed a comparable difference between performance in the presence of the two pure Pavlovian stimuli. Figure 12.5 shows that the pattern of test performance matched this prediction exactly, with no significant interaction between the type of training reinforcer (sucrose solution vs. food pellets) and the type of stimulus (Pavlovian vs. instrumental). This implies that the simple irrelevant incentive effect is entirely due to the association between the stimuli that accompany instrumental performance and the reinforcers, rather than to the causal relationship between the instrumental actions and the reinforcers.

The original students of the irrelevant incentive effect were unable to dissociate the Pavlovian and instrumental processes because they used mazes. A maze procedure inevitably confounds the instrumental and Pavlovian contingencies; not only is reinforcement dependent upon approaching the location of the reward in the maze, but it is also associated with the cues

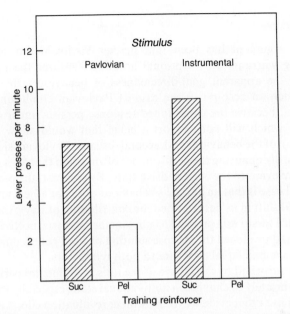

Fig. 12.5 Mean rates of lever pressing during an extinction test in the presence of either a Pavlovian conditioned stimulus or an instrumental discriminative stimulus. These stimuli had been associated with either the sucrose solution (Suc) or the food pellets (Pel) during training.

specifying that location. As a result intentionality was attributed to instrumental actions on the basis of latent learning phenomena, when, as it turns out, such an attribution is not warranted by an analysis of the training relationships underlying, at least, the irrelevant incentive effect. The effect does not depend upon the animal being provided with evidence that an instrumental action causes a reinforcer that is relevant or irrelevant to the test drive state, but rather upon simple exposure to an association between accompanying stimuli and the reinforcers.

The inappropriateness of an intentional account is highlighted by the irrationality of the outcome of our Pavlovian–instrumental transfer experiment. There is no way that the difference in instrumental performance under thirst produced by Pavlovian signals for sucrose and food pellets can be plausibly characterized as goal-directed, especially given the fact that the animals had reason to believe that the instrumental action produced only a reinforcer, food pellets, that was irrelevant to the test drive state. This difference is best explained by simply assuming that Pavlovian signals for a relevant reinforcer exert a general activating effect on any pre-potent action tendencies, an account that further highlights the mechanistic nature of this form of conditioning.

Changing desires

So far my argument has been that neither Pavlovian nor instrumental conditioning warrants an intentional account whatever the intentionality manifest in the apparent goal-directedness of behaviours they support. I dismissed such an account in the case of Pavlovian conditioning for two reasons; first, because the conditioned response persists under an omission contingency which will not support a belief that would allow a purposive interpretation of the behaviour and, second, because Pavlovian signals appear to be capable of enhancing the performance of an action that does not lead to a goal that is relevant to the current drive state. By contrast, the problem in the instrumental case is that an animal's behaviour does not adjust appropriately to a supposed shift in its desires when the contribution of Pavlovian processes is controlled. Thirsty rats press a lever at similar rates irrespective of whether that action had produced the sucrose solution or food pellets during training when they have had equal exposure to both reinforcers.

I was very surprised by the failure of the rat's instrumental performance to adjust appropriately to changes in motivational state, especially in view of the fact that we have other evidence for reinforcer revaluation effects mediated by the instrumental contingency (Adams and Dickinson 1981; Colwill and Rescorla 1985). The Colwill and Rescorla studies are particularly instructive in the present case. Like us, they initially trained their rats to press a lever and pull a chain for two different rewards before independently devaluing one of the rewards by establishing an aversion to it. When subsequently they tested the propensity of the animals to press the lever, in contrast to our irrelevant incentive results, performance of this action was reduced when the training reinforcer for lever pressing had been devalued, a finding that is clearly in accord with an intentional account of instrumental performance. This discrepancy between the outcomes of reinforcer revaluation using aversion and drive shift procedures led us to re-examine the premises upon which the irrelevant incentive procedure is taken to be a test of the intentional status of instrumental action.

The intentional interpretation of our standard irrelevant incentive effect must assume something like the following: under hunger the animal has two distinct and equally strong desires, namely that 'delivery of the sucrose solution occurs' and that 'delivery of a food pellet occurs', whereas under thirst the desire for the sucrose solution must be, at least, stronger than that for the food pellets. Moreover, this account must assume that this change in the relative strength of the desires is brought about simply by a shift in drive state. But why should such a shift change the animals' desires? Our animals never had the opportunity to consume the two reinforcers under thirst and therefore had no experience upon which to base a relative evaluation. Testing for the intentionality of instrumental actions by the standard irrelevant incentive procedure is predicated upon the assumption that desires automatically change in response to drive shifts, an assumption that was probably bolstered by the success of this procedure. But we have now seen that the standard effect is not goal-directed in character but rather is mediated by a non-intentional Pavlovian system. Up to now I have interpreted this conclusion as casting doubt upon the intentional status of instrumental actions in animals, but it could equally well be taken as a challenge to the assumption that drive shifts *per se* alter desires.

In fact a closer reading of the major intentional theory of conditioning reveals that Tolman would not have anticipated an automatic adjustment in the desire for a reinforcer in response to a drive shift. For Tolman (1949*a*, 1849*b*) the desire for a reinforcer, or what he called the 'valence' of the reinforcer, was determined by the current drive state and the 'cathexis' attached to the reinforcer. The cathexis of a reinforcer is a belief about the value of the reinforcer in a given drive state that is based upon prior consummatory experience with the reinforcer in that drive state. In other words, according to Tolman, animals have to learn about the value of a reinforcer under a particular drive state before a shift to that state will bring about a desire for the reinforcer. This analysis of the origins of basic desires would not anticipate an irrelevant incentive effect mediated by the instrumental contingency unless the animals had previously experienced the reinforcers under the test drive state, and in this connection it is interesting to note that a number of the classic demonstrations of the effect did give such experience (e.g. Christie 1951; Thistlewaite 1952). By contrast, our subjects never had the opportunity to consume the sucrose solution and the food pellets while thirsty prior to the test, and so, in terms of this theory, it is not surprising that we failed to detect the goal-directedness of lever pressing on test.

The obvious prediction from this analysis is that if we were, in fact, to give animals the appropriate consummatory experience, we should observe an irrelevant incentive effect mediated by the instrumental contingency. Consequently, in a further study we trained hungry rats on the concurrent lever-press chain-pull schedule with the sucrose solution acting as the reinforcer for one action and the food pellets for the other in a counterbalanced assignment. After performance was established, the lever and chain were withdrawn and the drive state was alternated daily between hunger and thirst for 10 days. During this phase half of the animals received free or non-contingent presentations of the sucrose solution and food pellets on days when they were thirsty. Because neither the lever nor the chain was present during this non-contingent training, the rewards delivered during this stage could not have exerted any direct reinforcing effect on these instrumental actions. However, this experience should have allowed the animals to acquire the cathexes appropriate for a state of thirst. Thus we should expect these animals to have had a greater desire for the sucrose solution than for the food pellets when they were thirsty once again on test. By contrast, the remaining animals, which received the non-contingent rewards on days when they were hungry, should not have had the opportunity to acquire cathexes for the two reinforcers appropriate to being thirsty. Following this non-contingent training, the lever and chain were reinserted and the animals retrained under hunger to press the lever and pull the chain to ensure that both actions were performed at comparable rates in the two groups prior to test. In this test the chain was removed and lever pressing was tested without any rewards under thirst.

If control of the irrelevant incentive effect by the instrumental contingency depends upon previous acquisition of the appropriate cathexes for the reinforcers, we should not expect to have observed an effect in the control animals that received non-contingent presentations of the reinforcers under hunger. They had no opportunity to find out about the relative values of the rewards when thirsty. Figure 12.6 bears out this expectation; the performance of rats which received non-contingent training under hunger was unaffected by the type reward used to reinforce lever pressing. By contrast, the animals that had non-contingent experience of the reinforcers under thirst pressed more when this action had been reinforced by the sucrose solution. It would appear that knowledge of an instrumental contingency can mediate the effects

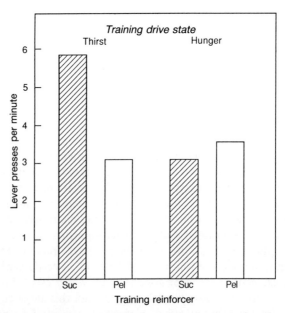

Fig. 12.6   Mean rates of lever pressing during the extinction test following reinforcement by either the sucrose solution (Suc) or food pellets (Pel.) During training the animals had received non-contingent presentations of the reinforcers under either thirst or hunger.

a drive shift on performance, but only if the animals have had previous experience of the training reinforcers under the new motivational state.

So it turns out that instrumental behaviour will support an intentional characterization in terms of beliefs and desires after all. Not only do we perceive manifest intentionality in instrumental action, its goal-directedness does depend upon experiencing the evidence that would support a belief about the consequences of the action, namely the action-reinforcer contingency, rather than some other feature of the instrumental training procedures. Moreover, this purposiveness is preserved across operations that should alter the desire for the reinforcer.

Conclusions

Perhaps the most significant feature of mental states is that they have content, in that they exhibit a psychological relationship to states of affairs and objects in the environment. Under normal circumstances our actions often appear to manifest the intentionality of our mental states in their goal-directed character. By this we mean that the performance of an action is rational and comprehensible in terms of the content of mental states where that content reflects the contingencies involving the action and the value we place upon its consequences. Thus if there is a positive contingency between an action on our part and an outcome, supporting the belief that the action causes this outcome, and if we are in the relevant motivational state and have had the appropriate experience with the outcome to support a desire for it, then the execution of the action under these circumstances is intelligible in terms of the content of these mental states. Clearly, the preference for this intentional explanation of our own behaviour reflects the fact that it allows us to understand the harmony that typically exists between the content of our mental states and the goal-directedness of our actions.

The problem of explaining the accord between mental states and behaviour does not arise, of course, in the case of other animals. What recommends an intentional explanation to us is that their actions, like our own, often appear to be goal-directed under conditions that would support the content of the appropriate mental states. To maintain such an intentional account, however, we must demonstrate empirically that the purposive nature of the action really does depend upon conditions that supply the appropriate content for beliefs and desires. As we saw, in the case of Pavlovian conditioning, this is not so. Whatever the manifest intentionality of the rat's approach response, it persisted when the conditions were changed, so that they would not support the appropriate belief about the consequences of this action. Moreover, when in the analysis of the simple irrelevant incentive effect we arranged for a stimulus to predict the free delivery of the sucrose solution, its effect upon instrumental performance was not rationally related to what this stimulus signalled. There is no obvious reason why the belief that this stimulus signals the delivery of the sucrose solution should enhance the performance of an action under thirst that had previously produced food pellets, and yet this is what it did.

At first sight it may appear that the question of concordance between belief conditions and the goal-directedness of behaviour does not arise in the case of instrumental actions, for they are by definition actions that are modified appropriately by their consequences. But if an intentional account is to have any explanatory power, it must be capable of predicting alterations in behaviour across changes in the conditions supporting the content of beliefs and desires. By demonstrating an irrelevant incentive effect mediated by the instrumental contingency, we have shown that an intentional account can anticipate the behavioural changes produced by an alteration in the conditions for desires (see Dickinson (1985, in press) and Colwill and Rescorla (1986) for reviews of other evidence supporting this conclusion).

In summary, then, it appears that the instrumental actions of, at least, some animals will support an intentional interpretation. But it should not be assumed from this conclusion that all aspects of such actions can be characterized in these terms. In fact, our analysis of the irrelevant incentive effect has confirmed that instrumental performance can be modulated by a non-intentional influence arising from the Pavlovian properties of the accompanying stimuli. This is surely but one of many such influences. Furthermore, it is clear that under certain training schedules instrumental actions loose their purposive character (see Dickinson 1985, in press); their execution is unaffected by shifts in desires and they exhibit the properties of habits, simply elicited by the appropriate stimuli.

While it may be true that instrumental conditioning will bear an intentional interpretation, why should one wish to espouse such an explanation in the case of animal behaviour rather than a mechanistic account or a functional explanation in terms of computational and information-processing systems? With animals we are not faced with the problem of explaining the nature of direct knowledge of mental states nor the concordance of this knowledge with behaviour, and moreover there is little doubt that a mechanistic or functional system could be made to simulate the intentionality of instrumental actions. It is true that at the time they were first investigated latent learning phenomena, such as the irrelevant incentive effect, presented insuperable problems for the stimulus-response theories of the time, but now there would be no difficulty, at least in principle, in endowing a mechanism with the capacity to simulate intentionality. It is trivially easy, for instance, to write a PROLOG program that enables a computer to produce a symbolic output that the programmer could interpret as demonstrating the irrelevant incentive effect.

There seem to me to be at least two reasons for adhering to the intentional stance at this stage in psychological theorizing. First, it leads us to ask significant questions about instrumental actions that would not necessarily be addressed from alternative theoretical perspectives. In the present case, questions about the role of the instrumental contingency and prior experience with the reinforcer in the motivational control of instrumental behaviour arose directly from viewing such actions as intentional. Second, the intentional stance draws an important psychological distinction between reflexive or elicited behaviour, such as Pavlovian responses, and the rational and goal-directed nature of instrumental activities. It is not immediately obvious how a mechanistic or functional theory would preserve this distinction.

Finally, it would be disingenuous if I did not acknowledge that the common intentionality shown by my own actions and those of certain other animals leads me to attribute mental states to these animals. If this anthropomorphic attribution is in fact correct, then any mechanistic or functional account faces the same problems with animal mentality as it does with our own. More important in the present context, however, is the fact that the demonstration of this common intentionality in behaviour provides empirical justification for the claim that an internalized form of natural language cannot provide the sole representational medium of cognition; if the implications of this commonality are accepted, then some other form of representation must be capable of carrying the content of mental states such as beliefs and desire.

But this argument cannot be based upon simple observation or informal analysis of animal behaviour. It is not sufficient to appeal to the manifest intentionality of behaviour, as many still do (e.g. Griffin 1984), in making cognitive attributions to animals, however complex and adaptive a behavioural competence may be. What I hope has become clear from the analysis of the irrelevant incentive effect presented in this chapter is that processes, such as that underlying Pavlovian conditioning, that warrant no more than a mechanistic account can endow behaviour with apparent intentionality. It has required a relatively sophisticated behavioural analysis to reveal that even simple instrumental actions can be rational and goal-directed.

Acknowledgements

The work reported in this chapter was supported by a grant from the UK Science and Engineering Research Council. I should like to thank Paula Durlach, Cecelia Heyes, Nick Mackintosh, and John Pearce for their useful comments on an earlier draft.

References

Adams, C. D. and Dickinson, A. (1981). Instrumental responding following reinforcer devaluation. *Quarterly Journal of Experimental Psychology*, **33B**, 109–12.

Amundson, R. (1986). The unknown epistemology of E. C. Tolman. *British Journal of Psychology*, **77**, 525–31.

Brentano, F. (1973). *Psychology from an empirical standpoint*. Routledge and Kegan Paul, Andover, Hants.

Christie, R. (1951). The role of drive discrimination in learning under irrelevant motivation. *Journal of Experimental Psychology*, **42**, 13–19.

Colwill, R. C. and Rescorla, R. A. (1985). Postconditioning devaluation of a reinforcer affects instrumental responding. *Journal of Experimental Psychology: Animal Behaviour Processes*, **11**, 120–32.

—— and —— (1986). Associative structures in instrumental conditioning. In *The psychology of learning and motivation, Vol. 20*, (ed. G. H. Bower), pp. 55–104. Academic Press, London.

Dennett, D. C. (1979). *Brainstorms*. Harvester Press, Brighton, Sussex.

Dickinson, A. (1985). Actions and habits: the development of behavioural autonomy. *Philosophical Transactions of the Royal Society (London)*, **B308**, 67–78.

—— (1986). Re-examination of the role of the instrumental contingency in the sodium-appetite irrelevant incentive effect. *Quarterly Journal of Experimental Psychology*, **38B**, 161–72.

—— (in press). The expectancy theory of animal conditioning. In *Contemporary learning theories*, (ed. S. B. Klein and R. R. Mowrer). Laurence Erlbuam Associates, Hillsdale, NJ.

—— and Dawson, G. R. (1986). Irrelevant incentive effect based upon a transition from thirst to hunger. Unpublished manuscript.

—— and —— (1987a). The role of the instrumental contingency in the motivational control of performance. *Quarterly Journal of Experimental Psychology*, **39B**, 77–93.

—— and —— (1987b). Pavlovian processes in the motivational control of instrumental performance. *Quarterly Journal of Experimental Psychology*, **39B**, 201–13.

—— and Nicholas, D. J. (1983). Irrelevant incentive learning during instrumental conditioning: the role of drive-reinforcer and response-reinforcer relationships. *Quarterly Journal of Experimental Psychology*, **35B**, 249–63.

Fabre, J. H. (1916). *The hunting wasps*. Hodder and Stoughton, London.

Fodor, J. A. (1976). *The language of thought*. Harvester Press, Brighton, Sussex.

Griffin, D. R. (1984). *Animal thinking*. Harvard University Press.

Good, J. and Still, A. (1986). Tolman and the tradition of direct perception. *British Journal of Psychology*, **77**, 533–9.

Holland, P. C. (1979). Differential effects of omission contingencies on various components of Pavlovian appetitive responding in rats. *Journal of Experimental Psychology: Animal Behavior Process*, **5**, 178–93.

—— and Straub, J. J. (1979). Differential effects of two ways of devaluing the unconditioned stimulus after Pavlovian appetitive conditioning. *Journal of Experimental Psychology: Animal Behaviour Processes*, **5**, 65–78.

Irwin, F. W. (1971). *Intentional behavior and motivation: a cognitive theory*. Lippincott, Philadelphia, PA.

Michotte, A. (1963). *The perception of causality*. Methuen, Andover, Hants.

Pavlov, I. P. (1927). *Conditioned reflexes*. Oxford University Press.

Premack, D. (1988). Minds with and without language. In *Thought without language*, (ed. L. Weiskrantz), pp. 46–65. Oxford University Press.

Rescorla, R. A. and Solomon, R. L. (1967). Two-process learning theory: relationship between Pavlovian conditioning and instrumental learning. *Psychological Review*, **74**, 151–82.

Searle, J. R. (1983). *Intentionality*. Cambridge University Press.

Seligman, M. E. P. and Johnston, J. C. (1973). A cognitive theory of avoidance learning. In *Contemporary approaches to conditioning and learning*, (ed. F. J. McGuigan and D. B. Lumsden), pp. 69–110, Winston, Washington, DC.

Thistlewaite, D. (1952). Conditions of irrelevant incentive learning. *Journal of Comparative and Physiological Psychology*, **45**, 517–25.

Tolman, E. C. (1932). *Purposive behaviour in animals and men*. Appleton-Century-Crofts, New York.

—— (1949*a*). There is more than one kind of learning. *Psychological Review*, **56**, 144–55.

—— (1949*b*). The nature and functioning of wants. *Psychological Review*, **56**, 357–69.

—— (1951). *Collected papers in psychology*. University of California Press.

—— (1959). Principles of purposive behaviour. In *Psychology: a study of a science. Vol. 2*, (ed. S. Koch), pp. 92–157. McGraw, New York.

Zener, K. (1937). The significance of behavior accompanying conditioned salivary secretion for theories of the conditioned response. *American Journal of Psychology*, **50**, 384–403.

Discussion, Section D

Implicit processing

Kertesz offered another example of implicit knowledge in aphasia, namely the automatic correction of anomalous sentences revealing knowledge of syntax even though the sentences are not comprehended. Furthermore, the patient is not aware of the anomalous nature of the stimulus sentence (he mentioned seeing two such patients recently). *Schacter* replied that the observations are interesting, '. . . but like several of the phenomena discussed in our chapter, it is not clear whether this example should be characterized as an implicit/ explicit dissociation. Perhaps these patients have explicit knowledge of syntax and lack explicit knowledge of semantics'.

Bisiach also described other kinds of patients, who may be verbally and explicitly aware of their illness but none the less behave as if they are not; for example, they may try to stand and walk even though they know they are hemiplegic. *Schacter* wondered whether such patients were truly aware of their deficit, or simply supplying a learned verbal response? 'However, if one accepts that they are aware of their deficits, this dissociation would appear to be quite different from the ones I have been discussing—it falls into the general category of dissociations between awareness and knowledge on the one hand, and action or behaviour on the other. People often possess knowledge that is not expressed in behaviour'. Important issues were raised here, but he thought they were fundamentally different from those he had discussed.

The possible link with 'infantile amnesia' (i.e. the inability to remember events from early childhood) was raised by *Leslie*. *Schacter* thought that there was indeed '. . . an intriguing possibility that very young children store information in a form that is later accessible implicitly but not explicitly. Hence materials from the beginning of life may not be available to conscious recollection'. He added that, of course, there were a host of other possible hypotheses.

Gazzaniga thought the dissociation in amnesic patients between intact priming and poor recognition was extraordinary, and wondered whether task difficulty might be an important factor—in particular, '. . . whether the test for implicit knowledge (i.e. provision of three-letter stems), being more difficult than the explicit recognition, activates the attention of the patient and thereby

results in superior performance?' *Schacter* offered three reasons why he
thought this was not so. 'First, if increasing the difficulty of the task actually
helped amnesic patients . . . they should perform even better on explicit recall
tests, which are presumably more difficult than stem completion tests. But
they perform disastrously on explicit recall tests. Second, we can produce
similar dissociations in normal subjects through various experimental
manipulations, and it is doubtful that arousal or activation of attention plays
a significant role here. Third, one could easily argue that *recognition* is a more
difficult task (and, by your reasoning, more attention-activating) than stem
completion. Recognition requires the subject to "think back" to the study
episode, whereas stem completion does not'. He concluded that it was unlikely
that heightened attention could account for the dissociation.

The important question of the possible relationship between 'implicit/
explicit' and 'conscious/unconscious' was raised by *Caramazza*, who suggested that the distinction between 'conscious' and 'unconscious' was '. . .
mere relabelling of the data. Thus, to use one of your [*Schacter*'s] examples . . .
the fact that some patients may show semantic priming but not be able to
judge two words to be semantically related does not, in any obvious way, show
a conscious/unconscious processing distinction'.

Schacter replied at length and asserted that '. . . no claim is being made that
performance of a task that taps implicit knowledge is any less "conscious"
than performance of a task that taps explicit knowledge. . . . What is not
conscious in certain cases, however, is the knowledge that is expressed in task
performance. To take the example that you cited, it is clear that both the
semantic relatedness and lexical decision tasks require conscious processing.
On the latter task, however, the patient expresses knowledge that he is
apparently not aware that he possesses—i.e. knowledge concerning the
semantic relations between two words. . . . It is the knowledge expressed in
task performance, rather than the carrying out of the task itself, that one
would want to characterize as implicit or perhaps "unconscious", although
the latter term is so loaded with surplus meaning that it is best avoided'.

At a more general level, he went on to say that, at this stage, he considered
the implicit/explicit distinction to be more descriptive than explanatory:
'Since the business of examining it in neuropsychological syndromes is a
relatively new one, the first task is to characterize and describe the phenomena
adequate. We have really just begun in this attempt'.

Multiple memory systems and imprinting

Fabrigoule and *Spelke* asked for more clarification about imprinting. The
former wanted to know whether imprinting in natural circumstances involved
both predispositions and the learning of individual features: 'If for some
reason chicks are first exposed to some other object does this learning cancel

the predisposition?' *Horn* replied that it did not. The two processes interact (cf. Johnson *et al.* 1985). *Spelke* asked about the limits of the set of objects or other stimuli to which a chick will imprint. *Horn* said that there was a wide range of '. . . visually conspicuous objects, though some are more effective than others. Size, colour, shape, contrast, the presence of absence of movement, as well as its direction, all influence the effectiveness. . . . In young ducklings objects smaller than a matchbox are ignored or pursued by them as food, and are relatively ineffective as imprinting stimuli (Fabricius and Boyd 1952)'.

Chapouthier mentioned his work on '. . . imprinting using a rather different system, in which chicks are required to follow a moving decoy. . . . We found differences in the optic tectum. Could we suppose that the optic tectum is related to visuo–motor integration whereas IHMV is related to the cognitive aspect of imprinting?' *Horn* considered this view to be entirely plausible.

Other participants pursued the link between imprinting and other processes and different species. *Young* put the broad issue quite directly: 'Obviously, imprinting and visual recognition in the chick form topics of interest in their own right. But can we use such work as anything other than an analogy in attempting to understand human visual recognition?' *Horn* replied: 'It is essential to be cautious when attempting to relate recognition processes in chicks to . . . humans. However, chicks, like human infants have predispositions for faces [Johnson and Horn, in press; Young, chapter 4, this volume], and chicks, like infants learn to recognize individuals [Johnson and Horn, 1987]. It may well be that the underlying neural mechanisms of these processes in chicks are fundamentally different from those in humans. It is also possible, however, that there are continuities. We need to find out. If there prove to be continuities, we should not perhaps be too surprised: there are after all continuities between humans and other animals at the biochemical and cellular levels, and upwards to the level of behaviour'.

Mounoud followed up the question of the predisposition for human faces by infants, and said that it takes at least two to three months for an infant to learn about the individual. He asked whether this could be related to findings on the chick. *Horn*'s reply was that '. . . chicks learn to recognize individuals quite quickly—after a few hours of exposure on the day after hatching [Johnson and Horn 1987]; so the time course is very different from that in humans. This difference does not, of course, preclude the possibility that similar neural mechanisms are involved'.

Weiskrantz raised the question of how one can distinguish recognition, in the sense of a stimulus being familiar as having been seen on a particular recent occasion, from recognition of an object being part of a visual repertoire of meaningful objects. He also asked *Horn* if he would speculate about homologies between systems in the bird brain and corresponding systems in the mammalian brain that are involved in discrimination vs. recognition memory.

Horn replied: 'These two kinds of recognition may correspond to (i) the recognition which involves mediational processes (see pp. 283–5) and (ii) the recognition which is implied by a habit (see p. 284). It is difficult to dissociate these different forms of recognition, but we have attempted to do so. IMHV appears to be implicated in the former kind of recognition (see pp. 285–9), it may not be necessary for the latter kind of recognition (see pp. 283–4), and I do not know which parts of the chick brain are so implicated. I have suggested elsewhere that IMHV may be homologous with the pre-frontal and cingulate cortex of primates [Horn 1985]'.

Intentionality in animals

A number of participants wanted further specification of 'intentionality'. *Butterworth*, for example, said that it is possible to isolate many different levels of intentionality from a developmental point of view: 'Dewey, in his famous paper on the reflex arc concept . . . seems to define the mechanistic concept in intentional terms. Piaget distinguishes in his circular reactions between 'goal-directed' and 'intentional' in terms of the point in the action sequence at which the goal is inserted. . . . It is also possible to think of deliberate actions carried out with foresight as another class of intentional acts. Which, if any, of these levels of intentionality applies here?

Dickinson said that he agreed about several levels, and he should have made this point in this contribution. 'Although the magazine approach of rats under a Pavlovian contingency is not intentional with respect to the goal of acquiring food, it may well be goal-directed with respect to achieving proximity to the magazine; the animals may well be able to alter their route to the magazine to avoid obstacles, etc. [but see Hershberger (1986) for evidence that even simple approach behaviour is not always intentional even on this level of analysis]. The significance of approach acquisition in the presence of the conditioned stimulus is that it is not intentional with respect to the goal specified by the conditioned procedure, namely access to the reinforcer.

Dickinson continued: 'It is generally recognized that actions and responses in conditioning procedures are typically defined in terms of the achievement of some goal or state of affairs, such as pressing the level or pulling the chain. This means that a mechanistic account of the conditioning . . . may involve terms that are potentially intentional at another level of analysis; thus it seems to me to be legitimate to talk about "activation" or "elicitation" of magazine approach or level processing, which are goal-defined responses, when attempting to give a mechanistic account in relation to the goal that is manipulated by the conditioning schedule, the reinforcer'. He went on to say that he was not clear how his view of levels of intentionality mapped on to distinctions drawn by Piaget, who did not, as far as he was aware, consider the adaption of instrumental actions to motivationally induced changes in the value of goals. Likewise he had little to say about the concept of acts said to have intentionality and 'forethought' in relation to explanations in terms of mental states, such as beliefs and desires, but '. . . perhaps one could relate the two concepts within a theory of practical inference by viewing deliberation and forethought as referring to a process of inference operating on the content of the mental states to produce an action'.

A question raised by *Schacter* was directed to the relationship between priming and computation, which he understood *Dickinson* to consider as 'mechanistic' and not sufficient for intentional states: 'Was it possible to say anything more about the nature of the cognitive processes that underly intentional states?'

Dickinson replied that he wished to make it clear that he did not wish to give the impression that he regarded 'computation' as 'mechanistic': 'As I understand it, the problem with a computational theory of mental states, and for that matter of intentional behaviour, is how to endow the symbols in such an account with representational power for the agent. This problem is what led me to say that a computer program could simulate intentionality rather than instantiate it. Perhaps if we could satisfactorily turn the computer into a robot, then the problem would be solved, at least for intentional behaviour even if not for mental states. But cleverer minds than mine have struggled with this problem'. As for making general claims about the nature and form of the representations that carry the content of intentional states, I can do little more than rehearse, for instance, Fodor's (1976) claims for a "language of thought" or Bisiach's arguments (Chapter 18, this volume) for "reduced" or "bounded" analogue representations. To elaborate within particular claims about the content of representations within particular domains would, of course, go beyond the possible scope of my answer'.

There were a number of questions about experiments with reinforcer devaluation. For example, *Fabrigoule* said that, in his 1980 book, *Dickinson* accepted animals' ability to acquire representations of relations between events, or between their actions and events, and described these as cognitive processes: 'Do you now restrict the term "cognitive" to the case in which you find intentionality? It is difficult, for example, to see how a non-cognitive process could mediate the type of integration of information . . . found in reinforcer devaluation studies'.

Dickinson said he had no clear answer, but if pushed he would probably wish to restrict the term "cognitive" to mental states and processes involving representation: 'At first sight, this definition appears to commit me to the view that mechanistic explanations can be cognitive. This is because, along with many others, I have claimed in various places (including here) that Pavlovian conditioning, although mechanistic in character, is mediated by the activation of a reinforcer representation, a claim motivated by the outcome of devaluation studies'. But he went on to confess that he had doubts about whether such mediation in Pavlovian conditioning is properly characterized as a representation: 'In order for an element in a psychological theory to merit the term "representation", it seems to me that its role in the theory should depend upon its serving as a representational function for the agent. And it is not clear to me that the so-called reinforcer representations in a mechanistic theory of Pavlovian conditioning have this function; all they in fact do is to transmit excitation in a way that allows the target of this excitation to be altered by reinforcer devaluation through establishing a new excitatory connection from this element. The element may well be a reinforcer representation for the theorist, but it is not clear that it is for the animal. This restriction on the concept would seem to entail that the term "cognitive" be limited to intentional mental states (i.e. mental states that exert their effects by virtue of their representational content through, for instance, an inference process that operates upon this content) and the behavioural expressions of such states'.

On a related but more specific point about devaluation experiments, *Neuenschwander* commented that she understood *Dickinson*'s interpretation of his experiments, '. . . but I don't see clearly how you interpret devaluation experiments. After overtraining, animals seem to get what you call habits, that is, they are less sensitive to devaluation of the reinforcer; so do you think that they lost intentionality even if they still perform the action?' *Dickinson* answered: 'Yes, exactly so. The fact that the performance of an overtrained action is, under certain circumstances, impervious to reinforcer devaluation [see Dickinson 1985] means that the action is not related rationally to the desires supported by the current states of affairs. The reinforcer devaluation should reduce the desire for this reward and yet performance continues unabated. Just as Pavlovian conditioning fails to meet the criterion for intentionality because the conditioned response does not adjust to a schedule that should have altered the animal's belief about the consequences of this action, so overtrained instrumental conditioning fails because it is insensitive to conditions that should have altered the animal's desire for the reinforcer'.

Finally, *Weiskrantz* asked what, if anything, was added to his explanation of 'intentionality' by using the term 'natural language', to which *Dickinson* replied: 'If the behaviour of animals warrants the attribution of intentional mental states, then the content of such states must be capable of being carried by representations other than some internalized form of natural language. This is not to say, of course, that natural language (or, for that matter, even artificial languages and symbolic systems) does not play a role in human cognition, but simply that linguistic competence is not necessary for cognition'. But, in discussion with *Caramazza*, he stressed 'Clearly, I should argue that the question of whether a particular class of actions warrants an intentional account is an empirical issue; indeed, I had hoped that the studies reported here are testimony to this fact'.

References

Dickinson, A. (1980). *Contemporary animal learning theory.* Cambridge University Press.

—— (1985). Actions and habits: the development of behavioural autonomy. *Philosophical Transactions of the Royal Society (London)*, **B308,** 67–78.

Fabricius, E. and Boyd, H. (1952). Experiments on the following reactions of ducklings. *Wildfowl Trust Annual Report,* **6,** 84–9.

Fodor, J. A. (1976). *The language of thought.* Harvester Press, Brighton, Sussex.

Hershberger, W. A. (1986). An approach through the looking-glass. *Animal Learning and Behavior,* **14,** 443–51.

Horn, G. (1985). *Memory, imprinting and the brain.* Oxford University Press.

Johnson, M. H. and Horn, G. (1987). The role of a restricted region of the chick forebrain in the recognition of individual conspecifics. *Behavioural Brain Research,* **23,** 269–75.

—— and —— (in press). Developmental of filial preferences in the dark-reared chick. *Animal Behaviour.*

——, Bolhuis, J., and Horn, G. (1985). Interaction between acquired preferences and development predispositions during imprinting. *Animal Behaviour,* **33,** 1000–6.

Section E

Shapes, space, and memory

Editorial to Section E

Negotiations by other creatures with the spatial world and the objects within it are the source of much of our information about their concepts, prototypes, and schemas (as well as for the creatures themselves). It is also a rich mine for skillful and rewarding investigations, a mine with an inexhaustible potential. This classical area is being continuously renewed by novel discoveries.

A useful and scholarly review of historical and contemporary research on primate shape and space perception is contained in *Bresard's* chapter. Because it analyses many of the separate factors involved, it serves as a convenient entrée into the broader field as a whole, including both human and sub-primate mammalian. She considers questions of the storage of visual prototypes of objects, cross-modal transfer, colour, spatial frames and displacements within them, cognitive maps based on either egocentric or allocentric space, and spatial transforms, including some of the results from her own original research on 'mental rotation' by apes. The review also forms direct bridges with findings with other species, including both pigeon and human, on mental rotation of shapes. Her analysis leads her, in common with a number of the other participants, to favour a modular interpretation of perception.

Within such a framework, specific and seminal lines of enquiry are reported by *Diamond* and *Thinus-Blanc*. *Diamond* is concerned with the difficulty that human infants with the 'A—not B' problem, that is, the tendency for them to continue to select spatial position A, previously correct, even when the correct position at which an attractive object has been placed is visibly switched to B. She detects the close similarity of such a task with delayed response and related tasks conventionally administered to monkeys. Because it has long been known that adult monkeys are also severely deficient in such a task if they have dorsolateral frontal lobe lesions, she puts forward the reasonable view that emergence of the correct strategy developmentally in infants depends upon the gradual maturation of the frontal lobes. She summarizes novel evidence with infant monkeys as well as with human infants showing closely similar developmental progressions for delayed response as well as for other types of 'frontal' tasks, such as object retrieval via a visual detour, which reinforce the evidence for a frontal lobe specialization. A reasonable interpretation is put forward that the mechanisms involve the development of inhibition. Just as with adult patients with frontal lobe lesions, who 'know' what is correct in clinical diagnostic tests (such as the Wisconsin card-sorting test), they nevertheless persevere in making prior responses that are no longer correct. Just the same is advanced for the 'A—not B' infants: their eye movements reveal correct knowledge but the infants cannot suppress their reaching behaviour. *Diamond's* study represents a rare and important convergence of knowledge, not only across species, but across three disciplines—behavioural analysis, human and monkey development, and neuroscience.

Thinus-Blanc, too, is concerned with spatial memory and negotiation, but at the level of environmental maps and within the context of natural situations, where the problems of adaptation can be severe. 'Let us imagine', she remarks, 'a world without any maps, road signs, or tourist offices; in short, without any information transmitted by language or writing. Such is the animal's universe, which may also contain hostile elements such as predators. Therefore, an accurate localization of the nest or burrow, of the places abounding in food, etc., are prerequisites for survival. For these reasons, paradoxical though they may seem, the animal offers us a better model than the human in the study of the cognitive mechanisms involved in spatial orientiation. Spatial intelligence is becoming increasingly unnecessary in man, and, according to the laws of evolution, it should be extinct in a few thousand years!' She proceeds to review a variety of original studies by her and her colleagues using a number of species and different custom-designed situations, ranging from dogs retrieving in large fields to hamsters carrying out detour problems in more laboratory-scaled settings. She concludes from several of these systematic studies that animals can reorganize previous acquired spatial information as environmental representations and that they do so in a way that is independent of temporal ordering. She also relates processes involved in the formation of 'cognitive maps' with parallel evidence from habituation and exploration, and in this way also provides a conceptual link with the infant habituation research presented in Section C.

13

Differences between adult and infant cognition: is the crucial variable presence or absence of language?

ADELE DIAMOND

How does 'thought without language' differ from 'thought with language'? Do they differ? Do certain cognitive skills or strategies rely on language so that they would be impossible without language?

One way to try to address these questions is to look at infants in the first year of life, who, for the most part, do not have language.[1] Does their thinking differ from that of adults in fundamental ways?

The answer is by no means clear. Infants sometimes seem to show very sophisticated abilities, such as abstraction, generalization, problem-solving, and planning; that is, infants sometimes show behaviours that are analogous to the very highest abilities of which adults pride themselves. On the other hand, bright, mature adults sometimes show the same 'dumb' behaviours seen in infants—e.g. failure to show transfer of training, absence of systematic hypothesis testing or planning, rigidity, and perseveration. Is there no fundamental difference between the way infants and adults think? Or, are analogies misleading so that seemingly similar behaviours are really fundamentally different? When infants do not seem to be able to do something, is it a problem of communication (i.e. it is hard for us to tell them what we would like them to do) or is it a problem of infants' lack of cognitive ability?

My own research suggests that there are important differences in how the mind of the infant and the adult works. That research links some of the developmental changes between 6–12 months of age to maturation of frontal cortex. In fundamental ways, the behaviour of infants below 9–12 months resembles that of adults with frontal cortex damage. Adults with damage of frontal cortex have language, however. Thus, my work suggests that, yes, infants organize experience and action in different ways from adults, but that

[1] It is an interesting, and somewhat open, question how much language infants have below one year. Some infants say their first word as early as eight or nine months, and children understand much earlier than they speak.

this difference may not be due to the fact that adults have language and infants do not.

The hypothesis that developmental changes between 6–12 months might be related to maturation of frontal cortex had seemed plausible because of (a) the similarity of Piaget's AB̄ task (Piaget 1954) to 'delayed response' (DR), and (b) the overwhelming evidence linking DR to frontal cortex function.

Similarity of AB̄ and delayed response

AB̄ is one of the classic markers of developmental change during the second half of the first year of life. An infant watches as a toy is hidden in one of two identical wells, a delay of 0–10 sec is imposed, then the infant is allowed to reach. Infants under $7\frac{1}{2}$ months cannot uncover a hidden object and so cannot be tested on AB̄. Infants of $7\frac{1}{2}$–11 months usually find the toy at the first well (A). When side of hiding is reversed to B, however, they reach back to A (Diamond 1985; Fox et al. 1979; Gratch and Landers 1971). Hence the name 'A, not B'. Since the task was originally devised in the 1930s it has been used extensively with infants.

DR is the classic test for prefrontal cortex function in non-human primates. Since Jacobsen first introduced the test for this purpose in 1935, it has been used extensively. In DR, as on AB̄, the subject watches as a desired object is hidden in one of two identical wells,[2] a delay of 0–10 sec is imposed, then the subject is allowed to reach. Within-trial procedures are exactly the same on the two tasks. DR and AB̄ differ only in how side of hiding is varied over trials. In DR, side of hiding is varied randomly; in AB̄ the reward is consistently hidden on one side until the subject is correct, then side of hiding is reversed and the procedure repeated.

The performance of infants from $7\frac{1}{2}$–9 months on AB̄ matches, in considerable detail, that of monkeys with prefrontal cortex lesions on DR. At delays as brief as 1–2 sec, infants fail AB̄ and frontally lesioned monkeys fail DR (infants: Diamond 1985; Evans 1973; Gratch et al. 1974; monkeys: Battig et al. 1960; Fuster and Alexander 1971; Goldman and Rosvold 1970; Harlow et al. 1952). This is true whether the hiding places differ in left–right location (infants: Diamond 1985; Gratch and Landers 1971; monkeys: Goldman and Rosvold 1970; Harlow et al. 1952) or in up–down location (infants: Butterworth 1976; monkeys: Fuster 1980). Both groups succeed when there is a 0 sec delay (infants: Gratch et al. 1974; Harris 1973; monkeys: Battig et al. 1960; Fuster and Alexander 1971; Goldman and Rosvold 1970; Harlow et al. 1952) or when they are allowed to keep looking at, or orienting their body toward, the correct well during the delay (infants: Cornell 1979; Diamond 1985; Fox et al. 1979; monkeys: Battig et al. 1960; Miles and Blomquist 1960;

[2] On DR, the subjects have been non-human primates and the desired object, food. On AB̄, the subjects have been infants and the desired object, a toy.

Pinsker and French 1967). Both are able to learn to associate a landmark with the correct well, and to use that information to reach correctly even at long delays (*infants*: Butterworth *et al.* 1982; Diamond unpublished thesis, 1983; *monkeys*: Pohl 1973).

Another task closely linked to frontal cortex function is 'spatial reversal'. Here, side of hiding is varied as on AB̄: the reward is always hidden on one side until the subject is correct, then side of hiding is reversed and the procedure repeated. The difference between spatial reversal and AB̄ is that in spatial reversal the subject does not see where the reward is hidden, whereas in AB̄ and DR hiding is done in full view.

Spatial reversal requires the subject to deduce where the reward is hidden on the basis of feedback. Initially, the reward is always hidden in the same place. Animals with frontal cortex damage have no difficulty learning this initial spatial discrimination (e.g. Goldman and Rosvold 1970; Gross and Weiskrantz 1962). However, when side of hiding is reversed frontally operated animals are impaired. They persist in reaching to the previously correct place (e.g. Butter 1969; Butters *et al.* 1969; Goldman and Rosvold 1970; Mishkin *et al.* 1969).[3]

This is very similar to the pattern of performance of infants on AB̄: they are correct at the first place the reward is hidden, but when side of hiding is reversed errors appear; infants persist in reaching to the previously correct place (Diamond 1985; Gratch *et al.* 1974; Harris 1973).

Failure on DR and spatial reversal is the hallmark of lesions to dorsolateral prefrontal cortex. AB̄ appears to be a composite of DR and spatial reversal: identical to DR on within-trial procedures and identical to spatial reversal on between-trial procedures.

Evidence linking delayed response to prefrontal cortex

DR performance in the monkey has been consistently shown to depend upon frontal cortex function by virtually every known anatomical, physiological, and pharmacological technique. Moreover, it has been consistently linked to a specific subregion within frontal cortex, the dorsolateral prefrontal region, the critical locus within that site being the principal sulcus (Butters *et al.* 1969; Goldman and Rosvold 1970). The link between DR and prefrontal cortex was first demonstrated by Jacobsen (1935, 1936), and scores of studies using ablation procedures have replicated the finding that animals fail DR following

---

[3] The Wisconsin card-sorting test was designed to be an adaptation of spatial reversal appropriate for human adults (Berg 1948; Grant and Berg 1948). The subject is required to deduce the correct criterion (colour, shape, or number) for sorting a deck of cards on the basis of feedback. Adult patients with frontal lobe damage learn the initial sorting criterion normally but, when the criterion is switched, they are impaired; they persist in sorting according to the criterion that was previously correct (Milner 1963, 1964; Drewe 1974).

bilateral lesions of prefrontal cortex (major reviews include Fuster 1980; Markowitsch and Pritzel 1977; Nauta 1971; Rosenkilde 1979).

Equally large ablations elsewhere in the brain, e.g. parietal cortex, do not produce deficits on DR (e.g. Jacobsen 1936; Meyer *et al*. 1951). Lesions of prefrontal cortex which produce deficits on DR do not produce deficits on other tasks, such as visual discrimination (e.g. Harlow and Dagnon 1943; Jacobsen 1936; Pohl 1973). In short, DR appears to be sensitive to damage specifically to prefrontal cortex, and damage to prefrontal cortex produces deficits only on specific tasks, such as DR.

These results have been replicated with techniques that enable experimenters to interrupt functioning of a localized neural region temporarily and reversibly. Thus DR has also been linked to the frontal lobe using *localized cooling* (Alexander and Goldman 1978; Bauer and Fuster 1976; Fuster and Alexander 1970), *localized electrical stimulation* (Stamm 1969; Stamm and Rosen 1969; Weiskrantz *et al*. 1962), and *localized dopamine depletion* (depleted using 6-OHDA, deficits reversed by L-Dopa) (Brozoski *et al*. 1979).

Inferring function from dysfunction can be problematic. It is important that the link between DR and prefrontal cortex has been confirmed by techniques that assess patterns of functioning in the intact brain: *surface-negative steady potential shifts* (Stamm 1969; Stamm and Rosen 1969), *single unit recording* (Fuster 1973; Fuster and Alexander 1971; Niki 1974), and *2-deoxyglucose metabolic labelling* (Bugbee and Goldman-Rakic 1981).

All of this work taken together, representing as it does such diverse experimental approaches, makes the link between DR and prefrontal cortex essentially incontrovertible.

Since AB̄ and DR are so similar and the evidence so convincingly links DR to frontal lobe function, it was hypothesized that maturation of the frontal lobe might underlie some of the cognitive advances between 6–12 months. This was tested using AB̄, DR, and another task, object retrieval, which, although also linked to the frontal lobe, appears to share little or none of the task requirements seen in AB̄ or DR. (Object retrieval is a transparent barrier task, where the subject must make a detour to reach a visible goal; nothing is hidden.) The line of inquiry involved studying the developmental progression of performance on these tasks in the human infant and infant monkey, the effects of brain lesions on performance of these tasks in the infant and adult monkey, and the relation between developmental progression on these tasks and brain maturation in the infant monkey.

Results with human infants on AB̄

Twenty-five full-term infants (11 male, 14 female) were studied longitudinally, with testing every two weeks from 6–12 months. Another 84 children were tested only once at ages between 6 and 12 months. The testing apparatus

consisted of a table with embedded wells. All subjects were tested individually
in the laboratory. An infant was seated on the parent's lap facing the testing
table, equidistant from the wells. The experimenter was seated across the
table, facing parent and child. A trial began with the experimenter holding up
a toy to catch the infant's attention. As the subject watched, the experimenter
slowly hid the toy in one of two wells. Particular care was taken to ensure that
the subject observed this. Both wells were covered simultaneously, and a brief
delay imposed. Subjects were prevented from straining, turning, or looking at
a well during the delay. Parents were instructed to look straight ahead and to
restrain the infant's arms and torso gently but firmly. Visual fixation of the
wells was broken by the experimenter calling to the infant during the delay and
counting aloud, which caused the infant to look up. After the delay, the
subject was allowed to reach. A reach was defined as the removal of a cover.

Confirming and extending previous work (Fox *et al.* 1979; Gratch and
Landers 1971), a developmental progression in AB̄ performance was found in
infants between $7\frac{1}{2}$ and 12 months (Diamond 1985). The delay needed to
produce the AB̄ error increased continuously at an average rate of about 2 sec
per month (see Fig. 13.1). At $7\frac{1}{2}$–9 months, the characteristic AB̄ error pattern
occurred at delays of 2–5 sec. By 12 months, infants reached correctly at delays
as long as 10 sec.

Although delay remained constant across trials, performance did not.

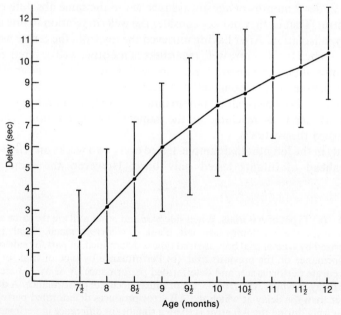

Fig. 13.1 Delay at which the AB̄ occurred by age. (From Diamond 1985.)

Infants erred on only certain classes of trials (reversal trials and repeat trials following errors), while in the same session, at the same delay, they reached correctly on another class of trials (repeat trials following correct reaches) (Diamond 1985). This is the classic error pattern from which the name AB̄ is derived, for infants are correct at 'A' but they are not correct when side of hiding changes to 'B' (see Fig. 13.2).

All children made the AB̄ error throughout the months of testing. At each age, errors disappeared when delay was reduced 2–3 sec, and performance deteriorated when delay was increased 2–3 sec above the level producing the AB̄ error. Thus, at $7\frac{1}{2}$–9 months a 10 sec delay produced deteriorated, random performance, with errors equally distributed over trials instead of in the AB̄ error pattern. By 12 months, infants reached correctly even at delays as long as 10 sec.

The AB̄ testing table contained three wells arranged in a semicircle, although only two wells were used on each trial. The wells used were always adjacent and the infant was also seated equidistant from the wells used. The three-well arrangement was needed for testing sequences such as the following: The toy is hidden in the centre well, the centre and left wells are covered, and the infant correctly retrieves the toy from the centre well. Then the centre and right well are covered. If the infant reaches to the centre well that would be a reach to the same absolute position, whereas if the infant reaches to the right well that would be a reach to the same relative position. Infants under 9 months of age always reached to the same absolute position (the centre). That is, they did not consider the wells in relation to one another but only in isolation. After having retrieved the toy from the centre well, they always reached to the centre well, regardless of the other well covered. Starting at 9 months, infants began to consider the wells in relation to one another and began reaching to the same relative position. Preference for the relative position never became predominant in infants from 9–12 months of age but it became as likely as reaching to the same absolute position (Diamond, unpublished thesis, 1983).

Infants in the longitudinal sample, tested every two weeks on AB̄, were 2–4 weeks ahead of infants tested only once. However, the same general

Fig. 13.2 (a) Types of AB̄ trials. When side hide and other well are the same as on the previous trial, these columns are left blank. √=correct reach. Trial 1 is not characterized by type of trial because trial type is determined, in part, by side of hiding and performance on the previous trial. (b) Performance by type of trial for the AB̄ error, accurate performance, and deteriorated performance. A delay 2–3 sec shorter than the delay at which AB̄ error occurs produces accurate performance. A delay 2–3 sec longer than the delay at which the AB̄ error produces deteriorated performance. Note that only during the AB̄ error is there a significant difference in performance by type of trial. (From Diamond 1985.)

				Type of trial		
Trial no.	Side hide	Other well	Reach	Repeat trial following correct reach	Reversal trial following correct reach	Repeat trial following error
1	L	C	✓			
2			✓	X		
3	C	L	errs	X		
4			errs			X
5			✓			X
6			✓	X		
7	L	C	errs		X	
8			✓			X
9			✓	X		

(a)   etc.

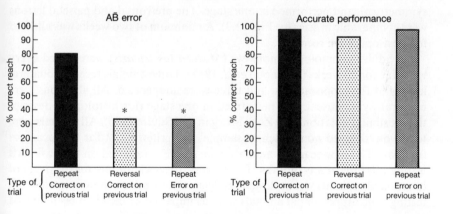

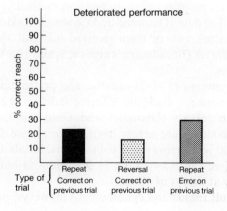

developmental progression was found in infants tested cross-sectionally or longitudinally(Diamond 1985, in prep.).

Results with monkeys on AB̄

The same AB̄ task administered to the infants was administered to the monkeys. The only differences were as follows: (1) a testing tray was used rather than a table, (2) food was hidden instead of a toy, (3) visual fixation was broken by lowering an opaque screen rather than by calling to the subject and counting aloud, and (4) monkeys were not physically restrained from moving during the delay (although if they tried to position cue this habit was broken).

Nine adult rhesus monkeys (*Macaca mulatta*) were tested every weekday for 15 weeks (Diamond and Goldman-Rakic 1983). Prior to testing, three animals received bilateral lesions of dorsolateral prefrontal cortex (Broadmann's areas 8, 9 and 10), three received bilateral parietal cortex lesions (Broadmann's area 7), and three were unoperated. All ablations were bilateral, symmetrical, and performed in one stage. The prefrontal and parietal lesions were comparable in size (see Fig. 13.3). A minimum of two weeks was allowed for post-operative recovery.

Six adult cynomologus monkeys (*Macaca fascicularis*) were tested every weekday for 20 weeks (Diamond *et al.* 1987). Three animals received bilateral lesions of the hippocampus, and three were unoperated. All ablations were bilateral, symmetrical, and performed in one stage (for histological description of similar ablations, see Zola-Morgan and Squire 1986). All animals were tested on 'delayed non-match to sample', the criterial test for hippocampal function. The hippocampal animals were severely impaired on this task. AB̄ testing was done many months after surgery; to check for possible recovery of function all animals were retested on delayed non-match to sample after AB̄ testing. The hippocampal animals were as impaired as they had been on first testing.

Four infant rhesus monkeys were studied longitudinally, with testing every weekday from 40–150 days (Diamond and Goldman-Rakic 1986). At the end of testing ($4\frac{1}{2}$ months), two of them received bilateral ablations of dorsolateral prefrontal cortex (Broadmann's areas 8, 9, and 10). They were retested on AB̄ at 5 months.

Infant rhesus monkeys of $1\frac{1}{2}$–$2\frac{1}{2}$ months, and prefrontally operated adult and infant rhesus monkeys, made the AB̄ error at delays of 2–5 sec, as do $7\frac{1}{2}$–9-month-old human infants (Diamond and Goldman-Rakic 1983, 1986). Although delay was constant across trials, performance differed systematically by type of trial with errors restricted to reversal trials and to repeat trials following errors (see Fig. 13.4). Like $7\frac{1}{2}$–9-month-old human infants, they reached randomly at delays of 10 sec.

Unoperated adult rhesus and cynomologus monkeys, parietally operated

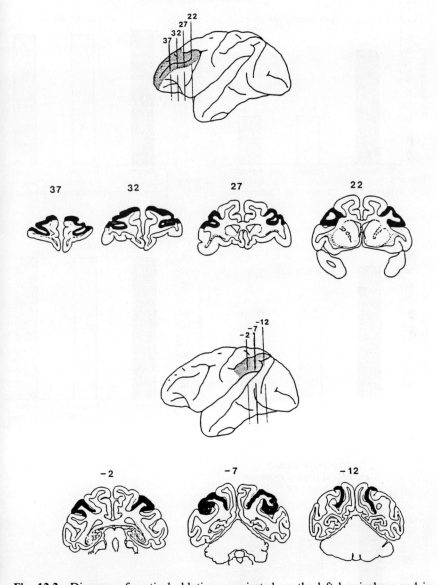

Fig. 13.3 Diagram of cortical ablations, projected on the left hemisphere and in coronal sections. Dorsolateral prefrontal site is shown above and parietal site below. (From Diamond and Goldman-Rakic, in prep.)

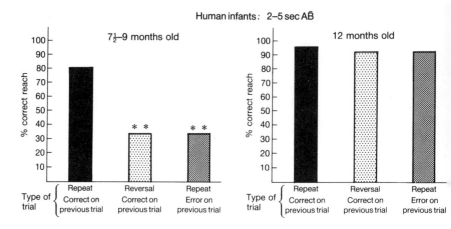

Human infants: 2–5 sec AB̄

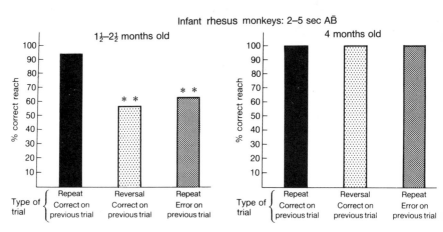

Infant rhesus monkeys: 2–5 sec AB̄

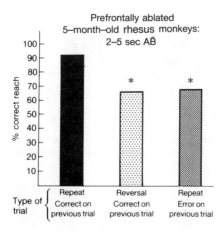

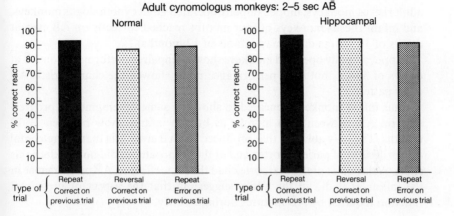

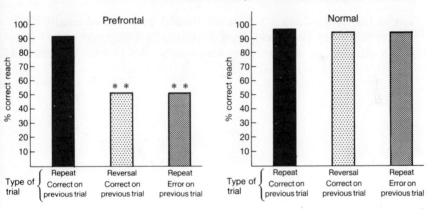

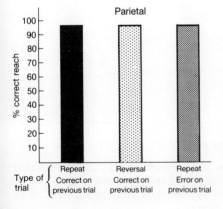

Fig. 13.4 Pattern of performance across trials on A$\bar{\text{B}}$ at delays of 2–5 sec in human infants, infant rhesus monkeys (intact and frontally operated), adult cynomolgus monkeys (unoperated and hippocampally operated), and adult rhesus monkeys (unoperated, frontally operated, and parietally operated).

adult rhesus monkeys, hippocampally operated adult cynomologus monkeys, and infant rhesus monkeys of four months reached correctly on AB̄ even at delays of 10 sec (as do human infants of 12 months).

Hippocampally operated monkeys showed impaired performance on AB̄ at delays of 30 sec, but their performance never showed the characteristic AB̄ error pattern.

Thus infant monkeys appeared to show the same developmental progression on AB̄ between 1½–4 months as human infants show between 7½–12 months. The only ablation that produced the AB̄ error was that of prefrontal cortex; lesions of parietal cortex and of the hippocampus did not produce this effect. Ablation of prefrontal cortex had the same effect on AB̄ performance in the infant as it did in the adult, suggesting that the aspect of prefrontal function required by AB̄ matures during infancy.

Results with human infants on delayed response

Twelve full-term infants (six male, six female) were studied longitudinally, with testing every two weeks from 7–12 months (Diamond and Doar, in prep.). Another 40 children were tested only once at ages between 8–12

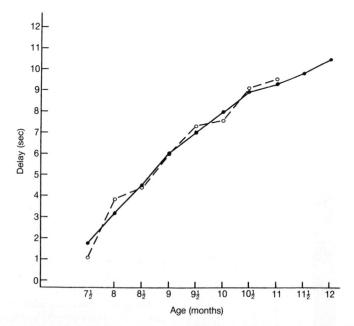

Fig. 13.5   Delay at which performance on DR in human infants was below criterion by age, superimposed over the delay at which the AB̄ error occurred by age. Criterion on DR = 88 per cent correct (at least 14 of 16 trials correct). Dash line = DR. Solid line = AB̄. (From Diamond and Doar, in prep.)

months. The testing apparatus and procedure were the same as that used for AB̄ with human infants, except that side of hiding was varied randomly over trials by a predetermined schedule. A testing session consisted of 16 trials. Criterion for correct performance was 14 correct reaches (88 per cent).

The developmental progression for DR performance is given in Fig. 13.5, superimposed over the developmental progression for AB̄ performance. The curves are virtually identical, even though AB̄ testing was done at Harvard University with babies from the Boston area, DR testing was done at Washington University with babies from the St Louis area, different testers administered AB̄ and DR, and the DR testers were blind to the earlier AB̄ results. In all respects, the results for DR are comparable to those for AB̄: (a) excellent performance on repeat trials following correct reaches; errors confined to reversals following correct reaches and repeat trials following errors; (b) infants tested only once lagged 2–4 weeks behind infants tested longitudinally, but the form of their performance was the same; (c) large individual differences between infants of the same age; and (d) boys lagged 2–4 weeks behind the girls.

This completes the AB̄–DR story. Monkeys with prefrontal cortex lesions perform on AB̄ as do 7½–9-month-old human infants. Human infants of 7½–9 months fail DR under the same conditions as do monkeys with lesions of prefrontal cortex. The performance of human infants on DR mirrors their performance on AB̄.

Results with human infants on object retrieval

'Object retrieval' (OR) is a detour task with the goal object inside a rectangular box open on one side. Three Plexiglas boxes were used for human infant testing: (a) transparent, $6'' \times 6'' \times 2''$, (b) transparent, $4\frac{1}{2}'' \times 4\frac{1}{2}'' \times 2\frac{1}{2}''$, and (c) opaque, $4\frac{1}{2}'' \times 2\frac{1}{2}'' \times 2\frac{1}{2}''$.

As with AB̄, all subjects were tested individually in the laboratory. Each infant was seated on the parent's lap facing the testing table and experimenter. A trial began with the experimenter placing a toy in one of the boxes. The infant had simply to retrieve the toy. No time limit was imposed. A trial ended with retrieval or when the infant refused to try any longer. Considerable freedom of movement was permitted and, if an infant became distracted, the experimenter tapped the box or toy to regain attention. The experimenter held the back of the box throughout each trial to prevent the infant from simply lifting the box off the toy.

Experimental variables included: (a) side of box which was open (front, top, left, or right), (b) distance of toy from opening (ranging from partially outside the box to deep inside the box), and (c) position of box on the testing surface (near front edge of table or far; far to the left, at the midline, or far to the right). The bait was always visible when a transparent box was used, but the experimental variables jointly determined whether the toy was seen through a closed side of the box or through the opening. Order of conditions was counterbalanced across testing sessions.

The idea for OR came from a task on which Moll and Kuypers (1977) had demonstrated impairments in monkeys following lesions of the frontal lobe:[4] food could be seen beneath the centre of a transparent floor plate, but the only route to the food was through a hole in the plate's side. Monkeys with frontal lobe lesions only reached straight for the food at the centre of the plate, although normal monkeys and those with lesions elsewhere had no difficulty making the appropriate detour. When a unilateral frontal lobe lesion was combined with a commissurotomy, the hand contralateral to the lesion persisted in reaching at the plate's centre, while the hand connected to the intact hemisphere *of the same monkey* reached through the hole to the food!

The same 25 infants tested longitudinally on A$\bar{\text{B}}$ were tested on OR during the same bi-weekly sessions. The 84 children in the cross-sectional sample were tested on both A$\bar{\text{B}}$ and OR in the same session (Diamond 1981).

Infants were found to pass though a clear, tightly age-related series of phases in the performance of OR. All infants progressed through the same sequence of phases, in the same order, at approximately the same age (see Fig. 13.6). So rarely did infants deviate from this that the sequence of development fits a Guttman scale with a coefficient of reproducibility of 0.93. There was a small effect of repeated testing (infants in the cross-sectional sample lagged approximately 2–4 weeks behind infants tested longitudinally), but the same phases were found in the same order.

Infants of $6\frac{1}{2}$–7 months, like the monkeys with frontal lobe lesions studied by Moll and Kuypers (1977), were unable to retrieve the reward if they saw it through a closed side. They banged and scratched with considerable effort and persistence, but if their line of sight did not change they tried no other route to the toy. They insisted on reaching directly to where they saw the toy. The tendency to be guided only by visual information was so strong that it overrode available tactile information and the effect of repeated reinforcement. This is impressive because we know that infants at this age, and younger, will react to tactile information and we know that their behaviour can be shaped by reinforcement (e.g. Lipsitt *et al.* 1966; Rovee-Collier and Fagan 1981). So totally controlled was their reach by their line of sight that a fraction of an inch difference in the height of the box or in how close the box was to the baby made the difference between success and failure—everything depended upon whether the infant was looking through the opening. Even if an infant's hand was already inside the box *en route* to the toy, if line of sight changed the infant withdrew the hand and reached to the side through which he now saw the toy.

The first advance on OR was seen at $7\frac{1}{2}$–8 months. It was a small change and

[4] The lesions were large, extending from dorsolateral prefrontal cortex into supplementary motor and premotor cortex, terminating in the rostral part of the precentral gyrus.

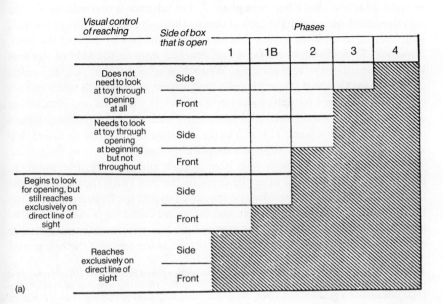

(a)

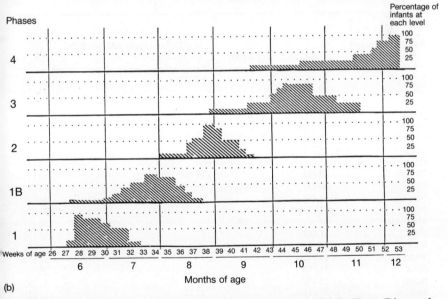

(b)

Fig. 13.6 (a) Characterization of the phases in performance of OR. (From Diamond 1981.) (b) Histograms of the age distributions for the OR phases. Based on performance with the transparent box by the 25 infants studied longitudinally. (From Diamond 1981.)

so is called phase 1B, rather than phase 2. The advance is that infants, for the first time, took active steps to look at the toy through different sides of the box, (e.g. leaning to look through a different side of the box or moving the box). However, $7\frac{1}{2}$–8 month-old-infants still reached only at the side of the box through which they were looking. When line of sight changed, the reach changed too. Onset of phase 1B coincided almost exactly with when infants could first uncover a hidden object (see Table 13.1). Phase 1B and uncovering an object require a more active, or less passive and reactive, orientation than is seen in younger infants. This marks the first time infants take an active step to change the situation with which they are presented.

The means–end behaviour seen here is quite rudimentary. For example, infants were permitted to raise the front of the box (with the experimenter holding the back of the box down on the table) so that the front opening of the bottomless box became quite large and the infant could see in. Often, a $7\frac{1}{2}$–8-month-old infant would raise the front of the box with both hands, remove one hand from the box, and attempt to reach for the toy, but the box would

Table 13.1 *Age at which the 25 infants studied longitudinally entered Phase 1B on OR and could first uncover a hidden object. (Five infants were not yet ready for A$\bar{B}$ testing with two wells when they could first uncover a hidden object.) Note the striking similarity in age of entering Phase 1B and age of onset of A$\bar{B}$ error*

Age (in weeks) of first appearance of:	Phase 1B, object retrieval	Able to find totally hidden object, one hiding place	A$\bar{B}$ error
Jack	35 (3) =	35 (3)	37 (5)
Lyndsey	33 (2) =		33 (2)
Tyler	36 (2)		38 (4)
Jamie	34 =		34
Emily	34 (2) =		34 (2)
Rachel	32 (4)		30 (6)
Brian	28 (3) =		28 (3)
Ryan	33 (1) =		33 (1)
James	28 (5)	28 (5)	30 (5)
Erin	30 (3)		32 (4)
Sarah	34 (6) =		34 (6)
Julia	33 (2) =		33 (2)
Mariama	34		36 (3)
Kate	31 (6)		33 (5)
Rusty	35 (6)		33 (5)
Todd	39 (4) =		35 (1)
Nina	31		29
Isabel	32 (5) =		32 (5)
Jennine	31 (4) =	31 (4)	33 (2)
Jane	34 (5) =		34 (5)
Bobby	33 (2) =		33 (2)
Graham	34 (2) =		34 (2)
Blair	35 (4) =	35 (4)	37 (3)
Michael	34		36 (4)
Chrissy	32 (6) =	32 (6)	34 (4)

come down halting the reach. The reach would halt and go back to the box top because once the box was down the infant saw the toy through the box top rather than through the open front, and reaches were made at this age only at the side through which the infant was looking. But why did the box come down; after all, the second hand was still holding on? The problem here was that when the infants lowered one hand to reach for the toy, they had great difficulty *not* lowering the other. They would repeatedly try to raise the front of the box, but the hand left to hold up the box repeatedly failed at its task. With both hands in the raised position, when one was lowered, the other came down too.[5]

At $8\frac{1}{2}$–9 months (phase 2), the first separation of line of sight and line of reach occurred. Infants leaned and looked through the front opening of the box, sat up, then reached into the front while looking through the top of the box. For the first time, the memory of having looked into the opening was sufficient. For the first time, infants could look through one side and reach through another. (This is reminiscent of Millar and Schaffer's (1972, 1973) finding on an operant conditioning task requiring infants to push a lever in order to see a light display. Even 6-month-old infants succeeded when the lights and lever were in the same visual field, but not until 9 months could they look one place and reach another.) If an infant had not looked into the opening on that trial, he would still not reach there, but having looked in, line of sight through the opening no longer needed to be maintained.

At $8\frac{1}{2}$–9 months, the problem of raising the box was also solved sequentially. The infant first raised the box, both hands came down, and then the infant reached in and retrieved the toy.

Between phases 1 and 4 there was an explosion in the number of sides of the box to which infants reached. Whereas $6\frac{1}{2}$–7-month-old infants often reached to only one side of the box throughout a trial, an $8\frac{1}{2}$–9-month-old might show the following sequence of reaches over a trial: front, top, left, front, top, left, front, top, front, top, front, top, left, top, right opening. Infants no longer restricted themselves to one side of the box, but, going to the other extreme, made many more reaches than necessary. They kept returning to sides of the box to which they had already reached and found closed.

Performance with the opening at the left or right of the box always lagged one phase behind performance at the front. Hence, at $8\frac{1}{2}$–9 months, infants showed phase 1B performance when the opening was on the left or right of the

---

[5] A similar observation was made by Bruner (1969). Here the task consisted of a box with a transparent lid mounted on sliding ball bushings. To retrieve the toy, the child had to slide the lid up its track, which was tilted 30° from the horizontal and would fall back down if not held. 'A seven month old has great difficulty holding the panel with one hand while reaching underneath with the other. Indeed, the first compromise solutions to the problem consist of pushing the panel up with both hands, then attempting to free one hand in order to slip it under the panel. One notes how often the infant fails because the two hands operate in concert' (Bruner 1969, p. 222).

box: they leaned and looked in the opening and needed to maintain this line of sight during the reach. This leaning and looking to the left or right was accompanied by an 'awkward reach', i.e. a reach with the hand contralateral to the opening. Reaching thus with the hand farthest from the opening made the action maximally contorted and awkward.

By $9\frac{1}{2}$–11 months (phase 3), infants succeeded when the front of the box was open without looking into the opening at all. They were able to raise the box with one hand and reach in with the other, or raise the box with both hands, lower one hand, and *keep the box raised* with the other. When the opening was on the left or right side of the box, $9\frac{1}{2}$–11-month-old infants still needed to look in the opening, but they could then sit up, look through the top, and reach through the side. Awkward reaches disappeared.

Four of the 25 infants followed longitudinally departed from the typical picture of phase 3. They reached to the left- or right-side opening *without* first looking in through that side. However, these four infants all failed to get their hand inside the opening. They misreached, going too high or too far, etc. For example, one child kept getting her thumb stuck on the top edge of the opening. To try to help her out, the experimenter tipped the box to enlarge the size of the opening, but then she reached much higher yet and still got her thumb stuck on the top edge of the opening! It was as if, although most infants appeared to attend only to vision, ignoring available tactile information, these four infants attended only to touch, ignoring the available visual information. They seemed to search for the opening the way a blind person would, by feeling for the edge. Therefore, when the opening was made very large, they still went for the edge.

Finally, by 11–12 months (phase 4), infants were perfect on OR. They did not need to look in the opening on any side to succeed. Their performance was efficient, quick, and accurate. Number of sides of the box to which infants reached returned almost to the low levels seen in phase 1, not because they reached to only one side of the box as did phase 1 infants but because one-year-old infants rarely returned to a side to which they had reached and found closed. A single touch, or look, sufficed to tell them whether a side was open or closed. They attended to both visual and tactile information. They would reach simultaneously to different sides of the box, and whichever was open they would enter. Younger children, too, reached with both hands, but typically both of their hands reached to the same side; now the hands were used to get two different pieces of information.

To determine side preferences, all infants tested on AB̄ and OR were also presented with five pairs of identical objects. A similar age progression is seen here. By 12 months, infants often reached simultaneously for both objects. Younger infants almost never did so. When younger infants used both hands they reached with both hands for the same object (Table 13.2).

Once infants were old enough to retrieve a hidden object (approximately $7\frac{1}{2}$

Table 13.2 *Percentage of simultaneous
reaches for both objects when presented
with five identical pairs of objects*

Age (months)	% reaches for both objects
5	0
6	3
7	7
8	18
9	21
10	28
11	44
12	61

Based on the 25 infants studied longitudinally.

months) they were also tested with an opaque box. At each age, performance
was one phase ahead on the opaque box compared with the transparent box
(Diamond 1981). Thus, when infants could not see the toy at the outset of trial,
they performed *better* than when they could. Bruner et al., (unpublished
manuscript, 1969) and Lockman (1984) report similar results with an opaque
wall vs. a transparent wall. This counterintuitive finding that the task was
easier when infants could not see their goal can be understood in light of the
fact that when the box was opaque infants did not need to resist reaching
along their line of sight; they could not see the toy through the box.

Testing on both OR and AB̄, thus, yielded clear age-related patterns of
improvement over a rather brief time period in all children. Although OR and
AB̄ are quite different tasks, improvement on each occurred over the same age
range. Since different experiences would seem to have been necessary for
mastery of these quite different tasks, the fact that improvement on both is
seen over the same age period suggests that these improvements are, at least in
part, maturationally based.

Results with monkeys on object retrieval

The same OR task administered to human infants was administered to rhesus
and cynomolgus monkeys. These were the same animals tested on AB̄. The
only differences in OR procedure were: (1) food was placed in the box instead
of a toy, and (2) the experimenter held the box in place by a locking device
hidden underneath the testing surface instead of by holding onto the back of
the box. The Plexiglas boxes used with adult monkeys were: (a) transparent,
$5'' \times 5'' \times 2''$, and (b) transparent, $3'' \times 3'' \times 2\frac{1}{2}''$. The Plexiglas box used for
infant monkey testing was transparent, $3'' \times 3'' \times 2\frac{1}{2}''$.

Adult rhesus monkeys with prefrontal lesions and infant rhesus monkeys of $1\frac{1}{2}$–$2\frac{1}{2}$ months showed the same pattern of performance on OR as did $7\frac{1}{2}$–9-month-old human infants (phases 1B and 2) (Diamond and Goldman-Rakic 1985, 1986). No monkeys displayed phase 1 behaviour as they all actively tried to look through more than one side of the OR box. Whereas human infants below $7\frac{1}{2}$ months rather passively accepted the task as presented, infant monkeys of even $1\frac{1}{2}$ months moved quite a bit. (Monkeys below the age of $1\frac{1}{2}$ months cannot reach and retrieve a piece of food and so cannot be tested on OR). Monkeys are more advanced at birth than are humans and very shortly become quite mobile and agile.

Human infants of $7\frac{1}{2}$–9 months, frontally operated monkeys, and infant monkeys of $1\frac{1}{2}$–$2\frac{1}{2}$ months all needed to have seen the bait through the opening of the box in order to reach in and retrieve it. When the bait (toy for children, food for monkeys) was partially out of the box they reached for it straight away, but, if in so doing they accidentally pushed the bait inside the box, they could no longer retrieve it. Deserting the opening, they tried to reach through the transparent wall of the box through which they now saw the bait, even though they had pushed the bait inside the box themselves (see Fig. 13.7)!

Frontally operated adult animals and $1\frac{1}{2}$–$2\frac{1}{2}$-month-old infant monkeys also reached repeatedly to sides they had tried and found closed like human infants at phase 2 on OR. Their approach to the problem appeared more frantic than systematic.

Monkeys with frontal lobe lesions and infant monkeys of 2–$2\frac{1}{2}$ months also showed the 'awkward reach': they reached to the left side of the box with their right hand and to the right side of the box with their left hand, seeming to make the task maximally difficult for themselves (see Fig. 13.8).

In contrast, human infants of 11–12 months, unoperated adult rhesus and cynomologus monkeys, parietally operated adult rhesus monkeys, hippocampally operated adult cynomologus monkeys, and 4-month-old infant rhesus monkeys succeeded on all trials straightaway. They did not need to have looked through the opening and they reached into the left or right side effortlessly with the hand nearest the opening (see Fig. 13.9). A single touch served to tell them whether a side was open or closed; they did not persist at a closed side and did not return to sides already tried and found to be closed.

Thus, infant monkeys appeared to show a similar developmental progression on OR between $1\frac{1}{2}$–4 months as do human infants between $7\frac{1}{2}$–12 months. In the monkey this progression was truncated, however. Human infants progressed through stages 1, 1B, 2, 3, and 4. Infant monkeys progressed from stage 1B–2 to stage 4. Consistent with the more rapid post-natal development of the monkey, this progression took 5–6 months in humans but only 2–3 months in the monkey.

On the surface, OR and $A\bar{B}$ appear to share little in common. OR is a detour task, where the bait is always visible. In $A\bar{B}$ the bait is hidden. However, the

Infant
monkey
1½ months

Human
infant
7½ months

Prefrontal
monkey

Fig. 13.7 Failure after pushing the toy inside the box themselves. Frame 1: Bait is partially out of box, S reaches immediately for the part that is sticking out of the box. Frame 2: S accidentally pushes bait into the box. Once bait is inside the box, S is unable to retrieve it, even though S was touching the bait. Frame 3: S withdraws hand from opening and goes to the side of the box through which he sees the bait. Frame 4: S looks at bait through front of box and reaches to the front. Frame 5: Unable to retrieve the bait, S gives up. (From Diamond and Goldman-Rakic 1985).

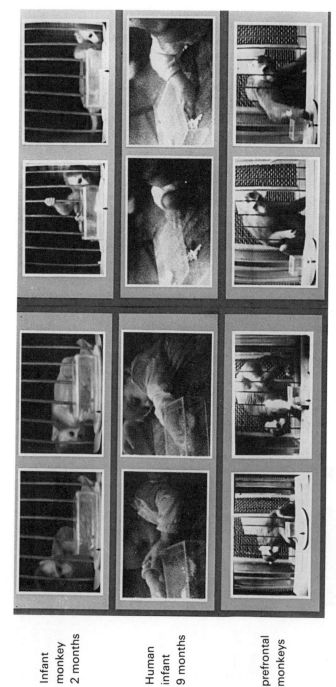

Infant
monkey
2 months

Human
infant
9 months

prefrontal
monkeys

Fig. 13.8 The awkward reach. Frame 1: S leans and looks at bait through opening of box. Frame 2: S reaches in awkwardly with the far hand. Frame 3: Opening is on the other side. Performance is the same. S leans and looks into the opening. Frame 4: S reaches in awkwardly with the far hand. (From Diamond and Goldman-Rakic 1985.)

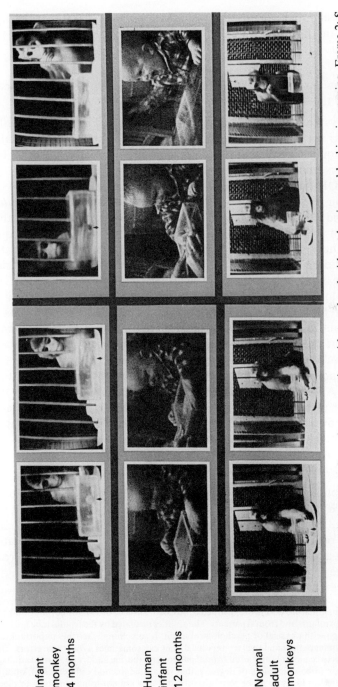

Infant
monkey
4 months

Human
infant
12 months

Normal
adult
monkeys

Fig. 13.9   Mature performance. Frame 1: S reaches to opening with near hand without leaning and looking in opening. Frame 2: S retrieves bait quickly and efficiently. Frame 3: Opening is on the other; performance is the same. S looks through top of the box and reaches into opening with the near hand. Frame 4: Success!

fact that human and simian infants improve on both tasks over the same period and the fact that both tasks have been linked to the frontal lobe suggests that they probably require common abilities.

Abilities required by AB̄ and object retrieval: insights from the function subserved by the frontal lobe

In what ways are the behaviours of infants below 9–12 months described above similar to the behaviours of adults with frontal lobe damage? What do these behaviours suggest about how the mind of an infant or a frontal lobe patient differs from that of a normal adult?[6]

AB̄ and DR have usually been thought to be measures of memory or perseveration (e.g. *memory*: Fox *et al.* 1979; Jacobsen 1936; *perseveration*: Bremner and Bryant 1977; Mishkin 1964). However, neither of these interpretations works very well for OR. OR does not appear to require memory as the box is transparent. Instead of infants perseveratively repeating what they did on the previous trial, they *fail* to repeat the previous trial's performance if a change is made in the variables controlling line of sight. For example, following three successful retrievals from the *front* of the box, if the box is moved forward 1 inch and the toy moved $\frac{1}{2}$ inch deeper into the box (so that the infant now sees the toy through the top), infants below $8\frac{1}{2}$ months reach only at the top of the box on this trial, although the perseverative response would be to reach at the front. Infants fail by not repeating their previous response (Diamond 1981). Thus, if a common explanation is to be sought for AB̄ and OR performance, it must be something other than forgetting or perseveration. Two general abilities are proposed: (a) relating information over space or time, integrating two or more pieces of information, and (b) inhibition of predominant action tendencies.

Relating information separated in space or time

OR requires the subject to relate the box opening to the bait over a spatial separation. When bait and opening are superimposed (as when the bait is in the opening, partially out of the box) even the youngest infants and prefrontally operated monkeys succeed. However, as the spatial separation between bait and opening widens, the age at which infants succeed progressively increases.

AB̄ requires the subject to relate two *temporally* separated events—cue and

---

[6] When normal, mature adults are distracted, stressed, rushed, or exhausted, they make the same errors as do infants and frontal patients. The abilities mediated by the frontal lobe are fragile and the first to go with physical or psychological insult. If something is terribly important to an infant or to a frontal patient and they try very hard, they can sometimes avoid these errors. Thus, the differences between infants and adult frontal patients, on the one hand, and normal adults, on the other, appear to be differences of degree rather than fundamental differences of kind; e.g. normal adults are less likely to make certain errors, but they are not totally immune to them.

response. The subject watches as a bait is hidden in one of two identical wells, a brief delay follows, then the subject is allowed to reach. When there is no delay between hiding and retrieval even the youngest infants and prefrontally operated monkeys succeed. However, as the time interval between hiding and retrieval increases, the age at which infants succeed progressively increases. Here, memory is conceived as one aspect of the ability to relate information over a separation.

The development of the ability to relate or integrate two or more items is an ever-present theme in the age progression in OR performance. It is seen in the development of the ability (a) to reach through one side of the box while looking through a different side, (b) to attend to both visual and tactile information, and (c) to do different things with the two hands. When infants reach through the side they are looking, they can almost always reach the toy by a straight route. When they look through one side and reach through another, their reach is almost always two-directional, as when an infant sits up and looks through the top and then reaches away from the midline to get to the left or right opening and then directs the reach back toward the midline to get the toy. Here one sees the development of the ability to integrate two movements in opposing directions (see Fig. 13.9 above).

Frontal patients are impaired on delayed comparison tasks where they must indicate whether a test stimulus is the same colour or sound as a target stimulus presented seconds before. They are not impaired, however, when no delay is imposed (Prisko, cited in Milner 1974). This is very reminiscent of results with infants on AB̄.

Tasks that require the simultaneous use of multiple facts prove very difficult for adults with frontal cortex damage. For example, they can solve mathematical problems such as: 'What is 30 divided by 2?' and 'What is 15 times 5?' But they cannot solve: 'If the price of two packages is $30, what is the price of five packages?' (Barbizet 1970). Frontal patients also have unusually severe difficulty doing two things at once or attending to more than one thing at a time. When they are shown a pictorial scene suggesting a story, they typically fixate on one detail in the picture, missing the suggested story (Nichols and Hunt 1940).

Relating items in a sequence is also a problem. An expert cook, following frontal lobectomy, can still measure, pour, sift, and knead, but may not be able to put the ingredients together to bake a loaf of bread or to make a multi-course meal. Frontal patients have great difficulty keeping track of a temporal sequence. They can remember which of two pictures they saw before (unlike temporal lobe patients who cannot), but they cannot remember which of two pictures they saw most recently (Corsi, cited in Milner 1974). When shown a page of words or pictures and instructed to touch all stimuli, one at a time, in any order, but without repeating a choice, frontal patients touch some stimuli more than once, never managing to touch them all (Petrides and Milner 1982). They do not perseverate; rather they simply fail to sample all stimuli systematically. This is reminiscent of the behaviour of 8–9-month-old infants who fail to systematically check all sides of the box; they reach back repeatedly to sides they have tried and found closed.

Inhibiting prepotent responses

In OR, the tendency to reach straight to a visible target must be inhibited. Subjects must instead reach around to the opening. Results when the box is opaque provide particularly strong evidence here: infants performed better with the opaque box, where the toy could not be seen through a closed side. When the toy could be seen through a closed side, there was a very strong tendency to reach there. The opaque box presented no such conflict, because the toy could only be seen through the opening.

Inhibition is also required when infants raise the front of the OR box and then try to lower one hand to reach in, while the other hand holding onto the box remains raised. Problems inhibiting their eagerness and enthusiasm for the toy may also contribute to why infants do not approach the task more systematically. Schaffer *et al.* (1972) report that, although infants of at least 6 months indicate visually (through habituation and dishabituation of looking) that they can tell whether or not they have seen an object before, until 9 months of age they reach impulsively for all objects. At 9 months, behavioural inhibition to the novel appears, i.e. the latency to reach for a new object becomes significantly longer than the latency to reach to the familiar.

In A$\bar{\text{B}}$, a conditioned tendency or 'habit' to reach to 'A' (where the subject was rewarded) must be inhibited when the bait is hidden at 'B'. Indeed, infants may sometimes reach back to 'A' on the A$\bar{\text{B}}$ task even when they know the toy's location, because of difficulty inhibiting this habitual response. Thus, even when the toy is *visible* at B, errors sometimes occur, as when the covers are transparent, and occasionally when there is no cover at all (Butterworth 1977; Harris 1974). Often, infants will uncover A, *not look in*, then reach immediately to B and retrieve the toy (Diamond 1985). It is as if they know the toy is at B even though they reach first to A. Most telling, occasionally an infant will look directly at B before, and throughout, the reach, even as that infant's hand goes to A.[7] If visual fixation were the dependent measure, the infant would be scored as correct on such trials (see Fig. 13.10).

This is reminiscent of the performance of frontal patients on the Wisconsin card sort: after being rewarded for sorting the cards by one criterion, frontal patients have difficulty sorting the cards by a new rule. However, these patients can sometimes tell you the new rule as they continue to sort the cards incorrectly. Indeed, they sometimes say, as they are sorting the cards by the

---

[7] This is a rare occurrence because looking and reaching are usually closely tied in infants. However, it has been observed in many different laboratories and when it occurs it is particularly impressive because such dissociation of looking and reaching is so rare.

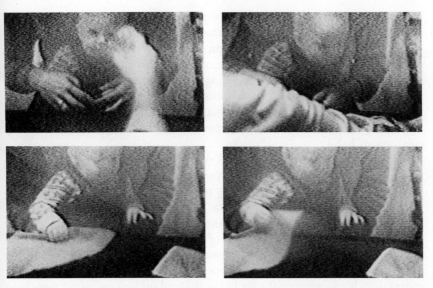

Fig. 13.10 Instance of an infant looking at B while reaching to A. Infant had successfully retrieved toy at A. Side of hiding is now reversed to B. Top row: Infant clearly sees the hiding. Following a brief delay, he was allowed to reach. Bottom row: Although infant is looking fixedly at B, his hand goes back to A.

old criterion, 'This is wrong, and this is wrong. . .' (Luria and Homskaya 1964; Milner 1964; Nauta 1971).[8] Infants cannot tell you the correct answer verbally, but looking at A even as they reach to B may be the non-verbal equivalent. Improved performance may mark the emergence of the ability to resist making the predominant response, the emergence of the ability to exercise choice.

In AB̄ and the Wisconsin card sort, an initial response is strengthened by reinforcement. This effect of reinforcement on a response is evident in infants soon after birth (Sameroff 1971; Rovee-Collier 1986) and in the simplest organisms (e.g. Kandel 1979). It is early developing (in phylogeny and ontogeny) and robust, capable of surviving considerable neurological insult. A more fragile and later developing ability is the capacity to *resist* a

---

[8] Such dissociations between frontal patients' verbal and motor behaviour are common. One such example is provided by Teuber: '[The patient] has in many ways what people call a classical frontal lobe syndrome. . . . He was put to work in the garden where he was assigned to another man who was digging ditches; our patient had a big pair of shears with which to cut roots. . . . And while a ditch was opened, a huge thing appeared; four black strands lying side by side. The patient was standing there, and the subsequent episode was described by both the patient and his companion. He said, 'Ha ha, it's not a root. It looks like a root (going through the motions of cutting). It looks like a root. It's not a root. Why are the fire alarms ringing?' By cutting the strands he had shorted out all the cables that led to the alarms all over the camp' (Teuber, in discussion of Konorski and Lawicka 1964, pp. 287–288).

predominant response, whether it is innately strong or has been strengthened by reinforcement. It is this ability that is required when the correct well changes in AB̄ or the correct criterion changes in the Wisconsin card sort. Although instinctual and habitual responses are very strong, even in humans, we are capable, with effort, of breaking a habit, whereas organisms without frontal cortex may have no such option. The ability to resist the strongest response of the moment endows humans with extraordinary flexibility and freedom to choose and control our actions. It gives us the option of not being creatures of habit.

Adults have yet to be tested on OR or a similar task, but there is evidence that vision exerts a pull on the behaviour of frontal patients similar to that seen in infants. Vision exerts a strong pull in all of us (e.g. Rock and Harris 1967), but most of us with intact frontal lobes are able to inhibit or counteract this tendency when necessary. For example, when asked to hold up a finger when the examiner makes a fist, most of us might be tempted to copy what we see but would manage to follow the instructions. A frontal patient, on the other hand, upon seeing the fist, makes a fist, even though he may repeat the instructions back correctly (Luria 1973). A standard task requires a patient to hold up two fingers when the examiner holds up one finger, and to extend a single finger in response to the examiner's two. Patients with frontal damage cannot resist mimicking what they see and so fail the task (for other examples of echopraxia, see Luria 1966).

This can also be seen in tasks that do not involve vision. For example, although instructed to give a long squeeze to a short tone and a short squeeze to a long tone, frontal patients match the duration of the squeeze to the tone, even though they can repeat the instructions correctly (Marushevskii 1959, cited in Luria 1966).

Problems in the inhibitory control of behaviour occur in all areas of life for frontal patients. Socially, they are 'disinhibited', meaning that they lack the usual inhibitions about saying or doing inappropriate things (such as talking about sex in public). Frontal patients are easily distracted by irrelevant, but firmly established, connections. They are pulled by this free association or that. This makes it extremely difficult to obtain even a simple personal history from such patients because of the many associations to that history.

Frontal patients are also especially sensitive to proactive interference.[9] It is as if earlier occurrences are not properly inhibited or damped down. On the delayed comparison tasks of Prisko mentioned above, frontal patients could perform well if trial-unique stimuli were used. However, when stimuli recurred over the trials (so that subjects had to remember whether they had seen a stimulus on the current trial or a previous one), frontal patients were impaired.

---

[9] Sensitivity to proactive interference has been associated with amnesia, but that is only because many amnesics also have frontal lobe disorders. Moscovitch (1982) has elegantly shown that amnesics without frontal symptoms show normal release from proactive interference, whereas frontal patients without amnesia are abnormally sensitive to proactive interference.

This is reminiscent of the A$\bar{\text{B}}$ error: on trials at B infants are unable to inhibit proactive interference from the trials at A.

One of the classic tests diagnostic of frontal lobe function is the Stroop test. Here, the names of colours are printed in the ink of another colour (e.g. the word 'blue' is printed in red ink). Patients are instructed to report the colour of the ink as they look through the list of words. The customary response when reading, however, is to ignore the ink and attend to the meaning of the word. Frontal patients fail the test; they recite the words and not the colour of the ink (Perret 1974).

Problems of inhibition are often problems at the output end. Instead of reflecting deficits in thinking, they reflect deficits in gaining control of one's behaviour so that it reflects what one is thinking. Infants and frontal lobe patients give some indications that they know more than they can often express in their behaviour. Frontal patients give such indications verbally; infants do so with their eyes. We have seen this in A$\bar{\text{B}}$ and in the work of Schaffer *et al.* (1972). It can also be seen in an elegant habituation–dishabituation experiment by Baillargéon *et al.* (1985). Using looking, rather than reaching, as their dependent measure, Baillargéon *et al.* demonstrated that 5-month-old infants appear to know that an object hidden behind a screen is still there. Yet, it is not until at least 2 months later that they will reach behind a screen for a hidden object or will uncover an object. Using reaching as their indicator, investigators had concluded that infants below $7\frac{1}{2}$ months did not know that a hidden object continued to exist. Baillargéon *et al.*'s work suggests that infants know the object is there but cannot use this to guide their reaching behaviour.

Visual habituation is an automatic response, whereas lifting a cover to get what is underneath would seem to require more explicit planning. As discussed earlier, infants below $7\frac{1}{2}$–8 months react automatically and unreflectively to their world. Thus, for example, I would predict that infants younger than $7\frac{1}{2}$–8 months should succeed at delayed non-match to sample but would fail delayed *match* to sample at the same delays, using trial-unique stimuli for each. In both of these tasks, the subject is first shown a model, a delay follows, then the subject is given a choice of an object that matches the model or another object. By the age infants can first reach for an object (5–6 months) they show a reliable preference for the new over the familiar (e.g. Fagan 1970; Fantz 1964; Rose *et al.* 1982). Delayed non-match to sample (which rewards reaching for the non-match) would capitalize on infants' natural tendency to reach to the new, provided they can remember what they have already seen. Delayed match to sample (which rewards reaching to the match), however, would require infants not only to remember what they have seen, but to inhibit their natural tendency to reach to the new stimulus.[10] This combination of requirements (memory plus inhibition) depends, I suggest,

[10] It is critical that trial-unique stimuli be used because when the same stimuli are used over trials no stimulus is new, i.e., unfamiliar.

upon frontal cortex, and will be beyond the ability of infants below 9–12 months of age.

References

Alexander, G. E. and Goldman, P. S. (1978). Functional development of the dorsolateral prefrontal cortex: an analysis utilizing reversible cryogenic depression. *Brain Research*, **143**, 233–50.

Baillargéon, R., Spelke, E. S., and Wasserman, S. (1986). Object permanence in five-month-old infants. *Cognition*, **20**, 191–208.

Barbizet, J. (1970). Prolonged organic amnesias. In *Human memory and its pathology*, (ed. J. Barbizet), pp. 25–93. W. H. Freeman and Co., San Francisco.

Battig, K., Rosvold, H. E., and Mishkin, M. (1960). Comparison of the effects of frontal and caudate lesions on delayed response and alternation in monkeys. *Journal of Comparative and Physiological Psychology*, **4**, 400–4.

Bauer, R. H. and Fuster, J. M. (1976). Delayed-matching and delayed-response deficit from cooling dorsolateral prefrontal cortex in monkeys. *Journal of Comparative and Physiological Psychology*, **90**, 293–302.

Berg, E. A. (1948). A simple objective technique for measuring flexibility in thinking. *Journal of Genetic Psychology*, **39**, 15–22.

Bourgeois, J.-P., Goldman-Rakic, P.S., and Rakic, P. (1985). Synaptogenesis in the prefrontal cortex: quantitative EM analysis in pre- and postnatal rhesus monkeys. *Society for Neuroscience Abstracts*, **11**, 501.

Bremner, J. G. and Bryant, P. E. (1977) Place versus response as the basis of spatial errors made by young children. *Journal of Experimental Child Psychology*, **23**, 162–71.

Brozoski, T., Brown, R. M., Rosvold, H. E., and Goldman, P. S. (1979). Cognitive deficit caused by depletion of dopamine in prefrontal cortex of rhesus monkey. *Science*, **205**, 929–31.

Bruner, J. (1969). The origins of problem-solving strategies in skill acquisition. Paper presented at the 19th International Congress of Psychology, London.

—— Kaye, K, and Lyons, K. (1969). The growth of human manual intelligence: III. The development of detour reaching. Unpublished manuscript, Center for Cognitive Studies, Harvard University.

Bugbee, N. M. and Goldman-Rakic, P. S. (1981). Functional 2-deoxyglucose mapping in association cortex: prefrontal activation in monkeys performing a cognitive task. *Society for Neuroscience Abstracts*, **7**, 416.

Butter, C. M. (1969). Perseveration in extinction and in discrimination reversal tasks following selective frontal ablations in *Macaca mulatta*. *Physiology and Behavior*, **4**, 163–71.

Butters, N., Pandya, D., Sanders, K., and Dye, P. (1969). Behavioral deficits in monkeys after selective lesions within the middle third of sulcus principalis. *Journal of Comparative and Physiological Psychology*, **76**, 8–14.

Butterworth, G. (1976). Asymmetrical search errors in infancy. *Child Development*, **47**, 864–7.

—— (1977). Object disappearance and error in Piaget's Stage IV task. *Journal of Experimental Child Psychology*, **23**, 391–401.

—— Jarrett, N., and Hicks, L. (1982). Spatiotemporal identity in infancy: perceptual competence or conceptual deficit? *Developmental Psychology*, **18**, 435–49.

Cornell, E. H. (1979). The effects of cue reliability on infants' manual search. *Journal of Experimental Child Psychology*, **28**, 81–91.

Crawford, M. P., Fulton, J. F., Jacobsen, C. F., and Wolfe, J. B. (1948). Frontal lobe ablation in chimpanzee: a resume of 'Becky' and 'Lucy'. *A.M.A. Research Publications of Association for Research in Nervous and Mental Disease*, **27**, 3–58.

Diamond, A. (1981). Retrieval of an object from an open box: the development of visual-tactile control of reaching in the first year of life. *Society for Research in Child Development Abstracts*, **3**, 78.

—— (1983). Behaviour changes between 6 to 12 months of age: what can they tell us about how the mind of the infant is changing? Unpublished Ph.D. thesis. Harvard University.

—— (1985). The development of the ability to use recall to guide action, as indicated by infants' performance on AB̄. *Child Development*, **56**, 868–83.

—— (in prep.). The developmental progression in AB̄ performance: comparison of cross-sectional and longitudinal results.

—— and Doar, B. (in prep.). The developmental progression in human infants' performance on delayed response.

—— and Goldman-Rakic, P. S. (1983). Comparison of performance on a Piagetian object permanence task in human infants and rhesus monkeys: evidence for involvement of prefrontal cortex. *Neuroscience Abstracts (Part I)*, **9**, 641.

—— and —— (1985). Evidence for involvement of prefrontal cortex in cognitive changes during the first year of life: comparison of human infants and rhesus monkeys on a detour task with transparent barrier. *Society for Neuroscience Abstracts (Part II)*, **11**, 832.

—— and —— (1986). Comparative development in human infants and infant rhesus monkeys of cognitive functions that depend on prefrontal cortex. *Society for Neuroscience Abstracts*, **12**, 742.

—— and —— (in prep.). Comparison of human infants and rhesus monkeys on Piaget's AB̄ task: evidence for dependence on dorsolateral prefrontal cortex.

—— Zola-Morgan, S., and Squire, L. R. (1987). Performance of monkeys with hippocampal ablations on Piaget's AB̄ task. *Society for Neuroscience Abstracts*, **13**, 206.

Drewe, E. A. (1974). The effect of type and area of brain lesion on Wisconsin Card Sorting Test performance. *Cortex*, **10**, 159–70.

Evans, W. F. (1973). *The stage IV error in Piaget's theory of concept development.* Unpublished Ph.D. thesis, University of Houston.

Fagan, J. F. (1970). Memory in the infant. *Journal of Experimental Child Psychology*, **9**, 217–26.

Fantz, R. L. (1964). Visual experience in infants: decreased attention to familiar patterns relative to novel ones. *Science*, **146**, 668–70.

Fox, N., Kagan, J., and Weiskopf, S. (1979). The growth of memory during infancy. *Genetic Psychology Monographs*, **99**, 91–130.

Fuster, J.M. (1973). Unit activity in prefrontal cortex during delay-response performance: neuronal correlates of transient memory. *Journal of Neurophysiology*, **36**, 61–78.

—— (1980). *The prefrontal cortex*. Raven Press, New York.

—— and Alexander, G. E. (1970). Delayed response deficit by cryogenic depression of frontal cortex. *Brain Research*, **20**, 85–90.

—— and —— (1971). Neuron activity related to short-term memory. *Science*, **173**, 652–54.

Goldman, P. S. and Rosvold, H. E. (1970). Localization of function within the dorsolateral prefrontal cortex of the rhesus monkey. *Experimental Neurology*, **27**, 291–304.

Grant, D. A. and Berg, E. A. (1948). A behavioral analysis of degree of reinforcement and ease of shifting to new responses in Weigl-type card-sorting problem. *Journal of Experimental Psychology*, **38**, 404–11.

Gratch, G. and Landers, W. (1971). Stage IV of Piaget's theory of infants' object concepts: a longitudinal study. *Child Development*, **42**, 359–72.

—— Appel, K. J., Evans, W. F., LeCompte, G. K., and Wright, N. A. (1974). Piaget's stage IV object concept error: evidence for forgetting or object conception? *Child Development*, **45**, 71–7.

Gross, C. G. and Weiskrantz, L. (1962). Evidence for dissociation of impairment on auditory discrimination and delayed response following lateral frontal lesions in monkeys. *Experimental Neurology*, **5**, 453–76.

Harlow, H. F. and Dagnon, J. (1943). Problem solution by monkeys following bilateral removal of prefrontal areas: I. Discrimination and discrimination reversal problems. *Journal of Experimental Psychology*, **32**, 351–6.

—— Davis, R. T., Settlage, P. H., and Meyer, D. R. (1952). Analysis of frontal and posterior association syndromes in brain-damaged monkeys. *Journal of Comparative Physiology and Psychology*, **54**, 419–29.

Harris, P. L. (1973). Perseverative errors in search by young infants. *Child Development*, **44**, 29–33.

—— (1974). Perseverative search at a visibly empty place by young infants. *Journal of Experimental Child Psychology*, **18**, 535–42.

Jacobsen, C. F. (1935). Functions of frontal association areas in primates. *Archives of Neurology and Psychiatry*, **33**, 558–60.

—— (1936). Studies of cerebral functions in primates. I. The function of the frontal association areas in monkeys. *Comparative Psychology Monographs*, **13**, 1–60.

—— Wolfe, J. B., and Jackson, T. A. (1935). An experimental analysis of the frontal association areas in primates. *Journal of Nervous and Mental Disease*, **82**, 1–14.

Kandel, E. R. (1979). Cellular insights into behavior and learning. *Harvey Lecture*, **73**, 19–92.

Konorski, J. and Lawicka, W. (1964). Analysis of errors by prefrontal animals on the delayed response test. In *The frontal granular cortex and behavior*, (ed. J. M. Warren and K. Akert), pp. 271–312. McGraw-Hill, New York.

Lipsitt, L. P., Kaye, H., and Bosack, T. N. (1966). Enhancement of neonatal sucking through reinforcement. *Journal of Experimental Child Psychology*, **32**, 1–10.

Lockman, J. J. (1984). The development of detour ability during infancy. *Child Development*, **55**, 482–91.

Luria, A. R. (1966). *The higher cortical functions in man*. Basic Books, New York.

—— (1973). *The working brain*. Basic Books, New York.

—— and Homskaya, E. D. (1964). Disturbance in the regulative role of speech with frontal lobe lesions. In *The frontal granular cortex and behavior*, (ed. J. M. Warren and K. Akert), pp. 353–71. McGraw-Hill, New York.

Markowitsch, H. J. and Pritzel, M. (1977). Comparative analysis of prefrontal learning functions in rats, cats, and monkeys. *Psychological Bulletin*, **84**, 817–37.

Meyer, D. R., Harlow, H. F., and Settlage, P. H. (1951). A survey of delayed response performance by normal and brain-damaged monkeys. *Journal of Comparative and Physiological Psychology*, **44**, 17–25.

Miles, R. C. and Blomquist, A. (1960). Frontal lesions and behavioral deficits in monkey. *Journal of Neurophysiology*, **23**, 471–84.

Millar, W. S. and Schaffer, H. R. (1972). The influence of spatially displaced feedback on infant operant conditioning. *Journal of Experimental Child Psychology*, **14**, 442–53.

—— and Schaffer, H. R., (1973). Visual-manipulative response strategies in infant operant conditioning with spatially displaced feedback. *British Journal of Psychology*, **64**, 546–52.

Milner, B. (1963). Effects of brain lesions on card sorting. *Archives of Neurology*, **9**, 90–100.

—— (1964). Some effects of frontal lobectomy in man. In *The frontal granular cortex and behavior*, (ed. J. M. Warren and K. Akert), pp. 313–34. McGraw-Hill, New York.

—— (1974). Hemispheric specialization: scope and limits. In *The neurosciences: third study program*, (ed. F. O. Schmitt and F. G. Worden), pp. 75–89. MIT Press, Cambridge, Massachusetts.

Mishkin, M. (1964). Perseveration of central sets after frontal lesions in monkeys. In *The frontal granular cortex and behavior*. (ed. J. M. Warren and K. Akert), pp. 219–41. McGraw-Hill, New York.

—— Vest, B., Waxler, M., and Rosvold, H. E. (1969). A reexamination of the effects of frontal lesions on object alternation. *Neuropsychologia*, **7**, 357–64.

Moll, L. and Kuypers, H. G. J. M. (1977). Premotor cortical ablations in monkeys: contralateral changes in visually guided reaching behavior. *Science*, **198**, 317–19.

Moscovitch, M. (1982). Multiple dissociations of function in amnesia. In *Human memory and amnesia*, (ed. L. S. Cermak), pp. 337–70. Lawrence Erlbaum Associates, Hillsdale, NJ.

Nauta, W. J. H. (1971). The problem of the frontal lobe: a reinterpretation. *Journal of Psychiatric Research*, **8**, 167–87.

Nichols, I. C. and Hunt, J. McV. (1940). A case of partial bilateral frontal lobectomy: a psychopathological study. *American Journal of Psychiatry*, **96**, 1063–87.

Niki, H. (1974). Differential activity of prefrontal units during right and left delayed response trials. *Brain Research*, **70**, 346–49.

Perret, E. (1974). The left frontal lobe of man and the suppression of habitual responses in verbal categorical behaviour. *Neuropsychologia*, **16**, 527–37.

Petrides, M. and Milner, B. (1982). Deficits on subject-ordered tasks after frontal- and temporal-lobe lesions in man. *Neuropsychologia*, **20**, 249–62.

Piaget, J. (1954). *The construction of reality in the child*. Basic Books, New York.

Pinsker, H. M. and French, G. M. (1967). Indirect delayed reactions under various testing conditions in normal and midlateral frontal monkeys. *Neuropsychologia*, **5**, 13–24.

Pohl, W. (1973). Dissociation of spatial discrimination deficits following frontal and parietal lesions in monkeys. *Journal of Comparative and Physiological Psychology*, **82**, 227–39.

Rock, I. and Harris, C. S. (1967). Vision and touch. *Scientific American*, 269–80.

Rose, S. A., Gottfried, A. W., Melloy-Carminar, P. and Bridger, W. H. (1982). Familiarity and novelty preferences in infant recognition memory: implications for information processing. *Developmental Psychology*, **18**, 704–13.

Rosenkilde, C. E. (1979). Functional heterogeneity of the prefrontal cortex in the monkey: a review. *Behavioral and Neural Biology*, **25**, 301–45.

Rovee-Collier, C. (1986). The rise and fall of infant classical conditioning research: its promise for the study of early development. In *Advances in infancy research, Vol. 4*, (ed. L.P. Lipsitt and C. Rovee-Collier), pp. 139–59. Ablex, Norwood, New Jersey.

—— and Fagan, J. W. (1981). The retrieval of memory in early infancy. In *Advances in infancy research Vol. 2*, (ed. L. P. Lipsitt), pp. 226–54. Ablex, Norwood, NJ.

Sameroff, A. J. (1971). Can conditioned responses be established in the newborn infant: 1971? *Developmental Psychology*, **5**, 1–12.

Schaffer, H. R., Greenwood, A., and Parry, M. H. (1972). The onset of wariness. *Child Development*, **43**, 165–75.

Stamm, J. S. (1969). Electrical stimulation of monkeys' prefrontal cortex during delayed response performance. *Journal of Comparative and Physiological Psychology*, **67**, 535–46.

—— and Rosen, S. C. (1969). Electrical stimulation and steady potential shifts in prefrontal cortex during delayed response performance by monkeys. *Acta Biologicae Experimentalis*, **29**, 385–99.

Weiskrantz, L., Mihailovic, L., and Gross, C. G. (1962). Effects of stimulation of frontal cortex and hippocampus on behavior in the monkey. *Brain*, **85**, 487–504.

Zola-Morgan, S. and Squire, L. R. (1986). Memory impairment in monkeys following lesions limited to the hippocampus. *Behavioral Neuroscience*, **100**, 155–60.

14

Animal spatial cognition
CATHERINE THINUS-BLANC

The theoretical problem of comparing man and animal is frequently tackled in articles about cognitive mechanisms and animal intelligence (cf., for example, d'Amato and Salmon 1984; Premack 1979; Weiskrantz 1985), whereas the characteristics of the 'natural' situations met by both are rarely discussed. This point goes beyond the mere question of methodology and deserves to be highlighted, at least in terms of spatial cognition. In natural conditions, animals live and have to move about in extremely difficult environments, in contrast to the 'assisted' situations that constitute human beings' everyday life, at least in our Western civilizations. Let us imagine a world with restricted possibilities of communication with other people, without any maps, road signs, or tourist offices, in short, without any information transmitted by language or writing. Such is the animal's universe, which may also contain hostile elements such as predators. Therefore, an accurate localization of the nest or burrow, of the places abounding in food, etc., are prerequisites for survival. For these reasons, paradoxical though they may seem, the animal offers us a better model than the human in the study of the cognitive mechanisms involved in spatial orientation. Spatial intelligence is becoming increasingly unnecessary in man, and, according to the laws of evolution, it should be extinct in a few thousand years!

But, what is animal cognition? This psychological concept is vague and has a multiplicity of meanings. According to Neisser (1976, p. 1), 'Cognition is the activity of knowing: the acquisition, organization and use of knowledge'. In fact, apart from describing the initial phases of information-processing, the term usually refers to the ultimate and more elaborated phase of representations.

As we will see later, both phases are closely interdependent, the information-processing being controlled by representations. A cognitive activity is possible without any previous abstraction, however, and the result of cognitive processing may not always be stored and represented.

The nature of what is represented is another factor of differentiation. For example, the information necessary to perform an oriented complex displacement can be stored and represented as a list of instructions or as responses to a sequence of stimuli ('turn right at this cue, turn left at that one, etc.'). This is far simpler than storing the representation of the environment in the form of 'cognitive maps' (Tolman 1948). These different means of performing accurate complex displacements refer to O'Keefe and Nadel's (1978) 'taxon' and 'locale' systems and to Dickinson's (1980) 'procedural' and 'declarative' memory, respectively, each system being defined by the authors in terms of distinctive characteristics and properties.

In this chapter, I shall consider some spatial behaviours, in animals, which cannot be explained (at least at present) without referring to cognitive maps, i.e. to an allocentrically organized representation of environmental features. The time is over when Hull's and Tolman's followers disputed about the existence of spatial representations in animals. Nowadays the study of those behaviours based upon cognitive representations focus rather upon their critical features and properties, which is a more appropriate and effective way of understanding the structure and function of these abstract and unobservable entities which are the psychological processes. Nevertheless, it is far from easy to characterize the psychological processes underlying some spatial behaviours. In the first section, a representative example of this problem will be discussed. However, putting aside my own pessimistic view, I shall present in the second section some examples of behaviours which strongly argue in favour of spatial representations. Then, in the third section, the role of exploration as a fundamental and essential cognitive activity will be debated. Finally, in the last section, some hypotheses about reciprocal relationships between representations and exploration will be proposed.

How do we characterize spatial behaviours?

In their reference books, *The hippocampus as a cognitive map*, O'Keefe and Nadel (1978) define two classes of mechanisms likely to be separately involved in oriented displacements: a 'taxon system' and a 'locale system'. The first system involves the perceptually guided behaviours that reduce the distance between the subject and a goal which is indicated by a cue, as does the use of 'routes' that '. . . direct attention to particular objects or specify turns within egocentric space' (1978, p. 83). A route is composed of several segments resulting from a series of reorientations of the body axis (or responses) to a sequence of stimuli. The second system refers to the set up and use of environmental representations corresponding to the 'cognitive maps' defined by Tolman (1948). O'Keefe and Nadel also define the respective properties of these systems. In the case of the 'taxon system' they talk in terms of the rigidity of the routes and the lack of resistance to a loss of information due to the low informative level of the maps, which thereby result in rapid displacements since there is no need to choose between several ways. As for the 'locale system', they refer to the plasticity of the maps and their resistance to a loss of information because of a very high informative level, which thereby produces longer displacements because there is more information to process and a choice between many pathways.

Although intuitively acceptable, these properties are hypothetical and have never been systematically tested. Apart from this testing, there is also the problem concerning the nature of the system to which a given behaviour actually belongs. The designing of experimental situations which are supposed to yield the psychological process under study does not guarantee the emergence of this process, as illustrated by the following example. The experiment was conducted on cats (Poucet 1985) in a cross-maze. The four arms of the maze were strictly identical, three of them served as starting points, and the reward was placed at the end of the fourth so that it could not be perceived from any point of the apparatus. The maze was placed into a 'cue-controlled' environment and the only available information for locating the goal was a salient visual cue. For one of the two groups of cats, this cue was placed just above the goal ('guidance' situation); for the other group it was 180° from the goal ('mapping' situation). In the latter case, the cats had to work out or 'infer' the position of the goal by reference to the cue. The difficulty was increased by the use of three different starting points which were pseudo randomly alternated. This experiment is very similar to O'Keefe and Conway's (1980) study in rats showing that hippocampal lesions selectively impaired 'mapping' performances. The aim of Poucet's study was to quantify and analyse the behavioural manifestations associated with the choice of the correct path: head and body movements, place of occurrence and duration of the stops, latency times, etc. This study was conducted with the hope of being able to predict the type of mechanisms which would be involved in such and such a spatial task in other situations. Needless to say there was no doubt as to the processes involved in each of these situations, the 'taxon' system being used in the 'guidance' situation, the 'locale' system in the 'mapping' one.

Within the 'mapping' group, five subjects out of six made their choice when still in the starting arm (see Fig. 14.1), spending a long time at that place with many head movements directed towards the cue and the goal. One subject (A) behaved differently and stopped at the choice point only, where it displayed many head movements and body turns. It is interesting to note that during subsequent short-cut and delayed response (DR) tests, only the non-conforming cat out of the six subjects of the 'mapping' group failed to take the shorter path and to reach the goal directly after the indicative cue had been removed. The most parsimonious conclusion is that the correct performance of this particular animal was based upon different mechanisms to those used by the other subjects of the 'mapping' group. This same lack of adaptability was a characteristic of all the cats from the 'guidance' group.

This particularity is of course anecdotal since it concerns only one subject, but it draws our attention to the fact that unexpected and efficient strategies

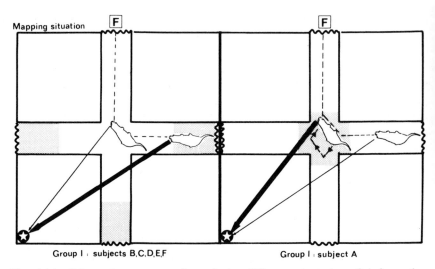

Mapping situation

Group I : subjects B,C,D,E,F

Group I : subject A

Fig. 14.1 Schematic representation of the different strategies of information gathering in the 'mapping situation'. (Reproduced from Poucet (1985) by kind permission of the Experimental Psychology Society.)

can be used by animals in situations designed to yield other means of fulfilling the task. In this case, the abberant subject's behaviour suggests that he had used a 're-orientation' strategy ('taxon' system), according to O'Keefe and Nadel's (1978) definition; i.e. the route to the goal was found by positioning the body in a constant manner by reference to the cue.

In a follow-up experiment conducted in hamsters by Poucet and Scotto (1987) the animals were obliged to use a given strategy instead of being free to choose. The principle of the apparatus was the same as that used for the previous 'mapping' situation, but the possibility of picking up the relevant information to localize the goal was limited to the starting point for one group and to the central crossroad for another group. A third control group could perceive the cue from any part of the apparatus (Fig. 14.2). After the hamsters from the three groups had reached the learning criterion with similar numbers of trials, they were submitted to DR tests. The delays between the moment they could perceive the relevant cue and the moment that they were allowed to respond varied from 30 sec to 15 min. Only the performances of the subjects which could perceive the cue only from the central choice point were affected by the delay.

These results suggest that the non-conforming cat's spontaneous adoption of a 'reorientation' strategy, on the one hand, or the elimination of the difficulty caused by the different starting points in the hamster experiment, on the other hand, is correlated with a deterioration of the DR test performances. It is true that this correlation *per se* has no explicative value, but it can be

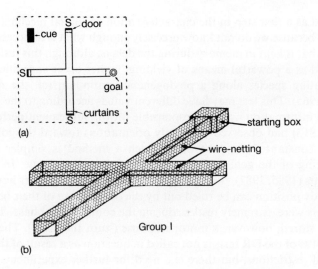

(a)

(b) Group I

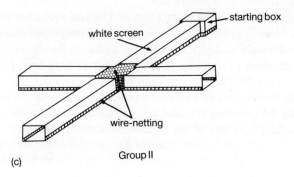

(c) Group II

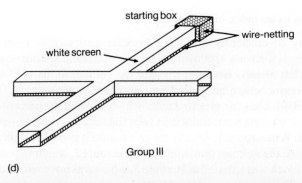

(d) Group III

Fig. 14.2 (a) Overview of the experimental area showing the relative locations of the cue, the goal, and the starting points. (b), (c), (d) devices used for groups A, C, and S, respectively. The starting box was removable so that it could be placed at several points. (Reproduced from Poucet and Scotto 1987).

considered as a first step in the characterization of spatial mechanisms. It is only such because we do not know precisely enough what is a success in a DR test and what is kept in memory during the delays, although this test has been considered as a powerful means of yielding 'higher order capacities' and of differentiating species along a phylogenetic continuum (cf. the review by Fletcher 1965). This test may have different values according to the nature of the stored information which is responsible for the subsequent performance. Hunter (1913) had observed that body orientations toward the goal in rats remained constant during the delay. Such a method is simpler than the remembering of the goal position or that of the relevant cue. In Poucet's experiments (1985, 1987), the possibility of the cats and hamsters having used a fixed body position can be ruled out by the observation of their behaviour: the subjects were extremely restless during the confinement phase. They may also have stored, however, a motor response ('turn this way'). The psychological status of the DR tests is not called in question as a result of the above-mentioned restrictions, but there is a need for further experiments to bring some nuances to their interpretation.

Such being the case, the interpretation of DR test success converges with O'Keefe and Nadel's (1978) hypothesis about the properties associated with the 'taxon' and 'locale' systems, respectively, and with the classical conception of cognitive psychology in terms of the plasticity of high-level psychological mechanisms. Therefore it appears reasonable to consider the above-mentioned spatial performances as based upon environmental representations. The following experiments are also good arguments in favour of cognitive maps due to the properties of the studied behaviours. However, because of limited cognitive capacities or in virtue of a 'cognitive economy principle', we should remember that animals may use some tricks or strategies which may be unknown to us (at present) to move around efficiently.

Adaptation as an index of spatial cognition

The ability to efficiently modify a familiar pathway in response to new possibilities is a strong argument in favour of animal spatial cognition. This argument has already been put forward by Tolman in his 1948 article about cognitive maps, where he quoted an important experiment by Tolman and Honzik (1930). Using an elevated maze which allowed the perception of extra-apparatus cues, rats were trained to take the correct route to reach the food (Fig. 14.3). When route 1, usually taken because it is the most direct one, was blocked at A, the animals immediately chose route 2, which bypasses block A. When the block was situated at B, route 3, which was not preferred previously, was taken. This simple experiment is an elegant example of adaptability to the contingencies of the environment and of the adequate use of spatial information.

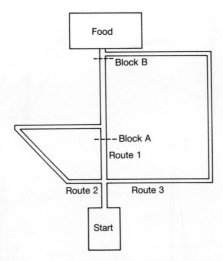

Fig. 14.3   Schema of the maze used by Tolman and Honzik (1930).

Since Kohler's (1925) pioneer studies in monkeys detour experiments have proven to be a good way of testing intelligence and spatial abilities in animals and also in infants (cf. Diamond 1988). However, according to Hull (1938; cited by Rashotte 1987), detour ability (as for most spatial performances) could be accounted for in terms of stimulus responses, i.e. without referring to spatial representations and to a reorganization of the information within the representation itself as assumed by Lewin (1933) and Tolman (1932). In Hull's explicative system, after several unsuccessful attempts to pass a barrier separating itself from a goal, the subject loses interest in this direct but unpracticable way; other ones are tried, until, by trial and error, the subject finds the one leading to the goal, although it implies moving away from the goal first. One of Hull's predictions is that, when the two detours around the barrier are of different lengths, the subject will choose that one which implies the smaller 'angular deviation' from the straight direction of the goal, even if it is the longer one lengthwise. In fact, the results obtained from two experiments conducted by our team on dogs and cats (Chapuis *et al.* 1983; Poucet *et al.* 1983) are in keeping with Hull's prediction, though only when the goal could be directly perceived through a transparent barrier at the starting point. The prediction was not confirmed when the reward was hidden by an opaque screen.

The four situations represented in Fig. 14.4 have been used for the two species under study with size modifications adapted to each of them. In addition to the nature of the barrier (opaque or transparent), two other variables were manipulated: the length and the angular deviation of the two

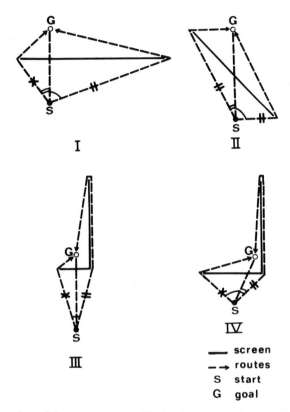

Fig. 14.4 Overview of the apparatus used in the detour experiments. (Adapted from Chapuis *et al.* (1983) by kind permission of the Experimental Psychology Society.)

practicable paths; this last variable was measured by the angle formed by the path at the starting point and the straight-line direction of the goal. In situation I, the two paths differ with regard to both the length and 'angular deviation', the shorter path making the smaller angle. In situation II, the two paths differ in 'angular deviation', the lengths being equal. The reverse is the case in situation III. Finally, situation IV represents a conflict situation: the shorter path makes the greater angle with the direction of the goal, the longer one making the smaller angle. The tests were preceeded by a phase of forced exploration of the two paths and of the food behind the barrier. The experiment was conducted outdoors with dogs and indoors with cats.

Both species preferred the shorter and less deviant path in situation I with both kinds of barrier. In situation II, the cats chose the less divergent no matter which type of barrier was used, whereas the dogs displayed a preference for the less-divergent path only when the goal could be seen from the starting point. A similar result was obtained in situation III where cats preferred the shorter path with both kinds of barrier whereas this preference appeared in dogs in the 'hidden goal' situation only. The most interesting result, however, is that obtained in the conflict situation (IV): when the goal was hidden, the subjects from the two species displayed a significant preference for the shorter path, which was also the most divergent from the straight-line direction of the goal. This preference disappeared with the transparent barrier, although the animals had the possibility of perceiving the longer extremity of the screen that defined the longer of the two paths. It should be added that in a similar experiment conducted in horses by Chapuis (1987), no significant preference was found in the conflict situation; otherwise the data were the same as those obtained with the dogs.

These results converge with Hull's (1938) prediction, although the actual confirmation is far from striking. When the goal can be perceived, the behaviour of both cats and dogs appears to be under the dominance of this attractive perception and narrowly organized along a subject–goal axis. The aim is to diverge as little as possible from this axis, even if, in some cases, this process leads to a non-optimal solution. I tend to agree with Hull (1938) and Rashotte (1987) to the extent that such behaviour can be accounted for in terms of stimulus response. Moreover, an improvement of performance over the trials is predictable within this theoretical framework, since animals might learn to differentiate the advantage of the shorter path by trial and error. In contrast the behaviourist explanation fails to account for the immediate choice of the best-adapted solution when the goal is hidden. The only interpretation is that in this case the whole situation is taken into account and represented by the animals. It is important to note that the same subjects were submitted to the two situations (visible and hidden goal), the trials being varied. Therefore, at the moment of the last tests with the visible goal, the animals had already constituted a representation of the situation, but were prevented from using it since they were strongly influenced by the salience of what they perceived.

These data point to the modulation of attentional processes involved in spatial behaviours. Attention can be drawn externally by distracting or attracting factors or by internal factors such as expectation or anticipation based upon previously acquired knowledge. The predominance of one or the other modulating factor might characterize the level of spatial behaviours displayed, as in the above detour experiment. This distinction will be discussed further in the following section.

Another form of adaptability is an animal's capacity to display 'innovative' behaviours, i.e. to discover new but efficient spatial solutions. This capacity is one of the properties of the cognitive maps as defined by Tolman (1948). In my team we have conducted some experiments showing that hamsters and dogs are able to display such innovative behaviours provided they have previously been given a sufficient amount of exploratory experience. In the hamster experiment (Chapuis *et al.* in press), two spaces, each consisting of two baited tables linked by a runway, were explored separately by the animals (Fig. 14.5(a)). In a second phase, half of the subjects were provided with a connecting pathway between the two spaces (Fig. 14.5(b)). All the animals were finally submitted to a short-cut test: they were shown a piece of food in one of the spaces and then they were placed in the other space (Fig. 14.5(c)). In order to get to the food, they could choose between the longer familiar pathway and two shorter new pathways. In comparison with a control group

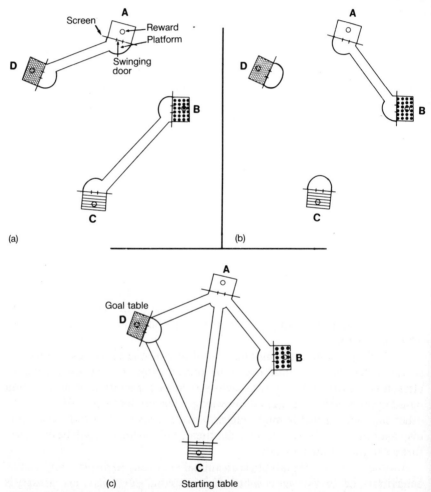

Fig. 14.5   Schematic representation of the apparatus for the three phases (a), (b), (c) of the short-cut experiment. (From Chapuis *et al.* 1987). (Reprinted by kind permission of the Psychonomic Society.)

which did not undergo the second phase, the experimental group displayed a
significant preference for the short-cut that did not cross either the linking
path with which they were familiar or either of the two distant runways which
they had already explored.

Although relying upon a different procedure and with a different species,
the following study with dogs yields similar innovative capacities (Chapuis
and Varlet 1987). The experiment was conducted outdoors in a meadow. The
animals (Alsatian dogs) were first taken on a leash along the path ADB,
represented in Fig. 14.6. They were shown pieces of meat at points A and B but
were not allowed to eat them. The task consisted of finding the food hidden at
A and B when released from D. The three points A, B and D were far enough
apart to prevent the animals from seeing the reward. Furthermore, the field
was covered with bushes and plants. Control trials were conducted at the end
of the experiment without food to ascertain that the animals were not guided

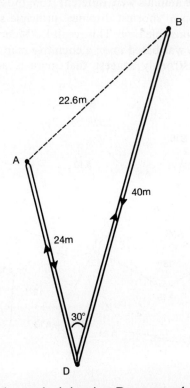

Fig. 14.6 Schema of the standard situation: D corresponds to the starting point, A
and B to the food points. DA-AD-DB-BD vectors (solid) represent exploratory runs
(dogs on the leash), and AB segment (dotted) the optimally oriented task run.
(Reproduced from Chapuis and Varlet (1987) by kind permission of the Experimental
Psychology Society.)

by olfactive cues, and the experiment was also carried out in different parts of the meadow.

In 96 per cent of the trials, the animals went directly from A to B rather than returning to the starting point and taking the familiar pathway. Examples of the paths taken are represented in Fig. 14.7.

As in the hamster experiment, the choice of a new solution involves covering a part of the field never experienced before, and this choice represents the best means of getting to the food as quickly as possible.

Following in the same vein are Menzel's experiments with chimpanzees (1978; also discussed by Brésard 1988). Pieces of fruit were hidden by the experimenter at 18 different points in an open outdoor field. The experimenter carried the animal around the field so that it could observe where the food was located. Then the animal was let free to collect the hidden pieces of food. Almost all the pieces were found by the end of the trial; more interestingly, the paths followed by the animals were different from those of the experimenter and were based upon a 'shortest distance' principle so that the food was collected in the least possible time. This result led Menzel (1978) to conclude that the performance was based upon a cognitive map of the situation.

All these results strongly suggest that animals are able to link and

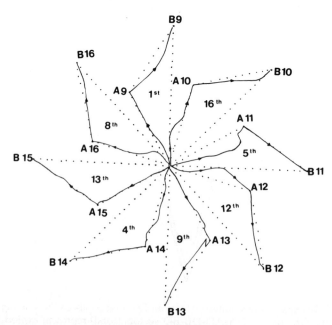

Fig. 14.7 Examples of some trials performed by one dog at eight different places of the field. (Reproduced from Chapuis and Varlet (1987) by kind permission of the Experimental Psychology Society.)

reorganize information, sometimes acquired at different times, in order to innovate efficient and adapted solutions. In a recent paper, Ellen (1987) argued in this sense: 'Since the animal uses its past learning concerning the spatial relationships in a novel manner, it would seem that there has been a reorganization at the time of the response expression of the stored cognitive structure' (p. 23).

The possibility of reorganizing previously acquired spatial information proves that the subject is not limited to acquiring this information on a purely temporal scale. Space is simultaneous and independent of time. The common association space–time is in fact related to the subject's spatial experience being arranged along a temporal continuum. The data from the above experiments imply that the spatial experience during which the maps have been constituted is independent of time; thus the different places and their relationships need not be directly associated with the linking pathways which have been previously explored. This means that the subject has the choice of other pathways if the familiar one is blocked in any way. On the other hand, spatial knowledge and any resulting displacements may depend on the sequence in which the information is collected, as in O'Keefe and Nadel's (1978) 'routes'. A segment of any route forms part of a sequence, and before and after it there are other segments. As for the spatial aspect of the routes, this refers to the positioning of the body with regard to the cues or landmark's and involves several small parts of space which are more or less related and which are recorded with reference to the subject itself. The places and the routes which link them constitute a rigid and unified whole.

Granted this interpretation of animals' performances, we now need to explain how spatial representations are constituted. In the following section several experimental arguments are presented which show that exploratory behaviour is a crucial phase in the set up of these representations; I also propose some hypotheses in an endeavour to explain this cognitive function of exploration.

Exploration: an interface between the real world and its representation

In some of the experiments discussed above, the actual test was preceded by a phase of exploration (Chapuis et al. 1983; Chapuis and Varlet 1987; Poucet et al. 1983). In another study (Chapuis et al. 1987) the success of the task was closely related to whether or not the subject had had the possibility of exploring the pathway which linked the two subspaces. This beneficial effect of exploratory activity was first investigated by Maier (1932), who, although not involved in the well-known Hull–Tolman controversy, was a pioneer of cognitive psychology.

In one of Maier's (1932) experiments, rats were allowed to explore the 'three-table' apparatus which consisted of three tables and interconnecting runways (see Fig. 14.8). This exploration, however, was unidirectional and fragmented; one day the animals ran X–Y several times, finding food at Y; the following day, they ran Y–Z, the food being at Z, and the third day Z–X was run with food at X. During the test, the animals were shown the food on one of the tables, X, for example, and for a few seconds they were allowed to eat a small part of it. They were then released from Y. The aim of the exercise was to return directly to the table where they had just been fed by running a leg (Y–X) of the apparatus in a direction they had not taken before. A screen with a door before each table prevented the animals from seeing from one table to another. Unlike a control group which had been allowed to freely explore each leg of the apparatus, those animals submitted to an unidirectional and fragmented exploration failed to choose the shorter path during the first test trials but ran along the longer one in the direction they were familiar with.

In another experiment, the legs X–Z and X–Y could be explored in both directions and in a second pre-test phase animals run Z–X–Y for food. Only the third leg was run unidirectionally (Y–Z). During the tests, animals were fed at Y and placed at Z. Therefore, the optimal choice corresponded to the path Z–Y which had not been explored in that direction before. Unlike the previous experiment, a large number of rats chose immediately the shorter path.

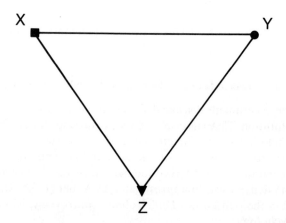

Fig. 14.8   Schema of the 'three-table-task' apparatus.

These results have several implications. First they illustrate the respective properties of the different systems of orientation discussed in the preceding sections: dependence on the sequence in which information has been collected (X–Y, Y–Z, Z–X) in the first experiment, independence with regard to time, and choice of a new solution in the second one. Furthermore, they point to the fact that bi-directional displacements appear to be a prerequisite for the setting up of spatial relationships. This point will be discussed in detail later in this section.

Since the time of Maier's (1932) investigations, his 'three-table test' has been extensively used in the study of spatial problem-solving capacities in intact and brain-lesioned animals. For example, in an experiment conducted by Ellen *et al.* (1984), rats were allowed to freely explore either one or two tables of the apparatus and their corresponding runways on successive days. Only those animals which had been presented with pairs of tables and their interconnecting runways were able to solve the problem. No rat that explored only one table and runway per day succeeded in the task.

These experiments, like many others, demonstrate that a minimal amount of exploration is necessary for the animals to solve the problem. More direct evidence of the functional role of exploration in the setting up of spatial relationships has been provided with rats by Corman and Shafer (1968) and in gerbils by Cheal (1978), Wilz and Bolton (1971), and Thinus-Blanc and Ingle (1985). In the first two experiments, animals were allowed to explore an open field containing several objects. After habituation of exploratory activity, the objects were re-arranged. This change induced a renewal of exploratory activity in rats and gerbils. In fact, the novelty was related, not to the intrinsical characteristics of the objects, but to their spatial relationships. In Thinus-Blanc and Ingle's (1985) experiment, gerbils were given five short trials of exploration in a rectangular open field containing one object A and a striped pattern (Fig. 14.9). The field was covered with a translucent top to prevent the animals from using extra-apparatus cues. The door of introduction was door 1. For the test trial, a second object identical to the first (including olfactory marks since both objects had been used alternatively during the habituation phase) was placed equidistant to the striped pattern. The animals were introduced through door 2 to prevent them from forming a relationship between the proximity of the door of introduction and the 'new' object. The results show that during this test trial the animals made far more contacts with the object that was 'new' according to its position with regards to the striped pattern. This result suggests that during the previous phase of familiarization the gerbils had set up the accurate spatial relationship between the object and the pattern.

As a result of these data, we have been led to make a more systematic investigation of the nature of the spatial features spontaneously encoded by animals during exploration. As in the above experiments and in many studies

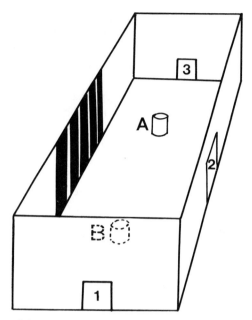

Fig. 14.9   Schema of the open field with the two objects. The 'old' subject is in position A during the first five trials; the 'new' object is in position B in the sixth trial. (Reprinted from Thinus-Blanc and Ingle (1985) by kind permission of the American Psychological Association.)

with babies (cf. Cohen 1988), we have used a procedure based upon the decrease of exploratory activity over time (habituation) and its reactivation following a change. The principle of this series of experiments is the following: if after habituation a spatial change induces a renewal of exploration, this change must have been detected by referring to an 'internal model' or map of the previous situation which no longer exists. Therefore, by studying different reactions to several kinds of rearrangements, it should be possible to yield some of the spatial parameters encoded in the 'internal model'.

Animals (hamsters) are submitted to three 15-minute sessions of exploration in a circular open field containing four different objects and a conspicuous striped pattern. The sessions are separated by about 6–8 hour intervals. For the experimental groups, the arrangement of the objects remains the same during all three sessions; for the other groups, a change is introduced in the third session, that is, after habituation has occurred. The number and duration of the contacts with the objects are recorded via a video system.

This study is still in progress but the results already obtained have been recorded elsewhere (Poucet *et al.* 1986; Thinus-Blanc 1987; Thinus-Blanc *et al.* 1987). Briefly, we have recorded three types of reactions to the change:

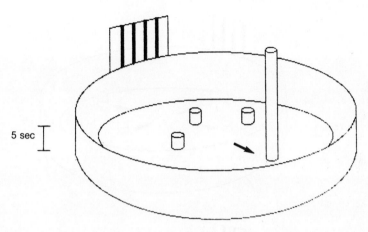

Fig. 14.10   Example of a change that induces a selective displaced re-exploration of the object.

1. Re-exploration is selectively directed towards the actually displaced object. An example of such a situation is represented in Fig. 14.10. In the initial arrangement, the four objects form a square. For the test, one of them is set apart from the others.

2. Re-exploration is directed toward all the objects, whether or not they have been displaced, as if the situation were entirely new. An example is represented in Fig. 14.11. The initial arrangement, which was the same as that in Fig. 14.10, defines a triangle during the test.

3. No renewal of exploratory reactions is observed, as is the case in the

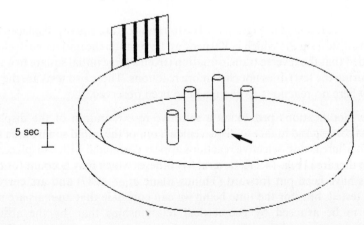

Fig. 14.11   Example of a change that induces a generalized re-exploration of the objects.

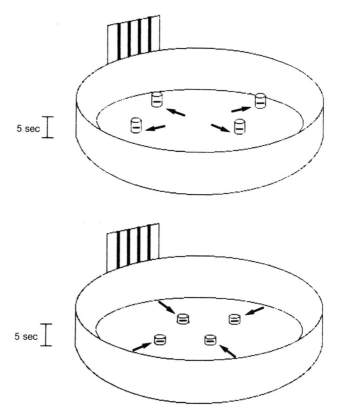

Fig. 14.12 Schemas of the two object displacements that do not elicit a renewal of exploration.

situation represented in Fig. 14.12. The four objects are equally displaced so as to constitute a square which is 300 per cent larger than the initial one. It should be added that the reverse transformation (from a large initial square to a small one during the test) does not elicit more reactions. These two tests are the only ones where no reactions to change have been observed.

The modifications provoking a selective re-exploration of the displaced objects correspond in fact to displacements out of the initial square area (Fig. 14.10), whereas non-selective reactions appear correlated with a displacement within this area (Fig. 14.11). Several hypotheses which may account for these results have been put forward (Thinus-Blanc *et al.* 1987) and are currently being tested, but, for the time being we can conclude that animals are more likely to be aroused by geometrical relationships than by the absolute distances between objects. Furthermore, the environmental framework does not appear to be encoded by the subjects in their internal model of the situation; otherwise they would have accurately detected and reacted to any change by refering to this stable environmental information. This neglect may be related to a lack of salience of the striped pattern which was the only diversity in what was otherwise a visually homogeneous environment, or it may also be related to the fact that only spontaneous behaviour was studied; the use of extra-apparatus cues was not required to localize a goal.

As a result of this survey, it can be reasonably concluded that exploration is a cognitive activity which leads to the constitution of maps or internal models of the investigated situations. Even if more information is acquired during the course of subsequent learning in the laboratory, or under eco-ethological pressures in natural conditions, this first confrontation with novelty would seem to be crucial. Such a functional value is inconsistent with the apparent lack of organization of exploratory activity. The nature of the exploratory process itself is still obscure even though we are becoming more informed in terms of the results of exploration. At this stage we can only speculate about the evolution of the psychological processes involved in habituation. For my part, I shall consider three parameters along which this evolution can be hypothetically defined: attention, space, and time.

Attention

I must point out that attention will be discussed in terms of its relationships with perceptual processes, in other words as '. . . a system for routing information and for control of priorities' (Posner 1980, p. 9) or as '. . . the selective aspect of perception and response' (Treisman 1969, p. 283).

From the point of view of attention, the evolution of exploratory activity can be described as a progressive modification of the respective role of external and internal modulating factors of attention. When the subject starts exploring, its attention is fully drawn by the novelty of the surrounding stimuli. The impact of these stimuli depends on their 'remarkability', which is determined by the previous experience of the subject and by his innate equipment for perceiving and taking these stimuli into account. But, as this information is gathered and processed, a certain object comes to be associated with a certain place and is expected to be there. At this point, attention is controlled by internal factors, that is, by knowledge, and shifts from playing an undifferenciated role to a selective and anticipatory one. The adaptive advantage of this progressive change is that it releases the 'novelty detector' aspect of attention in case of unexpected events.

Space

Spatial knowledge acquired during exploration is characterized by the stability of objects and places with regard to a moving subject. The animal's investigatory displacements that are apparently erratic might still contribute to the picking out of spatial invariants. Let us consider two objects A and B contained in a field; as the subject moves in this field he is met with changing sensory stimulations and different vistas of the objects, and proprioceptive stimulations correlative with the displacements between and around these objects are produced. Hence, exploratory activity has a structuring function and corresponds to an actual manipulation of space. In everyday life we are used to holding and manipulating an object when we do not know its use; for example, we turn it to see all sides of it. In the same way, the animal (or the infant) which moves and explores restructures space by means of its own displacement, setting up spatial relationships that lead, as during the handling of an object, to the final notion of a spatial object which has been built up by perceptual and motor activity. The distinctive feature of this spatial exploratory activity is that the subject itself is moving around.

Time

In the preceding section (p. 376) I have frequently underlined that the use of spatial representations or cognitive maps implies a breaking away from the time-course element of information collection. It is quite understandable that running the same pathway unidirectionally several times as in the first Maier (1932) experiment, and thus being submitted to the repetition of a fixed sequence of stimuli, may lead to the use of 'routes' and prevent, or be unsufficient for, the constitution of maps. On the other hand, the large number of comings and goings during exploration, in addition to the spatial function discussed above, might prevent the animals from the repetition of the same pattern of stimulations. The multiple back-and-forth displacements, observed in even the most structured mazes, would prevent the emergence of a temporal structure by 'cancelling' the effects of sequential experiences. Therefore, paradoxically, the apparent disorganization of exploratory behaviour might perform this spatial function.

It should be added that the temporal dimension is nevertheless present in the use of spatial representations, but on quite a different level. At the moment of making a choice, for example, the subject submitted to a spatial task uses the information acquired in the past, but a correct choice also implies a projection into the future, that is, an anticipation of the issue of this choice according to the chosen pattern of displacements. This projection into the future characterizes high-level cognitive processes according to Miller *et al.* (1960). These authors refer to 'plans' which are the links between representation and action.

Exploration and representations: reciprocal links?

The above discussion concerned unidirectional relationships between exploration and spatial maps. Neisser (1976), in his book *Cognition and reality*, proposes a model of reciprocal relationships, which rekindles, if need be, interest in exploration and attributes to the 'cognitive maps' a dynamic function. This author defines a 'cycle' made up from three elements: the present environment, the representation or 'schema' of the present environment, and the perceptual exploration. Neisser replaces the term 'cognitive maps' by that of 'schemata' or 'orienting schemata' because they correspond better to the function of such representations conceived as '. . . active information seeking structures' (p. 111). Perceptual exploration is a means of sampling the actual environment, and the effect of this sampling is to constitute or reinforce the representation of this environment. But it is the 'schema' of this environment which directs the perceptual exploration. According to Neisser, this cycle is 'embedded' in another one, corresponding to larger temporal and spatial scales and made up from the actual world (or potentially available information), the 'cognitive map' of the world, and locomotion and action. It should be noted that, in this case, Neisser uses the term 'cognitive maps' because they are not supposed to guide action and exploration; they are simply part of the knowledge of the individual.

This model calls for several remarks. First, 'perceptual exploration', although not defined by Neisser (1976), is spoken of in general terms. It appears to concern perceptual activity in general rather than specific reactions to novelty. Second, the model does not account for the case when the 'schema' of a present situation is not yet constituted, as in all the above experiments. However, it has the incontestable value of proposing a dynamic conception of spatial representations which are discussed only too often '. . . as if they were mental pictures of the environment that could be examined at leisure by the mind's eye while the mind's owner reclined in his armchair' (1976, p. 110). I have discussed this old-fashioned idea elsewhere (Thinus-Blanc 1984, 1987).

I have attempted to modify Neisser's model in order to adapt it to the case when a situation is totally new, and to incorporate it into a more comprehensive view of spatial cognition and related behaviours (Fig. 14.13).

First of all, as we have seen throughout this discussion, exploratory activity can lead to at least two types of spatial knowledge. If exploration is insufficient or if the subject's cognitive capacities are limited, it will lead to a 'procedural memory' or '*mode d'emploi*' of space; the resulting behaviour is the use of 'routes'. Provided a sufficient amount of exploration is carried out, this activity will lead to the setting up of cognitive maps allowing spatial performances and actual oriented displacements. This is a first function of the so-called maps. I shall consider that a second one is to guide, as Neisser has assumed, exploratory activity, even if a situation is totally new, i.e. even if a 'schema' of the present environment does not exist. The hypothesis maintains that the set of spatial representations accumulated during previous experiences constitutes a system for extracting spatial invariants and therefore

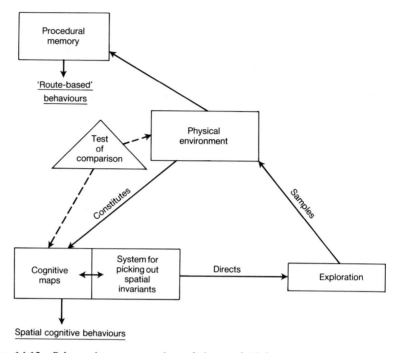

Fig. 14.13 Schematic representation of the twofold function of spatial representations.

organizes exploratory activity whatever the degree of familiarity with the situation. This degree might be defined by a comparison test between the perception of a present given situation and the spatial maps already constituted. According to O'Keefe and Nadel (1978), hippocampal 'match-mismatch' cells are devoted to performing this comparison. A slight modification of a familiar situation would give rise simply to an updating of the 'internal model' by exploratory activity, whereas a large discrepancy between previous maps and the present environment would lead to a complete mapping (or remapping) by exploratory activity.

A first stage to test this hypothesis would be to investigate, using fine and sophisticated recording methods, the animals' behaviour during exploration to try to find out some regularities. This task might be facilitated by comparing the behaviour of animals which have been reared from birth in spatially different conditions. Would they display other patterns of exploration? Similarly, the above hypotheses referring to the three-fold evolution of exploratory behaviour can be easily tested by, for example, submitting animals to repeated sequences of forced exploration.

I hasten to add that in adapting this formulation from that by Neisser

(1976), I do not presume that it shall be explanatory. My aim is to define the reciprocal links between exploratory activity and spatial knowledge and to contribute to the design of further experiments. In addition, if the hypothesis about the organizing role of spatial representations is eventually verified, then Tolman's (1948) concept of 'cognitive maps', which underlies many of the above studies, would be invested with an operational and heuristical status. That was not the case when defining 'cognitive maps' in terms of static images of the world.

References

Brésard, B. (1988). Primate cognition of space and shapes. In *Thought without language*, (ed. L. Weiskrantz), pp. 396–415. Oxford University Press.

Chapuis, N. (1987). Detour and shortcut abilities in several species of mammals. In *Cognitive processes in animal and man* (ed. P. Ellen and C. Thinus-Blanc), pp. 97–106. Martinus Nijhoff, The Hague.

—— and Varlet, C. (1987). Shortcut by dogs in natural surroundings. *Quarterly Journal of Experimental Psychology*, **39B**, 49–64.

——, Thinus-Blanc, C., and Poucet, B. (1983). Dissociation of mechanisms involved in dogs' oriented displacements. *Quarterly Journal of Experimental Psychology*, **35B**, 213–19.

——, Durup, M., and Thinus-Blanc, C. (1987). The role of exploratory experience in a shortcut task by golden hamsters (Mesocricetus auratus). *Animal Learning and Behaviour*, **15**, 174–8.

Cheal, M. L. (1978). Stimulus-elicited investigation in the mongolian gerbil (Meriones unguiculatus). *Journal of Biological Psychology*, **20**, 26–32.

Cohen, L. B. (1988). An information-processing approach to infant cognitive development. In *Thought without language*, (ed. L. Weiskrantz), pp. 211–28. Oxford University Press.

Corman, C. D. and Shafer, J. N. (1968). Open-field activity and exploratory behaviour. *Brain Research*, **5**, 469–76.

D'Amato, M. R. and Salmon, D. P. (1984). Cognitive processes in cebus monkeys. In *Animal cognition*, (ed. H. L. Roitblat, T. G. Bever, and H. S. Terrace), pp. 149–70. Lawrence Erlbaum Associates, Hillsdale, NJ.

Diamond, A. (1988). Differences between adult and infant cognition: is the crucial variable presence or absence of language. In *Thought without language* (ed. L. Weiskrantz), pp. 337–70. Oxford University Press.

Dickinson, A. (1980). *Contemporary animal learning theory*. Cambridge University Press.

Ellen, P. (1987). Cognitive mechanisms in animal problem-solving. In *Cognitive processes in animal and man*, (ed. P. Ellen and C. Thinus-Blanc), pp. 20–35. Martinus Nijhoff, The Hague.

——, Soteres, B. J., and Wages, C. (1984). Problem solving in the rat. *Animal Learning and Behaviour*, **12**, 232–7.

Fletcher, H. J. (1965). The delayed-response problem. In *Behavior of non-human primates. Vol. 1*, (ed. A. M. Schrier, H. F. Harlow and F. Stollnitz), pp. 129–65. Academic Press, New York.

Hull, C. L. (1938). The goal-gradient hypothesis applied to some 'field-force' problems in the behavior of young children. *Psychological Review*, **45**, 271–99.

Hunter, W. S. (1913). The delayed reaction in animals and children. *Behavior Monographs*, **2**(1).

Köhler, W. (1925). *The mentality of apes*. Harcourt, Brace and World, New York.

Lewin, K. (1933). Vectors, cognitive processes, and Mr. Tolman's criticism. *Journal of General Psychology*, **8**, 318–45.

Maier, N. R. F. (1932). A study of orientation in the rat. *Journal of Comparative Psychology*, **14**, 387–99.

Menzel, E. W. (1978). Cognitive mapping in chimpanzees. In *Cognitive processes in animal behaviour*, (ed. S. H. Hulse, H. Fowler, and W. K. Honig), pp. 375–422. Lawrence Erlbaum Associates, Hillsdale, NJ.

Miller, G. A., Galanter, E., and Pribram, K. H. (1960). Plans and the structure of behavior. Holt, Rinehart and Winston, New York.

Neisser, U. (1976). *Cognition and reality*. W. H. Freeman, San Francisco, CA.

O'Keefe, J. and Conway, D. H. (1980). On the trail of the hippocampal engram. *Physiological Psychology*, **8**, 229–38.

—— and Nadel, L. (1978). *The hippocampus as a cognitive map*. Oxford University Press.

Posner, M. I. (1980). Orienting of attention. *Quarterly Journal of Experimental Psychology*, **32**, 3–35.

Poucet, B. (1985). Spatial behaviour of cats in cue-controlled environments. *Quarterly Journal of Experimental Psychology*, **37B**, 155–79.

—— and Scotto, G. (1987). Memory properties of spatial behaviour in cats and hamsters. In *Cognitive processes in animal and man*, (ed. P. Ellen and C. Thinus-Blanc), pp. 135–46. Martinus Nijhoff, The Hague.

——, Thinus-Blanc, C., and Chapuis, N. (1983). Route-planning in cats related to the visibility of the goal. *Animal Behaviour*, **31**, 594–99.

——, Durup, M., Chapuis, N., and Thinus-Blanc, C. (1986). A study of exploration as an index of spatial knowledge in hamsters. *Animal Learning and Behavior*, **14**, 93–100.

Premack, D. (1979). Capacités de représentations et accessibilité du savoir. Le cas des chimpanzés. In *Théories du language, théories de l'apprentissage*, (ed. M. Piatelli-Palmarini), pp. 302–23. Editions du Seuil, Paris.

Rashotte, M. (1987). Behavior in relation to objects in space: some learning theoretic perspectives. In *Cognitive processes in animal and man*, (ed. P. Ellen and C. Thinus-Blanc), pp. 39–53. Martinus Nijhoff, The Hague.

Thinus-Blanc, C. (1984). A propos des cartes cognitives chez l'animal: examen critique de l'hypothèse de Tolman. *Cahiers de Psychology Cognitive*, **4**, 537–58.

—— (1987). The cognitive map concept and its consequences. In *Cognitive processes in animal and man*, (ed. P. Ellen and C. Thinus-Blanc), pp. 1–19. Martinus Nijhoff, The Hague.

—— and Ingle, D. (1985). Spatial behavior in gerbils (Meriones unguiculatus). *Journal of Comparative Psychology*, **99**, 311–15.

——, Bouzouba, L., Chaix, N., Chapuis, N., Durup, B., and Poucet, B. (1987). A study of spatial parameters encoded during exploration in hamsters. *Journal of Experimental Psychology; Animal Behavior Processes*, **13**, 418–27.

Tolman, E. C. (1932). Lewin's concept of vectors. *Journal of General Psychology*, **7**, 3–15.

—— (1948). Cognitive maps in rats and men. *Psychological Review*, **55**, 189–208.

—— and Honzik, C. H. (1930). Degrees of hunger reward and non-reward on maze learning in rats. *University California Publications in Psychology*, **4**, 241–56.

Treisman, A. M. (1969). Strategies and models of selective attention. *Psychological Review*, **76**, 282–299.

Weiskrantz, L. (1985). Categorization, cleverness and consciousness. In *Animal intelligence*, (ed. L. Weiskrantz), pp. 1–19, Clarendon Press, Oxford.

Wilz, K. and Bolton, R. L. (1971). Exploratory behaviour in response to the spatial rearrangement of familiar stimuli. *Psychonomic Science*, **24**, 117–18.

15

Primate cognition of space and shapes
BERNADETTE BRÉSARD

Shapes and locations pose cognitive problems because of the differences in geometry and sensory information. The geometry of solid objects differs from that of plaited or knotted strings as it does from that of bodies or leaves. Sensory information on objects or localities, visual and tactile data for example, involves differing geometric problems. Furthermore, transformations resulting from displacement of the observer's own body are not the same as those resulting from displacement of the objects observed. Investigation of the information retained in the memory and the composition of this information to recognize shapes or places can be used to compare cognitive organization by determining which problems can be solved by the processing methods of various animal species.

These questions have been studied for over a century, since Helmholtz, the gestalt theory, and Gibson's work, with particular accent on visual perception. However, work on the mechanism of passage from the initial input described by Fourier transforms to representations of recognizable shapes began only recently (Marr 1982; Hoffman and Richards 1984). The problem of intermodal relations is still more complex owing to the differences between geometries and the recognition of intermodal categorical characters. Research into mental construction of places in primates reveals some of their cognitive capacities and limits.

A target can be located through three types of data. It may be distinguished by its shape if the other objects differ by their shape, by features or identifying marks such as colour, or by its position among a set of identical objects. These methods involve three distinct analytical processes. Investigation of the ways in which these cues are treated when they are used singly or in conjunction to identify a target permits comparison of the performance in each modality and in combined modalities.

Remembering and reasoning about shapes and spatial facts by primates can be divided into four subtopics:

(1) objects as shapes in stereometric space, patterns in *planimetric* space, or groups of local landmarks in *two-dimensional* space;

(2) features of landmarks or characteristics of objects such as colour;

(3) spaces as frames of reference and localizations with respect to egocentric space as determined by the subject's own body, or with respect to allocentric space or an *object-centred* frame as determined by external referants;

(4) relations between locations and geometrical transformations in *allocentric* space.

These subtopics are discussed in the following four sections.

Objects as shapes or patterns

Primates can categorize and recognize an object despite differences caused by its being viewed from different angles or being identified by different sensory modalities. The problem is more difficult if information on shape transformation or data from distinct senses are not memorized simultaneously at least once but are presented independently.

Storage of an object-centred visual prototype by rhesus monkeys (*Macaca mulatta*) has been demonstrated by Weiskrantz and Saunders (1984). Six concrete plain positive objects were presented with transformations of orientation, size, and enlightment. The monkeys store a 'prototype' of a visual object and

. . . store it in a form that is accessible to and independent of (within limits) various transforms. . . . An adequate prototype would be a prerequisite both for further association being formed between the object and meaningful rewards and punishment—and hence the recognition of food *qua* food is impaired—and also for being "addressed" by various transforms of the object—and hence the transform deficit' (p. 1013).

Recognition of forms in different modalities is cognitively different from *cross-modal* transfer (Ettlinger 1976). Forms coded by touch in the dark are recognized visually in the light. Chimpanzees, even juveniles, recognize visually shapes of stereometric objects memorized haptically. They can recognize a solid form memorized haptically in a drawing or photograph even after a 20 sec delay (Davenport *et al.* 1973, 1975). However, chimpanzees do not always recognize solid objects in photographs of the objects (Winner and Ettlinger 1979).

Rhesus monkeys can learn the shapes of positive edible solid objects and those of distasteful negative objects in the dark haptically and can then recognize these objects visually in the light (Cowey and Weiskrantz 1975; Weiskrantz and Cowey 1975). However, they find it difficult to recognize the haptic form presented in the visual form of a drawing and full-sized colour photograph of similar objects (Malone *et al.* 1980). In this experiment, pre-training was bimodal, the object stimuli could be seen and touched. Either the monkeys 'perceived the photographs as objects from the beginning but had difficulty mastering the matching-to-sample procedure, or they had first to learn the equivalence between photographs and objects' (1980, p. 696). Photographs, fixed planimetric representations, have a geometry different from the representation resulting from the projective perspective of a perception obtained by mobile regard in *three-dimensions* (Marr and Nishihara 1976).

The success in cross-modality matching of the storage from touch and the storage from vision of an object implies that both visual and tactile parts of this object belong to the same prototype representation. It could be that storage of certain parts from the privileged orientation in three-dimensional space that are perceptively best recognized is a condition of the coding as 'prototype'. However, even in the chimpanzee, representation of forms and patterns poses the same problems.

Shapes of *three-dimensional* solid objects can fit into hollowed-out shapes in a *solid surface* (form board) in which they can be encased, as a key can be fitted in a keyhole. If a plane surface is separated with a curve into two distinct areas, the outlines of the inside area of each shape created appear different from the same origin-curve (Rubin 1921; Attneave 1974). Chimpanzees and orangutans are known to insert rigid objects such as sticks in large-enough hollowed openings. But how do they judge the relation between the *hollow* shapes and the orientation of the corresponding solid shapes? The problem is not only to recognize the shape of an object or to recognize an opening of hollowed shape, but also to distinguish between individual hollowed shapes and between these and a solid encasable shape.

Yerkes notes (Yerkes and Yerkes 1929, pp. 316–17) that Garner in 1905 and Furness in 1911 tried to teach young chimpanzees to encase geometrical blocks in form boards. Although the animals progressively learned to encase the more different blocks, they went on confusing others: 'The simple square, the oblong and the lozenge are invariably shifted from one hole to another all over the board' (p. 317).

A chimpanzee, Chloé, which could select the correct key to put in a lock from a bunch of keys, and an orang-utan, Doudou, were given the task of encasing, one after the other, geometrically shaped solids (cylinder, cube, prism, right-angled parallelepiped) in the corresponding openings of a form board (round, square, triangular, right-angled split) (Brésard, in prep.). Both apes always applied the appropriate faces of the solid objects that they had in their hands to any of the openings in the form board indifferently. They tried to encase these objects in the hollows, the chimpanzee using her hands. the orang-utan using his mouth. However, both had great difficulty recognizing the hollow openings by their similarity to the solid forms of the blocks to be encased and the two animals treated the blocks in the same way. The

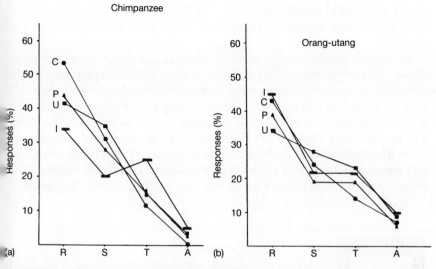

Fig. 15.1 Responses (%) of (a) chimpanzee and (b) orang-utan with solid objects (Line C and circles = cylinder; line U and squares = cube; line P and triangles = prism; line I and bars = parallelepiped) on each hollowed shape (R = round, S = square, T = triangular, A = right-angled split). Both apes give higher response rates for the cylinder on the round opening, the cube on the square opening, the parallelepiped on the right-angled split. But that is not true of the prism on the triangular opening.

chimpanzee and the orang-utan both showed the following order of preference for the forms: round, square, triangular, and right-angled split (see Fig. 15.1).

Indeed, the infinite number of symmetries of the cylinder increased the success rate and may be sufficient to explain why this shape was more often applied to the correct hollow. There is no evidence to suggest that the correspondence between the two shapes was better established. The cylinder encasement success rate was comparable in both species: chimpanzee 53.8 per cent, orang-utan, 48.8 per cent. However, both animals also applied the cylinder to the square (30.7 and 23.8 per cent) and the triangle (11.5 and 14 per cent) (Fig. 15.1). The chimpanzee was able to encase the right-angled parallelepiped but not the prism, which implies that encasement success rate was not the only criterion for application of the forms to the openings in the board.

This experiment demonstrates that, while apes can distinguish solid objects from each other, hollowed shapes from each other, and solid objects from hollowed shapes, it cannot be said that they can recognize which *particular* solid form corresponds to *a given* hollowed shape. It appears that they cannot establish the correspondence between the orientation of the face of the solid and the orientation of the hollowed shape. Nor can they distinguish similar geometrical shapes: cylinder, square, and particularly prism (Fig. 15.1). It would seem that in addition to global recognition of the shape of the solids, a comparison of the geometrical features of these and the hollowed shapes is required.

The chimpanzee learned to distinguish simple two-dimensional geometric shapes when these were clearly different. Yet, in another experiment, where the animal was presented with patterns whose external outlines were identical, such as 'schematic faces' with a 'sad or smiling mouth' (see Fig. 15.2), the performance remained at chance level during numerous trials and matching was not obtained (Brésard 1985b). It may be supposed that these shapes cannot be discriminated at the global level because of their similar outlines, and neither can they be at the local level of features inside the outline. This evokes the interaction between global and local levels of a form which depends

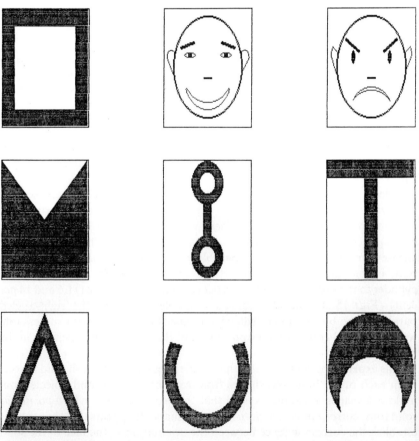

Fig. 15.2   Simple geometrical figures and patterns named 'schematic faces'.

upon the relative visibility or quality of form information in humans (Hoffman 1980).

In another experiment, the probe patterns to be matched by the chimpanzee differed by an angular *rotation* of 0°, 45°, 90°, 225°, 270°, 315° from sample items which were always presented in a 'vertical' position (Brésard 1985*b*). The two figures in each of these experiments were symmetrical configurations of orthogonal lines (T, or including a V), or curved lines (U). The animal succeeded whatever the angular deviations. Furthermore, the response times (RTs) were correlated for perpendicular angulations and, separately, for diagonal angulations (Brésard 1985*b*). In these cases, nevertheless, mental rotation cannot be assumed to be involved in recognition. This is to be considered together with the results in man. Shepard and Metzler (1971) noted results suggesting rotated mental images. However, with low educational level subjects, Baldy (1986) did not note any correlation between angular differences and latencies.

In a fourth experiment, the chimpanzee was asked to match dissymetric patterns composed of orthogonal lines (see Fig. 15.3). These patterns and

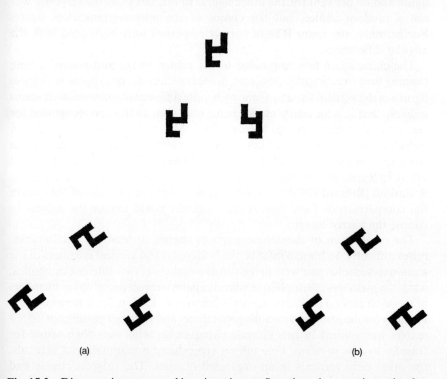

(a)   (b)

Fig. 15.3 Dissymetric pattern and its mirror image. Sample and comparison stimulus at 0°. Left (a) and right (b) situations of the comparison stimuli at 45°.

paradigms are analogous to those used by Hollard and Delius (1982) with pigeons and humans. The two shapes were randomly successively dispatched in following matching trials series. The sample item and the two matches, one identical to the sample and the other symmetrical with respect to one plane ('*mirror image*'), were first presented in the same position with vertical and horizontal lines. In this first series, the chimpanzee's choice were initially random (the frequencies were equal) and the series was given until the chimpanzee chose the identical item. The criterion was 90 per cent success for each one of the two shapes and this was obtained after more than 6000 trials. Throughout these trials, the RTs were approximately similar.

In the next series, the figures, the probe item, and the sample items, were presented either in the same position as in the first series, that is, at $0°$, or rotated through $45°$ or $90°$, according to a random order. For $0°$, one error was obtained in 144 trials with one of the figures, and 21 errors, i.e. 14.6 per cent, with the other figure. The error rate increased for the *diagonal* ($45°$) inclination: 6 per cent errors for the first figure, 30.5 per cent for the other figure. For the $90°$ presentation, the error rate was 49 per cent for the first figure and 80 per cent for the other figure. In this last case, the response was not a random choice, but the choice of the mirror-symmetrical figure. Furthermore, the mean RTs of correct responses were correlated with the angular differences.

The chimpanzee first responded to the mirror image and needed a long training time to extinguish this error. Since the effect did not appear with these figures in the vertical situation, nor with quite different *discriminanda*, it seems unlikely that it is an *oddity* choice behaviour such as the one recognized for real objects (Davenport and Menzel 1960). Mirror equivalences in animals, including the pigeon and monkeys, have been attributed to perception by the two halves of the visual field (Corballis and Beale 1976; Brown and Ettlinger 1983). In this situation, the RTs to the obliques are correlated with the angular deviations (Brésard 1985b). One may suppose that the difficulty of obliques in the comparison of these figures seen together could induce the subject to choose the mirror image.

The recognition of the *oblique* parts of shapes, at least the planimetrics, raises difficulty. In human infants 'the horizontal and vertical members of the main-axis stimulus pair were perceived as members of two different categories, while the members of the oblique stimulus pairs were all perceived as members of the same general oblique category' (Quinn *et al.* 1985, p. 302). Reproductive memory for diagonal and non-diagonal three- and four-cell patterns in a 3×3 matrix was studied in two juvenile chimpanzees who were then tested for transfer to new patterns. One subject reproduced horizontals and verticals, the other only verticals in an organized manner. The subjects clearly had difficulty reproducing the diagonal patterns, and, when successful, the diagonal was reproduced in random sequences. There did not seem to be any confusion between figures, as the difficulties were apparently related to a way of processing proceeding by local features.

Difficulty in the recognition of *two-* and *three-dimensional forms* may not be due to the same inadequacies of modular processing. Two-dimensional shapes (pictures, drawings, or patterns on a display unit) were presented at different angles which were kept immobile in the plane of presentation, unlike holograms. The orthogonal and oblique planimetric lines correspond then to the projective visual perception of outline forms in real space. The figures and patterns were not processed as shapes of objects or were so processed with difficulty. Comparisons of solid blocks and of hollowed shapes appeared to present different problems. Man also has difficulty with this correspondence between concave and convex outlines in planimetric space. The perceptive problem of obliques and mirror-image is also a general difficulty.

Coloured landmarks

Can *colours* in goal-seeking situations be used as features specifying a place?

Monkeys can distinguish planometric mixtures of simple forms and colours as well as man. By using coloured pictures that were difficult to name or describe to compare the performance of man and macaque, Ringo *et al.* (1986) lessened the linguistic and experimental advantage of the human subjects. The monkeys (two *Macaca nemestrina*) were presented with stimuli which were readily distinguishable on the basis of form and colour. When the difficult-to-name material was utilized, the performance of man and monkey was similar.

Chimpanzees have been trained by Essock (1977) and Matsuzawa (1985) to use symbols (drawings, figures) to 'name' chips of 11 different colour sets representing up to 40 hues. The chimpanzee named the various portions of the Munsell colour 'space' as consistently as a human under the same conditions. The colours for which the chimpanzee did not use a single name were not the same as the focal points for principal colour names used by humans. These experiments suggest that chimpanzees are capable of describing the perceptual world by using arbitrary codes. Furthermore, the colours that chimpanzees group around the *prototypical* ones are the same as the basic colours unequivocally named in various human languages (Berlin and Kay 1969; Rosch 1973).

Furthermore, monkeys are capable of retention, of recalling the sample colour, not from a visual trace, but indirectly, from a trace of the coded response associated with it. Gaffan (1977) tried to find out if monkeys could remember stimuli not only directly through visual traces of colour, but also indirectly, through a response-coded trace. In bidimensional presentation, either on screens or on enlighted quadrants, the coloured samples are well perceived and well memorized in matching situations, even after delays of up to 10 sec in monkeys (*Macaca mulatta*). Gaffan compared this recall of colours with a different task in which the same subjects learn to respond by touching panels with no colour cues, after touching the panel bearing the colour samples. They were required to touch the panel corresponding to stimulus colour. In this retention test, the monkeys could not only recall the sample colour directly, from a visual trace, but indirectly, from a trace of the recall response associated with it. This cognitive processing between direct code storage and storage related to a different base seems to be analogous to the one evoked by Conrad (1962) between letters and speech.

The inverse problem is different: can monkeys and apes not only recall the target place directly, from a localization trace, but also indirectly, from a trace of the colour associated with it, and thus decide the motor response? W. Köhler and Tinklepaugh (see Tinklepaugh 1932, p. 239) found that two untrained monkeys (*Macacus cynomolgus* and *Macacus rhesus*) responded more easily on the basis of position than of colour, size, or shape of the food container. Food was placed in one of three containers of different sizes, shapes, or colours. Then, in view of the subjects, the containers were shifted about in position. Yerkes and Yerkes (reported by Tinklepaugh 1932, p. 239) demonstrated that their four chimpanzees in a delayed experiment were at first entirely unable to adjust; i.e. to shift at once from places to colours only. In a five to eight object array, two of the symmetrically placed objects bore a landmark *coloured* yellow or green (Brésard, unpublished thesis, 1984). In these two subjects, the rate of location errors in a line after rotation did not decrease if the coloured cues were added to the containers. Two types of error were observed:

(1) An error involving the two symmetrical colours; in this case, the subject located the two landmarks, but confused the two colours.

(2) An error involving the container with the landmark and the adjacent container without a landmark. In this case, the subject did not appear to detect the coloured mark. The response suggested that the yellow or green colour of an object in a constant place in the line was abstractly coded as 'yellow' only, and not integrated in a kind of 'place' entity which would codify the object and its place in the line together.

When stereometric targets could be located *only* by the colour features, colour could be used as a landmark of the target. A chimpanzee and an orang-utan were immediately able to locate a green cup differing only in colour when the position of the cups was not fixed (Brésard, unpublished thesis, 1984).

Two hypotheses, which are not mutually exclusive, can be proposed to explain these findings. In the first hypothesis, place and form are coded directly from analysers involved in the recalling of localization in the cognitive map, but landmarks such as colour are not. What would then be memorized in the first case would be the relative character of the colour with respect to the apparatus. In the other case, with individual displacement of each box, colour would become an absolute—and not a relative—landmark with respect to a location on the tray. The second hypothesis is that place and colour information are checked in different modules and that there may be some independence between the two types of data, allowing some location and colour errors (Treisman 1986).

Spatial frame for displacements and relocation

The processing of representations of locations and relations among addresses in the cognitive map involves different frames of reference: the organization of personal *body displacements* with respect to places in the surroundings and object displacement in object-centred space.

Monkeys and apes are able to memorize a set of target locations, but do not show the same cognitive recognition of relations between places to reach those targets when they are displaced. The cognitive problems of target recognition and relocation between different sets of places can be used to examine the different ways of processing egocentric vs. allocentric frames of reference. This has been studied in delayed response experiments (Tinklepaugh 1932) on two macaques (*Macacus cynomolgus* and *Macacus rhesus*) and two chimpanzees.

In the first experiment with chimpanzees, each subject was successively led to different rooms in the laboratory (up to 10 rooms). The animals located the targets during the tour, when lures were placed in one of two distinct containers. In a second experiment, up to 16 pairs of containers were set around a 20-foot-radius circle in one room. The chimpanzee, placed in the centre of the circle, could see the lures being hidden, successively, in one of each pair of similar containers. He had to successively go from the central starting stool towards each pair of containers. Both chimpanzees could memorize the pairs of containers in up to 10 different rooms and, in the circle situation, both could manage up to 15 pairs and one subject could manage 16. Yet with intervals of 24 hours between baiting and the time of response testing, memory seemed to fail entirely.

The circle experiment was also carried out with five adult humans and four children aged from seven to nine years. Only two of the adults reached the highest levels of the chimpanzees' performance (16 and 15 successes). The childrens' performance remained at chance level.

The two macaques were submitted to the same two experiments. In the first one, with five rooms, 10 series of five trials were carried out. They achieved four and five correct responses, respectively, in seven of these (binomial test, $p = 0.11$). In the circle experiment, if they succeeded with four pairs of containers (binomial test, $p = 0.062$), with eight pairs in one of 10 series, seven correct responses (binomial test, $p = 0.035$) were obtained. The global result of all series was 45 per cent of correct responses for the cynomolgus and 53 per cent for the rhesus. Unlike the chimpanzees, if, after an error, the monkeys were given the opportunity to correct themselves, they made the same error again.

When the chimpanzees were presented with a different order for the run of the 10 rooms, they achieved eight to 10 correct responses in these 10 trials. When they were given a different starting point for eight pairs of containers in the circle, their performance remained high as well (69 per cent for one chimpanzee and 88 per cent for the other). In both experiments, the results indicate that their choices were based upon cues separate and apart from serial relations. For the circle experiment, in most cases the chimpanzees seem to have made their choices before leaving the centre of the circle. They started directly towards the container of their choice and they usually appeared surprised and disturbed if they turned up an empty container. After choosing from one pair, they hesitated before progressing from the centre towards the next pair.

Recognition of each one of the *places* did not enable the monkeys to recognize the relations between the locations of the rooms. After leaving a room, they had to be taken to the next one by the experimenter. On the contrary, the chimpanzees not only achieved better recognition of a higher number of pairs of containers in different locations, but they themselves took the initiative of going from one room to the next, or from the centre of the circle to the next pair of containers.

When the subject can or must move from a first room or from a first pair of containers to a second, it must shift from an initial perception or representation to a second perception or representation of the location of the target after a transformation. Recognizing the set of pairs of containers seems to pose a different problem to that of moving from one room to another, or from shifting the observer's starting point. There is no evidence that cognitive maps or frames of reference are represented according to the same processes in chimpanzees and monkeys.

Chimpanzees were able to memorize and recognize a set of places independently from the order of the initial journey in the '*travelling salesman*' combinatorial problem (Menzel 1973). One of six young chimpanzees was carried during a journey where food was hidden in 18 different places. The chimpanzee, which saw the food being hidden, found almost all of it, but by an optimal path different from the carriage path. The choice of path to the places visited was more economical both in terms of distance and of preference if foods were of different value. Consequently, the frame of reference seems not to depend only on the subject's position. It appears to be allocentric. The chimpanzee used displacement properties in a familiar environment for his journey in this optimized choice of 18 places. He kept track of the locations of stationary objects according to a cognitive 'survey' map between analogous representations of surrounding spatial information. At each place where the subject arrived, he could anticipate a part of his future locations on the best next goal-seeking path (Schutzenberger 1954).

One may wonder if this modular spatial representation is in place at birth and if it is complete independently of the experiments. A 17-month-old female *gorilla* (Visalberghi 1986) could no longer locate which out of four places on the top of a square was the target after a 90°, 180°, or 270° displacement. This gorilla showed that it was capable of encoding and recognizing a spatial location when it was presented again from the same perspective. However, the gorilla did not evidence an ability to compensate for a rotation that shifts its perspective. Rather, during the experiment she developed a 'tour strategy', searching successively all the bowls beginning from the right-proximal one and proceeding counterclockwise. These modules seem fully functional only after some cognitive development.

Relocation and recognition after transformations in the space of places

The knowledge of places in the space where the subject is corresponds to a representation of the environment where these places are fixed and where the relations between these places are steady. It is probably the same if the target objects are perceived during the subject's displacements. The cognitive maps appear then as not requiring transformations between the places by keeping only a part of the relations between the information from the cognitive maps and the information to construct. The only transformations which have been considered so far concern information about the order of places to choose in the cognitive map where their relative situations are stable, as in the 'travelling salesman' problem. How are transformations of the relations among places recognized? How is information compounded in order to build up the place in the cognitive map after transformation?

In a set of experiments on *representation* of *spatial transformations* in the space of objects' locations, *rotations* through two different axes in the *projective perspective* were compared (Brésard, unpublished thesis, 1984, 1985*a*).

The first horizontal axis was in a frontal plane with regard to the subject. With a 180° rotation, the places were symmetrically situated and the distance of each object from the subject was unchanged. The second horizontal axis was in the sagittal median plane with regard to the subject. With a 180° rotation, the distances and intervals were not maintained in the projective perspective of the visual perception.

Two juvenile captive-born apes, a five-year-old male *orang-utan*, Doudou, and a three-and-a-half-year-old female *chimpanzee*, Chloé, were the subjects of these experiments. They were shown a line of five to nine equidistant identical boxes set upon a tray (55 cm × 35 cm) in front of them. One target box was randomly baited, then the line was covered with a cloth and the tray rotated. The apes could have a global perception of the tray during the rotation but they could not see the line of boxes. The same line was presented in nine consecutive trials.

Two experiments was performed: rotation of the subject around a fixed tray and rotation of the tray supporting the boxes in sight of the seated ape. The *sagittal* proximo-distal perspective *gradient* was compared to the *frontal* left-right symmetry of the line of boxes. In the frontal rotation, the initial perception of the line of boxes was the same as the perception of the line at arrival, since the right and left places were symmetrical. In the sagittal configuration of the line, the decreasing intervals between the proximal and distal containers in projective depth perception were reversed after the 180° rotation. Large intervals at the start looked shorter at arrival and, conversely, short intervals at the start looked larger at arrival (see Fig. 15.4).

The results show that the subjects could find the target box after the rotation of the tray as well as after the rotation of their own body. The two sets of results were not significantly different. Thus the apes represent these rotations in the object-centred cognitive map as well as in the ego-centred cognitive map.

In 180° rotations, the subjects' rate of success was statistically significant and very high. In the series of nine trials, both subjects achieved 100 per cent success with five-container lines. When the number of containers increased up to eight, the success rate remained significant (binomial probability < 0.02 for both subjects); the errors mostly were with the neighbouring container of the target.

In the frontal rotation tests, performance was significantly better than the sagittal rotation tests. In the 180° saggital rotation tests, the error responses were staggered one step towards the distal part of the line at arrival, i.e. the

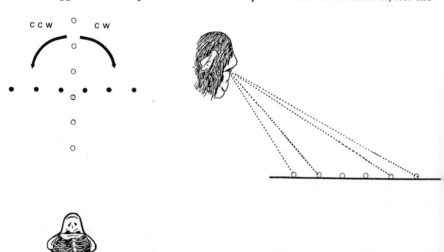

(a)   (b)

Fig. 15.4 (a) Clockwise (cw) and counterclockwise (ccw) rotations of a line of containers. (b) Projective perspective gradient in depth of the sagittal line of containers.

proximal part at the start. In the projective perspective seen at the start the places seem closer than they are in metric geometry. The errors in the choice of target corresponded to the gradient. If both the target and its one-step-nearer box are considered together, there is no statistical difference between the responses in frontal and sagittal rotations.

To determine in the object-centred cognitive map what refers to start and to arrival representations, respectively, in the choice responses given by the subjects, clock- and counterclockwise 90° rotations of the initially frontal or sagittal line were added to the frontal and sagittal 180° rotations. In the 90° rotations, the arrangement of the boxes at arrival after a clockwise was the reverse of the arrangement after a counterclockwise rotation. The left extremity of the frontal starting line became the distal extremity of the sagittal line at arrival after a 90° clockwise rotation and the proximal extremity at arrival after a counterclockwise rotation. In the 90° rotation of a sagittal starting line, the proximal extremity was at the left after a clockwise rotation and at the right after a counterclockwise rotation.

In a series of nine successive trials involving 90° rotations, the results were equivalent for the clockwise and counterclockwise rotation. This implies that the apes observed not only the rule governing box-line rotation but also the rule governing clockwise or counterclockwise rotation. The sagittal gradient errors, particularly in the chimpanzee, were in an identical proportion in the sagittal-start 90° rotation and in the 180° rotation. The gradient-related errors were symmetrically situated left and right at arrival after the sagittal-start 90° rotation.

In a third experiment, with the chimpanzee, a 10 sec *delay* was imposed after the 180° rotation of the tray before the cloth was removed and the animal allowed to respond.

The errors increased, particularly those involving the extremal distal places of the sagittal line. These boxes were correctly identified in all cases when there was no delay. With the delay, the end places were one-step-staggered. This post-rotation delay extends the gradient effect up to the terminal box, although this extremity is referable to the edge of the tray. The difference between the distal extremal place of the experiments with and without a post-rotation delay was significant (Fisher, $p = 0.05$).

The results of these three experiments suggest the hypothesis that the subjects proceed by mental image, as has been shown in man (Shepard and Cooper 1982; Corballis and McLaren 1982). *Mental images* are suggested by the following facts. In the sagittal situation, the subjects' errors are linked to the perceptive perspective gradient at start. The errors are not at arrival. The subjects take into account the direction of rotation in the 90° rotation. Rules or algorithms of representation other than mental imagery would be very complicated in these cases. In the 180° frontal rotation, the place in the line at the start can be located with respect to a lateral reference, the wall on the right for instance, permitting processing of the rotation according to an egocentric frame. However, this is not possible for the 180° sagittal rotation, and *a fortiori* the 90° rotation.

The increase of the subject-centred apparent perspective gradient with the time delay bears upon information kept in memory, since the line is covered. It is reminiscent of the perspective distortions between mental imagery and real space in man (Pinker and Finke 1980): 'The subjects had mentally rotated their images ahead of their manual rotation of the cylinder' (Finke 1986, p. 79).

In a fourth experiment, the information on location was temporarily separated from the information on rotation. A 10 sec delay was introduced between information about the place where the lure was put and information about rotation of the line. The rate of correct responses decreased significantly with regard to the three previous experiments. Two kinds of errors frequently occurred. First, inverted responses, where the subject did not take the rotation into account but only the initial place. Second, constant responses, where the subject did not take the place or rotation into account, and chose the same box from trial to trial. The results of this pre-rotation delay show that rotation is frequently not compounded with the representation of the target place and only the target place is encoded. The mental imagery of the rotation of the line and the memory of the target place can be compounded for the response only if the traces required are not temporally separated

The delay shows that the composition of this information on place and rotation in the representational process is possible only if the traces of the information are not temporally separated. The first type of information is more persistent than the second type. Yet the constant responses show that even the trace of the information to be compounded cannot be recalled any more. This is then different from the post-composition delay which deletes neither type of information.

In another set of experiments (Brésard, unpublished thesis, 1984), the same subjects had to compound three different types of information: the place in the line, the frontwards–backwards *translation* of the tray over the seated subject's head, and spontaneous rotation of the subject when he is looking at the tray in its translation displacement. The same tray with a line of containers is carried behind the seated animal, by a forwards–backwards and reverse translation over its head (see Fig. 15.5).

The subject spontaneously turned through 180° in order to face the tray again. This situation combines rotation of the subject and translation of the tray. The task is much more difficult than in the previous experiments. Even with as few as three containers, the sagittal line produced failure in both subjects. In the case of the frontal line, the orang-utan succeeded in nine consecutive trials with three containers but the chimpanzee failed. The translation was performed near a wall that could be used as an external

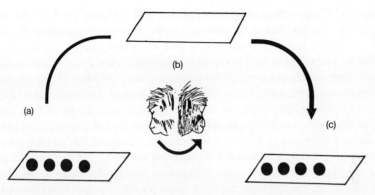

Fig. 15.5 Translation of the tray over the head and simultaneous 180° rotation of the ape: (a) start; (b) translation of the tray and rotation of the subject; (c) arrival.

referential in the frontal case: 'the container is the nearest to the wall' or 'the container is the farthest from the wall' or 'the container is between the two others'. This experiment shows the difficulty involved in representing the passage of the line from the front to the back of the subject. It also demonstrates the difficulty of compounding information on the subject's rotation and the translation of the tray. These items of information, own body rotation and tray displacement, which are both easily represented if independent, are not compoundable when they are simultaneous, even in simple cases.

If the *translation* is done from left to right, or vice versa, in front of the subject, the movement of the head to look at the tray displacement does not create any problems. It seems that it is the rotation of the body which is not compoundable with the translation of the line situated on the tray. Representation of place location on the cognitive map space appears to be possible either for own-body displacements towards the target or for target displacement in sight of the subject, but not for both. The frame of reference of the tray appears different from the frame of reference of the surroundings. Either the latter is ignored or the frames of reference are not compoundable.

The transformations considered so far maintain the *metric geometry* of the space. An experiment by Yerkes preserves only the *order relations* independently of the metric of the target places. This transformation was used in a multiple choice situation with an *orang-utan* (Yerkes and Yerkes 1929, p. 184–7). The problem required recognition of a place which was stable only in its relation to other open places in a line of nine open and closed places. The first problem, 'first box at the subject's left', was solved suddenly after a long period of failure without any progress. After a set of massively incorrect trials (10 a day for eight days), the subject succeeded in all subsequent trials for two days. He was then given the second problem: 'the second box at his right'.

Despite 1380 trials, the orang-utan failed to find the solution. A third problem was given, 'the first box at the animal's right'. Instead he tended to choose the box which was second from the right and, therefore, correct for the previous problem. The orang-utan's performance differed from those of two monkeys, which made steady progress in this multiple-choice problem. Their mean error curves have a continuous slope, whereas the slope of the orang-utan's curve is at first horizontal and then, for the first problem only, abruptly falls to zero.

The order relation here appears to be independent of the relations between places and distances in the memorial representation of the set of boxes. The number and distance between the cages are constant. From one trial to the next, the places of the open cages change and then the distances between them. The metric of the distance between open places changes from one trial to another. Only the *order relation* among the open boxes is conserved.

It may seem that the insight in the first problem corresponds to the discovery of a rule applicable to the representation of the boxes as a whole: 'there are no more open boxes at the subject's left'. However, this discovery is not transferable to the second problem: 'the second box from the right end'. The long period of failures without any progress shows that the previous rule is only a local one; that is, applied to the trials of the second problem. The orang-utan did not extract the subset of open boxes from the line to find the rule proposed. Instead he seemed to build a representation of the target based on the whole set of boxes, which could be the frame of reference of his cognitive map. However, the way the orang-utan used this also shows that the knowledge of the trials appears to be compositions of information relative to a cognitive map different from those used by monkeys in Yerkes' experiments. The representation of the order relation among open cages appears different from the representation of the places in the metric alignment. Yet it appears to interfere with the frame of reference of this metric alignment.

When the subject is moving towards the target, the cognitive maps do not raise any problem and can be stored in long-term memory. As seen above with the rotations, correct transformation of place requires composition of information that it is difficult to keep in memory. When the subject does not direct its movement towards the memorized target but follows it in the translation displacement, the results suggest that the own-body rotation is not compounded with the translation. Hence the information is functionally characterized both by content and by the conditions in which it is collected for the process of composition. In still more complex transformations, such as the order of places, apes do not seem to be able to process the composition. Their failures reflect both difficulty in the collection of information and difficulty in compounding the information. The difference between own-body rotation and place rotation, although both transformations can be managed, is marked by the fact that in the first case information was stored in long-term memory while in the other a 10 sec wait prevented compounding of information. The two processing methods are probably different. This shift from some ways of processing to others is associated with phylogenesis (monkeys and apes) and maybe with ontogenesis (young gorilla).

Conclusion

Cognitive space can be defined through places, shapes, or landmarks. It seems as if the processing of these different types of information is dependent on different systems which can be presented as *modules* in Fodor's (1983) sense. On the one hand the processing of colours appears to be independent of the processing of the other information. On the other hand, information on colours appears to be usable only if it does not have to be compounded with data on shapes and places. Shapes and places do not appear independent of movement, at least in the memorization of the prototypes, but colours do not seem to be related to displacement. The cognitive maps in primates, at least in apes, can represent an egocentric or an allocentric space, which implies that they are constructed from the relations among places as well as from the relations of the subject to the places. Cognitive maps of geometric environmental space at visible distances can be constructed. The problem is to determine how the modules and routines (Ullman 1984) that are used to build up cognitive maps and to treat parts, forms, and other information enable development of compositions leading to a shift to other methods of processing transformations of shape and space.

Acknowledgements

F. Doumenge provided support and apes, as well as the Primate Research Institute of Kyoto University, where part of the work was done. F. Bresson gave helpful suggestions, and Fondation Thiers is gratefully acknowledged for its grants.

References

Attneave, F. (1974) Multistability in perception. *Scientific American*, **225**, 63–71.
Baldy, R. (1986). Comparaison de dessins de volumes en perspective cavalière par des sujets adultes de bas niveau de formation. *Archives de Psychologie*, **54**, 271–85.
Berlin, B. and Kay, P. (1969). *Basic colour terms: their universality and evolution*. University of California Press.
Brésard, B. (1984). Contribution à une éthologie cognitive: rotations mentales et prévalences latérales chez deux anthropoïdes (*Pan* et *Pongo*). Unpublished Ph.D. thesis, Université Pierre et Marie Curie—Museum d'Histoire Naturelle, Paris.
—— (1985a). Ethologie cognitive des anthropoïdes: quelques orientations actuelles. *Annales de la Fondation Fyssen*, **1**, 45–53.
—— (1985b). Mental rotation and some coding processes in two juvenile apes (orang-utan and chimpanzee). Unpublished manuscript, Kyoto University.
—— in prep. Apes fitting of solid blocks in a hollowed form-board.

Brown J. V. and Ettlinger, G. (1983). Intermanual transfer of mirror-image discrimination by monkeys. *Quarterly Journal of Experimental Psychology*, **35B**, 119–24.

Cheng, K. (1986). A purely geometric module in the rat's spatial representation. *Cognition*, **23**, 149–78.

Conrad, R. (1962). Acoustic confusions in immediate memory. *British Journal of Psychology*, **29**, 75–84.

Corballis, M. C. and Beale, I. L. (1976). *The psychology of left and right*. Lawrence Erlbaum Associates, Hillsdale, NJ.

—— and McLaren, R. (1982). Interaction between perceived and imagined rotation. *Journal of Experimental Psychology: Human Perception and Performance*, **8**, 215–24.

Cowey, A. and Weiskrantz, L. (1975). Demonstration of cross-modal matching in rhesus monkeys, *Macaca mulatta*. *Neuropsychologia*, **13**, 117–20.

Davenport, R. K. Jr. and Menzel, E. W. Jr. (1960). Oddity preference in the chimpanzee. *Psychological Reports*, **7**, 523–6.

——, Rogers, C. M., and Russell, I. S. (1973). Cross-modal perception in apes. *Neuropsychologia*, **11**, 21–8.

——, Rogers, C. M., and Russell, I. S. (1975). Cross-modal perception in apes: altered visual cues and delay. *Neuropsychologia*, **13**, 229–35.

Essock, S. M. (1977). Color perception on color classification. In *Language learning by a chimpanzee*, (ed. D. M. Rumbaug), pp. 207–24. Academic Press, New York.

Ettlinger, G. (1976). The transfer of information between the sense modalities: a neuropsychological review. In *Memory and transfer of information*, (ed. H. P. Zippel), pp. 43–64. Plenum, New York.

Finke, R. A. (1986). Mental imagery and the visual system. *Scientific American*, **254**, 88–95.

Fodor, J. A. (1983). *Modularity of wind*. MIT Press, Cambridge, MA.

Gaffan, D. (1977). Response coding in recall of colours by monkeys. *Quarterly Journal of Experimental Psychology*, **29**, 597–605.

Hoffman, D. D. and Richards, W. A. (1984). Parts of recognition. *Cognition*, **18**, 65–96.

Hoffman, J. E. (1980). Interaction between global and local levels of a form. *Journal of Experimental Psychology: Human Perception and Performance*, **6**, 222–34.

Holland, V. D. and Delius, J. D. (1982). Rotational invariance in visual pattern recognition by pigeons and humans. *Science*, **218**, 804–6.

Malone, D. R., Tolan, J. C., and Rogers, C. M. (1980). Cross-modal matching of objects and photographs in the monkey. *Neuropsychologia*, **18**, 693–7.

Marr, D. (1982). *Vision*. W. H. Freeman, San Francisco, CA.

—— and Nishihara, H. K. (1978). Representation and recognition of the spatial organisation of three-dimensional shapes. *Proceedings of the Royal Society of London*, **200**, 269–94.

Matsuzawa, T. (1985). Colour naming and classification in a chimpanzee (*Pan troglodytes*). *Journal of Human Evolution*, **14**, 283–91.

Menzel, E. W. (1973). Chimpanzee spatial memory organization. *Science*, **182**, 943–5.

Pinker, S. F. and Finke, R. A. (1980). Emergent two-dimensional patterns in images rotated in depth. *Journal of Experimental Psychology: Human Perception and Performance*, **6**, 244–64.

Quinn, P. C., Siqueland, E. R., and Bomba, P. C. (1985). Delayed recognition memory for orientation by human infants. *Journal of Experimental Child Psychology*, **40**, 293–303.

Ringo, J. L., Lewine, J. D., and Doty, R. W. (1986). Comparable performance by man and macaque on memory for pictures. *Neuropsychologia*, **24**, 711–17.

Rosch, E. (1973). Natural categories. *Cognitive Psychology*, **4**, 328–50.

Rubin, E. (1921). *Visuell wahrgenommene Figuren. Studies in Psychologisher Analyse.* Gyldendaske Boghandel, Copenhagen.

Schutzenberger, M. P. (1954). A tentative classification of goal-seeking behaviours. *British Journal of Psychiatry*, **100**, 97–102.

Shepard, R. N. and Cooper, L. A. (1982). *Mental images and their transformations.* MIT Press, Cambridge, MA.

—— and Metzler, J. (1971). Mental rotation of tri-dimensional objects. *Science*, **171**, 701–3.

Tinklepaugh, O. L. (1932). Multiple delayed reaction with chimpanzees and monkeys. *Journal of Comparative Physiological Psychology*, **13**, 207–24.

Treisman, A. (1986). Properties, parts and objects. In *Handbook of perception and performance: Vol. 2*, (ed. K. Boff, L. Kaufman, and J. Thomas), pp. 35.1–35.70. John Wiley and Sons, New York.

Ullman, S. (1984). Visual routines. *Cognition*, **18**, 97–159.

Vauclair, J., Rollins, H. A., and Nadler, R. D. (1983). Reproductive memory for diagonal and nondiagonal patterns in chimpanzee. *Behavioral Processes*, **8**, 289–300.

Visalberghi, E. (1986). Aspects of space representation in an infant gorilla, In *Current perspectives in primate social dynamics*, (ed. D. M. Taub and F. A. King), pp. 445–52. Van Nostrand Reinhold, New York.

Weiskrantz, L. and Cowey, A. (1975). Cross-modal matching in the rhesus monkey using a single pair of stimuli. *Neuropsychologia*, **13**, 257–61.

—— and Saunders, R. C. (1984). Impairments of visual object transforms in monkeys. *Brain*, **107**, 1033–72.

Winner, E. and Ettlinger, G. (1979). Do chimpanzees recognize photographs as representations of objects? *Neuropsychologia*, **17**, 413–20.

Yerkes, R. M. and Yerkes, A. W. (1929). *The great apes: a study of anthropoid life.* Yale University Press, New Haven, Conn.

Discussion, Section E

Brain maturation and A–not B

A number of questions were directed to both the specificity and the generality of maturational explanations. *Gazzaniga* asked whether such an explanation will deal with all 'developmental mysteries'; is psychological theory unnecessary? *Diamond* replied, 'of course not. Brain maturation can set the lower limits; it can explain why an ability is not seen before a certain age, but cross-cultural research (Cole and Scribner 1974; Rogoff and Mistry 1984) amply demonstrates the effect of experience on the development of cognitive skills and style'. She went on to say that here strategy has been to draw upon *two* research literatures, the developmental, and the clinical and research literature concerning brain function. 'First, I tried to demonstrate that frontal lobe maturation might underlie some of the developmental changes between $7\frac{1}{2}$–12 months. Then I said, 'OK, given that might be true, what insights can we gain into the meaning of these changes from what is known about frontal lobe functions? This strategy can be applied in the opposite direction as well; the developmental literature should be used to help us unravel the mysteries of brain function'. In reply to a question from *Caramazza* as to the definition of 'frontal function', she added that the frontal lobe hypothesis generates predictions, such as that infants of $7\frac{1}{2}$–9 months and monkeys with lesions of dorsolateral prefrontal cortex will pass delayed match to sample but fail delayed non-match to sample'.

Weiskrantz asked if there is actual neurological evidence of gradual maturation of prefrontal cortex. *Diamond* summarized some relevant evidence: 'The density of synaptic contacts across all layers of dorsolateral prefrontal cortex increases during the first 2–$2\frac{1}{2}$ post-natal months in the macaque and then declines (Bourgeois *et al.* 1985). Synaptic density is much higher in prefrontal cortex during the first year of life than it is in the adult. Decline, or pruning back, is associated with maturation. This maturational profile is consistent with the behavioural improvement observed on A—not B and object retrieval between $1\frac{1}{2}$–2 months and 4 months. Increase in dopamine levels with age is another important maturational change . . . during this time period. Dopamine is more highly concentrated in prefrontal cortex than in any other cortical area. When dorsolateral prefrontal cortex in the adult macaque is depleted of dopamine, the animal fails delayed response and returns to normal after the levels are restored (Brozoski *et al.* 1979). Dopamine levels in the brain of the macaque increase during the first months of life, and are close to adult levels at 5 months of age (Brown *et al.* 1979)'.

Sergent pointed out that some of the deficits following frontal lobe damage are dissociable, especially orbitofrontal vs. dorsolateral frontal vs. mesial frontal. Also, failure on Wisconsin card sort can occur without failure on the Stroop test. Given this, what kind of deficit should be attributed to the youngest children? *Diamond*'s answer was that dorsolateral frontal cortex was probably the critical site for A—not B: 'We found deficits on object retrieval after dorsolateral prefrontal lesions but we also found recovery of function. I think dorsolateral prefrontal cortex is implicated in object retrieval but I'm not sure if other areas of frontal cortex might not be as much or more involved'.

At $7\frac{1}{2}$–8 months of age, *Butterworth* pointed out, infants are said first to be able to use indirect means to acquire a goal, i.e. uncover a hidden object, detour around a barrier. He asked what area of brain might be involved in the changes. *Diamond* said that the answer depends on how these changes are conceptualized: 'If you conceptualize it as translation of knowledge into action and inhibition of reflexes, then premotor cortex is implicated. If you conceptualize the change as being able to organize actions into the correct sequence, then supplementary cortex is implicated. If you conceptualize it as a move from implicit to explicit (automatic to planned) then the medial frontal-hippocampal system is implicated'.

Sergent referred to the report that using looking rather than reaching yields different results with the infants. The frontal lobes probably contribute to the control of visual fixation. Is the difficulty with the youngest infants one of motor co-ordination? *Diamond* replied that she thought that in part the visual response is sometimes automatic while reaching involves intentionality. 'I have suggested that visual habituation [as in Baillargéon's (1986) task] is automatic while uncovering a hidden object requires planning. In A—not B and Wisconsin card sort I think there is competition between the tendency to repeat a rewarded motor response and more recent remembered information. Occasionally that conflict can be demonstrated by the child looking at the correct place but reaching back to the old one.'

Weiskrantz asked about analogous (or homologous) frontal deficits in adult human patients. *Diamond* said that A—not B had not been tested on patients with restricted frontal lesions. Amnesic patients who also had frontal signs did have a deficit (Schacter *et al.* 1986), but the delays used were very long and the amnesia made the deficit more complex. But Freedman and Oscar-Berman (1986) found that human adults with prefrontal cortex damage fail delayed response at delays of 0–60 seconds. They found that performance on delayed response was correlated with performance on Wisconsin card sort, 'as it should be, since they are both measures of dorsolateral prefrontal function'.

Kertesz asked for an explanation of 'awkward reach'. *Diamond* considered that it was a secondary result of the need to look in the opening; when an infant leans over to look in the side of the box the hand ipsilateral to the opening is caught underneath the body: 'Infants below $8\frac{1}{2}$–9 months do not move their bodies to look in either side of the box and so fail when the sides are open. Nine-month-olds succeed by leaning and looking and reaching with the awkward hand. By $10\frac{1}{2}$ months, infants are able to lean and look in the opening, then sit up straight, look in the top, and reach through the side with the hand nearest the opening. The awkward reach is only seen when infants lean and look'.

Schacter enquired about the distribution of errors on the B trials. Were they random or perseverative to A? A related point stemmed from the finding of Cummings and Bjork (1983) that when multiple hiding places are used infants do not necessarily return to A. What were the implications for *Diamond's* view? She replied that the finding was fully consistent with her position: 'Most studies of A—not B have used only two wells, so reaching errors can only be reaches to A. Cummings and Bjork used multiple wells. A memory interpretation would predict errors randomly distributed around B. The interpretation I offer predicts that errors will always be in the direction of A. My interpretation is that infants have difficulty fighting the tendency to reach back to A. Hence reaches should be deflected toward A; they do not need to be specifically at A. Cummings and Bjork used six wells, with well 2 as A and well 5 as B. Although 65 per cent of the infants erred on the B trial, none reached to the side of B away from A (well 6).'

Koenig asked, in relation to the work on different species, whether the same behaviours necessarily mean the same things and are dependent on the same area of the brain. *Diamond* said it was a very good question, too infrequently asked. Similar behaviours can reflect different processes and depend on different parts of the brain. But 'it becomes more likely that they mean the same thing and depend on the same area of the brain, the more parameters on which they match and the more identical the circumstances under which they are elicited. For example, in comparing human infants and prefrontal monkeys we have looked not only at their overall success rate but on the form of their behaviour (e.g. the conditions under which they err, and what their errors look like). Second, we have not used analogous tests, but the same tests, with experimental variables, such as delay, equal in the two subject groups'.

Cognitive maps and environmental space

Dickinson referred to the distinction by O'Keefe and Nadel (1978) between cognitive maps and guidance systems. Did *Thinus-Blanc's* results (exploration in the open field) discriminate these two systems? She replied that to answer 'yes' one additional result would be needed: 'Each subject of this exploration experiment was placed at the same location of the apparatus (at the periphery) at the beginning of each session. Therefore it is possible that the novelty detection took place from this particular location. If so, the 'internal model' of the situation would be egocentrically referred and would not be a cognitive map in the sense meant by O'Keefe and Nadel, ourselves, and many others. . . . The animal can only see an alignment of objects in a definite order from left to right. The arrangement would be different when perceived from another point of the periphery. Before reaching a definite conclusion about an actual spatial map it would be necessary to ascertain whether the outcome is the same whatever the place of introduction in the apparatus'.

Sergent asked about transfer of perceptive relations to a new environment: 'Have you tried in your open field study for the animal to explore a given spatial relationship and then test them in a completely new environment with different distractors but the same spatial relationships of the relevant target location?' *Thinus-Blanc* said that they intended to do this experiment in the near future. But there was a problem: 'It is nearly certain that new objects, even in the same spatial configuration, will elicit a renewal of exploration simply because they are unfamiliar objects. A control group might partly guard against a misinterpretation. More interestingly, the method that Dr Cohen presented to study categorization in babies could be used with animals too. They would be submitted during habituation to the same spatial relationships with different objects each time. The occurrence of habituation would demonstrate categorization of spatial relationships in animals, the control situation being, for example, to confront the animals with a new configuration of familiar objects'.

Pearce wondered about the rationale for the linking experiment, and whether it could be explained in terms of the model. The experiment, replied *Thinus-Blanc*, was an extension of the study by Maier, 'showing that bidirectional exploration of one leg of the triangular apparatus allowed the shortcut performance on another leg. . . . There appears to be a "generalization" of spatial relationships established in a restricted part of space to the whole apparatus. Our linking experiment was an even more crucial test of such generalization since the short cut is a pathway never experienced before. Its choice corresponds to a new and original solution. The model I presented at the end of the chapter (adapted from Neisser 1976) emphasizes the role of exploratory behaviour in the establishment of maps or spatial representations. A major property of such maps (e.g. according to O'Keefe and Nadel 1978) is to allow inferences of unknown pathways, i.e. the choice of equivalent but unfamiliar pathways. Therefore the linking experiment, showing the beneficial effect of exploratory behaviour on the choice of a short cut, fits in with this model.

Cohen asked about specific methodological details in the arrangement of objects. Was there a condition in which the arrangement was changed so that they did not form a square? This was an important control for the relationship between novelty and exploratory behaviour. *Thinus-Blanc* said that if he meant that the lack of recovery of exploration might be related to the displacement of the four objects (not the case in all the other tests) and not to the conservation of the square shape, 'we have not done such a control and you are right to underline this point. What I can say is that the behaviour of the subjects was quantitatively and qualitatively the same as when nothing changed during the third session (control groups). We did not observe fear or startle reactions likely to be seen when animals are confronted with a large and stressing novelty'. *Cohen* continued by asking about the nature of the representation. It was unclear: were the animals forming representations of distance or angle information or actual spatial mapping of the entire gestalt? *Thinus-Blanc* said the issue was related to the point raised by *Dickinson*: 'If the spatial relationships are not dependent on a particular location or perspective, if they are allocentrically organized, I don't see any conflict between an "actual spatial mapping of entire gestalt figures" and the fact that this mapping also contains information relating to angles and distances'.

Weiskrantz asked whether any modern experimental work had been done on the old claim by Lloyd Morgan (1900, p. 143) that a dog had great difficulty in negotiating a narrow spatial gap (e.g. a gap in a railing or vertical grill) with a stick in its mouth (cf. Weiskrantz 1985, p. 8). *Thinus-Blanc* said she knew of no such work: 'When we carry a very large parcel, for example, we are able to evaluate accurately whether or not we will go through a door. Do animals evaluate as quickly and accurately? Or do they need some learning? This task could represent an interesting test of insight'.

Primate object and space perception

Thinus-Blanc asked whether there are any data on monkeys similar to that on infants, comparing performance when the tray is rotated as against when the subject moves around the tray itself (Acredolo 1978). *Brésard* said it is still open at what age such an ability appears. In the Visalberghi (1986) experiment with her gorilla, the young ape's response was egocentric, in Piaget's sense, as in Acredolo's experiments. But conditions involving active displacements of the subject's own body as against displacements of the objects have not been compared systematically at the same age. Referring to her own work, 'as I said, using a hidden tray, the orang-utan and chimpanzee I used processed the rotations of their own body and rotations of the objects in the same way. Another experiment I did not mention used visible boxes, and the results were the same. In those experiments, at least, the same frame of reference is used by the apes at a juvenile age, whether the objects are visible or invisible, or whether the body rotates or the objects rotate. As I said, the problem is different when the same subject turns himself while staring at the moving target. In this case, the combination of the two rotations is not possible, but that does not mean that a different module is involved. What depends on age is a different question from what the specific abilities of the species are for cognitive mapping'.

Hinde asked if there is a possible link with Koehler's experiment on counting without naming numbers. It was claimed that birds could transfer a number from one modality to another. *Brésard* said that there had been very few studies on the importance of sensory modality in counting behaviour in animals. 'The counting behaviour studied by Koehler (1937, 1956, 1960) in several species of birds (pigeons, parakeets, jackdaws, crows, magpies, grey parrots, amazonas) and a mammal (squirrel) used both simultaneous and successive presentation of stimuli, the latter in the visual or the auditory modalities. The reports, although sporadically anecdotal and unsystematic, were similar for these different conditions.

'Four-month-old human infants discriminate between visual arrays which differ only in having four or five elements (Treiber and Wilcox 1984). Infants use "subitizing", a rapid and direct simultaneous perceptual judgement of number content without actually counting (Starkey and Cooper 1980; Mandler and Shebo 1982). At least in the simultaneous visual situation with Koehler's subjects, the process was also probably that of subitizing.

'Koehler also used a transfer paradigm, presenting stimuli simultaneously and requiring the birds to respond in a successive way either in the visual or auditory modalities, and vice versa. The results were analogous to the previous ones. Presenting an auditory chord and requiring a response to simultaneous visual stimuli, a parrot could only manage one or two elements. The same bird was able to give a successive visuo-motor counting response to a temporal series of tones up to four, but it failed to give an instantaneous subitizing response to the same stimuli when required to discriminate the number of elements in them.

'There are also temporal counting experiments in which rats learn to respond only to a definite number of stimuli in Pavlovian conditioning (Davis and Memmott 1982) or by pushing a lever 'n' times in an operant conditioning situation (Mechner 1958).

'In all the experiments with chimpanzees the animals were required simultaneously to match visual symbols ("naming") with small numbers of visual items (one to six). The aim was to prevent the apes from responding to specific factors such as colour, size, shape, and spatial arrangement (Ferster 1964; Hayes and Nissen 1971; Dooley and Gill 1977; Matsuzawa 1985). The process involved is probably subitizing (McGonigle 1985) or acquired canonical patterns (Mandler and Shebo 1982). Similar experiments have been conducted with monkeys (Hicks 1956; Thomas *et al.* 1980).

'In general, there seems to be a difference in kind between subitizing and temporal counting, and this difference is more important than whether the auditory or visual modality is used. It is unknown how numerosity—and *a fortiori* the number concept—might arise out of subitizing or temporal counting in a single organism'.

References

Acredolo, L. P. (1978). Development of spatial orientation in infancy. *Developmental Psychology*, **14**, 224–34.

Baillargéon, R. (1986). Representing the existence and the location of hidden objects: object permanence in 6- and 8-month-old infants. *Cognition*, **23**, 21–42.

Bourgeois, J. P., Goldman-Rakic, P. S., and Rakic, P. (1985). Synaptogenesis in the prefrontal cortex: quantitative EM analysis in pre- and postnatal rhesus monkeys. *Society for Neuroscience Abstracts*, **11**, 501.

Brown, R. M., Crane, A. M., and Goldman, P. S. (1979). Regional distribution of monoamines in the cerebral cortex and subcortical structures of the rhesus monkey: concentrations and *in vivo* synthesis rate. *Brain Research*, **168**, 133–50.

Brozoski, T., Brown, R. M., Rosvold, H. E., and Goldman, P. S. (1979). Cognitive deficit caused by depletion of dopamine in prefrontal cortex of rhesus monkey. *Science*, **205**, 929–31.

Cole, M. and Scribner, S. (1974). *Culture and thought*. John Wiley and Sons, New York.

Cummings, E. M. and Bjork, E. L. (1983). Search behaviour on multi-choice hiding tasks: evidence for an objective conception of space in infancy. *International Journal of Behavioural Development*, **1**, 71–88.

Davis, H. and Memmott, J. (1982). Counting behaviour in animals: a critical evaluation. *Psychological Bulletin*, **92**, 547–71.

Dooley, G. B. and Gill, T. V. (1977). Acquisition and use of mathematical skills by a linguistic chimpanzee. In *Language learning by a chimpanzee. The Lana project*, (ed. D. M. Rumbaugh), pp. 247–60. Academic Press, New York.

Ferster, C. B. (1964). Arithmetic behaviour in chimpanzees. *Scientific American*, **210**, 98–106.

Freedman, M. and Oscar-Berman, M. (1986). Bilateral frontal lobe disease and selective delayed response deficits in humans. *Behavioral Neuroscience*, **100**, 337–42.

Hayes, K. J. and Nissen, C. H. (1971). Higher mental functions of a home-raised chimpanzee. In *Behaviour of nonhuman primates, vol. 4*, (ed. A. M. Schrier and F. Stollnitz), pp. 59–115. Academic Press, New York.

Hicks, L. H. (1956). An analysis of number concept formation in the rhesus monkey. *Journal of Comparative and Physiological Psychology*, **49**, 212–18.

Koehler, O. (1937). Können Tauben 'zahlen'? *Zeitschrift für Tierpsychologie*, **1**, 39–48.

—— (1955). Zählende Vögel und vergleichende Verhaltensforschung. *Acta XI Congressus internationalis ornithologici, 1954*, pp. 588–98. Birkhauser Verlag, Basel.

—— (1960). Le denombrement chez les animaux. *Journal de Psychologie normale et pathologique*, **57**, 45–58.

McGonigle, B. (1985). Can apes learn to count? *Nature*, **315**, 16–17.

Mandler, G. and Shebo, B. J. (1982). Subitizing: an analysis of its component processes. *Journal of Experimental Psychology: General*, **111**, 1–22.

Matsuzawa, T. (1985). Use of numbers of a chimpanzee. *Nature*, **315**, 57–9.

Mechner, F. (1958). Probability relations within response sequences under ratio reinforcement. *Journal of the Experimental Analysis of Behavior*, **1**, 109–21.

Morgan, C. Lloyd (1900). *Animal behaviour*. Edward Arnold, London.

Neisser, U. (1976). *Cognition and reality*. W. H. Freeman, San Francisco, CA.

O'Keefe, J. and Nadel, L. (1978). *The hippocampus as a cognitive map*. Oxford University Press.

Rogoff, B. and Mistry, J. (1984). Memory development in cultural context. In *Cognitive learning and memory in children*, (ed. M. Pressley and C. J. Brainerd), pp. 117–42. Springer-Verlag, NewYork.

Schacter, D. L., Moscovitch, M., Tulving, E., McLachan, D. R., and Freedman, M. (1986). Mnemonic precedence in amnesic patients: an analogue of the AB̄ error in infants? *Child Development*, **57**, 816–23.

Starkey, P. and Cooper, R. G. Jr. (1980). Perception of numbers of infants. *Science*, **210**, 1033–5.

Thomas, R. K., Fowlkes, D., and Vickery, J. D. (1980). Conceptual numerousness judgments by squirrel monkeys. *American Journal of Psychology*, **93**, 247–57.

Treiber, F. and Wilcox, S. (1984). Discrimination of number by infants. *Infant Behavior and Development*, **7**, 93–100.

Visalberghi, E. (1986). Aspects of space representation in an infant gorilla. In *Current perspectives in primate social dynamics*, (ed. D. M. Taub and F. A. King), pp. 445–52. Van Nostrand Reinhold, New York.

Weiskrantz, L. (1985). Introduction: categorization, cleverness and consciousness. *Philosophical Transactions of the Royal Society (London)*, B, **308**, 3–19.

Section F

Verbal/non-verbal interactions
and independence

Editorial to Section F

Whatever the nature of non-verbal reflection or cognition, it is typically intertwined with linguistic content. As already noted, extremists among philosophers would even maintain that, without such a content, human thought could not exist. The evidence from brain damage provides an important source of evidence about the interaction between thought and language as well as their potential independence. All three chapters in this section deal with such material, but converge on the question from very different directions.

One modern line of research that has become very well-known focuses on patients in whom the two cerebral hemispheres have been surgically severed to control the spread of paryoxysmal electrical outbursts resulting in epileptic convulsions. In such patients it is possible to direct sensory information selectively either to the left or right hemisphere (e.g. by projecting the visual image either to the right or left half-field of the retina), and to study their capacities in relative isolation from the other hemisphere. *Gazzaniga*, one of the pioneers of such research, discusses the (now) conventional view that the left hemisphere is typically in control of language, and the right hemisphere in control of non-verbal, perceptual processes. He concludes that the conventional view should be replaced by a modular account that, while it distinguishes between verbal and non-verbal, is not simply tied to hemisphere differences as such nor, for that matter, to a simple verbal/non-verbal dichotomy. The 'split-brain' patient population under scrutiny is still a small one, but even so there is considerable variance in what the right hemispheres can do in different patients. He concludes that the component modules are spread through-out and across various loci. It is worth noting, in passing, that the commissural separation between hemispheres does not create isolation at the level of the midbrain, and the possibility for interaction at that level affecting cortical activity in both hemispheres may have a bearing on the results. As regards the broad characterization of the two hemispheres, given the clear evidence for left hemisphere dominance for speech, he suggests that it typically becomes involved in 'additional processing' in response to stimuli directed to it in such patients, which can actually be a disadvantage for those inputs for which such processing is inappropriate, especially perceptual inputs for which verbalization is difficult. The left hemisphere is a kind of cognitive fusspot. In such circumstances, the same input to the right hemisphere is dealt with more speedily and effectively because it is not burdened with ineffective and surplus efforts. He gives a number of examples of such effects, in characteristically stimulating construction.

The complementary approach to the study of cerebral specialization, whether within or between hemispheres, derives from the study of patients with focal brain lesions. These need not be complicated by long histories of epilepsy and a backdrop of neurological disturbance prior to the critical lesion, as in the 'split-brain' field, although they carry other complications. *Kertesz* reviews a field that has long attracted attention in connexion with language and non-linguistic intelligence. Because patients can be rendered literally speechless and/or incomprehending of speech or written language (by, typically, focal left-hemisphere lesions), the question can be asked about the quality and scale of their residual intellectual capabilities in the absence of language. The issue is complicated, of course, by the extent to which the brain itself might not segregate the relevant control processes anatomically, even if they were independent in principle, so that the lesion would have more than a single effect. Therefore, in addition to group studies, investigations of relatively 'pure' single cases can sometimes be especially illuminating as to what dissociations might be possible, even if not common. *Kertesz* takes us through a number of cases and issues. As regards group studies, he concludes that, while non-verbal tasks of logical thinking *are* commonly affected in aphasia, this is associated primarily with comprehension deficits rather than aphasia *per se*, and moreover the loss is no greater than with right-hemisphere damage, which leaves language largely intact. From single case studies, he illustrates that in a few but significant number of individuals there is preserved non-verbal intellectual performance in the face of a severe language deficit.

Bisiach examines the implications of particular, specially chosen, cases to consider the deep question of the form and character of mental representations. He has long been interested in patients who lose part of their mental representation of space, as in his now classical studies of 'unilateral neglect'. It long has been known that patients with focal damage to the right posterior cortex (in the parietal lobe) are apt to ignore perceptually the objects in the left halves of their visual fields which are plainly there to see. This is not because they are blind; neglect is the appropriate term. The crucial step that *Bisiach* took was to establish that these patients may also ignore the left-half of remembered *images* of familiar scenes. For example, they only report the right half of a famous cathedral square from memory, depending upon the direction from which they are examining the image. He argues here for an analogical, as opposed to a propositional, structure of mental representations. He advances the hypothesis of 'a strict and uneliminable dependence of language upon the cognitive blue-print supplied by the mental structures which preserve the analogue organization of peripheral sensory mechanisms'. One verbal interview with a brain-damaged patient, who failed to acknowledge the paralysis on one side of the body and a visual field defect, is quoted at length by *Bisiach*; it is especially revealing in support of his position. In such an example, it is the analogical non-linguistic experience that drives language, not vice versa. He extends this to a general conclusion about the analogical character of normal thought: 'Language divorced from thought has no effective residual competence of its own'. *Bisiach's* paper is both provocative and powerful, and brings well-chosen clinical material to bear directly on the fundamental theme of the symposium.

16

The dynamics of cerebral specialization and modular interactions
MICHAEL S. GAZZANIGA

Introduction

When given the assignment to study the brain and to learn about how brain processes produce any aspect of our cognitive life, the researcher is naturally overjoyed when evidence develops that suggests particular brain structures do particular things. The richness of what particular brain areas might or might not do can be no greater than the claims of how complex the cognitive system is viewed to be by cognitive psychologists. Thus, if language and thought are supposed to be one and the same, then the neuropsychologist's task is no more difficult than finding the brain area that serves or is involved in this integrated function. If, on the other hand, language and thought are maintained to be distinct different systems, then the brain scientist looks for at least two different patterns of brain lesions that might affect the representations of these functions. If the cognitive psychologist has come to view the workings of cognition to be even more complicated and far more 'modular', then the task of those interested in how and where the brain subserves these functions is correspondingly more complex. In the recent past, cognitive views that were imported to brain science were exceedingly simple. For example, the dichotomy of analytic vs. holistic (or some other similar characterization) was emphasized and with it that the left brain was analytic and the right brain holistic.

These simple dichotomies and the brain evidence that supported these views has played an important role in reaffirming the idea that cognitive processes might be traced to brain processes (Levy *et al.*, 1972). At the same time, advances in cognitive theory as well as new empirical studies on brain-altered patients has called for the need for a new way to conceptualize how brain and cognitive activities are related that is more consistent with a more modular or componential view of brain and psychological function (Kosslyn 1983; Gazzaniga 1985). In what follows I will attempt to summarize the new view with special emphasis on studies with split-brain patients.

General background

It has been known for almost a century that the left hemisphere of the human brain is specialized for language functions. Damage to the left cerebral hemisphere can cause severe disruption of language processes whereas right-hemisphere damage produces little if any disruption in language-processing. While it is also known that some left-handers have language more prominently distributed in their right hemispheres, the vast majority of humans are left dominant, with current calculations suggesting that over 95 per cent of the general population respects this organization (Rasmussen and Milner 1977).

It was of great interest when clinical observations and experimental studies began to suggest that the right hemisphere was also making major contributions to cognition. A wide number of studies began to suggest a right-hemisphere specialization for non-verbal functions such as those involved in perceptual memory of hard-to-name stimuli. Studies on patients with unilateral brain lesions were the first to reveal this remarkable observation (Milner 1974) and these studies were bolstered by observations on split-brain patients where the right brain seemed more efficient than the left brain at carrying out a wide variety of visuo–motor (Gazzaniga et al. 1965) and tactile spatial tasks. The split-brain studies were widely interpreted as suggesting that one could come to think about right-brain versus left-brain cognition, since disconnection of the cerebral hemispheres gave rise to patients who had co-active but separate modes of responding to similar stimuli (Levy et al. 1972). It now appears that this simple dichotomous view of cerebral function needs to be radically changed. With the advent of more split-brain patients for testing, a more complex pattern of results suggests that the distribution of cerebral skills is highly varied. Coincident with these new discoveries, a wealth of reports in cognitive theory have argued for the broad concepts of modularity in the sense of componential analysis. Many of these general concepts have proven helpful when considering the recent neuropsychological data.

The concept of modularity has been used in many different ways. For some it refers to the idea that a mental process can be broken down into its component parts and that these parts of modules reside in particular brain structures (Kosslyn 1983). In practice it may be difficult to isolate one module from another, given their proximity and given the size of symptom-producing lesions in humans. None the less, traditional experimental approaches which use reaction time and error data have provided a broad framework for considering the modularity point of view. Recent analyses of patients undergoing only partial callosal section have also shed light on how specific neural systems appear to be in the kinds and types of information they encode (Gazzaniga 1988a, b). Additionally, research on animals, in particular on animal visual systems, has also provided support for the idea of modularity. Here, using largely anatomical and electrophysiological techniques, visual processes such as motion detection, colour detection, and other primary features of visual perception are localized to different brain structures with the different channels beginning to be identified in the retina and continuing into association cortex. With these advances in animal research where experimental methods allow for controlled intervention and specificity, the concept of modularity takes on added importance (see Zeki 1988).

Still others have come to use the term of modularity to refer to quite different ideas. Minsky (1987) uses the term to refer to the fact that even the simplest of behaviours, i.e. the act of picking up an object, has dozens if not hundreds of component parts or agents that toil to accomplish the goal. This view has been derived from considering the task of building an artifact that behaves like an intelligent agent. This enlightening enterprise has uncovered the easy assumptions of simpler models wholly based on empirical data derived from living organisms. The term of modularity has also been used in yet another context by Fodor (1983). Here, modules are viewed as independent 'vertical' systems in the cognitive system, each with their own memories, computational features, and values. These ideas are not what is intended when considering the following.

The concept of modularity, in the componential sense, has many implications for neuropsychology. With dozens if not hundreds to thousands to billions of components, it seems highly unlikely that their distribution in the brain would be constant and exact, given the high degree of variation known to exist in the human brain. Indeed, the distribution of components known to be active in a particular mental act may vary not only within a cerebral hemisphere but also between the hemispheres. I will report data that suggests this is the case. The modularity view also suggests that a particular patient may show a plethora of dissociations that might truly be enlightening in the search for evidence about the nature of components of a larger mental activity. At the same time, single case and group studies can also be misleading in the search for the components of mental activity. Much of the right-brain cognition story is to be told here and I will present my views. Finally, the modular view mandates that cognition is a product of a constellation of components that are interacting in a variety of ways using most of the cerebrum. To talk of left-brain or right-brain thinking is like talking about the top half vs. the bottom half of a computer. It is the integrated brain that generates our cognition, and how we process a particular piece of information on far more variables than what our left or right brain is doing with the stimulus.

Pre- and post-operative evaluation of commissurotomy patients

Studies on split-brain patients have been weak on the quantification of pre- vs. post-operative results of both standard and non-standard tests of cerebral function. This issue becomes of crucial importance when considering the capacities of a disconnected hemisphere, and in trying to understand factors involved in cerebral specialization. For example, it has recently come to light that most commissurotomy patients have little if any language in their right hemispheres (Gazzaniga 1983). These patients also have an exaggerated incapacity to carry out the simplest activities in their disconnected right brain, including so-called right-hemisphere tasks. Consider case D.R., a right-handed 38-year-old female who had experienced intractable idiopathic complex partial seizures which began at the age of 18. They were occurring many times a day in spite of optimal doses of available anticonvulsant medications. Neurological examinations revealed no abnormality. She had a verbal IQ of 114 and a performance IQ of 100. A CT scan showed a low-density lesion in the region of the quadrigeminal cistern on the left which was considered compatible with a teratoma or lipoma. She underwent complete section of the corpus callosum except for some possible sparing in the rostrum. No mass was seen on partial exploration of the quadrigiminal.

Post-operatively, case D.R. who is easily able to carry out picture–picture matches with the right hemisphere, is unable to perform a face matching task with the right hemisphere that other split-brain patients perform more efficiently from the right than left brain (Gazzaniga and Smylie 1983). This pattern of results in cases like D.R. raises the question of what the right hemisphere is contributing to cognitive processes prior to the disconnecting surgery (Fig. 16.1). Could it be that this kind of right hemisphere was

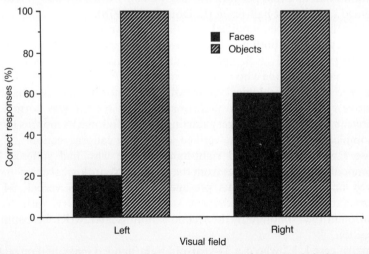

Fig. 16.1   Case D.R. was easily able to carry out match-to-sample judgements from either hemisphere on line drawings of everyday objects such as apples, books, bicycles etc. On the more challenging facial recognition test, however, only her left hemisphere performed above chance.

contributing nothing to cognitive processes when the two hemispheres were connected? Or, could it be that overall capacity would be reduced following commissurotomy on all cognitive–perceptual tasks? Or, could it be that there would be great variation in the competence of each separated hemisphere, a pattern of pre- vs. post-operative results that would suggest not only variation in the patterns of cerebral specialization but also that specific mental tasks were componential in nature with the various components potentially dissociable from one another.

Prior to our pre- and post-operative tests, the patients that have been reported in the literature generated the view of 'either/or' for cerebral specialization. While there was no argument that the left brain was always specialized and superior for language processes, there were some stunning demonstrations of right-brain superiority for some visuo-constructional tasks (Gazzaniga et al. 1962, 1965). The first case, W.J. of the California series, was able to put the Kohs blocks together with his left hand not with his right hand. This same crisp response was seen in the early testing of case P.S. from the East Coast series (Gazzaniga and LeDoux 1978). Other cases were equivocal on this test and it was presumed that, when good performance was seen with the right hand, the right hemisphere was contributing to the solution by controlling the right hand through ipsilateral motor systems (Bogen and Gazzaniga 1965). This reasoning was verified in subsequent tests on P.S., who began to show that each hand was equally capable at the task. However, when the design to be performed was lateralized to one or the other hemisphere, it was found that he could perform the task well only when the design had been presented to the right half-brain (LeDoux et al. 1978).

This picture has been modified with the appearance of new cases and new studies that examine both pre- and post-operative capacities. Case D.R. and three others, cases J.J., E.S., and L.L., are illustrative. Case J.J. is a 26-year-old right-handed female who had intractable multifocal seizures which began at the age of 7. Neurological examination was normal along with a pre-operative verbal IQ of 85 and performance IQ of 63. CT was normal. She underwent staged callosal surgery starting in 1984 followed 8 months later by the complete section. MRI has verified a complete callosal section.

Case E.S. is a 30-year-old right-handed male who had suffered from multimodal, multifocal seizures from the age of 6. Neurological exam and CT showed no abnormalities. His pre-operative WAIS was verbal, 94 and performance, 69. He, too, underwent staged callosal surgery, with the first operation in 1984 followed by the second 8 months later. MRI has confirmed the section.

Finally, case L.L., who is a 34-year-old right-handed male, had intractable partial complex seizures which began at the age of 4. At the age of 20 a right temporal lobectomy was carried out, but to no avail. Subsequently, EEG evaluation showed bilateral temporal and frontal paroxysmal slow activity.

He had a verbal IQ of 89 and a performance IQ of 86. His CT revealed only the right temporal lobectomy. His callosum was sectioned in two stages approximately a year apart.

Comparison of response capacity (speed of solution) and accuracy for the block design test shows the right hand to be frequently impaired after callosal surgery, which would be expected from the early pattern of results (see Fig. 16.2). What is of interest, however, was the discovery that the left hand was equally impaired on the task when compared to the pre-operative level of performance. In previous cases that have gained the most attention, the post-operative performance of the left hand was fast and accurate. It is as if the surgery disrupted the capacity of both hemispheres to perform the task, a result that suggests that the right and left hemispheres were both contributing factors to the normal execution of this task.

It is also of interest to note in Fig. 16.2 the post-operative scores of J.J. and E.S. Both of these patients had the callosum sectioned in two stages, first the anterior one-half then the posterior half. In E.S. the first section did not disrupt the inter-operative performance with the right hand, while the same surgery in J.J. did disrupt performance. It was only after the full section that E.S. showed the more frequently observed bilateral impairment. This finding underlines that the deficits observed are not due to general capacity problem

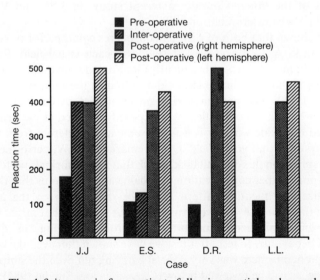

Fig. 16.2 The deficits seen in four patients following partial and complete callosal section. In these cases only D.R. has shown any evidence of right-hemisphere language. All four were impaired on their block design performance following full callosal section, thereby suggest that both hemispheres were contributing to performing the task pre-operatively.

following callosal surgery. It also suggests how specific the callosum seems to be in the encoding of information. In E.S. the critical fibres happened not to be included in the first surgery while in J.J. they were included. Where the surgeon stops in the first stage is, of course, arbitrary.

When the foregoing findings are considered in light of results on patients such as W.J. and P.S., who were clearly capable of carrying out the task with only one hand, they suggest that the whole capacity to solve this kind of mental task can reside in one hemisphere and need not involve brain systems shared between the two hemispheres. However, since the number of cases that reveal this strict unilateral superiority are infrequent, it must be concluded that this is not the normal pattern. Moreover, it suggests that in the normal brain a variety of modules or components are involved in this particular act and that their distribution varies.

Post-operative variability for cognitive tasks

As new tests are continually being developed and applied to the currently studied patients, pre-operative comparisons are not always possible, However, these studies can be revealing when considering the issue of hemisphere variability. We are discovering that a given test may find one patient performing better out of one hemisphere, and another patient performing better out of the other. Consider a recent study on J.W. and V.P. on a sequential pattern discrimination task.

We had shown that both of J.W.'s hemispheres could perform well on the following task. A 3×3 grid was presented to each visual field. Each grid, consisting of nine cells, was subsequently illuminated such that four cells were sequentially highlighted in the left field and four in the right (Holtzman and Gazzaniga 1985). The pattern varied on each trial. After each field was illuminated one or the other field was exposed to a second pattern and the subject had to decide whether it was the same as or different from the prior pattern viewed in that visual field. Quite remarkably, J.W. performed well in each hemisphere on this difficult task, a task that found normals performing at chance. Upon further consideration, it became apparent to us that the ability to recognize a sequential pattern might be different from the ability to reproduce the sequence. We were casting about for tests that might correlate with the left-hemisphere superiority for problem-solving, in short, for intelligent behaviour. In test after test we have shown that even the language-robust right hemisphere was very poor at carrying out even the simplest kind of inference, as will be reviewed below (Gazzaniga and Smylie 1984). Could a key element in problem-solving be the ability to carry out simple sequential activities?

We modified and simplified the task. The two 3×3 grids were presented, one to each field; however, only one grid was highlighted with the four

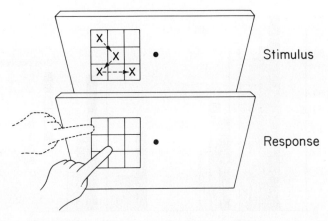

Fig. 16.3 In this test four of the nine cells were illuminated for 100 msec and in a particular sequence that varied on each trial. After each stimulus train, the subject was required to point to each illuminated cell in the proper sequence. In scoring, the spatial response had to be correct within the sequence.

elements of the sequences (Fig. 16.3). After stimulus presentation, either the left or right hand reproduced the sequence by pointing to appropriate cells, in sequence, on the computer display screen. Thus, if the left field was stimulated the left hand would respond, and if the right field was stimulated the right hand would respond. We tested J.W. first and found a striking difference between the fields (Fig. 16.4). The left hemisphere could perform the task while the right hemisphere did poorly. We thought we had a test that correlated with greater computational capacity. Then we ran V.P., who also has poor computational skills in her right hemisphere despite a more robust right-hemisphere language system than J.W.'s. V.P. could perform the task better with her right hemisphere than her left! The robustness of this effect can not be overemphasized. Whatever this task is tapping into, it is drawing upon capacities present in the left brain in J.W. and in the right in V.P. These resources may be present with superior problem-solving skills or inferior skills. In short, their location varies and is associated with factors that have not yet been identified. It would also follow from the implications of the other pre-operative studies that other patients may be impaired on this task in both hemispheres following callosal disconnection.

These results point out the large variability that exists in how functions other than language sort out in terms of their physical representation. The cortical network appears to be highly dynamic during development and susceptible to many influences. As an example of this, new studies suggest that the brain processes active in the establishment of the left-hemisphere's superior computational capacities are in part driven by brain processes in the right hemisphere during the first year of life (Nass *et al.* 1985). Right-sided

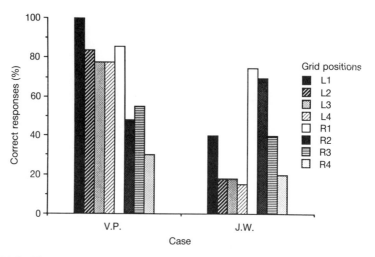

Fig. 16.4 The results for cases V.P. and J.W. on the grid sequencing task. The left hemisphere of V.P. was superior to the right, while for case J.W. the opposite was true.

lesions after the first year of life do not have the same negative effect on left-sided computational capacity and are more consistent with adult lateralization patterns. Additionally, the new anatomical work by Goldman-Rakic (1983) also illustrates how early brain damage can affect the final distribution of nerve fibre systems, which in turn could reflect different cortical representations for cognitive skills. In short, the pathologic data point out the dynamic way in which the brain develops its final cortical networks and raises the possibility that a variety of epigenetic factors may contribute to the established adults patterns of cortical connectivity.

The 'what' of lateral specialization

The foregoing suggests that the adult pattern of cerebral specialization varies, with the set of capacities seen for one hemisphere in one person being quite different for another. In this light it would seem that in the normal connected brain it becomes nonsensical to talk about left-brain and right-brain cognition. There are networks committed to certain mental activities, and the components involved in any mental skill are interconnected by both within and between hemisphere cortical connections. The location of these components with respect to right-brain and left-brain processes may be inconsequential. This is not to say, of course, that there are not people who are perceived to be more analytic or more intuitive than others. It simply says that tying those mental strategies to a simple, dichotomous brain lateralization story is wishful, not to mention useless, when trying to figure out what these various mental phenomena truly reflect.

Still, this view leaves unanswered why superior performance on a task can be seen by the right or left hemisphere, as revealed through studying patients with focal disease or patients with callosal disconnection. Current thinking sorts out commonly reported phenomena into two general categories: perceptual-based and manipulation-based. The perceptually based phenomena associated with right-hemisphere superiority may merely reflect that the left hemisphere is attempting to carry out more operations on the stimulus than is the right hemisphere. That 'what' of lateralization in this case would reflect a relatively uninteresting by-product of the logic of left-hemisphere strategies, relative to those used in the right.

A second class of tests, tasks that require manipulations of items, can also exist as a skill seemingly present in one half-brain and not in the other. For these tasks, no matter what coaxing or accommodation is given in the inferior hemisphere, superior performance is still seen in one hemisphere. Tasks, such as block design, which require mapping of sensory information onto motor systems are more commonly illustrated than explained. In the few split-brain cases where this specialization has been seen, there is a 'what' to explain. Why did all the components necessary to execute these tasks settle into one hemisphere? But, before describing some studies on both of these topics, it is helpful to consider a feature of split-brain patients that may be important in understanding aspects of the 'what' of lateralization.

The famous patients, cases L.B. and N.G. of the California series, and cases P.S., J.W., and V.P. of the East Coast series, are all patients who have some kind of right-hemisphere language capacity. These are the very same cases that show the most robust so-called right-hemisphere superior skills, Some of the less-frequently studied California patients, such as cases A.A. and R.Y., have also shown some evidence of possessing a very rudimentary right-hemisphere lexicon, as recently reported by Hamilton *et al.* (1986). These two patients also have shown some weak effects of right-hemisphere specialization (Milner and Taylor 1973). Other patients who have demonstrated no language capacity of any kind have revealed no evidence of these specialized abilities; e.g. cases E.B., S.F., L.L., and P.K. of the East Coast series. This suggests that, following commissurotomy, the presence of certain language abilities may determine whether or not the right hemisphere will be able to perform perceptual or manipulo-spatial tasks. This variable language competence may provide an executive capacity that allows sensory computations to be mapped onto the motor system. The suggestion is that some aspect of language function correlates somewhat with executive capacity, although not always. The isolated right hemisphere that lacks executive capacity may be more 'locked in' than incapable of processing at least the sensory aspects of the information in question. To borrow a computer metaphor, it is as if the data base may be there, but not the controllers that would allow for its use.

Some preliminary findings on case D.R. made in collaboration with Marta

Kutas and Steven Hillyard illustrate this point. In an oddball, P300 paradigm, a target word from a fruit category appeared embedded with a 20 per cent probability in a list of other objects. Case D.R.'s right hemisphere illicited a P300 response to the target stimuli. Yet, in a behavioural paradigm where the right hemisphere responded to these same types of words by pointing to a corresponding picture, near-chance performance was seen. This clearly indicates that certain processes related to lexical access are present and functioning. Yet, expression of this capacity falters when called upon to do so in a forced-choice matching task.

Perceptual studies

It has been noted for some time that patients with right-hemisphere lesions as opposed to left-hemisphere lesions show a greater impairment on facial discrimination tasks. We have shown in split-brain patients that the right hemisphere is superior to the left in a facial discrimination task (Gazzaniga and Smylie 1984). This same study gave the clue for why the human disconnected right hemisphere sometimes shows a superior performance for perceptual stimuli. Some faces used in this study were highly dissimilar and some were highly similar. There was no difference in performance on the dissimilar faces. Hemisphere differences were apparent for only highly similar faces. Since the differences between these faces could not be described verbally, the left hemisphere lost its competitive edge by allocating resources to the naming enterprise rather than by simply solving the problem perceptually. The right hemisphere is not compelled to name and simply proceeds, with all of its resources, to remember the faces *qua* faces.

We have recently examined this issue in case J.W. (Gazzaniga *et al.* 1986). Our stimuli were a set of hard-to-name colours. On a given trial a coloured rectangle was presented in one visual field followed by either the same or different colour being presented in the same point in spaces as the first stimulus. Five different colours were used in all, which were generated on the Apple IIE using a colour graphics system that was capable of producing a wide range (254) of subtly different colours to choose from. There were two inter-stimulus interval (ISI) conditions. In the fast condition, the two colour patches were presented with an interval of 180 msec. In the slow condition the interval was 1000 msec. The stimuli randomly appeared in either the left or right visual field. In an experimental run the first block of 40 trials utilized a slow ISI, followed by 40 trials with a fast ISI, followed by a block with slow ISI trials. There were two response buttons and the task was simply to respond by tapping the 'yes' button if they were the same and the 'no' button if they were not.

The results revealed no significant difference in error rate between the two hemispheres, but a highly significant difference in reaction times when the two coloured stimuli were separated in presentation by 1000 msec. In this condition the left brain was up to 250 msec slower than the right in carrying out the judgement ($p < 0.005$). However, there was no difference in reaction time between the two hemispheres with a 180 msec ISI.

The results are consistent with the view that each hemisphere is equally capable of performing a discrimination on a hard-to-name stimulus. The demand for quick response allows each half-brain to solve the problem in a perceptual domain before the judgement can be penetrated by verbal coding processes. If, on the other hand, the judgement is made after the left hemisphere's verbal coding processes have automatically activated, the overall left-hemisphere response slows down due to carrying out this additional processing. When this occurs, the left hemisphere appears less capable than the right on this type of task, but I would argue that interpretation was more apparent than real.

The wide variety of so-called right-hemisphere tasks that almost always consist of hard-to-name stimuli are really not eliciting brain processes that are structurally located in the right as opposed to the left hemisphere. The superior performance is a relative matter, being more the product of the left hemisphere's attempt to do more with a stimulus than it is being asked to do. This important consideration finds one reconsidering most claims of right-hemisphere superiority as being in effect illusionary and the product of test designs and procedures.

Consistent with this view are other studies carried out in collaboration with Marta Kutas and Steven Hillyard. We have been examining the P300 response in the split-brain patients. In a long series of tests using a variety of measures, one finding emerges. The P300 in response to an oddball stimulus set that is lateralized to one hemisphere or the other is generally larger in the right than in the left hemisphere. Before considering this pattern of results, it is interesting to consider the seminal experiment of Klein et al. (1984). These investigators showed variations in the P300 response as a function of subjects' musical knowledge. The classic stimulus sequence used to elicit the P300 was comprised of a series of tones in which a low probability odd tone was embedded. The note the non-musician perceives as odd is perceived as, say, B flat by the musician, and Donchin and colleagues found that musicians did not generate P300 waves to tones they could identify even though those tones were odd for the particular sequence. In short, if a stimulus is classifiable, which is to say nameable, the P300 response is reduced. If it is not nameable, the P300 wave is triggered. In this light, it is not surprising that the P300 wave is always disportionately larger over the right hemisphere. This pattern, which has been seen in virtually every split-brain, including all the patients with some language representation in the right hemisphere, may well reflect the fact that the right hemisphere does not automatically code or name stimuli. It accepts each stimulus on its own terms, can build up an expectancy for it appearing again, and then is inordinately surprised when a different stimulus appears. The left hemisphere reacts to the low probability stimulus by naming it or classifying it and thereby eliminates the P300 response. Needless to say, this pattern of results is also consistent with the view that the right hemisphere is not specialized for perceptual processing *per se*. It only appears that way because it does not illicit processing strategies that interfere with a simple perceptual judgement.

Manipulo-spatial studies

There is a set of tests that seems to bring out hemisphere superiorities in some of the patients. The block design test from the WAIS, already reviewed, is one such test. Here the simple task of arranging some red and white blocks to match those of a pattern can find the left hemisphere performing unbelievably poorly while the right triumphs. However, as already pointed out in other patients, both will appear impaired, and in still others the left hemisphere, in addition to speaking and thinking, performs this task in a superior way. The same pattern of results is also seen for other tests such as the nonsense wire figure test. Yet, for both tests, the prevalent picture would be that the skill seems frequently localized to the right hemisphere. When the capacity happens to be lateralized in this way, it should be easier to analyse than when the processes involved are shared between the two half-brains. The question is, what is it?

The components of the block design task have not yet been identified. We do know that a patient who demonstrates a right hemisphere superiority for this kind of task can show no superiority on the perceptual aspects of the task. If a picture of the block design pattern is flashed to either hemisphere, each can easily find the match from a series of pictures. And since each hand is demonstrably dextrous, the right for writing and the left for this kind of task, the crucial link must be in the mapping of the sensory message onto the capable motor system. It remains for future research to understand this superiority in performance when it is seen in one hemisphere.

Right hemisphere capacities: windows on modularity

The foregoing clearly illustrates how many disconnected right hemispheres simply respond at the most basic level, if at all; studies on these right hemispheres may only be illuminating as pre-operative tests begin to reveal how the whole brain apparently carries out some activities that the disconnected left or right brain can not do with efficiency. As already noted, more sensory capacities may be present in the post-operative right hemisphere but appear to be 'locked in'. Our most recent example of this again comes from case D.R., a new patient who evidences some weak right-hemisphere language

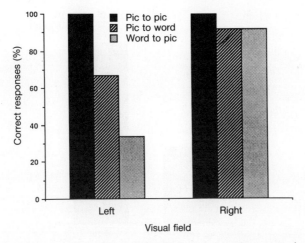

Fig. 16.5   Language capacity of case D.R. While her capacity to match pictures was very good for each half-brain, her language skills appeared more intact in only her left hemisphere. None the less, some language capacity was observed in her right hemisphere.

(Fig. 16.5). Yet, even though her right hemisphere has an excellent ability to match pictures, she cannot carry out a same/different judgement within the right hemisphere (Fig. 16.6). Responding in an associative way is different than responding in a computational way with these simple right hemispheres.

There are, however, the famous right hemispheres, the cases that have considerable language capacity. Still, even in these cases, what we find, time and time again, is evidence of limited capacity that is best characterized as not being able to compute using the information from two different variables (Gazzaniga and Smylie 1984). Our benchmark for most of these studies is case J.W. He has an NMR-verified full callosal split and shows no interactions between the hemispheres with perceptual stimuli. Case V.P. has some remaining fibres in the region of the splenium and in the rostrum which sometimes seem to interact to allow for interhemispheric integration of information, making it difficult to determine, on tasks where interactions are seen, which hemisphere is solving a task. Case P.S., as previously reported, has developed elaborate phonetically based strategies for cross-communication in the presence of a full NMR-verified callosal section (Gazzaniga et al. 1982), that appear as effective as those seen in the California case L.B. (Gazzaniga and Hillyard 1971). It becomes difficult to assess in such cases which hemisphere is active in a problem-solving task. In the following, then, we will consider a series of tests run on J.W. in collaboration with Stephen Kosslyn and his colleagues.

In an initial set of studies, we reported that the right hemisphere of J.W. was

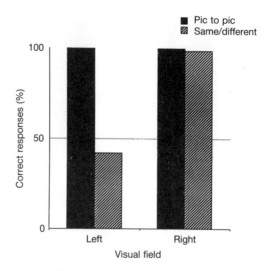

Fig. 16.6 Perceptual cognitive profile for case D.R. She was easily able to match a picture that was lateralized to the right hemisphere from a set of over 10 presented in free view. If, however, the task required her to judge whether two pictures presented to the right hemisphere were same or different, the right hemisphere was unable to carry out the task.

impaired in its ability to judge whether the lower case version of a flashed upper case letter possessed certain features (Farah *et al.* 1985). The task requires the subject to generate an image of the presented stimulus and to make certain judgements concerning its make-up, such as whether the lower case version has a stem such as a 'b' as opposed to an 'a'. The right hemisphere could point to a lower case version of the letter if an upper case version was presented. If a lower case version was presented it could easily judge whether or not it had a stem. It could not, however, generate a mental image and then read from the image the feature it needed to 'see' to make the correct response.

Yet, in follow-up tests, J.W.'s right hemisphere was easily capable of judging whether a mouse was smaller than a rat, but was poor at telling whether or not a German shepherd's ears stick above the top of its head, skills that point to other aspects of the imaginal process (Kosslyn *et al.* 1985). In addition, J.W.'s right hemisphere can draw out appropriate pictures to flashed words such as 'Texas'. He can even correctly draw a picture of Texas if the command is to 'Draw what you see upside down'. Or, if the lateralized word is 'apple' and the command is 'Draw a piece of it', he can perform accurately. Certainly, this suggests some kind of capacity—some kind of special skill exists with respect to imagery production. While it is an open question whether imaging is involved in drawing, the studies to date seem to suggest that, when a task requires a two-step process of generating an image and then ascertaining parts of the image, the right hemisphere fails the challenge. A further study carried out on J.W. illustrates the point.

J.W. was flashed the name of a state either to the left or right hemisphere. When the stimulus appeared for the left hemisphere, he simply named it. Following presentation of the stimulus to the right hemisphere, he was asked what he saw, then asked to point to where it was on the imaginary map of the USA represented by the blank video-monitor screen, and finally he was asked to draw out the state. As can be seen from Fig. 16.7, J.W. was unable to name left-field stimuli, but quite able to point to the correct position on a map of the USA and quite able to draw the correct shape. In follow-up tests, carried out with Van Kleeck (1987), where a more stringent criterion was adopted, the accuracy of his knowledge about location of states was found to be greater in the left hemisphere than in the right. Still, the right half-brain had good knowledge about location of the states. It also had the capacity to correctly react to relational words such as 'left', 'right', 'above', and 'below'. When these words were presented to the right hemisphere, it performed perfectly at pointing to the correct position relative to a reference point on the screen. Yet, when the right hemisphere was asked to judge whether a particular state was to the left or right or above or below another, it failed on the task (Fig. 16.8). In this task the examiner would say 'Is Pennsylvania to the west of' and then New York would be flashed to either the left or right hemisphere. It is as if the right hemisphere cannot take knowledge it has and use it in a problem-solving setting.

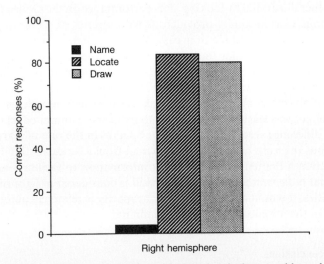

Fig. 16.7 Names of states presented to the right hemisphere could not be named, thereby confirming the disconnection and the fact that J.W.'s right hemisphere does not speak. However, the right hemisphere could draw the shape of the state and point to where it would appear on an 'imagined' outline of the USA.

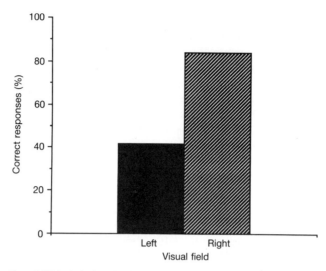

Fig. 16.8   Case J.W.'s right hemisphere was poor at judging whether a particular state was to the left, right, above, or below another, even though it has been established that the right hemisphere had a good spatial sense of where each state was on an imaginary outline of the USA.

Perhaps the dilemma of what an advanced right hemisphere can and cannot do is further illustrated by looking at its performance on the Gollen figure test. Dr Susanne Corkin kindly provided us with a series of pictures, graded in perceptual clarity from difficult to easy. We administered the test to each half-brain of J.W. by altering the usual format. Either a half-brain saw only animals, or it saw objects. The tests were run a month apart. In the first session the right hemisphere was exposed to the set of animal stimuli while the left saw a series of objects. A month later the task was reversed. In both instances, the set of animals was learned more quickly than the more unlimited set of objects, with no difference seen between the hemispheres in the rate of learning (Fig. 16.9). Thus the right hemisphere can extract from a series of stimuli that it is calling upon a limited set and use that information to facilitate subsequent perceptual judgements. Yet when this skill is considered in light of its other incapacities, it would appear that such a capacity is relatively automatic and goes on in the absence of generative planning.

Interim conclusions

It is difficult to overdescribe the riveting experience of observing a right hemisphere perform or fail to perform many of the tasks that I have related. There is a certain eerie quality to watching a hand draw or point to places when the left brain of the patient does not in fact know under what command the left motor system is responding. When the data comes pouring out and when differences in performance are seen between the two hemispheres, it is only natural to start to talk and think of hemispheric specialization. As someone who has warned against the tendency time and time again, I find myself doing it, which brings me to my point. We are talking about only a few right hemispheres in split-brain research, and when we talk about them we need to be mindful of all the things most isolated right hemispheres cannot do, which in turn should make us mindful that in normal connected brains both hemispheres must participate in many information-processing tasks. The new concept of modularity in the sense of componential processes liberates one from simple dichotomies and instead focuses attention on isolating and identifying the various components active in any given mental activity. The new studies reveal not only how the two hemispheres can be interdependent, in that component processes that are necessary for various activities are located in different half-brains, but also that this distribution may well reflect the more normal brain architecture.

This line of thought raises the question of what the value might be in carrying out lateralization studies in normal, intact brains. When superior performance is seen in one visual field through reaction time or error analysis,

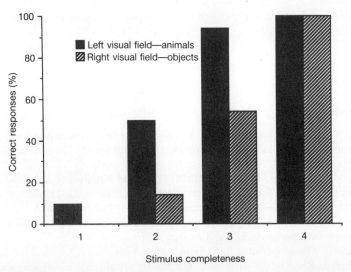

Fig. 16.9 Results of right-hemisphere performance on case J.W. The right hemisphere benefited from being exposed to a limited set of stimuli when compared to the performance of the left on an unlimited set. The same was true for the left hemisphere when tested a month later.

does it reflect superior capacity of a half-brain or does it reflect a host of other processes? I would argue on the basis of the split-brain work, that most if not all studies reflect that the small effects observed relate to the fact that the left dominant hemisphere is attempting to carry out additional processing of the stimulus, which in turn can give left-field presentations an apparent advantage. When viewed in this light, laterality work on normals is not of great interest. It does not point out possible structural differences that may exist between the two brains, a possibility that if true would be of great interest.

Finally, the working hypothesis of modularity, again in the componential sense, is helpful when considering a host of neuropsychological observations. In the present context, the view helps in understanding the right hemisphere of case J.W. It seems abundantly clear that mental capacity A does not predict the presence of mental capacity B. There seems to be a relative independence between capacities, and the dynamics of brain development can establish the components or submodules of a capacity in a variety of brain areas.

Acknowledgments

I would like to thank Drs Alexander Reeves and David Roberts for their continued support and interest in studying many of their patients. I would also like to thank Lynn Bohi, Barbara Duncan, and Charlotte Smylie for their assistance in carrying out many of the neuropsychological tests. This research was aided by USPHS Grant No. 5PO1 NS 17778.

References

Bogen, J. E., and Gazzaniga, M. S. (1965). Cerebral commissurotomy: minor hemisphere dominance for certain visuospatial functions. *Journal of Neurosurgery*, **23**, 394–9.

Farah, M., Gazzaniga, M. S., Holtzman, J. D., and Kosslyn, S. M. (1985). A left hemisphere basis for visual imagery? *Neuropsychologia*, **23**, 119–20.

Fodor, J. (1983). *The modularity of mind*. MIT Press, Cambridge, MA.

Gazzaniga, M. S. (1983). Right hemisphere language following brain bisection: a twenty-year perspective. *The American Psychologist*, **38**, 525–37.

—— (1985). *The social brain*. Basic Books, New York.

—— (1988*a*). Brain modularity: towards a philosophy of conscious experience. (ed. E. Bisiach and A. Marcel), Oxford University Press.

—— (1988*b*). Interhemispheric interactions. In *Neurobiology of neocortex*, (ed. R. Rakic and W. Singer). John Wiley and Sons, New York.

—— and Hillyard, S. A. (1971). Language and speech capacity of the right hemisphere. *Neuropsychologia*, **9**, 273–80.

—— and LeDoux, J. E. (1978). *The integrated mind*. Plenum Press, New York.

—— and Smylie, C. S. (1983). Facial recognition and brain asymmetries: clues to underlying mechanisms. *Annals of Neurology*, **13**, 536–40.

—— and —— (1984). Dissociation of language and cognition: a psychological profile of two disconnected right hemispheres. *Brain*, **107**, 145–53.

—— and —— (1986). Right hemisphere superiorities: more apparent than real? *Society for Neuroscience Abstracts*.

—— Bogen, J. E., and Sperry, R. W. (1962). Some functional effects of sectioning the cerebral hemispheres in man. *Proceedings of the National Academy of Sciences*, **48**, 1765–9.

—— —— and —— (1965). Observations on visual perception after disconnection of the cerebral hemispheres in man. *Brain*, **88**, 221–36.

—— Sidtis, J. J. Volpe, B. T., Smylie, C. S., Holtzman, J. D., and Wilson, D. H. (1982). Evidence of para-callosal transfer after callosal section: a possible consequence of bilateral language. *Brain*, **105**, 53–63.

—— Van Patten, C., and Marta, K. (in prep.).

Goldman-Rakic, P. S. (1983). Development and plasticity of primate frontal association cortex. In *The organization of the cerebral cortex*, (ed. F. O. Schmidt, F. G. Worden, G. Aldeman, and S. G. Dennis), pp. 69–87. MIT Press, Cambridge, MA.

Hamilton, C., Nargeot, M. C., Vermeire, B. A., and Bogen, J. E. (1986). Comprehension of language by the right hemisphere. *Society of Neuroscience Abstracts*, **22**, 721.

Holtzman, J. E. and Gazzaniga, M. S. (1985). Enhanced dual task performance following callosal commissurotomy in humans. *Neuropsychologia*, **23**, 315–21.

Klein, M., Cole, M. G. H., and Donchin, E. (1984). People with absolute pitch process tones without producing a P300. *Science*, **223**, 1306–9.

Kosslyn, S. M. (1983). *Ghosts in the mind's machine*. W. W. Norton, New York.

——, Holtzman, J. D., Farrah, M. J., and Gazzaniga, M. S. (1985). A computational analysis of mental image generation: evidence from functional dissociations in split-brain patients. *Journal of Experimental Psychology: General*, **114**, 311–41.

LeDoux, J. E., Wilson, D. H., and Gazzaniga, M. S. (1978). Block design performance following callosal sectioning: observations on functional recovery. *Archives of Neurology*, **35**, 506–8.

Levy, J., Trevarthen, C., and Sperry, R. W. (1972). Perception of bilateral chimeric figures following hemispheric deconnection. *Brain*, **95**, 61–78.

Milner, B. (1974). Hemispheric specialization: scope and limits. In *The neurosciences: third study program*, (ed. F. O. Schmidt and F. G. Worden), pp. 75–89. MIT Press, Cambridge, MA.

—— and Taylor, L. (1977). Right hemisphere superiority in tactile pattern-recognition after cerebral commissurotomy: evidence for nonverbal memory. *Neuropsychologia*, **10**, 1–15.

Minsky, M. (1987). *The society of mind*. Simon and Shuster, New York.

Nass, R., Koch, D., and Janowski, J. (1985). The differential effects of left versus right brain injury on intelligence. *Annals of Neurology*, **18**, 393.

Rasmussen, T. and B. Milner. (1977) The role of early brain damage in determining the lateralization of cerebral speech functions. In *Evolution and lateralization of the brain*, (ed. S. Dimond and D. Blizard), pp. 355–69. New York Academy of Science.

Zeki, S. (1988). Anatomical guides to the functional organisation of the visual cortex. In *Neurobiology of neocortex*, (ed. P. Rakic and W. Singer). John Wiley and Sons, New York.

17

Cognitive function in severe aphasia

ANDREW KERTESZ

There is often a striking discrepancy between the severely impaired language of aphasics and their well-preserved non-verbal behaviour. Their reactions to complex environmental situations are often remarkably appropriate, suggesting that some of their thought processes or intelligence remains intact. Examining abnormal behaviour gives us a special opportunity to observe a double dissociation between thought and language. The opposite dissociation of language from intelligence occurs in certain cases of mental retardation where verbal ability may be well preserved, even excessive, yet intelligence, and problem-solving is impoverished. A similar phenomenon is observed in early stages of dementia where language, especially syntactic and phonological aspects, remain well preserved and memory and cognition can be impaired significantly.

Most philosophers agree that thought is a precursor of language, but, as Whitehead expressed it, 'language is not the essence of thought'. However, without language the retention of thought, the easy recall of thought, the interweaving of thought into higher complexity, and the communication of thought are all greatly limited. Language modifies and shapes our thinking process in a very significant fashion. There are two philosophical camps: on one hand, the dualists, regarding language and general intelligence as being separate, including Bergson, Berkeley, Schopenhauer, Binet, Hebb, Piaget; and, on the other, the monists, believing in the unity of language and thought, having such notables as Plato, Leibnitz, J. S. Mill, and Ribot.

The basic issue of duality or unity of language and intelligence is also complicated by regarding language as a special sort of intelligence. We are therefore at a serious risk that we are asking the wrong question, when we ask; 'Do aphasics have loss of intelligence?' If language is considered by some a special form of intelligence, then by definition they are inseparable. Many psychologists will argue that any central process that underlies behaviour, such as attention, discrimination, memory, ideation, imagery, language, logic, or problem-solving, is intelligence. Somewhat in conflict, however, is the evidence that most men consider animals intelligent, even though they have no language. However, there are differences of opinion in either direction. The extreme position, which obviously differs from the main tenor of this conference, states quite forcefully that thought depends on language, at least in man. Descartes argued that, in all probability, animals do not think. This has been further elaborated by Viaud (1960): 'Animals do not think conceptually and logically because they do not talk'. Chomsky also thought that language was specific and essentially independent of intelligence. Premack (1971), on the other hand, believes that chimpanzees can acquire a reading and writing vocabulary and have an understanding of world class concepts and rudimentary sentence structure. One of the major problems with the animal, particularly in primate language experiments, is that linguists cannot agree on the definition of language. Among the many different operational definitions of language are the design features of language, such as semanticity, displacement, and productivity (Hockett 1963), or sentence creation (Terrace 1979). Language is purposive in that it aims to communicate something. It is propositional if it transmits information. It is also syntactic because it has internal organization. Some of these animals were claimed to perform at the level of a 'semiotic illusion' or the 'Clever Hans effect' (Terrace 1981). Clever Hans was the counting horse whose secret of solving mathematical problems was revealed to be related to the trainer's cue when it should stop clopping its foot on the ground. The expectation that apes will learn human language is probably over-simplistic. It is more likely that animal communication, although also a form of communication, is less prototypical than human language. However, the argument continues about the 'linguistic Rubicon' or the sharp divide between what is regarded as a uniquely human attribute, language, and the complex communication of animals.

There are also divergent views of intelligence. It is often considered a basic property of cognitive existence, a 'general capacity to solve new problems' (Claparède 1917). The other view is that intelligence is multidimensional and its measurement depends entirely on the tasks chosen. There are those who believe that, in addition to a central integrative process, there are various capacities, such as language, memory, constructional ability, visuo-spatial orientation, calculation, etc. These are, functionally and biologically, closely related but distinguishable from the central integrating process or general intelligence. Fodor's (1983) theory of modularity, for instance, considers language a cognitive operation that can be distinguished from a central, integrative process.

Finkelnburg (1876), Jackson (1878), Goldstein (1917), and many others called attention to the symbolic processing underlying language functions of various modalities, such as speech, written codes, and sign language. Marie (1906) firmly believed that aphasic impairment always entailed the loss of some intelligence and was fond of demonstrating this with the example of the French chef who could not make an omelette after he became aphasic.

Jackson (1878) emphasized that a severe aphasic is speechless, but not wordless, and that he can understand words and evoke images. He said that words were not essential for thought but at the same time conceptual thought necessitates symbols.

McFie and Piercy (1952) demonstrated intellectual deficits in left-brain-damaged individuals but found no correlation with aphasia. Tissot *et al.* (1963) found that constructional apraxia correlated more with intelligence deficit than language disturbance. Zangwill (1964, 1969) stated that intelligence may remain at a high level in severe aphasia. He also had an example of a speechless chef who, on the other hand, had produced an excellent omelette and functioned in his profession even though he remained severely expressively aphasic. He studied the performance of a few global aphasics who performed well on Raven's matrices. Piercy (1964), however, reviewed this issue and concluded that aphasia is generally accompanied by intellectual impairment. Teuber (1964) found that aphasics were deficient on a complex conditioned reaction task, designed for experiments requiring no verbal instructions.

Non-verbal intelligence is often assessed by tasks that go beyond perceptual stimuli, but which involve mental operations of processing and innovation of spatial information. These tasks of spatial thinking include finding figures concealed in a complex pattern, imaging in a picture in a reverse perspective, and deducing rules of spatial nature from spatial arrangements of the stimuli. The range of intellectual activities involved is not purely spatial; interpretation is far from simple. Many of these tasks demand a prolonged inspection of the stimuli. Some of the tests require verbal explanation. They also assume that scanning and discrimination of stimuli are intact. Even if the elementary perceptual abilities are preserved, the tasks themselves represent several factors of spatial ability. One of them is shown to be related to spatial visualization and the other one to spatial orientation. On the non-verbal tests of intelligence, Raven's coloured progressive matrices (RCPM) are considered to be heavily loaded in the G-factor, in addition to a specific spatial factor.

RCPM consist of two-dimensional visual patterns of graded complexity, out of which a smaller area is missing (Raven, 1965). This smaller area is presented to the patient along with five other similar patterns. For the correct choice, the patient is scored. Maximum score is 36. The test is similar to a jigsaw puzzle, except that the patterns are mostly meaningless, although the colours and many of the geometric figures are verbalizable. Studies of aphasics revealed a general severity effect of the aphasia on non-verbal performance tests. Global aphasics tend to perform worse on the RCPM (Archibald *et al.* 1967; Kertesz and McCabe 1975), but when only mild or so-called testable aphasics are selected no differences in performance are found between motor or sensory types (Orgass *et al.* 1972), nor in the performance on the non-verbal portion of the Wechsler Adult Intelligence Scale (WAIS)

(Maly *et al.* 1977). In our first study of RCPM, we found that impaired non-verbal intelligence correlated best with poor comprehension (Kertesz and McCabe 1975). We found that global, Wernicke's, and transcortical sensory aphasics (all with poor comprehension) perform worse on the RCPM than Broca's and transcortical motor aphasics of comparable severity. The reason for the difference in performance, therefore, is not only severity but specifically the degree of comprehension deficit which was the main distinguishing feature in typology. There could be other associated factors, such as lesion location and lesion size, but these would be reflected in the general severity or the comprehension deficit as well. Subsequently, Gainotti *et al.* (1986) confirmed the importance of comprehension deficit in the aphasic performance on RCPM. There are, however, left-hemisphere lesions that impair the performance on RCPM but they do not produce a language deficit (Arrigoni and DeRenzi 1964). Since RCPM are a visuo-spatial task, damage to more posterior, parieto-occipital areas to the brain could easily produce a performance deficit without interfering with language. Nevertheless, this does not necessarily prove the independence of visuo-spatial intelligence and language, but only suggests that both of these elements of cognition are required to solve these tasks.

Other cognitive processes, such as drawing or construction of visuo-spatially determined material, are also correlated well with performance on RCPM. Constructional ability has been shown to be a function of both hemispheres (Arrigoni and DeRenzi 1964). DeRenzi and Faglioni (1965) found that performance on RCPM was impaired just about equally by left- and right-hemisphere lesions, contradicting somewhat a former paper stating that the deficit was worse with left-hemisphere damage (Arrigoni and DeRenzi 1964) and that of Piercy and Smyth (1962), who found performance on RCPM to be more affected by right-sided lesions.

A study by Basso *et al.* (1981) used RCPM and the WAIS and found only a 'loose' connection between aphasia and impaired intelligence. The correlation with lesion size was also low, but they used a variety of time-to-onset intervals and therefore the factor of recovery would be confounded and so diminish the correlation. They felt that the area crucial for intelligence overlapped, but did not coincide with that of language in the left hemisphere.

Borod *et al.* (1982) examined intelligence in aphasics using the WAIS performance, creating a subscore for spatial organization and another for 'verbalizability'. Although global aphasics performed worse than other aphasics groups, their mean performance IQ was 80.6. They also found that constructional apraxia, auditory comprehension, and overall severity correlated best with performance IQ. Auditory comprehension affected the verbalizable subtests such as picture arrangement and completion but had no effect on the spatial organization subtests, such as object assembly and block design. They postulated that constructional apraxia taps into a more general cognitive functioning in a population with aphasia. There are several problems with these conclusions, such as the variable difficulty level of the tasks and the issue of whether there is really such a thing as a non-verbalizable subtest of the WAIS. In other words, the differences may be related more to the spatial characteristic or difficulty level of constructional tasks rather than to their non-verbal nature.

An important issue that needs to be clarified is the arguably verbal component of almost all of the so-called non-verbal tests of intelligence. RCPM, for instance, are designed for children as a non-verbal measure of reasoning by analogy (Raven 1965). They require no language output or praxis and can be performed by relatively young children without any verbal instruction. They are correlated well with verbal tests of intelligence, such as the WAIS (Hall 1957; Talland 1965; Urmer et al. 1960). Thus, for all these reasons, they would appear well suited for exploring the residual intellectual capacities or deficits of aphasics.

A considerable amount of internal verbalization was postulated to occur in normal individuals in processing of RCPM task (Arrigoni and DeRenzi 1964). Zaidel and Sperry (1973) looked at this problem of verbal mediation in commissurotomized patients performing RCPM. The subjects were allowed to look at the task with free vision but the response was separate from each hemisphere tested through palpation. The left-hand–right-hemisphere combination was a better, faster, albeit a silent, performer. The right-hand–left-hemisphere processing was slow and associated with verbal labelling. Costa (1976) suggested that various parts of RCPM represent selective sensitivity to a verbal component or the non-verbal spatial element of the task. Part A involves problems of increasing perceptual difficulty and part B requires the deduction of analogies.

Messerli and Tissot (1974) examined aphasics based on Piaget's concepts of intelligence, such as tests of conservation of physical qualities, mental image, space perspectives, classification, and formal logic, in addition to the usual tests of intelligence, the WAIS and RCPM. They felt that some aphasics found certain tests, such as the classification test, difficult because these required verbal mediation. They did not think that this was the same as an impairment of conceptual thinking, because on tests of conservation of physical qualities, formal logic, and the matrices the aphasics performed well. They felt that the operativity of intelligence was not disturbed but that the instrumentality, that is, language, was defective. Verbalization may affect problem-solving at the level of comprehending instructions or the conditions of the task. It may also occur at the level of processing because of the need for verbal feedback to proceed with the performance. Verbalization plays an important role in encoding and short-term memory that is necessary for the success of intelligent behaviour. In connection with verbal behaviour during non-verbal tests, it was observed by many investigators that aphasics attempt to verbalize some of the components of the task rather than perform them. This curious phenomenon suggested that subvocal verbalization may go on in normal subjects attempting the task, but surfaces as an overt verbalization due to disinhibition in aphasia.

The clinical observations of severe global aphasics indicate that, after the patient becomes alert and the hemiplegia recovers enough for ambulation, the patient can usually dress and take care of the activities of daily living. He appears to be correctly oriented and he clearly recognizes familiar persons and objects. The retention of normal non-verbal actions, reactions, and facial expressions are in great contrast with the severe loss of language.

We have examined 75 globally affected stroke aphasics whose language was non-functional by definition. In our classification, global aphasics must be non-fluent (a score of 4/10, or less) and their comprehension has to be 3.9/10, or less, on the Western aphasia battery (Kertesz 1982). All of these patients were examined in the acute stage between 14–45 days of onset, most of them exactly at two weeks, and the few who could not co-operate for a one-hour examination were postponed up to the limit of six weeks. Only those patients who had the complete aphasia test and RCPM are considered here. We also had 19 age-matched, non-brain-damaged controls whose performance on RCPM (× 24.8, SD 6.6) was a guide for determining cut-off points for aphasic performance. This is the same as the average of Levinson's (1959) normal population. Nine of the 75 patients had a performance of 18.2 or better, which was the mean − 1 SD of the normal controls, and an additional six achieved a score of 11.6 or better, which was the mean − 2 SD of normals.

The following dissociations are detailed in individual cases with high RCPM scores among global aphasics.

(1) E.S., an 80-year-old woman, had a stroke resulting in global aphasia with an aphasia quotient (AQ) of 6.9/100, had a comprehension score of 3.05/ 10, with better than chance yes/no responses (45/60), and a praxis score of 19/ 60, and she was indeed able to perform some of the commands even though most of the scores were given for imitation. She also had a score of 8/14 on reading sentence commands which required a non-verbal pointing response. She scored 6/6 in letter matching but only 1/6 in a picture–word matching task. A CT scan shows a fronto-parietal lesion, as well as occipital involvement, which accounts for her hemianopia. She demonstrates that an elderly patient with a devastatingly large destruction of the language area can still have a slight but significant amount of residual comprehension and ability to pay attention to visual stimuli and understand the task requirements.

(2) S.M., a 56-year-old man, was very alert during examination but his only utterance was singing and clicking his tongue, 'tsh, tsh'. He had an AQ of 3.1. He gestured, indicating somewhat meaningfully that he could do the tasks, and often smiled at the examiner. His responses to personally relevant yes/no

questions were correct by appropriate nodding, but he had a great deal more difficulty with more abstract questions. He could not write but he was able to copy. His ability to calculate as assessed by a multiple choice questionnaire was surprisingly good. Although he took a longer time than usual, his block design tasks were properly done. His praxis score was also 34/100, mostly on imitation. He demonstrated very clearly the dissociation between axial movements and distal movements on command, being able to stand up, turn around, walk forward, and to show how boxers stand, much better than limb and buccofacial movements. He had severe hemiplegia, the right arm being more affected than the leg, but he was able to walk six weeks after his stroke. He could play Chinese chequers, take care of his toilet needs, and he could feed himself, as well as dress himself.

(3) E.B., a 62-year-old woman, became aphasic and hemiparetic on the right side following a subarachnoid haemorrhage from a middle cerebral artery aneurysm. She had surgery 17 days after onset, following which she was globally aphasic. Initially, testing was conducted one month post-onset and two weeks post-surgery. Her AQ was 18.2, comprehension only 2.1/10, but she answered correctly on the personally relevant section of the yes/no questions, doing poorly on word discrimination and on sentences. She was able to read at 33.5/100. Her spontaneous speech output was very non-fluent but at times she produced automatic sentences, such as 'That is about all there is', and the occasional incomplete propositional sentence, such as 'It may be just from being . . .', unusually good for a global aphasic.

A CT with contrast showed enhancement of the left insular region, the fronto-parietal operculum and the posterior temporo-parietal regions. In addition there was a subdural haematoma obliterating the sulci in the fronto-parietal area, higher in the convexity. The infarct was considered to be related to vasospasm, secondary to the subarachnoid haemorrhage.

She showed remarkable recovery three months post-onset, her AQ reaching 52.2. Her speech was more propositional, although with still a considerable amount of word finding difficulty, but her comprehension improved to 7.1 (Broca's aphasia). RCPM score was 30. At eight months post-onset she showed further recovery, comprehension of 8.8, and an AQ of 70.8. Her comprehension and even her reading were at a higher level than most global aphasics, even at the initial examination. She was classified as a mild anomic aphasic. Her initial depression of language function may be related to the added factors of subarachnoid haemorrhage, brain oedema, and compression by haematoma. The treatment of the aneurysm and the absorption of blood results in faster and more complete recovery than in strokes. Her infarct did not extend to the parieto-temporal region.

(4) B.C., a 38-year-old woman, had a stroke in August 1981. Her first test and CAT scan were conducted 15 days after her stroke, showing an AQ of 7.6.

Comprehension for the yes/no test was 45/60, word discrimination 23/60, reading 24/100, and block design 6/9. Her lesion was fronto-central, involving the basal ganglia, but sparing Wernicke's area partially. It did not extend as far back as the usual global lesions do. Her subsequent testing was at three months post-stroke, which showed a good recovery AQ of 36.7, yes/no comprehension 60/60, word discrimination 44/60, sentence comprehension 60/80, and she achieved a total comprehension of 5.95/10. Further improvement resulted in scores of 44/100 (reading) 9/9 (block design) 23/30 (drawing), and 22 RCPM. She was now classified as Broca's aphasia.

(5) G.H., a 69-year-old woman, was tested nine days after her stroke, showing an AQ of 14.4. She had low volume and whispered utterances, often a single word and an occasional incomplete sentence with several semantic paraphasias. She could not name or repeat and cueing did not facilitate word retrieval. Her yes/no comprehension was 21/60, but word discrimination was only 4/60, and sentence comprehension 4/80, giving her a poor comprehension of 1.45. Testing two weeks post-onset showed similar results, except for the rather good performance on Raven's Matrices of 21, and comprehension, which also improved with a significant increase in the auditory word recognition (19/60) and sequential commands (15/80). She had more paraphasia and perseveration than the average global patient. A CT scan showed a left fronto-temporal infarct and an MRI confirmed the sparing of Wernicke's area to a considerable degree.

(6) R.H., a 48-year-old man, was seen two weeks after a stroke, which left him with severe global aphasia, showing an AQ of 5.2, with his spontaneous speech being mainly expletives. Comprehension was severely impaired for word discrimination and complex commands, but he responded on the yes/no questions 39/60 which raised his comprehension level to 2.5/10. His performance was very poor in everything else except block design where he was able to score 7/9. He was retested three months post-stroke. His improved comprehension at 5.5 placed him in the Broca's group. Although his fluency was still very poor, he was only able to say single words. His AQ was still low, at 25.5, but his RCPM score was 27, above the mean of normal populations; calculation was 24/24, praxis 30/60, and reading 35/100. The CT scan showed an infarct from the level of the anterior horn to the posterior aspects of the insula and involved the subcortical structures anteriorly. On six months and at one year follow-up he still had Broca's aphasia. His comprehension of complex commands remained moderately impaired.

(7) L.S., a 42-year-old woman, developed right hemiplegia and global aphasia from a left carotid occlusion, showing an AQ of 8.3. She was seen two weeks after her stroke when she had only stereotypic utterances but scored relatively high on the yes/no comprehension task on questions concerning

personal information (30/60). She did better than chance on pointing to objects and obeyed a few of the simple commands. This gave her a comprehension score of 3.15 and an AQ of 8.3. In a praxis test she was able to do a few items on imitation. Eye closure was preserved and also object use on transitive movements. She was retested four years later when she still had severe global aphasia with her scores essentially unchanged, except that her drawing was severely impaired even four years after her stroke with inability to draw angles, oversimplification, and clock agraphia. Her CT showed an extensive infarction from the posterior frontal region to the occipital lobe.

(8) F.L., a 72-year-old man, was seen two weeks after the onset of his severe global aphasia with stereotypic utterances. He showed an AQ of 13.9. His initial hemiplegia recovered within days. His comprehension was 3.75/10, reading 32/100, praxis of 39/60, block design 9/9, and calculation of 16/24. Three months post-stroke he produced telegraphic, agrammatic speech. His repetition, naming, and reading improved and his AQ rose to a remarkable 67.6 from the initial 13.9. He performed normally in the praxis test, block design, calculation, and RCPM, with some errors on the drawing scores. At six months he was still Broca's aphasic with a rather halting, spontaneous speech. A year after his stroke his AQ improved further to 79/100 and he had only a mild anomic aphasia with some hesitation. His comprehension was 8.9/10, reading 89/100, and naming and wording finding 7.8/10. His CT scan showed a large frontal, and a smaller temporo-occipital, lesion, similar to other reports in the literature of a double lesion with sparing of the central region that can produce global aphasia without hemiplegia (Van Horn and Hawes 1982; Ferro 1983; Tranel *et al.* 1987).

When one looks at the overall population of aphasics, one finds that performance on non-verbal tasks is indeed impaired and the impairment is commensurate with the comprehension deficit and not with the degree of speechlessness. Whether this is related to an actual cognitive impairment, a disturbance of symbolic thought, or to a neighbourhood effect of these non-verbal tasks being affected by the same lesion that affects the substrate of language remains controversial. The relative preservation of non-verbal performance in the severely affected aphasics presented here argues for a dissociable process of language and high-level thought. This is supported by the clinical observations of non-verbal activities of these patients.

Poor performance in non-verbal tests could be ascribed to a disturbance of symbolic function or a 'Grundstörung', or an impairment of 'abstract attitude'. There is no doubt that the majority of severely affected aphasics indeed perform poorly in a variety of tasks that are non-verbal. However, these low scores indicate an impaired capacity to perform formalized tasks rather than everyday activity that remains. The complexity of residual non-verbal thought is beyond easy reach at present. Some of the interesting observations were made by aphasics who recovered, some of them with considerable knowledge and insight. Lordat (1843), Professor of Medicine in Montpellier, recalled after recovery that he continued to think, even when he could not say anything. Many of these descriptions, however, indicate that words are also unavailable to the aphasic at a silent level, that the loss of speech does not remain restricted to the use of symbols in discourse, but also to the loss of inner speech and to some extent the loss of reasoning.

Inner speech (endophasy) is not identical with subvocal or silent speech. It appears to be more amorphous than an articulated utterance and it probably does not have grammar to the extent that propositional speech has. Inner speech is intransitive and not intended for communication. It is more concerned with the sense of words or semantics than with phonetics and there is predominance of sense over meaning, sentence over word, and context over sentence. Images and thoughts in words are interwoven but eventually distinguishable (Critchley 1970). Semantic processing of a very high or abstract level is not easily separable from a cognitive process. Day-dreaming appears to occur through mental images without words. At any moment, however, either by a deliberate act of integration or by focusing attention on the content, the process is crystallized in unspoken words focusing into 'inner speech'. Examples of 'naked', non-verbal, yet focused, thought would be mathematical thinking, music composition, and non-verbal problem-solving. Bergson's dichotomy of knowledge distinguishing symbolic or intuitive components is a similar concept.

Modern cognitive psychology has postulated many pre-language stages in just about every aspect of language operations, including phonology, syntax, and semantics. Instead of 'inner' speech, the words 'logogen' and 'output buffer' are used to denote certain stages that are postulated to take place before the actualization of language output. There are many single case studies that indicate a certain stage of linguistic processing which can be impaired selectively. Some of the cognitive studies show that concepts of objects or entities may be quite intact, yet the anomic aphasic is unable to evoke them. It can be demonstrated that these patients, in fact, have the word forms and can distinguish them from non-words; that is, they have a mental lexicon. It also seems that there are different processing stages for written and verbal language and, because of their differential impairment, it is assumed that even the subvocal or intermediary stages are independent. Patients with phonological alexia, for instance, are unable to read nonsense words, but they can certainly repeat them when they hear them. Others with the so-called deep dyslexia syndrome cannot generate the correct target, but produce semantic errors similar to the semantic paraphasias used by some aphasics. These also represent examples of thought processes where a written word may evoke the meaning of words without being able to elicit the corresponding spoken word form.

A practical aspect of the deficit or the preservation of intelligence in severe aphasia is the legal consideration of the aspects or testamentary capacity of aphasics. Critchley (1961) expresses reservations concerning the ability of aphasics to understand the nuance of legal expression. However, the judgement and the knowledge of what is right and wrong is probably preserved in most aphasics. Certainly the visual identification of a suspect can be carried out by even a global aphasic who witnessed a crime. Occupational competence is another related problem. Formal studies of occupational competence by Newcombe (1969) indicated that left-hemisphere-damaged patients recover to the same extent as right-hemisphere-damaged individuals concerning their eventual return to gainful occupation. These head-injured groups were also examined on RCPM and no difference in the performance was found between the two groups of right- and left-brain-damaged individuals.

In addition to the actual test scores, the performance of aphasics on a non-verbal task has been observed to reveal disturbances of conceptual thinking. Some patients repeatedly persevered in their errors, they did not seem to learn from their mistakes, and did not recognize even successful choices. The strategies of performance differed from those of right-hemisphere-damaged individuals. The quantitation of these operative parameters was very difficult (Voinescu and Gheorghita 1974).

In summary, (1) non-verbal tasks of logical thinking or visuo-spatial problem-solving are affected in aphasia but not to a much greater extent than in right-hemisphere damage; (2) the impairment is correlated best with comprehension deficit in the overall aphasia population; (3) mild aphasics with still significant language disturbance, such as anomia or difficulty with semantic access, can perform non-verbal intelligence tasks very well; (4) the dissociation of a severe language deficit, including impaired comprehension, from preserved non-verbal performance in a few but a significant number of individuals, is evidence in favour of the duality of language and high-level thought.

References

Archibald, Y., Wepman, J., and Jones, L. V. (1967). Nonverbal cognitive performance in aphasic and non-aphasic brain-damaged patients. *Cortex*, **3**, 275–94.

Arrigoni, G. and DeRenzi, E. (1964). Constructional apraxia and hemispheric locus of lesion. *Cortex*, **1**, 170–97.

Basso, A., Capitani, E., Luzzatti, C., and Spinnler, H. (1981). Intelligence and left hemisphere disease: role of aphasia, apraxia and size of lesion. *Brain*, **104**, 721–34.

Borod, J. C., Carper, M., and Goodglass, H. (1982). WAIS performance IQ in aphasia as a function of auditory comprehension and constructional apraxia. *Cortex*, **18**, 199–210.

Claparède, E. (1917). La psychologie de l'intelligence. *Scientia*, **22**, 353–68.

Costa, L. D. (1976). Intertest variability on the Raven Coloured Progressive Matrices as an indicator of specific ability deficit in brain lesioned patients. *Cortex*, **12**, 31–40.

Critchley, M. (1961). Testamentary capacity in aphasia. *Neurology*, **11**, 749–54.

—— (1970). *Aphasiology and other aspects of language*. Edward Arnold, London.

DeRenzi, E. and Faglioni, P. (1965). The comparative efficiency of intelligence and vigilance tests in detecting hemispheric cerebral damage. *Cortex*, **1**, 410–33.

Ferro, J. M. (1983). Global aphasia without hemiparesis. *Neurology*, **33**, 1106.

Finkelnburg, F. (1876). Ueber Aphasie und Asymbolie nebst Versuch einer Theorie der Sprachbildung. *Archiv Psychiatrie*, **6**.

Fodor, J. A. (1983). *The modularity of mind*. MIT Press, Cambridge, MA.

Gainotti, G., d'Erme, P., Villa, G., and Caltagirone, C. (1986). Focal brain lesions and intelligence: a study with a new version of Raven's Colored Matrices. *Journal of Clinical and Experimental Neuropsychology*, **8**, 37–50.

Goldstein, K. (1917). *Die transkortikalen Aphasien*. G. Fischer, Jena.

Hall, J. C. (1957). Correlation of modified form of Raven's Progressive Matrices (1938) with the Wechsler Adult Intelligence Scale. *Journal of Consulting Psychology*, **21**, 23–6.

Hockett, C. F. (1963). The problem of universals in language. In *Universals of language*, (2nd edn), (ed. J. H. Greenberg), pp. 1–22. MIT Press, Cambridge, MA.

Jackson, H. J. (1878). On affections of speech from disease of of the brain. *Brain*, **1**, 304–30.

Kertesz, A. (1982). *The Western Aphasia Battery*. Grune and Stratton, New York.

—— and McCabe, P. (1975). Intelligence and aphasia: performance of aphasics on Raven's Coloured Progressive Matrices (RCPM). *Brain and Language*, **2**, 387–95.

Levinson, B. M. (1959). A comparison of the Coloured Progressive Matrices (CPM) with the Wechsler Adult Intelligence Scale (WAIS) in a normal aged white male population. *Journal of Clinical Psychology*, **15**, 288–91.

Lordat, J. (1843). Analyse de la parole pour servir à la théorie de divers as d'alalie et de paralalie (de mutisme et d'imperfection du parler) que les nosologistes ont mal connus. *Journal de la Societe de Medecine Pratique de Montpellier*, **7**, 333–53, 417–33.

McFie, J. and Piercy, M. F. (1952). Intellectual impairment with localized cerebral lesions. *Brain*, **75**, 292–311.

Maly, J., Turnheim, M., Heiss, W. D., and Gloning, K. (1977). Brain perfusion and neuropsychological test scores: a correlation study in aphasics. *Brain and Language*. **4**, 78–94.

Marie, P. (1906). Revision de la question de l'aphasie: la troisieme circonvolution frontale gauche ne joue aucun role special dans la fonction du langage. *Seminaires de Medecin*, **21**, 241–7.

Messerli, P. and Tissot. R. (1974). Operational capacity and aphasia. In *Neurolinguistics 2—intelligence and aphasia*, (ed. Y. Lebrun and R. Hoops), pp. 66–71. Swets and Zeitlinger BV, Amsterdam.

Newcombe, F. (1969). *Missile wounds of the brain*. Oxford University Press.

Orgass, B., Hartje, W., Kerschensteiner, M., and Poeck, K. (1972). Aphasie und nichtsprachliche intelligenz. *Nervenarzt*, **43**, 623–7.

Piercy, M. (1964). Effects of cerebral lesions on intellectual functions: a review of current research trends. *British Journal of Psychiatry*, **110**, 310–52.

—— and Smyth, V. O. G. (1962). Right hemisphere dominance for certain nonverbal intellectual skills. *Brain*, **85**, 775–89.

Premack, D. (1971). Language in chimpanzee? *Science*, **172**, 808–822.

Raven, J. C. (1965). *Guide to using the coloured progressive matrices*. H. K. Lewis, London.

Talland, G. A. (1965). *Deranged memory*. Academic Press, New York.

Terrace, H. (1979). *Nim: a chimpanzee who learned sign language.* Washington Square Press, New York.

—— (1981). A report to an academy. In The Clever Hans phenomenon: communication with horses, whales, apes and people. *Annals of the New York Academy of Sciences*, **364**, 94–11.

Teuber, H. L. (1964). The riddle of frontal lobe function in man. In *The frontal granular cortex and behaviour*, (ed. J. M. Warren and K. Akert), pp. 416–41. McGraw-Hill, New York.

Tissot, R., Lhermitte, F., and Ducarne, B. (1963). Etat intellectual des aphasiques. Essai d'une nouvelle approche à travers des épreuves perceptives et opératoires. *L'Encéphale*, **52**, 285–320.

Tranel, D., Biller, J., Damasio, H., Adams, H. P., Jr., and Cornell, S. H. (1987). Global aphasia without hemiparesis. *Archives of Neurology*, **44**, 304–8.

Urmer, A. H., Morris, A. B., and Wendland, L. U. (1960). The effect of brain damage on Raven's Progressive Matrices. *Journal of Clinical Psychology*, **16**, 182–5.

Van Horn, G. and Hawes, A. (1982). Global aphasia without hemiparesis: a sign of embolic encephalopathy. *Neurology*, **32**, 403–6.

Viaud, G. (1960). L'intelligence des animaux. *Les Cahiers Rationalistes*, **184**, 4–14.

Voinescu, I., and Gheorghita, N. (1974). Thinking by aphasics. In *Neurolinguistics 2— intelligence and aphasia*, (ed. Y. Lebrun and R. Hoops), pp. 76–80. Swets and Zeitlinger BV, Amsterdam.

Zaidel, D. and Sperry, R. W. (1973). Performance on the Raven's Colored Progressive Matrices test by subjects with cerebral commissurotomy. *Cortex*, **9**, 34–9.

Zangwill, O. L. (1964). Intelligence in aphasia. In *Ciba Foundation Symposium: Disorders of language*, (ed. A. V. S. DeReuck and M. O'Connor), pp. 261–74. Churchill, London.

—— (1969). Intellectual status in aphasia. In *Handbook of clinical neurology, Vol. 4: Disorders of speech, perception, and symbolic behaviour*, (ed. P. J. Vinken and G. W. Bruyn), pp. 105–11. North-Holland, Amsterdam.

18

Language without thought

EDOARDO BISIACH

'... *words are but the signs of ideas.*'
Samuel Johnson (1709–1784)

'*Language is not simply a reporting device for experience but a defining framework for it.*'
Benjamin Whorf (1897–1941)

Introduction

I will approach the topic circuitously and try to draw some inferences about *thought without language* by showing what happens in *language without thought*, where by 'thought' I refer exclusively to non-linguistic representations, expressly conceived as neurodynamic structures bearing information (about actual or simulated states of affairs in the world) in active memory.

Part, at least, of these structures are assumed to correspond to (indeed, to be the same as) the ill-defined category of the so-called 'intensional states' which constitute the content of phenomenal, i.e. subjective, experience.

The indeterminacy of the last statement is due to a twofold incertitude: (1) it is not clear to me whether the concept of cognitive representation should or should not include mental structures which, as in the case of implicit knowledge (see Schacter 1988), shape the content of active memory though being themselves sometimes unable to surface into awareness; (2) criteria for consciousness are relativistic and sometimes conflicting (Bisiach, in press *a*). Although not of primary concern here, these issues constitute an uneliminable accompaniment to what follows.

Language and unilateral misrepresentation of the environment

Focal damage to the human brain may result in impaired representation of one side of the environment, more precisely, of the side contralateral to the damaged hemisphere. Lack of space precludes even a summary exposition of the varied phenomenology of the disorder, of anatomo-clinical correlations, of the results of animal experimentation, and of the various explanations offered for the syndrome. Formal treatments can be found in recent neuropsychology textbooks, e.g. Heilman and Valenstein (1985), and an overview of recent research and speculation is provided by the volume recently edited by Jeannerod (1987). For present purposes, it is sufficient to say that the commonest form in which the disorder manifests itself, known as 'unilateral neglect of space', may be approximately described as a failure to perceive, and to direct activity to one side of the environment, including one half of the body itself.

As will later be shown, there are other, less-frequent but highly informative kinds of unilateral misrepresentation. A common feature present in neglect and these other phenomena is that, as a rule, they occur in severe form only in the acute or subacute stages of an illness affecting the language-incompetent (or less—competent) hemisphere. It follows that the misrepresented side of the environment is usually the left, and, most important, that the lesion may not involve language centres.

At first sight, some aspects of the behaviour of neglect patients might appear susceptible to interpretation in terms of an impairment of relatively peripheral mechanisms processing inflowing or outflowing information, or of low-level (i.e. non-cognitive) mechanisms directing attention in outer space. As already suggested by Zingerle (1913), however, the disorder seems to be much more deeply rooted in the core of the cognitive machinery. My associates and I have provided empirical support for this idea through a series of investigations (for a review, see Bisiach and Berti 1987), and, as I will presently show, our findings have been confirmed and significantly enlarged upon by other researchers.

The basic datum emerged from this line of enquiry, on which I will ground my present arguments, is the occurrence of neglect at the level of imaginative processes inferred from patients' verbal reports. If you ask these patients to describe their mental image of a complex object from a definite vantage point, you may find indications of an impaired representation of the side contralateral to the lesion. Thus, when describing the appearance of a familiar place, our left-hemineglect patients omitted salient particulars located on the left side of the imaginary line of sight. Most important, these particulars were afterwards reported when the patients had to describe the same place from the opposite view point. Conversely, details which the patients had reported a few instants earlier from the right side of their image were neglected in the description of the reversed perspective, into the left half of which they were to fit (Bisiach and Luzzatti 1978; Bisiach et al. 1981). Similarly, patient J.L., studied by Barbut and Gazzaniga (1987), was asked to imagine looking at California from New York and to report the states lying between his vantage point and the target of his mind's eye (California). He named only 10 states, all located to the right: the representation of the side contralateral to his brain lesion—a right parietal infarction—was empty!

The topological correspondence between impaired area of mental images and impaired area of nervous tissue, from which my associates and I argued for an analogue (as opposed to 'propositional' or 'abstract') structure of mental representations (Bisiach *et al.* 1985; Bisiach and Berti 1987), can also be observed in tasks which do not involve descriptive responses. For example, same–different judgements to pairs of visual stimuli have been found to fail, in neglect patients, if differences in configuration appeared in the side contralateral to the brain lesion. This happened both in a condition in which the stimuli were stationary and exposed to unrestrained sight and in another condition in which they moved in either horizontal directions behind a stationary vertical slit (Bisiach *et al.* 1979; Ogden 1985). In the latter condition, an explanation of the findings in terms of sensory disorders contralateral to the brain lesion or disorders of attention in outer space would obviously be wrong, since neglect, in this case, relates to one side of a mental representation constructed from segments which had been perceived with equal clarity in central vision. For present purposes, however, the above referred instances in which hemineglect was inferred from the missing part of a verbal report are specifically relevant. The reason is evident; the pathological behaviour, in this case, clarifies the role and mutual relationships of two kinds of representation: namely, of the non-symbolic analogue and of its linguistic counterpart. Leaving aside for the moment the elusive issue of abstract thought, these are indeed the two subjects involved in speculations about thought and language.

Now, the occurrence of space-related pathological constraints affecting mental representations of the analogue type after focal impairment of neural space may rouse no wonder; on the contrary, it is a proof of the actual existence of this kind of representation. Less obvious is the fact that verbal representation alone could not fill the imaginal gap. This suggests that language *per se* cannot be considered an autonomous form of representation, in the sense that it has no independent data base of its own: all representation (originally) missing in the analogue mode is (derivatively) missing in the verbal mode as well.

The hypothesis of a strict and uneliminable dependence of language upon the cognitive blue-print supplied by the mental structures which preserve the analogue organization of peripheral sensory mechanisms is especially urged by some instances in which unilateral neglect is present within the domain of linguistic items themselves. Evidence of this kind is still exceptional, but it comes from two independent sources which strongly corroborate one another. Patient O.R.F., reported by Baxter and Warrington (1983), not only showed left-sided neglect in outer space in the form of a neglect dyslexia, but he also misspelled the left half of words, both forwards and backwards. The same phenomenon was observed by Barbut and Gazzaniga (in press) in their patient J.L. The behaviour of this patient was even more striking. On writing words to dictation he would begin from the last letter and proceed backwards from right to left, often leaving out some of the leftmost letters. After having thus written B-UE for BLUE, he was asked to write the same word in a mirror-reversed way; the missing letter was thereby recovered, as if the beginning of the word could adequately be represented if mentally projected onto the unimpaired right half of space.

It must be noted that O.R.F. and J.L. were exceptional also in that both of them were to some extent aware of their disorder: O.R.F. described attempting to spell as reading off an image in which the letters on the right side were clearer than those on the left; J.L. was able to tell how many letters were missing (or wrong) at the beginning of words he had written. This is theoretically relevant, since it suggests that (1) it is not the left side of an absolute representation of egocentric space, but the mental representation of objects, in so far as it fills that part of space, which is altered in these two patients, and (2) that the disorder could hardly be exaplained away as resulting from impaired 'attention' to the side of environmental or mental space contralateral to the brain lesion.

A further and even more revealing hint at possible constaints imposed on language by non-linguistic cognitive processes is supplied by the most peculiar disorder which affected spontaneous speech in patient J.L. and which manifested itself in omissions or substitutions of the first phonemes of a word. For example, he would say 'bulance' for 'ambulance' or 'portant' for 'important'. The obvious similarity of this disfunctional pattern to those which characterize neglect dyslexia, neglect dysgraphia, and neglect misspelling forces us to consider the radical hypothesis of an implicit dependence of language on a visuo-spatial analogue. This would hold true also in those cases in which explicit reliance on this analogue does not appear to be due to particular task demands; spontaneous speech, indeed, seems to be far from implying operations in outer or mental space such as those obviously or arguably involved in reading, writing, and spelling.

Although it is still far from clear to what extent the unusual symptomatology observed in O.R.L. and J.L. depended on the rare coincidence of dysphasic and visuo-spatial disorders in the two patients, both of whom had some degree of sinistrality, it would be a mistake, in my opinion, to underestimate its relevance for an understanding of the interaction between linguistic and non-linguistic cognitive activities.

It is not only the negative aspects of the syndrome of unilateral misrepresentation caused by pathological events located in the linguistically incompetent (or less-competent) hemisphere which provides insight into functional relationships between language and non-verbal thought processes. Besides mere hemineglect, there are in fact well-known instances in which *productive* aspects of unilateral misrepresentation may be observed. In the verbal domain these range from elementary pathological completion to enlarged fabulation.

The former is typically seen in neglect dyslexia, and consists of substitutions or additions at the beginning of words, so that—to take recent examples from Ellis *et al.* (in press)—*train* is read as 'brain' and *right* as 'bright'. The latter manifests itself in some patients' delusory narrative related to the left (contralesional) side of the environment (Zingerle 1913), or, much more frequently, to the left side of the body; in which case the term 'somato-paraphrenia' is applied, after Gerstmann (1942).

As will presently be shown, the apparent entanglement of verbal and non-verbal phases of thought in the production of such aberrant aspects of behaviour, the pathological involvement of the patient's beliefs and awareness relative to *one* side of ego-centred space, and the firm resistance of the symptoms to any kind of persuasion constitute both a challenge and a possible clue in facing some of the problems connected with the subject matter of this volume.

Central to the symptomatology of unilateral misrepresentation is anosognosia, ranging from tacit awareness to explicit denial of neurological disorders affecting the side contralateral to the brain lesion, such as hemiplegia and hemianopia.

My associates and I have recently incorporated such forms of anosognosia and those related to global disfunction of individual sensory analysers—such as anosognosia for cortical deafness or cortical blindness (Anton 1899)—into a unitary treatment (Bisiach *et al.* 1985). We have developed a model of non-verbal cognitive processes, which I will not describe here since it is not directly relevant to a discussion concerning the interface between verbal and non-verbal thought processes. I will limit myself to mentioning the two essential features of the model: (1) thought processes preserve vestiges of the modularity of sensory channels; (2) the control function is not the prerogative of a unitized, hierarchically superordinate module, endowed with a map of its sensory specific tributary districts, but is decentralized and distributed across the various sensory analysers. The latter are structured as sensory analogues in which patterns of activity, fed either by bottom-up or top-down input, may be generated, corresponding to sensory driven and mental representation, respectively.

These two features—relative modularity and lack of separate omniscient control functions—may account for the appearance of encapsulated cognitive disorders, such as selective anosognosia and related phenomena following global or even circumscribed impairment in the highest quarters of individual sensory channels. Outside the decayed branch, cognitive processes may remain unaltered, but totally unable to influence pathological ideation.

However, an interview reported in Bisiach *et al.* (1985) may help to provide a concrete illustration of the disorders at issue, and a better introduction to further arguments concerning the vicissitudes to which language is subjected if stripped of a proper non-verbal representational basis. P.R., a 74-year-old painter, admitted to our department following the sudden development of a right temporo-occipito-parietal haematoma, had a left hemiplegia and a left hemianopia and was severely anosognosic to both. In spite of some sluggishness, no intellectual impairment was apparent either to the attending clinicians or to his family. Detailed information about remote events of clinical relevance was provided by the patient himself and checked for accuracy with his wife; curiously, he only failed to mention the history of a *left* inguinal herniation.

Examiner:	Do you know where you are?
Patient:	In a hospital.
Examiner:	Why are you in a hospital?
Patient:	Something went wrong.
Examiner:	What went wrong? [No reply]. Is your left arm all right?
Patient:	Yes.
Examiner:	Give me your left hand.
Patient:	Here you are [without performing any movement].
Examiner:	Where is it?
Patient:	[Still motionless] Here, in front of you.

The examiner ostentatiously raises his forefinger in the patient's right (unimpaired) visual field and asks: 'Grasp my finger with your left hand . . . Well? Can't you move your left arm at all?'

Patient:	[Hesitates] Just give me time to proceed from thought to action.
Examiner:	Why don't you need any time to proceed from thought to action when you use your right hand? Maybe you *can't* move your left hand?
Patient:	I can move it all right. Only, . . . sometimes there are illogical reactions in behaviour; some positive and some negative . . . .

The examiner, placing the patient's left hand in the patient's right visual field, asks: 'Whose hand is this?'

Patient:	Your hand.

The examiner then places the patient's left hand between his own hands, and asks: 'Whose hands are these?'

Patient:	Your hands.
Examiner:	How many of them?
Patient:	Three.
Examiner:	Ever seen a man with *three* hands?
Patient:	A hand is the extremity of an arm. Since you have three arms it follows that you must have three hands.

The examiner then places his hand in the patient's right visual field, and says: 'Put your left hand against mine'.

Patient:	Here you are.
Examiner:	But I don't see it and *you* don't either!

Patient: [After prolonged hesitation] You see, doctor, the fact that the hand didn't move might mean that *I* don't want to raise it. My words may astonish you, but there are bizarre phenomena. My not moving my hand might be due to the fact that if I keep from performing this movement I might be in a position to make movements which would otherwise be impossible. I am well aware of the fact that this seems illogical and uncanny. Indeed, this obscurity is repugnant to my mind, which is very rational. I hope I'm not boring you, doctor, with my apparently odd talk'.

To take P.R.'s verbal behaviour as *bona fide* evidence of what language can and cannot do without a proper non-verbal representational basis, it is first necessary to argue against the hypothesis that his behaviour could have arisen either (1) from a dysfunction of the verbal system itself or (2) as a merely linguistic expletive product filling up a non-verbal representational vacuum.

Since, as regularly happens with patients showing this kind of symptomatology, the linguistically competent hemisphere was not directly affected in patient P.R. by the lesion, an actual disorder of language might only be envisaged by evoking some sort of diaschisis, that is, secondary pathological changes occurring in an area of nervous tissue due to special connectivities normally existing between this area and the area harbouring the primary pathological process (cf. Feeney and Baron 1986). Leaving out considerations relative to the plausibility of such a diaschisis in the present instance, however, attributing a disordered representation of a circumscribed area of space (in this case, of the patient's left upper limb) to a selective disorder of language would imply the oxymoronic admission that indications of analogue functioning can be found in what constitutes the symbolic, non-analogue system *par excellence*. Moreover, explicit denial of the illness and somato-paraphrenic delusions are obviously manifestations of the same underlying disorders, which, in some instances, may be seen in non-verbal behaviour; as first remarked by Anton (1899), indeed, non-verbal behaviour may betray a substantial lack of representation of the illness, even when the patient appears to be verbally aware of his disability (see Bisiach (in press *a*) for a discussion of this dissociation).

These arguments also apply to the hypothesis that confabulations such as those observed in patient P.R. might constitute an autochthonous product of the speech area, released by disconnection of this area from other brain structures. In addition, the circumstance (already noted by Zingerle 1913) that conveying information about the illness directly to the patient's verbal system through non-interrupted pathways—i.e. through verbal communication from the examiner—may be totally ineffective upon delusional utterances, or instigate verbal trickery as in patient P.R., militates against this hypothesis.

Pathological verbal behaviour in anosognosia seems therefore to originate in an upstream disorder of a disintegrative, as opposed to dissociative, kind; in other words, the speech area of the patient suffering from this disorder is neither impaired nor disconnected: it is misfed.

For a proper evaluation of verbal disorders found in association with anosognosia and related clinical manifestations it is also necessary to clear one's mind of more fanciful and misleading ideas which might distort interpretive efforts. Behaviour such as that observed in patient P.R., in fact, might suggest an explanation in terms of 'psychodynamic' reaction to the negative condition into which the patient has fallen. On this view, patients showing anosognosia and related disorders would seek refuge from the illness by denying its existence, in almost the same way in which patients suffering from conversion hysteria are said to seek refuge from social threats in the illness itself. Regardless of whether this might actually be the case in those instances in which the denial concerns diseases unrelated to focal brain damage, a psychodynamic explanation of anosognosia for the disabling consequences of a brain lesion—i.e. of the syndrome established by the early teachings of Anton (1899) and Babinski (1914, 1918)—suffers from a nearly total lack of plausibility. A series of counterarguments concur to undermine it:

(1) As a rule, anosognosia appears at the very onset of the illness, when the patient's vigilance is still clouded, and often fades away in the following few hours or days during which the patient comes to realize all the ominous consequences of his new situation; the time course of a psychodynamic repression would indeed be more likely to parallel this evolution, rather than constituting its mirror image.

(2) Normally, full awareness of impairments as invalidating as those which may develop together with an anosognosic condition is preserved if, as in the case of hemiplegia due to capsular lesion, the nervous system is damaged at a relatively peripheral level.

(3) It is well known that, for reasons which cannot possibly be discussed here, anosognosia related to hemiplegia, with extremely rare exceptions, only appears when the illness afflicts the left half of the body in right-handers and has therefore less-severe consequences than if the right limbs had been involved.

(4) Anosognosia is selective: a patient with more than one disorder due to brain damage may be agnosic for one of them and not for another; Anton's (1899) patient Ursula Mercz., for example, although completely anosognosic about her cortical blindness, was fully cognizant of her dysphasia.

(5) As already mentioned, a patient may verbally admit (either spontaneously or in compliance with the examiner's diagnosis) being afflicted, e.g. with hemiplegia, although ignoring it altogether in planning and programming his motor activities.

(6) Finally, some preliminary findings by my colleagues and myself (Cappa *et al.*, in press) suggest that severe anosognosia for left hemiplegia may in some instances be alleviated by caloric vestibular stimulation ipsilateral (or inhibition contralateral) to the side of the brain lesion, as is known to happen with unilateral neglect (Rubens 1985); this observation, if confirmed, would deprive the psychodynamic explanation of anosognosia of any residue of credibility.

Briefly I will add that any attempt to refer the ethiology of anosognosia and related disorders to general intellectual impairment, besides being dismantled by the above arguments, is also invalidated by clinical histories such as that of patient P.R. Finally, it has also been remarked that even severe mental deterioration does not necessarily imply anosognosia for a disorder ensuing from local brain damage (Angelergues *et al.* 1960).

The interplay of language and thought

In the foregoing section, data from clinical investigation have been reviewed, on which two independent, but interrelated, claims were based: (1) cognitive representations have analogue properties; (2) language does not qualify as an autonomous representational system. In other words, the second claim denies intrinsic representational competence outside those structures which, by virtue of their analogue properties, detain the actual thought data base. Language can only operate with these structures on-line; it remains silent if not fed by them and malfunctions in a passive, uncontrolled way if misfed.

There remain, however, two open questions:

A. Does language merely constitute an instrument for the communication of thought? Assuming that this is not the case and that language interplays on-line with non-linguistic phases of thought, how crucial is its role? What kind of cognitive skills—lacking in non-verbal thought—might it contribute?

B. Has language reverberated through developmental stages on thought, thus determining lasting changes in the structure of the latter?

I do not consider myself in a position to formulate and defend complete answers to these questions. What follows, therefore, is admittedly tentative and meant to solicit clarification of some aspects of the problem, rather than to provide a comprehensive and coherent view of the latter: though adhering, were it only as a dialectic trick, to the two above stated claims derived from study of unilateral misrepresentation, I am wary of rigid, one-sided solutions which may leave important issues bogged down in sterile controversies.

The uncertain definition and ascription of the so-called 'abstract' cognitive structures, and the problem of the interaction between verbal and non-verbal components of thought

The focus of concern is here twofold. One issue relates (a) to the properties which characterize the content of thought processes at a level of processing which, for some reasons, is termed 'abstract', and (b) to the classification of such processes relative to a verbal vs. non-verbal dichotomy. The other issue, even more problematic, is that of extricating the propositional function of cognitive representations from other, supposedly inadequate components. Both issues are crucial to any attempt at developing neuropsychological models of the transition from non-verbal to verbal thought processes or vice versa. The first, however, is worth preliminary consideration, for it seems comparatively more tractable and settling it might help clarify the second.

The property of abstractness is often taken for granted (and left with no further qualification) with reference to putative phases of representation which are conceived as neither obviously sensory bound nor linguistic. As such, the concept is indeterminate and its usefulness dubious or null. To step beyond vague intuitions, it is therefore necessary to consider some positive proposals about the way so-called 'abstract' representations might depart from the iconicity characterizing earlier processing stages. The simplest of such proposals relates to some sort of *reduction* of original experience. The process of reduction is aptly illustrated by Woodworth's (1915, p. 27) parable of the photographer who, on attempting to take a picture of a particular scene, discovered that he was without sensitive plates. He therefore resorted to the expedient of tracing the image projected by the scene on the ground glass of his camera. He found afterwards that his drawing differed from a photograph of the scene in that it only preserved 'the facts to which he had definitely reacted'. An impoverishment of this kind, according to Harnad (1982, p. 192), is a necessary condition for further cognitive processing of representations; whence his aphorism 'No induction without reduction'.

As noted by Woodworth (1915), a representation does not undergo reduction in a random way, but following principles which proceed, at least in part, from top-down instructions and involve meaningful parsing of the content of representations. Reduction, therefore, has much in common with another proposal concerning the extraction of a set of relevant features from the literal record characterizing earlier phases of representational processes. I am referring to the organization, within the frame of a representation, of *structures* such as those considered by Hinton (1979). A good example, suggested by Hinton himself, are the upright and inverted tripods which emerge if one rotates one's mental image of a Necker cube, so that two opposite corners lie on the same perpendicular.

Of course, there are incremental levels of structuring; from instances of perceptual grouping operating over raw sensory material to cognitive chunking of meaningful units, as the encoding of binary digits into octal bytes, in Pribram's (1982) example. A representation undergoing incremental transformations through reduction and structuring may indeed be said to become more and more 'abstract'. This does not at all mean, however, that it abandons its analogue structure to turn into a linguistic one, free of any trace of its sensory origin.

The last statement, of course, is only valid under a qualified acceptance of the term 'analogue'. This term, if applied to the relation between information-processing activities in the brain and the outer world, may be taken as corresponding to Shepard's (e.g. 1975) second-order isomorphism. Unlike first-order isomorphism (which cannot, of course, apply, e.g. to the representation of colours in the nervous tissue), second-order isomorphism does not relate to the similarity between represented and representing properties (A, A'), but to the similarity of the relationships existing within pairs of represented properties and within the corresponding pairs of representing properties [(A,B), (A',B')].

An analogue conception of mental representation, however, needs not necessarily imply that all relations within the represented object be preserved in the representing medium. In other words, the analogue structure of representation is not at all superseded once the latter has undergone (putative) reduction. Likewise, parsing of a representation into meaningful components, as in Hinton's (1979) example, does not imply any departure from the analogue mode; on the contrary, it presupposes it, for unanticipated gestalten such as the two tripods embedded in the mentally rotated cube cannot emerge *ex vacuo* or merely linguistically.

The existence of abstract representations of a non-analogue character is questioned by the above reviewed instances of representational neglect. Moreover, as already argued elsewhere (Bisiach *et al.* 1985; Bisiach and Berti, in press *a*), the phenomena of unilateral neglect suggest that the analogue medium of mental representation is not a cognitively inert scratch-pad, but incorporates mechanisms of cognitive processing. This is also suggested by instances in which meaningful components of a representation are globally neglected or globally spared as units, contrary to what would happen if they were passive icons laid down on the sensory analogue like paint on canvas for the benefit of some putative spectator (Bisiach and Berti, in press *b*). This phenomenon could be interpreted in the framework of the cell assembly theory, perhaps in the same way in which a similar phenomenon could be interpreted: namely, the unitary disappearance of meaningful segments of stabilized retinal images. As noted by Paivio (1982), indeed, the cell assembly theory is probably 'the earliest explicit componential-hierarchical-network model of mental representations'.

A defender of imageless thought might still try to save the idea of abstract— in the sense of totally non-sensuous—representational contents at the level of deep representation. Something of the sort has already been done by

Woodworth (1915). However, in declaring himself 'inclined to believe that a new thought [that is, a thought *in statu nascendi*] is characteristically imageless, and that it attaches itself secondarily to a word or other convenient symbol' (p. 6), he was evidently referring to phenomenal experience, hardly a firm ground for his argument. Of course, there is long-term information which remains available to cognitive activities, although it may not surface in active memory if the portion of the representational medium which should accept it is impaired. Thus, in neglect patients, long-term visual memory of a particular scene, unaddressable by working-memory processes in the impaired sector of the ego-centred representational frame, may still be activated if its contents are redirected to fit the analogue in its intact field. Does deep representation of this kind deserve being considered a constituent of thought? Although in some respects this is only a matter of stipulation, I am inclined to think it does, at least to the extent that it participates in thought processes in the guise of implicit knowledge. Anyway, as argued elsewhere (Bisiach and Berti, in press *b*), there is reason to believe that even idle states of knowledge have an analogue structure, which is in contrast with the idea that, at least in certain stages, thought might be altogether imageless.

Abstracting the (functionally) more flexible notion of analogue from the idea of a raw representational icon paves the way for envisaging thought processes running on a merely imaginal basis. Premack (1983, pp. 136–7) gives an example of feasible elaboration of the imaginal code made by a 'language'-trained chimpanzee to solve a complex match-to-sample problem. He questions, however, the possibility of disposing of an 'abstract' (in the sense of non-imaginal) code in cognitive tasks involving judgements about relations between objects which go beyond the immediate appearances. Such an abstract code, he claims, is necessary in order to match (as his trained chimpanzee Sarah did) $\frac{1}{4}$ apple to a $\frac{1}{4}$-filled cylinder (p. 120) or to judge that the relation key/lock is the same as the relation opener/can (p. 136).

Although Premack notes that the abstract code is commonly equated with language (1983, p. 126), contrary to the opinion of some of his commentators I failed to see any strong commitment to such a view in his paper. It must also be considered that, since trained animals are able to appreciate the similarity of the above-mentioned relations, explaining their ability on a linguistic basis would give rise to foundational issues concerning language. These I prefer to avoid, here, by simply asserting—as several commentators did in *The Behavioral and Brain Sciences* issue in which Premack's article appeared—that the necessity of non-imaginal forms of representation for comparing relationships such as those considered by Premack is far from being apparent. Non-imaginal representation, in fact, has never been ostensibly proven nor is it required by known contradictions incurred by pro-imaginal suggestions.

Since parsimony seems to impel renunciation of imageless representation, the notion of 'abstractness', which Premack rightly wishes to maintain (1983, p. 126), might be reformulated to connotate the most sophisticated *processes* in which (not necessarily refined) elements of originally sensory specific neural codes are extracted and activated; such processes might include some in which *analogue representations* are applied to the *representation of analogies*, as in the key/lock, opener/can example.

One reason for doubting the necessity of any substantial refining of representational items involved in such processes is that the latter seem to be far from being sharply demarcated from one another and can only be qualified with reference to concrete situations; they also seem to require mobilization of a great deal of prior knowledge which is likely to be recruited, or however exploited, in all its richness of detail, regardless of what proportion of these details proves relevant to the task at hand. Think, for example, of what is dropped and what is added in the transition from one to another of a series of analogies such as: key/lock–opener/can–corkscrew/bottle–screwdriver/screw–etc.

On the other hand, suggesting that a crowd of unanalysed representations might participate *en masse* in single acts of thought does not deny the likelihood of forms of neural activity capturing some essence, as it were, of all implicit knowledge recruited at a given moment. Hebb's (1949) concept of higher order cell assemblies is a reasonable model for this hypothetical activity. Higher order cell assemblies might generate representational codes such as those which transmit information about figural stimuli from one hemisphere to the other in commissurotomized patients (Gazzaniga, in press; Cronin-Golomb 1986). As argued by Cronin-Golomb, such information has lost all character of literal iconicity and cannot itself surface into 'verbal' awareness, though becoming available to the recipient hemisphere for categorical matches of various degrees of abstractness, such as *shoe/sock, fish/mallard*, and *envelope/telephone*.

Analogues and propositions

Analogues have been contrasted to propositions (e.g. Pylyshyn 1984). The usual (stronger) claim is that the latter, but not the former, qualify as cognitive structures. As already mentioned, my colleagues and I have repeatedly argued, against this view, that analogues are fully entitled to being regarded as having an executive role in thought processes (Bisiach *et al.* 1985; Bisiach and Berti 1987, in press *a*). I will not reiterate our arguments here. Rather, I will focus on the weaker claim that, whatever their cognitive functions, analogues, contrary to propositions, do lack a fundamental one.

What a proposition is in any natural or artificial language is pretty obvious. What is not so obvious is whether the *propositional function* inherent in statements such as 'Caesar crossed the Rubicon' should of necessity be carried out only by language or language-like structures.

Harnad (1982) maintains that the propositional function cannot be ascribed to analogues, in so far as they are viewed as *unreduced* bearers ('unbounded engrams') of an indefinitely large amount of information, of which only a part is relevant to single propositions. Propositions, therefore, should rather be regarded as instantiated by *reduced* representations ('bounded engrams'). As argued before, however, the substantive aspects of the analogue mode of representation—as contrasted to the linguistic—are not lost in reduced representation; Harnad himself seems to admit this when he writes that 'perhaps it is not unreasonable to suppose that abstract properties and relations have *structural* characteristics that are, as such, amenable in principle to an iconic representation' (p. 198). Further on, Harnad makes the following claim: 'Whereas in the bounded case the propositional information is decoded as something proposed or claimed concerning category relations, in the unbounded case the information is merely construed as the *apposition* of (the unbounded engrams of) the object and the predicate' (p. 202). The term 'apposition' is here borrowed from Bogen (1969), who used it to signify mere juxtaposition and comparison of representations: a process which in his view might constitute a peculiar capacity of the right hemisphere.

I am inclined to think that here indeed lies the crux of the matter. Should we really posit that thought processes cannot directly proceed from raw representation (unreduced icons, 'unbounded engrams'), since these require interpretation? Should we even assume, as hinted by Harnad (1982, p. 198), that language must play a role in this interpretation?

Much of the controversy over mental images hinges upon their alleged intrinsic ambiguity, whence the presumed necessity of some sort of non-imaginal process operating upon them in order to capture meaning. Regardless of the fact that the argument can rebound against the ambiguity of sentences, my opinion is that, whatever imaginal representation be summoned to active memory, it is always summoned under a particular meaning which is not conferred to it by an inner scribe, but is intrinsic and immediate; it only depends on the context created by extant representational activity of the brain, even in the absence of any verbal component (Bisiach and Berti, in press *a*). I take this position since it appears logically coherent, parsimonious, and in agreement with what still constitutes—if only for want of better alternatives— the best model of representational activity in the brain: the cell assembly (Hebb 1949, 1968).

If one admits that analogue processes are the primary bearers of interpreted representational content, that they have *intrinsic*, as opposed to *derived*, intensionality, as Searle (1980) would put it, then one also has to admit that they possess first-person capability of instantiating the propositional function.

Whether or not this capability should only be ascribed to abstract analogues (in the above defined sense of reduced or bounded representations) is a different question, to which, however, I am not inclined to accept too restrictive solutions. The reason why I am not so inclined is that what distinguishes mental states corresponding to propositions such as 'Caesar crossed the Rubicon' and 'Caesar crossed the Mississippi', what determines the degree of belief implicit in each of them, seems to be inherent in a wealth of prior knowledge which might be recruited unselectively, diffusely, and unsteadily. This is suggested (with all due reservations!) by introspection and might have a neural basis in the spread of activity through jittery cell assembly patterns.

Albeit somewhat loosely, information thus structured might be viewed as already satisfying the criteria for propositionality and, as hinted by Premack in the above-mentioned paper (1983, p. 162), form the basis for much of our ordinary reasoning, if not for more constrained and controlled computations such as required by formal logic. The inability to take advantage of this kind of information in the impaired area of the analogue medium into which it should have surfaced leads to disorders of reasoning, which, as happened with our patient P.R., cannot be amended by computation over putative abstract representations, free from the constraint imposed by the analogue structure on more concrete sensory like representations. Asked, during the above reported interview, to point to the right side of his bed, P.R. reacted quite adequately; however, when asked to point to the left side, after some hesitation he answered: 'If this is the right side [the external, right surface of the right bed-rail], this [the inner, left surface of the same bed-rail] must be the left'! This constitutes a further instance of what language without appropriate thought may express!

As suggested by Pinker (1984, p. 55), 'we might store a relatively uncommitted, literal record of the appearance of objects from which we can compute properties that we could not anticipate the need for knowing when we initially saw the object'. I hypothesize that it is indeed this surplus of information—neglected in Woodworth's (1915) metaphor—this intrinsic, unreduced intensionality of analogue representations, that feeds the stream of non-verbal thought in all its richness.

Language-based contributions to thought

Once it has been argued that abstract representations need not necessarily be linguistic, but are more likely to be special purpose excerpts from an imaginal data base of which they preserve the fundamental characteristics which define an analogue structure, the next step is to ask what role, if any, might be played by language in thought processes. Introspectively, the counterpoint of inner speech in a train of thought seems in general to consist, as Vygotsky (1954) remarked, of units, an imaginary record of which would appear elliptic, asyntactical, and meaningless to an external reader. According to him (p. 37), this is due to the fact that inner speech omits what is obvious to the speaker himself. But *what is omitted* is most likely to be indeed the fundamental, non-linguistic component of thought. Should we therefore interpret the phenomenological fragmentariness of inner speech as suggesting a passive, sporadic entailment of linguistic structures by fundamentally non-verbal thought processes, a sort of epiphenomenal resonance of the latter in the instrument they have at their disposal for overt communication? My guess is that in many, perhaps in most instances, this is indeed the case. Not in all instances, since I think it would be too rash and quite unjustified to deny any functional role of language in thought.

The acquisition of native language evolves more or less *pari passu* with the acquisition of all knowledge which enters our thoughts. Linguistic icons have been laid down alongside the non-linguistic icons of objects, situations, and events to which they related. As such, linguistic icons might act as keystones supporting the assemblage of independent representations, and specifying the nature of their relations, in a compound act of thought. In terms of neural activity, this might take the form of an interaction of cell assemblies such as that diagrammed by Hebb (1949, Fig. 16, p. 131).

By 'linguistic icons', I literally mean sensori–motor representations of natural language items, the neuropsychological reality of which is suggested by the previously mentioned observations of Baxter and Warrington (1983) and of Barbut and Gazzaniga (in press). It might be objected that, by so doing, I downgrade inner language. This may be true, but to the best of my ability this is what I can conceive so far.

Long-term modification of thought by language

Although Vygotsky is often credited with having shown how introversion of speech shapes thought processes, in particular those which apply to problem-solving activity, the evidence on which this conviction is based is far from compelling. Vygotsky is obviously right in emphasizing the role of social intercourse—largely based on verbal communication—in the development of thought, but from this to the inference that egocentric speech turns out therefore to constitute the essential framework of adult thought would indeed be similar to an act of faith. Omitting considerations based on problem-solving activities performed by children lacking language skills due to sensory impairment (Furth 1971), thinking implies the manipulation of an enormous amount of prior knowledge. Cognitive science—largely due to its renewed interest in biological systems—has come to realize the necessity of devising parallel models for processing this form of knowledge (e.g. Fahlman 1981); inner speech, inasmuch as it is a sequential process, is simply unable to cope with the task.

In spite of this broad assumption, however, it is reasonable to admit that the development of language as a highly sophisticated tool for the communication of thought is most likely to reverberate around thought itself. It might contribute to the structuring of the latter in a form which, though originally suited for the translation of thought into linguistic expressions, constitutes an advantageous arrangement for a better adaptation of thought to the individual's goals (for a recent discussion of this point, see Oatley, in press).

Although itself a product of thought, language adds considerably to our environment and therefore to its representation in the nervous system; as Wittgenstein (1953, p. 12) noted, language is 'as much a part of our natural history as walking, eating, drinking, playing'. In this sense, it does not remain peripheral to thought, which, on the contrary, it permeates. Vygotsky expressed his agreement with the opinion of other authors that the child has no innate awareness of the symbolic relation between words and their referents and that words appear to him as intrinsic properties of objects rather than as signs (p. 48). With the subsequent abstraction of language from concrete instances of objects and relations, words and phrases might be instrumental in favouring the 'abstraction' of the entities previously referred to as 'reduced' analogues or 'bounded engrams', or, in Hebb's (1968) terms, favouring the constitution of higher order cell assemblies.

I do not see, however, any reason for asserting that this role of natural language in humans is radically different from the role which might be played by any other sophisticated form of non-verbal communication in humans as well as in subhumans. Premack's (1983) results demonstrate that lasting and most remarkable modifications of thought can be obtained in chimpanzees through extensive training in tasks which exemplify elementary forms of abstract thinking.

Another way in which language skills and the introversion of the child's ego-centred speech contribute to the shape of adult thought processes might be to help channelling and sequencing parallel processes into that line to which concepts such as deliberate attention and control apply. Under this aspect too, however, the question remains as to how primary and crucial this contribution is. In a recent review of hemispheric dominance in decision-making activities (Bisiach, in press *b*), I left this question open: the observed left-hemisphere dominance in tasks in which the decision is likely to require some kind of rehearsal of the underlying algorithm on each trial might either be interpreted as being due to involvement of language-mediated skills or to left-hemisphere-specific pre-verbal factors—e.g. a predisposition to engage in sequential processes—upon which the development of a left-hemisphere competence for language might be contingent.

Conclusions

Miller (1978) remarked, with reference to the disambiguation of equivocal sentences, that 'practical knowledge must play an important role in most of the uses we make of language' (p. 306). As noted before, the amount of prior knowledge supporting even the most elementary act of thought is such as to require a parallel form of processing. Nothing forbids assuming that before their organization into speech some linguistic items might also be handled in parallel. Words and phrases, however, convey less than the actual content of cognitive representation. Moreover, it is unconceivable that all knowledge about the world be recast, and subsequently manipulated, in the form of sentences or sentence-like structures only.

The investigation of unilateral misrepresentation due to lesions of the right hemisphere—'dyschiria' in Zingerle's (1913) terminology—has shown the neuropsychological reality of analogue representations such as those posited by Shepard and associates (e.g. Shepard 1975) and by Kosslyn and associates (e.g. Kosslyn 1980), as well as their full cognitive qualification.

The study of these disorders also suggests that language divorced from thought has no effective residual competence of its own. This does not mean that we must view the right hemisphere, lesions of which are responsible for the occurrence of the syndrome of unilateral misrepresentation, as excelling over the left in non-verbal cognitive processes. For all we know, the different consequences of left- and right-hemisphere lesions, as far as the contralateral representation of the environment is concerned, are not due to different processing modes, but probably to a different neural implementation of the spatial analogue subserving representation (Bisiach and Berti 1987). Indeed, recent reviews (Ley 1983; Ehrlichman and Barrett 1983; Paivio, in press) have failed to evidence firm indications of radical hemispheric asymmetries in imagery functions (see, however, Farah (1984) and Kosslyn *et al.* (1985) concerning some aspects of image generation, and Bisiach and Berti (in press *b*) for a discussion of their data and arguments).

Whatever the extent to which the thesis developed in this chapter will prove to have understated the role of language in cognitive activities, nobody is likely to deny that language has definite limits in its expressive capacity. On the occasion of the recent, delightful exhibition 'Vienna 1900' at The Museum of Modern Art, New York, Utley (1986) has reminded us how acutely such limits were felt around the turn of the century by members of the Viennese intelligentsia such as Robert Musil, Arthur Schnitzler, Hugo von Hoffmann-stahl, and Fritz Mauthner. The philosophical predicament of the latter culminated in the idea of a 'suicide of language', which was indeed accomplished by Hugo von Hoffmannstahl. That scepticism, with its romantic overtones, still seems to hang over Wittgenstein's '*Philosophical investigations*', in which language is essentially represented as one of the games our minds play through life.

References

Angelergues, R., de Ajuriaguerra, J. and Hécaen, H. (1960). La négation de la cécité au cours des lésions cérébrales. *Journal de Psychologie*, **4**, 381–404.

Anton, G. (1899). Ueber die Selbstwahrnehmung der Herderkrankungen des Gehirns durch den Kranken bei Rindenblindheit und Rindentaubheit. *Archiv. für Psychiatrie und Nervenkrankheiten*, **32**, 86–127.

Babinski, J. (1914). Contribution à l'étude des troubles mentaux dans l'hémiplégie organique cérébrale (Anosognosie). *Revue Neurologique*, **27**, 845–8.

—— (1918). Anosognosie. *Revue Neurologique*, **31**, 365–7.

Barbut, D. and Gazzaniga, M. S. (1987). Disturbances in conceptual space involving language and speech. *Brain*, **110**, 1487–96.

Baxter, D. M. and Warrington, E. K. (1983). Neglect dysgraphia. *Journal of Neurology, Neurosurgery and Psychiatry*, **46**, 1073–78.

Bisiach, E. (in press *a*). The (haunted) brain and consciousness. In *Consciousness in contemporary science*, (ed. A. J. Marcel and E. Bisiach). Oxford University Press.

—— (in press *b*). Hemispheric interaction and dominance for decision-making. In *Festschrift for Alexandr Romanovich Luria*, (ed. E. Goldberg). IRBN Press, New York.

—— and Berti, A. (1987). Dyschiria. An attempt at its systemic explanation. In *Neurophysiological and neuropsychological aspects of spatial neglect*, (ed. M. Jeannerod), pp. 183–201. North-Holland, Amsterdam.

—— and —— (in press *a*). Waking images and neural activity. In *Psychophysiology of mental imagery: theory, research and application*, (ed. A. Sheikh and R. G. Kunzendorf). Baywood Publishing, Farmingdale, NY.

—— and —— (in press *b*). Unilateral misrepresentation of distributed information: paradoxes and puzzles. In *The neuropsychology of visual perception*, (ed. J. W. Brown). IRBN Press, New York.

—— Berti, A., and Vallar, G. (1985). Analogical and logical disorders underlying unilateral neglect of space. In *Attention and performance XI*, (ed. M. I. Posner and O. S. M. Marin), pp. 239–46. Lawrence Erlbaum Associates, Hillsdale, NJ.

—— Capitani, E., Luzzatti, C., and Perani, D. (1981). Brain and conscious representation of outside reality. *Neuropsychologia*, **19**, 543–51.

—— and Luzzatti, C. (1978). Unilateral neglect of representational space. *Cortex*, **14**, 129–33.

——, —— and Perani, D. (1979). Unilateral neglect, representational schema and consciousness. *Brain*, **102**, 609–18.

——, Meregalli, S., and Berti, A. (1985). Mechanisms of production-control and belief-fixation in human visuo-spatial processing: clinical evidence from hemispatial neglect. Paper presented at the eighth symposium on quantitative analyses of behaviour, at Harvard University: pattern recognition and concepts in animals, people and machines.

Bogen, J. E. (1969). The other side of the brain III: an appositional mind. *Bulletin of the Los Angeles Neurological Society*, **34**, 135–62.

Cappa, S., Sterzi, R., Vallar, G., and Bisiach, E. (in press). Remission of hemineglect during vestibular stimulation. *Neuropsychologia*.

Cronin-Golomb, A. (1986). Subcortical transfer of cognitive information in subjects with complete forebrain commissurotomy. *Cortex*, **22**, 499–519.

Ehrlichman, H. and Barrett, J. (1983). Right hemisphere specialization for mental imagery: a review of the evidence. *Brain and Cognition*, **2**, 55–76.

Ellis, A. W., Flude, B. M., and Young, A. (in press). 'Neglect dyslexia' and the early visual processing of letters in words and nonwords. *Cognitive Neuropsychology*.

Fahlman, S. E. (1981). Representing implicit knowledge. In *Parallel models of associative memory*, (ed. G. E. Hinton and J. A. Anderson), pp. 145–59. Lawrence Erlbaum Ass, Hillsdale, NJ.

Farah, M. J. (1984). The neurological basis of mental imagery: a componential analysis. *Cognition*, **18**, 245–72.

Feeney, D. M. and Baron. J.-C. (1986). Diaschisis. *Stroke*, **17**, 817–30.

Furth, H. (1971). Linguistic deficiency and thinking: research with deaf subjects, 1964–1969. *Psychological Bulletin*, **76**, 53–72.

Gazzaniga, M. S. (in press). Brain modularity: towards a philosophy of conscious experience. In *Consciousness in contemporary science*, (ed. A. J. Marcel and E. Bisiach). Oxford University Press.

Gerstmann, J. (1942). Problem of imperception of disease and of impaired body territories with organic lesions. Relation to body scheme and its disorders. *Archives of Neurology and Psychiatry*, **48**, 890–913.

Harnad, S. (1982). Metaphor and mental duality. In *Language, mind, and brain*, (ed. T. W. Simon and R. J. Scholes), pp. 189–211. Lawrence Erlbaum Associates, Hillsdale, NJ.

Hebb, D. O. (1949). *The organization of behaviour*. John Wiley, New York.

—— (1968). Concerning imagery. *The Psychological Review*, **75**, 466–72.

Heilman, K. M. and Valenstein, E. (1985). *Clinical neuropsychology*, (2nd edn). Oxford University Press.

Hinton, G. (1979). Some demonstrations of the effects of structural descriptions in mental imagery. *Cognitive Science*, **3**, 231–50.

Jeannerod, M. (ed.) (1987). *Neurophysiological and neuropsychological aspects of spatial neglect*. North-Holland, Amsterdam.

Kosslyn, S. M. (1980). *Image and mind*. Harvard University Press.

——, Holtzman, J. D., Farah, M. J., and Gazzaniga, M. S. (1985). A computational analysis of mental image generation: evidence from functional dissociations in split-brain patients. *Journal of Experimental Psychology: General*, **114**, 311–41.

Ley, R. C. (1983). Cerebral laterality and imagery. In *Imagery. Current theory, research, and application*, (ed. A. A. Sheikh), pp. 252–87. John Wiley, New York.

Miller, G. A. (1978). Practical and lexical knowledge. In *Cognition and categorization*, (ed. E. Rosch and B. B. Lloyd), pp. 305–19. Lawrence Erlbaum Associates, Hillsdale, NJ.

Oatley, K. (in press). On changing one's mind: a possible function of consciousness. In *Consciousness in contemporary science*, (ed. A. J. Marcel and E. Bisiach). Oxford University Press.

Ogden, J. A. (1985). Contralesional neglect of constructed visual images in right and left brain-damaged patients. *Neuropsychologia*, **23**, 273–7.

Paivio A. (1982). The Hebbian perspective on mind-brain relations. *Canadian Journal of Psychology*, **36**, 543–7.

—— (in press). A dual coding perspective on imagery and the brain. In *The neuropsychology of visual perception*, (ed. J. W. Brown). IRBN Press, New York.

Pinker, S. (1984). Visual cognition: an introduction. *Cognition*, **18**, 1–63.

Premack, D. (1983). The codes of man and beasts. *The Behavioral and Brain Sciences*, **6**, 125–67.

Pribram, K. H. (1982). Computations and representations. In *Language, mind, and brain*, (ed. T. W. Simon and R. J. Scholes), pp. 213–24. Lawrence Erlbaum Associates, Hillsdale, NJ.

Pylyshyn, Z. W. (1984). *Computation and cognition*. MIT Press, Cambridge, MA.

Rubens, A. B. (1985). Caloric stimulation and unilateral visual neglect. *Neurology*, **35**, 1019–24.

Schacter, D. L., McAndrews, M. P., and Moscovitch, M. (1988). Access to consciousness: dissociations between implicit and explicit knowledge in neuropsychological syndromes. In *Thought without language*, (ed. L. Weiskrantz), pp. 242–78. Oxford University Press.

Searle, J. R. (1980). Minds, brains, and programs. *The Behavioral and Brain Sciences*, **3**, 417–57.

Shepard, R. N. (1975). Form, formation and transformation of internal representations. In *Information processing and cognition: the Loyola symposium*, (ed. R. L. Solso), pp. 87–122. Lawrence Erlbaum Associates, Hillsdale, NJ.

Utley, G. (1986). Fritz Mauthner 1849–1923. In *Vienna 1900*. (The Museum of Modern Art, New York), p. 4. The Star-Ledger, Newark, NJ.

Vygotsky, L. S. (1954) *Pensiero e linguaggio*, (trans. A. F. Costa *et al.*). Giunti-Barbera, Firenze.

Wittgenstein, L. (1953). *Philosophical investigations*, (trans. G. E. M. Anscombe). Blackwell Scientific Publications, Oxford.

Woodworth, R. S. (1915). A revision of imageless thought. *The Psychological Review*, **22**, 1–27.

Zingerle, H. (1913). Ueber Stoerungen der Wahrnehmung des eigenen Koerpers bei organischen Gehirnerkrankungen. *Monatschrift für Psychiatrie und Neurologie*, **34**, 13–36.

Discussion, Section F

Split-brain phenomena and hemispheric specialization

The question arose as to just how much specialization *Gazzaniga* was allowing. *Horn* commented that, while he was strongly in sympathy with the views about the integrative functions of the corpus callosum, he was not clear about whether there was a claim for no hemispheric specialization: 'Partial or complete hemispherectomy may be performed in the absence of chronic underlying pathology, for example, after severe cerebral trauma. In those cases involving left hemispherectomy, there are some reports of substantial residual function. These functions could not have developed slowly prior to the operation, since there was no prior pathology. How does one account for the performance of these patients?' *Gazzaniga* replied: 'There is clear specialization when it comes to language. Most members of our species have their language processes in the left hemisphere. When it comes to the large category of other skills that are purported to be specialized and lateralized, I am suggesting there may well be some specialization, although not as much as is commonly argued, but that the distribution of the systems and subsystems that support those processes varies from individual to individual. . . . As for the hemispherectomy cases, reading that literature makes one occasionally surprised if you expect nothing out of the spared hemisphere. Equally often one is surprised to see how little these isolated hemispheres can do'.

On a related point, *Young* put the question, 'If you hold strongly a view in which functional components are distributed across the cerebral hemispheres and interaction is necessary to support cognitive performance, might it not be the case that the commissurotomy operation is dissociating specialized right-hemisphere capacities from the control processes to support them? If so, is the split-brain operation going to be able to inform us about cerebral hemisphere specialization?' To this *Gazzaniga* replied that his chapter also makes the first point, but '. . . as to the split-brain patients, they have never been the kind one wants to study for simple brain and behaviour correlations on the issue of lateralization. As more patients begin to be studied, however, and as we are able to compare pre- and post-operative tests, I think they become enormously instructive on the many processes that are involved in cerebral lateralization phenomena'.

Weiskrantz asked for the differences in outcome and variance between split-brain and focal damage studies. *Gazzaniga* said it was a key question: 'Of course, there is tremendous variation in the focal picture, as can be seen from Dr Kertesz's paper. Very few neuropsychological studies are consecutive case studies. Variation would pop out in such studies and the standard picture that is commonly taught would be quite different if consecutive case studies were the rule'. But in answer to a further question from *Schacter* on a similar point, *Gazzaniga* said that work from the split-brain field complements that from focal damage evidence: 'The earlier belief of ours and others that the isolated right hemisphere is the purest way to study lateral specialization needs to be revised. Again the variation we are now seeing leads one to this view'.

The comparison of surgical patients with cases of congenital agenesis of the corpus callosum was raised by *Butterworth*. He asked whether there was variation in hemispheric cognitive function in such cases, and also whether they differ in important ways from the adult surgical cases. *Gazzaniga* said that, regarding the second question, the patients '. . . studied to date, for the most part, have been quite different. Most seem to transfer information, visual, auditory, and to a lesser extent tactile, between the hemispheres with impunity. It has been suggested the remaining anterior commissure is larger in these patients. This was demonstrably not the case in one patient with total absence of the corpus callosum who has come to autopsy and been examined by Dr Carol Petito and me. However, this patient was not studied prior to his death. It is likely that other reported cases, in fact, do not have full callosal absence. Yet, because of the basic fact that transfer takes place with ease, it is difficult to answer your other question'.

Anticipating a point that arose in his own paper, *Kertesz* asked whether some of the deficits seen in the isolated right hemisphere could be related to a failure to understand the task. *Gazzaniga* said that there is always that possibility: 'However, we walk through each test, first showing all parameters in full field of vision. We administer practice trials and have the subjects respond with each hand until they are responding perfectly. The general format of all tests are well known to the subjects and, in other tests using virtually the same format but simpler stimuli, the right hemispheres of these patients can usually perform well. Additionally, on some tasks, although impoverished, the right hemisphere performs above chance, indicating that something about the nature of the task was successfully communicated'.

Diamond pursued *Gazzaniga*'s claim that 'the same function can be subserved by different neural regions, or that a deficit found in one patient may not be found in another patient with similar brain damage but may be found in another patient with damage to a very different part of the brain. You state that this is consistent with current notions of brain anatomy and organization'. She asked for elaboration of this point. *Gazzaniga* said that it is an extrapolation of some of the anatomical work by Goldman-Rakic (1981), who has reported, as mentioned in his chapter, that early focal lesions can produce anomalous callosal connexions: 'It is assumed these new and aberrant connexions would carry functional freight with them. Now these studies, while fascinating, are difficult to carry out and there are potential problems. However, I am also thinking of the general view that has emerged in the past 10 years that cortical development involves exuberant growth, a concept introduced by Innocenti (1981). He discovered that cortical networks develop with many more fibres than are ultimately seen in the adult brain. A good percentage of the fibres die off. What determines which fibres stay is a fascinating question.'

Aphasia and non-verbal intelligence

The relation between language impairments and gesture comprehension was raised by *Bisiach*, who asked: 'Is it a linguistic factor or a question of anatomical contiguity? Were there any conspicuous dissociations? *Kertesz* replied: 'Gesture comprehension in aphasics tends to parallel verbal comprehension, although we did not study this in this particular population. Some gestures are iconic and have symbolic content; therefore I think impairment is related to its association with linguistic or semantic conceptualization'.

Schacter asked about imagery: 'Were any of the aphasic groups capable of imagery or imagistic thinking?' *Kertesz* said that he has not studied imagery in this group of patients and it would be difficult because of their severely restricted output: 'However, indirectly, from their performance on Raven's matrices one has to assume that if it is not a verbal performance then it must be through visual imagery'. [See also the interesting work by Kosslyn *et al.* (1985) on deficits in imagery—ed.]

Weiskrantz asked whether just one single 'pure' case of dissociation between thought and language would be adequate to settle the issue of quality, and was perhaps better than a group correlation? *Kertesz* replied that the cases presented '. . . were indeed single cases and each of them showed a significant dissociation between thought and language. The group statistics for the severely affected aphasics were shown only to compare the degree of impairment in the usually globally affected patients and these special cases where the non-verbal performance as measured by Raven's matrices was preserved'. [A striking single case in whom there was good preservation of non-verbal cognitive skills in the face of severe loss of verbal capacity (an academic scientist who sustained severe head injury) has recently been published (Newcombe 1987, pp. 135–7). Although unable to perform better than a 4- or 5-year-old child on verbal tests of comprehension, and with severe jargon dysphasia, he performed normally or above average on non-verbal tests, viz. Advanced Progressive Matrices, short-term memory, long-term maze learning, and visual 'closure'.—ed.]

Butterworth noticed a possible resemblance between the drawings of *Kertesz*'s patients and the drawings of children, at the earlier scribbling state. He asked if there were any ideas of a possible connexion. *Kertesz* said that he agreed that the similarity is striking, but he had not studied it systematically: 'Unfortunately drawing is so variable between individuals and some normal adults have very primitive drawings, resembling children's drawings. These global patients, however, have a very severely affected drawing ability that is perseverative and consists of round loops and scribbling, as you indicated. One can assume that some sort of regression has taken place to an earlier stage of primitive motor output disconnected from mental representation'.

Schacter asked about memory impairments in the various aphasic groups. *Kertesz* answered: 'We have observed severe global amnesia for periods of months in cases of severely affected global aphasics who then subsequently recover comprehension enough to let us know that they have no memory for the initial hospitalization and for months after that. This global amnesia for severe aphasia indicates that much of our episodic memory is verbal in nature'.

Unilateral neglect and analogical mental representations

Sergeant raised the still puzzling question of why unilateral neglect is found much more commonly after right- than left-hemisphere lesions in clinical patients. *Bisiach* replied: 'Neurophysiological evidence [cf. Rizzolatti *et al.* 1981] suggests that in the monkey space representation is bilateral, although skewed within each hemisphere; that is, on each side of egocentric space the most peripheral areas rely heavily on the contralateral cortex and minimally on the ipsilateral. There is no reason to believe that such a bilateral representation should not be preserved in man. In the human brain, however, the skewedness is likely to be *asymmetrical*, since lesions of the left hemisphere may only cause minor forms of hemineglect (at least this is the prevailing opinion). Otherwise stated, in man one side of egocentric space—the left—is likely to rely on the opposite hemisphere much more than does the right side of space'.

Kertesz added a comment, and said there were a number of possible answers. One was that right-hemisphere dominance for attention might emerge as a compensation for the left hemisphere's dominance for language. A second was a similar factor for left-hemisphere motor dominance. He also said that he had evidence for representational neglect by giving a test to brain-damaged patients in which they had to remember pictures of objects in a horizontal row. They tended to recall them correctly immediately but neglected the ones to the left with delayed recall. *Bisiach* noted that these findings were parallel to those of Heilman *et al.* (1974), in the auditory modality, '. . . although less susceptible to an interpretation in terms of sensory disorders contralateral to the lesion. The selective forgetting of left-sided items might, however, be explained in terms of hemi-attention; that is, of a weaker encoding of these items, sufficient for immediate but not delayed recall'. [Also cf. discussion of hemineglect, pp. 258-9.—ed.]

Changeux raised the question of the possible extension of analogical representations to abstract concepts: 'If I understand your point about analogical representations, abstract concepts might also be coded by neuronal assemblies as "images". Does the equivalent of the neglect you describe for representation of space exist for abstract concepts? Would lesions, for instance in the prefrontal cortex, affect the programming of complex time sequences? What about musical perception, execution, or even creation?' *Bisiach* conceded that '. . . hemineglect of representational space has so far been inferred from performance on tasks explicitly or implicitly that require imagery and a definite imaginary vantage point. Whether abstract concepts might or might not be handled in an analogue format in the spared area of the "representational scratch-pad" is an interesting question, but still unsettled empirically. However, P.R.'s difficulty concerning the left side of his bed may suggest, indeed, a disorder at a conceptual level. Concerning cognitive functions related to musical activities, my hypothesis implies that they might be disrupted by a disorder of a time analogue as well as of a space analogue. I have no data about the former, but, concerning the latter, Erminio Capitani and I made an informal observation in the patient N.V., the first patient in whom we found indications of representational neglect (Bisiach and Luzzatti 1978). N.V. (who was a lawyer by profession) suffered from a right temporo-parietal haematoma, the symptoms of which were severe extrapersonal hemineglect and *negligence motrice* (that is, his left arm seldom became involved in any activity, even though it was hardly, if at all, paretic). As he was a skilled pianist, we asked him to play some pieces on a harmonium we were able to find in the hospital. We observed that whatever he played, he persistently ignored the lower pentagram, offering no replies to our remarks about that. After one of us set N.V.'s left hand on the left side of the keyboard, he went on playing with his right hand, quite unaffected by the terribly discordant sounds he too must have heard'.

The relationship of putative analogical representations to language received concentrated discussion. *Caramazza* referred to *Bisiach*'s claim that language does not have an autonomous representational status: 'More specifically, you have argued that mental representations are only given in "analogical" form. How can such a notion account for *any* of the "known" facts about language? That is, in what sense can there be an analogical representation for *grammar*?'

Bisiach replied: 'Implicit in my working hypothesis is the suggestion that rather than looking for an analogue representation for grammar we should ask, for example, what changes in non-linguistic representation underlie purportedly *equivalent* utterances, such as "John loves Mary" and "Mary is loved by John". Active and passive transformations of the same sentence can arbitrary be defined as being equivalent within a formal system that does not take into account the utterer's knowledge and intentions, the context, etc. But this does not imply that they are psychologically or neurologically equivalent. Although "John loves Mary" logically implies that "Mary is loved by John", the deictic polarity of the cognitive processes underlying the two propositions is conceivably quite dissimilar; whence the evolution of two different forms of verbal expression. The idea of the primacy of non-verbal representation advanced in my chapter should be evaluated by keeping in mind that analogues are not to be conceived of as frozen, uninterpreted pictures in the head, but as carriers of both the semantic and the syntactical aspects of mental representation'.

Leslie continued the discussion, following on from the points raised by *Caramazza*: 'Over the last 20 years or so, the proposition that the syntactic forms of language can be generated from a semantic base has been intensively studied by linguists. The attempt to construct a generative semantic theory collapsed in the face of fundamental problems. Given this, the claim that the syntactic forms of language can be reduced to semantic representations must be viewed with considerable skepticism unless these fundamental problems can somehow be overcome'. *Bisiach* replied that *Leslie*'s comment was '. . . both frustrating and stimulating. It is frustrating since it exposes my lamentable ignorance of recent developments in psycholinguistics. I had set hopes in what I thought was a winning movement, destined to bring together linguistics, psychology, and cognitive neurosciences. On receiving such bad news, I have nothing to reply and have much to worry about, given the effort necessary to go through a substantial amount of unfamiliar literature in order to update my knowledge of the subject. To be frank, however, I cannot conceal my suspicion that if attempts to give linguistics a semantic basis actually were wrecked, this was because of insufficient realism, that is, because of vestiges of certain autistic tendencies which characterized earlier linguistic approaches. If so, one can be optimistic if one considers that cross-disciplinary interaction in the study of the mind is still in its infancy, a definite proof of which is the exciting feeling, so widespread among the participants in this symposium, of having found new horizons'.

References

Bisiach, E. and Luzzatti, C. (1978). Unilateral neglect of representation space. *Cortex*, **14**, 129–33.
Heilman, K. M., Watson, R. T., and Shulman, H. M. (1974). A unilateral memory defect. *Journal of Neurology, Neurosurgery, and Psychiatry*, **37**, 790–3.
Goldman-Rakic, P. S. (1981). Development and plasticity of primate frontal

association cortex. In *Organization of the cerebral cortex*, (ed. F. O. Schmidt, F. G. Worden, G. Aldleman, and S. G. Dennis), pp. 69–87. M.I.T. Press, Cambridge, MA.

Innocenti, G. M. (1981). Growth and reshaping of axons in the establishment of visual callosal connections. *Science*, **212**, 824–7.

Kosslyn, S., Holtzman, J. D., Farrah, M. J., and Gazzaniga, M. S. (1985). A computational analysis of mental image generation: evidence from functional dissociations in split-brain patients. *Journal of Experimental Psychology: General*, **114**, 311–41.

Newcombe, F. (1987). Psychometric and behavioural evidence: scope, limitations, and ecological validy. In *Neurobehavioral recovery from head injury*, (ed. H. S. Levin, J. Grafman and H. M. Eisenberg), pp. 129–45. Oxford University Press.

Rizzolatti, G., Scandolara, C., Matelli, M., and Gentilucci, M. (1981). Afferent properties of periarcuate neurons in macaque monkeys. II. Visual responses. *Behavioural Brain Research*, **2**, 147–63.

Section G

Dyslexia and a mathematicians's
experience

Editorial to Section G

This short section consists of only one chapter. It approaches the subject of this symposium not through experimental enquiry but through personal experience. *Jansons* is a young university mathematician. He is also dyslexic—he has severe difficulty in reading and writing, although not in speaking. Accordingly, he did not submit a written paper; his talk to the symposium was tape-recorded, transcribed, and edited by Barbara Weiskrantz. The written text was then finally prepared by Mrs Jansons. It is an account, all too brief, of his experiences in school as well as a description of the way he thinks about mathematics.

We do not know much about the technical profile of *Jansons'* form of developmental dyslexia. It is clear that he has severe difficulties in translating the visual appearance of a word into sound, and vice versa. From this and other comments it seems that his difficulties are probably similar to those that are characteristic of 'phonological dyslexia' (cf. Coltheart 1982; Marshall 1984; Ellis 1985), in which there is a problem with converting letter groups into sounds. But the neuropsychological label is not important here, although the fact that reading (and writing) skills themselves can be fractionated and that there are several forms of dyslexia is important evidence for a number of potentially independent processes. That is, not only can verbal and non-verbal processes be dissociated in neuropsychology, as we have seen, but verbal processes themselves are inferred to be compounded of several parallel routes in normal reading. But whatever the particular linguistic difficulties may be here, we have a clear exposition of the severe trials they caused in his education and how his thinking nevertheless developed to an unusual level.

Nor does it matter here whether developmental dyslexias are or are not causally or neurologically linked to the extensively studied dissociable 'acquired' dyslexias, i.e. resulting from brain damage. This is an important if somewhat contentious question (cf. Bryant and Impey 1986), but irrelevant to our theme, as is the issue of whether there could be a congenital link, commented on by *Jansons* himself in the discussion. What matters is the independence of his powers of thinking from his particular linguistic difficulties. Whatever the origin or explanation of these difficulties, *Jansons'* account should be a powerful object lesson for educators. Were it not for a few dedicated teachers, his mother, and the backing of an experienced psychologist (Prof. Oliver Zangwill), no doubt he would have been condemned in school to continue doing the 'trivial crafts' in the class for slow children to which he had been assigned.

In one sense, the dyslexia itself might be irrelevant to our theme, because unquestionably his *spoken* language is certainly good. If he can speak in words, why does he not think in words? It is hard to believe that his reading problems did not, at the very least, bias him towards a mode of thinking that was free of such troublesome entities as he was encountering in his schooling. There probably is a more fundamental link, which it would be interesting to explore in severely dyslexic persons more widely. But, whatever the explanation, he found from an early age 'that many things were easier to think about without language. This usually, but not always, meant thinking in terms of pictures and was particularly true when trying to make or understand intricate mechanisms'. He describes how his mathematical ideas are put into visual form, or otherwise are not fully understood by him. He also considers some of his non-verbal thought to be non-visual, e.g. to embody tactile imagery. [This and, for example, the use of colour to code space is reminiscent of the sensory transforms of Luria's (1968) 'mnemonist'.] Without the benefit of the black-board diagrams and the like that *Jansons* uses with his students, and the necessary mathematical background, it is difficult to comprehend the precise form or pattern of thinking, but the general message is clear enough.

The personal account not only shows how powerful gifts can be developed despite a particularly severe form of language handicap, but also makes one wonder how many other persons' skills have been overlooked or even suppressed in similar conditions. It also raises the question of the preferred or characteristic modes of thought of other gifted persons. It is interesting how little verbal mediation appears in the accounts of Einstein's thinking in Wertheimer's (1945) classic, *Productive thinking.* Indeed, Einstein remarked to Wertheimer that his 'thoughts [concerned with the triple sets of axioms contrasted in the Einstein–Infeld book] did not come in any verbal formulation. I very rarely think in words at all. A thought comes, and I may try to express it in words afterwards'. This was 'merely a later formulation of the subject matter, just a question of how the thing could afterwards best be written'. When Wertheimer remarked that 'many report that their thinking is always in words, he [Einstein] only laughed' (p. 184). A survey and analysis of creative mathematical thinking in these terms would be of some interest. But returning to the example at hand, here, as in many of the other examples discussed in this symposium, striking evidence emerges of cognitive operations displayed in relative isolation from linguistic skills when the latter are absent, undeveloped, or dissociated from them.

References

Bryant, P. and Impey, L. (1986). The similarities between normal readers and developmental and acquired dyslexics. *Cognition*, **24**, 121–37.

Coltheart, M. (1982). The psycholinguistic analysis of acquired dyslexias: some illustrations. In *The neuropsychology of cognitive function*, (ed. D. E. Broadbent and L. Weiskrantz), pp. 151–64. The Royal Society, London.

Ellis, A. W. (1985). The cognitive neuropsychology of developmental (and acquired) dyslexia: a critical survey. *Cognitive Neuropsychology*, **2**, 169–205.

Luria, A. R. (1968). *The mind of a mnemonist.* Basic Books, New York.

Marshall, J. C. (1984). Towards a rational taxonomy of developmental dyslexia. In *Dyslexia: a global issue*, (ed. R. N. Malatesha and H. A. Whitaker), pp. 45–58. Martinus Nijhoff, The Hague.

Wertheimer, M. (1945). *Productive thinking.* Harper and Row, New York.

19

A personal view of dyslexia and of thought without language

KALVIS M. JANSONS

Before I started school I spent most of my time exploring some aspect of science or technology. I learnt a lot from television, particularly from nature programmes, and would look for interesting animals and plants around me wherever I was. My mother tried to teach me a little basic reading and writing before I went to school, although progress was slow. However, at that time we did not think that there was anything to worry about and I looked forward to the time when I would go to school because I enjoyed learning new things and acquiring new skills.

After being at school for a few years, however, I found that, although I certainly seemed to be more intelligent than all of the other children there, they were able to learn to read more easily than me. So after school, my mother would give me extra lessons, which resulted in the headaches I already got at school becoming worse. At first we thought it could be an eye problem, but when my eyes were tested they were found to be very good, and in any case I did not have the same difficulty with numbers or intricate diagrams.

As time went on, my ability to read and write lagged further and further behind my knowledge and intelligence. Although some teachers really did make a special effort to get me over these difficulties, by the time I was about 10 it was generally believed by the staff at my school that I was of below average intelligence, in spite of the fact that my general knowledge and ability to answer questions in class were not equalled by any of the other children. At that time I enjoyed drawing and painting, particularly the animals, plants, and scenery that I saw around me. However, when I showed my teachers the pictures I had drawn in my spare time, they did not believe that they could be my own work.

Eventually I was put in a special class for slow children, where I learnt little that was of interest to me and spent most of my time doing trivial crafts again and again. However, my interest in furthering my understanding of the natural world was as strong as ever. I spent my spare time learning about many aspects of physics, chemistry, and biology, together with my brother, two years younger, who had similar interests. He was doing very well at school and was usually top of his class in everything.

My mother became quite anxious as the time approached for me to take the 11 plus examination, as she had gone to grammar school and wanted my brother and me to have the same quality of education. She spent a lot of time trying to minimize my reading and writing difficulties but with little success. I failed the examination quite dramatically as I was only able to read a few of the questions and was then almost unable to write even the shortest answers. There were a few arithmetic questions which I could do although I lacked practice as I had been taught with very slow children.

So, at the age of 11, I went to a local secondary modern school, where, at least to begin with, I was able to study biology, chemistry, and physics all as individual subjects. However, I was soon prevented from doing physics by a teacher who thought I knew nothing, mainly due to my attempts to point out when he was wrong. If he had only consulted his reference books he may have had quite a different opinion of my ability.

One subject that I enjoyed at this school, to my surprise, was history, and I did quite well in it as I had an understanding teacher. However, good teachers were rare, and it was clear that I would not win a university place if I continued there.

My mother tried to get my reading and writing problems recognized as being an isolated weakness, and it was around this time that I saw a television programme on dyslexia and convinced my mother that this was probably an appropriate term for my own difficulties. The grammar school I failed to get a place at had merged with a neighbouring secondary modern school to become a new comprehensive school, and eventually my mother succeeded in getting me transferred there where we believed the teachers would be better. Although this was certainly true, many were reluctant to believe that I was much more intelligent than my previous school had given me credit for. For a while I had remedial English lessons with a psychologist at Peterborough Hospital, who believed it to be important for me to accept that I did have a low intelligence, although she claimed this did not mean I could not have a fulfilled life. Not surprisingly these English lessons were not a great success.

Eventually my mother and I made contact with the first person who really seemed to understand my difficulties: Prof. Oliver Zangwill of the Department of Psychology at Cambridge University. He seemed to have no difficulty at all in seeing that I was very intelligent. His backing helped to convince some people that my problem ought to be taken seriously, and at 14 I started yet another school, namely Millfield in Somerset. This school had an extremely good remedial English department run by Mr Lynn Lewis. For most of my time at that school, more than a third of my timetable was remedial English, most of these lessons being with Lewis himself. It is impossible to describe exactly what was different about Lewis's English lessons compared with those

I had had previously, but they certainly were worthwhile since I began to improve. However, there were clearly some very important differences between his attitude and that of my earlier teachers. First, he believed that I was intelligent and that it was not ridiculous for me to want to go to university. Second, he never promised a complete cure; he set realistic targets for me and made it clear that I would always have to work much harder than most people. In short, he was very believable.

For my first year at Millfield, I was in a very low mathematics class and I was not studying physics. One of my maths teachers seemed to appreciate that I was bored with maths, not because I could not do it but because it was not stretching me enough, so I was moved up to one of the higher maths classes taught by the head of department, Mr Sherlock. He was an extremely good teacher and soon I became much more interested in maths than I was in either biology or chemistry. The very compact notation, which I had no trouble in reading or writing, excited me and allowed me to play around with mathematical ideas for a long time after reading only a very small amount. Soon I became one of the best mathematics students in the school as it was such an easy subject to learn. In some cases the best mathematical ideas of a century could be condensed into a chapter. A little after starting to study maths further than arithmetic I was also able to start physics, which was taught by a very enthusiastic teacher called Dr Hanna.

I took O levels in maths, additional maths, physics, chemistry, biology, engineering drawing, and English, and, although it had been arranged for me to have extra time in these examinations to compensate for the dyslexia, in most cases I did not take this. My grades, however, were proportional to the amount of reading and writing involved in the examination, the only failure being in English. In O level maths, for example, it is very easy to guess what is required from the maths in the question and it is easy for an examiner to see that you are using the correct method even when very few words are used.

I took the Cambridge Entrance Examination a year before my A levels. The questions were very varied and it was important to read them carefully. We tried to arrange for these examinations to be read to me, but that request was turned down. However, the first examination drained me to the extent that I was almost incapable of reading or writing at all, so the rest of the papers were read to me and the technical problems that this created had to be sorted out later. I successfully got a place at King's College, Cambridge to read maths, in spite of having no language qualification at all. I went on to do A levels in pure maths, applied maths, and physics, but more reading and writing was involved than at O level which made the examinations much more of a struggle

At this time I thought my problems were over as I had achieved so much compared with what was expected of me by my early teachers. For the first few weeks at Cambridge, I tried to take notes in lectures, but I could not keep up at all even when taking the briefest notes, and while trying to do so I was unable to follow what was being said. So soon I tried to remember the lectures without taking any notes. This was not as difficult as it might seem as over the years I had developed an extremely good memory to deal with the difficulties of getting new ideas to think about. I could not afford to forget. The college did allow me free photocopying and I photocopied lecture notes of other students. These were rarely useful, though, as I find it harder to read even neat handwriting than I do printed text. I was helped by having many other maths students around to talk to and many people would volunteer to read anything I needed. But listening to anything read aloud when you need to learn every detail is actually very tiring, so I could only cope with this for up to a few hours each day.

There was no problem in having the examinations read to me at Cambridge which meant that I achieved middle seconds at the end of each of my three undergraduate years. Although this grade would not normally be considered good enough to go on to do the postgraduate course in maths called Part III, because of my special reading and writing difficulties I was able to take this course. Because the examination was very much harder than the undergraduate ones, many people ran out of ideas well before they ran out of time. So even though I worked slowly, because I still had to have the questions read to me and it took a long time to write even brief answers, using the full time of the examination I obtained a Distinction and I started a Ph.D. in fluid mechanics under the supervision of Dr John Rallison.

Rallison was an exceptionally good supervisor in many respects: he allowed me as much freedom as I wanted while doing my Ph.D. and he had a very healthy attitude towards my reading and writing difficulties, as well as being a talented mathematician himself. Many people around did not think I would be able to complete a Ph.D. because of these difficulties, but, like me, Rallison believed in dealing with problems when they arose and not wasting time and energy attempting to see too far into the future. My research went very well and after the first year I had finished the piece of work that had been planned for my Ph.D. To some extent this was because the problem turned out to be a little more straightforward than might have been expected. However, it did give me the time and confidence to try a much more difficult problem, which after one more year led to my being made a Fellow of King's College; I finished my Ph.D. thesis during the first year of my Fellowship. Both my Fellowship essay and Ph.D. thesis were dictated to the person who is now my wife. Three-and-a-half years into my Fellowship I became a lecturer in mathematics at University College London.

I still have serious reading and writing difficulties, but have developed a large number of coping strategies which enable me to do everything expected of a normal person in my position, although it always involves me in much more effort (sometimes by orders of magnitude) than others. One thing that has helped a lot has been a microcomputer with a sophisticated word processor, spelling checker, and thesaurus. Lectures are written out completely beforehand, using a small subset of the English language and highlighting difficult words; the mathematics which comes much more easily is included in a brief form. I can then copy the lectures directly onto the blackboard word for word, expanding only the maths. Sometimes I take advantage of the ability of most people to correct errors automatically by using intentionally ambiguous characters. As far as I know, none of the students have spotted this.

From an early age I found that many things were easier to think about without language. This usually, but not always, meant thinking in terms of pictures and was particularly true when trying to make or understand intricate mechanisms. It is also the way that my father thinks about things. I soon found it reasonably easy to create images in my mind and to manipulate them and, although I do not have a photographic memory, I developed a very good visual memory. For example, in building Meccano models (an engineering-based construction toy) I would often try out many possible arrangements in my mind before any assembling of the pieces.

To me, abstract pictures and diagrams feel more important than words. For example, in maths I never feel that I fully understand something unless I have found a way of visualizing the system, although this is not usually a substitute for mathematical symbolism. Many of my original mathematical ideas begin with some form of visualization and, once that seems to be a sound model of the system I am analysing, the analysis usually falls into place. Occasionally this fails to happen and then I return to and modify the visual model.

This is not the way that all mathematicians work, but for many some sort of visualization is important and certainly a deep intuition of some form is vital.

The first examples class I was asked to give to the undergraduates at University College involved working out the total resistance of a network of resistors. It turned out that the students were intended to translate the problem into algebra, after spotting the obvious symmetries of the network, and to solve the problem algebraically. However, I manipulated the resistor network by mentally cutting, folding, and reconnecting it in a way that would clearly not change the overall resistance, thus reducing a complicated network to a simple one which could be solved immediately to give a numerical answer. At each stage, I drew a diagram on the black-board for the benefit of the students to explain the method. The process of reducing the complicated network to the simple one was completely non-verbal, though just as precise as the algebra for which it was a substitute.

The reaction of the students divided them into two groups. Two-thirds of them were very impressed with my method as they could see that not only was the argument shorter but they also felt it to be more elegant and natural than their own. The remaining one-third were only impressed with the speed with which I solved the problem but did not feel they would be able to generalize the argument to solve similar problems. Maybe the division was essentially between those that found some sort of visualization easy and those that did not.

Examples of how visualization is important in my research are far too complex to describe to non-mathematicians. However, to give an idea of how abstract notions are visualized it is important to realize that these are often defined recursively, in the same way as algebra develops complicated ideas from simple ones and, when complicated expressions become too difficult to manage, new notions are introduced to simplify them.

It would be a mistake to believe, however, that non-verbal thought has to involve pictures. For example, three-dimensional space can be equally well represented in what I often think of as a tactile world. If I am trying to remember a complicated knot when no rope is available, I usually imagine the finger movements involved and the feel of the knot being tied without picturing it in my mind or moving my hands at all. Knots are examples of things that are extremely hard to describe and remember in words, and people who attempt to do so usually forget them very quickly and are poor at spotting similarities between complicated knots. Another familiar representation comes from the idea of shutting ones eyes in a familiar room. There is no need to visualize the room; knowing exactly where objects are is not related to the senses at all, and furniture can be rearranged in the mind without ever picturing it. These representations of space can also be used in maths together with other non-verbal representations which seem to have no relation at all to real space.

Although, of course, words are important for mathematicians, many mathematicians find it very difficult to communicate ideas solely in terms of them and conversations often take place at a blackboard where ideas can be summarized with simple diagrams and a few symbols to indicate the structure of equations.

I feel I should apologize to any mathematician reading this since I can only describe parts of mathematics which border on common experience, and this always leads to an unbalanced view to some extent. For example, when describing applied mathematics to a non-mathematician, one is forced to talk about the physics, rather than the techniques and arguments which revealed it, and the same will be true of my description of the role of non-verbal thought in mathematics.

Discussion, Section G

Mathematical thinking and language

Various questions were concerned with the comprehension and interpretation of written mathematical symbols, and the relation to language. Thus, *Changeux* asked *Jansons* how he read mathematical books. Did he have trouble reading mathematical symbols? *Jansons* said he usually found it possible to read a mathematics book or paper by 'reading the equations and occasionally looking for key words in the text. I have no trouble at all in reading mathematical symbols'. *Dehaene* continued: 'Numbers are usually considered to be symbols, especially when they have multidigital representation. Do you see numbers as quantities?' The reply was: 'Interpreting numbers expressed in digital form is a much more systematic process than decoding words and *it is not necessary at any stage to relate a digit or a sequence of digits to a sound* [italics added—ed.]. I have no trouble with arithmetic, although like most mathematicians do very little and avoid it where possible. Of course, in mathematics a number does usually represent a single quantity, something which is not true for a telephone number, for example'.

The same questioner asked whether *Jansons* could view multidimensional space. He replied: 'I generally find it easy to visualize three-dimensional space, and often in mathematics spaces of more than three dimensions are formed as the products of smaller spaces where it is often more useful to think of the components separately. However, to answer your question, I cannot usefully visualize four-dimensional space–time as used in special relativity, for example, although in solving problems it is often only necessary to consider slices of this space, bringing the dimension down three or less. Sometimes it is convenient to represent a spatial dimension as a shade or colour in a lower dimensional space. For example, redness could indicate position in the fourth dimension'.

Caramazza queried the relevance of a reading difficulty to 'thought without language', and said: 'I think it is a mistake to equate reading and writing ability with language. It is quite obvious to all of us that your mastery of the English language surpasses many speakers' knowledge of the language. So that, in fact, you have language in a sense in which linguists and ecologists say is language. So the question then really is: What does reading and writing contribute to thinking processes—apparently not very much?' *Jansons* replied: 'One point I should like to make is that a lot of my mathematics is done completely without words of any kind. For example, when I determined the total resistance of a network of resistors for my students, that was originally solved in my mind by silent manipulation of the figure. Thought is not necessarily hindered by reading and writing difficulties, but the availability of things to think about is'.

The dyslexic condition

Several questions were directed towards obtaining a more detailed picture of the dyslexic condition in this instance. *Kertesz* asked *Jansons* whether he read by sounding out the words or by reading the word pattern? And 'what if you come across a word that seems strange or does not fit in the sentence?' *Jansons* said: 'An increasing number of words are recognized as a whole and these will often not translate into sounds in my mind when reading. I find it extremely difficult to decode new words or translate them into sounds, although I will often guess their meaning from context'. What difficulties were there, asked *Schacter*, in writing papers for publication? *Jansons* answered that he was very much helped by the sophisticated word processor he described in his talk, 'although writing of papers is slow and tiring, and sometimes I still have to dictate parts of them'.

Sergent questioned whether he had trouble telling left from right? 'For the first six years of my life', said *Jansons*, 'I was essentially ambidextrous and I have always had trouble telling right from left, as do my father and brother. Often when I try to recall a scene I find it difficult to determine whether it or its mirror image is the correct representation, unless there is some cue like traffic or road signs'.

Gazzaniga asked whether *Jansons'* father was dyslexic. The reply was: 'Although he claims that no Latvian is dyslexic, he has great trouble in reading and writing (worse than me)'. Had any cytogenetic tests been carried out, 'because there is some evidence that there is a marker of the twenty-first chromosome indicating dyslexia, which is familiarly traceable?' *Jansons* said that he had had none of the tests.

Premack asked whether it was not the case that Geschwind had data 'in which asthma, maths, genius, and myopia were correlated in the male?' *Horn* elaborated: 'One of that constellation of symptoms, besides asthma which Kalvis evidently did have, was migraine, and you mentioned that you did have migraine after a certain time. I wonder whether you had it at all commonly, and on which side of your head? Geschwind's story is that migraine is one part of the symptomatology of the dyslexic condition'. [The reference is Geschwind and Galaburda 1985—ed.] *Jansons* said he does have frequent migraines, 'which are usually the result of excessive reading or writing. The pain is almost always symmetrical. These headaches can also be caused and are made worse by some periodic patterns (either temporal or spatial periodicity)'.

Reference

Geshwind, N. and Galaburda, A. M. (1985). Cerebral lateralization. Biological mechanisms, associations, and pathology: a hypothesis and a program for research. *Archives of Neurology*, **42**, 428–59, 521–52, 634–54.

20

Afterthoughts

After any symposium one is apt to wish to proceed almost immediately to a follow-up symposium on the same topic. That is especially true of one such as this, where the three groups had never before come together to discuss the common theme, and hardly anyone's research had ventured into all three domains. But in any symposium worthy of its name, one is fully occupied during it in absorbing a new set of findings and ideas, and digestion is only setting in as one leaves the meeting. Later one can provide discussion with proper nourishment.

After the event, then, and with the written scripts before one, what thoughts occur to one about conclusions? That some fascinating, sometimes quite surprising, evidence emerged about cognitive capabilities that can and do exist in the absence of language is clear enough. The procedures, the facts they generated, and their various implications for further research are also evident. That techniques or approaches used in one domain might well transfer with profit to other domains can also be appreciated. This is hardly the place to try to offer a compendium, even if one were able to do so. But what about 'thought' or 'thinking'? Are there any general conclusions to have emerged? Perhaps one skeleton on to which to hang some suggestions is to appeal to common parlance in the use of the word *think*. In everyday speech the word arises in phrases such as 'think *of*', 'think *through*', 'think *in*'.

That there can be mental *content*, a capacity to 'think of' in the absence of language, and in a form that has external reference, would not seem to be in doubt from a large variety of evidence presented here. The pre-linguistic infant can understand where a hidden object is, images can be conjured up which are impossible to code verbally, the chimpanzee can have an abstract understanding of a ratio, the right hemisphere can handle non-verbal material categorically, the rat can have an intention, and so forth. Elsewhere, Terrace (1985) attributes 'representations' of learned sequences to the pigeon: the bird can compare the relation between non-adjacent elements in the sequences of responses to a set of colours and also have knowledge of the ordinal position of a particular element. Precisely how one incorporates such content into one's formal, theoretical psychological explanations is a separate question, about which there is no shortage of protagonists.

To 'think through', in the sense of reflection, putting separate items of information together, to consider implications, is slightly more difficult, but again the evidence can be seen. Animals can put separate items of spatial information together to concoct a direct route. Impressively, the chimpanzee can add two ratios of physically unlike items to match a third quantity, again physically different. In an earlier period, from which we have not quite emerged, when pronouncements could be made authoritatively from the armchair, Romanes commented on yet another group of people he considered to be without language, the 'uneducated deaf' who lacked 'finger language' (and, in Victorian times, were socially deprived). He concluded that 'from the mental condition of the uneducated deaf-mutes we learn the important lesson that, in the absence of language, the mind of man is almost on a level with the mind of a brute in respect of its power of forming abstract ideas'. Indeed, they (and presumably also animals) . . . 'cannot attain to ideas of even the *lowest* degree of abstraction' (see Weiskrantz 1985, p. 9). What would he say about the ratio-adding chimpanzee? Or indeed, of much of the other material in this symposium?

Another intrepid commentator (and experimenter) on animal behaviour, Hobhouse, said . . . 'none of my animals (with the possible exception now and again of the monkeys) showed the least understanding of the how or why of their actions. . . . What Jack [Hobhouse's dog] or the elephant knew was, crudely that they had to push a bolt. . . . The reason why . . . they obviously never grasped' (1901, p. 235). We have heard that in experiments on devaluation of reward there is a consequential effect on *subsequent* behaviour contingent on that reward. The spatial detour experiments, or the mental rotation experiments, and many others, would also seem to imply an understanding of 'why', at least in the sense that in these, too, there is not an automatic and inflexible connection between an action and a consequence. And, as we heard, some aphasic patients can demonstrate normal non-verbal logical sequencing. Whether the infant has such a capacity to 'think through' is not clear from the evidence, but it would be rash to exclude the possibility, especially as they seem to make inferences about the status of a hidden object.

To 'think in'—that is another matter. Clearly many of us think in words. It would appear that some persons can think only in them. But to say that there can be no other medium of thinking hardly follows. It is curious that the one of the heated debates in psychology at the turn of the century was whether thought could be 'imageless'. The Wurzburg School concluded, from analysis of introspective accounts, that some thought could be. But what was *not* in doubt was that thought could be rich in imagery. The argument stemmed precisely because imagery was considered to account for much of the content of thought, to constitute one of its elements. The focus of the debate appears to have shifted, almost unnoticeably, from whether thought can be imageless to whether it can be wordless.

Well, if thinking of, thinking through, and thinking in are open to non-linguistic modes, what advantages does language confer on thinking? As an independent system, in and of itself, perhaps none. There certainly can be language without thought, and if there is nothing to talk about there is nothing to be gained in listening. Clearly, that there are advantages for thinking cannot be in any doubt, but what are they? That it allows communication, and hence cultural transmission, is obviously a colossal benefit in adaptive terms. But beyond that? It might be considered that to 'think through' in propositional terms might be a powerful advantage, as indeed it is, and clearly language lends itself easily to such an exercise. But we have a suggestion from the final presentation that this need not be pursued 'in words' to be creative in advanced mathematics. We even have more than a hint that words can actually impede cognition if the material is non-verbal. The benefits of cultural transmission can be colossal, but callosal transmission can be harmful, we are told.

Animals, infants, and aphasic patients might be able to indicate that they know why, and know how, but they can rarely, if ever, communicate this, or anything else, outside of their direct negotiations with their physical environment. The adaptive advantages of having such information are beyond calculation. The power to communicate with words entails, inevitably, both the capacity and the need to abstract, and that language provides a quantum leap for powers of abstract thinking is obvious and not controversial. It does indeed allow a world, a universe, (even, said Romanes, a supernatural) to be constructed and elaborated, and one with not only a past but a future. That much can be granted. But the question still remains: In thinking *of* and thinking *through*, and even in thinking *in* with a non-syntactic symbolic system, is there any difference in principle between thought without and with language that is qualitative rather than quantitative? It bears thinking about.

References

Hobhouse, L. T. (1901). *Mind in evolution*. Macmillan, London.
Terrace, H. S. (1985). Animal cognition: thinking without language. *Philosophical Transactions of the Royal Society (London)*, **B308**, 113–28.
Weiskrantz, L. (1985). Categorization, cleverness, and consciousness. *Philosophical Transactions of the Royal Society (London)*, **B308**, 3–19.

Author index

Acredolo, L. P. 420, *422*
Adams, C. D. 318, *323*
Adams, H. P. Jr. 459, *463*
Albert, M. L. 80, *100*
Alegria, J. 34, *41*
Alexander, G. E. 338, 340, *368*
Allen, M. 85, *100*
Allen, N. 90, *105*
Allport, A. 88, *100*
Alvarado, M.C. 283, *303*
Amin, D. 123, *129*
Anderson, J. R. 56, *64*, 147
Andrewsky, E. L. 256, 257, *272*
Angelergues, R. 83, 90, *103*, 472, *481*
Anstis, S. M. 196, *210*
Antell, S. G. 216, *227*, 233, *236*
Anton, G. 468, 470, 471, *482*
Archibald, Y. 453, *461*
Arrigoni, G. 454, 455, *461*
Ashmead, D. H. 31, *42*
Assal, G. 82, *100*
Attneave, F. 398. *413*

Baars, B. J. 270, *272*
Babinski, J. 471, *482*
Baddeley, A. D. 108, 112, *128*, 245, 262, 263, *272*
Baillargéon, R. 176, 177, *182*, 194, 195, *209*, 365, 417, *422*
Baldwin, J. M. 5, *23*
Barbizet, J. 361, *366*
Barbur, J. L. 248, *272*
Barbut, D. 465, 466, 479, *482*
Baron, J.-C. 470, *483*
Barrett, J. 481, *482*
Basso, A. 454, *461*
Bateson, P. P. G. 281, 283, 284, 285, 286, 293, *300*, *302*
Battig, K. 338, *366*
Bauer, R. M. 94, *100*, 262, 263, 340, *366*
Baxter, D. M. 466, 479, *482*
Beale, I. L. 402, *414*
Beauvois, M-F. 80, *100*
Becker, C. A. 257, *277*
Becker, J. 245, *275*

Bekedam, D. J. 69, *71*
Bender, M. B. 249, *272*
Bennett, E. L. 282, *303*
Benton, A. L. 83, 90, *100*, 123, *130*
Berger, T. W. 289, *300*
Beritashvili, I. S. 300, *301*
Berlin, B. 403, *413*
Berlucchi, G. 120, *130*
Berryman, R. 151, *153*
Bertelson, P. 120, 121, *128*
Bertenthal, B. I. 217, *227*
Berti, A. 465, 466, 468, 474, 475, 476, 477, 481, *482*
Best, C. T. 40, *42*
Bever, T. G. 33, *41*
Biller, J. 459, *463*
Bion, P. J. 86, *107*
Bisiach, E. 30, 258, 259, 262, 263, 265, *272*, 464, 465, 466, 470, 472, 474, 475, 476, 477, 481, *482*, 489
Bjork, E. L. 418, *422*
Blanc-Garin, J. 81, *100*
Blomquist, A. 338, *369*
Blumstein, S. E. 94, *104*, 257, 263, *272*, 275
Boakes, R. A. 151, *155*
Bogen, J. E. 83, *103*, 434, 439, *449*, 477, *482*
Bolhuis, J. J. 290, 291, 292, 294, *301*, 328, *332*
Bomba, P. C. 221, 225, *227*, 402, *415*
Born, W. S. 171, *184*
Bornstein, B. 90, *100*
Borton, R. 178, *183*
Borod, J. C. 454, *461*
Bosack, T. N. 350, *369*
Bourgeois, J. P. 416, *422*
Bouzouba, L. 388, *394*
Bower, G. H. 112, *128*
Bower, T. G. R. 30, 31, *41*, *44*, 176, *182*, 196, *209*, 362
Boyd, H. 328, *332*
Boyes-Braem, P. 80, *105*
Bradshaw, J. L. 112, 120, *128*
Braine, M. D. 32, *41*
Brand, N. 86, *100*
Bransford, J. D. 133, *154*
Bremner, J. G. 360, *366*

Subject index

A—not B
  abilities required by object retrieval
      and 360–6
  brain maturation and 416–8
  dorsolateral prefrontal cortex and 417–8
  in infants 335, 336
  results with infants on 340–4
  similarity of delayed response and 338–9
abstract cognitive structures and verbal and
      non-verbal thought 472–6
'abstract' structures
  mental representations and 466
adaptation to reality 26
adaptive mechanisms, habituation, memory
      systems and 213
affective stimuli 68
agnosia
  implicit/explicit dissociation and 260–1
  object 80
  visual 80
agraphia 254–5
alexia
  left hemisphere lesions and 83
  lip reading and 88
  phonological 460
  pure 79
  without agraphia 254–5, 263–4
allocentric frames of reference, egocentric
      versus 405
allocentric space, locations and geometrical
      transformations in 397
amazonas, modality transfer in 421
amnesia
  'A—not B' and 417
  IMHV lesioned chicks and human 285
  implicit/explicit dissociation and 243–7,
      267, 268, 282
  implicit knowledge and infantile 326
  learning and 239
  priming and 93, 262, 326
  proactive interference and 344 (note)
  prosopagnosia and 99
analogies, in apes 56, 63, 70
analogue
  abstract representation and 473–6
  anosognosia and 470–1
  structure of mental representation 466
  propositions and 476–8
anencephaly 69

animals
  Cartesian view of 279
  categorization 158–60, 226
  cognition xiii
  conditioning and intentionality 305–23
  exploration in animal spatial
      cognition 383–99
  habituation studies 213, 229
  human cognitive capacities and 280
  human thought and consciousness
      and 296–300
  self awareness and 299–300
  spatial cognition 371–93
angular displacement 14
angular relations and perceptual
      integration 214–6
angular rotation of shapes 401
anomia 267
anosognosia,unilateral misrepresentation in
      468–72
apes
  analogies and 56
  hemispheric specialization and 39
  intentionality and 305
  memory for target location in 405–7
  neoteny 47
  meta-cognition and 55–6
  picture-objects and 50–2
aphasia
  Broca's 255, 256, 261, 266, 268
  cerebral specialization and 428
  cognitive function in severe 451–61
  constructional apraxia and 454–5
  day-dreaming and 460
  global 453, 456
  implicit/explicit knowledge and 255–8
  implicit linguistic knowledge and 256–7,
      326
  inner speech and 459–60
  non-verbal intelligence and 487–8
  non-verbal tests and 459, 461
  optic 80
  semantic priming in 263
  Wernicke's 255–8, 261, 266, 268
apraxia, constructional 452, 454–5
attention
  manual pointing and 19
  spatial cognition and 389
audition, temporal frequencies and 157